Coconut-Peach Cobbler with Bourbon-Pecan Ice Cream, page 208

*Grilled Thai Chicken Salad
with Mango and Ginger,
page 191*

Sausage-Pepper Pizza,
page 313

3

Party Favor, page 156

Cooking Light®

ANNUAL RECIPES 2000

Oxmoor House®

©1999 by Oxmoor House, Inc.
Book Division of Southern Progress Corporation
P.O. Box 2463, Birmingham, Alabama 35201 .

Library of Congress Catalog Number: 96-71335
ISBN: 0-8487-1910-7
ISSN: 1091-3645

Printed in the United States of America
Second printing 2000

Be sure to check with your health-care provider
before making any changes in your diet.

Oxmoor House, Inc.

Editor-in-Chief: Nancy Fitzpatrick Wyatt
Senior Foods Editor: Katherine M. Eakin
Senior Editor, Copy and Homes: Olivia Kindig Wells
Art Director: James Boone

Cooking Light® Annual Recipes 2000

Editor: Adrienne S. Davis
Foods Editor: Anne C. Cain, M.S., M.P.H., R.D.
Copy Editors: Donna Baldone, Jacqueline B. Giovanelli
Editorial Assistant: Heather Averett
Publishing Systems Administrator: Rick Tucker
Director, Production and Distribution: Phillip Lee
Associate Production Manager: Vanessa C. Richardson
Production Assistant: Faye Porter Bonner

Contributors
Designer: Carol Damsky
Indexer: Mary Ann Laurens

Cooking Light®

Vice President, Editor: Doug Crichton
Executive Editors: Nathalie Dearing, Rod Davis
Managing Editor: Billy R. Sims
Senior Editors: Ellen Templeton Carroll, M.S., R.D. (Projects),
    Lisa Delaney (Healthy Living), Jill G. Melton, M.S., R.D. (Food)
Food Editors: Mary S. Creel, M.S., R.D.,
    Maureen Callahan, M.S., R.D.
Editorial Coordinator: Carol C. Noe
Associate Editors: John DeMers, Polly Pabor Linthicum,
    Kerri Westenberg
Assistant Editors: Melissa Ewey, Krista Ackerbloom Yates, M.S., R.D.
Beauty Editor: Martha Schindler
Editor-at-Large: Graham Kerr
Art Director: Susan Waldrip Dendy
Assistant Art Director: Lori Bianchi Nichols
Designers: Maya Metz Logue, Paul T. Marince
Photographers: Becky Luigart-Stayner, Randy Mayor
Photo Stylists: Lydia E. DeGaris, Mary Catherine Muir,
    Fonda Shaia
Assistant Photo Stylist: Jan Gautro
Test Kitchens Director: Rebecca J. Pate
Food Stylist: Kellie Gerber Kelley
Test Kitchens Staff: Martha Condra, Missy Frechette,
    Leigh Fran Jones, M. Kathleen Kanen, John Kirkpatrick,
    Julie Walton
Copy Chief: Tim W. Jackson
Copy Editors: Lisa C. Bailey, Ritchey Halphen
Production Editors: Hazel R. Eddins, Liz Rhoades
Office Manager: Stacey L. Strawn
Editorial Assistants: Su Reid, Joyce McCann Swisdak, Ann Taylor

WE'RE HERE FOR YOU!

We at Oxmoor House are dedicated to serving you with reliable
information that expands your imagination and enriches your
life. We welcome your comments and suggestions. Please write
us at:

Oxmoor House, Inc.
Editor, Cooking Light® Annual Recipes
2100 Lakeshore Drive
Birmingham, AL 35209

To order additional publications, call 1-205-877-6560.

Cover: *Easy Lemon Squares (page 105)*

Back cover, clockwise: *California Crepe Rolls (page 99),
Patrick Sage-y Crusted Lamb Loin with Angel Hair Pancake
and Broken Hearts of Palm-Teardrop Tomato Salad (page 54),
Strawberries Romanoff Sundaes (page 111), and Italian Bean
Salad with Escarole (page 171)*

CONTENTS

Our Year at *Cooking Light*®

Dear Readers,

Thanks for inviting *Cooking Light* into your kitchen—the most important room in any home. We've got plenty of ideas for making the most of the time you spend there, especially when it comes to recipes. This cookbook includes every single recipe that appeared in *Cooking Light* magazine in 1999—more than 750 in all! And they're easy to find and use, because of our triple index system, easy-to-follow layouts, and other touches such as "Our Favorite Recipes" (page 11).

Some of the highlights that made 1999, and thus this cookbook, so special are:

- 99 Quick & Easy Ways to be a Better Cook in 1999. This feature helped people around the world start a new year on the right food, speaking in culinary terms. Now it can do the same for you, whether you're seeing it here as a reminder or for the first time (page 14).

- Renowned cookbook author Deborah Madison signed on as the magazine's "Inspired Vegetarian" columnist in 1999, and she has taken our meatless dishes to new heights of flavorful innovation.

- Readers have asked us for years to help inspire them with their gardening. So we worked with a family to design, plant, tend, and harvest a home garden. We showcased the spectacular results in a three-part series in 1999, and have recapped it for you here (pages 44, 159, and 215). Happy planting, cooking, and eating!

- We teamed up with TBS Superstation's *Dinner & a Movie* for a Superchef Cookoff that created deliciously offbeat recipes such as Patrick Sage-y Crusted Lamb Loin with Angel Hair Pancake and Broken Hearts of Palm-Teardrop Tomato Salad (page 54). (The chefs' recipe titles have to somehow playfully reflect the movie *Ghost*.) And you'll love Pair-o-Normal Game Hens with "Break on Through to the Other Side" of Mango Salsa (page 55).

- The recipe contests didn't end there, either. We also joined *Healthy Choice* for a $16,000 5 O'Clock Challenge recipe contest that climaxed at our GrandStand '99 food-and-fitness festival in Atlanta. We showcased the winner and two runners-up here (see page 235).

- *Cooking Light* also worked with Bayville, New York, to plan a healthier millennium than the one everyone was leaving. Our entire October issue explored the good things to come, and you won't miss a one with this cookbook (beginning on page 241).

- For the holidays, you'll find a step-by-step countdown for The Big Dinner that leaves nothing to anxiety-stricken last minutes (page 301). And just maybe you'll create special memories of your own with the December recipes that framed special moments in the lives of our authors (beginning on page 321).

All in all, 1999 was a fabulous way to leave a millennium, and I hope you enjoy this year-2000 edition of the *Cooking Light Annual Recipes* series. Even more important, I hope this cookbook helps you enter the new epoch on the firm footing of active good health.

Best Regards,

Vice President/Editor

Our Favorite Recipes

A recipe has to be pretty impressive to make it into the pages of *Cooking Light* magazine. After all, each recipe is tested several times by our Test Kitchens staff and food editors, who judge its merits on many factors: taste, ease of preparation, broadness of appeal, relevancy to today's way of eating, and that indefinable quality we call "yum factor." Of all the recipes we approved in 1999, we've highlighted the following outstanding examples. These are the recipes that *Cooking Light* staffers most like to make at home for family and friends, and those that generated the most reader excitement. We think of them as the most delicious of the delicious.

◆ **CINNAMON-BUN BREAD** (page 20): With its swirl of cinnamon and raisins and a powdered sugar-vanilla glaze, this bread is reminiscent of cinnamon rolls—but tastes even better.

◆ **CREAMY TWO-CHEESE POTATOES GRATIN** (page 70): Begin with a creamy, no-fail cheese sauce, add garlic and Parmesan cheese to boost the flavor, and you've got a lightened classic that you're bound to make again and again.

◆ **DOUBLE-MUSHROOM BREAD PUDDING** (page 71): Not just for dessert anymore, bread pudding becomes a hearty main dish with a double dose of mushrooms: portobello and cremini. Consider this a new comfort food.

◆ **SMOKED-GOUDA RISOTTO WITH SPINACH AND MUSH-ROOMS** (page 118): This recipe took top honors in our annual chefs' competition with cheese as the featured ingredient. The smoky gouda and earthy wild mushrooms are indeed a winning combination.

◆ **ASIAGO DIP WITH CROSTINI** (page 134): Sharp, pungent Asiago cheese and sweet sun-dried tomatoes pair up in this creamy cheese dip. Spread it on crostini (Italian for "little toasts") for terrific party fare.

◆ **SPINACH CALZONES WITH BLUE CHEESE** (page 138): Blue cheese melts into a filling of fresh spinach and mushrooms in this vegetarian calzone. Calling for refrigerated pizza crust and only six ingredients, this recipe is a breeze to make.

◆ **TURKISH LAMB, FIG, AND MINT KEBABS** (page 170): Dried figs and lamb, marinated with mint and spices, form a perfect Mediterranean medley. This unexpected combination sounds exotic, but all the ingredients are readily available.

◆ **GREEK CHICKEN WITH CAPERS AND RAISINS IN FETA SAUCE** (page 172): Chicken is topped with a remarkable sauce of onions, garlic, lemon, raisins, capers, and warm feta cheese. The dish is so beautiful and has such a deep flavor, you'd never guess it was a cinch to make.

◆ **CURRIED CHICKEN WITH PLUMS AND GINGER** (page 179): A key ingredient in this recipe is crystallized or candied ginger, which lends a sweet and piquant taste. A nice golden crust coats chicken thighs drizzled with a sauce that includes sautéed red plums.

◆ **FIERY THAI BEEF SALAD** (page 192): When you want a light dinner, try this easy-to-prepare main-dish salad. The flavor—derived from fiery chiles, lime juice, cilantro, garlic, mint, and lemon grass—is so vibrant it'll make a Thai fan out of anyone.

◆ **FRENCH TOAST-PEACH COBBLER** (page 194): Biscuit topping gives way to bread dipped in an egg batter for this fabulous, fun cobbler. Fresh, ripe peaches produce a luscious syrup. This recipe is a pure, plate-licking dessert.

◆ **ADOBO-MARINATED PORK TENDERLOIN WITH GRILLED PINEAPPLE SALSA** (page 206): The tangy marinade called adobo—made with garlic, cumin, and lime—turns pork into a spectacular entrée. Grilling slightly caramelizes the pineapple and brings out its inherent sweetness.

◆ **NEW ORLEANS-STYLE BARBECUED SHRIMP WITH CANE-SYRUP GLAZE** (page 207): The flavor combination of sweet and hot never tasted so good. Keep the grill fired up; these little goodies are completely addictive.

◆ **HONEYED APPLE TORTE** (page 209): This buttery cake is filled with moist apples and covered with a cinnamon-sugar topping. The taste is entirely decadent.

◆ **CHEDDAR-POTATO BREAD** (page 265): You'll find little pockets of Cheddar cheese throughout this yeast bread. Toast a slice, and the heat will melt the cheese. It's a wonderful accompaniment with a hearty soup.

◆ **OLD-FASHIONED CARAMEL LAYER CAKE** (page 332): The fine texture and simple flavor of this cake pair with a rich caramel frosting to create one of our favorite cakes of the year. This sure-hit will be one of your favorites, too.

HOW TO USE IT AND WHY Glance at the end of any *Cooking Light* recipe, and you'll see how committed we are to helping you make the best of today's light cooking. With five registered dietitians, five Test Kitchens professionals, three chefs, and a computer system that analyzes every ingredient we use, *Cooking Light* gives you authoritative dietary detail like no other magazine. We go to such lengths so you can see how our recipes fit into your healthy eating plan. If you're trying to lose weight, the calorie and fat figures will help most. But if you're keeping a close eye on the sodium, cholesterol, and saturated fat in your diet, we provide those numbers, too. Many women don't get enough iron or calcium; we can also help there. Finally, there's a fiber analysis for those of us who don't get enough roughage.

What it means and how we get there: We list calories, protein, fat, fiber, iron, and sodium at the end of each recipe, but there are a few things we abbreviate for space.

- *sat* for saturated fat
- *g* for gram
- *CHOL* for cholesterol
- *mono* for monounsaturated fat
- *CARB* for carbohydrates
- *poly* for polyunsaturated fat
- *mg* for milligram
- *CALC* for calcium

We get numbers for those categories based on a few assumptions: When we give a range for an ingredient, we calculate the lesser amount. Some alcohol calories evaporate during heating; we reflect that. And only the amount of marinade absorbed by the food is calculated.

Your Daily Nutrition Guide

	WOMEN AGES 25 TO 50	WOMEN OVER 50	MEN OVER 24
Calories	2,000	2,000 or less	2,700
Protein	50g	50g or less	63g
Fat	67g or less	67g or less	90g or less
Saturated Fat	22g or less	22g or less	30g or less
Carbohydrates	299g	299g	405g
Fiber	25g to 35g	25g to 35g	25g to 35g
Cholesterol	300mg or less	300mg or less	300mg or less
Iron	15mg	10mg	10mg
Sodium	2,400mg or less	2,400mg or less	2,400mg or less
Calcium	1,000mg	1,200mg	1,000mg

Calorie requirements vary according to your size, weight, and level of activity. This chart is a good general guide; additional nutrients are needed during some stages of life. For example, children's calorie and protein needs are based on height and vary greatly as they grow. Compared to adults, teenagers require less protein but more calcium and slightly more iron. Pregnant or breast-feeding women need more protein, calories, and calcium. Also, the need for iron increases during pregnancy but returns to normal after birth.

JANUARY · FEBRUARY

99 Quick & Easy Ways
to be a Better Cook
in 1999

What you need to know to take charge of your kitchen.

You've resolved to become a better cook. But how? You want to know, for instance, what professional cooks consider the most essential ingredients and tools in their kitchens. What shortcuts they've discovered over the years. What some secrets of their successes are.

And, perhaps most important, how they stay content in the kitchen day in and day out.

Let us help. We posed these questions and other practical queries to our Test Kitchens staff, Food Editors, and Contributors, as well as to cooking instructors and recipe developers around the country. The results were impressive—and vast. So in addition to some special recipes that make the best use of them, we bring you 99 quick-and-easy ways to be a better cook. To score a perfect 100, just add yourself.

TOOLS NO KITCHEN SHOULD BE WITHOUT

1. High-quality chef's knife
2. Heavy 10-inch nonstick skillet
3. Cutting board
4. Vegetable peeler
5. Oven thermometer
6. Stainless-steel whisk
7. Colander
8. Stainless-steel box grater
9. Pepper mill

INGREDIENTS WORTH THE SPLURGE

1. Freshest seafood available
2. Parmigiano-Reggiano cheese
3. Good extra-virgin olive oil
4. Imported olives
5. Vanilla bean
6. Gourmet greens
7. Dried mushrooms
8. Good coffee
9. Pine nuts

BEST BOOKS FOR COOKS

1. For the beginner: *Light Basics* (William Morrow & Co., 1999), by Martha Rose Shulman
2. For the hip: *Canyon Ranch Cooking* (HarperCollins, 1998), by Jeanne Jones
3. For the sweet: *Chocolate and the Art of Low-Fat Desserts* (Warner Books, 1994), by Alice Medrich
4. For the spicy: *Steven Raichlen's Healthy Latin Cooking* (Rodale Press, 1998), by Steven Raichlen
5. For the meatless: *Vegetarian Cooking for Everyone* (Broadway Books, 1997), by Deborah Madison
6. For the gourmet: *Fresh & Fast* (Chapters, 1996), by Marie Simmons
7. For the committed: *The American Dietetic Association's Complete Food and Nutrition Guide* (Chronimed, 1996), by Roberta Larson Duyff
8. For the globetrotter: *Healthy Indian Cooking* (Stewart, Tabori & Chang, 1998), by Shehzad Husain
9. For the homebody: *Down-Home Wholesome* (NAL-Dutton, 1995), by Danella Carter

(SHHH!) COOL KITCHEN SECRETS

1. When sautéing, get your pan good and hot.
2. Toast nuts to bring out their flavor.
3. If you overbrown garlic, throw it away and start over.
4. A little chopped fresh parsley enhances the flavor of almost any savory dish.
5. Pat chicken breasts dry before sautéing to help them brown.
6. Use your hands!
7. Cut bread, bagels, and tomatoes, using a serrated knife.
8. Roll lemons and limes on the counter before squeezing to extract the most juice.
9. Use zip-top bags to marinate, dredge, and store foods; to degrease sauces; and as a substitute for a pastry bag.

SUREFIRE SHORTCUTS

1. Chop fresh herbs in a measuring cup, using scissors.

2. Use an egg slicer to cut mushrooms and strawberries.

3. Use bottled minced garlic.

4. Freeze extra chopped onion and bell pepper for future use. They keep up to 2 months.

5. Buy precut vegetables and fruit at a salad bar.

6. Quick-drain yogurt on paper towels.

7. To peel ginger quickly, use the side of a square wooden chopstick or a spoon.

8. Use a mini food processor or electric food chopper to chop vegetables.

9. Use your microwave.

ALL-TIME GREAT SUBSTITUTES

1. 1 tablespoon balsamic or red wine vinegar for ¼ cup red wine

2. Parmesan cheese for Asiago

3. Plain low-fat yogurt for sour cream or buttermilk

4. Cottage cheese for ricotta

5. Angel-hair pasta or linguine for Asian noodles

6. Worcestershire sauce for fish sauce

7. 3 tablespoons egg substitute for 1 large egg white

8. ½ teaspoon turmeric for ⅛ teaspoon saffron

9. 3 tablespoons cocoa plus 1 tablespoon butter for 1 ounce semisweet chocolate

WAYS TO CHILL IN THE KITCHEN

1. Enjoy a little wine while you cook.

2. Tackle only one new dish per meal.

3. Keep an ongoing grocery list and photos of the people from item 9 on the fridge.

4. Wear comfortable shoes and clothes.

5. Turn on music.

6. Laugh at your mistakes—and learn from them.

7. Persuade somebody else to wash the dishes.

8. Be messy; you can always clean up the mess.

9. Cook with your friends, kids, or mate whenever possible.

EASY WAYS TO DRESS UP YOUR DINNER

1. Serve one-dish meals in shallow pasta bowls.

2. Garnish with fresh herbs cut in sprigs.

3. Try putting sauce under food rather than on top of it.

4. Slice chicken breast, pork tenderloin, or flank steak, and fan on plate.

5. Dine by candlelight.

6. Arrange food on a bed of greens.

7. Sprinkle herbs or spices around the edge of the plate.

8. Garnish desserts with powdered sugar, cocoa, chopped fruit, or whole berries.

9. Wipe plate edges free of splatters prior to serving.

FAST 'N' FRIENDLY CONVENIENCE ITEMS

1. Near East-flavored couscous

2. Frozen chopped spinach

3. Gerhard's gourmet reduced-fat sausages

4. Ready-to-eat roasted skinned, boned chicken breasts

5. Prewashed greens in a bag

6. Preshredded reduced-fat cheese

7. Bottled roasted red bell peppers

8. Boboli pizza crusts

9. Prepared pesto

THINGS YOU DIDN'T KNOW YOU NEEDED

1. Ice-cream maker

2. Food processor

3. Salad spinner

4. Stand-up mixer

5. Kitchen scale

6. Heat-resistant spatulas

7. Mortar and pestle

8. Instant-read thermometer

9. Pizza stone

PANTRY MUST-HAVES

1. Fat-free, less-sodium chicken broth

2. Fresh garlic

3. Canned diced tomatoes

4. Balsamic vinegar

5. Dried pasta

6. Basmati rice

7. Canned garbanzo beans

8. Low-sodium soy sauce

9. Olive oil

Continued

Sizzling Steak with Roasted Vegetables

(pictured on page 38)

Zip-top bags *simplify the marinating process.*

Marinade:

⅓ cup dry red wine
¼ cup beef broth
2 tablespoons balsamic vinegar
1 tablespoon brown sugar
¼ teaspoon coarsely ground black
    pepper
3 garlic cloves, minced
4 (4-ounce) beef tenderloin steaks
    (1 inch thick)

Roasted vegetables:

1 cup (1-inch) pieces red bell
    pepper
1 cup (1-inch) pieces yellow bell
    pepper
2 teaspoons vegetable oil
12 small red potatoes, quartered
    (about 1½ pounds)
3 shallots, halved
¼ teaspoon salt

Remaining ingredients:

2 teaspoons coarsely ground
    black pepper
½ teaspoon salt
1 teaspoon vegetable oil
1 teaspoon prepared horseradish

1. To prepare marinade, combine first 6 ingredients in a large zip-top plastic bag. Add steaks to bag, and seal. Marinate in refrigerator 2 hours, turning occasionally.
2. Preheat oven to 400°.
3. To prepare roasted vegetables, combine bell peppers, 2 teaspoons oil, potatoes, shallots, and ¼ teaspoon salt in a 13 x 9-inch baking dish. Bake at 400° for 45 minutes or until potatoes are tender, stirring occasionally.
4. Remove steaks from bag, reserving marinade. Sprinkle 2 teaspoons black pepper and ½ teaspoon salt evenly over both sides of steaks. Heat 1 teaspoon oil in a large nonstick skillet over medium-high heat. Add steaks, and sauté 3 minutes on each side or until desired degree of doneness. Remove steaks from pan. Add reserved marinade to skillet, and boil 1 minute, scraping skillet to loosen browned bits. Stir in horseradish. Pour sauce over steaks and vegetables. Yield: 4 servings (serving size: 1 steak, 1 cup vegetables, and 2 tablespoons sauce).

CALORIES 379 (27% from fat); FAT 11.4g (sat 3.7g, mono 3.9g, poly 2.3g); PROTEIN 29g; CARB 37.4g; FIBER 4.7g; CHOL 73mg; IRON 7.1mg; SODIUM 620mg; CALC 49mg

Peppered Chicken-and-Shrimp Jambalaya

Streamline preparation with our suggested ***pantry staples.***

1 tablespoon olive oil
½ pound skinned, boned chicken
    breasts, diced
6 ounces turkey kielbasa, halved
    lengthwise and sliced (about
    1½ cups)
1½ cups finely chopped onion
½ cup diced red bell pepper
½ cup diced green bell pepper
½ cup diced yellow bell pepper
1½ cups uncooked long-grain rice
½ teaspoon dried thyme
½ teaspoon black pepper
¼ teaspoon ground red pepper
1 cup water
2 (16-ounce) cans fat-free,
    less-sodium chicken broth
2 (14.5-ounce) cans diced
    tomatoes, undrained
½ pound medium shrimp, peeled
    and deveined
½ teaspoon hot sauce
¼ cup chopped fresh parsley

1. Heat oil in a Dutch oven over medium heat. Add chicken, kielbasa, onion, and bell peppers; sauté 5 minutes or until vegetables are tender. Add rice; sauté 2 minutes. Add thyme, black pepper, and ground red pepper; sauté 1 minute. Add water, broth, and tomatoes; bring to a boil over medium-high heat. Cover, reduce heat to medium-low, and simmer 15 minutes. Add shrimp and hot sauce; cover and cook 5 minutes or until shrimp are done. Remove from heat; stir in parsley. Yield: 6 servings (serving size: 2 cups).

CALORIES 374 (16% from fat); FAT 6.6g (sat 2g, mono 2.8g, poly 1.3g); PROTEIN 26g; CARB 51.3g; FIBER 3g; CHOL 65mg; IRON 7.9mg; SODIUM 919mg; CALC 95mg

Spiced Tuna with Mediterranean Wine Sauce

Fresh tuna, ***Parmigiano-Reggiano cheese,*** *and* ***high-quality olive oil*** *add great flavor.*

1 cup dry white wine, divided
8 sun-dried tomato halves,
    packed without oil
1 tablespoon orange juice
2 teaspoons fennel seeds
1 teaspoon black peppercorns
1 tablespoon olive oil, divided
½ teaspoon salt, divided
½ teaspoon grated orange rind
2 garlic cloves, crushed
4 (6-ounce) tuna steaks (about
    1 inch thick)
Cooking spray
3 tablespoons chopped pitted
    Greek olives
¼ teaspoon coarsely ground black
    pepper
2 cups hot cooked angel hair
    (4 ounces uncooked pasta)
¼ cup (1 ounce) grated
    Parmigiano-Reggiano cheese

1. Combine ½ cup wine and tomato halves in a 1-cup glass measure. Cover with plastic wrap, and vent. Microwave at HIGH 1½ minutes or until mixture boils; let stand, covered, 15 minutes. Strain tomatoes through a sieve into a bowl, reserving liquid; chop tomatoes. Add tomatoes, ½ cup wine, and orange juice to reserved tomato liquid.
2. Place fennel seeds and peppercorns in a spice or coffee grinder; process until finely ground. Pour into a small bowl; stir in 1 teaspoon oil, ¼ teaspoon salt, orange rind, and garlic. Spread spice mixture evenly over 1 side

of tuna steaks. Heat 1 teaspoon oil in a large nonstick skillet coated with cooking spray over medium-high heat; add steaks, crust sides down, to skillet. Cook 5 minutes on each side or until fish is medium-rare or desired degree of doneness. Remove from heat; keep warm. Add wine mixture, ¼ teaspoon salt, olives, and black pepper to skillet; cook until reduced to ½ cup (about 3 minutes). Combine pasta, 1 teaspoon oil, and cheese in a bowl; toss well. Serve tuna over pasta; drizzle with wine sauce. Yield: 4 servings (serving size: 5 ounces tuna, ½ cup pasta, and 2 tablespoons wine sauce).

CALORIES 439 (31% from fat); FAT 15.1g (sat 4g, mono 6g, poly 3.5g); PROTEIN 46.9g; CARB 26.7g; FIBER 1.7g; CHOL 69mg; IRON 4.1mg; SODIUM 620mg; CALC 122mg

WINTER-FRUIT TART WITH CARAMEL ICE CREAM

*Make this duet in a snap with an **electric ice-cream maker** and a **food processor**.*

Fruit mixture:

1½ cups sliced dried apricots (about 8 ounces)
1½ cups water
1¼ cups coarsely chopped dried apple (about 4 ounces)
½ cup golden raisins
½ cup amaretto (almond-flavored liqueur) or apple juice
⅓ cup packed brown sugar
1 tablespoon butter or stick margarine
2 teaspoons vanilla extract

Crust:

1¾ cups all-purpose flour
1 tablespoon granulated sugar
½ teaspoon ground cinnamon
¼ teaspoon salt
6 tablespoons chilled butter or stick margarine, cut into small pieces
4 to 5 tablespoons ice water
Cooking spray
Caramel Ice Cream

1. Combine first 6 ingredients in a medium saucepan. Bring to a boil; cook 1 minute. Remove from heat. Stir in 1 tablespoon butter and vanilla; cover and let stand 10 minutes.
2. Preheat oven to 375°.
3. Lightly spoon flour into dry measuring cups, and level with a knife. Place flour, granulated sugar, cinnamon, and salt in a food processor; pulse 3 times or until combined. Add chilled butter; pulse 10 times or until mixture resembles coarse meal. With processor on, add ice water through food chute, processing just until combined (do not form a ball).
4. Gently press mixture into a 4-inch circle on heavy-duty plastic wrap; cover with additional plastic wrap. Roll dough, still covered, into a 14-inch circle; freeze 5 minutes or until plastic wrap can be easily removed. Remove top sheet of plastic wrap; invert and fit dough into a 10-inch pie plate or quiche dish coated with cooking spray, allowing dough to extend over edge of dish. Remove plastic wrap. Spoon fruit mixture into pastry. Fold dough over fruit mixture, pressing gently to seal (pastry will partially cover fruit mixture). Coat dough with cooking spray.
5. Bake at 375° for 50 minutes or until pastry is crisp (shield fruit with foil if it begins to burn). Serve warm with Caramel Ice Cream. Yield: 12 servings (serving size: 1 wedge and ¼ cup ice cream).

CALORIES 317 (23% from fat); FAT 8.1g (sat 2g, mono 3.3g, poly 2.2g); PROTEIN 4.6g; CARB 58.1g; FIBER 2.5g; CHOL 5mg; IRON 2.1mg; SODIUM 188mg; CALC 86mg

Caramel Ice Cream:

4 cups 2% reduced-fat milk
2 teaspoons vanilla extract
1 (10-ounce) jar caramel topping

1. Combine all ingredients in a bowl.
2. Pour mixture into the freezer can of an ice-cream freezer, and freeze according to manufacturer's instructions. Spoon ice cream into a freezer-safe container; cover and freeze 1 hour or until firm. Yield: 6 cups (serving size: ¼ cup).

CALORIES 59 (17% from fat); FAT 1.1g (sat 0.6g, mono 0.3g, poly 0g); PROTEIN 1.6g; CARB 10.2g; FIBER 0g; CHOL 5mg; IRON 0mg; SODIUM 48mg; CALC 61mg

ORIENTAL FLANK STEAK WITH ASPARAGUS AND WILD-RICE PILAF

*A **sharp chef's knife** lets you cut the steak into the thin strips that carry the flavors in this peppery entrée.*

16 asparagus spears
⅓ cup low-sodium soy sauce
¼ cup dry sherry
½ teaspoon black pepper
⅛ teaspoon ground red pepper
1 garlic clove, minced
1 (1-pound) flank steak or boned top round steak
4 cups sliced spinach
2 cups cooked wild rice
½ cup finely chopped celery
2 teaspoons dark sesame oil
⅔ cup chopped green onions

1. Snap off tough ends of asparagus. Cook asparagus in boiling water 2 minutes or until crisp-tender. Drain well, and chill.
2. Combine soy sauce and next 4 ingredients. Set aside ⅓ cup soy sauce mixture. Place remaining soy sauce mixture, asparagus, and steak in a zip-top plastic bag; seal. Marinate in refrigerator 1 hour, turning occasionally.
3. Remove asparagus and steak from bag, and discard marinade. Place a grill pan over medium-high heat until hot. Add asparagus and steak, and cook steak 3 minutes on each side or until desired degree of doneness, turning asparagus as needed. Place steak on a platter, and cover with foil. Let stand 5 minutes. Cut steak diagonally across grain into thin slices.
4. Combine ⅓ cup reserved soy sauce mixture, spinach, rice, celery, oil, and onions; toss to coat. Divide asparagus, steak, and wild-rice pilaf evenly among 4 plates. Yield: 4 servings (serving size: 4 asparagus spears, 3 ounces steak, and 1 cup wild-rice pilaf).

CALORIES 362 (39% from fat); FAT 15.5g (sat 5.9g, mono 6.3g, poly 1.6g); PROTEIN 28.9g; CARB 26.7g; FIBER 5.5g; CHOL 60mg; IRON 5mg; SODIUM 427mg; CALC 97mg

Easier Than You Think

All you need for wholesome, homemade yeast bread is your hands—and an appetite for the best loaf you'll ever slice.

"All my life I've relished good bread and loved the resilience of dough in my hands, the relaxed rhythm of kneading, the fragrance of baking, the beautiful even-grained cross-section of a well-risen loaf," James Beard once wrote. And anyone who's had the experience knows the feeling.

We're sure you'll find making bread by hand a rewarding experience; however, all these recipes (except the Cinnamon-Bun Bread, page 20) can be made in a bread machine. Simply follow the manufacturer's instructions for placing ingredients in the bread pan and selecting the right cycle.

HOMEMADE WHITE BREAD

1 package dry yeast (about 2¼ teaspoons)
1 tablespoon sugar
1⅔ cups warm fat-free milk (100° to 110°)
2 tablespoons butter or stick margarine, melted
4¾ cups all-purpose flour, divided
1½ teaspoons salt
 Cooking spray

1. Dissolve yeast and sugar in warm milk in a large bowl; let stand 5 minutes. Stir in butter. Lightly spoon flour into dry measuring cups; level with a knife. Add 4¼ cups flour and salt to yeast mixture; stir until blended. Turn dough out onto a floured surface. Knead until smooth and elastic (about 10 minutes); add enough of remaining flour, 1 tablespoon at a time, to prevent dough from sticking to hands (dough will feel tacky).

2. Place dough in a large bowl coated with cooking spray, turning to coat top. Cover and let rise in a warm place (85°), free from drafts, 1 hour or until doubled in size. Punch dough down; let rest 5 minutes. Roll into a 14 x 7-inch rectangle on a floured surface. Roll up rectangle tightly, starting with a short edge, pressing firmly to eliminate air pockets; pinch seam and ends to seal. Place roll, seam side down, in a 9 x 5-inch loaf pan coated with cooking spray. Cover and let rise 1 hour or until doubled in size.

3. Preheat oven to 350°.

4. Uncover dough. Bake at 350° for 45 minutes or until loaf is browned on bottom and sounds hollow when tapped. Remove loaf from pan, and cool on a wire rack. Yield: 1 loaf, 16 servings (serving size: 1 slice).

CALORIES 162 (11% from fat); FAT 1.9g (sat 0.4g, mono 0.7g, poly 0.6g); PROTEIN 4.9g; CARB 30.5g; FIBER 1.1g; CHOL 1mg; IRON 1.8mg; SODIUM 219mg; CALC 38mg

Cheese-Bread Variation:

You can use almost any kind of cheese in this bread; make sure it's one with a strong flavor. Extra-sharp Cheddar, Parmesan, or Romano are great choices.

Add 1 cup (4 ounces) shredded reduced-fat extra-sharp Cheddar cheese with the 4¼ cups flour and salt. Proceed with recipe.

CALORIES 176 (17% from fat); FAT 3.3g (sat 1.2g, mono 1.1g, poly 0.6g); PROTEIN 6.8g; CARB 29.3g; FIBER 1.1g; CHOL 5mg; IRON 1.7mg; SODIUM 301mg; CALC 100mg

Herb-Bread Variation:

Add ½ cup grated Parmesan cheese, 1 teaspoon each of onion flakes, dried oregano, and dried basil, and ½ teaspoon each of garlic powder and coarsely ground black pepper with the 4¼ cups flour and salt. Proceed with recipe.

CALORIES 175 (14% from fat); FAT 2.7g (sat 0.9g, mono 0.9g, poly 0.6g); PROTEIN 6g; CARB 30.9g; FIBER 1.2g; CHOL 2mg; IRON 2mg; SODIUM 297mg; CALC 76mg

ANADAMA BREAD

1 package dry yeast (about 2¼ teaspoons)
¼ cup molasses
1¼ cups warm water (100° to 110°)
2 tablespoons butter or stick margarine, melted
3½ cups all-purpose flour, divided
¾ cup stone-ground cornmeal
2 teaspoons salt
 Cooking spray

1. Dissolve yeast and molasses in warm water in a large bowl, and let stand 5 minutes. Stir in butter. Lightly spoon flour into dry measuring cups, and level with a knife. Add 3 cups flour, cornmeal, and salt to yeast mixture; stir until blended. Turn dough out onto a lightly floured surface. Knead until smooth and elastic (about 8 minutes), adding enough of remaining flour, 1 tablespoon at a time, to prevent dough from sticking to hands (dough will feel tacky).

2. Place dough in a large bowl coated with cooking spray, turning to coat top. Cover and let rise in a warm place (85°), free from drafts, 1 hour or until doubled in size. Punch dough down; let rest 5 minutes. Roll into a 14 x 7-inch rectangle on a floured surface. Roll up rectangle tightly, starting with a short edge, pressing firmly to eliminate air pockets; pinch seam and ends to seal. Place roll, seam side down, in a 9 x 5-inch loaf pan coated with cooking spray. Cover and let rise 1 hour or until doubled in size.

3. Preheat oven to 350°.

4. Uncover dough. Bake at 350° for 45 minutes or until loaf is browned on bottom and sounds hollow when tapped. Remove from pan; cool on a wire rack. Yield: 1 loaf, 16 servings (serving size: 1 slice).

CALORIES 148 (12% from fat); FAT 2g (sat 0.4g, mono 0.7g, poly 0.7g); PROTEIN 3.5g; CARB 28.9g; FIBER 1.5g; CHOL 0mg; IRON 1.8mg; SODIUM 314mg; CALC 16mg

❶ Proofing the Yeast

Making sure that your yeast is alive, a process known as proofing, is the most crucial step in baking bread. That's because if the yeast is dead, it can't leaven your bread. Live yeast will swell and foam (or activate) a few minutes after it's stirred into the warm liquid.

❷ Making the Dough

To make the initial bread dough, add most of the flour to the liquid ingredients all at once, and stir just until the mixture is combined. (Be sure to save some of the flour for kneading.) Then dump the dough onto a floured surface, and you're ready to knead.

❸ Kneading the Dough

Knead your dough with authority—push it out with the heels of your hands, fold it over, give it a quarter-turn, and repeat. You may not use all of the remaining flour—in fact, try to use as little of it as possible. After about 10 minutes of kneading, the dough should be smooth and elastic but still feel tacky.

❹ The First Rising

Place the dough in a large bowl because during this rising, the dough will double in size. During the rising, cover the bowl with a slightly damp lightweight dish towel.

❺ The Touch Test

To tell when the dough has risen enough, simply press a finger into it. If an impression remains, the dough is ready. If the dough springs back, it needs more rising time.

❻ Punching It Down

Punch the dough down to deflate it. Then turn the dough out onto a floured surface for rolling.

❼ Rolling It Out

To shape the bread, begin by rolling it out. Lift the rolling pin up slightly as you near each end of the rectangular shape.

❽ Rolling It Up

You're almost there, but remember: Rolling up the dough, or shaping, is just as important as rolling it out. The purpose is to eliminate air bubbles, giving a better crumb—or texture—to the bread. To accomplish this, roll the dough tightly, pressing firmly as you go.

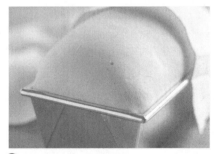

❾ The Second Rising

Once you roll up the dough and place it in a loaf pan, let it rise a second time. Watch carefully. If the dough rises too much and starts to fall, the bread will be dense. To avoid this problem, check the dough to be sure it has not begun to deflate. Once it's doubled in size, the dough is ready to bake.

WHOLE-WHEAT WALNUT BREAD

1 package dry yeast (about
    2¼ teaspoons)
¼ cup honey
1¾ cups warm water (100° to
    110°)
2 tablespoons plain low-fat
    yogurt or low-fat sour cream
2 tablespoons vegetable oil
3 cups all-purpose flour, divided
2 cups whole-wheat flour
⅓ cup coarsely chopped walnuts
    or pecans, toasted
2 teaspoons salt
    Cooking spray

1. Dissolve yeast and honey in warm water in a large bowl; let stand 5 minutes. Stir in yogurt and oil. Lightly spoon flours into dry measuring cups; level with a knife. Add 2½ cups all-purpose flour, whole-wheat flour, walnuts, and salt to yeast mixture; stir until blended. Turn dough out onto a lightly floured surface. Knead until smooth and elastic (about 10 minutes); add enough of remaining flour, 1 tablespoon at a time, to prevent dough from sticking to hands (dough will feel tacky).
2. Place dough in a large bowl coated with cooking spray, turning to coat top. Cover and let rise in a warm place (85°), free from drafts, 1 hour or until doubled in size. Punch dough down; let rest 5 minutes. Roll into a 14 x 7-inch rectangle on a floured surface. Roll up rectangle tightly, starting with a short edge, pressing firmly to eliminate air pockets; pinch seam and ends to seal. Place roll, seam side down, in a 9 x 5-inch loaf pan coated with cooking spray. Cover and let rise 30 minutes or until doubled in size.
3. Preheat oven to 350°.
4. Uncover dough. Bake at 350° for 45 minutes or until loaf is browned on bottom and sounds hollow when tapped. Remove from pan; cool on a wire rack. Yield: 1 loaf, 16 servings (serving size: 1 slice).

CALORIES 186 (18% from fat); FAT 3.8g (sat 0.5g, mono 0.9g, poly 2g); PROTEIN 5.4g; CARB 33.7g; FIBER 2.8g; CHOL 0mg; IRON 1.8mg; SODIUM 296mg; CALC 14mg

CINNAMON-BUN BREAD

(pictured on page 38)

Reminiscent of cinnamon rolls, this bread received the highest rating in our Test Kitchens.

Bread:

1 package dry yeast (about
    2¼ teaspoons)
¼ cup granulated sugar, divided
1⅔ cups warm fat-free milk
    (100° to 110°)
¼ cup butter or stick margarine,
    melted
4 teaspoons vanilla extract
2 large egg yolks
5 cups all-purpose flour, divided
2 teaspoons salt
    Cooking spray
⅔ cup packed brown sugar
2 teaspoons ground cinnamon
½ cup apricot preserves, melted

Glaze:

1 tablespoon butter or stick
    margarine, softened
1 cup sifted powdered sugar
1 tablespoon fat-free milk
½ teaspoon vanilla extract

1. To prepare bread, dissolve yeast and 1 tablespoon granulated sugar in warm milk in a large bowl; let stand 5 minutes. Stir in ¼ cup butter, vanilla, and egg yolks. Lightly spoon flour into dry measuring cups, and level with a knife. Add 4½ cups flour, 3 tablespoons granulated sugar, and salt to yeast mixture; stir to form a soft dough. Turn dough out onto a floured surface. Knead until smooth and elastic (about 10 minutes); add enough of remaining flour, 1 tablespoon at a time, to prevent dough from sticking to hands (dough will feel tacky).
2. Place dough in a large bowl coated with cooking spray, turning to coat top. Cover and let rise in a warm place (85°), free from drafts, 1 hour or until doubled in size. Punch dough down, and let rest 5 minutes. Divide in half.

Working with one portion at a time (cover remaining dough to keep from drying), roll each portion into a 14 x 7-inch rectangle on a floured surface. Combine brown sugar and cinnamon. Sprinkle each dough portion with half of brown sugar mixture, leaving ½-inch borders. Roll up each dough rectangle tightly, starting with a short edge, pressing firmly to eliminate air pockets, and pinch seams and ends to seal. Cut each dough roll crosswise into 3 pieces. Place 3 pieces, cut sides up, into each of 2 (8 x 4-inch) loaf pans coated with cooking spray. Cover and let rise 30 minutes or until dough is doubled in size.
3. Preheat oven to 350°.
4. Uncover dough, and bake at 350° for 35 minutes or until loaves are browned on bottoms and sound hollow when tapped. Cool in pans 10 minutes on a wire rack, and remove from pans. Brush tops of loaves with melted preserves. Cool loaves on rack.
5. To prepare glaze, beat 1 tablespoon butter at low speed of a mixer until creamy. Add powdered sugar, 1 tablespoon milk, and ½ teaspoon vanilla, beating just until blended. Spread over tops of loaves. Yield: 2 loaves, 12 servings per loaf (serving size: 1 slice).

CALORIES 198 (15% from fat); FAT 3.2g (sat 0.7g, mono 1.3g, poly 0.9g); PROTEIN 3.7g; CARB 38.5g; FIBER 0.9g; CHOL 19mg; IRON 1.5mg; SODIUM 239mg; CALC 38mg

PICKING A PAN

The type of pan you use to bake your bread does make a difference in the final product. We tested all our recipes in shiny metal loaf pans. If you're using a dark metal loaf pan or a glass dish, lower the oven temperature by 25°.

Romancing the Soup

The popular sopas *and* caldos *of Mexico are the stuff of nourishing meals and lasting memories.*

So central are soups to Mexican cooking that many home-style Mexican restaurants, even when they've run out of most menu items, will still offer you a beautifully prepared bowl of soup whipped up from an omnipresent meat-based stock. Indeed, soups are the measure of a serious restaurant in Mexico. Soups often launch a *comida corrida* (elaborate meal), much like salad in the United States.

Mexican soups easily translate into substantial and healthful one-dish meals. Their ingredients are simple and accessible, from dried chiles to the basic staples of the American diet. Beans, rice, corn, and light sour cream plump up aromatic broths into full dinners. Soft corn tortillas, cut into strips and baked crisp in the oven, make guiltless garnishes.

CHICKEN STOCK

- 8 cups water
- 1 teaspoon salt
- 1 (3½-pound) chicken
- 1 medium onion, unpeeled and sliced
- 1 medium tomato, sliced
- 6 garlic cloves, sliced
- 3 bay leaves
- 1 tablespoon cider vinegar

1. Combine first 7 ingredients in a large Dutch oven; cover and bring to a boil over medium heat. Reduce heat; simmer 40 minutes or until chicken is done. Remove chicken from cooking liquid; cool. Remove chicken from bones; reserve meat for another use. Return bones and skin to cooking liquid; stir in vinegar. Cover and simmer 1 hour. Strain stock through a sieve into a large bowl; discard solids. Cover and chill stock 8 hours. Skim solidified fat from surface of stock; discard. Yield: 8 cups (serving size: 1 cup).

CALORIES 26 (35% from fat); FAT 1g (sat 0.3g, mono 0.3g, poly 0.2g); PROTEIN 4g; CARB 0.1g; FIBER 0g; CHOL 12mg; IRON 0.2mg; SODIUM 304mg; CALC 2mg

SOPA CALDOSA

This popular soup from the Oaxaca region of Mexico features chorizo *(pronounced chor-EE-zoh), a coarsely ground pork sausage flavored with chili powder, garlic, and other seasonings. We use a simple, homemade Mexican Chorizo that's easy to put together. You can substitute a soft commercial chorizo that's found in most supermarkets, but it will be higher in fat.*

- 2 bacon slices, cut into ½-inch pieces
- 8 cups thinly sliced green cabbage (about 1 pound)
- 1 cup chopped onion
- 1 garlic clove, minced
- 5 cups Chicken Stock (see recipe) or 2½ (16-ounce) cans fat-free, less-sodium chicken broth
- 1 (15½-ounce) can chickpeas (garbanzo beans), drained
- 1 (14.5-ounce) can whole tomatoes, undrained and chopped
- Mexican Chorizo
- 3 tablespoons chopped fresh parsley

1. Cook bacon pieces in a large Dutch oven over medium-high heat until crisp. Add cabbage, onion, and garlic; sauté 10 minutes. Add Chicken Stock, chickpeas, and tomatoes. Bring to a boil; reduce heat, and simmer 10 minutes. Ladle soup into each of 6 bowls; top with Mexican Chorizo and parsley. Yield: 6 servings (serving size: 1⅓ cups soup, ¼ cup Mexican Chorizo, and 1½ teaspoons parsley).

CALORIES 236 (29% from fat); FAT 7.6g (sat 2.1g, mono 2.8g, poly 1.9g); PROTEIN 18.6g; CARB 25.4g; FIBER 5.2g; CHOL 35mg; IRON 3.5mg; SODIUM 655mg; CALC 101mg

Mexican Chorizo:

- ½ pound boned pork loin
- 2 tablespoons cider vinegar
- 1 tablespoon chili powder
- 1½ teaspoons paprika
- 1 teaspoon vegetable oil
- ½ teaspoon sugar
- ½ teaspoon dried oregano
- ½ teaspoon ground cumin
- ¼ teaspoon salt
- 1 garlic clove, crushed

1. Trim fat from pork. Combine all ingredients in a food processor, and pulse until well-blended. Place mixture in a zip-top bag; seal and marinate in refrigerator 8 hours or overnight.
2. Place a medium skillet over medium-high heat until hot. Add pork mixture; cook 5 minutes or until done, stirring to crumble. Yield: 1½ cups (serving size: ¼ cup).

TALK SOUP

Sopas (soups) range from thick, creamy purees to delicate broths, but *caldos* (broths) are always stock-based. *Sopa seca* (dry soup), which you'll find on many Mexican menus, is not actually sopa at all, but rice or pasta cooked in broth. And then there's *menudo* (tripe soup). Legions of tequila-lovers swear by *menudo's* curative powers on a hangover.

SOPA RANCHERA

Soup:

- 1 teaspoon vegetable oil
- 1 cup chopped onion
- ½ teaspoon dried oregano
- ½ teaspoon ground cumin
- 1 garlic clove, minced
- 6 cups Chicken Stock (page 21) or 3 (16-ounce) cans fat-free, less-sodium chicken broth
- 1¾ cups cubed peeled baking potato
- 1 (15-ounce) can chickpeas (garbanzo beans), drained
- 2 cups shredded cooked chicken breast (about 8 ounces)
- 1 cup frozen whole-kernel corn, thawed
- ¾ teaspoon salt
- 1 zucchini, quartered lengthwise and sliced (about 1½ cups)
- 1 cup diced tomato
- ⅓ cup chopped fresh cilantro

Toppings:

- ⅔ cup finely chopped onion
- ⅔ cup chopped fresh cilantro
- ⅔ cup low-fat sour cream
- ⅔ cup (2½ ounces) shredded queso quesadilla cheese or reduced-fat Monterey Jack cheese
- 10 lime wedges

1. To prepare soup, heat oil in a large Dutch oven over medium-high heat. Add 1 cup onion; sauté 3 minutes. Add oregano, cumin, and garlic; sauté 1 minute. Add Chicken Stock, potato, and chickpeas; bring to a boil, and cook 5 minutes. Add chicken, corn, salt, and zucchini; cook 5 minutes. Stir in tomato and ⅓ cup cilantro; cook 2 minutes.
2. Ladle 1 cup soup into each of 10 bowls, and top each with 1 tablespoon finely chopped onion, 1 tablespoon cilantro, 1 tablespoon sour cream, and 1 tablespoon cheese. Serve with lime wedges. Yield: 10 servings.

CALORIES 208 (31% from fat); FAT 7.2g (sat 2.9g, mono 2.2g, poly 1.3g); PROTEIN 16.1g; CARB 21.2g; FIBER 3g; CHOL 39mg; IRON 2.2mg; SODIUM 498mg; CALC 119mg

CORN TORTILLA SOUP

Soup:

- 2 onions, peeled and quartered
- 2 tomatoes, cored and quartered
- 1 teaspoon vegetable oil
- 1½ teaspoons dried oregano
- 1½ teaspoons ground cumin
- 2 garlic cloves, minced
- 6 cups Chicken Stock (page 21) or 3 (16-ounce) cans fat-free, less-sodium chicken broth
- ½ teaspoon salt

Toppings:

- 3 (6-inch) corn tortillas, cut into ¼-inch strips
- 1½ cups shredded cooked chicken breast (about 6 ounces)
- ½ cup (2 ounces) shredded part-skim Oaxaca cheese or reduced-fat Monterey Jack cheese
- 6 lime wedges

1. To prepare soup, combine onion and tomato in a blender or food processor; process until smooth. Heat oil in a Dutch oven over medium-high heat until hot. Add oregano, cumin, and garlic, and sauté 10 seconds. Add pureed onion mixture to pan (mixture will boil vigorously), and cook 1 minute. Stir in Chicken Stock and salt; bring to a boil. Reduce heat, and simmer 15 minutes.
2. Preheat oven to 350°.
3. To prepare tortilla strips, place in a single layer on a jelly-roll pan. Bake at 350° for 12 minutes or until tortilla strips are toasted.
4. Ladle soup into each of 6 bowls, and top with baked tortilla strips, shredded chicken, and cheese. Serve with lime wedges. Yield: 6 servings (serving size: 1⅓ cups soup, ¼ cup chicken, about 3 tablespoons tortilla strips, and about 1 tablespoon cheese).

CALORIES 165 (30% from fat); FAT 5.5g (sat 2.1g, mono 1.6g, poly 1.1g); PROTEIN 17g; CARB 12.6g; FIBER 2.2g; CHOL 41mg; IRON 1.5mg; SODIUM 608mg; CALC 118mg

SEAFOOD CHILPACHOLE

This favorite soup (pronounced CHIL-pa-CHOL) from the Veracruz region along the Gulf of Mexico is the essence of practicality, generally made not from any one type of seafood, but with whatever is fresh and available at the time.

- 1 pound unpeeled medium shrimp
- 7 cups Chicken Stock (page 21) or 3½ (16-ounce) cans fat-free, less-sodium chicken broth
- 3 garlic cloves, sliced
- 2 (6-inch) corn tortillas
- ½ teaspoon salt
- ½ teaspoon dried oregano
- 1 (14.5-ounce) can whole tomatoes, undrained
- 1 onion, quartered
- 1 drained canned chipotle chile in adobo sauce
- 1 teaspoon vegetable oil
- 1 pound red snapper or other firm white fish fillets, cut into 1-inch pieces
- 7 lime wedges

1. Peel shrimp, reserving shells. Cut shrimp in half lengthwise; cover and chill. Combine reserved shrimp shells, Chicken Stock, and garlic in a large saucepan. Bring mixture to a simmer, and cook 15 minutes. Strain through a colander into a bowl, reserving broth mixture. Discard shrimp shells. Return broth mixture to saucepan.
2. Add tortillas to broth mixture; let stand 10 seconds or until soft. Remove tortillas from broth. Place tortillas, salt, and next 4 ingredients in a blender; process until well-blended. Heat oil in a large nonstick skillet over medium-high heat; add tortilla mixture. Cook 5 minutes, stirring frequently. Stir tortilla mixture into broth mixture. Bring to a boil; add shrimp and fish. Reduce heat; simmer 3 minutes or until seafood is done. Serve with lime wedges. Yield: 7 servings (serving size: 1½ cups).

CALORIES 185 (18% from fat); FAT 3.7g (sat 0.8g, mono 0.9g, poly 1.3g); PROTEIN 28.4g; CARB 8.3g; FIBER 1.1g; CHOL 110mg; IRON 2.1mg; SODIUM 702mg; CALC 83mg

BLACK-BEAN SOUP

Creamy bean soups of this type are served all over Mexico. Crunchy toppings add textural contrast that's pleasing to the eyes as well as the taste buds.

Soup:

- 1 pound dried black beans
- 2 bacon slices, cut into ½-inch pieces
- 1 cup chopped onion
- 1 teaspoon dried thyme
- 3 garlic cloves, sliced
- 2 bay leaves
- 5 cups Chicken Stock (page 21) or 2½ (16-ounce) cans fat-free, less-sodium chicken broth
- 3 cups water
- ½ teaspoon salt

Toppings:

- 3 (6-inch) corn tortillas, cut into ¼-inch strips
- 6 tablespoons low-fat sour cream
- 6 tablespoons minced fresh onion
- 6 lime wedges

1. To prepare soup, sort and wash beans; place in a large Dutch oven. Cover with water to 2 inches above beans; bring to a boil, and cook 2 minutes. Remove from heat; cover and let stand 1 hour. Drain.
2. Cook bacon in pan over medium heat until crisp. Remove bacon from pan. Add chopped onion, thyme, garlic, and bay leaves to bacon drippings in pan; sauté for 4 minutes. Add beans, bacon, Chicken Stock, and 3 cups water to pan. Bring to a boil; reduce heat, and simmer 1½ hours, stirring occasionally. Add salt, and simmer 30 minutes or until beans are tender. Discard bay leaves. Place half of bean mixture in a blender or food processor; process until smooth. Pour bean puree into a large bowl. Repeat procedure with remaining bean mixture. Add to bowl.
3. Preheat oven to 350°.
4. To prepare tortilla strips, place strips in a single layer on a jelly-roll pan.

Bake at 350° for 12 minutes or until tortilla strips are toasted.
5. Ladle soup into each of 6 bowls, and top with tortilla strips, sour cream, and minced onion. Serve with lime wedges. Yield: 6 servings (serving size: 1½ cups soup, about 3 tablespoons tortilla strips, 1 tablespoon sour cream, and 1 tablespoon minced onion).

CALORIES 360 (12% from fat); FAT 5.3g (sat 2.1g, mono 1.5g, poly 1.1g); PROTEIN 22.1g; CARB 58.5g; FIBER 11.4g; CHOL 18mg; IRON 4.5mg; SODIUM 520mg; CALC 148mg

CORN-POBLANO SOUP WITH SALSA VERDE

Salsa verde (green sauce) is added to this soup in Mexico to produce a vibrant color and to complement the underlying flavor of the roasted poblanos.

- 2 large poblano chiles (about 8 ounces)
- 2 teaspoons butter or stick margarine, divided
- ½ cup chopped onion
- 1 garlic clove, minced
- ½ cup evaporated fat-free milk
- 2 tablespoons cornstarch
- 2 (10-ounce) packages frozen whole-kernel corn, thawed
- 4 cups Chicken Stock (page 21) or 2 (16-ounce) cans fat-free, less-sodium chicken broth
- ¼ cup (2 ounces) ⅓-less-fat cream cheese
- ¾ teaspoon salt
- ¼ teaspoon black pepper
- 7 tablespoons Salsa Verde

1. Preheat broiler.
2. Place chiles on a foil-lined baking sheet, and broil 10 minutes or until chiles are blackened, turning occasionally. Place chiles in a zip-top plastic bag; seal. Let stand 15 minutes. Peel chiles; cut in half lengthwise, discarding seeds and membranes. Cut into ½-inch pieces; set aside.
3. Heat 1 teaspoon butter in a small skillet over medium heat. Add onion

and garlic; sauté 5 minutes. Remove from heat.
4. Combine onion mixture, milk, cornstarch, and corn in a blender or food processor; process until smooth.
5. Heat 1 teaspoon butter in a large saucepan over medium-high heat. Add corn mixture to pan (mixture will boil vigorously), and cook for 3 minutes. Add Chicken Stock, and bring to a boil. Stir in chiles, cream cheese, salt, and pepper; reduce heat, and cook for 5 minutes or until cheese melts. Serve with Salsa Verde. Yield: 7 servings (serving size: 1 cup soup and 1 tablespoon salsa).

CALORIES 147 (20% from fat); FAT 3.2g (sat 1.2g, mono 1.2g, poly 0.5g); PROTEIN 7.6g; CARB 25g; FIBER 2.8g; CHOL 12mg; IRON 0.8mg; SODIUM 549mg; CALC 78mg

Salsa Verde:

- 6 tomatillos (about 8 ounces)
- 1 jalapeño pepper
- ¼ teaspoon salt
- 1 garlic clove, sliced
- Cooking spray
- ¼ cup water
- ¼ cup minced fresh cilantro

1. Discard husks and stems from tomatillos. Place tomatillos and jalapeño in a saucepan; cover with water, and bring to a boil. Cook 15 minutes or until tender, and drain.
2. Combine tomatillos, jalapeño, salt, and garlic in a blender or food processor; process until smooth.
3. Place a nonstick skillet coated with cooking spray over medium-high heat until hot. Pour tomatillo mixture into pan (mixture will boil vigorously), and cook 2 minutes. Add ¼ cup water; cook 1 minute or until thoroughly heated. Stir in cilantro. Yield: ½ cup (serving size: 1 tablespoon).

CALORIES 5 (18% from fat); FAT 0.1g; PROTEIN 0.2g; CARB 0.9g; FIBER 0.2g; CHOL 0mg; IRON 0.1mg; SODIUM 39mg; CALC 4mg

SOPA DE AJO

This simple garlic soup relies on a procedure similar to that used to make egg drop soup. Mashing the garlic into a paste with paprika and ground cumin intensifies the flavor in the broth.

- 1 teaspoon olive oil
- 6 garlic cloves
- 1 tablespoon paprika
- ¼ teaspoon ground cumin
- 6 cups Chicken Stock (page 21) or 3 (16-ounce) cans fat-free, less-sodium chicken broth
- 1 chipotle chile (or a dried ancho or pasilla chile)
- 2 large eggs, lightly beaten
- 5 (1-ounce) slices diagonally cut French bread (about 1 inch thick), toasted
- 1¼ cups diced tomato
- 5 tablespoons sliced green onions
- 5 tablespoons (1¼ ounces) shredded Manchego cheese or reduced-fat Monterey Jack cheese

1. Heat oil in a large Dutch oven over medium heat. Add garlic; sauté 5 minutes or until golden. Remove garlic from pan. Combine garlic, paprika, and cumin in a small bowl; mash with a fork until smooth.

2. Return garlic mixture to pan, and add Chicken Stock and chile. Bring to a simmer over medium heat, and cook 10 minutes. Discard chile. Slowly pour beaten eggs into soup, stirring constantly. Immediately remove from heat. Place 1 bread slice in each of 5 soup bowls, and top each bread slice with ¼ cup tomato and 1 tablespoon green onions. Ladle 1 cup soup into each bowl; sprinkle each serving with 1 tablespoon cheese. Yield: 5 servings.

CALORIES 216 (16% from fat); FAT 6.9g (sat 2.2g, mono 2.6g, poly 1.2g); PROTEIN 13.4g; CARB 23.3g; FIBER 1.6g; CHOL 109mg; IRON 2mg; SODIUM 633mg; CALC 100mg

LIGHTEN UP

Special Delivery

Post Office Supervisor Dan Mayo asked us to lighten a favorite rice pudding.

Dan's dessert is one punishing pudding. But by reducing the butter, switching from whole to reduced-fat milk, and using low-fat sour cream for the heavy stuff, we knocked off nearly 13 grams of fat and more than 80 calories per serving.

BEFORE & AFTER	
SERVING SIZE	
¾ cup	
CALORIES	
401	316
FAT	
20.8g	7.9g
PERCENT OF TOTAL CALORIES	
47%	23%
CHOLESTEROL	
88mg	44mg

RICE PUDDING

If you want a more traditional rice pudding, replace the amaretto with ¼ cup water (no almond extract), and increase the vanilla extract to 1 tablespoon.

- 8 cups 2% reduced-fat milk
- 1 cup sugar
- 2 tablespoons butter or stick margarine
- 1½ cups uncooked long-grain rice
- ¼ teaspoon salt
- 1 large egg
- ½ cup golden raisins
- ¼ cup amaretto (almond-flavored liqueur) or ¼ cup water and ½ teaspoon almond extract
- 1½ teaspoons vanilla extract
- 1 (8-ounce) carton low-fat sour cream
- Ground cinnamon (optional)

1. Combine first 3 ingredients in a heavy Dutch oven; bring to a simmer over medium-high heat (about 15 minutes). Stir in rice and salt; reduce heat to medium, and cook 45 minutes or until rice is tender. Stir occasionally, about every 5 to 10 minutes initially, and then as pudding begins to thicken, watch and stir every few minutes to prevent sticking. Do not boil. Place egg in a bowl; gradually add 1 cup hot rice mixture to egg, stirring constantly with a whisk. Return egg mixture to pan; cook 1 minute. Remove from heat. Add raisins, amaretto, vanilla, and sour cream; stir well. Sprinkle with cinnamon, if desired. Yield: 12 servings (serving size: ¾ cup).

CALORIES 316 (23% from fat); FAT 7.9g (sat 4.8g, mono 2.3g, poly 0.4g); PROTEIN 8.4g; CARB 50.7g; FIBER 0.6g; CHOL 44mg; IRON 1.3mg; SODIUM 165mg; CALC 231mg

PUDDING PATIENCE

The cooking time for this rice pudding may seem unusually long, but have patience. To achieve the creamy texture that makes this dessert special, the milk and rice must be brought to a simmer slowly to prevent scorching, and then cooked at a simmer for 45 minutes to coax the relatively small amount of rice to absorb the liquid. Stir the pudding initially every five or 10 minutes. Then, as the rice swells with milk and the mixture thickens, stir it nearly constantly. Be sure to adjust the heat, if necessary, in order to keep the pudding at a constant simmer.

What's Love Got to Do With It?

Do men and women have different ideas about making Valentine's Day dinners for each other? To find out, we went to two of our favorite TV hosts—Annabelle Gurwitch and Paul Gilmartin of TBS Superstation's Dinner & a Movie.

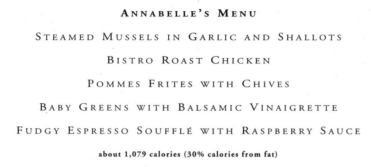

STEAMED MUSSELS IN GARLIC AND SHALLOTS

- 1 teaspoon olive oil
- ⅓ cup minced shallots
- 2 garlic cloves, minced
- 1 cup Riesling or other slightly sweet white wine
- 12 mussels (about 8 ounces), scrubbed and debearded
- 2 teaspoons chopped fresh thyme

1. Heat oil in a large nonstick skillet over medium heat. Add shallots and garlic; sauté 3 minutes, stirring occasionally. Add wine, and bring to a simmer. Add mussels; cover and cook 6 minutes or until shells open. Discard any unopened shells. Divide mussels evenly between 2 shallow dishes, and sprinkle with chopped thyme. Yield: 2 servings (serving size: 6 mussels and ⅓ cup sauce).

CALORIES 132 (30% from fat); FAT 4.4g (sat 0.7g, mono 2.2g, poly 0.8g); PROTEIN 12.5g; CARB 10.7g; FIBER 0.3g; CHOL 27mg; IRON 4.2mg; SODIUM 189mg; CALC 43mg

BISTRO ROAST CHICKEN

Serve the roasted heads of garlic on the side. Squeeze out the pulp and use it as a spread on baguette slices or as a condiment for the chicken.

- 2 chicken leg quarters (about 1½ pounds)
- 1 tablespoon chopped fresh or 1 teaspoon dried basil
- 1 tablespoon chopped fresh or 1 teaspoon dried thyme
- 1 tablespoon chopped fresh or 1 teaspoon dried rosemary, crushed
- 2 teaspoons olive oil
- ½ teaspoon salt
- ¼ teaspoon black pepper
- 2 whole garlic heads

1. Preheat oven to 375°.
2. Rinse chicken with cold water; pat dry. Trim excess fat. Loosen skin from thigh and leg by inserting fingers, gently pushing between skin and meat. Combine basil and next 5 ingredients. Rub herb mixture under loosened skin. Place chicken on a broiler pan. Insert meat thermometer into meaty part of thigh, making sure not to touch bone.
3. Remove white papery skin from garlic heads (do not peel or separate cloves). Wrap each head separately in foil; place on broiler pan with chicken. Bake at 375° for 45 minutes. Increase oven temperature to 450° (do not remove chicken from oven). Bake 30 minutes or until thermometer registers 180°. Cover chicken loosely with foil; let stand 10 minutes. Discard skin. Yield: 2 servings (serving size: 1 leg quarter and 1 garlic head).

CALORIES 358 (38% from fat); FAT 15.2g (sat 3.5g, mono 7g, poly 2.9g); PROTEIN 33.7g; CARB 22.4g; FIBER 1.3g; CHOL 100mg; IRON 4mg; SODIUM 682mg; CALC 165mg

POMMES FRITES WITH CHIVES

You can cook these potatoes with the Bistro Roast Chicken, (see recipe) during the last 30 minutes. Simply place the baking sheet on a lower rack in your oven.

- ¾ pound Yukon gold or red potatoes, cut into 3 x ¼-inch sticks
- 2 teaspoons olive oil
- 2 teaspoons chopped fresh or ½ teaspoon dried thyme
- ¼ teaspoon garlic salt
- Cooking spray
- 1 tablespoon chopped fresh chives

1. Preheat oven to 450°.
2. Combine first 4 ingredients in a large zip-top plastic bag; seal and shake to coat. Arrange potatoes in a single layer on a baking sheet coated with cooking spray.
3. Bake at 450° for 30 minutes, turning once. Toss potatoes with chopped chives. Yield: 2 servings (serving size: 1 cup).

CALORIES 230 (20% from fat); FAT 5g (sat 0.7g, mono 3.3g, poly 0.5g); PROTEIN 3.8g; CARB 43.2g; FIBER 3.2g; CHOL 0mg; IRON 2.8mg; SODIUM 275mg; CALC 28mg

Baby Greens with Balsamic Vinaigrette

1 garlic clove, halved
6 (½-inch-thick) slices French bread baguette
2 tablespoons balsamic vinegar
1 tablespoon water
2 teaspoons minced shallot
2 teaspoons olive oil
¼ teaspoon black pepper
⅛ teaspoon salt
8 cups gourmet salad greens

1. Preheat oven to 400°.
2. Rub garlic on one side of each bread slice, and place bread on a baking sheet. Bake at 400° for 4 minutes on each side or until golden.
3. Combine vinegar and next 5 ingredients in a small jar. Cover tightly, and shake vigorously. Combine vinaigrette and greens, and toss well. Serve salad with garlic croutons. Yield: 2 servings (serving size: 2 cups salad and 3 croutons).

CALORIES 163 (30% from fat); FAT 5.5g (sat 0.9g, mono 3.6g, poly 0.9g); PROTEIN 6.4g; CARB 22.4g; FIBER 4.6g; CHOL 1mg; IRON 3.4mg; SODIUM 330mg; CALC 98mg

Fudgy Espresso Soufflé with Raspberry Sauce

When this soufflé falls, it turns into a dense fudge cake.

½ cup unsweetened cocoa
6 tablespoons hot water
1 tablespoon instant espresso or 2 tablespoons instant coffee granules
2 tablespoons butter or stick margarine
3 tablespoons all-purpose flour
¾ cup 1% low-fat milk
¼ cup sugar
⅛ teaspoon salt
4 large egg whites
3 tablespoons sugar
Cooking spray
Raspberry Sauce

1. Preheat oven to 375°.
2. Combine first 3 ingredients, stirring until smooth. Set aside.
3. Melt butter in a small heavy saucepan over medium heat. Add flour; cook 1 minute, stirring constantly with a whisk. Gradually add milk, ¼ cup sugar, and salt; cook 3 minutes or until thick, stirring constantly. Remove from heat; stir in cocoa mixture. Spoon into a large bowl; cool slightly.
4. Beat egg whites at high speed of a mixer until foamy. Add 3 tablespoons sugar, 1 tablespoon at a time, beating until stiff peaks form. Gently fold 1 cup egg white mixture into cocoa mixture; gently fold in remaining egg white mixture. Spoon into a 1½-quart soufflé dish coated with cooking spray.
5. Bake at 375° for 45 minutes or until puffy and set. Serve warm with Raspberry Sauce. Yield: 6 servings (serving size: 1 wedge and 2 tablespoons sauce).

CALORIES 196 (24% from fat); FAT 5.2g (sat 1.5g, mono 1.8g, poly 1.3g); PROTEIN 6.2g; CARB 31.3g; FIBER 1.8g; CHOL 2mg; IRON 1.8mg; SODIUM 149mg; CALC 61mg

Raspberry Sauce:

This sauce is quite versatile. You can make it ahead, cover, and refrigerate. Serve it cold or at room temperature.

1 (10-ounce) package frozen raspberries in syrup, thawed and undrained
2 tablespoons water
2 teaspoons cornstarch

1. Drain raspberries, reserving syrup. Press raspberries through a sieve into a bowl, reserving puree; discard seeds. Combine water and cornstarch in a saucepan; stir until blended. Stir in reserved raspberry syrup and puree; bring to a boil, and cook 1 minute, stirring constantly. Pour into a bowl; cool. Yield: ¾ cup (serving size: 2 tablespoons).

Crispy Mozzarella Sticks Marinara

4 (3 x ½ x ½-inch) sticks part-skim mozzarella cheese (about 3 ounces)
2 teaspoons commercial pesto
4 sheets frozen phyllo dough, thawed
Olive oil-flavored cooking spray
¼ cup fat-free tomato-and-basil marinara sauce

1. Preheat oven to 400°.
2. Coat cheese with pesto.
3. Cut phyllo sheets in half crosswise to form 8 (13 x 9-inch) rectangles. Place 1 sheet on a work surface (cover remaining dough to keep from drying); coat with cooking spray. Place 1 sheet on top of first sheet. Fold in half crosswise to form a 9 x 6½-inch rectangle.
4. Place 1 stick of cheese at center of a short end of rectangle; fold long sides of phyllo over cheese, and coat with cooking spray. Starting with filled end, roll up phyllo. Coat with cooking spray. Place on a baking sheet coated with cooking spray. Repeat with remaining phyllo and cheese. Bake at 400° for 12 minutes or until golden brown.
5. Heat marinara sauce in a saucepan over medium-low heat. Serve sauce with cheese sticks. Yield: 2 servings (serving size: 2 cheese sticks and 2 tablespoons sauce).

CALORIES 275 (41% from fat); FAT 12.4g (sat 5.1g, mono 4.1g, poly 1.9g); PROTEIN 14.1g; CARB 25.1g; FIBER 0.2g; CHOL 25mg; IRON 2.3mg; SODIUM 439mg; CALC 318mg

POSOLE WITH TURKEY AND HEART-SHAPED CHIPOTLE GORDITAS

(pictured on page 39)

A gordita is a thick corn tortilla. Because gorditas are more practical to make in larger quantities, this recipe makes enough for two meals.

Gorditas:
- ⅔ cup masa harina or cornmeal
- ⅓ cup all-purpose flour
- 1 teaspoon baking powder
- ¼ teaspoon salt
- ⅓ cup water
- 1½ tablespoons vegetable oil
- 1½ teaspoons minced, seeded, canned chipotle chile in adobo sauce
- **Cooking spray**

Posole:
- 1½ teaspoons vegetable oil
- 1 cup chopped onion
- 4 garlic cloves, minced
- ¾ pound turkey tenderloin, cut into ¾-inch pieces
- 1 tablespoon adobo sauce (from canned chipotle chile)
- 1 (16-ounce) can fat-free, less-sodium chicken broth, divided
- 1 tablespoon all-purpose flour
- 1 (15.5-ounce) can white hominy, rinsed and drained
- 2 poblano chiles, seeded and chopped
- 3 tablespoons chopped fresh cilantro

1. Preheat oven to 400°.
2. To prepare gorditas, combine first 4 ingredients. Stir in water, 1½ tablespoons oil, and chipotle chile. Turn out onto a lightly floured surface; roll dough to a ¼-inch thickness. Cut with a sharp (1½-inch) heart-shaped cookie cutter into 12 gorditas. Place gorditas on a baking sheet coated with cooking spray; discard any remaining dough. Bake at 400° for 8 minutes. Reserve 6 gorditas for another use; refrigerate in an airtight container up to 1 week.
3. To prepare posole, heat 1½ teaspoons oil in a Dutch oven over medium heat. Add onion and garlic; sauté 5 minutes. Combine turkey and 1 tablespoon adobo sauce, tossing well to coat. Add turkey mixture to pan; sauté 3 minutes. Combine ¼ cup broth and 1 tablespoon flour. Add broth mixture, remaining broth, hominy, and poblano chiles to pan; bring to a boil. Reduce heat; simmer 15 minutes. Remove 2½ cups posole for another use; refrigerate in an airtight container up to 1 week, or freeze up to 3 months.
4. Arrange 6 gorditas on top of posole in pan; cover and simmer 5 minutes. Spoon 1¼ cups posole into each of 2 bowls, and top each serving with 3 gorditas. Sprinkle with cilantro. Yield: 2 servings.

CALORIES 373 (24% from fat); FAT 10g (sat 1.9g, mono 2.7g, poly 4.4g); PROTEIN 26.7g; CARB 42.2g; FIBER 3.9g; CHOL 51mg; IRON 4.1mg; SODIUM 770mg; CALC 147mg

"PAIR" SALAD WITH PEPPERCORN VINAIGRETTE

- 1 tablespoon honey
- 1 tablespoon raspberry or red wine vinegar
- 2 teaspoons Dijon mustard
- ¼ teaspoon freshly ground black pepper
- 4 large red leaf lettuce leaves
- 2 cups trimmed watercress
- 1 large ripe Comice pear, cored and sliced
- 2 tablespoons chopped walnuts, toasted

1. Combine first 4 ingredients in a small bowl; stir with a whisk. Arrange 2 lettuce leaves and 1 cup watercress on each of 2 salad plates. Top each serving with pear slices and 1 tablespoon chopped walnuts. Drizzle peppercorn vinaigrette over salads. Yield: 2 servings.

CALORIES 162 (29% from fat); FAT 5.3g (sat 0.3g, mono 1.1g, poly 3.1g); PROTEIN 3.5g; CARB 28.4g; FIBER 4.6g; CHOL 0mg; IRON 0.9mg; SODIUM 167mg; CALC 67mg

MARINATED STRAWBERRIES WITH MANGO SORBET

(pictured on page 40)

- 1½ cups sliced strawberries
- 1 tablespoon powdered sugar
- 2 teaspoons chopped fresh mint
- 1 cup mango sorbet or lime sherbet
- **Fresh mint sprigs (optional)**

1. Combine first 3 ingredients in a bowl. Cover strawberry mixture, and chill 2 hours. Spoon ½ cup strawberry mixture into each of 2 dessert bowls, and top each serving with ½ cup mango sorbet. Garnish with mint sprigs, if desired. Yield: 2 servings.

CALORIES 152 (8% from fat); FAT 1.3g (sat 0.5g, mono 0.3g, poly 0.3g); PROTEIN 1.6g; CARB 35.3g; FIBER 2.9g; CHOL 0mg; IRON 0.5mg; SODIUM 68mg; CALC 55mg

PAUL'S VALENTINE'S DAY DINNER ADVICE

1. *Don't get in over your head.* Stick to the recipes and ingredients that you know instead of trying a new or complicated recipe that may or may not impress your date.

2. *Use fresh ingredients.* For a few extra dollars or cents, your food will taste so much better. The difference between dried and fresh spices is incredible.

3. *Prepare.* If something can be done ahead of time without sacrificing the quality of the food, do it.

4. *Stick with a time line.* You may cook everything perfectly, but bad time management may leave something cooling off on the counter because you didn't plan what recipes should be made first and last.

5. *Dishes.* Relax and don't ruin the romantic mood by immediately doing the dishes.

Twice as Nice

Turning the first night's rave review into the second night's spectacular sequel makes weeknight dinner planning half as necessary—and twice as tasty.

At the end of the day, say, 5 o'clock, how functional is your brain? Are you thinking clearly, approaching dinner from an organized, well-planned perspective? Here's a solution: Extend pre-thinking a step further and plan two meals at once. It's not lazy; it's efficient. The trick is envisioning first-night dishes good in their own right but also convertible to the equally spectacular second meal you get out of them. Or put it this way: A good roasted chicken is very nice indeed, but to also end up with Enchiladas Verdes is twice as nice—spectacular, in fact.

To get the most from meals, make one recipe, and then use what's left another night for a new dish.

MAPLE-GLAZED ROASTED SALMON

¼ cup grated peeled fresh ginger
¼ cup rice vinegar or white wine vinegar
¼ cup maple syrup
1 (2½-pound) salmon fillet
6 shallots, halved lengthwise
½ teaspoon salt
¼ teaspoon black pepper
2 tablespoons maple syrup, divided
Chopped fresh parsley (optional)

1. Combine first 3 ingredients in a large platter. Add fish, skin side up, to ginger mixture. Cover and marinate in refrigerator 20 minutes. Remove fish from marinade; pat dry with paper towel to remove excess marinade.
2. Preheat oven to 450°.
3. Place a baking sheet in oven 5 minutes. Place shallots and fish, skin side down, on baking sheet; sprinkle with salt and pepper. Brush fish with 1 tablespoon syrup. Bake at 450° for 10 minutes. Brush with 1 tablespoon syrup; bake an additional 7 minutes or until fish flakes easily when tested with a fork. Sprinkle with parsley, if desired. Yield: 6 servings (serving size: 5 ounces fish and 2 shallot halves).

CALORIES 342 (41% from fat); FAT 15.6g (sat 2.7g, mono 7.5g, poly 3.4g); PROTEIN 38.8g; CARB 9g; FIBER 0g; CHOL 123mg; IRON 1mg; SODIUM 284mg; CALC 19mg

FINNISH SALMON-POTATO CHOWDER

Reserve 2 servings of the Maple-Glazed Roasted Salmon (see recipe), to make this chowder.

1 teaspoon butter or stick margarine
3 cups chopped onion
½ teaspoon celery salt
¼ cup all-purpose flour
1 (8-ounce) bottle clam juice
4 cups cubed peeled baking potato
1½ cups thinly sliced carrot
3½ cups 1% low-fat milk
10 ounces Maple-Glazed Roasted Salmon (see recipe)
2 tablespoons chopped fresh or 2 teaspoons dried dill
¼ teaspoon Worcestershire sauce

1. Melt butter in a Dutch oven over medium heat. Add chopped onion, and sauté for 5 minutes. Sprinkle onion mixture with celery salt. Stir in flour, and cook for 1 minute, stirring constantly. Gradually add clam juice. Bring mixture to a boil, and cook 1 minute or until thick, stirring constantly. Add potato cubes and carrot slices, and stir in milk. Bring to a boil; reduce heat, and simmer 10 minutes. Break Maple-Glazed Roasted Salmon into chunks; add salmon, chopped dill, and Worcestershire sauce to pan. Bring chowder to a boil; reduce heat, and simmer for 10 minutes or until potato is tender. Yield: 6 servings (serving size: 1½ cups).

CALORIES 311 (22% from fat); FAT 7.7g (sat 2g, mono 3.3g, poly 1.5g); PROTEIN 21.6g; CARB 39.1g; FIBER 4.2g; CHOL 47mg; IRON 1.9mg; SODIUM 386mg; CALC 224mg

DOUBLE-HERB ROASTED CHICKEN AND POTATOES

(pictured on page 39)

1 (5½-pound) roasting chicken
3 tablespoons chopped fresh or 1 tablespoon dried oregano, divided
2 garlic cloves, minced
8 fresh basil leaves
Cooking spray
8 red potatoes, quartered lengthwise
¼ teaspoon salt
¼ to ½ teaspoon black pepper

1. Preheat oven to 450°.
2. Remove and discard giblets and neck from chicken. Rinse chicken with cold water; pat dry. Trim excess fat. Starting at neck cavity, loosen skin from breast and drumsticks by inserting fingers, gently pushing between skin and meat.
3. Combine 2 tablespoons chopped oregano and garlic. Rub seasoning mixture under loosened chicken skin of breast and drumsticks. Carefully place basil leaves under loosened skin. Tie ends of legs with cord. Lift wing tips up and over back; tuck under chicken.
4. Place chicken, breast side up, on a broiler pan coated with cooking spray. Pierce skin several times with a meat fork. Arrange potatoes on rack around chicken. Coat chicken and potatoes with cooking spray, and sprinkle with 1 tablespoon oregano, salt, and pepper. Insert a meat thermometer into meaty part of thigh, making sure not to touch bone. Bake at 450° for 30 minutes. Reduce oven temperature to 350° (do not remove chicken from oven); bake an additional 45 minutes or until thermometer registers 180°. Cover chicken loosely with foil; let stand 10 minutes. Discard skin. Remove chicken from pan; place on a serving platter. Serve with roasted potatoes. Yield: 8 servings (serving size: 3 ounces chicken and 4 potato wedges).

CALORIES 249 (24% from fat); FAT 6.5g (sat 1.8g, mono 2.3g, poly 1.5g); PROTEIN 27.2g; CARB 19.4g; FIBER 2.1g; CHOL 76mg; IRON 2.7mg; SODIUM 155mg; CALC 37mg

Enchiladas Verdes

If you eat all of the Double-Herb Roasted Chicken (see recipe on previous page), *use a prepackaged rotisserie chicken (in the meat section of the supermarket) instead.*

Salsa verde:

 1 pound tomatillos (about 15)
 1¼ cups fat-free, less-sodium chicken broth
 ¼ teaspoon salt
 1 jalapeño pepper, seeded and chopped

Filling:

 2½ cups shredded Double-Herb Roasted Chicken (about 12 ounces) (see recipe on previous page)
 ½ cup (2 ounces) shredded asadero cheese or Asiago cheese
 ⅓ cup finely chopped onion
 ⅓ cup minced fresh cilantro
 ⅓ cup fat-free, less-sodium chicken broth
 ⅓ cup fat-free sour cream
 1 tablespoon fresh lime juice
 ½ teaspoon ground cumin
 ¼ teaspoon salt
 ⅛ teaspoon black pepper

Remaining ingredients:

 Cooking spray
 8 (6-inch) corn tortillas
 ¼ cup fat-free sour cream
 Sliced jalapeño pepper (optional)

1. To prepare salsa verde, discard husks and stems from tomatillos; cut into quarters. Combine tomatillos, 1¼ cups broth, ¼ teaspoon salt, and chopped jalapeño in a saucepan over medium heat. Bring to a boil; reduce heat, and simmer 15 minutes or until tomatillos are tender. Cool slightly. Place salsa verde in a blender or food processor, and process until smooth or mash with a potato masher. Place a large nonstick skillet over medium-high heat until hot.

Add salsa verde; cook until reduced to 2 cups (about 1 minute).
2. Preheat oven to 400°.
3. To prepare enchilada filling, combine chicken and next 9 ingredients in a large bowl.
4. Spread ½ cup salsa verde in bottom of a 13 x 9-inch baking dish coated with cooking spray. Warm tortillas according to package directions. Spoon about ⅓ cup chicken mixture down center of each tortilla; roll up. Arrange enchiladas, seam sides down, crosswise in dish. Pour remaining salsa verde evenly over enchiladas. Cover and bake at 400° for 10 minutes or until thoroughly heated. Serve with sour cream, and garnish with sliced jalapeño, if desired. Yield: 4 servings (serving size: 2 enchiladas and 1 tablespoon sour cream).

CALORIES 386 (27% from fat); FAT 11.5g (sat 3.9g, mono 3.4g, poly 2.3g); PROTEIN 36.5g; CARB 38.9g; FIBER 4.8g; CHOL 86mg; IRON 2.9mg; SODIUM 841mg; CALC 205mg

Loaded Baked Potatoes

(pictured on page 37)

This simple-but-delicious dish does double-duty as the basis of our Baked-Potato Soup (see recipe). *Just make sure to save half of the recipe (or four stuffed potato halves) for the soup.*

 4 large baking potatoes (about 12 ounces each)
 ½ cup 1% low-fat milk
 ⅓ cup (3 ounces) ⅓-less-fat cream cheese, softened
 ½ cup (2 ounces) crumbled feta cheese
 2 tablespoons minced fresh or 2 teaspoons dried oregano
 ½ teaspoon salt
 ¼ teaspoon black pepper
 ¼ cup thinly sliced green onions
 2 bacon slices, cooked and crumbled

1. Preheat oven to 400°.
2. Pierce potatoes with a fork; bake at 400° for 1 hour or until tender.

Cool slightly. Cut each potato in half lengthwise; scoop out pulp into a large bowl, leaving ¼-inch-thick shells. Mash pulp with a potato masher. Add milk and cream cheese to mashed potato in bowl, and stir with a whisk. Add feta cheese, oregano, salt, and pepper; stir well.
3. Spoon potato mixture into shells. Place on a baking sheet; bake at 400° for 15 minutes or until thoroughly heated. Sprinkle each serving with 1½ teaspoons green onions; top with bacon. Yield: 8 servings (serving size: 1 potato half).

CALORIES 251 (19% from fat); FAT 5.3g (sat 3.1g, mono 1.5g, poly 0.3g); PROTEIN 7g; CARB 44.7g; FIBER 3.2g; CHOL 17mg; IRON 2.7mg; SODIUM 320mg; CALC 87mg

Baked-Potato Soup

 2 teaspoons butter or stick margarine
 1 cup chopped onion
 ½ cup diced celery
 2 garlic cloves, minced
 1 bay leaf
 1½ cups 1% low-fat milk
 ½ teaspoon chopped fresh or ⅛ teaspoon dried thyme
 ¼ teaspoon salt
 ¼ teaspoon black pepper
 2 Loaded Baked Potatoes (4 stuffed halves), chopped (see recipe)
 1 (16-ounce) can fat-free, less-sodium chicken broth
 ¼ cup thinly sliced green onions

1. Melt butter in a Dutch oven over medium heat. Add onion and celery; sauté 3 minutes. Add garlic and bay leaf; sauté 2 minutes. Add milk and next 5 ingredients; bring to a boil. Reduce heat; simmer 10 minutes. Ladle soup into 4 bowls; top each serving with 1 tablespoon green onions. Yield: 4 servings (serving size: 1¼ cups).

CALORIES 340 (22% from fat); FAT 8.3g (sat 4.1g, mono 2.7g, poly 1g); PROTEIN 12.4g; CARB 54.9g; FIBER 4.5g; CHOL 21mg; IRON 3.1mg; SODIUM 790mg; CALC 224mg

SHRIMP-AND-RICE STUFFED TOMATOES

The 4 cups of leftover rice can be put to good use in our Snow Pea-and-Pork Fried Rice (see recipe).

1¾ cups uncooked long-grain rice
4 large ripe tomatoes (about 3 pounds)
1 teaspoon olive oil
1 cup chopped onion
1 garlic clove, minced
½ cup (2 ounces) crumbled feta cheese
2 tablespoons chopped fresh or 2 teaspoons dried oregano
1 tablespoon fresh lemon juice
½ teaspoon salt
⅛ teaspoon black pepper
½ pound medium shrimp, peeled and deveined
½ cup hot water

1. Cook rice according to package directions, omitting salt and fat. Place 2 cups cooked rice in a large bowl; set aside. Refrigerate remaining rice in an airtight container for another use.
2. Preheat oven to 350°.
3. Cut tops off tomatoes, and reserve. Carefully scoop out tomato pulp, leaving shells intact; reserve ½ cup pulp. Discard remaining pulp.
4. Heat oil in a medium nonstick skillet over medium-high heat. Add onion; sauté 3 minutes. Add garlic; sauté 1 minute. Add reserved ½ cup tomato pulp; cook 5 minutes or until liquid evaporates. Add onion mixture, cheese, and next 5 ingredients to 2 cups rice.
5. Place tomato shells in an 8-inch square baking dish. Divide rice mixture evenly among tomato shells; replace tomato tops. Add hot water to baking dish. Bake at 350° for 40 minutes or until tomatoes are tender and rice mixture is thoroughly heated. Serve warm or chilled. Yield: 4 servings.

CALORIES 269 (19% from fat); FAT 5.8g (sat 2.5g, mono 1.7g, poly 0.8g); PROTEIN 15.2g; CARB 40.4g; FIBER 4.2g; CHOL 77mg; IRON 3.5mg; SODIUM 535mg; CALC 136mg

SNOW PEA-AND-PORK FRIED RICE

2 (4-ounce) boned center-cut loin pork chops
1 tablespoon low-sodium soy sauce
1 tablespoon dry sherry
2 large egg whites
1 large egg
Cooking spray
2 teaspoons dark sesame oil, divided
2 cups vertically sliced onion
2 cups snow peas
2 cups sliced mushrooms
1 tablespoon minced peeled fresh ginger
2 garlic cloves, minced
4 cups cooked long-grain rice, chilled
¼ teaspoon salt
⅓ cup chopped green onions

1. Trim fat from pork chops; cut pork into 2 x ¼-inch strips. Combine pork, soy sauce, and sherry; cover and marinate in refrigerator 30 minutes. Drain; discard sherry mixture.
2. Combine egg whites and egg in a medium bowl; stir well with a whisk. Place a large nonstick skillet or wok coated with cooking spray over medium-high heat until hot. Add egg mixture; cook 2 minutes or until egg is done. Remove egg mixture from skillet.
3. Add ½ teaspoon oil to skillet. Add pork; stir-fry 2 minutes or until done. Remove pork from skillet; keep warm. Add ½ teaspoon oil to skillet. Add sliced onion and snow peas; stir-fry 2 minutes. Add mushrooms, ginger, and garlic; stir-fry 1 minute. Remove onion mixture from skillet, and keep warm.
4. Add 1 teaspoon oil to skillet; add rice, and cook 1 minute without stirring. Stir in egg mixture, pork, onion mixture, and salt; stir-fry 1 minute or until thoroughly heated. Sprinkle each serving with about 1 tablespoon green onions. Yield: 5 servings (serving size: 2 cups).

CALORIES 345 (17% from fat); FAT 6.7g (sat 1.8g, mono 2.6g, poly 1.4g); PROTEIN 18.8g; CARB 50.7g; FIBER 3.7g; CHOL 73mg; IRON 3.7mg; SODIUM 236mg; CALC 67mg

AMERICANA POT ROAST

The leftover broth and beef from this pot roast provide the foundation for our Cozy Shepherd's Pie (see recipe on next page).

Cooking spray
1 (4-pound) boned rump roast
6 cups (¼-inch-thick) sliced onion (about 3 medium)
2 tablespoons Hungarian sweet paprika
½ teaspoon dried basil
½ teaspoon dried oregano
½ teaspoon dried thyme
3 garlic cloves, crushed
½ cup water
½ cup dry red wine or 2 tablespoons red wine vinegar
1 (14¼-ounce) can low-salt beef broth
6 small red potatoes (about 1 pound)
½ teaspoon salt
¼ teaspoon black pepper
6 carrots, cut into 1½-inch-thick pieces (about 1 pound)

1. Preheat oven to 300°.
2. Place a Dutch oven coated with cooking spray over medium-high heat until hot. Add roast, browning on all sides. Remove from pan; reduce heat to medium. Add onion to pan; sauté 10 minutes. Add paprika, basil, oregano, thyme, and garlic; sauté 1 minute. Add water, wine, and broth; bring to a boil. Peel a ½-inch strip around each potato. Stir in salt, pepper, carrot, and potatoes. Return roast to pan. Cover and bake at 300° for 2 hours. Turn roast; cover and bake an additional hour or until tender. Serve roast with vegetables and broth. Yield: 10 servings (serving size: 3 ounces beef, ⅔ cup vegetables, and ¼ cup broth).

CALORIES 237 (22% from fat); FAT 5.7g (sat 1.9g, mono 2.1g, poly 0.4g); PROTEIN 30.1g; CARB 15.7g; FIBER 3g; CHOL 76mg; IRON 3.8mg; SODIUM 354mg; CALC 38mg

Cozy Shepherd's Pie

Make this shepherd's pie ahead, and freeze after assembling. Thaw in the refrigerator overnight, and bake as directed.

Potato topping:

- 2 pounds peeled baking potatoes, cut into 1-inch pieces (about 4 cups)
- ½ cup low-fat sour cream
- ¼ cup 1% low-fat milk
- 2 teaspoons chopped fresh or ½ teaspoon dried rubbed sage
- 1 teaspoon butter or stick margarine
- ½ teaspoon salt
- ⅛ teaspoon black pepper

Filling:

- 2 teaspoons olive oil
- 2 cups diced carrot
- 6 cups quartered mushrooms (about 1½ pounds)
- 1 tablespoon chopped fresh or 1 teaspoon dried rubbed sage
- 1 garlic clove, minced
- ¼ cup all-purpose flour
- 1¼ cups Americana Pot Roast broth (see recipe on previous page) or low-salt beef broth
- ½ cup dry red wine
- 2 tablespoons tomato paste
- 1 tablespoon red wine vinegar
- 3 cups diced Americana Pot Roast or cooked roast beef (about 12 ounces)
- ½ teaspoon paprika

1. To prepare potato topping, place potatoes in a saucepan; cover with water. Bring to a boil; cook 20 minutes or until very tender. Drain. Place potatoes, sour cream, and next 5 ingredients in a large bowl, and beat at medium speed of a mixer until smooth. Keep warm.
2. Preheat oven to 375°.
3. To prepare filling, heat oil in a large nonstick skillet over medium-high heat. Add carrot; sauté 7 minutes. Add mushrooms; sauté 5 minutes. Add 1 tablespoon sage and garlic; sauté 2 minutes. Sprinkle with flour; cook 2 minutes, stirring until well-blended. Add broth and wine; bring to a boil. Stir in tomato paste and vinegar. Add pot roast; cook 2 minutes. Spoon meat mixture into a 2-quart casserole.
4. Spread potato topping over meat mixture; sprinkle with paprika. Bake at 375° for 45 minutes or until golden brown. Yield: 8 servings (serving size: about 1 cup).

CALORIES 228 (26% from fat); FAT 6.6g (sat 2.4g, mono 2.6g, poly 0.6g); PROTEIN 18.5g; CARB 24.5g; FIBER 3.1g; CHOL 45mg; IRON 3.1mg; SODIUM 330mg; CALC 50mg

INSPIRED VEGETARIAN

The "It" Dish of Winter

Who says a rib-sticking cold-weather stew needs meat? Nobody who tries one of these.

Undoubtedly the biggest difficulty with preparing vegetarian food, especially when one is starting out cooking that way, is figuring out the entrée. The following recipes are all main-dish vegetable stews.

Quick Mushroom Stock

- 1½ cups hot water
- ¼ cup dried porcini mushrooms (about ¼ ounce)
- 2 teaspoons olive oil
- 1½ cups chopped onion
- 1 cup sliced cremini mushrooms
- ½ cup chopped carrot
- 1 garlic clove, sliced
- ½ cup dry red wine
- 1 tablespoon all-purpose flour
- 1 tablespoon chopped fresh or 1 teaspoon dried marjoram
- 2 teaspoons tomato paste
- 1 teaspoon red wine vinegar
- ¼ teaspoon salt
- ¼ teaspoon black pepper

1. Combine water and porcini mushrooms in a small bowl, and let stand for 20 minutes.
2. Heat olive oil in a small saucepan over medium-high heat. Add onion, cremini mushrooms, carrot, and garlic; sauté 10 minutes or until onion is browned. Reduce heat to medium. Stir in wine, flour, marjoram, and tomato paste. Cover and cook 3 minutes or until mixture is syrupy. Add porcini mixture, vinegar, salt, and pepper; cook 20 minutes. Strain through a sieve into a bowl. Discard solids. Yield: ¾ cup.

CALORIES 92 (46% from fat); FAT 4.7g (sat 0.7g, mono 3.4g, poly 0.5g); PROTEIN 1.8g; CARB 11.5g; FIBER 1g; CHOL 0mg; IRON 1.9mg; SODIUM 603mg; CALC 33mg

---

MUSHROOM STOCK— WORTH THE EXTRA STEP

This stock is made much like the Portobello-Mushroom Stew (page 32). In fact, you might even think you've made a mistake when you begin on your main dish because they're so similar. While the stock does add an extra step, the big flavor it produces is well worth it.

Also, the stock can be used anywhere you want a boost of mushroom—a mushroom-barley soup, a sauté, or in a mushroom-flavored béchamel sauce for a lasagna. If you find yourself mushroom-rich but without a plan, make the stock, and then freeze it for later use.

Browning the stock vegetables in a little oil is a very important step. The heat of the oil is what makes them caramelize, hence the dark, rich color and flavor.

PORTOBELLO-MUSHROOM STEW

This reliable stew is best made with the Quick Mushroom Stock *(page 31), but water can be substituted. Serve with rice pilaf, soft polenta, or mashed potatoes.*

  2 tablespoons olive oil, divided
  2 cups chopped onion
  1 teaspoon dried rosemary
  ¼ teaspoon crushed red pepper
  4 cups (½-inch-thick) sliced portobello mushrooms (about ½ pound)
  5 cups sliced button mushrooms (about 1 pound)
  1 cup water
  3 tablespoons tomato paste
  1 teaspoon sherry vinegar
  ¾ cup Quick Mushroom Stock (page 31) or water
  2 garlic cloves, minced
  2 tablespoons chopped fresh parsley
  ¼ teaspoon salt
  ¼ teaspoon black pepper
  4 cups cooked wild-rice pilaf (such as Uncle Ben's Wild Blend or Lundberg's Wehani Rice Pilaf)

1. Heat 1 tablespoon oil in a large skillet over medium heat. Add onion and rosemary; sauté 12 minutes or until browned. Stir in red pepper; remove from pan.
2. Heat 1½ teaspoons oil in skillet over medium heat. Add portobello mushrooms; sauté 5 minutes. Add to onion mixture. Heat 1½ teaspoons oil in skillet over medium heat. Add button mushrooms; sauté 5 minutes. Return onion mixture to skillet. Stir in 1 cup water and next 4 ingredients, and simmer 15 minutes. Stir in parsley, salt, and black pepper. Serve with rice. Yield: 4 servings (serving size: ¾ cup stew and 1 cup rice).

CALORIES 371 (23% from fat); FAT 9.5g (sat 1.4g, mono 6.1g, poly 1.2g); PROTEIN 10.4g; CARB 65.9g; FIBER 5.9g; CHOL 0mg; IRON 3.7mg; SODIUM 470mg; CALC 72mg

WINTER-VEGETABLE STEW WITH SUNCHOKES

Sunchokes have an edible thin skin and a nutty-flavored white flesh that's sweet and crunchy.

  2 tablespoons olive oil
  2 cups chopped onion
  ¼ teaspoon dried thyme
  6 garlic cloves, minced
  2 bay leaves
  2 cups (2-inch-thick) sliced carrot
  1 cup (2-inch-thick) sliced celery
  ½ teaspoon salt
  ¼ teaspoon black pepper
  ⅛ teaspoon ground nutmeg
  ½ pound sunchokes (Jerusalem artichokes), cut into ½-inch-thick pieces (about 2 cups)
  4 peeled red potatoes, quartered (about 1 pound)
  1 cup dry red wine
  1 tablespoon all-purpose flour
  1 tablespoon tomato paste
  1 cup water
Chopped fresh parsley (optional)

1. Heat olive oil in a Dutch oven over medium heat. Add onion, thyme, garlic, and bay leaves, and cook 12 minutes or until onion begins to brown. Add carrot and next 6 ingredients, and cook 5 minutes. Add wine, and bring to a boil. Reduce heat; simmer until wine is reduced to ½ cup (about 5 minutes). Stir in flour and tomato paste with a whisk; cover and cook 2 minutes. Stir in water; bring to a boil. Cover, reduce heat, and simmer 30 minutes or until carrot is tender. Garnish with chopped parsley, if desired. Yield: 4 servings (serving size: 1 cup).

CALORIES 289 (23% from fat); FAT 7.3g (sat 1g, mono 5g, poly 0.8g); PROTEIN 6.4g; CARB 52.3g; FIBER 6.7g; CHOL 0mg; IRON 4.8mg; SODIUM 357mg; CALC 82mg

THAI TOFU-AND-WINTER SQUASH STEW

  2 tablespoons roasted-peanut oil (such as Loriva) or vegetable oil, divided
  2 cups thinly sliced leeks (about 3 small)
  1 tablespoon minced peeled fresh ginger
  ¾ to 1½ teaspoons finely chopped seeded serrano chile
  2 garlic cloves, minced
  3 tablespoons less-sodium mushroom-flavored soy sauce (such as House of Tsang) or low-sodium soy sauce
  1 tablespoon curry powder
  1 teaspoon brown sugar
  3 cups water
  2 cups (½-inch) cubed peeled butternut squash (about 1 pound)
  ½ teaspoon salt
  1 (14-ounce) can light coconut milk
  1 (12.3-ounce) package reduced-fat firm tofu, drained and cut into ½-inch cubes
  1 tablespoon fresh lime juice
  5 cups hot cooked basmati or other long-grain rice
  ¼ cup finely chopped unsalted, dry-roasted peanuts
  ¼ cup chopped fresh cilantro

1. Heat 1 tablespoon oil in a Dutch oven over medium-high heat. Add leeks; sauté 3 minutes. Add ginger, serrano chile, and garlic, and sauté 1 minute. Stir in soy sauce, curry, and sugar. Add water, squash, salt, and coconut milk; bring to a boil. Reduce heat; simmer 15 minutes.
2. Heat 1 tablespoon oil in a large nonstick skillet over medium-high heat. Add tofu; sauté 12 minutes or until golden brown. Add tofu and lime juice to squash mixture. Serve over rice; sprinkle evenly with peanuts and cilantro. Yield: 5 servings (serving size: 1¼ cups stew and 1 cup rice).

CALORIES 476 (27% from fat); FAT 14.5g (sat 5.8g, mono 3.6g, poly 4.3g); PROTEIN 13.1g; CARB 74.7g; FIBER 3.9g; CHOL 0mg; IRON 4.5mg; SODIUM 512mg; CALC 138mg

White Bean-and-Vegetable Stew in Red Wine Sauce

We've taken liberties with a French recipe, expanding it into a hearty winter bean-and-vegetable stew. While olive oil is always splendid with beans, butter gives this dish its silky texture.

    2   cups dried cannellini or other
          white beans (about 12 ounces)
    1   onion, peeled
    2   whole cloves
    8   cups water
    6   tablespoons chopped fresh
          parsley, divided
    ½   cup diced celery
    ½   cup diced carrot
    1   teaspoon salt
    ¼   teaspoon dried thyme
    2   bay leaves
    2   cups thinly sliced leeks
    2   cups (1-inch) cubed peeled
          celeriac (celery root) or
          2 cups sliced celery
    1   cup (2-inch-thick) sliced carrot
    ¼   teaspoon black pepper
    1   garlic clove, minced
    4   tablespoons chilled butter or
          stick margarine, divided
    ⅔   cup diced shallots
    1   cup dry red wine

1. Sort and wash beans; place in a large Dutch oven. Cover with water to 2 inches above beans; bring to a boil, and cook 2 minutes. Remove from heat; cover and let stand 1 hour. Drain beans, and discard soaking liquid. Return beans to pan.
2. Cut onion in half. Stud 1 onion half with cloves; dice remaining onion half. Add clove-studded onion, diced onion, 8 cups water, ¼ cup parsley, ½ cup diced celery, and next 4 ingredients to beans; bring to a boil. Cover, reduce heat, and simmer 30 minutes. Discard clove-studded onion and bay leaves. Add leeks, celeriac, and sliced carrot; bring to a boil. Cover, reduce heat, and simmer 30 minutes or until sliced carrot is tender. Drain bean mixture in a colander over a bowl, reserving 1½ cups liquid. Return bean mixture to pan. Stir in pepper and garlic.

3. Melt 2 tablespoons butter in a medium skillet over medium heat. Add shallots; sauté 3 minutes. Add wine, and bring to a boil. Reduce heat, and simmer until liquid almost evaporates (about 8 minutes). Remove from heat. Cut 2 tablespoons butter into small pieces, and add wine mixture, stirring until well-blended. Gently stir butter mixture into bean mixture. Stir in reserved cooking liquid, and simmer gently 5 minutes. Garnish with 2 tablespoons chopped parsley. Yield: 6 servings (serving size: 1½ cups).

Note: Celeriac (seh-LER-ay-ak), also called celery root, is a knobby, brown-skinned root vegetable that you can find in most markets from September through May. You can substitute regular celery if you prefer a milder flavor.

CALORIES 343 (23% from fat); FAT 8.8g (sat 5.1g, mono 2.3g, poly 0.8g); PROTEIN 15.6g; CARB 54g; FIBER 27g; CHOL 21mg; IRON 5.1mg; SODIUM 561mg; CALC 179mg

---

What You See Is What You Eat

Stews are naturally rather shapeless, but a few simple tips let you give them form and visual appeal—and we do eat with our eyes.

First, cut your vegetables into large, neat-looking pieces. That gives the eye something to focus on. Large pieces are also quicker to prepare—the time just goes into the cooking.

Stews look especially attractive served in a pasta plate—a wide, shallow bowl with a rim, which frames and gives them definition.

Also, use the starchy accompaniments—a heap of mashed potatoes, a mound of rice, triangles of grilled polenta, or garlic-rubbed toasted country bread—to provide a visual center or accent, as well as a textural one.

AT LAST

So Many Smiths, So Little Time

It was Smiths who made America great. Or a great many Smiths that made America. There was actually a Granny Smith. But she was an apple.

Stuffed Granny Smiths with Maple Sauce

    ¾   cup dried sweet cherries
    ¾   cup packed brown sugar
    ¼   cup coarsely chopped walnuts
    2½ teaspoons pumpkin-pie spice
    8   Granny Smith apples (about 3
          pounds)
    1   cup apple juice
    ½   cup maple syrup
    1   tablespoon butter or stick
          margarine, melted

1. Preheat oven to 350°.
2. Combine first 4 ingredients in a small bowl.
3. Core apples three-fourths of the way through. (Do not cut through bottom.) Peel top half of each apple. Fill apples with cherry mixture. Place apples in a 12-inch cast-iron or heavy ovenproof skillet. Add apple juice to skillet. Combine maple syrup and butter; pour over apples. Cover; bake at 350° for 40 minutes. Uncover; baste apples with juices from pan. Bake, uncovered, an additional 25 minutes or until tender. Serve with sauce. Yield: 8 servings (serving size: 1 apple and 2 tablespoons sauce).

Note: Apples can also be baked in a 13 x 9-inch baking dish.

CALORIES 307 (13% from fat); FAT 4.4g (sat 1.2g, mono 0.9g, poly 1.7g); PROTEIN 1.7g; CARB 69.5g; FIBER 5.7g; CHOL 4mg; IRON 1.5mg; SODIUM 29mg; CALC 56mg

Nantucket, Bite-by-Bike

A two-wheel tour of this tiny Massachusetts island takes a culinary turn en route to a fresh twist on active travel.

The first in a series of what are billed as "Moveable Feasts" by the luxury cycling/walking-tour outfitter Butterfield & Robinson, this effort to appeal to the fitness-and-food-minded represents the convergence of two tourism trends—the soaring popularity of active travel and of travel containing an educational component. That's the model B&R is following in employing cookbook author Sarah Leah Chase to host its Moveable Feast in Nantucket.

SWORDFISH PORTUGAISE

We cut back a bit on the olive oil in this recipe. (From Nantucket Open-House Cookbook, *©1987 by Sarah Leah Chase; used with permission of Workman Publishing Co., Inc., New York; all rights reserved.)*

- 6 (6-ounce) swordfish steaks or other firm white fish such as mahimahi (about 1½ inches thick)
- ¼ cup fresh lemon juice
- ½ teaspoon salt, divided
- ¼ teaspoon black pepper
- 1½ tablespoons olive oil
- 2 cups chopped yellow onion
- 4 garlic cloves, minced
- 2 cups chopped seeded tomato (about 3 large)
- ¾ cup dry white wine
- ½ cup dry sherry
- ½ cup tomato paste
- 1 tablespoon brown sugar
- ½ cup chopped fresh cilantro
- ⅛ teaspoon black pepper
- 6 lemon slices

1. Preheat oven to 375°.
2. Arrange fish in a single layer in a 13 x 9-inch baking dish. Pour lemon juice over fish; sprinkle with ¼ teaspoon salt and ¼ teaspoon pepper. Cover and refrigerate.
3. Heat oil in large nonstick skillet over medium-high heat. Add onion and garlic; sauté 10 minutes or until browned, stirring frequently. Stir in tomato and next 4 ingredients. Bring to a boil; simmer 15 minutes, stirring frequently. Stir in ¼ teaspoon salt, cilantro, and ⅛ teaspoon pepper.
4. Pour tomato mixture over fish; top with lemon slices. Cover and bake at 375° for 30 minutes. Yield: 6 servings (serving size: 5 ounces fish and about ⅔ cup sauce).

CALORIES 307 (31% from fat); FAT 10.7g (sat 2.4g, mono 5.2g, poly 2.1g); PROTEIN 36.1g; CARB 16.4g; FIBER 3g; CHOL 66mg; IRON 3mg; SODIUM 378mg; CALC 46mg

The Spice is Right

Burned out on supersweet holiday desserts? A spice cake may be what you're craving.

The holidays are great, but two months of gobbling Halloween candy, Thanksgiving pies, and Christmas cookies make you welcome the return of a little moderation. Still, going cold turkey on desserts can be painful. To ease back into your regular routine, you need something that's light and not too sweet—such as spice cake.

With vibrant seasonings such as cinnamon, clove, nutmeg, and allspice supplying ample flavor, a spice cake doesn't need a fat-filled frosting to satisfy the post-dinner craving. In fact, many of the best spice cakes don't come with a topping at all.

PEAR-WALNUT UPSIDE-DOWN CAKE

- 1 cup all-purpose flour
- ¼ cup packed brown sugar
- 1 teaspoon baking powder
- 1 teaspoon ground cinnamon
- 1 teaspoon ground ginger
- ½ teaspoon baking soda
- ¼ teaspoon salt
- ¼ teaspoon ground cloves
- ½ cup low-fat buttermilk
- ¼ cup egg substitute or 2 large egg whites
- ¼ cup butter or stick margarine, melted
- ¼ cup molasses
- 1 tablespoon butter or stick margarine
- ⅓ cup packed brown sugar
- 3 tablespoons chopped walnuts
- 2 peeled Bosc or Comice pears, cored and thinly sliced lengthwise

1. Preheat oven to 375°.
2. Lightly spoon flour into a dry measuring cup; level with a knife. Combine flour, sugar, and next 6 ingredients in a bowl. Combine buttermilk, egg substitute, ¼ cup butter, and molasses in a bowl. Add to flour mixture, stirring until smooth.
3. Melt 1 tablespoon butter in a 9-inch cast-iron skillet. Stir in ⅓ cup brown sugar, and cook over medium heat 1 minute. Remove from heat; sprinkle with walnuts.
4. Place pear slices in bottom of skillet. Pour batter over pear slices, and bake at 375° for 30 minutes or until a wooden pick inserted in center comes out clean. Cool in pan 10 minutes on a wire rack; invert cake onto a serving plate. Serve warm or at room temperature. Yield: 8 servings (serving size: 1 wedge).

CALORIES 263 (32% from fat); FAT 9.3g (sat 1.8g, mono 3.6g, poly 3.9g); PROTEIN 3.9g; CARB 42.5g; FIBER 1.8g; CHOL 0mg; IRON 2mg; SODIUM 342mg; CALC 105mg

PRUNE-SPICE CAKE WITH CREAM CHEESE FROSTING

Cake:

Cooking spray
4 teaspoons all-purpose flour
1 cup chopped pitted prunes
¾ cup water
1 cup packed brown sugar
½ cup butter or stick margarine, softened
½ cup egg substitute or 3 large egg whites
2 cups all-purpose flour
1½ teaspoons ground cinnamon
1 teaspoon baking soda
1 teaspoon baking powder
1 teaspoon ground nutmeg
1 teaspoon ground allspice
½ teaspoon salt
⅔ cup low-fat buttermilk

Frosting:

¼ cup (2 ounces) ⅓-less-fat cream cheese
3 tablespoons butter or stick margarine
1 tablespoon grated lemon rind
1 tablespoon fat-free milk
1½ teaspoons vanilla extract
3 cups sifted powdered sugar

1. Preheat oven to 350°.
2. To prepare cake, coat 2 (8-inch) round cake pans with cooking spray; dust each with 2 teaspoons flour.
3. Place prunes and water in a small saucepan, and bring to a boil. Remove from heat; cover and let stand 10 minutes. Drain.
4. Beat brown sugar and ½ cup butter at medium speed of a mixer until well-blended. Add egg substitute; beat well.
5. Lightly spoon 2 cups flour into dry measuring cups; level with a knife. Combine flour, cinnamon, and next 5 ingredients in a bowl. Add flour mixture to sugar mixture alternately with buttermilk, beginning and ending with flour mixture. Fold in prunes. Pour batter into prepared cake pans. Bake at 350° for 30 minutes or until a wooden pick inserted in center comes out clean.

Cool in pans 10 minutes; remove from pans. Cool completely on a wire rack.
6. To prepare frosting, beat cream cheese and 3 tablespoons butter at medium speed until smooth. Add rind, milk, and vanilla, and beat well. Gradually add powdered sugar, beating until smooth. Place 1 cake layer on a plate; spread top with half of frosting. Top with remaining cake layer. Spread remaining frosting over top of cake. (Do not spread frosting on sides of cake.) Yield: 16 servings (serving size: 1 slice).

CALORIES 322 (26% from fat); FAT 9.3g (sat 5.6g, mono 2.6g, poly 0.4g); PROTEIN 3.6g; CARB 57.8g; FIBER 1.5g; CHOL 24mg; IRON 1.7mg; SODIUM 301mg; CALC 64mg

SUGAR-AND-SPICE CAKE

Cooking spray
2⅔ cups plus 2 teaspoons all-purpose flour, divided
1 teaspoon baking powder
1 teaspoon baking soda
1 teaspoon ground cinnamon
½ teaspoon salt
½ teaspoon ground cloves
2 large egg whites
2 cups packed brown sugar, divided
6 tablespoons butter or stick margarine, softened
2 large eggs
2 large egg whites
1 teaspoon vanilla extract
⅔ cup low-fat buttermilk
¼ cup chopped walnuts

1. Preheat oven to 350°.
2. Coat a 13 x 9-inch baking pan with cooking spray; dust with 2 teaspoons flour.
3. Lightly spoon 2⅔ cups flour into dry measuring cups, and level with a knife. Combine flour, baking powder, and next 4 ingredients in a bowl.
4. Beat 2 egg whites at high speed until soft peaks form. Gradually add ½ cup brown sugar, 1 tablespoon at a time, beating until stiff peaks form.
5. Beat butter and 1½ cups brown sugar at medium speed of a mixer until well-blended. Add eggs, 2 egg whites,

and vanilla; beat well. Add flour mixture to butter mixture alternately with buttermilk, beginning and ending with flour mixture. Pour batter into prepared pan. Carefully spread egg white mixture over batter. Sprinkle with walnuts. Bake at 350° for 35 minutes or until a wooden pick inserted in center comes out clean. Cool completely on a wire rack. Yield: 16 servings (serving size: 1 piece).

CALORIES 250 (23% from fat); FAT 6.5g (sat 3.1g, mono 1.8g, poly 1.1g); PROTEIN 4.7g; CARB 44g; FIBER 0.7g; CHOL 39mg; IRON 1.8mg; SODIUM 264mg; CALC 64mg

PUMPKIN-PECAN COFFEE CAKE

1 teaspoon butter or stick margarine
¼ cup regular oats
3 tablespoons brown sugar
3 tablespoons chopped pecans
3 tablespoons butter or stick margarine, softened
⅓ cup granulated sugar
¼ cup packed brown sugar
1 large egg
1¼ cups all-purpose flour
1 teaspoon baking powder
1 teaspoon pumpkin-pie spice
½ teaspoon baking soda
½ cup canned pumpkin
½ cup low-fat buttermilk

1. Preheat oven to 350°.
2. Melt 1 teaspoon butter in bottom of a 9-inch round cake pan. Combine oats, 3 tablespoons brown sugar, and pecans. Sprinkle oat mixture over bottom of pan, and set aside.
3. Beat 3 tablespoons butter, granulated sugar, and ¼ cup brown sugar at medium speed of a mixer until well-blended (about 4 minutes). Add egg, and beat well. Spoon flour into dry measuring cups, and level with a knife. Combine flour, baking powder, pumpkin-pie spice, and baking soda. Add flour mixture to butter mixture alternately with pumpkin and buttermilk, beginning and ending with flour mixture.

Continued

4. Spoon batter evenly over oat mixture in prepared pan. Bake at 350° for 40 minutes or until a wooden pick inserted in center comes out clean. Cool in pan 5 minutes, and invert cake onto a serving plate. Serve warm or at room temperature. Yield: 8 servings (serving size: 1 wedge).

CALORIES 236 (30% from fat); FAT 7.9g (sat 1.4g, mono 3.6g, poly 2.2g); PROTEIN 4.2g; CARB 37.8g; FIBER 1.6g; CHOL 41mg; IRON 1.7mg; SODIUM 217mg; CALC 77mg

KENTUCKY SPICED STACK CAKE

This traditional American cake is popular wherever apples are dried for winter storage, specifically throughout Appalachia and in parts of the Midwest. Some variations have as many as six layers.

Filling:

3¼ cups water
 ½ cup packed brown sugar
 ¼ cup bourbon or apple juice
  1 teaspoon vanilla extract
  2 (6-ounce) packages dried apples

Cake:

 ½ cup vegetable shortening
  1 cup packed brown sugar
 ⅓ cup molasses
  1 teaspoon vanilla extract
  3 large eggs
2¼ cups all-purpose flour
1¼ teaspoons baking soda
 ½ teaspoon ground nutmeg
 ½ teaspoon ground cinnamon
 ½ teaspoon ground allspice
 ¼ teaspoon salt
 ¾ cup low-fat buttermilk
    Cooking spray
  1 teaspoon powdered sugar

1. To prepare filling, combine first 5 ingredients in a large saucepan, and bring to a boil. Cover, reduce heat, and simmer 35 minutes or until liquid is nearly absorbed. Place apple mixture in a food processor; pulse 8 or 9 times or until mixture has consistency of a chunky puree. Set aside.
2. Preheat oven to 350°.
3. To prepare cake, beat shortening and 1 cup brown sugar at medium speed of a mixer until light and fluffy. Add molasses, 1 teaspoon vanilla, and eggs; beat well.
4. Lightly spoon flour into dry measuring cups, and level with a knife. Combine flour and next 5 ingredients in a bowl. Add flour mixture to sugar mixture alternately with buttermilk, beginning and ending with flour mixture.
5. Pour batter into a 12-cup Bundt pan coated with cooking spray. Bake at 350° for 40 minutes or until a wooden pick inserted in center comes out clean. Cool 10 minutes in pan. Remove from pan; cool completely on a wire rack.
6. Split cake into thirds horizontally, using a serrated knife. Place bottom layer, cut side up, on a serving platter; spread with half of filling. Top with middle cake layer. Spread cake with remaining filling; top with remaining cake layer. Sift powdered sugar over top of cake. Yield: 16 servings (serving size: 1 slice).

CALORIES 281 (22% from fat); FAT 6.8g (sat 1.8g, mono 2.2g, poly 1.8g); PROTEIN 3.7g; CARB 53.1g; FIBER 1.1g; CHOL 41mg; IRON 2mg; SODIUM 183mg; CALC 57mg

Loaded Baked Potatoes, page 29

Cinnamon-Bun Bread, page 20

Sizzling Steak with Roasted Vegetables, page 16

*Double-Herb Roasted Chicken and
Potatoes, page 28*

*Posole with Turkey and Heart-Shaped
Chipotle Gorditas, page 27*

Balsamic-Glazed Tuna, page 41

Marinated Strawberries with Mango Sorbet, page 27

Fast Fish

You know its reputation for health and flavor, but fish also can be one of the speediest meals in your weeknight dinner rotation.

Confronted with a numbing number of types and forms of seafood, many opt for the familiarity of poultry or meat. But there's a way past that. Learn to recognize two quick-cooking cuts of a handful of popular fish varieties—fillets and steaks.

Also, when you buy fish, remember the golden rule: Choose what's freshest, and cook it that day or the next. The fish's flesh should appear firm and unblemished. And it should not have a "fishy" smell—bad fish smells bad. Many times the quickest and easiest way to decide, however, is to ask.

BALSAMIC-GLAZED TUNA

(pictured on page 40)

Preparation time: 15 minutes
Cooking time: 10 minutes

Cooking spray
1¼ teaspoons coarsely ground
     black pepper
¼   teaspoon salt
4   (6-ounce) tuna steaks (about
     ¾ inch thick)
¼   cup fat-free, less-sodium
     chicken broth
1   tablespoon balsamic vinegar
4   teaspoons dark brown sugar
1   tablespoon low-sodium soy
     sauce
½   teaspoon cornstarch
¼   cup diagonally sliced green
     onions

1. Place a grill pan coated with cooking spray over medium-high heat until hot. Sprinkle pepper and salt over fish. Place fish in grill pan; cook 3 minutes on each side or until medium-rare or desired degree of doneness. Remove from heat.
2. Combine broth, vinegar, sugar, soy sauce, and cornstarch in a small saucepan. Bring to a boil; cook 1 minute, stirring constantly. Spoon glaze over fish; top with green onions. Yield: 4 servings (serving size: 1 steak and 1 tablespoon glaze).

CALORIES 266 (29% from fat); FAT 8.5g (sat 2.2g, mono 2.3g, poly 2.9g); PROTEIN 40.3g; CARB 4.6g; FIBER 0.3g; CHOL 65mg; IRON 2.2mg; SODIUM 366mg; CALC 11mg

CURRY-CHUTNEY SNAPPER

Preparation time: 5 minutes
Cooking time: 11 minutes

2   tablespoons all-purpose flour
2   teaspoons curry powder
¼   teaspoon salt
4   (6-ounce) red snapper or
     mahimahi fillets
1   tablespoon butter or stick
     margarine
½   cup fat-free, less-sodium
     chicken broth
¼   cup mango chutney
¼   teaspoon hot sauce
2   tablespoons minced fresh
     cilantro

1. Combine first 3 ingredients in a shallow dish. Dredge fish in flour mixture. Melt butter in a large nonstick skillet over medium-high heat. Add fish; cook 3 minutes on each side or until fish flakes easily when tested with a fork. Remove from skillet; keep warm.
2. Add broth, chutney, and hot sauce to skillet; bring to a boil. Cook 1 minute, stirring constantly. Spoon sauce over fish; sprinkle with cilantro. Yield: 4 servings (serving size: 1 fillet and 2 tablespoons sauce).

CALORIES 257 (19% from fat); FAT 5.3g (sat 1.1g, mono 1.8g, poly 1.7g); PROTEIN 36.1g; CARB 14.4g; FIBER 0.5g; CHOL 63mg; IRON 1.1mg; SODIUM 386mg; CALC 69mg

SEA BASS PROVENÇALE

Preparation time: 14 minutes
Cooking time: 16 minutes

2   teaspoons olive oil
2   garlic cloves, minced and
     divided
1½ cups diced tomato
⅓   cup chopped pitted kalamata
     olives
¼   cup chopped fresh parsley,
     divided
¼   cup water
1   tablespoon capers
4   (6-ounce) sea bass or striped
     bass fillets
2   teaspoons fresh lemon juice
¼   teaspoon black pepper
¼   teaspoon salt
1   tablespoon grated lemon rind

1. Heat oil in a large nonstick skillet over medium-high heat. Add 1 garlic clove; sauté 30 seconds. Stir in tomato, olives, 2 tablespoons parsley, water, and capers, and bring to a boil. Cover, reduce heat to medium, and cook 5 minutes. Add fillets, and sprinkle with lemon juice, pepper, and salt. Cover and cook 10 minutes or until fish flakes easily when tested with a fork; remove from heat.
2. Combine 1 garlic clove, 2 tablespoons parsley, and lemon rind. Spoon ⅔ cup tomato mixture onto each of 4 plates; top each portion with 1 fillet, and sprinkle with 1 tablespoon parsley mixture. Yield: 4 servings.

CALORIES 217 (29% from fat); FAT 7.1g (sat 1.4g, mono 3.3g, poly 1.8g); PROTEIN 32.4g; CARB 5.3g; FIBER 1.5g; CHOL 70mg; IRON 1.5mg; SODIUM 463mg; CALC 41mg

FISH FACTS

How you cook a fish depends more on the texture of the fish than the size. Dense and sturdy fish, such as salmon, can be prepared almost any way; a softer-textured fish, such as red snapper, should be baked or sautéed because it tends to fall apart when grilled or steamed.

Salmon with White Wine-Mustard Sauce

Preparation time: 5 minutes
Cooking time: 19 minutes

¼ teaspoon salt, divided
⅛ teaspoon black pepper
4 (6-ounce) salmon fillets (about 1 inch thick)
1 tablespoon butter or stick margarine, divided
3 tablespoons minced shallots
2 tablespoons dry white wine
¾ cup fat-free, less-sodium chicken broth
1 tablespoon Dijon mustard
¾ teaspoon cornstarch
4 teaspoons minced fresh tarragon

1. Sprinkle ⅛ teaspoon salt and pepper over fish. Melt 1½ teaspoons butter in a large nonstick skillet over medium-high heat. Add fish, and cook 7 minutes on each side or until fish flakes easily when tested with a fork. Remove from skillet, and keep warm.
2. Melt 1½ teaspoons butter in skillet over medium heat. Add shallots, and sauté 1 minute or until tender. Add wine, and cook 30 seconds. Combine ⅛ teaspoon salt, broth, Dijon mustard, and cornstarch, and stir with a whisk. Add to skillet, and bring to a boil. Reduce heat, and simmer until reduced to ¾ cup (about 1 minute). Spoon sauce over fish, and sprinkle with tarragon. Yield: 4 servings (serving size: 1 fillet and 3 tablespoons sauce).

CALORIES 318 (48% from fat); FAT 17.1g (sat 3g, mono 8g, poly 4g); PROTEIN 35.7g; CARB 2.4g; FIBER 0.1g; CHOL 111mg; IRON 0.9mg; SODIUM 467mg; CALC 16mg

Tilapia with Sherry-Mushroom Sauce

Preparation time: 10 minutes
Cooking time: 15 minutes

¼ teaspoon salt, divided
1½ pounds tilapia fillets
1 tablespoon butter or stick margarine, divided
4 cups thinly sliced mushrooms
⅛ teaspoon black pepper
2 tablespoons dry sherry
⅔ cup fat-free, less-sodium chicken broth
¼ cup fat-free milk
1 teaspoon cornstarch

1. Sprinkle ⅛ teaspoon salt over fillets. Melt 1½ teaspoons butter in a large nonstick skillet over medium-high heat. Add fillets, and sauté 4 minutes on each side or until fish flakes easily when tested with a fork. Remove fillets from skillet, and keep warm.
2. Melt 1½ teaspoons butter in skillet. Add ⅛ teaspoon salt, mushroom slices, and pepper; sauté 4 minutes or until golden. Add sherry, and cook 30 seconds, stirring constantly.
3. Combine broth, milk, and cornstarch, and stir with a whisk. Add broth mixture to skillet, and bring to a boil, stirring constantly. Reduce heat to medium, and cook 1 minute. Spoon sauce over fish. Yield: 4 servings (serving size: 5 ounces fish and ⅓ cup sauce).

CALORIES 355 (12% from fat); FAT 4.7g (sat 1.1g, mono 1.6g, poly 1.7g); PROTEIN 31.1g; CARB 47.3g; FIBER 1g; CHOL 75mg; IRON 1mg; SODIUM 481mg; CALC 26mg

Carolina Catfish Sandwiches

Preparation time: 5 minutes
Cooking time: 9 minutes

3 tablespoons yellow cornmeal
2 tablespoons all-purpose flour
2 teaspoons Cajun seasoning
4 (6-ounce) catfish fillets
1 tablespoon butter or stick margarine
Cooking spray
2½ cups packaged cabbage-and-carrot coleslaw
2 tablespoons light coleslaw dressing (such as Marzetti)
4 (2½-ounce) hoagie rolls with sesame seeds

1. Combine first 3 ingredients in a shallow dish. Dredge catfish fillets in cornmeal mixture.
2. Melt butter in a large nonstick skillet coated with cooking spray over medium-high heat. Add catfish fillets, and cook 5 minutes on each side or until fish flakes easily when tested with a fork. Remove catfish fillets from heat, and keep warm.
3. Combine coleslaw and dressing. Cut hoagie rolls in half horizontally, and spoon ½ cup slaw over bottom halves of rolls. Top each half of roll with 1 fillet and top of a roll. Yield: 4 servings.

CALORIES 497 (26% from fat); FAT 14.4g (sat 3g, mono 5.3g, poly 4.4g); PROTEIN 38.6g; CARB 50.6g; FIBER 3.1g; CHOL 107mg; IRON 3.8mg; SODIUM 1,194mg; CALC 145mg

MARCH

How Does Your Garden Grow? Part I

A home garden makes every meal memorable and gives you plenty of outdoor fun in the bargain.

We want to show you, step-by-step, how to create a home garden of your own, and how easy it is. So, we hooked up with master gardeners Melanie and Buddy Colvin and the Burpee seed company to start and track a home garden. We followed the Colvins, tracking the progress of their garden, from planning to harvest, in each of three stages: early spring, summer, and autumn. Learn not only how to plant a garden but why doing so can be such an integral part of a healthy lifestyle—and what incredible recipes, brimming with freshness, can result. We've provided the recipes below as well as in Part II (page 159) and Part III (page 215).

ORZO WITH PESTO AND PEAS

Arugula, an aromatic salad green with a peppery mustard flavor, gives this easy-to-make pesto its distinctive flavor. Add fresh shelled peas and pasta, and you have a unique spring side dish.

Pesto:

- 2 tablespoons coarsely chopped walnuts
- 1 garlic clove, peeled
- 1½ cups torn spinach
- 1½ cups trimmed arugula
- 3 tablespoons grated Parmesan cheese
- 2 tablespoons water
- 1 teaspoon lemon juice
- ½ teaspoon salt
- ¼ teaspoon black pepper
- 1½ tablespoons olive oil

Remaining ingredients:

- 2 cups hot cooked orzo (about 1 cup uncooked rice-shaped pasta)
- 1 cup shelled green peas (about ¾ pound unshelled green peas)

1. To prepare pesto, drop walnuts and garlic through food chute with food processor on; process until minced. Add spinach and next 6 ingredients; process until finely minced. With food processor on, slowly pour oil through food chute; process until well-blended.
2. Combine pesto, orzo, and peas in a large bowl, and toss well. Yield: 8 servings (serving size: ½ cup).

CALORIES 141 (30% from fat); FAT 4.7g (sat 0.8g, mono 2.3g, poly 1.2g); PROTEIN 5.5g; CARB 19.7g; FIBER 1.7g; CHOL 1mg; IRON 1.5mg; SODIUM 194mg; CALC 58mg

MESCLUN WITH GRILLED ONION, APPLE, AND GRUYÈRE CHEESE

Cooking spray
- 8 (¼-inch-thick) slices onion
- 1 teaspoon sugar, divided
- 6 cups gourmet salad greens
- 1 cup sliced Fuji or Gala apple
- ¼ cup (1 ounce) grated Gruyère cheese
- 1 tablespoon water
- 1 tablespoon white wine vinegar
- 1 teaspoon olive oil
- ¼ teaspoon salt
- ¼ teaspoon black pepper

1. Place a large nonstick skillet coated with cooking spray over medium heat. Carefully arrange 4 onion slices in skillet, and sprinkle with ½ teaspoon sugar; sauté 4 minutes on each side or until golden brown. Wipe skillet; repeat procedure with remaining onion slices and ½ teaspoon sugar.
2. Combine salad greens, apple, and cheese. Combine water, vinegar, oil, salt, and pepper; pour vinegar mixture over salad greens mixture, tossing to coat. Divide salad evenly among 4 plates; top each serving with onion slices. Yield: 4 servings (serving size: 1½ cups salad and 2 onion slices).

CALORIES 86 (41% from fat); FAT 3.9g (sat 1.5g, mono 1.6g, poly 0.4g); PROTEIN 3.9g; CARB 9.8g; FIBER 2.8g; CHOL 8mg; IRON 1.1mg; SODIUM 178mg; CALC 110mg

SPRING-VEGETABLE PIZZA

- 1 teaspoon olive oil
- 2 cups thinly sliced leek (about 2 large)
- 1½ cups (1-inch) sliced asparagus (about 1 pound)
- 1½ teaspoons chopped fresh or ½ teaspoon dried sage
- ¼ teaspoon salt
- ¼ teaspoon black pepper
- 3 cups torn spinach
- 1 (10-ounce) Italian cheese-flavored pizza crust (such as Boboli)
- ¼ cup (2 ounces) goat cheese

1. Preheat oven to 450°.
2. Heat oil in a nonstick skillet over medium-high heat. Add leek and asparagus; sauté 5 minutes or until lightly browned. Stir in sage, salt, and pepper.
3. Arrange spinach over crust; leave a 1-inch border. Top with leek mixture; sprinkle with cheese. Place on a baking sheet. Bake at 450° for 10 minutes. Cut into 8 slices. Yield: 4 servings (serving size: 2 slices).

CALORIES 310 (30% from fat); FAT 10.3g (sat 4.8g, mono 2.8g, poly 2.5g); PROTEIN 13.2g; CARB 42g; FIBER 4.4g; CHOL 16mg; IRON 4.2mg; SODIUM 776mg; CALC 360mg

RISOTTO WITH PEAS AND SHRIMP

2 (8-ounce) bottles clam juice
3 cups water
1 tablespoon olive oil
¼ cup minced shallots
1½ cups uncooked Arborio rice or other short-grain rice
⅓ cup dry white wine
¾ pound medium shrimp, peeled and deveined
1 cup (½-inch) diagonally sliced snow peas
1 cup shelled green peas (about ¾ pound unshelled green peas)
¼ cup (1 ounce) grated fresh Parmesan cheese
1½ teaspoons chopped fresh or ½ teaspoon dried thyme
1 teaspoon grated lemon rind
¼ teaspoon black pepper

1. Bring clam juice and water to a simmer in a medium saucepan (do not boil). Keep warm over low heat.
2. Heat oil in a large saucepan over medium heat; add shallots, and cook 1 minute. Add rice; cook 1 minute, stirring constantly. Stir in wine; cook 1 minute. Stir in ½ cup juice mixture; cook 2 minutes or until liquid is nearly absorbed, stirring constantly. Add remaining juice mixture, ½ cup at a time, stirring constantly until each portion of juice mixture is absorbed before adding the next (about 20 minutes total). Stir in shrimp, snow peas, and green peas; cook 4 minutes or until shrimp are done, stirring constantly. Remove from heat; stir in cheese and remaining ingredients. Yield: 6 servings (serving size: 1 cup).

CALORIES 302 (14% from fat); FAT 4.6g (sat 1.3g, mono 2.2g, poly 0.6g); PROTEIN 16.1g; CARB 47.3g; FIBER 2.3g; CHOL 68mg; IRON 4.2mg; SODIUM 306mg; CALC 111mg

Growing Your Spring Vegetables

Lettuce:

Leaf or romaine lettuce types are easier to grow than heading types. Be sure to pick some of the red-leaf selections to add color to the garden (and the salad). In early spring, sow seeds two weeks before the average date of last frost, or buy transplants when they appear in the garden shops. Plant outdoors, and cover when frost threatens. Begin harvesting in a month. Melanie's favorite selections include Burpee's Gourmet Blend, Buttercrunch, and Green Ice.

Onions:

Frost tolerance varies among onions. In general, plant bulb onions from sets or seedlings four to six weeks before the average date of last frost. Bunching (green) onions are grown for their foliage and don't produce large bulbs. Set them out two weeks before the average date of last frost. Onions are ready to harvest within four to eight weeks.

Root Crops:

Carrots, radishes, beets, and turnips are frost-tolerant and grown from seed. Sow seeds in early spring two weeks before the average date of last frost. Keep the soil evenly moist, watering in the absence of rain. When seedlings reach 2 inches high, thin them to 4 to 6 inches apart. Harvest in four to eight weeks. For especially tender vegetables, grow "baby" selections such as Little Ball beets, Thumbelina carrots, and Tokyo Cross Hybrid turnips. Melanie also likes Easter Egg radishes (pink, white, or red) and daikon radishes such as Burpee's Summer Cross Hybrid.

Edible Podded Peas:

These are frost-tolerant and grown from seed. Sow outdoors four to six weeks before the average date of last frost. Keep seeds evenly moist, watering in the absence of rain. Use a trellis or fence to support vining types. Harvest in six to eight weeks. For a great-tasting pea that's easy to grow, try Super Sugar Snaps.

Spring Greens:

Spinach, Swiss chard, and arugula can be enjoyed raw in salads or cooked in stir-fry dishes. They're easy to grow from seed or transplants. Sow the seeds of these spring greens four weeks before the average date of last frost, or set out transplants two weeks before the same date. Melanie likes Bloomsdale Longstanding spinach and Bright Lights Swiss chard.

Spring Herbs:

Cool-season herbs such as dill, cilantro, and parsley can be started outdoors in the early spring from seeds or transplants. All three are frost-tolerant. With dill and cilantro, however, it's best to stagger plantings. If starting with transplants, set them out two to four weeks before the average date of last frost. Begin harvesting within four to eight weeks, cutting no more than one-third of the foliage at a time. Dill and cilantro will flower and go to seed when the weather turns hot, so keep flowers pinched off to prolong leaf production. Parsley will survive the heat of the summer and perk up again in the cool fall weather.

GLAZED TURNIPS WITH CHIVES

 1 teaspoon butter or stick
    margarine
 4 cups (3-inch) julienne-cut
    turnips (about 1½ pounds)
 1 tablespoon water
 ¼ teaspoon salt
 ¼ teaspoon black pepper
 2 tablespoons brown sugar
 4 teaspoons chopped fresh chives

1. Melt butter in a nonstick skillet over medium heat. Add turnips, water, salt, and pepper; toss to combine. Cover and cook 5 minutes or until turnips are crisp-tender; stir in sugar. Increase temperature to medium-high; cook, uncovered, 10 minutes or until golden brown, stirring mixture occasionally. Sprinkle salad with chives. Yield: 4 servings (serving size: about ½ cup).

CALORIES 61 (16% from fat); FAT 1.1g (sat 0.2g, mono 0.4g, poly 0.4g); PROTEIN 1.1g; CARB 12.7g; FIBER 2.4g; CHOL 0mg; IRON 0.5mg; SODIUM 247mg; CALC 45mg

ROASTED BEETS-AND-MANGO SALAD

 2 large beets (about ¾ pound),
    trimmed
 ¼ cup orange juice, divided
 2 tablespoons lime juice, divided
 ¼ teaspoon black pepper, divided
 1 tablespoon honey mustard
 2 teaspoons olive oil
 ⅛ teaspoon salt
 6 cups gourmet salad greens
 1 cup diced peeled ripe mango
    (about 2 mangoes)

1. Preheat oven to 425°.
2. Place beets in a baking dish, and bake at 425° for 1 hour and 10 minutes or until tender. Cool beets. Combine 2 tablespoons orange juice, 1 tablespoon lime juice, and ⅛ teaspoon pepper. Peel beets; cut each into 8 wedges. Toss beets with orange juice mixture.
3. Combine 2 tablespoons orange juice, 1 tablespoon lime juice, ⅛ teaspoon pepper, mustard, oil, and salt. Combine salad greens and diced mango. Drizzle with mustard mixture, and toss well to coat. Divide salad evenly among 4 plates, and top with beet wedges. Yield: 4 servings (serving size: 1½ cups salad and 4 beet wedges).

CALORIES 109 (24% from fat); FAT 2.9g (sat 0.4g, mono 1.9g, poly 0.4g); PROTEIN 3.3g; CARB 19.8g; FIBER 2.8g; CHOL 0mg; IRON 1.8mg; SODIUM 193mg; CALC 54mg

LEMONY RICE SALAD WITH CARROTS AND RADISHES

 2 tablespoons water
 1 teaspoon grated lemon rind
 2 tablespoons fresh lemon juice
 1 tablespoon olive oil
 2 teaspoons chopped fresh or
    ½ teaspoon dried thyme
 ½ teaspoon salt
 ¼ teaspoon black pepper
 2 cups hot cooked long-grain rice
 ¾ cup shredded carrot
 ¾ cup shredded radish
 ¼ cup golden raisins
 3 tablespoons chopped walnuts,
    toasted

1. Combine first 7 ingredients in a small bowl.
2. Combine rice and remaining 4 ingredients; drizzle with lemon mixture, and toss well. Serve warm or at room temperature. Yield: 4 servings (serving size: 1 cup).

CALORIES 223 (28% from fat); FAT 7g (sat 0.7g, mono 3.3g, poly 2.5g); PROTEIN 4.2g; CARB 37.5g; FIBER 2.2g; CHOL 0mg; IRON 1.6mg; SODIUM 307mg; CALC 33mg

CHICKEN-BULGUR SALAD WITH SPRING VEGETABLES

 ¾ cup uncooked bulgur or
    cracked wheat
 1 cup boiling water
 1 tablespoon olive oil
 1¼ cups (1-inch) diagonally sliced
    asparagus
 1 cup diagonally sliced snow
    peas
 ½ cup diced red onion
 1½ cups shredded cooked chicken
    breast (about 6 ounces)
 ¼ cup finely chopped fresh
    cilantro
 ¼ cup finely chopped fresh
    parsley
 ½ cup fat-free, less-sodium
    chicken broth
 2 tablespoons fresh lime juice
 2 tablespoons finely chopped
    seeded jalapeño peppers
 ¼ teaspoon salt
 ¼ teaspoon black pepper
 6 cups gourmet salad greens

1. Combine bulgur and water in a large bowl. Cover and let stand 30 minutes.
2. Heat oil in a nonstick skillet over medium-high heat. Add asparagus, peas, and onion; sauté 4 minutes. Add asparagus mixture, chicken, cilantro, and parsley to bulgur mixture.
3. Combine broth and next 4 ingredients. Pour over bulgur mixture; toss to coat. Arrange greens on 4 plates; top with bulgur mixture. Yield: 4 servings (serving size: 1½ cups salad greens and 1½ cups bulgur mixture).

CALORIES 246 (21% from fat); FAT 5.7g (sat 1g, mono 3.1g, poly 0.9g); PROTEIN 20.7g; CARB 30.2g; FIBER 8.9g; CHOL 36mg; IRON 3.7mg; SODIUM 257mg; CALC 87mg

Health Nuts

Heart-healthy and full of nutrients, nuts are back from banishment. Scientists are now discovering that nuts can do your body good.

In a scientific study, published in 1992, on the dietary habits and heart health of 27,000 California Seventh-Day Adventists, researchers at Loma Linda University's Center for Health Research looked at 65 different food items to see which, if any, most affected coronary health. Not so surprisingly, nuts virtually led the pack.

Turns out the prevailing conventional wisdom had gotten it backward. People who noshed nuts five or more times a week were 53% less likely to die from heart disease when compared to those who avoided eating nuts.

The more research evolves, the more we see how these tasty and plentiful food sources, when eaten in small amounts, work their magic. A few of the likeliest mechanisms include:

Good-fat content. Generally, one-fourth cup of any nut contains about 20 grams of fat. The fat in nuts, however, is highly monounsaturated—the same form found in abundance in heart-healthy olive oil and canola oil. Nuts are also rich in polyunsaturated fat, the other form known to lower cholesterol levels. Nuts contain relatively modest amounts of artery-clogging saturated fat.

Omega-3 fatty acids. Like mackerel, salmon, and other cold-water fish, nuts tend to be high in omega-3 fatty acids. This complex biomolecule may help reduce the risk of strokes and heart attacks.

Nutrient density. Nuts are full of micronutrients such as vitamin E, folic acid, niacin, copper, magnesium, potassium, flavonoids, and isoflavones.

PORK, CASHEW, AND GREEN BEAN STIR-FRY

¼ cup low-sodium soy sauce
2 teaspoons cornstarch
1 pound pork tenderloin, cut into ¼-inch-thick slices
4 cups (2-inch) cut green beans (about 1 pound)
2 teaspoons dark sesame oil
Cooking spray
1 to 2 tablespoons minced peeled fresh ginger
2 garlic cloves, minced
¼ cup fat-free, less-sodium chicken broth
2 cups hot cooked rice
¼ cup chopped unsalted cashews, toasted

1. Combine soy sauce and cornstarch in a medium bowl, and add pork, stirring to coat. Cover and chill.
2. Place beans in a large saucepan of boiling water, and cook 5 minutes. Drain beans; plunge into ice water. Drain.
3. Heat oil in a large nonstick skillet coated with cooking spray over medium-high heat. Add ginger and garlic; sauté 1 minute. Add pork mixture; stir-fry 1½ minutes. Stir in green beans; stir-fry 1½ minutes or until pork is done. Stir in broth; reduce heat, and simmer 2 minutes. Serve over rice; sprinkle with cashews. Yield: 4 servings (serving size: 1 cup stir-fry mixture, ½ cup rice, and 1 tablespoon cashews).

CALORIES 349 (25% from fat); FAT 9.7g (sat 2.2g, mono 4.6g, poly 2.1g); PROTEIN 29.5g; CARB 34.5g; FIBER 3.3g; CHOL 74mg; IRON 4.1mg; SODIUM 463mg; CALC 73mg

PERSIAN POACHED PEARS

Because the poached pears need to chill before they can be stuffed, you may want to start preparing this recipe early in the day.

4 large Bosc pears
1 cup water
1 cup dry white wine
2 tablespoons sugar
2 tablespoons honey
4 dried apricots
2 (3 x ½-inch) lemon rind strips
1 (3-inch) piece vanilla bean, split lengthwise, or 1 teaspoon vanilla extract
1 whole clove
4 reduced-calorie vanilla wafers, crushed
5 tablespoons coarsely chopped pistachios, toasted and divided

1. Peel and core pears, leaving stems intact. Slice about ¼ inch from base of each pear so it will sit flat.
2. Combine water and next 7 ingredients in a large saucepan; bring to a boil. Add pears; cover, reduce heat, and simmer 10 minutes or until tender. Remove pears and apricots from cooking liquid, using a slotted spoon; chill pears and apricots. Bring cooking liquid to a boil; cook until reduced to 1 cup (about 15 minutes). Strain cooking liquid through a sieve over a bowl; discard solids. Chill.
3. Chop apricots. Combine apricots, wafer crumbs, and 1 tablespoon pistachios. Stuff about 2 tablespoons apricot mixture into each pear cavity. Place a pear in each of 4 bowls. Spoon ¼ cup syrup over each pear; sprinkle each with 1 tablespoon pistachios. Yield: 4 servings.
Note: Use a melon baller to core pears.

CALORIES 251 (22% from fat); FAT 6g (sat 0.7g, mono 3.4g, poly 0.9g); PROTEIN 3.4g; CARB 51.5g; FIBER 6.0g; CHOL 0mg; IRON 1.7mg; SODIUM 24mg; CALC 41mg

HAZELNUT-FIG QUICK BREAD

(pictured on page 57)

Sprinkling nuts on top of the batter before it bakes, rather than mixing them in, helps concentrate the nut flavor.

⅓ cup hazelnuts
¾ cup fresh orange juice
1 cup chopped dried figs
½ cup sugar
2 tablespoons vegetable oil
1 tablespoon grated orange rind
1 large egg
1 large egg white
1½ cups all-purpose flour
1½ teaspoons baking soda
¼ teaspoon salt
Cooking spray

1. Preheat oven to 350°.
2. Place hazelnuts on a baking sheet. Bake at 350° for 15 minutes, stirring once. Turn nuts out onto a towel. Roll up towel; rub off skins. Chop nuts.
3. Bring orange juice to a boil; pour over figs in a bowl. Let stand 15 minutes. Combine sugar, oil, rind, egg, and egg white; stir well with a whisk. Stir into fig mixture.
4. Lightly spoon flour into dry measuring cups; level with a knife. Combine flour, baking soda, and salt in a large bowl; make a well in center of mixture. Add fig mixture to flour mixture, stirring just until moist. Spoon batter into an 8 x 4-inch loaf pan coated with cooking spray; sprinkle with nuts. Bake at 350° for 45 minutes or until a wooden pick inserted in center comes out clean. Cool 10 minutes in pan on a wire rack; remove from pan. Cool completely on wire rack. Yield: 12 servings.

CALORIES 178 (27% from fat); FAT 5.4g (sat 0.8g, mono 2.7g, poly 1.5g); PROTEIN 3.4g; CARB 30.4g; FIBER 2.6g; CHOL 18mg; IRON 1.2mg; SODIUM 218mg; CALC 31mg

FRUIT 'N NUT GRANOLA

4 cups regular oats
½ cup sliced almonds
1 teaspoon ground cinnamon
¼ teaspoon salt
⅓ cup honey
⅓ cup molasses
⅓ cup water
2 tablespoons vegetable oil
Cooking spray
1 cup chopped pitted dates
1 cup raisins

1. Preheat oven to 325°.
2. Combine first 4 ingredients in a large bowl.
3. Combine honey, molasses, water, and oil in a medium saucepan; bring to a boil. Remove from heat; pour over oat mixture, stirring well to coat. Spoon mixture onto a jelly-roll pan coated with cooking spray; spread evenly. Bake at 325° for 40 minutes or until lightly toasted, stirring every 10 minutes. Remove from oven; stir in dates and raisins. Cool completely. Store in an airtight container. Yield: 6 cups (serving size: ½ cup).

CALORIES 277 (20% from fat); FAT 6.2g (sat 1g, mono 2.6g, poly 2.2g); PROTEIN 5.8g; CARB 53.4g; FIBER 5.2g; CHOL 0mg; IRON 2.2mg; SODIUM 56mg; CALC 56mg

WALNUT-SPICE COOKIES

2 cups all-purpose flour
½ cup sifted powdered sugar
2¼ teaspoons baking powder
1 teaspoon pumpkin-pie spice
¼ teaspoon salt
1 cup packed dark brown sugar
3 tablespoons vegetable oil
2 tablespoons molasses
3 large egg whites
¾ cup chopped walnuts, toasted
Cooking spray

1. Preheat oven to 350°.
2. Lightly spoon flour into dry measuring cups; level with a knife. Combine flour and next 4 ingredients in a medium bowl. Combine brown sugar, oil, molasses, and egg whites in a large bowl, stirring well with a whisk. Add flour mixture; stir until well-blended. Stir in walnuts. Drop by level tablespoons 2 inches apart onto baking sheets coated with cooking spray. Bake at 350° for 10 minutes. Cool 3 minutes on pans. Remove from pans; cool on wire racks. Yield: 3 dozen (serving size: 1 cookie).

CALORIES 85 (29% from fat); FAT 2.7g (sat 0.3g, mono 0.7g, poly 1.6g); PROTEIN 1.6g; CARB 14.1g; FIBER 0.4g; CHOL 0mg; IRON 0.6mg; SODIUM 24mg; CALC 27mg

---

A TOAST TO NUTS

One of the best ways to bring out the flavor in any kind of nut is to toast it. Heating helps release flavor compounds that make a richer, more intense nut taste. To toast, just place whole or chopped nuts in a shallow pan or on a baking sheet, and bake at 350° for 6 to 8 minutes. Be sure to watch them carefully; they can go from toasted to burned very quickly.

CHICKEN TETRAZZINI WITH ALMONDS

 1 tablespoon butter or stick margarine
 2 cups presliced mushrooms
 ¼ cup chopped shallots
 ⅓ cup all-purpose flour
 2 cups 2% reduced-fat milk
 2 cups fat-free, less-sodium chicken broth
 ⅓ cup sherry
 2 cups chopped cooked chicken breast (about ½ pound)
 ½ cup grated Parmesan cheese
 4 cups hot cooked spaghetti (about 8 ounces uncooked pasta)
 ½ cup slivered almonds, toasted
 ¼ teaspoon salt
 ½ teaspoon black pepper
 ⅛ teaspoon ground nutmeg
Cooking spray
 2 tablespoons grated Parmesan cheese

1. Preheat oven to 350°.
2. Melt butter in a saucepan over medium heat. Add mushrooms and shallots; sauté 5 minutes. Stir in flour. Gradually add milk, broth, and sherry; stir with a whisk until blended. Bring to a boil; reduce heat. Simmer 8 minutes, stirring constantly. Stir in chicken and ½ cup cheese; cook 1 minute. Remove from heat; add pasta, nuts, salt, pepper, and nutmeg. Spoon into a 3-quart casserole coated with cooking spray; top with 2 tablespoons cheese. Bake at 350° for 40 minutes. Let stand 5 minutes. Yield: 6 servings (serving size: about 1¼ cups).

CALORIES 380 (29% from fat); FAT 12.1g (sat 3.6g, mono 5.1g, poly 2.6g); PROTEIN 26.3g; CARB 40.9g; FIBER 3g; CHOL 43mg; IRON 2.9mg; SODIUM 384mg; CALC 259mg

APPLESAUCE-PECAN CRUMB CAKE

 1½ cups all-purpose flour
 ½ cup packed brown sugar
 1 teaspoon baking powder
 ½ teaspoon baking soda
 ½ teaspoon salt
 ¼ teaspoon ground nutmeg
 ½ cup low-fat buttermilk
 ½ cup applesauce
 1 tablespoon butter or stick margarine, melted
 1 large egg
 1 large egg white
Cooking spray
 ⅓ cup chopped pecans
 ⅓ cup all-purpose flour
 ¼ cup packed brown sugar
 2 teaspoons butter or stick margarine, melted
 ½ teaspoon ground cinnamon

1. Preheat oven to 350°.
2. Lightly spoon flour into dry measuring cups; level with a knife. Combine 1½ cups flour and next 5 ingredients in a large bowl; make a well in center of mixture. Combine buttermilk and next 4 ingredients in a bowl; add to flour mixture, stirring just until moist.
3. Spoon batter into a 9-inch round cake pan coated with cooking spray. Combine pecans and remaining 4 ingredients in a small bowl; stir with a fork until mixture resembles coarse meal. Sprinkle evenly over top of cake. Bake at 350° for 35 minutes or until a wooden pick inserted in center comes out clean. Yield: 8 servings.

CALORIES 252 (24% from fat); FAT 6.7g (sat 1g, mono 3.4g, poly 1.8g); PROTEIN 4.9g; CARB 57.3g; FIBER 1.3g; CHOL 27mg; IRON 1.7mg; SODIUM 260mg; CALC 58mg

TEST YOUR NUT KNOWLEDGE

Match the following nuts (**almonds, hazelnuts, macadamias, pecans, and walnuts**) to the appropriate statement below.

1. Descriptions of these date back to 7,000 B.C., making them one of humankind's oldest known tree foods.

2. These are a close botanical cousin of cherries, peaches, and plums and are richer in calcium than other nuts.

3. This type grows on evergreen trees in rain forests. At 20 grams of fat per ounce, they're the fattiest nut.

4. The ancient Greeks and Romans used these medicinally.

5. These were a staple in the diet of many Native Americans living in the South. One ounce of these nuts carries as much zinc as an ounce of red meat.

Answers: 1. walnuts, 2. almonds, 3. macadamias, 4. hazelnuts, 5. pecans.

Source: Nutrition Reviews

Big Bowls

From the heart of Southeast Asia to the sidewalks of New York and the heartland of America, these noodle-and-broth mainstays are the one-dish supertrend of the century.

If the world of what we now call big bowls has a center, it's Southeast Asia. In countries such as Vietnam, Thailand, Cambodia, and Laos, these nearly tureen-size vessels—each comprising a single serving and containing meats, vegetables, delicious broths, steaming hot noodles, and a variety of condiments and flavors—have evolved to become among the most important and influential dishes in the Eastern tradition. The United States also may be joining the crowd as the spirit of the big bowl is being freely translated coast to coast.

Big bowls make your cooking life easier at almost every level. They are easy to make—usually under an hour for preparation. Because liquid is such a great carrier of aromas and tastes, big bowls are intensely flavored. And they almost always contain noodles—nearly everyone's favorite food and one of the most reasonably priced staples at your grocer's.

FRENCH ONION-BEEF BOWL

1½ pounds boned sirloin steak, thinly sliced
½ cup chopped fresh parsley
2 tablespoons balsamic vinegar
2 teaspoons chopped fresh or ½ teaspoon dried thyme
4 garlic cloves, crushed
1 tablespoon butter or stick margarine
6 cups vertically sliced onion (about 3 onions)
1 teaspoon sugar
3 tablespoons all-purpose flour
3 cups water
1 cup dry white wine
1 (16-ounce) can fat-free, less-sodium chicken broth
1 (10½-ounce) can beef consommé
1 tablespoon Worcestershire sauce
½ teaspoon black pepper
¼ teaspoon salt
4 cups hot cooked soba noodles (about 8 ounces uncooked buckwheat noodles)
2 cups garlic-flavored croutons
½ cup (2 ounces) shredded Gruyère or Jarlsberg cheese

1. Combine first 5 ingredients in a large zip-top plastic bag. Seal and marinate in refrigerator 1 to 4 hours.
2. Melt butter in a large Dutch oven over medium-high heat. Add onion and sugar, and cook 10 minutes or until golden brown, stirring frequently. Reduce heat to medium. Cover and cook 10 minutes, stirring frequently. Stir flour into onion mixture, and cook, uncovered, 2 minutes. Add water, wine, broth, and consommé, stirring with a whisk. Bring to a boil; partially cover, reduce heat, and simmer 20 minutes. Add beef mixture, Worcestershire, pepper, and salt; cook, uncovered, 5 minutes. Place noodles into 6 large bowls; top with broth mixture, croutons, and cheese. Yield: 6 servings (serving size: ⅔ cup noodles, about 1⅔ cups broth mixture, ⅓ cup croutons, and about 1 tablespoon cheese).

CALORIES 526 (25% from fat); FAT 14.9g (sat 6.1g, mono 5.4g, poly 2g); PROTEIN 37.7g; CARB 56.1g; FIBER 2.6g; CHOL 94mg; IRON 5.2mg; SODIUM 733mg; CALC 159mg

MINESTRONE BOWL

½ cup sun-dried tomatoes
2 cups boiling water
1 tablespoon olive oil
2 cups chopped lower-salt ham (about 8 ounces)
2 cups chopped onion
1 cup chopped carrot
1 cup chopped celery
5 garlic cloves, chopped
6 cups water
1 (14.5-ounce) can diced tomatoes, undrained
1 zucchini, halved lengthwise and sliced
1 (16-ounce) can cannellini beans or other white beans, rinsed and drained
¼ cup chopped fresh basil
¼ teaspoon salt
¾ teaspoon black pepper
3½ cups hot cooked linguine (about 7 ounces uncooked pasta)
¼ cup plus 2 teaspoons (about 1 ounce) grated fresh Parmesan cheese

1. Combine sun-dried tomatoes and boiling water in a bowl; let stand 30 minutes. Drain sun-dried tomatoes through a sieve into a bowl, reserving sun-dried tomatoes and soaking liquid. Cut sun-dried tomatoes into julienne strips.
2. Heat oil in a large Dutch oven over medium-high heat. Add sun-dried tomatoes, ham, and next 4 ingredients, and sauté 5 minutes. Add reserved soaking liquid, 6 cups water, and diced tomatoes; bring to a boil. Cover, reduce heat, and simmer 30 minutes. Add zucchini and beans; cook 5 minutes. Stir in basil, salt, and pepper. Place pasta into 7 large bowls; top with broth mixture and cheese. Yield: 7 servings (serving size: ½ cup pasta, 2 cups broth mixture, and 2 teaspoons cheese).

CALORIES 319 (21% from fat); FAT 7.4g (sat 2.1g, mono 3.3g, poly 1.4g); PROTEIN 17.1g; CARB 48.1g; FIBER 5.5g; CHOL 22mg; IRON 4mg; SODIUM 822mg; CALC 139mg

NEW ENGLAND PORK BOWL

Perciatelli is thick spaghetti with a hole in the center. It's heartier and stands up to the other ingredients in this dish, but you can substitute spaghetti, if desired.

¼ cup bourbon
¼ cup maple syrup
1 tablespoon Dijon mustard
½ teaspoon salt
½ teaspoon black pepper
5 garlic cloves, minced
1 pound boned pork loin, cut into thin strips
3 bacon slices, cut into ½-inch pieces
2 cups vertically sliced onion
1 cup thinly sliced leek (about 1 large)
2 cups (1-inch) cubed peeled sweet potato
2 cups water
3 (16-ounce) cans fat-free, less-sodium chicken broth
3 cups chopped spinach
4 cups hot cooked perciatelli (about 8 ounces uncooked tube-shaped spaghetti)
¾ cup (3 ounces) finely shredded white Cheddar cheese
6 tablespoons chopped green onions

1. Combine first 7 ingredients in a large zip-top plastic bag. Seal and marinate in refrigerator 4 to 24 hours, turning bag occasionally. Remove pork from bag, reserving marinade.
2. Cook bacon pieces in a large Dutch oven over medium-high heat until bacon is crisp. Remove bacon from pan, reserving bacon drippings in pan, and set bacon aside. Add half of pork to bacon drippings in pan; sauté 5 minutes, and remove pork from pan. Repeat procedure with remaining pork. Add sliced onion and leek to pan, and sauté 5 minutes. Add reserved marinade, pork, sweet potato, water, and broth; bring to a boil. Reduce heat, and simmer 10 minutes. Stir in cooked bacon and spinach, and cook 1 minute. Place pasta into 6 large bowls, and top with broth mixture, cheese, and green onions. Yield: 6 servings (serving size: ⅔ cup pasta, 2 cups broth mixture, 2 tablespoons cheese, and 1 tablespoon green onions).

CALORIES 478 (25% from fat); FAT 13.4g (sat 5.8g, mono 4.9g, poly 1.4g); PROTEIN 30.7g; CARB 57.3g; FIBER 4.5g; CHOL 63mg; IRON 4.1mg; SODIUM 983mg; CALC 189mg

VIETNAMESE BEEF-NOODLE BOWL

Marinating the beef 4 to 24 hours ahead can save preparation time later and add extra flavor.

8 cups water
2 (14¼-ounce) cans fat-free beef broth
3 whole star anise (optional)
2 (3-inch) cinnamon sticks
1 (1½-inch) piece peeled fresh ginger, sliced
4 ounces uncooked rice stick noodles or vermicelli
1½ pounds boned sirloin steak, thinly sliced
2½ tablespoons minced shallots
2 tablespoons sake (rice wine) or rice vinegar
1 tablespoon minced peeled fresh ginger
2 cups fresh bean sprouts
1 cup sliced fresh basil leaves
⅓ cup minced fresh cilantro
¼ cup minced green onions
3 tablespoons fish sauce
½ teaspoon salt
¼ teaspoon black pepper
1 teaspoon thinly sliced red chile (optional)
6 lime wedges (optional)

1. Combine first 5 ingredients in a large Dutch oven; bring to a boil. Reduce heat; simmer 30 minutes. Strain broth; discard solids. Return broth to pan.
2. Place rice noodles into a large bowl, and cover with hot water. Let stand 15 minutes; drain. Cook noodles in boiling water 1 minute or until tender; drain.
3. Combine beef, shallots, sake, and minced ginger in a large zip-top plastic bag; seal and marinate in refrigerator 10 minutes. Add beef mixture to broth in pan; bring to a boil. Reduce heat to medium; cook 3 minutes. Stir in bean sprouts and next 6 ingredients; cook 1 minute.
4. Place noodles into 6 large bowls; top with broth mixture. If desired, garnish with sliced chile and lime wedges. Yield: 6 servings (serving size: ½ cup noodles and 2 cups broth mixture).

CALORIES 264 (20% from fat); FAT 6g (sat 2.1g, mono 2.4g, poly 0.3g); PROTEIN 31.1g; CARB 20.8g; FIBER 1.2g; CHOL 70mg; IRON 4mg; SODIUM 967mg; CALC 35mg

SPICY PORTUGUESE BOWL

1 pound collard greens
½ pound chorizo or spicy sausage, cut into ½-inch-thick slices
3 cups chopped onion
6 garlic cloves, chopped
4 (16-ounce) cans fat-free, less-sodium chicken broth
1 (15-ounce) can navy beans, drained
¼ teaspoon black pepper
4 cups hot cooked fettuccine (about 8 ounces uncooked pasta)

1. Remove and discard stems from collard greens. Wash and pat dry; cut crosswise into 1-inch-wide strips.
2. Cook sausage in a large Dutch oven over medium heat until browned. Remove sausage from pan with a slotted spoon, reserving sausage drippings. Add onion and garlic to drippings in pan, and sauté 5 minutes or until tender. Add greens, sausage, and broth, and bring to a boil. Cover, reduce heat, and simmer 25 minutes or until greens are tender. Add beans and pepper, and cook 10 minutes. Place pasta in 6 large bowls, and top with broth mixture. Yield: 6 servings (serving size: ⅔ cup pasta and 1⅔ cups broth mixture).

CALORIES 386 (26% from fat); FAT 11.2g (sat 4g, mono 5.2g, poly 1.4g); PROTEIN 19.4g; CARB 52.9g; FIBER 6.7g; CHOL 23mg; IRON 3.8mg; SODIUM 1,033mg; CALC 204mg

CARIBBEAN SHRIMP BOWL

(pictured on page 59)

Marinated shrimp:

⅓ cup chopped fresh cilantro
3 tablespoons honey
1 tablespoon minced peeled fresh ginger
2 teaspoons grated lemon rind
2 teaspoons grated orange rind
2 teaspoons curry powder
¼ teaspoon ground red pepper
1½ pounds medium shrimp, peeled and deveined
Cooking spray

Broth mixture:

2 teaspoons vegetable oil
2 cups vertically sliced onion
4 garlic cloves, minced
1 jalapeño pepper, seeded and minced
2 cups (1-inch) cubed peeled butternut squash
2 cups water
2 teaspoons minced peeled fresh ginger
1 teaspoon chopped fresh or ¼ teaspoon dried thyme
3 (16-ounce) cans fat-free, less-sodium chicken broth
4 cups torn kale (about 1 small bunch)

Remaining ingredients:

4 cups hot cooked udon noodles (thick, round fresh Japanese wheat noodles) or spaghetti (about 8 ounces uncooked pasta)
2 tablespoons chopped fresh cilantro
2 tablespoons sliced jalapeño pepper rings
6 lime wedges

1. To prepare marinated shrimp, combine first 7 ingredients in a zip-top plastic bag. Add shrimp to bag; seal. Marinate in refrigerator 30 minutes, turning occasionally. Remove shrimp from bag. Place a large Dutch oven coated with cooking spray over medium-high heat until hot. Add shrimp; cook 3 minutes or until done. Remove from pan; set aside.

2. To prepare broth mixture, heat oil in pan over medium-high heat. Add onion, garlic, and minced jalapeño; sauté 4 minutes. Add squash and next 4 ingredients. Bring to a boil; cover, reduce heat, and simmer 10 minutes or until squash is tender. Add kale; cook 5 minutes.

3. Place noodles into 6 large bowls. Top with shrimp, broth mixture, 2 tablespoons cilantro, and sliced jalapeño. Serve with lime wedges. Yield: 6 servings (serving size: ⅔ cup noodles, ⅔ cup shrimp, 1⅔ cups broth mixture, 1 teaspoon chopped cilantro, 1 teaspoon sliced jalapeño, and 1 lime wedge).

CALORIES 383 (21% from fat); FAT 9g (sat 3.3g, mono 1.9g, poly 2.9g); PROTEIN 26.5g; CARB 50.3g; FIBER 3.2g; CHOL 133mg; IRON 4.8mg; SODIUM 1,245mg; CALC 160mg

JAPANESE PORK-NOODLE BOWL

6 cups water
3 cups (2-inch) sliced green onions (about 10)
2 cups (2-inch) julienne-cut carrot (about ½ pound)
1½ cups sake (rice wine)
½ cup low-sodium soy sauce
2 tablespoons sugar
½ teaspoon dried crushed red pepper
1 (1½-inch) piece peeled fresh ginger, sliced
1½ pounds boned pork loin, cut into ½-inch slices
1 (10-ounce) package fresh spinach, chopped (about 8 cups)
2½ cups hot cooked whole-wheat spaghetti (about 5 ounces uncooked pasta)

1. Combine first 8 ingredients in a large Dutch oven, and bring vegetable mixture to a boil. Partially cover, reduce heat, and simmer over low heat 20 minutes. Add pork. Bring mixture to a boil; cover, reduce heat, and simmer 35 minutes or until pork is tender. Remove ginger slices with a slotted spoon, and discard. Add spinach, and cook 1 minute or until wilted. Place spaghetti into each of 5 large bowls, and top with broth mixture. Yield: 5 servings (serving size: ½ cup spaghetti and 2¼ cups broth mixture).

CALORIES 385 (25% from fat); FAT 10.7g (sat 4g, mono 4.5g, poly 1.2g); PROTEIN 36g; CARB 35.9g; FIBER 8.2g; CHOL 78mg; IRON 5.9mg; SODIUM 938mg; CALC 140mg

---

BUILDING YOUR BOWL

Because the noodles and broth in big-bowl recipes are prepared separately, you don't want to dump them together before serving. Instead, combine them as you serve. It's easy.

1. After draining the cooked noodles, put some into each bowl.

2. Then ladle the broth mixture over the noodles.

3. Mix in whichever noodle toppings you've prepared, and you're ready to eat.

If you have leftovers, you should continue to keep the noodles and broth separate. Storing them in the same container may seem expedient, but the noodles will expand like sponges in the broth, and the flavor will be affected, too. When you're ready to re-serve, heat the noodles and broth separately in the microwave, and then combine them as you did originally.

Scene Stealer

Our Dinner & a Movie *Super Chef Cook-off brought 10 of the country's best chefs to New York City. But the winning recipes are just right for your own kitchen.*

What do you get if you take 10 of this country's most talented chefs, pit them against each other at the trendy Supper Club in Manhattan, and fill the room with media moguls and food experts? A good table, if you're lucky. And we were, as cohosts of TBS Superstation's first *Dinner & a Movie* Super Chef Cook-off—so far as we know the only culinary competition in the world in which chefs have to be up on their cinema as well as their cooking. The rules for this contest called for a recipe that was not only delicious and low in fat, but required an inspirational reference to the 1990 celluloid romance, *Ghost*. Odd, maybe, but what else would you expect from *Dinner & a Movie* co-hosts Annabelle Gurwitch and Paul Gilmartin? When the judging ended, the winner, Houston chef Claire Smith, had given us a tour-de-force version of clay-pot chicken that will taste as good on your table as it did in the bright lights of New York City.

The cook-off was about celebrating and eating, and as the merrymaking progressed, guests were invited to sample. Let it be said: Everything was excellent, including the donation of the $5,000 "Super Chef" prize in Smith's name to the antihunger organization Share Our Strength.

STEAMY CLAY-POT CHICKEN WITH TO-KILL-FOR EMBEZZLER'S PURSES

This winning dish from Claire Smith of Houston's Daily Review Café can also be made in a large Dutch oven. The Embezzler's Purses are superb, but it's not against the law to leave them out.

Broth:

- 1 cup chopped fresh cilantro
- 1 cup chopped plum tomato
- 2 tablespoons chopped red onion
- ½ cup fat-free, less-sodium chicken broth
- 2 garlic cloves, chopped
- 1 jalapeño pepper, seeded and chopped
- Dash of curry powder
- Dash of ground cumin
- Dash of chili powder

Chicken and vegetables:

- ¾ teaspoon salt, divided
- ½ teaspoon ground cumin
- ½ teaspoon ground coriander
- ¼ teaspoon black pepper
- ¼ teaspoon saffron threads
- ¼ teaspoon ground ginger
- 4 (4-ounce) skinned, boned chicken breast halves
- 1½ teaspoons olive oil
- 7 cups (1-inch) cubed peeled eggplant (about 1 pound)
- 1⅓ cups (1-inch) pieces red bell pepper
- ⅛ teaspoon black pepper
- 18 cherry tomatoes
- 8 red potatoes, halved
- Embezzler's Purses (optional)

1. Preheat oven to 375°.
2. To prepare broth, combine first 9 ingredients in a blender or food processor; process until smooth. Set aside.
3. To prepare chicken and vegetables, combine ½ teaspoon salt, ½ teaspoon cumin, and next 4 ingredients; rub spice mixture over chicken.
4. Heat olive oil in a large nonstick skillet over medium-high heat. Add chicken, and sauté 3 minutes on each side or until lightly browned. Remove from pan. Add eggplant and bell pepper to pan; sauté 2 minutes. Sprinkle with ¼ teaspoon salt and ⅛ teaspoon black pepper. Spoon eggplant mixture into a large clay pot or Dutch oven; top with cherry tomatoes and potatoes. Pour broth over vegetables; arrange chicken on top of vegetables. Cover and bake at 375° for 40 minutes or until potatoes are tender. Serve with Embezzler's Purses, if desired. Yield: 4 servings (serving size: 1 chicken breast half, 1½ cups vegetables, and 1 Embezzler's Purse).

CALORIES 298 (14% from fat); FAT 4.3g (sat 0.8g, mono 1.8g, poly 1g); PROTEIN 32.2g; CARB 34.8g; FIBER 8.3g; CHOL 66mg; IRON 4.9mg; SODIUM 606g; CALC 74mg

Embezzler's Purses:

These make great appetizers all by themselves.

- 8 green onion tops
- 2 teaspoons olive oil
- ¾ pound ground turkey
- 8 ounces packaged fresh spinach (about 4 cups)
- ½ cup (2 ounces) finely crumbled feta cheese
- ¼ cup pine nuts, toasted
- ¼ teaspoon salt
- ¼ teaspoon black pepper
- Dash of paprika
- Dash of ground cinnamon
- 4 sheets frozen phyllo dough, thawed
- 4 teaspoons butter or stick margarine, melted

1. Preheat oven to 375°.
2. Cook onion tops in boiling water 2 minutes. Drain and plunge into ice water; drain.
3. Heat oil in a nonstick skillet over medium-high heat. Sauté turkey 5 minutes or until done. Add spinach; cook until spinach wilts. Stir in cheese and next 5 ingredients; remove from heat.

Continued

4. Place 1 phyllo sheet on a large cutting board or work surface (cover remaining dough to keep from drying); lightly brush with 2 teaspoons butter. Top with a second phyllo sheet; cut into 4 squares. Spoon ⅓ cup turkey mixture in center of each square. Gather 4 corners of phyllo, and crimp to seal, forming a purse. Tie 1 green onion strip around top of each purse. Repeat with remaining phyllo, butter, turkey mixture, and green onion strips. Place purses on a baking sheet, and bake at 375° for 8 minutes or until golden brown. Yield: 8 purses (serving size: 1 purse).

CALORIES 160 (51% from fat); FAT 9g (sat 3.3g, mono 3g, poly 2g); PROTEIN 13.2g; CARB 7.7g; FIBER 1.5g; CHOL 39mg; IRON 2.4mg; SODIUM 272mg; CALC 79mg

PATRICK SAGE-Y CRUSTED LAMB LOIN WITH ANGEL HAIR PANCAKE AND BROKEN HEARTS OF PALM-TEARDROP TOMATO SALAD

(pictured on page 57)

The "People's Choice Award" was given to Marty Blitz of Mise en Place in Tampa, Florida, for this recipe. Don't be intimidated by the mushroom crust—it's easy to whirl dried porcini mushrooms in a clean coffee grinder. You can substitute a 12-ounce beef tenderloin or pork tenderloin for the lamb.

Salad:

    ¾ cup (½-inch) diagonally sliced canned hearts of palm (about 4)
    ⅓ cup vertically sliced red onion
    2 tablespoons thinly sliced fresh basil
    1½ tablespoons sherry vinegar
    1½ tablespoons olive oil
    ⅛ teaspoon salt
    ⅛ teaspoon black pepper
    9 teardrop or round cherry tomatoes, halved
    1 large garlic clove, minced

Pancakes:

    1½ tablespoons chopped fresh parsley
    ¼ teaspoon salt
    ¼ teaspoon black pepper
    3 large eggs
    3 cups cooked angel hair (about 6 ounces uncooked pasta)
    1 tablespoon olive oil, divided

Lamb:

    1 (0.35-ounce) package dried porcini mushrooms
    1 tablespoon minced fresh or 1 teaspoon dried rubbed sage
    ⅛ teaspoon salt
    ⅛ teaspoon black pepper
    1 (12-ounce) boned lamb loin
    1 teaspoon olive oil

1. Preheat oven to 400°.
2. To prepare salad, combine first 9 ingredients in a bowl; toss gently to coat. Set aside.
3. To prepare pancakes, combine parsley, ¼ teaspoon salt, ¼ teaspoon pepper, and eggs in a large bowl, stirring with a whisk. Add pasta; toss well to coat. Heat 1 teaspoon oil in a small nonstick skillet over medium-high heat. Add 1 cup pasta mixture; cook 1 minute on each side or until golden brown. Repeat procedure twice with 2 teaspoons oil and remaining pasta mixture; keep warm.
4. To prepare lamb, place mushrooms in a spice or coffee grinder, and process until finely ground. Combine 1 table-spoon ground mushrooms, sage, ⅛ teaspoon salt, and ⅛ teaspoon pepper, reserving remaining ground mushrooms for another use. Rub lamb with mushroom mixture. Heat 1 teaspoon oil in a large nonstick skillet over medium-high heat. Add lamb; sauté 1 minute on all sides. Insert a meat thermometer into thickest part of lamb. Wrap handle of skillet with foil if not ovenproof; place skillet in oven. Bake at 400° for 8 minutes or until meat thermometer registers 145° (medium-rare) to 160° (medium). Let stand 5 minutes before slicing.

5. Place 1 pancake on each of 3 serving plates; top each pancake with ¾ cup salad. Arrange 3 ounces lamb around each salad. Yield: 3 servings.

CALORIES 629 (40% from fat); FAT 27.7g (sat 6.5g, mono 15.2g, poly 2.9g); PROTEIN 41.2g; CARB 50.5g; FIBER 5.6g; CHOL 302mg; IRON 6.6mg; SODIUM 769mg; CALC 94mg

THE INVISIBLE SALMON WRAPPED IN GHOSTLY RICE PAPER LYING IN A TOMATO BLOOD PUDDLE ON BLACK BEAN PAVEMENT BY A BROCCOLI TREE

The title of this dish by Nora Pouillon of Nora in Washington, D.C., may twist your tongue, but the flavors will delight it.

Black-bean sauce:

    1 teaspoon vegetable oil
    1 cup finely chopped onion
    2 tablespoons finely chopped peeled fresh ginger
    3 garlic cloves, minced
    ½ cup dry sherry
    1 (14.5-ounce) can no-salt-added diced tomatoes, undrained
    ¼ cup Chinese fermented black beans
    1 tablespoon chopped fresh cilantro
    1 tablespoon chopped fresh mint
    1 tablespoon chopped fresh basil
    1 tablespoon fish sauce
    ¼ teaspoon black pepper

Salmon:

    4 (6-ounce) salmon fillets (about 1 inch thick), skinned
    ¼ teaspoon black pepper
    ⅛ teaspoon salt
    4 cilantro sprigs
    4 (8-inch) round sheets rice paper
    1½ teaspoons vegetable oil

Remaining ingredients:

    4 broccoli spears
    2 cups hot cooked short-grain rice

1. To prepare black-bean sauce, heat 1 teaspoon oil in a medium saucepan over medium-high heat. Add onion, ginger, and garlic; sauté 5 minutes or until tender. Stir in sherry. Bring to a boil; cook until reduced to ½ cup (about 2 minutes). Add tomatoes; reduce heat, and simmer 2 minutes. Stir in black beans and next 5 ingredients. Remove from heat.

2. To prepare salmon, sprinkle 1 side of fillet evenly with ¼ teaspoon pepper and salt. Gently press 1 cilantro sprig onto center of each fillet. Add hot water to a large shallow dish to a depth of 1 inch. Place 1 rice paper sheet in dish of water. Let stand 30 seconds. Remove sheet from water. Place sheet on a flat surface; let stand 30 seconds. Place 1 fillet, cilantro side down, in center of sheet. Fold edges of sheet over fillet; press seams to seal. Cover with a damp towel to prevent fish packet from drying. Repeat procedure with remaining rice paper sheets and fish. Heat 1½ teaspoons oil in a large nonstick skillet over medium-high heat. Add fish packets, cilantro sides down, to skillet, and cook 4 minutes on each side or until fish is done.

3. Steam broccoli, covered, 2 minutes or until crisp-tender.

4. Place 1 fish packet on each of 4 serving plates; spoon about ⅔ cup black-bean sauce around each fish packet. Arrange ½ cup rice and 1 broccoli spear on each plate. Yield: 4 servings.
Note: Bottled Chinese fermented black beans can be found in Asian markets.

CALORIES 518 (30% from fat); FAT 17.5g (sat 3.2g, mono 7.9g, poly 4.9g); PROTEIN 41.9g; CARB 47.3g; FIBER 3.7g; CHOL 111mg; IRON 3.8mg; SODIUM 780mg; CALC 119mg

PAIR-O-NORMAL GAME HENS WITH "BREAK ON THROUGH TO THE OTHER SIDE" OF MANGO SALSA

This recipe from Susan Goss of Zinfandel in Chicago is great on the grill.

Mango salsa:

    2   cups diced peeled mango
    ½   cup thinly sliced green onions
    ½   cup diced red bell pepper
    ¼   cup fresh lime juice
    2   teaspoons minced seeded
          jalapeño pepper
    2   teaspoons chopped fresh basil
    2   teaspoons chopped fresh mint
    2   teaspoons grated orange rind

Deviled seasoning paste:

    1   tablespoon Dijon mustard
    1   tablespoon honey
    1   teaspoon curry powder
    1   teaspoon dried oregano
    1   teaspoon grated orange rind
    1   teaspoon olive oil
    ½   teaspoon salt
    ¼   teaspoon ground red pepper
    ⅛   teaspoon black pepper
    2   (1¼-pound) Cornish hens

1. Preheat oven to 425°.
2. To prepare mango salsa, combine first 8 ingredients in a bowl; cover and chill.
3. To prepare deviled seasoning paste, combine mustard and next 8 ingredients in a small bowl. Remove and discard giblets and necks from hens. Rinse hens with cold water; pat dry. Starting at neck cavity, loosen skin from breasts by inserting fingers, gently pushing between skin and meat. Lift wing tips up and over back; tuck under hens. Rub deviled seasoning paste under loosened skin. Place hens, breast sides up, on a broiler pan. Bake at 425° for 35 minutes or until juices run clear. Split hens in half lengthwise. Discard skin. Serve with mango salsa. Yield: 4 servings (serving size: 1 hen half and about ⅔ cup salsa).

CALORIES 303 (29% from fat); FAT 9.7g (sat 2.4g, mono 3.8g, poly 2g); PROTEIN 31.8g; CARB 23.1g; FIBER 2.2g; CHOL 95mg; IRON 2.2mg; SODIUM 501mg; CALC 49mg

Cruising, with a Healthy Twist

This is one cruise with the perfect balance of learning and leisure—not to mention good food, good friends, and great scenery.

On the third-annual *Cooking Light* Ship Shape Cruise Adventure, a group of *Cooking Light* staffers and 280 readers spent the week aboard the *Galaxy,* a Celebrity Cruises ship, feasting on several meals prepared with *Cooking Light* recipes; going on exclusive shore excursions tailored to interests in food and fitness; and sitting in on as many as 10 editor-led seminars.

HONEY-CURRY GLAZED PINEAPPLE

This quick-and-easy recipe is a favorite of Hotel 1829 chef Matt Curry in St. Thomas, U.S. Virgin Islands. Serve as a dessert or a side dish with pork.

    1   pineapple, peeled and
          cut into 2-inch chunks
    ¼   cup honey
    1   tablespoon curry powder
    1   tablespoon vanilla extract
    ¼   cup light brown sugar
    ¼   cup Grand Marnier (orange-
          flavored liqueur)

1. Preheat oven to 500°.
2. Combine pineapple chunks, honey, curry, and vanilla in a bowl; toss well. Arrange on a baking sheet. Bake at 500° for 10 minutes. Sprinkle with brown sugar, and drizzle with Grand Marnier. Ignite pineapple with a long match, and let flames die down. Yield: 4 servings.

CALORIES 227 (5% from fat); FAT 1.2g (sat 0.1g, mono 0.2g, poly 0.4g); PROTEIN 1.1g; CARB 56.4g; FIBER 3.3g; CHOL 0mg; IRON 1.6mg; SODIUM 8mg; CALC 33mg

Gone But Not Forgotten

We lightened a luscious cheesecake recipe sent by a reader. Now if we could just find her ....

Reader Judy Chang would be ecstatic to learn that we'd lightened her rich sour cream cheesecake. But we can't locate her. Our letter was returned to sender.

We've preserved the richness of Judy's recipe by replacing regular cream cheese with low-fat cottage cheese and both light and fat-free cream cheeses. Our changes have dropped the fat level from nearly 36 grams of fat per serving to less than 10.

SOUR CREAM CHEESECAKE

Crust:

- 1 cup reduced-fat graham cracker crumbs (about 10 cookie sheets)
- ¼ cup sugar
- 2 tablespoons butter or stick margarine, melted
- Cooking spray

Filling:

- 1 cup 2% low-fat cottage cheese
- 1½ tablespoons vanilla extract
- ½ teaspoon salt
- 1 (8-ounce) block ⅓-less-fat cream cheese
- 1 (8-ounce) block fat-free cream cheese
- 3 large eggs
- 1 large egg white
- 1 cup sugar

Topping:

- 3 tablespoons sugar
- 1 teaspoon vanilla extract
- 1 (8-ounce) carton low-fat sour cream
- 1 (8-ounce) carton fat-free sour cream

1. Preheat oven to 350°.
2. To prepare crust, combine first 3 ingredients in a bowl. Firmly press crumb mixture into bottom and 2 inches up sides of a 9-inch springform pan coated with cooking spray. Bake at 350° for 10 minutes, and cool crust on a wire rack.
3. To prepare filling, combine cottage cheese and next 4 ingredients in a food processor; process 1 minute or until smooth. Add eggs and egg white, 1 at a time, pulsing after each addition. Add 1 cup sugar; process just until blended.
4. Pour cheese mixture into prepared crust, and bake at 350° for 50 minutes or until cheesecake is almost set. Remove cheesecake from oven, and let stand 10 minutes. Increase oven temperature to 450°.
5. To prepare topping, combine 3 tablespoons sugar and remaining 3 ingredients. Spread evenly over cheesecake. Bake cheesecake at 450° for 5 minutes or until set. Cool completely on wire rack. Cover and chill 8 hours. Yield: 12 servings (serving size: 1 slice).

CALORIES 300 (29% from fat); FAT 9.6g (sat 5.5g, mono 2.9g, poly 0.6g); PROTEIN 11.8g; CARB 38.9g; FIBER 0.4g; CHOL 83mg; IRON 0.7mg; SODIUM 508mg; CALC 128mg

BEFORE & AFTER	
SERVING SIZE	
1 slice	
CALORIES	
495	300
FAT	
35.9g	9.6g
PERCENT OF TOTAL CALORIES	
65%	29%
CHOLESTEROL	
167mg	83mg

Near-Miss Day

Life is full of narrow scrapes. You just gotta move on. Let the crumbs fall where they may and the dough drop where it will. Still, it never hurts to aim.

GIANT OATMEAL DROP COOKIES

- 1 cup packed dark brown sugar
- 2 tablespoons butter or stick margarine, softened
- ½ cup applesauce
- 1 large egg
- 1½ cups all-purpose flour
- 1½ cups regular oats
- 1 teaspoon baking soda
- 1 teaspoon ground cinnamon
- ¼ teaspoon salt
- ½ cup raisins
- ½ cup chopped walnuts
- 1½ teaspoons vanilla extract
- Cooking spray

1. Preheat oven to 350°.
2. Beat sugar and butter at medium speed of a mixer until well-blended (about 5 minutes). Add applesauce and egg; beat well. Lightly spoon flour into dry measuring cups; level with a knife. Combine flour, oats, soda, cinnamon, and salt. Add flour mixture to sugar mixture; beat at low speed until well-blended. Stir in raisins, walnuts, and vanilla. Using 3 level tablespoons per cookie, drop dough 2 inches apart onto baking sheets coated with cooking spray; flatten dough slightly. Bake at 350° for 10 to 15 minutes. Remove cookies from pans; cool on wire racks. Yield: 15 cookies (serving size: 1 cookie).

CALORIES 196 (23% from fat); FAT 4.9g (sat 1.3g, mono 1.3g, poly 1.9g); PROTEIN 4.2g; CARB 34.7g; FIBER 1.9g; CHOL 19mg; IRON 1.5mg; SODIUM 150mg; CALC 28mg

Patrick Sage-y Crusted Lamb Loin with Angel Hair Pancake and Broken Hearts of Palm-Teardrop Tomato Salad, page 54

Hazelnut-Fig Quick Bread, page 48

Skewered Singapore Chicken and Pineapple, page 67

Creamy Two-Cheese Potatoes Gratin, page 70

Caribbean Shrimp Bowl, page 52

*Make-Ahead
Cappuccino-Oreo
Trifles, page 73*

Sliced Lemon-Pistachio Chicken over Greens, page 64

So Many Mustards, So Little Time

If you think mustard comes in just yellow and works on buns only, you're missing about 999 flavorful alternatives and at least as many cooking adventures.

For some, mustard is the generic yellow stuff you squeeze out of plastic containers onto hot dogs at the ballpark. For others, it's the grocery store's sensory-overloading section with all the mustard choices—estimated at nearly 1,000 on the American market today.

Beyond serving it as a condiment, straight-up on sandwiches, or as a pretzel dip, cooks like to use prepared mustard to add flavor as well as to bind sauces and vinaigrettes. As mustard inventories swell—as many as 80 new mustard blends enter the market each year—creative cooks will keep scraping the jar for new recipes.

HONEY-MUSTARD PORK TENDERLOIN WITH KALE

Pork:

- 1 (1-pound) pork tenderloin
- ¼ cup stone-ground mustard
- 2 tablespoons honey
- 1 tablespoon sherry vinegar or white wine vinegar
- Cooking spray

Sauce:

- 2 tablespoons honey
- 1 tablespoon sherry vinegar or white wine vinegar
- ¾ cup fat-free, less-sodium chicken broth
- ¼ cup sherry
- 2 tablespoons minced shallot
- 1 tablespoon stone-ground mustard

Kale:

- 6 cups torn kale
- ¼ cup fat-free, less-sodium chicken broth
- 1 tablespoon stone-ground mustard
- 1 tablespoon minced shallot

1. To prepare pork, trim fat from pork. Combine pork and next 3 ingredients in a large zip-top plastic bag. Seal and marinate in refrigerator 2 hours, turning occasionally. Remove pork from bag, reserving marinade.
2. Preheat oven to 375°.
3. Place pork on a broiler pan coated with cooking spray. Insert a meat thermometer into thickest portion of pork. Bake at 375° for 40 minutes or until thermometer registers 160° (slightly pink). Let stand 10 minutes before slicing.
4. To prepare sauce, combine reserved marinade, 2 tablespoons honey, and next 5 ingredients in a small saucepan; bring to a boil. Reduce heat to medium; cook 15 minutes. Set aside.
5. To prepare kale, combine kale, ¼ cup chicken broth, 1 tablespoon mustard, and 1 tablespoon shallot in a large skillet over medium heat. Cover and cook 8 minutes or until tender. Yield: 4 servings (serving size: 3 ounces meat, 3 tablespoons sauce, and ½ cup kale).

CALORIES 287 (16% from fat); FAT 5.2g (sat 1.1g, mono 2.1g, poly 0.8g); PROTEIN 28.6g; CARB 31.5g; FIBER 1.8g; CHOL 74mg; IRON 3.8mg; SODIUM 634mg; CALC 175mg

MUSTARDY RED-FLANNEL HASH WITH SMOKED TURKEY

We prefer an old-fashioned whole-grain mustard—one of the most popular blends—to stand up to the strong flavors of this hearty dish.

- 1 teaspoon olive oil
- 1 cup diced onion
- 3 cups diced peeled red potato
- ¼ teaspoon black pepper
- 1 garlic clove, minced
- 1 cup drained diced canned beets
- 2 cups diced smoked turkey breast (about ¾ pound)
- 3 tablespoons water
- 3 tablespoons fat-free sour cream
- 3 tablespoons whole-grain mustard
- 2 teaspoons minced fresh or ½ teaspoon dried thyme

1. Heat oil in a large nonstick skillet over medium-high heat. Add diced onion, and sauté 5 minutes. Add diced potato, black pepper, and minced garlic, and cook 15 minutes, stirring frequently. Add diced beets, and sauté 5 minutes. Add smoked turkey breast, and sauté 1 minute. Combine water, sour cream, mustard, and thyme, and stir into turkey mixture. Remove from heat; cover and let stand 3 minutes. Yield: 4 servings (serving size: 1 cup).

CALORIES 246 (15% from fat); FAT 4g (sat 0.8g, mono 2.1g, poly 0.9g); PROTEIN 24.3g; CARB 29.3g; FIBER 3.2g; CHOL 48mg; IRON 1.9mg; SODIUM 927mg; CALC 48mg

CUTTING THE MUSTARD

If you would like to start your own mustard collection or want to order a jar of moutarde that your local grocer doesn't stock, call the Mount Horeb Mustard Museum at 800/438-6878. Or go to www.mustardweb.com for more information.

BISTRO CHICKEN WITH ROSEMARY-ROASTED POTATOES

4 (6-ounce) skinned chicken
    breast halves
¼ cup stone-ground mustard
1 tablespoon minced fresh or
    1 teaspoon dried thyme
1 tablespoon minced fresh or
    1 teaspoon dried marjoram
2 baking potatoes, each cut into
    8 wedges (about 1 pound)
1 tablespoon olive oil
½ teaspoon dried rosemary,
    crushed
¼ teaspoon salt
¼ teaspoon black pepper
Cooking spray
1 teaspoon olive oil
1⅓ cups chopped onion
¾ cup dry white wine
4 garlic cloves, minced
1 (16-ounce) can fat-free,
    less-sodium chicken broth
1½ teaspoons cornstarch
1 tablespoon water

1. Combine first 4 ingredients in a shallow dish. Cover and marinate in refrigerator 2 hours, turning occasionally.
2. Preheat oven to 450°.
3. Combine potatoes and next 4 ingredients in a medium bowl; toss well. Arrange potato mixture on a baking sheet coated with cooking spray. Bake at 450° for 30 minutes or until tender, stirring occasionally.
4. While potatoes are baking, prepare chicken. Heat 1 teaspoon oil in a large Dutch oven over medium-high heat. Add onion, and sauté 8 minutes, stirring frequently. Add wine, and bring to a boil. Stir in garlic. Place chicken, meat sides up, on top of onion. Add broth, and bring to a boil. Cover, reduce heat to medium, and cook 15 minutes or until chicken is done. Remove chicken from pan with a slotted spoon; keep warm. Bring broth mixture to a boil, and cook until reduced to 2 cups (about 15 minutes).

Combine cornstarch and water; add to pan, and bring to a boil. Cook 1 minute, stirring constantly. Pour sauce over chicken. Serve with roasted potatoes. Yield: 4 servings (serving size: 1 chicken breast half, about ⅓ cup sauce, and 4 potato wedges).

CALORIES 449 (21% from fat); FAT 10.6g (sat 2.1g, mono 6g, poly 1.7g); PROTEIN 46.8g; CARB 38.2g; FIBER 3.3g; CHOL 114mg; IRON 3.6mg; SODIUM 946mg; CALC 59mg

CARROTS WITH CASSIS MUSTARD AND RED ONIONS

Dijon, France, is famous not only for its mustard, but for crème de cassis, a black currant liqueur. This recipe calls for cassis mustard, a mixture of the two famous French ingredients. If a substitute is necessary, mix 2 tablespoons Dijon mustard with 2 teaspoons crème de cassis or grape juice.

1 teaspoon butter or stick
    margarine
2 cups vertically sliced red onion
3 cups (3-inch) julienne-cut
    carrot (about ¾ pound)
¼ cup water
2 tablespoons cassis mustard
    (such as Edmond Fallot)
1 tablespoon crème de cassis
    (black currant-flavored
    liqueur) or 2 tablespoons
    grape juice
¼ teaspoon salt
⅛ teaspoon black pepper

1. Melt butter in a medium nonstick skillet over medium-high heat. Add onion; cover and cook 3 minutes. Stir in carrot and water. Cover, reduce heat to medium-low, and cook 12 minutes or until tender. Stir in mustard and crème de cassis. Sprinkle with salt and pepper. Yield: 6 servings (serving size: ½ cup).

CALORIES 53 (19% from fat); FAT 1.1g (sat 0.2g, mono 0.3g, poly 0.3g); PROTEIN 1g; CARB 9.3g; FIBER 2.5g; CHOL 0mg; IRON 0.4mg; SODIUM 274mg; CALC 23mg

SEA BASS AND BRAISED LEEKS WITH MUSTARD SAUCE

Named after the French town where it has been made for centuries, Dijon mustard has a smooth, elegant texture and a taste suited to more subtle ingredients.

1 teaspoon olive oil
2 cups thinly sliced leek
    (about 2 large)
¼ teaspoon salt
⅛ teaspoon black pepper
4 cups (1-inch) diagonally sliced
    Belgian endive (about 3 heads)
3 garlic cloves, minced
Cooking spray
½ cup dry white wine
½ cup clam juice
¼ cup Dijon mustard, divided
1 teaspoon dried marjoram
4 (6-ounce) sea bass or grouper
    fillets

1. Preheat oven to 400°.
2. Heat oil in a large nonstick skillet over medium-high heat. Add leek; sauté 4 minutes. Stir in salt and pepper. Remove mixture from pan, and set aside. Add endive to pan. Sauté 9 minutes; stir occasionally. Add garlic, and cook 1 minute. Remove from heat; stir in leek mixture. Spoon into a 13 x 9-inch baking dish coated with cooking spray.
3. Combine wine, clam juice, and 2 tablespoons mustard in skillet; cook over medium-high heat until reduced to ⅔ cup (about 5 minutes). Remove from heat; stir in marjoram.
4. Spread 2 tablespoons mustard evenly over both sides of fillets. Arrange fillets on top of vegetables, and pour wine mixture over fillets. Cover and bake at 400° for 20 minutes or until fish flakes easily when tested with a fork. Yield: 4 servings (serving size: 1 fillet and ¾ cup vegetables).

CALORIES 267 (30% from fat); FAT 8.8g (sat 1.6g, mono 3.9g, poly 2.2g); PROTEIN 33.6g; CARB 10.9g; FIBER 0.7g; CHOL 116mg; IRON 4.1mg; SODIUM 791mg; CALC 180mg

Mustard-Spiced Cabbage and Cannellini Beans with Sausage

The coarse, almost crunchy, feel of whole-grain mustard is the perfect highlight for this peasantlike dish.

6   smoked turkey and duck
      sausages (such as Gerhard's)
      or turkey kielbasa, halved
      lengthwise (about 1¼ pounds)
1½ cups chopped onion
1   teaspoon fennel seeds, lightly
      crushed
1   teaspoon ground coriander
2   garlic cloves, minced
5   cups thinly sliced green cabbage
      (about 1½ pounds)
½   cup fat-free, less-sodium
      chicken broth
¼   cup whole-grain mustard
1   teaspoon chopped fresh or
      ¼ teaspoon dried thyme
½   teaspoon salt
1   (15-ounce) can cannellini
      beans, drained
Fresh thyme sprigs (optional)

1. Cook sausages in a large nonstick skillet over medium-high heat about 4 minutes on each side or until done. Remove from skillet; keep warm.
2. Add onion to skillet, and sauté 5 minutes or until tender. Add fennel seeds, coriander, and garlic; sauté 2 minutes. Add cabbage; cook 6 minutes. Add broth and mustard; cover and cook 10 minutes or until cabbage is tender. Stir in chopped thyme, salt, and beans; cook 5 minutes or until thoroughly heated. Garnish with thyme sprigs, if desired. Yield: 6 servings (serving size: 1 cup cabbage mixture and 2 sausage halves).

CALORIES 255 (29% from fat); FAT 8.3g (sat 2g, mono 3.4g, poly 2.3g); PROTEIN 20.2g; CARB 26.4g; FIBER 6.6g; CHOL 66mg; IRON 3.3mg; SODIUM 882mg; CALC 106mg

Celery Root-Watercress Salad with Creamy Dijon Dressing

Pommery lemon mustard could be used in place of Dijon in this zesty salad dressing.

⅓   cup fat-free sour cream
1   tablespoon minced shallot
1   tablespoon minced fresh or
      1 teaspoon dried tarragon
2   tablespoons Dijon mustard
2   tablespoons white wine vinegar
2   tablespoons water
1   garlic clove, minced
2   cups julienne-cut peeled
      celeriac (celery root, about 1½
      pounds)
6   cups coarsely chopped romaine
      lettuce (about 2 heads)
2   cups trimmed watercress
      (about 2 bunches)
3   tablespoons chopped walnuts,
      toasted

1. Combine first 7 ingredients in a bowl, and stir well with a whisk. Cover and chill.
2. Combine celeriac and 2 tablespoons dressing.
3. Combine celeriac mixture, lettuce, and watercress. Drizzle remaining dressing over salad; toss gently to coat. Spoon 1 cup salad onto each of 6 plates; sprinkle each serving with about 1 teaspoon walnuts. Yield: 6 servings.

CALORIES 73 (35% from fat); FAT 2.8g (sat 0.2g, mono 0.6g, poly 1.6g); PROTEIN 3.9g; CARB 8.5g; FIBER 2.2g; CHOL 0mg; IRON 1.2mg; SODIUM 220mg; CALC 63mg

Mustard History

The French recognized early on the use of the seeds of this hardy, leafy plant for cooking. By the 14th century, the city of Dijon had established itself as a mustard-production center, relying mostly on plants grown in the Burgundy region.

In 1853, the art of moutarde was advanced several notches when Maurice Grey came up with an efficient little machine that could both grind and sift mustard seeds. He subsequently hooked up with Auguste Poupon, and the rest is prepared-mustard history.

On a parallel course in England, Jeremiah Colman was perfecting his still-exemplary mustard powder; only later in the 19th century did the British enthusiasm for prepared mustards develop.

For Americans, on the other hand, French and English mustards were a not-so-readily acquired taste. We were converted at the beginning of this century when Francis French tweaked the pungent European recipes and toned them down to suit the American palate. His ubiquitous yellow version is still the mainstay for the company that bears his name, but a spirit of mustard adventurousness has definitely spread, so to speak, across the land.

Super Chicken

Scrumptious and superadaptable, chicken breasts are the ultimate heroes of the weeknight dinner table. A dynamic dozen are here at your command.

Can there be a cook alive for whom the humble chicken breast hasn't taken on the stature of superhero at suppertime? Chicken breasts are not only reliable and steadfast, they can morph into almost anything you can think of—as good stir-fried as they are simmering in sauce.

12 For Twelve

To give our 12 recipes the powerful flair that lifts them beyond the ordinary, we've brought in 12 special ingredients. You may want to add some of these items to your pantry or refrigerator for the recipes you choose.

1. Frozen artichoke hearts
2. Canned chipotle chiles
3. Bottled roasted red bell peppers
4. Port wine
5. Marsala wine
6. Fresh mint
7. Fresh ginger
8. Goat cheese
9. Pistachios
10. Oil-cured olives
11. Bottled chile paste with garlic
12. Anchovy paste

SLICED LEMON-PISTACHIO CHICKEN OVER GREENS

(pictured on page 60)

¾ cup cornflakes
2 tablespoons pistachios, toasted
1 teaspoon grated lemon rind
½ teaspoon salt, divided
½ teaspoon black pepper, divided
4 (4-ounce) skinned, boned chicken breast halves
1 tablespoon honey
Cooking spray
6 cups gourmet salad greens
1 tablespoon fresh lemon juice
1 teaspoon olive oil
Lemon wedges (optional)

1. Combine cornflakes, pistachios, rind, ¼ teaspoon salt, and ¼ teaspoon pepper in a food processor; pulse until coarsely ground. Place crumb mixture in a shallow dish.
2. Place each chicken breast half between 2 sheets of heavy-duty plastic wrap. Flatten to ¼-inch thickness, using a meat mallet or rolling pin. Brush chicken with honey. Dredge chicken in crumb mixture.
3. Heat a large nonstick skillet coated with cooking spray over medium heat. Add chicken, and sauté 5 minutes on each side or until done. Cut chicken into ½-inch strips; set aside.
4. Place salad greens in a large bowl. Combine ¼ teaspoon salt, ¼ teaspoon pepper, juice, and oil, and drizzle over salad greens, tossing gently to coat.
5. Divide salad greens and chicken evenly among 4 plates. Garnish with lemon wedges, if desired. Yield: 4 servings (serving size: 1½ cups salad and 1 chicken breast half).

CALORIES 217 (23% from fat); FAT 5.6g (sat 0.9g, mono 3g, poly 0.9g); PROTEIN 29.1g; CARB 12g; FIBER 2.2g; CHOL 66mg; IRON 2.5mg; SODIUM 427mg; CALC 53mg

STIR-FRIED CHICKEN AND VEGETABLES

2 tablespoons brown sugar
2 tablespoons chunky peanut butter
2 tablespoons white vinegar
2 tablespoons low-sodium soy sauce
1 teaspoon chile paste with garlic
¼ teaspoon salt
1 tablespoon dark sesame oil, divided
½ cup (1-inch) sliced green onions
2 teaspoons grated peeled fresh ginger
4 garlic cloves, minced
1 pound skinned, boned chicken breast, cut into ¼-inch-wide strips
4 cups thinly sliced bok choy (about 1 bunch)
1 cup thinly sliced red bell pepper
1 (8-ounce) can sliced water chestnuts, drained
2 cups hot cooked rice
2 tablespoons chopped unsalted, dry-roasted peanuts

1. Combine first 6 ingredients in a bowl, stirring with a whisk. Set aside.
2. Heat 2 teaspoons oil in a large nonstick skillet or wok over medium-high heat. Add onions, ginger, and garlic; stir-fry 2 minutes. Add chicken; stir-fry 5 minutes. Remove chicken mixture from skillet. Add 1 teaspoon oil to pan. Add bok choy, bell pepper, and water chestnuts; stir-fry 3 minutes. Add chicken mixture and peanut butter mixture to pan; stir-fry 2 minutes. Serve over rice; sprinkle with peanuts. Yield: 4 servings (serving size: 1½ cups stir-fry, ½ cup rice, and 1½ teaspoons peanuts).

CALORIES 406 (25% from fat); FAT 11.5g (sat 2g, mono 4.8g, poly 3.8g); PROTEIN 34.1g; CARB 42g; FIBER 2.7g; CHOL 66mg; IRON 3.6mg; SODIUM 573mg; CALC 126mg

SAUTÉED CHICKEN BREASTS WITH CHERRY-PORT SAUCE

    2 teaspoons olive oil
    ½ cup chopped red onion
    ½ teaspoon curry powder
    ¼ teaspoon ground cinnamon
    4 (4-ounce) skinned, boned
       chicken breast halves
    ¼ teaspoon salt
    ¼ teaspoon black pepper
    ⅓ cup ruby port or other sweet
       red wine
    ¼ cup fat-free, less-sodium
       chicken broth
    ¼ cup cherry preserves or seedless
       raspberry jam

1. Heat oil in a large nonstick skillet over medium-high heat. Add onion, curry, and cinnamon; sauté 2 minutes. Sprinkle chicken with salt and pepper, and add to skillet. Sauté 2 minutes on each side. Add port, broth, and preserves, stirring until preserves melt. Cover, reduce heat, and simmer 10 minutes or until chicken is done. Yield: 4 servings (serving size: 1 chicken breast half and 2 tablespoons sauce).

CALORIES 205 (17% from fat); FAT 3.8g (sat 0.7g, mono 2.1g, poly 0.5g); PROTEIN 26.9g; CARB 15.4g; FIBER 0.8g; CHOL 66mg; IRON 1.2mg; SODIUM 261mg; CALC 26mg

SPICED MARINATED CHICKEN

    ½ cup chopped fresh cilantro
    ¼ cup chopped fresh mint
    2 teaspoons ground cumin
    2 teaspoons fresh lime juice
    2 teaspoons vegetable oil
    ½ teaspoon ground red pepper
    ¼ teaspoon salt
    3 garlic cloves, minced
    4 (4-ounce) skinned, boned
       chicken breast halves
    Cooking spray

1. Place first 8 ingredients in a food processor, and pulse 2 or 3 times or until combined. Rub chicken with marinade, and place in a large zip-top plastic bag. Seal and marinate in refrigerator at least 15 minutes.

2. Prepare grill or broiler.
3. Remove chicken from bag; discard marinade. Place chicken on grill rack or broiler pan coated with cooking spray, and cook 6 minutes on each side or until done. Yield: 4 servings (serving size: 1 chicken breast half).

CALORIES 158 (24% from fat); FAT 4.2g (sat 0.8g, mono 1.2g, poly 1.5g); PROTEIN 26.8g; CARB 2g; FIBER 0.5g; CHOL 66mg; IRON 2mg; SODIUM 227mg; CALC 38mg

SAUCED CHICKEN BREASTS WITH APPLES AND ONIONS

    2 tablespoons all-purpose flour
    ¼ teaspoon salt
    ¼ teaspoon black pepper
    4 (4-ounce) skinned, boned
       chicken breast halves
    2 teaspoons olive oil, divided
    3 cups vertically sliced onion
    2½ cups sliced peeled Granny
       Smith apple (about 3 apples)
    1 teaspoon dried marjoram or
       ½ teaspoon dried rosemary
    1 cup apple cider or apple juice

1. Place first 3 ingredients in a zip-top plastic bag; add chicken. Seal and shake to coat. Heat 1 teaspoon oil in a large nonstick skillet over medium-high heat. Add chicken; sauté 2 minutes on each side. Remove from skillet, and keep warm.
2. Heat 1 teaspoon oil in skillet until hot. Add onion, and sauté 5 minutes or until lightly browned. Add apple and marjoram; sauté 5 minutes. Add chicken and cider; bring to a boil. Cover, reduce heat, and simmer 10 minutes or until chicken is done. Yield: 4 servings (serving size: 1 chicken breast half and ¾ cup sauce).

CALORIES 261 (14% from fat); FAT 4.1g (sat 0.8g, mono 2g, poly 0.7g); PROTEIN 27.8g; CARB 28g; FIBER 3.7g; CHOL 66mg; IRON 1.6mg; SODIUM 225mg; CALC 41mg

SMOKED CHICKEN WITH ROASTED-RED PEPPER SAUCE

Serve this dish with flour tortillas, if desired.

    2 bacon slices
    4 (4-ounce) skinned, boned
       chicken breast halves
    ¼ teaspoon salt
    ¼ teaspoon black pepper
    ½ cup chopped red onion
    ½ teaspoon ground coriander
    3 garlic cloves, minced
    1 drained canned chipotle chile
       in adobo sauce, diced
    1 cup salsa
    1 (7-ounce) bottle roasted red
       bell peppers, drained and
       sliced
    Chopped fresh cilantro (optional)

1. Cook bacon in a large nonstick skillet over medium-high heat until crisp. Remove bacon from skillet; crumble and set aside. Sprinkle chicken with salt and black pepper. Add chicken to bacon drippings in skillet; sauté 2 minutes on each side. Remove chicken from skillet. Add onion, coriander, garlic, and chile to skillet; sauté 3 minutes. Stir in salsa and bell peppers. Return chicken to skillet. Cover and cook over medium heat 12 minutes or until chicken is done. Sprinkle with crumbled bacon; garnish with cilantro, if desired. Yield: 4 servings (serving size: 1 chicken breast half and ½ cup sauce).

CALORIES 189 (18% from fat); FAT 3.7g (sat 1.1g, mono 1.3g, poly 0.6g); PROTEIN 28.8g; CARB 8.9g; FIBER 2.1g; CHOL 69mg; IRON 1.7mg; SODIUM 570mg; CALC 58mg

Stewed Chicken Niçoise

2 teaspoons olive oil
¼ cup minced shallots (about 3)
1½ teaspoons dried thyme
½ teaspoon anchovy paste
4 (4-ounce) skinned, boned
    chicken breast halves
¼ teaspoon black pepper
2 tablespoons all-purpose flour
2 cups diced red potato (about
    8 ounces)
1 cup (1-inch) cut green beans
    (about 4 ounces)
½ cup dry white wine
½ cup fat-free, less-sodium
    chicken broth
1 teaspoon sugar
1 (14½-ounce) can Italian-style
    stewed tomatoes, undrained
4 garlic cloves, minced
10 oil-cured or black olives, pitted
    and halved

1. Heat oil in a large nonstick skillet over medium-high heat. Add shallots, thyme, and anchovy paste; sauté 2 minutes. Sprinkle chicken with pepper, and dredge in flour. Add chicken to skillet, and sauté 2 minutes on each side. Add potato and next 6 ingredients, and bring to a boil. Cover, reduce heat, and simmer 20 minutes, stirring occasionally. Stir in olives; cover and simmer 15 minutes or until potato is tender. Yield: 4 servings (serving size: 1 chicken breast half and 1¼ cups sauce).

CALORIES 290 (16% from fat); FAT 5.2g (sat 0.9g, mono 2.8g, poly 0.8g); PROTEIN 31.1g; CARB 29.8g; FIBER 2.8g; CHOL 66mg; IRON 4.1mg; SODIUM 581mg; CALC 102mg

Seared Chicken and Peppers with Cilantro Sauce

½ cup picante sauce
4 (4-ounce) skinned, boned
    chicken breast halves
1 red bell pepper, quartered
    lengthwise
1 yellow bell pepper, quartered
    lengthwise
1 garlic clove, peeled
1 jalapeño pepper, seeded
1½ cups fresh cilantro leaves
1 tablespoon olive oil
1½ teaspoons all-purpose flour
⅓ cup fat-free, less-sodium
    chicken broth
¼ teaspoon salt
Cooking spray
Fresh cilantro sprigs (optional)

1. Combine first 4 ingredients in a large zip-top plastic bag; seal and marinate in refrigerator 20 minutes.
2. Prepare grill or broiler.
3. Drop garlic and jalapeño through food chute with food processor on, and process until minced. Add cilantro leaves; process until finely minced. Heat oil in a small saucepan over medium heat until hot. Add flour; cook 1 minute, stirring constantly with a whisk. Add cilantro mixture, broth, and salt; cook 4 minutes or until slightly thick, stirring occasionally. Remove from heat; keep warm.
4. Remove chicken and bell pepper pieces from bag, and reserve marinade. Place chicken and bell pepper pieces on grill rack or broiler pan coated with cooking spray. Cook 5 minutes on each side or until chicken is done, basting with marinade. Divide cilantro sauce evenly among 4 plates. Arrange chicken and bell pepper pieces on top of sauce. Garnish with cilantro sprigs, if desired. Yield: 4 servings (serving size: 1 chicken breast half, 2 bell pepper pieces, and about 1 tablespoon sauce).

CALORIES 189 (25% from fat); FAT 5.2g (sat 0.9g, mono 2.9g, poly 0.7g); PROTEIN 27.9g; CARB 6.7g; FIBER 1.7g; CHOL 66mg; IRON 3.1mg; SODIUM 607mg; CALC 55mg

Simmered Sicilian Chicken

2 tablespoons all-purpose flour
¼ teaspoon salt
¼ teaspoon black pepper
4 (4-ounce) skinned, boned
    chicken breast halves
2 teaspoons olive oil, divided
½ cup chopped onion
2 teaspoons dried oregano
¼ teaspoon dried crushed red pepper
4 garlic cloves, minced
⅔ cup fat-free, less-sodium
    chicken broth
⅓ cup sweet Marsala wine
½ cup pitted green olives,
    quartered
1 cup seedless red grapes, halved
3 cups hot cooked angel hair
    (about 6 ounces uncooked
    pasta)

1. Place first 3 ingredients in a zip-top plastic bag; add chicken. Seal and shake to coat.
2. Heat 1 teaspoon olive oil in a large nonstick skillet over medium-high heat. Add chicken; sauté 2 minutes on each side. Remove from skillet; keep warm.
3. Heat 1 teaspoon olive oil in skillet over medium-high heat. Add onion, oregano, red pepper, and garlic; sauté 3 minutes or until onion is tender. Stir in broth and Marsala wine; reduce heat, and simmer 1 minute. Add chicken and olives; cover and simmer 10 minutes. Add grapes; cover and simmer 10 minutes or until chicken is done. Serve over pasta. Yield: 4 servings (serving size: 1 chicken breast half, ¾ cup pasta, and ⅓ cup sauce).

CALORIES 358 (15% from fat); FAT 5.8g (sat 1g, mono 3g, poly 1g); PROTEIN 33g; CARB 42.1g; FIBER 3g; CHOL 66mg; IRON 3.6mg; SODIUM 456mg; CALC 63mg

STUFFED CHICKEN BREASTS WITH ARTICHOKE HEARTS AND GOAT CHEESE

2 teaspoons olive oil, divided
¾ cup frozen artichoke hearts, thawed and chopped
¼ cup minced shallots (about 3)
¼ cup (1 ounce) crumbled goat or feta cheese
1 teaspoon dried herbes de Provence or thyme, divided
¼ teaspoon salt, divided
¼ teaspoon black pepper, divided
4 (4-ounce) skinned, boned chicken breast halves
1 cup fat-free, less-sodium chicken broth
2 tablespoons fresh lemon juice
2 teaspoons cornstarch
Chopped fresh parsley (optional)
Lemon rind strips (optional)

1. Heat 1 teaspoon oil in a nonstick skillet over medium heat. Add artichokes and shallots; sauté 4 minutes. Remove from skillet; cool. Stir in cheese, ½ teaspoon herbes de Provence, ⅛ teaspoon salt, and ⅛ teaspoon pepper.
2. Cut a horizontal slit through thickest portion of each breast half to form a pocket. Stuff 2 tablespoons artichoke mixture into each pocket.
3. Heat 1 teaspoon oil in a large nonstick skillet over medium heat. Add chicken, and sprinkle with ⅛ teaspoon salt and ⅛ teaspoon pepper; sauté 6 minutes on each side or until done. Remove from skillet; keep warm. Add ½ teaspoon herbes de Provence and broth to skillet; bring to a boil. Combine juice and cornstarch; add to broth mixture, stirring with a whisk. Cook 1 minute or until thick. Return chicken to skillet; cover and cook 2 minutes or until thoroughly heated. If desired, garnish with parsley and lemon rind strips. Yield: 4 servings (serving size: 1 chicken breast half and 2 tablespoons sauce).

CALORIES 194 (25% from fat); FAT 5.3g (sat 1.8g, mono 2.3g, poly 0.6g); PROTEIN 29.2g; CARB 6.2g; FIBER 0.4g; CHOL 72mg; IRON 1.4mg; SODIUM 437mg; CALC 61mg

SMOTHERED CHICKEN IN MUSHROOM RAGOÛT

1 teaspoon olive oil
4 (4-ounce) skinned, boned chicken breast halves
¼ teaspoon black pepper
4 cups sliced cremini mushrooms (about 8 ounces)
4 cups thinly sliced shiitake mushroom caps (about 8 ounces)
2 cups chopped leeks
⅓ cup dry white wine
⅓ cup fat-free, less-sodium chicken broth
1 tablespoon sherry
¼ teaspoon salt
1 cup low-fat sour cream
4 cups hot cooked medium egg noodles (about 6 ounces uncooked noodles)
Freshly ground black pepper (optional)
Chopped fresh parsley (optional)

1. Heat olive oil in a large nonstick skillet over medium-high heat. Sprinkle chicken with ¼ teaspoon pepper. Add chicken to skillet, and sauté 6 minutes on each side. Remove from skillet, and keep warm.
2. Add mushrooms and leeks to skillet; sauté 8 minutes. Return chicken to skillet. Add wine, broth, sherry, and salt; cook 2 minutes or until chicken is done. Remove from heat; stir in sour cream. Serve over noodles; if desired, garnish with freshly ground black pepper and parsley. Yield: 4 servings (serving size: 1 chicken breast half, 1 cup noodles, and ¾ cup mushroom ragoût).

CALORIES 442 (25% from fat); FAT 12.1g (sat 5.5g, mono 3.8g, poly 1.5g); PROTEIN 37.4g; CARB 46g; FIBER 3.3g; CHOL 129mg; IRON 5.4mg; SODIUM 310mg; CALC 127mg

SKEWERED SINGAPORE CHICKEN AND PINEAPPLE

(pictured on page 58)

3 tablespoons brown sugar
3 tablespoons low-sodium soy sauce
2 tablespoons pineapple juice
4 teaspoons fresh lime juice
2 teaspoons grated peeled fresh ginger
2 teaspoons vegetable oil
1½ teaspoons curry powder
¼ teaspoon salt
3 garlic cloves, minced
1 pound skinned, boned chicken breast, cut into 32 bite-size pieces
1 cup (1-inch) pieces red bell pepper
1½ cups (1-inch) cubed fresh pineapple
Cooking spray
4 cups hot cooked rice

1. Prepare grill or broiler.
2. Combine first 9 ingredients in a large bowl. Add chicken and bell pepper, tossing to coat. Thread chicken, bell pepper, and pineapple alternately onto 8 (12-inch) skewers. Discard marinade. Place kebabs on grill rack or broiler pan coated with cooking spray; cook 10 minutes or until chicken is done, turning occasionally. Serve with rice. Yield: 4 servings (serving size: 2 skewers and 1 cup rice).

CALORIES 419 (7% from fat); FAT 3.4g (sat 0.6g, mono 0.7g, poly 1.1g); PROTEIN 31.3g; CARB 64g; FIBER 2.6g; CHOL 66mg; IRON 3.6mg; SODIUM 332mg; CALC 49mg

Five Easy Cheeses

Here are five lightened cheese sauces so simple they'll make you smile.

A cheese sauce is always welcome. That's also eternal good news for you because for all its dinnertime popularity, a cheese sauce—basically, a white sauce with cheese—is surprisingly easy to make. A lightened version is even easier, because you can skip the traditional white sauce's roux, which requires a combination of flour and butter. For the lighter version, just mix flour and low-fat milk, and then heat and add the cheese. The result is a sauce that's as creamy and delicious as the traditional version and just as versatile.

A MATTER OF BALANCE

You may notice that the sauces weigh in at more than 30% of calories from fat by themselves, but remember that they're not meant to be eaten alone. Combined with lean ingredients such as potatoes, pasta, and vegetables, each sauce becomes the foundation of a delicious, sensible dish.

CHEDDAR CHEESE SAUCE

¼ cup all-purpose flour
2 cups 1% low-fat milk
1¼ cups (5 ounces) shredded sharp Cheddar cheese

1. Lightly spoon flour into a dry measuring cup; level with a knife. Place flour in a medium, heavy saucepan; gradually add milk, stirring with a whisk until blended. Place over medium heat; cook until thick (about 8 minutes), stirring constantly. Remove from heat; add cheese, stirring until melted. Yield: 2 cups (serving size: ½ cup).

CALORIES 222 (53% from fat); FAT 13.1g (sat 8.3g, mono 3.7g, poly 0.4g); PROTEIN 13.6g; CARB 12.2g; FIBER 0.2g; CHOL 42mg; IRON 0.7mg; SODIUM 281mg; CALC 407mg

VARIATIONS:

Swiss Cheese Sauce:
Substitute 1 cup (4 ounces) shredded Swiss cheese for the shredded Cheddar cheese. Then proceed with the recipe.

CALORIES 186 (44% from fat); FAT 9.1g (sat 5.9g, mono 2.4g, poly 0.3g); PROTEIN 12.9g; CARB 12.7g; FIBER 0.2g; CHOL 31mg; IRON 0.5mg; SODIUM 135mg; CALC 424mg

Gruyère Cheese Sauce:
Substitute ¾ cup (3 ounces) shredded Gruyère cheese and ⅓ cup (about 1½ ounces) finely grated fresh Parmesan for the shredded Cheddar cheese. Then proceed with the recipe.

CALORIES 209 (47% from fat); FAT 11g (sat 6.6g, mono 3.3g, poly 0.5g); PROTEIN 14.9g; CARB 12.2g; FIBER 0.2g; CHOL 35mg; IRON 0.5mg; SODIUM 303mg; CALC 492mg

Asiago Cheese Sauce:
Substitute 1 cup (4 ounces) grated Asiago cheese for the shredded Cheddar cheese. Then proceed with the recipe.

CALORIES 191 (41% from fat); FAT 8.7g (sat 5.5g, mono 2.5g, poly 0.2g); PROTEIN 14.9g; CARB 12.7g; FIBER 0.2g; CHOL 24mg; IRON 0.7mg; SODIUM 515mg; CALC 487mg

Smoked Gouda Cheese Sauce:
Substitute ¾ cup (3 ounces) shredded smoked Gouda cheese for the shredded Cheddar cheese. Then proceed with the recipe.

CALORIES 155 (42% from fat); FAT 7.2g (sat 4.6g, mono 2g, poly 0.2g); PROTEIN 10.1g; CARB 12.3g; FIBER 0.2g; CHOL 29mg; IRON 0.5mg; SODIUM 235mg; CALC 300mg

MUSHROOM-GOUDA CHOWDER

½ cup dried porcini mushrooms (about ½ ounce)
1¼ cups boiling water
2 teaspoons butter or stick margarine
1½ cups sliced shiitake mushroom caps (about ¾ pound)
½ cup chopped shallots
2 garlic cloves, minced
1 cup diced peeled baking potato
1 cup fat-free, less-sodium chicken broth
½ teaspoon salt
¼ teaspoon dried thyme
¼ teaspoon freshly ground black pepper
½ cup hot Smoked Gouda Cheese Sauce (see recipe)
1 tablespoon sherry

1. Combine porcini mushrooms and boiling water in a bowl; cover and let stand 30 minutes. Drain porcini mushrooms in a colander over a bowl, reserving 1 cup liquid. Rinse and chop porcini mushrooms; set aside.
2. Melt butter in a large saucepan over medium-high heat. Add shiitake mushrooms, shallots, and garlic; sauté 6 minutes or until tender. Stir in porcini mushrooms, 1 cup reserved liquid, potato, and next 4 ingredients. Bring to a boil; cover, reduce heat, and simmer 10 minutes or until potato is tender. Stir in Smoked Gouda Cheese Sauce; cook 5 minutes or until thoroughly heated. Stir in sherry. Yield: 4 servings (serving size: 1 cup).

CALORIES 139 (27% from fat); FAT 4.2g (sat 2.4g, mono 1.1g, poly 0.3g); PROTEIN 6g; CARB 20.6g; FIBER 2.4g; CHOL 13mg; IRON 2mg; SODIUM 381mg; CALC 96mg

Desserts Doubly Delicious

Get extra use from popular cookies and candy bars by giving them dual duty in your favorite family sweets.

Trendy ice-cream and frozen-yogurt parlors got the idea a few years ago: Mix crumbled candy bars or crushed cookies into a light, flavorful base, and you've got a whole new creation.

All good ideas are worth tweaking, and this now-widespread technique also works wonderfully for countless other sweets. Heath bar in a crumb-cake batter, Butterfinger pie, and Oreo chunks in a cappuccino trifle. Lo, a pattern emerges. That it's low in fat is only part of the fun.

KIT KAT SLUSH

1 cup 1% low-fat chocolate milk
1 cup chocolate low-fat ice cream
2 (0.56-ounce) chocolate-covered crispy wafer bars (such as Kit Kat), chopped

1. Combine milk and ice cream in a blender; process just until smooth. Pour into a bowl; cover and freeze 3 hours or until frozen. Stir with a fork until slushy, and stir in wafer bars. Serve immediately. Yield: 4 servings (serving size: ½ cup).

CALORIES 120 (27% from fat); FAT 3.6g (sat 2.2g, mono 0.5g, poly 0.3g); PROTEIN 3.5g; CARB 18.5g; FIBER 0g; CHOL 5mg; IRON 0.2mg; SODIUM 64mg; CALC 112mg

MAKE-AHEAD CAPPUCCINO-OREO TRIFLES

(pictured on page 59)

½ cup sugar
¼ cup cornstarch
1 tablespoon instant coffee granules
1 large egg
2½ cups 1% low-fat milk
1 tablespoon Kahlúa (coffee-flavored liqueur)
16 reduced-fat cream-filled chocolate sandwich cookies (such as Reduced Fat Oreos), divided
1½ cups frozen reduced-calorie whipped topping, thawed

1. Combine first 4 ingredients in a bowl; stir well with a whisk. Cook milk in a heavy saucepan over medium-high heat to 180° or until tiny bubbles form around edge (do not boil). Gradually add hot milk to egg mixture, stirring constantly with a whisk. Return milk mixture to pan; cook over medium heat until thick (3 minutes), stirring constantly. Reduce heat to low, and cook 2 minutes. Remove from heat; stir in Kahlúa. Pour into a medium bowl; place bowl in a larger bowl of ice water, stirring occasionally until mixture is cool.
2. Coarsely chop 8 cookies; fold chopped cookies and whipped topping into pudding. Spoon about ½ cup cookie mixture into each of 8 small parfait glasses or 8 (6-ounce) custard cups. Cover and chill at least 2 hours or until cold. Top each serving with a cookie. Yield: 8 servings.

CALORIES 227 (21% from fat); FAT 5.4g (sat 3g, mono 1.5g, poly 0.3g); PROTEIN 5.1g; CARB 40.2g; FIBER 0.7g; CHOL 31mg; IRON 1.4mg; SODIUM 183mg; CALC 107mg

JUNIOR MINT BROWNIES

Cooking spray
¼ cup butter or stick margarine
32 (about 3 ounces) creamy, small-size mints in pure chocolate (such as Junior Mints)
1 cup all-purpose flour
¼ teaspoon baking soda
⅛ teaspoon salt
⅔ cup sugar
⅓ cup unsweetened cocoa
1 large egg
1 large egg white

1. Preheat oven to 350°.
2. Coat bottom of an 8-inch square baking pan with cooking spray.
3. Combine butter and mints in a 2-cup glass measure; microwave at HIGH 30 seconds or until soft. Stir until smooth, and set aside.
4. Lightly spoon flour into a dry measuring cup, and level with a knife. Combine flour, soda, and salt in a bowl. Combine sugar, cocoa, egg, and egg white in a large bowl; beat at medium speed of a mixer until well-blended. Add mint mixture, and beat well. Add flour mixture; beat at low speed just until blended. Pour batter into prepared pan. Bake at 350° for 20 minutes or until a wooden pick inserted in center comes out clean; cool completely on a wire rack. Yield: 16 brownies (serving size: 1 brownie).
Note: Substitute two large (1.5-ounce) mints or 6 miniature chocolate-covered peppermint patties (such as York) for 32 Junior Mints.

CALORIES 121 (29% from fat); FAT 3.9g (sat 1.1g, mono 1.4g, poly 1g); PROTEIN 2.1g; CARB 19.5g; FIBER 0.2g; CHOL 14mg; IRON 0.7mg; SODIUM 81mg; CALC 7mg

Frozen Butterfinger Pie

40 chocolate graham crackers
     (10 full cookie sheets)
1½ tablespoons butter or stick
     margarine, melted
 1   large egg white
     Cooking spray
 4   cups vanilla fat-free frozen
     yogurt
 3   tablespoons light-colored corn
     syrup
 3   tablespoons creamy peanut
     butter
 1   tablespoon fat-free milk
 1   (2.1-ounce) chocolate-covered
     crispy peanut-buttery candy
     bar (such as Butterfinger),
     chopped

1. Preheat oven to 350°.
2. Place graham crackers in a food processor; pulse until crumbly. Add butter and egg white; pulse until moist. Press crumb mixture into a 9-inch pie plate coated with cooking spray. Bake at 350° for 8 minutes; cool on a wire rack 15 minutes. Freeze 15 minutes.
3. Remove yogurt from freezer, and let stand at room temperature 15 minutes to soften. Spoon half of yogurt into prepared crust.
4. Combine corn syrup, peanut butter, and milk in a small bowl, stirring until smooth. Drizzle half of peanut butter mixture over yogurt in crust. Sprinkle with half of chopped candy bar. Repeat procedure with remaining yogurt, peanut butter mixture, and candy bar. Cover with plastic wrap, and freeze 3 hours or until firm. Yield: 9 servings (serving size: 1 wedge).

CALORIES 230 (30% from fat); FAT 7.6 g (sat 2.5g, mono 2.8g, poly 1.1g); PROTEIN 6.1g; CARB 36.6g; FIBER 1g; CHOL 5mg; IRON 1.4mg; SODIUM 221mg; CALC 104mg

Heath Bar-Marmalade Crumb Cake

 1   cup plus 2 tablespoons
     all-purpose flour
½   cup sugar
⅛   teaspoon salt
¼   cup chilled butter or stick
     margarine, cut into small
     pieces
 1   (1.4-ounce) English toffee
     candy bar (such as Heath or
     Skor), chopped
½   teaspoon baking powder
¼   teaspoon baking soda
½   cup plain fat-free yogurt
 1   tablespoon fat-free milk
 1   teaspoon grated orange rind
 1   teaspoon vanilla extract
 2   large egg whites
     Cooking spray
¼   cup orange marmalade

1. Preheat oven to 350°.
2. Lightly spoon flour into dry measuring cups, and level with a knife. Combine flour, sugar, and salt in a bowl; cut in butter with a pastry blender or 2 knives until mixture resembles coarse meal. Combine ⅓ cup flour mixture and candy bar for topping; set aside.
3. Stir baking powder and baking soda into remaining flour mixture in bowl; add yogurt and next 4 ingredients. Beat at medium speed of a mixer until blended. Spoon batter into an 8-inch round cake pan coated with cooking spray. Drop marmalade by teaspoonfuls onto batter; swirl together, using the tip of a knife. Sprinkle topping over batter. Bake at 350° for 35 minutes or until a wooden pick inserted in center comes out clean. Cool in pan on a wire rack. Yield: 8 servings (serving size: 1 wedge).

CALORIES 237 (30% from fat); FAT 7.8g (sat 4.8g, mono 1.9g, poly 0.5g); PROTEIN 3.8g; CARB 37g; FIBER 0.5g; CHOL 16mg; IRON 0.9mg; SODIUM 210mg; CALC 57mg

Biscotti with Raisinets

½   cup packed brown sugar
 3   tablespoons butter or stick
     margarine, softened
½   teaspoon vanilla extract
 1   large egg
 1   cup all-purpose flour
¾   teaspoon baking powder
⅛   teaspoon salt
¼   cup chocolate-covered raisins
     (such as Raisinets)
     Cooking spray

1. Preheat oven to 350°.
2. Beat first 3 ingredients at medium speed of a mixer 4 minutes or until well-blended. Add egg, and beat well. Lightly spoon flour into a dry measuring cup; level with a knife. Combine flour, baking powder, and salt; gradually add to sugar mixture, beating until well-blended. Stir in chocolate-covered raisins.
3. Turn dough out onto a lightly floured surface, and knead lightly 7 times. Shape dough into a 12-inch-long roll. Place roll on a baking sheet coated with cooking spray; flatten to ¾-inch thickness.
4. Bake at 350° for 25 minutes. Remove roll from baking sheet; cool 10 minutes on a wire rack. Cut roll diagonally into 20 (½-inch-wide) slices. Place, cut sides down, on baking sheet. Reduce oven temperature to 325°. Bake 10 minutes; turn biscotti over, and bake an additional 10 minutes (cookies will be slightly soft in center but will harden as they cool). Remove from baking sheet; cool completely on wire rack. Yield: 20 biscotti (serving size: 1 biscotto).

CALORIES 74 (30% from fat); FAT 2.5g (sat 1.4g, mono 0.7g, poly 0.1g); PROTEIN 1.1g; CARB 11.8g; FIBER 0.2g; CHOL 16mg; IRON 0.5mg; SODIUM 57mg; CALC 20mg

Using Their Noodles

Humble pasta is such a good beginning for creative, throw-together dishes.

GARLIC-LOVER'S PASTA

"My husband, Steve, loves garlic, and so do I. We make this dish at least once a week. The recipe has only a few ingredients so it goes together quite quickly."
—Nancy Howard, Bloomington, Indiana

- 2 tablespoons olive oil
- 5 garlic cloves, crushed
- 1 teaspoon dried basil
- ¼ teaspoon salt
- ¼ teaspoon black pepper
- ⅛ teaspoon dried crushed red pepper
- 1 (28-ounce) can Italian-style tomatoes, undrained and coarsely chopped
- 4 cups hot cooked linguine (about 8 ounces uncooked pasta)
- ¼ cup (1 ounce) grated fresh Parmesan cheese

1. Heat oil in a large nonstick skillet over medium heat. Add garlic; sauté 1 minute. Add basil, salt, peppers, and tomatoes; bring to a boil. Reduce heat, and simmer 10 minutes or until mixture starts to thicken. Serve over pasta; top with cheese. Yield: 4 servings (serving size: 1 cup pasta, ½ cup sauce, and 1 tablespoon cheese).

CALORIES 322 (27% from fat); FAT 9.6g (sat 2.2g, mono 5.6g, poly 1g); PROTEIN 11g; CARB 47.4g; FIBER 3.4g; CHOL 5mg; IRON 2.3mg; SODIUM 817mg; CALC 167mg

PASTA-AND-CHICKPEA SOUP WITH PESTO

"Moving from England to the United States meant leaving my favorite foods behind. But our family discovered a comfort food of our own in America— a re-invented English pasta soup."
—Sally Carter, Chicago, Illinois

- 1 tablespoon olive oil
- 2 cups chopped onion
- 1 cup sliced leek (about 1 small)
- 1 tablespoon chopped fresh or 1 teaspoon dried rosemary
- 2 garlic cloves, minced
- 4 cups chopped tomato (about 2 pounds)
- 3 cups water
- 1 (14½-ounce) can vegetable broth
- 1 (15-ounce) can chickpeas (garbanzo beans), undrained
- 1 cup diced zucchini
- ½ cup frozen petite green peas
- ½ cup frozen baby lima beans
- ½ cup frozen French-cut green beans
- ⅓ cup uncooked pastina (tiny star-shaped pasta) or any small pasta
- 2 tablespoons chopped fresh or 2 teaspoons dried parsley
- ¼ teaspoon black pepper
- 2 tablespoons commercial pesto
- 2 tablespoons (½ ounce) grated fresh Parmesan cheese

1. Heat oil in a large Dutch oven over medium heat. Add onion, leek, rosemary, and garlic, and sauté 10 minutes. Add tomato, water, broth, and chickpeas, and bring to a boil. Cover, reduce heat, and simmer 30 minutes. Add zucchini, peas, lima beans, and green beans; bring to a boil over medium-high heat. Reduce heat; simmer 10 minutes. Stir in pastina, parsley, and pepper, and cook 8 minutes. Spoon 1½ cups soup into each of 6 bowls; top each serving with 1 teaspoon pesto and 1 teaspoon cheese. Yield: 6 servings.

CALORIES 271 (25% from fat); FAT 7.5g (sat 1.8g, mono 4.1g, poly 1.3g); PROTEIN 10.5g; CARB 43.3g; FIBER 8.8g; CHOL 3mg; IRON 3.8mg; SODIUM 659mg; CALC 148mg

SANTA FE PASTA SAUCE

"I had a similar sauce once in a restaurant, and my mother and I re-created it at home."
—Linnea Keen, Canton, North Carolina

- 1 tablespoon olive oil
- ½ cup chopped onion
- 2 garlic cloves, minced
- 1 (16-ounce) jar salsa
- 1 (8-ounce) can tomato sauce
- 1 cup frozen whole-kernel corn
- ¾ cup canned black beans, rinsed and drained
- ⅓ cup chopped ripe olives
- ½ cup low-fat sour cream
- ½ teaspoon Creole seasoning (such as Louisiana)
- 4 (4-ounce) skinned, boned chicken breast halves
- Cooking spray
- 4 cups hot cooked fettuccine (about 8 ounces uncooked pasta)
- Sliced pickled jalapeño peppers (optional)

1. Heat oil in a large nonstick skillet over medium heat. Add onion and garlic, and sauté 5 minutes. Reduce heat to medium-low. Stir in salsa and tomato sauce; cook 20 minutes, stirring occasionally. Add corn and next 4 ingredients; cook 4 minutes or until thoroughly heated. Keep warm.
2. Prepare grill or broiler. Place chicken on a grill rack or broiler pan coated with cooking spray; cook 5 minutes on each side or until done. Slice chicken lengthwise into ½-inch-wide strips.
3. Spoon sauce over pasta. Top with grilled chicken strips, and garnish with sliced jalapeño peppers, if desired. Yield: 8 servings (serving size: ½ cup sauce, ½ cup pasta, and about 4 strips of grilled chicken).

CALORIES 302 (21% from fat); FAT 7.2g (sat 2.1g, mono 3g, poly 1.1g); PROTEIN 24.5g; CARB 34.6g; FIBER 3.8g; CHOL 54mg; IRON 2.8mg; SODIUM 592mg; CALC 73mg

RIGATONI WITH SPINACH AND BLUE CHEESE

"This is a combination of a lot of my favorite ingredients. It's also a sneaky way to get my family to eat stuff that's good for them."

—Suzette K. Hale, Camarillo, California

  1 teaspoon olive oil
 ¾ cup chopped onion
  4 garlic cloves, minced
  6 cups fresh spinach leaves, chopped
1⅓ cups chopped seeded tomato
 ½ cup fat-free, less-sodium chicken broth
  8 cups hot cooked rigatoni (about 16 ounces uncooked tube-shaped pasta)
 ½ cup (2 ounces) crumbled blue cheese
 ¼ cup pine nuts, toasted

1. Heat oil in a large nonstick skillet over medium heat. Add onion, and cook 20 minutes or until golden brown, stirring frequently. Add garlic, and sauté 1 minute. Add spinach, tomato, and broth; cook 3 minutes, stirring occasionally. Combine spinach mixture, pasta, cheese, and pine nuts in a large bowl; toss well to coat. Yield: 5 servings (serving size: 1½ cups).

CALORIES 432 (21% from fat); FAT 10.1g (sat 3.1g, mono 3.3g, poly 2.6g); PROTEIN 17.7g; CARB 69.8g; FIBER 7.5g; CHOL 9mg; IRON 5.9mg; SODIUM 267mg; CALC 155mg

CRAYFISH FETTUCCINE

"This is a local dish from southwestern Louisiana. Traditionally, it's made with heavy cream, one to two sticks of butter, and cheese. I lightened it, but my friends don't even know it's low in fat. They only know that it's good."

—Angela Sommers, Lafayette, Louisiana

  1 tablespoon reduced-calorie margarine
  2 cups chopped onion
  1 cup chopped green bell pepper
 ½ cup chopped celery
  3 garlic cloves, minced
 ¼ cup all-purpose flour
  1 (12-ounce) can evaporated fat-free milk
  1 (10-ounce) can diced tomatoes and green chiles, undrained
  4 cups hot cooked fettuccine (about 8 ounces uncooked pasta)
  1 cup (4 ounces) reduced-fat sharp Cheddar cheese
 ¼ cup grated Parmesan cheese
  1 pound cooked peeled crayfish or shrimp
 ¼ teaspoon salt
 ¼ teaspoon ground red pepper
 ¼ teaspoon black pepper

1. Preheat oven to 350°.
2. Melt margarine in a large nonstick skillet over medium-high heat until hot. Add onion, bell pepper, celery, and garlic; sauté 5 minutes. Stir in flour; cook 2 minutes. Stir in milk and tomatoes; cook 7 minutes or until thick. Stir in pasta and remaining ingredients. Spoon fettuccine mixture into a 13 x 9-inch baking dish; bake at 350° for 25 minutes. Yield: 6 servings (serving size: 1 cup).
Note: Look for packages of cooked peeled crayfish in the frozen-food section of many supermarkets.

CALORIES 407 (17% from fat); FAT 7.9g (sat 3.4g, mono 2.2g, poly 1.2g); PROTEIN 35.3g; CARB 46.6g; FIBER 3.3g; CHOL 152mg; IRON 4.7mg; SODIUM 642mg; CALC 428mg

RICOTTA FETTUCCINE ALFREDO WITH BROCCOLI

"This is my low-fat alternative to traditional Alfredo sauce. We like it more than the original version. And I'm Italian, so that's saying a lot."

—Linda L. Roswog, Falls Church, Virginia

  2 cups small broccoli florets
  2 tablespoons butter or stick margarine
  2 tablespoons all-purpose flour
  2 cups fat-free milk
 ⅔ cup (2½ ounces) part-skim ricotta cheese
 ½ cup grated Parmesan cheese
 ¼ teaspoon salt
 ¼ teaspoon coarsely ground black pepper
  4 cups hot cooked fettuccine (about 8 ounces uncooked pasta)
  2 tablespoons minced fresh parsley

1. Steam broccoli, covered, 3 minutes or until crisp-tender.
2. Melt butter in a saucepan over medium heat. Add flour, and cook 1 minute, stirring constantly. Gradually add milk, stirring with a whisk until blended. Cook 15 minutes or until thick, stirring constantly. Stir in cheeses, salt, and pepper, and cook 5 minutes or until cheese melts. Stir in broccoli and pasta. Sprinkle with parsley. Yield: 4 servings (serving size: 1½ cups).

CALORIES 421 (28% from fat); FAT 13.3g (sat 5.3g, mono 4.5g, poly 2.4g); PROTEIN 21.5g; CARB 53.6g; FIBER 3.8g; CHOL 23mg; IRON 3mg; SODIUM 529mg; CALC 437mg

APRIL

Home Cooking in the Low Country

The fateful merging of Africans and Europeans in the coastal Carolina plains resulted in a Creole cuisine whose healthy home-cooking style was the rage of its time. And of today.

In the 1800s, European settlers flocked to the Low Country to make their fortunes. As they settled, they forged a Creole cuisine spurred by the French traditions of the Huguenots; Mediterranean diet of the Sephardic Jews; German meat-curing skills; and English love of grains and puddings. However, the African slave was doing the cooking in Carolina. As a result, many Creole recipes are based on West African tradition.

FROGMORE STEW

This popular stew (named after the old town center on St. Helena Island) is really a boiled dinner made to showcase the bounty of the region. We've substituted lower fat turkey kielbasa for traditional Low Country smoked sausage, a spicy variety made with pork.

- 3 quarts water
- 1 (3-ounce) box crawfish, shrimp, and crab boil (such as Zatarain's)
- 1 pound turkey kielbasa, cut into 1-inch pieces
- 6 ears shucked corn, each cut crosswise into 4 pieces
- 2 pounds unpeeled medium shrimp

1. Bring water and seasoning bag to a boil in an 8-quart stock pot; cook 10 minutes. Add sausage; cook 5 minutes. Add corn; cook 5 minutes. Add shrimp; cook 3 minutes or until shrimp are done. Discard seasoning bag. Drain. Yield: 8 servings (serving size: 3 pieces corn, 2 sausage pieces, and ¼ pound shrimp).
Note: Open seasoning bag to disperse spices into water, if desired. Spices will adhere to shrimp and corn and add more color to the dish.

CALORIES 262 (29% from fat); FAT 8.3g (sat 3g, mono 3g, poly 1.6g); PROTEIN 28g; CARB 20.8g; FIBER 3g; CHOL 159mg; IRON 9.5mg; SODIUM 738mg; CALC 107mg

CRAB HOPPIN' JOHN

Hoppin' John, a humble dish of slow-cooked black-eyed peas served with rice, is thought by some to be the "national" dish of the Low Country. In this version of the Southern classic, we've substituted fresh crabmeat for the pork and transformed it into a main-dish salad.

- 1½ cups cooked long-grain rice
- 1 cup fresh or frozen black-eyed peas, cooked
- ½ cup chopped red onion
- ½ cup chopped celery
- ⅓ cup fresh lemon juice
- 2 tablespoons chopped fresh parsley
- 2 tablespoons extra-virgin olive oil
- ½ teaspoon salt
- ¼ teaspoon black pepper
- ½ pound lump crabmeat, shell pieces removed
- Dash of hot sauce
- 8 (¼-inch-thick) slices tomato

1. Combine first 11 ingredients in a large bowl, and toss gently to coat. Serve with tomato slices. Yield: 4 servings (serving size: 1¼ cups salad and 2 tomato slices).

CALORIES 269 (28% from fat); FAT 8.3g (sat 1.7g, mono 5.2g, poly 1.2g); PROTEIN 17.1g; CARB 31.8g; FIBER 2.2g; CHOL 57mg; IRON 2.2mg; SODIUM 470mg; CALC 95mg

CHICKEN COUNTRY CAPTAIN

The broth and chicken for this dish are cooked a day ahead and refrigerated to make it easier to skim off the fat. You can substitute a rotisserie chicken and canned broth (4½ cups). We recommend making the curry powder from scratch; it's crucial to the flavor.

Chicken:

- 3 quarts water
- 1 tablespoon chopped fresh parsley
- 1 tablespoon chopped fresh or 1 teaspoon dried thyme
- 1 tablespoon chopped fresh or 1 teaspoon dried oregano
- 3 celery stalks, cut into 3-inch pieces
- 2 carrots, cut into 3-inch pieces
- 1 large unpeeled onion, quartered
- 2 bay leaves
- 1 (3½-pound) chicken

Curry powder:

- 1½ teaspoons coriander seeds
- 1 teaspoon cumin seeds
- 1 teaspoon dried crushed red pepper
- 1 teaspoon ground turmeric
- ½ teaspoon black peppercorns
- ¼ teaspoon ground ginger
- 6 whole cloves
- 1 (3-inch) cinnamon stick, broken
- 1 bay leaf, crumbled

Remaining ingredients:

- 1 tablespoon olive oil
- 3 cups chopped onion
- 2½ cups chopped green bell pepper
- 2 garlic cloves, minced
- 1 (28-ounce) can diced tomatoes, undrained
- ½ cup currants
- ½ teaspoon salt
- 1½ cups uncooked long-grain rice
- ½ cup slivered almonds, toasted

1. To prepare chicken, combine first 9 ingredients in a stockpot; bring to a

boil. Reduce heat; simmer, uncovered, 1 hour. Remove from heat. Remove chicken from broth; place chicken in a bowl, and chill 15 minutes. Remove skin from chicken; remove chicken from bones, discarding skin and bones. Shred chicken with two forks; cover and chill. Strain broth through a sieve into a large bowl; discard solids. Cover and chill broth overnight. Skim fat from surface; discard. Reserve 4½ cups broth. Refrigerate remaining broth for another use.

2. To prepare curry powder, cook coriander and cumin seeds in a small skillet over medium heat 3 minutes or until toasted. Place seeds, red pepper, and next 6 ingredients in a spice or coffee grinder; process until finely ground.

3. Heat oil in a large Dutch oven over medium-high heat. Add chopped onion, bell pepper, and garlic; sauté 10 minutes. Combine curry powder and tomatoes in a blender or food processor; process until smooth. Add tomato mixture and 1½ cups reserved broth to pan; bring to a boil. Reduce heat; simmer 45 minutes, stirring occasionally. Stir in chicken and currants; cook until thoroughly heated.

4. Bring 3 cups reserved broth and salt to a boil in a saucepan. Add rice. Cover; reduce heat. Simmer 20 minutes or until liquid is absorbed. Remove from heat; fluff with a fork. Serve chicken mixture over rice; sprinkle with almonds. Yield: 8 servings (serving size: 1 cup chicken mixture, ¾ cup rice, and 1 tablespoon almonds).

Note: Store leftover broth in an airtight container and refrigerate up to 1 week or freeze up to 3 months.

CALORIES 386 (24% from fat); FAT 10.5g (sat 2g, mono 5.2g, poly 2.2g); PROTEIN 24.8g; CARB 49.2g; FIBER 4.2g; CHOL 57mg; IRON 4.5mg; SODIUM 371mg; CALC 91mg

---

> ### MENU SUGGESTION
>
> AWENDAW
>
> STEAMED GREEN BEANS
>
> *Pork cutlets with creamy mustard sauce**
>
> *Combine 4 (4-ounce) pork cutlets, ¾ cup fresh breadcrumbs, and ¼ cup chopped pecans in a zip-top bag; shake to coat. Bake at 400° for 25 minutes, turning once. Combine ¼ cup low-fat sour cream, 1 tablespoon fat-free milk, and 1 tablespoon Dijon mustard in a saucepan; cook and stir until warm. Spoon over pork. Serves 4.

AWENDAW

This classic spoon bread, named for an Indian settlement located north of Charleston, is typically served hot from the oven with butter and lots of shrimp. Like any spoon bread, it makes a nice side dish to pork, beef, or chicken.

    3 cups water
    ¾ teaspoon salt
    ¾ cup uncooked regular grits
    3 large eggs, lightly beaten
    1 large egg white, lightly beaten
    1 tablespoon butter or stick margarine
    2 cups fat-free milk
    ½ cup yellow cornmeal
       Cooking spray

1. Bring water and salt to a boil in a medium saucepan; gradually add grits, stirring constantly. Reduce heat, and simmer for 25 minutes or until thick, stirring occasionally.

2. Preheat oven to 375°.

3. Gradually add 1 cup hot grits to eggs and egg white in a bowl, stirring mixture constantly with a whisk. Return egg mixture to pan, stirring constantly with whisk. Add butter to mixture in pan, stirring until melted. Stir in milk and cornmeal, and remove from heat. Pour batter into a 2-quart

---

soufflé dish coated with cooking spray. Bake at 375° for 1 hour and 15 minutes or until set. Yield: 8 servings (serving size: 1 cup).

CALORIES 120 (29% from fat); FAT 3.8g (sat 1.6g, mono 1.2g, poly 0.4g); PROTEIN 6.4g; CARB 14.9g; FIBER 0.8g; CHOL 88mg; IRON 3.4mg; SODIUM 421mg; CALC 88mg

SHRIMP PILAU

No matter how you pronounce it, "PER-loe," "PER-loo," or "pee-LOE," the secret to this traditional rice dish is a good stock or broth. We flavored our pilau with shrimp shells, but Low Country cooks have been known to add a live crab to the broth for extra flavor.

Broth:

    1½ pounds unpeeled large shrimp
    6   cups water
    1   tablespoon chopped fresh or
        1 teaspoon dried thyme
    1   tablespoon chopped fresh or
        1 teaspoon dried oregano
    1   tablespoon chopped fresh
        parsley
    ½   teaspoon salt
    2   carrots with tops, each cut into
        3 pieces
    2   celery stalks, each cut into 3
        pieces
    1   onion, quartered

Pilau:

    3   tablespoons olive oil
    1½ cups chopped onion
    ½   teaspoon dried crushed red
        pepper
    1   (28-ounce) can whole tomatoes,
        undrained and chopped
    1½ cups uncooked long-grain rice
    ½   teaspoon salt
    3   tablespoons chopped fresh
        parsley

1. To prepare broth, peel shrimp, reserving shells. Cover and chill shrimp. Combine shrimp shells, water, and next 7 ingredients in a large Dutch oven;

Continued

bring to a boil. Reduce heat to medium; cook until reduced to 3 cups (about 40 minutes). Strain broth through a sieve into a bowl, and discard solids.

2. To prepare pilau, heat oil in pan over medium heat. Add chopped onion, and sauté 5 minutes. Stir in red pepper and tomatoes, and cook 5 minutes. Stir in broth, rice, and ½ teaspoon salt; bring to a boil. Cover, reduce heat, and simmer 20 minutes. Fluff rice with a fork. Stir in shrimp; cover and cook 3 minutes or until shrimp are done. Sprinkle with 3 tablespoons parsley. Yield: 6 servings (serving size: 1½ cups).

CALORIES 362 (22% from fat); FAT 8.9g (sat 1.3g, mono 5.4g, poly 1.4g); PROTEIN 22.4g; CARB 47.3g; FIBER 2.3g; CHOL 129mg; IRON 5.1mg; SODIUM 737mg; CALC 103mg

LEMONADE

Before interstate highways and air conditioning, U.S. 15 was a favored north-south route to the Low Country. The Pine Crest Restaurant in Walterboro, South Carolina, one of the most popular "watering holes" along the way, served up a thirst-quenching, one-of-a-kind lemonade.

1 cup sugar
6 lemons, halved
6 cups boiling water

1. Combine sugar and lemons in a 3-quart pitcher. Add water, stirring until sugar dissolves, and cool to room temperature. Remove lemons from pitcher. Squeeze juice from lemons into pitcher; discard lemons. Remove seeds with a slotted spoon. Serve over ice. Yield: 7 cups (serving size: 1 cup).

CALORIES 120 (0% from fat); FAT 0g; PROTEIN 0.1g; CARB 31.9g; FIBER 0g; CHOL 0mg; IRON 0mg; SODIUM 1mg; CALC 3mg

APPLE CHUTNEY

Nothing identifies Low Country cooking more than its extensive use of condiments, particularly homemade ones. This easy-to-make cooktop chutney can be prepared in about an hour. Serve it with country captain, country ham, or game.

13 cups chopped peeled Granny Smith or other tart apple (about 4 pounds)
3 cups chopped onion (about 1 pound)
2 cups raisins
2 cups packed brown sugar
2 cups cider vinegar
¼ cup finely chopped seeded jalapeño pepper
1 teaspoon mustard seeds

1. Combine all ingredients in a large nonaluminum Dutch oven or stockpot. Bring to a boil. Reduce heat; simmer 45 minutes or until most of liquid evaporates. Yield: 9½ cups (serving size: ¼ cup).
Note: Store chutney in an airtight container in refrigerator up to 2 weeks.

CALORIES 96 (2% from fat); FAT 0.2g (sat 0.1g, mono 0.1g, poly 0.1g); PROTEIN 0.5g; CARB 24.9g; FIBER 1.7g; CHOL 0mg; IRON 0.6mg; SODIUM 6mg; CALC 12mg

---

THE LOW COUNTRY PALATE

The Low Country gentry became so accustomed to all the exotic flavors of the tropics and West Africa that they were known to sequester dozens of potherbs in their kitchen gardens, ringed by citrus and bay trees. Some built orangeries for protection against winter.

And so it was—with their chutneys and smoked meats, coconuts and heavy use of spices—that the African cooks used their knowledge of naturally based cooking to engineer a healthful and exotic American Creole cuisine that seems modern even today.

A Stirring Discovery

Stir-frying comes from China, but it's becoming as much at home in America as apple pie.

Sure, stir-frying is fast, but it has also proved so popular and enduring because it's healthful and fun. In no time at all, ordinary foods—vegetables, rice or noodles, and some meat or seafood—take on a new, delicious life.

Traditionally, preparing a stir-fry meal took a lot of chopping, seasonings, and special equipment. Now it's easy, thanks to precut vegetables and meats. Flavored sauces and oils lighten the burden on your spice rack, and you don't even need a wok. A nonstick skillet, a spatula, some precut foods, a bottle of stir-fry sauce, and you're on your way.

EGG FOO YONG

Preparation time: 8 minutes
Cooking time: 10 minutes

1 cup (1 [3½-ounce] bag) uncooked instant rice (such as Success)
1½ teaspoons vegetable oil, divided
⅓ cup finely chopped green onions
¼ cup chopped 33%-less-sodium smoked, fully cooked ham
1 cup fresh bean sprouts, finely chopped
2 large eggs
2 large egg whites
1 tablespoon spicy stir-fry sauce (such as House of Tsang)
¼ teaspoon white pepper

1. Cook rice according to package directions; keep warm.
2. Heat ½ teaspoon oil in a large nonstick skillet over medium-high heat. Add onions and ham; stir-fry 1 minute. Add bean sprouts, and stir-fry 30 seconds. Remove from heat.

3. Combine eggs, egg whites, stir-fry sauce, and white pepper, and beat well. Stir in ham mixture. Heat ½ teaspoon oil in pan over medium-high heat, and pour half of egg mixture into pan. Cook 45 seconds on each side or until egg mixture is lightly browned. Remove from pan, and keep warm. Repeat with ½ teaspoon oil and remaining egg mixture. Serve over rice. Yield: 2 servings (serving size: 1 omelet and 1 cup rice).

CALORIES 408 (24% from fat); FAT 11g (sat 2.8g, mono 3.4g, poly 2.8g); PROTEIN 19.4g; CARB 57.6g; FIBER 2g; CHOL 234mg; IRON 3.4mg; SODIUM 584mg; CALC 68mg

ORANGE BEEF

(pictured on page 96)

Preparation time: 18 minutes
Cooking time: 12 minutes

1½ cups (1 [5¼-ounce] bag) uncooked instant rice (such as Success)
3 tablespoons orange juice
1 tablespoon rice vinegar
1 teaspoon cornstarch
1 teaspoon dark sesame oil
¼ teaspoon salt
⅛ teaspoon dried crushed red pepper
1 pound flank steak
1 teaspoon vegetable oil
1 tablespoon minced peeled fresh ginger
2 teaspoons grated orange rind
2 teaspoons bottled minced garlic
2 tablespoons lemon juice
2 tablespoons sherry
1 tablespoon low-sodium soy sauce
2 cups broccoli florets
½ cup diagonally sliced carrot
1 (8-ounce) can sliced water chestnuts, drained

1. Cook rice according to package directions, and keep warm.
2. Combine orange juice and next 5 ingredients; set aside.
3. Trim fat from steak, and cut into

thin slices. Heat vegetable oil in a large nonstick skillet until hot. Add ginger, orange rind, and garlic; sauté for 3 minutes or until lightly browned. Add beef, lemon juice, sherry, and soy sauce; stir-fry for 2 minutes. Add broccoli, carrot, and water chestnuts; stir-fry 3 minutes or until crisp-tender. Stir in orange juice mixture; stir-fry 2 minutes. Serve over rice. Yield: 4 servings (serving size: 1 cup stir-fry and ¾ cup rice).

CALORIES 461 (26% from fat); FAT 13.3g (sat 5g, mono 5.1g, poly 1.6g); PROTEIN 28g; CARB 57g; FIBER 3g; CHOL 57mg; IRON 4.5mg; SODIUM 374mg; CALC 61mg

KUNG PAO PORK

Preparation time: 10 minutes
Cooking time: 11 minutes
Marinating time: 5 minutes

Marinade:

1 (¾-pound) pork tenderloin
1 tablespoon minced peeled fresh ginger
1 tablespoon bottled minced garlic
1 teaspoon cornstarch
2 teaspoons low-sodium soy sauce
1 teaspoon water
1 teaspoon sake (rice wine)

Remaining ingredients:

1 (8-ounce) package Chinese-style plain noodles
1 tablespoon vegetable oil
2 cups (¼-inch) sliced green bell pepper
1 (8-ounce) package shredded carrot
¼ cup water
1½ tablespoons thinly sliced green onions
2 tablespoons chili garlic sauce
1 tablespoon lemon juice
¼ cup chopped dry-roasted peanuts

1. To prepare marinade, trim fat from pork, and cut into ½-inch-wide strips.

Combine pork, ginger, and next 5 ingredients, and let mixture stand 5 minutes.
2. Prepare noodles according to package directions, omitting salt; keep warm.
3. Heat oil in a large nonstick skillet over medium-high heat. Add pork mixture, and stir-fry for 3 minutes or until pork loses its pink color. Add bell pepper and carrot, and stir-fry 1 minute. Stir in ¼ cup water, onions, chili garlic sauce, and juice, and cook 2 minutes. Serve over noodles, and sprinkle with peanuts. Yield: 4 servings (serving size: 1 cup stir-fry, ¾ cup noodles, and 1 tablespoon nuts).

CALORIES 389 (25% from fat); FAT 11g (sat 2.1g, mono 4.3g, poly 3.7g); PROTEIN 27g; CARB 45.4g; FIBER 4.5g; CHOL 55mg; IRON 4mg; SODIUM 553mg; CALC 45mg

SHRIMP-CURRIED RICE

Preparation time: 5 minutes
Cooking time: 15 minutes

1½ cups (1 [5¼-ounce] bag) uncooked instant rice (such as Success)
1 teaspoon vegetable oil
½ pound large shrimp, peeled
2 garlic cloves, minced
1 cup frozen green peas, thawed
1 tablespoon curry powder
½ teaspoon salt
2 tablespoons chopped fresh cilantro
2 teaspoons dark sesame oil

1. Cook rice according to package directions, and cool.
2. Heat vegetable oil in a large nonstick skillet over medium-high heat. Add shrimp and garlic; sauté 2 minutes. Add peas, curry, and salt, and stir-fry 1 minute. Stir in rice; stir-fry 1 minute or until thoroughly heated. Sprinkle with cilantro and sesame oil. Yield: 3 servings (serving size: 1½ cups).

CALORIES 371 (15% from fat); FAT 6.2g (sat 0.9g, mono 2g, poly 2.5g); PROTEIN 18.6g; CARB 58.7g; FIBER 4g; CHOL 86mg; IRON 4mg; SODIUM 531mg; CALC 78mg

Cantonese Chicken Chow Mein

Preparation time: 15 minutes
Cooking time: 10 minutes

- 1 (8-ounce) package wide lo mein noodles
- 1 teaspoon vegetable oil
- 4 garlic cloves, minced
- 4 (4-ounce) skinned, boned chicken breast halves, cut into 1-inch strips
- 1 cup sliced shiitake mushroom caps
- 1½ tablespoons fish sauce
- 1 cup diagonally sliced green onions
- ½ cup water
- ¼ teaspoon white pepper
- 2 teaspoons dark sesame oil

1. Cook noodles according to package directions, omitting salt; keep warm.
2. Heat vegetable oil in a large nonstick skillet over medium-high heat. Add garlic; stir-fry 30 seconds. Add chicken; stir-fry 5 minutes. Stir in mushrooms and fish sauce; stir-fry 1 minute. Stir in lo mein noodles, onions, water, and pepper; cover and cook until thoroughly heated (about 2 minutes). Sprinkle with sesame oil. Yield: 4 servings (serving size: 1½ cups).

CALORIES 376 (12% from fat); FAT 5g (sat 0.9g, mono 1.6g, poly 1.9g); PROTEIN 32.5g; CARB 49g; FIBER 1.9g; CHOL 66mg; IRON 4.2mg; SODIUM 568mg; CALC 37mg

---

FOR TWO

A Winning Compromise

In the beef-or-chicken battle, a couple with two clever menus can make everything come up roses.

Both menus serve two people—saving you from the perilous reproportioning of six- or eight-serving recipes that has doomed many a meal.

MEDITERRANEAN MENU

LEMON-OLIVE CHICKEN
WITH MINTED COUSCOUS

GREEN BEAN-
AND-FETA SAUTÉ

FRESH MELON WITH
ORANGE SEGMENTS

about 770 calories
per serving
and 11 grams fat

13% calories from fat

LEMON-OLIVE CHICKEN WITH MINTED COUSCOUS

- 1 teaspoon olive oil, divided
- 2 (6-ounce) skinned chicken breast halves
- ½ cup thinly sliced onion, separated into rings
- 1 large garlic clove, minced
- 1 teaspoon all-purpose flour
- ½ teaspoon ground cumin
- ½ teaspoon ground cinnamon
- ¼ teaspoon paprika
- 1 (16-ounce) can fat-free, less-sodium chicken broth
- ½ cup water
- 4 lemon slices
- ⅔ cup drained canned chickpeas (garbanzo beans)
- ¼ cup sliced green olives
- Minted Couscous
- 2 teaspoons thinly sliced fresh mint leaves (optional)

1. Heat ½ teaspoon oil in a large non-stick skillet over medium-high heat. Add chicken; cook 4 minutes on each side or until browned. Remove chicken from pan; set aside.
2. Heat ½ teaspoon olive oil in pan over medium heat. Add onion and garlic, and sauté 3 minutes. Stir in flour, cumin, cinnamon, and paprika; sauté 30 seconds. Add broth and water; bring to a simmer. Add chicken and lemon slices; cover and simmer 30 minutes or until chicken is done. Stir in chickpeas and olives, and cook until thoroughly heated. Serve over Minted Couscous. Garnish with sliced mint leaves, if desired. Yield: 2 servings (serving size: 1 chicken breast half, 1 cup sauce, and 1 cup couscous).

CALORIES 390 (18% from fat); FAT 7.9g (sat 1.7g, mono 3.6g, poly 1.4g); PROTEIN 42.5g; CARB 38.1g; FIBER 4g; CHOL 81mg; IRON 4.4mg; SODIUM 1,136mg; CALC 96mg

Minted Couscous:

- ¾ cup water
- ½ teaspoon butter or stick margarine
- ¼ teaspoon salt
- ⅔ cup uncooked couscous
- 1 tablespoon chopped fresh mint

1. Bring water, butter, and salt to a boil in a medium saucepan, and gradually stir in couscous. Remove from heat; cover and let stand 5 minutes. Fluff with a fork, and stir in mint. Yield: 2 servings (serving size: 1 cup).

CALORIES 72 (14% from fat); FAT 1.1g (sat 0.6g, mono 0.3g, poly 0g); PROTEIN 2.4g; CARB 13.4g; FIBER 0.7g; CHOL 3mg; IRON 0.4mg; SODIUM 305mg; CALC 1mg

---

MEDITERRANEAN PANTRY

To capture the tastes of the Mediterranean, it's a good idea to add these ingredients to your pantry staples.

Top-quality olive oil
Chickpeas
Olives and artichokes
Couscous
Feta cheese

GREEN BEAN-AND-FETA SAUTÉ

Cooking spray
 1 cup (1-inch) cut green beans
   (about ½ pound)
 ½ cup chopped onion
 ½ cup (1-inch-thick) red bell
   pepper strips
Dash of dried crushed red pepper
 ½ cup drained canned quartered
   artichoke hearts
 ¼ cup canned vegetable broth or
   water
 2 teaspoons lemon juice
 2 tablespoons (½ ounce) finely
   crumbled feta cheese

1. Heat a large nonstick skillet coated with cooking spray over medium-high heat. Add green beans, onion, bell pepper, and crushed red pepper; sauté 3 minutes. Add artichokes and broth; cook until liquid is reduced to 2 tablespoons (about 30 seconds). Stir in lemon juice, and sprinkle with crumbled cheese. Yield: 2 servings (serving size: 1 cup).

CALORIES 86 (24% from fat); FAT 2.3g (sat 1.1g, mono 0.4g, poly 0.2g); PROTEIN 4.3g; CARB 14.6g; FIBER 2.4g; CHOL 6mg; IRON 1.5mg; SODIUM 543mg; CALC 84mg

FRESH MELON WITH ORANGE SEGMENTS

 2 large oranges
 3 cups cubed peeled honeydew
   melon
 ¼ cup honey
 1 teaspoon minced fresh mint

1. Grate 1 teaspoon rind from orange; peel and section oranges over a bowl, reserving juice. Combine grated orange rind, sections, juice, melon, honey, and mint in a large bowl; toss well. Yield: 2 servings (serving size: 1½ cups).

CALORIES 295 (2% from fat); FAT 0.5g (sat 0.2g, mono 0.1g, poly 0.1g); PROTEIN 2.8g; CARB 77.7g; FIBER 9.5g; CHOL 0mg; IRON 0.5mg; SODIUM 27mg; CALC 85mg

---

ASIAN MENU

HOISIN BEEF WITH
SHIITAKE MUSHROOM
SAUCE

HUNAN EGGPLANT

APRICOT-GLAZED
PINEAPPLE SUNDAE

about 740 calories
per serving
and 15 grams fat

18% calories from fat

HOISIN BEEF WITH SHIITAKE MUSHROOM SAUCE

 2 (4-ounce) beef tenderloin steaks
   (1 inch thick)
1½ tablespoons hoisin sauce
 1 tablespoon dry white wine
 1 teaspoon minced peeled fresh
   ginger
 2 garlic cloves, minced and
   divided
1½ cups water
 1 (0.5-ounce) package dried
   shiitake mushrooms (about
   ½ cup)
Cooking spray
 1 teaspoon dark sesame oil
 ⅔ cup sliced green onions
 2 cups hot cooked long-grain
   rice

1. Trim fat from steaks. Combine hoisin sauce, wine, ginger, and 1 garlic clove in a shallow dish. Add steaks; cover and marinate in refrigerator 2 hours, turning steaks occasionally.
2. Combine water and mushrooms in a small saucepan, and bring to a boil. Remove from heat; cover and let stand 30 minutes. Remove mushrooms from pan with a slotted spoon, reserving liquid. Discard mushroom stems; cut caps into quarters, and set aside. Bring mushroom liquid to a boil; cook until reduced to ⅓ cup (about 5 minutes). Remove from heat. Remove steaks from marinade. Add marinade to reduced mushroom liquid; set aside.
3. Prepare grill or broiler.

4. Place steaks on grill rack or broiler pan coated with cooking spray; cook 6 minutes on each side or until desired degree of doneness. Set aside, and keep warm.
5. Heat sesame oil in a nonstick skillet over medium-high heat. Add mushrooms, green onions, and 1 garlic clove; sauté 2 minutes. Add marinade mixture, and cook 2 minutes.
6. Cut steaks diagonally across grain into thin slices. Arrange steak on each of 2 plates, and top with mushroom sauce. Serve with cooked rice. Yield: 2 servings (serving size: 3 ounces steak, 1 cup rice, and ¼ cup sauce).

CALORIES 496 (20% from fat); FAT 10.9g (sat 3.4g, mono 4g, poly 1.3g); PROTEIN 30.2g; CARB 65.9g; FIBER 2.9g; CHOL 71mg; IRON 5.7mg; SODIUM 298mg; CALC 62mg

HUNAN EGGPLANT

Chinese cuisine from the Hunan province is known for its spiciness. This side dish uses crushed red pepper for a mild, mouth-friendly heat.

 1 (1-pound) eggplant, peeled and
   cut lengthwise into 1-inch-
   thick slices
 2 tablespoons canned vegetable
   broth or water
 1 tablespoon fresh lemon juice
 1 teaspoon dark sesame oil
 ½ teaspoon sugar
 ⅛ teaspoon salt
 1 tablespoon thinly sliced green
   onions
 ¼ teaspoon dried crushed red pepper
 2 garlic cloves, minced

1. Cut eggplant slices in half crosswise. Steam eggplant, covered, 5 minutes or until tender. Combine broth, juice, oil, sugar, and salt in a small saucepan; bring to a boil. Divide eggplant evenly between 2 plates; drizzle with 2 tablespoons sauce. Sprinkle with onions, pepper, and garlic. Yield: 2 servings.

CALORIES 81 (29% from fat); FAT 2.6g (sat 0.4g, mono 0.9g, poly 1g); PROTEIN 2.4g; CARB 14.9g; FIBER 2.9g; CHOL 0mg; IRON 1.1mg; SODIUM 218mg; CALC 75mg

APRICOT-GLAZED PINEAPPLE SUNDAE

4 (1-inch-thick) peeled fresh
   pineapple slices
2 tablespoons apricot preserves,
   melted
1 teaspoon sugar
Dash of ground cinnamon
1 cup vanilla low-fat frozen
   yogurt

1. Preheat broiler.
2. Place pineapple slices on a broiler pan. Brush pineapple with preserves; broil 6 minutes or until bubbly.
3. Combine sugar and cinnamon, and sprinkle over pineapple. Serve warm with frozen yogurt. Yield: 2 servings (serving size: 2 pineapple slices and ½ cup frozen yogurt).

CALORIES 161 (9% from fat); FAT 1.6g (sat 1g, mono 0g, poly 0.5g); PROTEIN 2.3g; CARB 35.8g; FIBER 0.2g; CHOL 7mg; IRON 0.1mg; SODIUM 39mg; CALC 78mg

---

ASIAN PANTRY

For Asian recipes, keep these ingredients on hand in your pantry.

Thai fish sauce, dark sesame oil,
or hoisin sauce
Fresh ginger
Fresh lemons and limes
Asian noodles
Exotic dry mushrooms

Take It Outside

Spring is the perfect time to invite friends over for a party because if you have a porch, you have friends, and if you have friends, you must feed them.

Porch. Party. The two are inseparable. Always have been. Always will be. Along with the kitchen, a porch is the one place at a party you can find a way to belong whether you know everybody or nobody. But a porch is better because it lacks appliances or dishware to knock over accidentally.

The other thing about porches is they're the perfect open-air cafés. In these surroundings, almost any kind of food tastes wonderful.

PORCH PARTY MENU FOR 6

HUMMUS WITH RASPBERRY VINEGAR

Pita wedges

Vegetable crudités

ARTICHOKE-AND-PASTA SALAD

ASPARAGUS AND
SUN-DRIED TOMATO VINAIGRETTE

FOCACCIA SANDWICH WITH SPRING GREENS

PIÑA COLADA GRANITA

HONEY-ALMOND COOKIES

GINGER LEMONADE

HUMMUS WITH RASPBERRY VINEGAR

Raspberry vinegar gives this hummus a little kick, but you can use any kind of vinegar you have on hand.

1 tablespoon olive oil
1½ cups diced onion
2 tablespoons raspberry vinegar
1 (15½-ounce) can chickpeas
   (garbanzo beans), undrained
1 tablespoon chopped fresh
   cilantro
½ teaspoon ground cumin
½ teaspoon coarsely ground black
   pepper
¼ teaspoon salt
Cilantro sprigs (optional)

1. Heat oil in a nonstick skillet over medium-high heat. Add onion, and sauté 5 minutes or until onion begins to brown. Add vinegar; bring to a boil, and cook 2 minutes or until vinegar evaporates. Cool to room temperature.
2. Drain chickpeas through a sieve over a bowl, reserving ¼ cup liquid. Place chickpeas and chopped cilantro in a food processor, and process until mixture resembles coarse meal. Add onion mixture, ¼ cup reserved liquid, cumin, pepper, and salt, and process until smooth. Garnish with cilantro sprigs, if desired. Yield: 2 cups (serving size: 2 tablespoons).

CALORIES 44 (27% from fat); FAT 1.3g (sat 0.2g, mono 0.8g, poly 0.3g); PROTEIN 1.9g; CARB 6.6g; FIBER 1g; CHOL 0mg; IRON 0.6mg; SODIUM 75mg; CALC 14mg

ARTICHOKE-AND-PASTA SALAD

1 (14-ounce) can artichoke
    hearts, drained and divided
1 tablespoon olive oil
1 tablespoon water
1 tablespoon lemon juice
½ teaspoon dried basil
¼ teaspoon dried oregano
¼ teaspoon black pepper
1 garlic clove, minced
3 cups cooked radiatore (about 5
    ounces uncooked short coiled
    pasta)
2 cups thinly sliced spinach
1 cup chopped seeded tomato
¼ cup (1 ounce) crumbled feta
    cheese

1. Combine 2 artichoke hearts, oil, and next 6 ingredients in a blender or food processor, and process until smooth.
2. Chop remaining artichoke hearts. Combine chopped artichokes, pasta, spinach, and chopped tomato in a large bowl. Pour pureed artichoke mixture over pasta mixture, and toss well to coat. Cover and chill 2 hours. Sprinkle with feta cheese. Yield: 6 servings (serving size: 1 cup).

CALORIES 153 (23% from fat); FAT 3.9g (sat 1.1g, mono 1.9g, poly 0.5g); PROTEIN 5.9g; CARB 24.9g; FIBER 1.8g; CHOL 4mg; IRON 2.2mg; SODIUM 137mg; CALC 70mg

ASPARAGUS AND SUN-DRIED TOMATO VINAIGRETTE

2 pounds fresh asparagus
⅓ cup sun-dried tomato sprinkles
¼ cup balsamic vinegar
1 tablespoon olive oil
¼ teaspoon salt
1 garlic clove, minced

1. Steam asparagus, covered, 4 minutes. Place in a shallow dish.
2. Combine tomato sprinkles and remaining 4 ingredients in a bowl. Spoon evenly over asparagus. Cover and chill 2 hours. Yield: 6 servings.

CALORIES 66 (35% from fat); FAT 2.6g (sat 0.4g, mono 1.7g, poly 0.4g); PROTEIN 4.1g; CARB 9.4g; FIBER 3.7g; CHOL 0mg; IRON 1.8mg; SODIUM 187mg; CALC 37mg

FOCACCIA SANDWICH WITH SPRING GREENS

This makes a giant focaccia sandwich that's cut into 6 servings.

Focaccia:

2 cups bread flour
½ teaspoon sugar
¼ teaspoon salt
1 package dry yeast (about 2¼
    teaspoons)
¾ cup very warm water (120° to
    130°)
Cooking spray
½ teaspoon olive oil
⅓ cup (1¼-inch) julienne-cut
    green onions
1 tablespoon (¼ ounce) grated
    fresh Parmesan cheese
¼ teaspoon black pepper

Sandwich:

4 ounces provolone or Havarti
    cheese, thinly sliced
8 (¼-inch-thick) slices tomato
3 cups gourmet salad greens
½ cup chopped green onions
2 tablespoons balsamic vinegar
1 tablespoon olive oil
¼ teaspoon salt
⅛ teaspoon black pepper

1. To prepare focaccia, lightly spoon flour into dry measuring cups; level with a knife. Place flour, sugar, ¼ teaspoon salt, and yeast in a food processor; pulse 2 times or until blended. With processor running, slowly add very warm water through food chute; process until dough forms a ball. Process an additional 30 seconds. Turn dough out onto a lightly floured surface, and knead lightly 4 or 5 times. Place dough in a large bowl coated with cooking spray, turning to coat top. Cover and let rise in a warm place (85°), free from drafts, 30 minutes or until doubled in size.
2. Punch dough down; let rest 5 minutes. Roll into a 13 x 9-inch rectangle on a lightly floured surface. Transfer dough to a 13 x 9-inch baking

pan coated with cooking spray; brush ½ teaspoon oil over dough. Cover and let rise 30 minutes or until puffy.
3. Preheat oven to 400°.
4. Uncover dough. Make indentations in top of dough, using the handle of a wooden spoon or your fingertips. Sprinkle ⅓ cup green onions, Parmesan cheese, and ¼ teaspoon pepper over dough, leaving a ½-inch border. Bake at 400° for 20 minutes or until lightly browned. Cool in pan on a wire rack.
5. To prepare sandwich, cut focaccia in half horizontally, using a serrated knife; place bottom layer, cut side up, on a flat surface. Arrange provolone cheese and tomato slices over bottom layer; top with salad greens and ½ cup green onions. Combine balsamic vinegar and remaining 3 ingredients in a small bowl, stirring well with a whisk. Drizzle vinaigrette over salad green mixture; top with remaining focaccia layer. Gently press sandwich together; cut into 6 equal portions. Yield: 6 servings (serving size: 1 [4-inch] square).

CALORIES 278 (29% from fat); FAT 9g (sat 3.9g, mono 3.5g, poly 0.8g); PROTEIN 12.1g; CARB 37g; FIBER 1.4g; CHOL 14mg; IRON 3mg; SODIUM 387mg; CALC 186mg

PIÑA COLADA GRANITA

1 (8-ounce) can pineapple chunks
    in juice, undrained
3 cups pineapple juice
½ cup cream of coconut
⅓ cup dark rum
2 tablespoons fresh lemon juice
1 teaspoon coconut extract
Mint sprigs (optional)

1. Place pineapple chunks in a blender or food processor, and process until smooth. Combine pineapple puree, 3 cups pineapple juice, and next 4 ingredients in a large bowl. Pour mixture into a 13 x 9-inch baking dish; cover and freeze at least 8 hours or until firm.
2. Remove frozen pineapple mixture from freezer. Scrape entire mixture with a fork until fluffy. Spoon mixture into a freezer-safe container; cover and

Continued

freeze up to 1 month. Garnish with mint sprigs, if desired. Yield: 16 servings (serving size: ½ cup).

CALORIES 75 (31% from fat); FAT 2.6g (sat 2.3g, mono 0.1g, poly 0g); PROTEIN 0.4g; CARB 9.3g; FIBER 0g; CHOL 0mg; IRON 0.3mg; SODIUM 1mg; CALC 10mg

HONEY-ALMOND COOKIES

2 cups all-purpose flour
½ teaspoon baking soda
⅛ teaspoon salt
⅓ cup sugar
⅓ cup honey
¼ cup butter or stick margarine, softened
2 tablespoons vegetable oil
1½ teaspoons vanilla extract
1 teaspoon almond extract
1 large egg white
Cooking spray
¼ cup sliced almonds, chopped

1. Lightly spoon flour into dry measuring cups; level with a knife. Combine flour, baking soda, and salt in a bowl. Combine sugar, honey, butter, and oil in a bowl; beat at medium speed of a mixer until well-blended. Add extracts and egg white to sugar mixture. Beat until well-blended. Stir in flour mixture (dough will be sticky).
2. Coat hands lightly with cooking spray; divide dough into 2 equal portions. Shape each portion into a 9-inch log. Wrap logs individually in plastic wrap; freeze 3 hours or until firm.
3. Preheat oven to 375°.

4. Cut each log into 24 (¼-inch) slices, and place 1 inch apart on baking sheets coated with cooking spray. Press almonds into cookies. Bake at 375° for 9 minutes. Cool 2 minutes or until firm. Remove cookies from pans; cool on wire racks. Yield: 4 dozen (serving size: 1 cookie).

CALORIES 49 (35% from fat); FAT 1.9g (sat 0.7g, mono 0.6g, poly 0.4g); PROTEIN 0.7g; CARB 7.4g; FIBER 0.2g; CHOL 3mg; IRON 0.3mg; SODIUM 30mg; CALC 3mg

GINGER LEMONADE

6 cups water, divided
1¼ cups sugar
¼ cup grated peeled fresh ginger
1¼ cups fresh lemon juice (about 7 large lemons)
¼ cup fresh lime juice
Lemon slices (optional)
Lime slices (optional)

1. Combine 1 cup water, sugar, and ginger in a small saucepan; bring to a boil, and cook 1 minute or until sugar dissolves, stirring occasionally. Remove from heat; cool.
2. Strain ginger mixture through a sieve into a pitcher, and discard solids. Add 5 cups water and juices, and stir well. Serve over ice, and garnish with lemon and lime slices, if desired. Yield: 8 servings (serving size: 1 cup).

CALORIES 133 (0% from fat); FAT 0g; PROTEIN 0.2g; CARB 35.2g; FIBER 0g; CHOL 0mg; IRON 0mg; SODIUM 1mg; CALC 4mg

READER RECIPES

Take Her Cake

BUTTERMILK-CHOCOLATE CAKE

"When a friend asked me to send in one of my chocolate recipes, I knew it had to be this cake."
—*Carol Hook, Newbury Park, California*

1 cup sugar
¼ cup butter or stick margarine, softened
½ teaspoon vanilla extract
2 large egg whites
1 large egg
1½ cups sifted cake flour
⅓ cup unsweetened cocoa
1½ teaspoons baking powder
¼ teaspoon salt
½ cup low-fat buttermilk
⅓ cup water
¼ teaspoon baking soda
Cooking spray
Chocolate Glaze

1. Preheat oven to 350°.
2. Beat sugar, butter, and vanilla in a large bowl at medium speed of a mixer until well-blended (about 5 minutes). Add egg whites and egg, 1 at a time, beating well after each addition. Lightly spoon flour into dry measuring cups; level with a knife. Combine flour, cocoa, baking powder, and salt in a small bowl, stirring well with a whisk. Combine buttermilk, water, and baking soda. Add flour mixture to sugar mixture alternately with buttermilk mixture, beginning and ending with flour mixture. Pour into a 9-inch round cake pan coated with cooking spray. Bake at 350° for 35 minutes or until a wooden pick inserted in center comes out clean. Cool in pan 10 minutes; remove from pan. Cool completely on a wire rack. Spread glaze over cake. Yield: 9 servings.

CALORIES 295 (21% from fat); FAT 7g (sat 1.8g, mono 2.6g, poly 1.8g); PROTEIN 5.1g; CARB 53.6g; FIBER 0g; CHOL 25mg; IRON 2.4mg; SODIUM 274mg; CALC 82mg

---

PORCH PARTY PLANNER

One week ahead
make granita
make focaccia (store in zip-top bag in freezer)
make lemonade
make vinaigrette for asparagus
make dressing for pasta salad

One day ahead
make hummus
make cookies (store in airtight container)

Morning of party
thaw focaccia

Two hours before party
steam asparagus and finish recipe
finish pasta salad

One hour before party
finish focaccia sandwich

Chocolate Glaze:

1 cup sifted powdered sugar
3 tablespoons unsweetened cocoa
2 tablespoons 1% low-fat milk
½ teaspoon butter or stick margarine, melted
½ teaspoon light-colored corn syrup

1. Combine all ingredients in a small bowl; stir well with a whisk until well-blended. Yield: ¾ cup.

BASIC BEAN-SOUP MIX

(pictured on page 94)

"When he lived at home, my son was forever making 15-bean soup from a package. The two of us came up with this variation."
—Joy Beck, Cincinnati, Ohio

Dried-bean mix:

1 pound dried kidney beans
1 pound dried yellow lentils
1 pound green split peas
1 pound dried black beans
1 pound dried black-eyed peas

Spice mix:

5 teaspoons salt
5 teaspoons dried basil
5 teaspoons dried rosemary
5 teaspoons dried marjoram
2½ teaspoons black pepper
1¼ teaspoons dried crushed red pepper
5 bay leaves

Additional soup ingredients for 1 packet dried-bean mix and 1 packet spice mix:

8 cups water
1 smoked ham hock (about ½ pound)
1 cup chopped onion
1 (14.5-ounce) can no-salt-added diced tomatoes, undrained

1. To prepare dried-bean mix, combine first 5 ingredients in a large bowl. Divide bean mixture into 5 equal portions (about 2½ cups each), and place in airtight containers.
2. To prepare spice mix, combine salt and next 6 ingredients in a bowl. Divide spice mix into 5 equal portions. Place in small airtight containers.
3. To prepare soup, sort and wash 1 portion dried-bean mix, and place in a large Dutch oven. Cover with water to 2 inches above beans; cover and let stand 8 hours. Drain.
4. Combine drained bean mixture, 8 cups water, and ham hock in a large Dutch oven; bring to a boil. Add 1 packet spice mix, onion, and tomatoes. Cover, reduce heat, and simmer 2 hours. Uncover; cook 1 hour. Discard bay leaf. Remove ham hock from soup. Remove meat from bone; shred meat with 2 forks. Return meat to soup. Yield: 6 servings (serving size: 1½ cups).

CALORIES 288 (14% from fat); FAT 4.5g (sat 1.9g, mono 1.1g, poly 1.1g); PROTEIN 18.4g; CARB 45.9g; FIBER 7.1g; CHOL 4mg; IRON 4.9mg; SODIUM 503mg; CALC 98mg

CRANBERRY-APPLE LIMEADE

"This fruit drink actually evolved from a cocktail I used to make using cranberry, orange, and apple juices. One day I ran out of orange juice and substituted limeade. Mix it with a bit of seltzer water to cut the sweetness."
—Laura Peverall, Pinehurst, North Carolina

¼ cup lime juice
2 (6-ounce) cans thawed limeade concentrate, undiluted
1 (48-ounce) bottle cranberry juice cocktail, chilled
1 (32-ounce) bottle apple juice, chilled

1. Combine all ingredients in a pitcher; stir well, and chill. Serve over ice. Yield: 3 quarts (serving size: 1 cup).

CALORIES 156 (1% from fat); FAT 0.1g (sat 0g, mono 0g, poly 0.1g); PROTEIN 0.1g; CARB 40.2g; FIBER 0.2g; CHOL 0mg; IRON 0.5mg; SODIUM 7mg; CALC 10mg

FRESH VEGETABLE SOUP

"This is my mother's recipe. I make a batch on Sundays. During the week, I reheat it for dinner in no time flat."
—Dorothy Duder, Burbank, California

2 tablespoons olive oil
2 cups chopped onion
5 garlic cloves, minced
2 cups chopped celery (about 4 stalks)
2 cups (2-inch) cut green beans (about ½ pound)
1½ cups fresh corn kernels (about 3 ears)
1 cup thinly sliced carrot
1 medium zucchini, halved lengthwise and sliced (about 1 cup)
1 teaspoon dried basil
1 teaspoon dried oregano
1 teaspoon dried rosemary
4 (14¼-ounce) cans fat-free beef broth
1 (15-ounce) can kidney beans, drained
4 cups chopped seeded tomato
⅔ cup uncooked elbow macaroni (about 3 ounces)
1 (8-ounce) can no-salt-added tomato sauce
2 cups shredded green cabbage
¾ teaspoon salt
¾ teaspoon black pepper
1 cup grated Parmesan cheese

1. Heat oil in a stockpot over medium-high heat. Add onion and garlic; sauté 2 minutes. Stir in celery and next 9 ingredients. Bring to a boil; cover, reduce heat, and simmer 30 minutes. Add tomato, macaroni, and tomato sauce. Bring to a boil; cover, reduce heat, and simmer 20 minutes or until pasta is done. Add cabbage, salt, and pepper; cook 5 minutes or until cabbage wilts. Serve with cheese. Yield: 8 servings (serving size: 2 cups soup and 2 tablespoons cheese).
Note: Refrigerate any remaining soup in an airtight container up to 1 week, or freeze up to 3 months.

CALORIES 272 (25% from fat); FAT 7.6g (sat 2.6g, mono 3.6g, poly 0.9g); PROTEIN 12.5g; CARB 39.4g; FIBER 6.4g; CHOL 8mg; IRON 3mg; SODIUM 529mg; CALC 213mg

MICHAEL'S WONDERFUL NACHOS GRANDE

"My husband, Michael, works magic with light food. I come home from work every night, and he has our dinner ready. This is one of his best recipes."

—Joy La Porte, Des Plaines, Illinois

  1 pound ground turkey
1½ cups chopped onion
  1 tablespoon water
  2 (15-ounce) cans turkey chili with beans
  1 (1.25-ounce) package reduced-sodium taco seasoning
  6 ounces fat-free baked tortilla chips (about 6 cups)
  ½ cup (2 ounces) shredded reduced-fat sharp Cheddar cheese
  2 tablespoons chopped seeded jalapeño pepper
1½ cups bottled salsa

1. Preheat oven to 350°.
2. Cook turkey, onion, and water in a large nonstick skillet over medium-high heat until browned, stirring to crumble. Add chili and taco seasoning; reduce heat, and simmer 10 minutes or until thoroughly heated.
3. Line a 13 x 9-inch baking pan with chips. Spoon turkey mixture over chips; top with cheese. Bake at 350° for 10 minutes or until cheese melts. Sprinkle with chopped jalapeño, and cut into 6 wedges; serve with salsa. Yield: 6 servings (serving size: 1 wedge and ¼ cup salsa).

CALORIES 428 (17% from fat); FAT 7.9g (sat 2.9g, mono 2.6g, poly 1.2g); PROTEIN 35g; CARB 54.8g; FIBER 8.3g; CHOL 73mg; IRON 3.4mg; SODIUM 839mg; CALC 190mg

CHICKEN AND DUMPLINGS

"This is one of those good everyday meals. It's easy and fast, and it uses ingredients that I almost always have in the cupboard. All you need to add are a salad and some bread to make a warm and filling meal."

—Linda Roswog, Falls Church, Virginia

Cooking spray
  1 pound skinned, boned chicken breast, cut into 1-inch pieces
  1 cup thinly sliced onion
  1 cup thinly sliced celery
  2 tablespoons all-purpose flour
3½ cups fat-free, less-sodium chicken broth
  2 cups (½-inch-thick) sliced carrot
  ¾ teaspoon dried thyme, divided
  ¼ teaspoon black pepper
  ¾ cup low-fat baking mix (such as Bisquick)
  5 tablespoons fat-free milk

1. Place a Dutch oven coated with cooking spray over medium-high heat until hot. Add chicken and onion; sauté for 10 minutes. Add celery, and sauté 2 minutes. Sprinkle chicken mixture with flour, and sauté 1 minute. Add broth, carrot, ½ teaspoon thyme, and pepper, stirring well with a whisk. Cover, reduce heat, and simmer 10 minutes, stirring occasionally.
2. Combine ¼ teaspoon thyme, baking mix, and milk in a small bowl. Drop dough by tablespoonfuls onto chicken mixture. Cover and cook over medium-low heat 15 minutes or until dumplings are done (do not boil). Yield: 4 servings (serving size: 1¾ cups).

CALORIES 290 (10% from fat); FAT 3.3g (sat 0.7g, mono 1.3g, poly 0.5g); PROTEIN 32.7g; CARB 30g; FIBER 3.5g; CHOL 66mg; IRON 2.6mg; SODIUM 802mg; CALC 98mg

CHICKEN SUPREME

"My mother used to make this recipe when I was growing up, and later I lightened it up. It isn't your typical bland chicken dish. It has a special pizazz that makes it great for dinner parties."

—Kristy Rea, Naples, Florida

  1 cup fat-free sour cream
  ¼ cup lemon juice
  1 teaspoon celery salt
  1 teaspoon paprika
  2 teaspoons Worcestershire sauce
  ½ teaspoon salt
  ½ teaspoon black pepper
  4 garlic cloves, minced
  6 (4-ounce) skinned, boned chicken breast halves
  ¾ cup dry breadcrumbs
Cooking spray
  3 tablespoons reduced-calorie stick margarine, melted and divided
  ¼ cup chopped fresh parsley

1. Combine first 8 ingredients in a large zip-top plastic bag. Add chicken; seal and marinate in refrigerator overnight. Remove chicken from bag; discard marinade.
2. Preheat oven to 325°.
3. Place breadcrumbs in a shallow dish. Dredge chicken in breadcrumbs. Place chicken in a 13 x 9-inch baking dish coated with cooking spray. Drizzle 1½ tablespoons margarine over chicken, and bake at 325° for 30 minutes. Pour 1½ tablespoons margarine over chicken, and bake for an additional 15 minutes or until done. Sprinkle chicken with chopped parsley. Yield: 6 servings.

CALORIES 245 (22% from fat); FAT 6g (sat 1.3g, mono 2.1g, poly 1.7g); PROTEIN 30.9g; CARB 14.8g; FIBER 0.8g; CHOL 66mg; IRON 2mg; SODIUM 834mg; CALC 57mg

Practicing What We Preach

Five of America's best chefs assembled for our GrandStand '99 festival, and we've picked their best dishes for you to try.

We spent months scouring the country for chefs whose innovative restaurants across America are dazzling customers by practicing what we preach: that light and healthy cooking can, and should, taste great. These chefs and thousands of our readers joined us in Atlanta for GrandStand '99—an unprecedented food, fun, and fitness festival.

PORK TENDERLOIN WITH DRIED-CHERRY CHUTNEY AND CARAMELIZED-ONION SAUCE

Bob Hurley of Napa Valley Grille in Yountville, California, serves this dish with a goat cheese-potato gratin. You'll have leftover Dried-Cherry Chutney, which goes great with ham, pork, or beef.

Marinade:

    1   cup thinly sliced onion
    ⅓   cup water
    3   tablespoons dry red wine
    2   tablespoons olive oil
    2   garlic cloves, crushed
    2   pounds pork tenderloin

Remaining ingredients:

    ¼   teaspoon black pepper
    ⅛   teaspoon salt
        Dried-Cherry Chutney
        Caramelized-Onion Sauce

1. To prepare marinade, combine first 5 ingredients in a large zip-top plastic bag; add pork to bag. Seal and marinate in refrigerator 8 hours. Remove pork from bag, discarding marinade.
2. Prepare grill, or preheat oven to 425°.
3. Sprinkle pork with pepper and salt. Insert a meat thermometer into thickest part of pork. Place pork on grill rack or broiler pan; grill or bake pork at 425° for 20 minutes or until thermometer registers 160° (slightly pink), turning pork occasionally. Cut into ¼-inch-thick slices. Serve with Dried-Cherry Chutney and Caramelized-Onion Sauce. Yield: 8 servings (serving size: 3 ounces pork, ⅓ cup chutney, and ¼ cup sauce).

CALORIES 484 (14% from fat); FAT 7.7g (sat 2.7g, mono 3.6g, poly 0.8g); PROTEIN 28.7g; CARB 77.7g; FIBER 2.6g; CHOL 86mg; IRON 2.6mg; SODIUM 334mg; CALC 60mg

Dried-Cherry Chutney:

If you don't have raspberry vinegar, just increase the red wine vinegar to 2 cups.

    4   cups dried tart cherries
    3   cups sugar
    2   cups water
    1½ cups red wine vinegar
    1   cup diced Vidalia or other
        sweet onion
    ½   cup raspberry vinegar
    2   tablespoons minced peeled
        fresh ginger
    1   tablespoon minced seeded
        jalapeño pepper
    2   teaspoons ground coriander
    1   teaspoon ground cardamom
    1   teaspoon ground cumin
    1   teaspoon grated orange rind
    3   whole cloves
    1   (3-inch) cinnamon stick

1. Combine all ingredients in a large saucepan, and bring to a boil. Reduce heat to medium, and cook, uncovered, until thick (about 1 hour), stirring occasionally. Discard cloves and cinnamon. Serve warm or at room temperature. Yield: 5 cups (servings size: ⅓ cup).
Note: Store leftover chutney in an airtight container in the refrigerator up to 2 weeks.

CALORIES 281 (1% from fat); FAT 0.2g (sat 0.1g, mono 0g, poly 0.1g); PROTEIN 1.5g; CARB 73g; FIBER 1.8g; CHOL 0mg; IRON 1.5mg; SODIUM 6mg; CALC 25mg

Caramelized-Onion Sauce:

    1   tablespoon butter or stick
        margarine
    3   cups thinly sliced onion
    1   cup dry red wine
    3   cups fat-free, less-sodium
        chicken broth
    ⅛   teaspoon salt
    ⅛   teaspoon black pepper

1. Melt butter in a large skillet over medium-high heat. Add onion; cook 5 minutes, stirring frequently. Continue cooking 15 minutes or until deep golden brown, stirring constantly. Add wine; cook 5 minutes or until liquid almost evaporates. Remove onion from skillet; finely chop onion. Return onion to skillet; stir in broth, salt, and pepper. Bring to a boil; cook until reduced to 2 cups (about 10 minutes). Yield: 2 cups (serving size: ¼ cup).

BEEF TENDERLOIN WITH YUKON GOLD POTATOES, CHILI-CURED ONIONS, AND HORSERADISH

The contrast of flavors in this dish from Tobias Lawry of Ajax Tavern in Aspen, Colorado, is phenomenal.

Onions:

    2   cups vertically sliced red onion
    ¼   cup fresh lemon juice
    1   tablespoon minced fresh basil
    2   teaspoons chili powder
    ¼   teaspoon salt
    ⅛   teaspoon ground red pepper

Continued

Potatoes:

4 cups sliced Yukon gold or red potato (about 1½ pounds)
1 tablespoon vegetable oil
½ teaspoon salt
¼ teaspoon freshly ground black pepper
Cooking spray

Horseradish cream:

⅔ cup low-fat sour cream
2 tablespoons fat-free milk
1 tablespoon prepared horseradish

Remaining ingredients:

1 (12-ounce) beef tenderloin
¼ teaspoon freshly ground black pepper
2 cups trimmed arugula
4 shavings fresh Parmesan cheese

1. To prepare onions, combine first 6 ingredients in a bowl; toss well. Let stand 2 hours, stirring occasionally.
2. Preheat oven to 450°.
3. To prepare potatoes, combine potato slices, oil, ½ teaspoon salt, and ¼ teaspoon black pepper in a bowl, and toss well to coat. Arrange potato slices in a single layer on a jelly-roll pan coated with cooking spray. Bake at 450° for 15 minutes. Turn potato slices over, and bake an additional 20 minutes or until tender and lightly browned.
4. To prepare horseradish cream, combine sour cream, milk, and horseradish; cover and chill.
5. Prepare grill, or preheat oven to 450°.
6. Rub tenderloin with ¼ teaspoon black pepper. Insert a meat thermometer into thickest part of tenderloin. Place tenderloin on a grill rack or a broiler pan coated with cooking spray, and grill or bake at 450° for 20 minutes or until meat thermometer registers 145° (medium-rare) or 160° (medium), turning every 5 minutes. Let stand 5 minutes; cut into 8 slices.
7. Drain onions in a colander over a bowl, reserving 1 tablespoon marinade; toss marinade with arugula.

8. Arrange 2 slices tenderloin, 1 cup potatoes, ½ cup arugula mixture, and ¼ cup onions on each of 4 plates; drizzle each serving with about 2½ tablespoons horseradish cream, and top with 1 cheese shaving. Yield: 4 servings.

CALORIES 385 (37% from fat); FAT 15.8g (sat 6.6g, mono 5g, poly 2.2g); PROTEIN 25.3g; CARB 36.6g; FIBER 3.9g; CHOL 71mg; IRON 3.8mg; SODIUM 519mg; CALC 165mg

MUSHROOM RAVIOLI WITH ROASTED-TOMATO SAUCE AND SHAVED PARMESAN CHEESE

Almost any combination of mushrooms will work in this easy dish from Jim Coleman of Philadelphia's Rittenhouse Hotel.

Ravioli:

1 tablespoon olive oil
1 cup sliced shiitake mushroom caps
1 cup sliced chanterelle mushroom caps
2 tablespoons chopped leek
2 tablespoons chopped shallot
¾ cup white wine
3 tablespoons chopped fresh chives
¼ teaspoon salt
¼ teaspoon black pepper
16 won ton wrappers
2 teaspoons cornstarch
6 cups water

Sauce:

4 tomatoes, cored and cut in half lengthwise (about 1¾ pounds)
1 tablespoon olive oil
1 cup chopped onion
4 garlic cloves, chopped
1 cup tomato juice
2 tablespoons chopped fresh basil
½ cup (2 ounces) shaved fresh Parmesan cheese
Fresh chive sprigs (optional)

1. Heat 1 tablespoon oil in a skillet over medium-high heat. Add mushrooms, leek, and shallot; cook 3 minutes. Stir in

wine and chives. Reduce heat; simmer 7 minutes or until liquid is evaporated. Sprinkle with salt and pepper.
2. Working with 1 won ton wrapper at a time (cover remaining wrappers with a damp towel to keep them from drying), spoon about 2 teaspoons mushroom mixture into center of each wrapper. Moisten edges of wrapper with water; bring 2 opposite corners together. Press edges together with a fork to seal, forming a triangle. Place ravioli on a large baking sheet sprinkled with cornstarch. Bring 6 cups water to a simmer in a large saucepan; add half of ravioli (cover remaining ravioli with a damp towel to keep them from drying). Cook 5 minutes or until done (do not boil). Remove ravioli with a slotted spoon. Keep warm. Repeat procedure with remaining ravioli.
3. Preheat broiler.
4. Place tomato halves, skin sides up, on a foil-lined baking sheet; flatten with hand. Broil 3 minutes or until blackened; peel. Heat 1 tablespoon oil in a saucepan over medium heat. Add onion and garlic; sauté 2 minutes. Stir in tomatoes, tomato juice, and basil; bring to a simmer. Place tomato mixture in a blender or food processor, and process 1 minute or until smooth. Spoon over ravioli; top with cheese. Garnish with chive sprigs, if desired. Yield: 4 servings (serving size: 4 ravioli, ½ cup sauce, and 2 tablespoons cheese).

CALORIES 289 (36% from fat); FAT 11.6g (sat 3.4g, mono 6.2g, poly 1.1g); PROTEIN 11.6g; CARB 37.1g; FIBER 3.1g; CHOL 13mg; IRON 3.1mg; SODIUM 796mg; CALC 202mg

THAI MARINATED-CHICKEN SALAD

Use prepackaged rotisserie chicken in this quick salad from Tim Creehan of Beach Walk Café in Destin, Florida.

1 tablespoon vegetable oil
1 cup quartered mushrooms
½ cup rice vinegar
½ cup low-sodium soy sauce
¼ cup pineapple juice
1 tablespoon chopped fresh mint
1 teaspoon minced peeled fresh ginger
1 teaspoon fish sauce
1 teaspoon dark sesame oil
¼ teaspoon chile paste
1 garlic clove, minced
4 cups chopped ready-to-eat roasted, skinned, boned chicken breasts (about 4 breasts)
4 cups thinly sliced napa (Chinese) cabbage
4 cups thinly sliced romaine lettuce
½ cup thinly sliced red cabbage
1 cup yellow or red bell pepper strips
1 (4-ounce) package alfalfa sprouts

1. Heat vegetable oil in a nonstick skillet over medium-high heat. Add mushrooms, and sauté 3 minutes. Combine mushrooms, vinegar, and next 8 ingredients in a large bowl. Add chicken, and toss to coat. Cover and refrigerate 30 minutes.
2. Combine napa cabbage, romaine, and red cabbage. Divide cabbage mixture evenly among 6 plates; top each serving with chicken mixture, bell pepper, and sprouts. Yield: 6 servings (serving size: 1⅓ cups cabbage mixture, ⅔ cup chicken mixture, about 3 tablespoons bell pepper, and ½ cup sprouts).

CALORIES 160 (29% from fat); FAT 5.2g (sat 1.2g, mono 1.6g, poly 2g); PROTEIN 21g; CARB 7.8g; FIBER 2.1g; CHOL 47mg; IRON 1.8mg; SODIUM 1,145mg; CALC 93mg

HALIBUT WITH CITRUS COUSCOUS, RED-ONION MARMALADE, AND CILANTRO-ALMOND SAUCE

This flavorful one-dish meal is from Greg Higgins of Higgins Restaurant and Bar in Portland, Oregon. You can substitute any firm-fleshed white fish for the halibut.

Marmalade:

¼ cup fresh orange juice
¼ cup port or other sweet red wine
2 tablespoons sugar
2 tablespoons red wine vinegar
1 cup vertically sliced red onion
1 teaspoon grated orange rind
⅛ teaspoon salt
Dash of black pepper

Sauce:

1½ cups chopped fresh cilantro
½ cup sliced almonds, toasted
¼ cup finely chopped seeded jalapeño pepper (about 2 large)
¼ cup fresh lime juice
3 tablespoons water
2 tablespoons honey
1 teaspoon ground cumin
¼ teaspoon salt
⅛ teaspoon black pepper
2 garlic cloves, peeled

Couscous:

¾ cup water
¼ teaspoon grated lemon rind
¼ teaspoon grated orange rind
2 tablespoons fresh lemon juice
2 tablespoons fresh orange juice
1 teaspoon chile paste (optional)
¼ teaspoon salt
¼ teaspoon curry powder
¼ teaspoon black pepper
2 garlic cloves, minced
1 cup uncooked couscous

Halibut:

1 tablespoon curry powder
½ teaspoon salt
4 (6-ounce) skinned halibut fillets (about 1 inch thick)
Cooking spray
2 cups gourmet salad greens

1. To prepare marmalade, combine first 4 ingredients in a small nonaluminum saucepan. Bring to a boil; cook until reduced to ½ cup (about 5 minutes). Add onion and 1 teaspoon orange rind; cook 5 minutes. Sprinkle with ⅛ teaspoon salt and dash of black pepper; set aside.
2. To prepare sauce, combine cilantro and next 9 ingredients in a blender or food processor; process until smooth.
3. To prepare couscous, bring ¾ cup water and next 9 ingredients to a boil in a medium saucepan; gradually stir in couscous. Remove from heat; cover and let stand for 5 minutes. Fluff with a fork.
4. To prepare halibut, combine curry and ½ teaspoon salt. Rub fillets with curry mixture. Lightly coat with cooking spray. Heat a large nonstick skillet over medium-high heat until hot. Add fillets, and sauté 4 minutes on each side or until fish flakes easily when tested with a fork. Place ½ cup salad greens on each of 4 plates, and top each serving with 1 cup couscous. Arrange fillets on couscous, and top each with 2 tablespoons marmalade. Spoon ¼ cup sauce around each serving. Yield: 4 servings.

CALORIES 428 (23% from fat); FAT 11.1g (sat 1.2g, mono 5.4g, poly 2.9g); PROTEIN 42.1g; CARB 42.4g; FIBER 4.9g; CHOL 80mg; IRON 5.2mg; SODIUM 804mg; CALC 192mg

Oops!

Erasers—who needs 'em? Pretty much all of civilization. Cooking, too, is very much in the correction business.

PERSONAL-DEDUCTION PIZZA

Our ingredient list is carved in pencil, not stone, so erase what you don't like and add what you prefer.

- 1 (10-ounce) can refrigerated pizza crust dough
- Cooking spray
- 1 teaspoon olive oil
- 1 cup green bell pepper strips
- 2 tablespoons water
- ⅔ cup canned crushed tomatoes
- 1 cup button mushrooms, thinly sliced (about 2 ounces)
- 1 (4-ounce) portobello mushroom cap, thinly sliced
- 1 teaspoon dried oregano
- ¼ teaspoon kosher salt
- 1 cup (4 ounces) thinly sliced fresh mozzarella cheese

1. Preheat oven to 425°.
2. Unroll pizza dough onto a baking sheet coated with cooking spray; fold under edges to form an 11-inch circle. Bake at 425° for 7 minutes.
3. Increase oven temperature to 475°.
4. Heat oil in a medium nonstick skillet over medium-high heat. Add bell pepper, and sauté 1 minute. Add 2 tablespoons water; cover, reduce heat to low, and cook 10 minutes or until bell pepper is soft. Spread tomatoes over dough, leaving a ½-inch border, and top with bell pepper and mushrooms. Sprinkle with oregano and salt. Bake pizza at 475° for 12 minutes. Top with cheese, and bake an additional 3 minutes or until cheese is melted. Yield: 6 servings.

CALORIES 197 (29% from fat); FAT 6.4g (sat 2.5g, mono 2.5g, poly 0.9g); PROTEIN 8.6g; CARB 26g; FIBER 1g; CHOL 15mg; IRON 1.9mg; SODIUM 522mg; CALC 113mg

Shipping News

From Arizona, Olive Mae Brass signaled "Mayday" for a 60-year-old French cake recipe from a luxury cruise liner.

We were there for the rescue. We've cut nearly 200 calories per slice and dropped the fat grams to less than 9 from the previously perilous 23.

NORMANDIE CAKE

(pictured on page 93)

Cake:

- 1½ cups granulated sugar, divided
- ¼ cup butter or stick margarine, softened
- 3 large egg yolks
- 1 tablespoon vanilla extract
- 2 ounces semisweet chocolate, melted and cooled
- 2 cups all-purpose flour
- 2 tablespoons unsweetened cocoa
- 1½ teaspoons baking powder
- ¼ teaspoon salt
- 1½ cups fat-free milk
- 3 large egg whites
- ¼ teaspoon cream of tartar
- Cooking spray

Icing:

- ½ cup packed brown sugar
- ½ cup fat-free milk
- ¼ cup butter or stick margarine
- 1 ounce semisweet chocolate, chopped
- 1 teaspoon vanilla extract
- 3 cups sifted powdered sugar
- 18 pecan halves

1. Preheat oven to 350°.
2. To prepare cake, beat 1¼ cups granulated sugar, ¼ cup butter, and egg yolks at high speed of a mixer until well-blended (about 5 minutes). Add 1 tablespoon vanilla and melted chocolate; beat well. Lightly spoon flour into dry measuring cups, and level with a knife. Combine flour, cocoa, baking powder, and salt, stirring well with a whisk. Add flour mixture to sugar mixture alternately with 1½ cups milk, beginning and ending with flour mixture.
3. Beat egg whites and cream of tartar at high speed until foamy, using clean, dry beaters. Gradually add ¼ cup granulated sugar, 1 tablespoon at a time; beat until stiff peaks form. Fold into batter. Pour into 2 (8-inch) round cake pans coated with cooking spray. Sharply tap pans once on counter to remove air bubbles. Bake at 350° for 40 minutes or until a wooden pick inserted in center comes out clean. Cool in pans 10 minutes on a wire rack; remove from pans. Cool completely on wire rack.
4. To prepare icing, combine brown sugar, ½ cup milk, ¼ cup butter, and 1 ounce chocolate in a small, heavy saucepan. Place over medium heat until chocolate melts, stirring occasionally with a whisk. Bring to a boil, and cook 7 minutes or until slightly thick. Pour into a bowl; cool to room temperature. Stir in 1 teaspoon vanilla. Add powdered sugar; beat well until combined.
5. Place 1 cake layer on a plate. Spread top with ½ cup icing, and top with other cake layer. Spread remaining icing over top and sides of cake. Arrange pecans on top. Yield 18 servings (serving size: 1 piece).

CALORIES 320 (24% from fat); FAT 8.6g (sat 4.6g, mono 2.9g, poly 0.6g); PROTEIN 4g; CARB 58.1g; FIBER 0.5g; CHOL 51mg; IRON 1.2mg; SODIUM 153mg; CALC 73mg

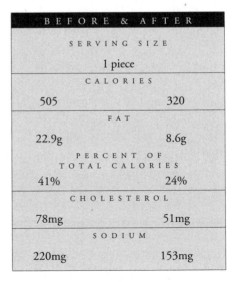

BEFORE & AFTER	
SERVING SIZE	
1 piece	
CALORIES	
505	320
FAT	
22.9g	8.6g
PERCENT OF TOTAL CALORIES	
41%	24%
CHOLESTEROL	
78mg	51mg
SODIUM	
220mg	153mg

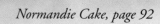

Normandie Cake, page 92

Basic Bean-Soup Mix, page 87

Cannellini Beans and Greens on Garlic Toast, page 104

California Crepe Rolls, page 99

Seriously Lemon Tart, page 106

Orange Beef, page 81

Spinach and Goat Cheese on Focaccia, page 103

Wrap 'N Roll

The name is fancy, but these easy-to-make crepes—the original wraps—are so practical, your weeknight menus may never be the same again.

BASIC CREPES

To make Cornmeal Crepes, add 2 tablespoons cornmeal with the flour and salt. A ¼-cup measure scoops and measures the batter at the same time; just remember to fill it only three-quarters full.

½ cup all-purpose flour
¼ teaspoon salt
¾ cup 1% low-fat milk
2 large egg whites
1 large egg

1. Lightly spoon flour into a dry measuring cup; level with a knife. Combine flour and salt in a bowl. Combine milk, egg whites, and egg in a bowl; stir well with a whisk. Gradually add to flour mixture, stirring with a whisk until smooth. Place an 8-inch crepe pan or nonstick skillet over medium heat until hot. Pour a scant ¼ cup batter into pan; quickly tilt pan in all directions so batter covers pan with a thin film. Cook about 1 to 2 minutes.
2. Carefully lift edge of crepe with a spatula to test for doneness. Crepe is ready to turn when it can be shaken loose from pan and the underside is lightly browned. Turn crepe over, and cook 15 seconds on other side.
3. Place crepe on a towel; cool. Repeat procedure until all of batter is used, stirring batter between crepes. Stack crepes between single layers of wax paper or paper towels to prevent sticking. Yield: 10 servings (serving size: 1 crepe).

CALORIES 41 (18% from fat); FAT 0.8g (sat 0.3g, mono 0.3g, poly 0.1g); PROTEIN 2.6g; CARB 5.8g; FIBER 0.2g; CHOL 23mg; IRON 0.4mg; SODIUM 85mg; CALC 26mg

MUSHROOM-CREPE CANNELLONI

Mushroom filling:

1 teaspoon olive oil
2 (8-ounce) packages mushrooms, coarsely chopped
1 teaspoon dried oregano
1 garlic clove, minced
¼ cup dry white wine
1 tablespoon tomato paste
1 teaspoon all-purpose flour
½ cup (2 ounces) part-skim ricotta cheese
1 tablespoon (¼ ounce) grated fresh Parmesan cheese
½ teaspoon salt
Dash of black pepper

Parmesan sauce:

3 tablespoons all-purpose flour
1¼ cups 1% low-fat milk
¼ teaspoon salt
⅛ teaspoon ground nutmeg
2 tablespoons (½ ounce) grated fresh Parmesan cheese

Cannelloni:

8 Basic Crepes (see recipe)
Cooking spray
1 (14.5-ounce) can no-salt-added diced tomatoes, drained
1 tablespoon (¼ ounce) grated fresh Parmesan cheese
Fresh chopped parsley (optional)

1. To prepare mushroom filling, heat oil in a large nonstick skillet over medium-high heat. Add mushrooms; cook 5 minutes, stirring occasionally. Add oregano and garlic; sauté 1 minute. Add wine, and cook 3 minutes or until liquid evaporates. Stir in tomato paste and 1 teaspoon flour. Remove from heat, and cool. Stir in ricotta cheese, 1 tablespoon Parmesan, ½ teaspoon salt, and black pepper.
2. To prepare Parmesan sauce, place 3 tablespoons flour in a small saucepan. Gradually add milk, stirring with a whisk until blended. Stir in ¼ teaspoon salt and nutmeg. Place over medium heat; cook until thick (about 3 minutes), stirring constantly. Remove from heat; stir in 2 tablespoons Parmesan, and keep warm.
3. Preheat oven to 425°.
4. To prepare cannelloni, spoon ¼ cup mushroom mixture in center of each crepe; roll up. Place, seam sides down, in 4 gratin dishes or in a 13 x 9-inch baking dish coated with cooking spray. Spoon half of tomatoes over crepes, and top with Parmesan sauce and remaining tomatoes. Sprinkle with 1 tablespoon Parmesan. Bake at 425° for 15 minutes. Turn broiler on (do not remove dish from oven); broil 3 minutes or until cheese is lightly browned. Garnish with parsley, if desired. Yield: 4 servings (serving size: 2 cannelloni).

CALORIES 266 (28% from fat); FAT 8.3g (sat 4.9g, mono 3.3g, poly 0.7g); PROTEIN 17.6g; CARB 31.8g; FIBER 2.3g; CHOL 63mg; IRON 3.4mg; SODIUM 832mg; CALC 353mg

DEMYSTIFYING CREPES

Do I have to use a crepe pan?
No, we tested our recipes in an 8-inch crepe pan and an 8-inch non-stick skillet, and came up with identical results. The most crucial element is size: A 7- or 8-inch skillet is a must. If the skillet is bigger, your crepes will be too thin; smaller, and they'll be too thick.

Do I have to oil the pan?
We found that a new nonstick skillet requires no oil at all. If you have an older nonstick skillet with a worn or scratched surface, use cooking spray.

I've read that crepe batter needs to rest for two hours. Is this true?
Traditionally, crepe recipes called for letting the batter rest for two hours to let the gluten from the flour relax, making a more tender crepe. We found no difference in the crepes that rested and those that didn't.

Why all the stirring?
While you make each crepe, the flour settles. Stirring the batter before you make the next crepe keeps the consistency you want for cooking.

Making crepes may sound intimidating, but nothing could be easier.
Combine flour, milk, and eggs, and then cook and flip—all in 20 minutes.

1 *Add the liquids to the flour mixture; whisk just until combined. Don't overstir—this will make the crepes tough.*

2 *The ideal crepe batter should be smooth, not lumpy, and about the consistency of heavy cream.*

3 *Heat your skillet, and then pour in the batter, tilting the pan to cover the bottom. It doesn't matter if your crepes are perfectly round, but you do want to cover most of the skillet or they'll be too small for the fillings.*

4 *Crepes cook very quickly. Check the bottom after about 1 minute. If the crepe is a speckled light brown, that side is ready. Flip the crepe over with a spatula, and cook only about 15 to 30 seconds on the other side.*

5 *Remove crepe to a towel or plate to cool. Proceed with other recipes. Or stack the crepes in wax paper or plastic wrap, place in a zip-top bag, and freeze up to 2 months. Crepes will keep up to 5 days in the refrigerator.*

MOO SHU PORK CREPES

In this traditional stir-fried dish, crepes replace the Chinese pancakes. Serve the crepes warm with commercial Chinese mustard or additional hoisin sauce.

  1 (0.5-ounce) package dried
     wood ear mushrooms or
     shiitake mushrooms
  2 cups boiling water
  ½ pound boned pork loin, cut
     into 2 x ¼-inch strips
  1 tablespoon low-sodium soy
     sauce
  1 tablespoon dry sherry
  1 teaspoon cornstarch
  1 teaspoon sugar
  1 teaspoon vegetable oil
  1 teaspoon grated peeled fresh
     ginger
1½ cups thinly sliced green
     cabbage
  3 tablespoons water
  1 cup sliced button mushrooms
  1 cup (1-inch) sliced green
     onions
  5 teaspoons hoisin sauce
 10 Basic Crepes (page 97)

1. Combine dried mushrooms and boiling water in a bowl; cover and let stand for 30 minutes or until tender. Drain mushrooms. Rinse and slice mushrooms, and set aside.
2. Combine pork and next 4 ingredients in a small bowl. Cover and marinate in refrigerator for 30 minutes.
3. Heat oil in a large nonstick skillet over medium-high heat. Add ginger, and sauté 30 seconds. Add pork mixture, and stir-fry 1 minute. Add cabbage and 3 tablespoons water, and stir-fry 2 minutes. Add wood ear mushrooms, button mushrooms, and onions; stir-fry 1 minute. Remove from heat.
4. Spread ½ teaspoon hoisin sauce over each crepe. Spoon about ⅓ cup pork mixture on lower third of each crepe. Fold in sides of crepes; roll up. Yield: 5 servings (serving size: 2 filled crepes).

CALORIES 213 (26% from fat); FAT 6.1g (sat 2g, mono 2.4g, poly 1.1g); PROTEIN 16.1g; CARB 22.1g; FIBER 1.9g; CHOL 73mg; IRON 1.9mg; SODIUM 409mg; CALC 85mg

CREAMY CREPES POBLANO

Using cornmeal crepes instead of corn tortillas adds an international fusion to this enchilada casserole.

  1 pound poblano chiles
     (about 6 chiles)
2½ cups water
  2 garlic cloves, thinly sliced
  2 bay leaves
  1 pound skinned, boned
     chicken breasts
  ⅓ cup all-purpose flour
  ¼ teaspoon salt
  1 cup 1% low-fat milk
  1 teaspoon butter or stick
     margarine
  1 teaspoon dried oregano
  1 teaspoon ground cumin
  1 garlic clove, minced
  ½ cup fresh corn kernels (about
     1 ear)
  ½ cup (2 ounces) shredded
     Monterey Jack cheese
  8 Cornmeal Crepes (page 97)
     Cooking spray
  1 cup diced tomato

1. Preheat broiler.
2. Place chiles on a foil-lined baking sheet; broil 10 minutes or until blackened, turning occasionally. Place in a zip-top plastic bag, and seal. Let stand 15 minutes. Peel chiles; cut in half lengthwise. Discard seeds and membranes; chop chiles, and set aside.
3. Bring water, sliced garlic, and bay leaves to a boil in a saucepan; add chicken. Reduce heat; simmer 20 minutes or until chicken is done. Remove chicken; cool. Strain broth through a colander into a bowl; discard solids. Reserve 1 cup broth. Shred chicken with 2 forks.
4. Preheat oven to 425°.
5. Combine flour and salt in a bowl; gradually add milk to flour mixture, stirring constantly with a whisk. Melt butter in a medium saucepan over medium heat; add oregano, cumin, and minced garlic, and sauté 1 minute. Add flour mixture and reserved 1 cup broth, and cook until thick (about 4 minutes), stirring constantly with

whisk. Remove 1 cup sauce; set aside. Add ½ cup chiles and corn to remaining sauce in pan; cook over medium-low heat 2 minutes. Remove from heat; stir in cheese. Combine chicken, reserved 1 cup sauce, and remaining ½ cup chiles in a bowl.
6. Spoon about ¼ cup chicken mixture down center of each crepe; roll up. Place crepes, seam sides down, in a 13 x 9-inch baking dish coated with cooking spray; spoon sauce over crepes. Bake at 425° for 15 minutes or until bubbly. Sprinkle with tomato. Yield: 4 servings (serving size: 2 filled crepes).
Note: Substitute two (4.5-ounce) cans of green chiles, drained and chopped, for poblano chiles.

CALORIES 390 (22% from fat); FAT 9.6g (sat 4.8g, mono 2.8g, poly 1g); PROTEIN 39.8g; CARB 35.1g; FIBER 2.9g; CHOL 128mg; IRON 3.3mg; SODIUM 567mg; CALC 268mg

CALIFORNIA CREPE ROLLS

(pictured on page 95)

In this version of the popular California roll, it's crucial to use short-grain rice that turns sticky when cooked.

1¾ cups water
  2 tablespoons rice vinegar
1½ tablespoons sugar
  ¼ teaspoon salt
  1 cup uncooked short-grain rice
  ¼ cup water, divided
  3 tablespoons low-sodium soy
     sauce
  1 tablespoon wasabi powder
 10 Basic Crepes (page 97)
 20 small spinach leaves
 30 medium shrimp, cooked and
     peeled
 20 (⅛-inch-thick) slices peeled
     avocado (about 1 avocado)
  5 teaspoons sesame seeds,
     toasted

1. Bring first 4 ingredients to a boil in a medium saucepan. Add rice; cover, reduce heat, and simmer 20 minutes or until liquid is absorbed. Cool slightly.

Continued

2. Combine 2 tablespoons water and soy sauce in a small bowl.

3. Combine 2 tablespoons water and wasabi powder in a small bowl.

4. Gently spread about ¼ cup rice mixture over 1 crepe using moist fingertips. Place 2 spinach leaves on lower third of crepe. Arrange 3 shrimp and 2 avocado slices over spinach. Sprinkle with ½ teaspoon sesame seeds. Roll up crepe jelly-roll fashion, pressing seam to seal. Cut roll crosswise into 4 slices. Repeat procedure with remaining crepes, rice mixture, spinach, shrimp, avocado slices, and sesame seeds. Serve with soy sauce mixture and wasabi sauce. Yield: 10 servings (serving size: 4 crepe slices, 1½ teaspoons soy sauce mixture, and about ½ teaspoon wasabi sauce).

CALORIES 201 (21% from fat); FAT 4.6g (sat 0.9g, mono 2g, poly 1g); PROTEIN 12.8g; CARB 26.5g; FIBER 1.2g; CHOL 80mg; IRON 2.8mg; SODIUM 379mg; CALC 73mg

ASIAN BEEF-CREPE ROLLS

Traditional spring rolls turn into crepe rolls when the rice paper is replaced by crepes, which are easier to roll up and eat. Serve these as appetizers. Cooked vermicelli can be substituted for the rice sticks.

Marinade:

1½ tablespoons fish sauce
1 tablespoon minced peeled fresh ginger
2 teaspoons sugar
1 (12-ounce) flank steak

Dipping sauce:

¼ cup chunky peanut butter
3 tablespoons fresh lime juice
2 tablespoons water
2 teaspoons fish sauce
1 teaspoon sugar

Remaining ingredients:

2 ounces uncooked rice sticks (rice flour noodles)
1 teaspoon vegetable oil
1 tablespoon fresh lime juice
½ teaspoon chile paste or dried crushed red pepper
10 small Boston lettuce leaves
10 Basic Crepes (page 97)
½ cup shredded carrot
30 thinly cut slices seeded cucumber
30 mint leaves
30 cilantro sprigs

1. To prepare marinade, combine fish sauce, minced ginger, and sugar in a large zip-top plastic bag. Trim fat from steak. Cut steak diagonally across grain into thin slices. Add steak to bag; seal bag, and marinate in refrigerator 2 hours. Remove steak from bag, and discard marinade.

2. To prepare dipping sauce, combine peanut butter and next 4 ingredients in a small bowl; stir with a whisk until blended. Set aside.

3. Place rice sticks in a medium saucepan; cover with hot water. Let stand 30 minutes. Bring to a boil, and cook 5 minutes. Drain; cut rice sticks into small pieces.

4. Heat oil in a large nonstick skillet over medium-high heat. Add beef, and stir-fry 2 minutes. Add rice sticks; cook 1 minute. Stir in 1 tablespoon lime juice and chile paste. Remove mixture from heat.

5. Place 1 lettuce leaf in center of 1 crepe, and top with ¼ cup beef mixture, about 1 tablespoon carrot, 3 cucumber slices, 3 mint leaves, and 3 cilantro sprigs. Fold in bottom of crepe, and roll up jelly-roll fashion starting at side. Repeat procedure with remaining lettuce, crepes, beef mixture, carrot, cucumber, mint, and cilantro. Cut each roll crosswise into 3 slices; arrange, cut sides up, on a plate. Serve with dipping sauce. Yield: 10 servings (serving size: 3 crepe slices and 1 tablespoon dipping sauce).

CALORIES 179 (39% from fat); FAT 7.8g (sat 2.4g, mono 3.3g, poly 1.4g); PROTEIN 12.3g; CARB 13.6g; FIBER 1g; CHOL 41mg; IRON 1.6mg; SODIUM 432mg; CALC 42mg

STACKED CREPE-SPINACH TORTE

This layered dish is similar to lasagna, with crepes replacing the pasta.

1 teaspoon olive oil
2 garlic cloves, minced
½ teaspoon dried basil
1 (14.5-ounce) can diced tomatoes, undrained
¾ cup fat-free ricotta cheese
¼ teaspoon salt
1 (10-ounce) package frozen chopped spinach, thawed, drained, and squeezed dry
7 Basic Crepes (page 97)
Cooking spray
½ cup (2 ounces) shredded provolone or fresh Parmesan cheese, divided

1. Preheat oven to 425°.

2. Heat oil in a large nonstick skillet over medium heat. Add garlic; sauté 1 minute. Add basil and tomatoes; bring to a boil. Cook 4 minutes or until most of liquid evaporates. Spoon into a bowl; reserve ¼ cup. Add ricotta cheese, salt, and spinach to remaining tomato mixture; stir well.

3. Place 1 crepe in a 9-inch pie plate coated with cooking spray; top with ⅓ cup spinach mixture and 1 tablespoon provolone cheese. Repeat layers, ending with a crepe. Spoon reserved ¼ cup tomato mixture over top; sprinkle with remaining cheese. Bake at 425° for 15 minutes or until thoroughly heated. Yield: 4 servings (serving size: 1 wedge).

CALORIES 221 (26% from fat); FAT 6.3g (sat 3.3g, mono 1.5g, poly 0.5g); PROTEIN 19.3g; CARB 22.6g; FIBER 3.4g; CHOL 66mg; IRON 3mg; SODIUM 691mg; CALC 371mg

Friends in Your Corner

Oranges, green veggies, and dried beans are even better when you realize how good they are for your body.

Folate, part of the B-vitamin family, is a powerful ally for your heart, pregnancies, resistance to disease, and maybe even memory.

In 1998, the Food and Drug Administration, convinced that expectant mothers are not familiar with folate, began requiring that folic acid—folate in vitamin-supplement form—be added to rice, pasta, bread, and flour.

Recent studies indicate that by lowering elevated levels of the amino-acid byproduct homocysteine in the bloodstream, folate may reduce the risk of heart attack.

Meanwhile, at the U.S. Department of Agriculture Human Nutrition Research Center on Aging at Tufts University, studies suggest possible links between folate consumption and decreased risks of colon cancer and types of memory loss in older people.

ASIAN ASPARAGUS-AND-ORANGE SALAD

2 oranges
1 tablespoon vegetable oil
6 cups (2-inch) diagonally sliced asparagus (about 2 pounds)
1 garlic clove, thinly sliced
2 teaspoons low-sodium soy sauce
¼ teaspoon dark sesame oil
1 tablespoon sesame seeds, toasted
Napa (Chinese) cabbage leaves (optional)

1. Peel and section oranges over a bowl, reserving 1 teaspoon juice. Set sections aside; discard membranes.
2. Heat vegetable oil in a large skillet over medium-high heat. Add asparagus and garlic; sauté 5 minutes. Remove from skillet.
3. Combine soy sauce and sesame oil; pour over asparagus mixture, tossing well. Cool to room temperature. Stir in sesame seeds, orange sections, and 1 teaspoon juice. Serve on cabbage leaves, if desired. Yield: 10 servings (serving size: ½ cup).
Note: Each serving provides 110 micrograms of folate.

CALORIES 46 (41% from fat); FAT 2.1g (sat 0.4g, mono 0.6g, poly 1g); PROTEIN 2.2g; CARB 6.2g; FIBER 2.5g; CHOL 0mg; IRON 0.9mg; SODIUM 34mg; CALC 34mg

SHRIMP-AND-CANNELLINI BEAN SALAD

Shrimp:

4 cups water
⅓ cup parsley sprigs
2 garlic cloves, peeled
1 onion, quartered
1 bay leaf
1½ pounds medium shrimp, peeled and deveined

Salad:

2 tablespoons extra-virgin olive oil
¼ teaspoon salt
¼ teaspoon black pepper
2 garlic cloves, minced
¾ cup diced red bell pepper
½ cup diced peeled avocado
½ cup minced fresh cilantro
¼ cup fresh lime juice
2 (15-ounce) cans cannellini beans or other white beans, rinsed and drained

1. To prepare shrimp, combine first 5 ingredients in a medium saucepan. Bring to a boil; add shrimp, and cook 3 minutes or until shrimp are done. Drain and rinse with cold water; cool. Discard onion, garlic, and herbs.
2. To prepare salad, combine oil, salt, black pepper, and minced garlic; stir well with a whisk. Add shrimp, bell pepper, and remaining ingredients, and toss well. Cover and chill 1 hour. Yield: 6 servings (serving size: 1⅓ cups).
Note: Each serving provides 84 micrograms of folate.

CALORIES 314 (30% from fat); FAT 10.4g (sat 1.5g, mono 5.3g, poly 2.4g); PROTEIN 26.3g; CARB 30.3g; FIBER 4.2g; CHOL 129mg; IRON 5.5mg; SODIUM 418mg; CALC 103mg

---

MENU SUGGESTION

LENTIL-AND-PANCETTA SOUP

Herb breadsticks *

*Unroll 1 (11-ounce) can refrigerated soft breadsticks; cut dough along perforations to form 12 breadsticks. Coat with cooking spray; sprinkle with 1 teaspoon paprika and ½ teaspoon Italian seasoning. Place on a baking sheet; bake at 425° for 11 minutes or until golden. Serves 4.

LENTIL-AND-PANCETTA SOUP

Pancetta (pan-CHEH-tuh) is an Italian bacon that's cured with salt and other spices. Wheat berries are sold in health-food stores with other hot cereals.

1 cup uncooked wheat berries
7 cups water
1 cup dried lentils
¾ cup chopped pancetta (about 3 ounces) or 3 bacon slices, chopped
2 teaspoons olive oil
1 cup chopped onion
¾ cup diced carrot
½ cup diced celery
4 cups coarsely chopped Swiss chard (about 6 ounces)
½ teaspoon salt
¼ teaspoon black pepper

1. Place wheat berries in a large saucepan; cover with water to 2 inches above

Continued

wheat berries. Bring to a boil; remove from heat. Cover; let stand 1 hour. Drain well; return wheat berries to pan.

2. Cover with water to 2 inches above wheat berries. Bring to a boil; reduce heat, and cook over medium-low heat, partially covered, 45 minutes or until tender. Drain; set aside.

3. Combine 7 cups water and lentils in pan. Bring to a boil; partially cover, reduce heat, and simmer 15 minutes. Add pancetta, and simmer 10 minutes or until lentils are tender. Drain lentil mixture in a colander over a bowl, reserving cooking liquid.

4. Heat oil in a large Dutch oven over medium-high heat. Add onion, carrot, and celery; sauté 8 minutes. Add Swiss chard, and cook 5 minutes, stirring frequently. Add reserved cooking liquid, salt, and pepper; bring to a boil. Stir in wheat berries and lentil mixture; cook 1 minute or until thoroughly heated. Yield: 9 servings (serving size: 1 cup).

Note: Each serving provides 99 micrograms of folate.

CALORIES 216 (29% from fat); FAT 7g (sat 2.2g, mono 3.3g, poly 0.9g); PROTEIN 10.5g; CARB 29.9g; FIBER 4.2g; CHOL 6mg; IRON 3.1mg; SODIUM 247mg; CALC 30mg

---

WHAT'S IN A NAME: FOLATE AND FOLIC ACID

Although folate and folic acid are both biochemical forms of the same B vitamin, they aren't exactly interchangeable. Studies show that the body absorbs folic acid, the form of the vitamin found in supplements, much more efficiently than folate, the form that's found in foods.

Dietary recommendations do take this factor into account. Daily requirements for adults are set at 400 micrograms of "dietary folate equivalents." Rather than agonize over terminology, just assume that you'll be getting at least some of that supply via breads and cereals, because by law they must now be fortified with folic acid. And aim to secure the rest from foods rich in folate such as spinach, legumes, and oranges.

HERB-ROASTED CHICKEN-AND-BEAN CASSEROLE

1 pound dried cranberry beans or pinto beans
2 quarts water
1 tablespoon chopped fresh or 1 teaspoon dried thyme, divided
3 garlic cloves, halved
4 bay leaves, divided
3 chicken drumsticks (about ¾ pound), skinned
3 chicken thighs (about ¾ pound), skinned
1¼ teaspoons salt, divided
½ teaspoon black pepper, divided
2 tablespoons olive oil, divided
1 cup diced carrot
1 cup chopped onion
¼ teaspoon ground cinnamon, divided
2 garlic cloves, minced
½ cup chopped fresh flat-leaf parsley
⅓ cup Italian-seasoned breadcrumbs

1. Sort and wash beans, and place in a large Dutch oven. Cover with water to 2 inches above beans; bring to a boil, and cook 2 minutes. Remove from heat; cover and let stand 1 hour. Drain beans, and discard liquid. Combine beans, 2 quarts water, 1½ teaspoons thyme, garlic halves, and 2 bay leaves in Dutch oven; bring to a boil. Partially cover, reduce heat, and simmer 1 hour or until almost tender. Drain bean mixture in a colander over a bowl, reserving 2 cups liquid. Discard 2 bay leaves.

2. Preheat oven to 350°.

3. Sprinkle chicken with ¼ teaspoon salt and ¼ teaspoon pepper.

4. Heat 1 tablespoon oil in a large nonstick skillet over medium-high heat. Add chicken; cook 4 minutes, browning on all sides. Remove chicken from skillet. Add 1½ teaspoons thyme, carrot, onion, ⅛ teaspoon cinnamon, and minced garlic to skillet; sauté 5 minutes or until tender.

5. Layer half of beans in bottom of Dutch oven. Add carrot mixture, chicken, and remaining beans. Add reserved 2 cups cooking liquid, 1 teaspoon salt, ¼ teaspoon pepper, and 2

---

bay leaves. Cover and bake at 350° for 1½ hours or until chicken and beans are tender, spooning cooking liquid over beans occasionally. Remove from oven; discard bay leaves.

6. Preheat broiler.

7. Combine 1 tablespoon olive oil, ⅛ teaspoon cinnamon, chopped parsley, and breadcrumbs, and toss well. Sprinkle parsley mixture over chicken and beans. Broil 2 minutes or until topping is lightly browned. Yield: 6 servings (serving size: 1 piece of chicken and 1 cup beans).

Note: Each serving provides 405 micrograms of folate.

CALORIES 423 (17% from fat); FAT 8.1g (sat 1.5g, mono 4.3g, poly 1.3g); PROTEIN 30.6g; CARB 58.2g; FIBER 10.6g; CHOL 52mg; IRON 6mg; SODIUM 735mg; CALC 131mg

---

SPINACH, RAISIN, PINE NUT, AND GARLIC-STUFFED PORK LOIN

¼ cup finely chopped raisins
2 tablespoons finely chopped pine nuts
2 garlic cloves, minced
2 (10-ounce) packages frozen chopped spinach, thawed, drained, and squeezed dry
¾ teaspoon salt, divided
½ teaspoon black pepper, divided
1 (2-pound) boned pork loin roast
2 bacon slices
Cooking spray
2 cups water

1. Preheat oven to 400°.

2. Combine chopped raisins, pine nuts, garlic, spinach, ½ teaspoon salt, and ¼ teaspoon pepper.

3. Unroll roast, and trim fat from pork. Slice pork lengthwise, cutting to, but not through, other side. Open the halves, laying pork flat. Slice each half lengthwise, cutting to, but not through, other side, and open flat. Place plastic wrap over pork, and flatten to an even thickness, using a meat mallet or rolling pin. Spread spinach

mixture down center of pork to within ½ inch of sides. Roll up pork, jelly-roll fashion, starting with a long side. Sprinkle with ¼ teaspoon salt and ¼ teaspoon pepper. Place bacon over pork. Secure at 2-inch intervals with heavy string. Place pork on a rack coated with cooking spray. Pour 2 cups water into a shallow roasting pan; place rack in pan. Insert a meat thermometer into thickest portion of pork. Bake at 400° for 1 hour or until thermometer registers 160° (slightly pink). Place pork on a platter; cover and let stand 10 minutes before slicing. Cut into 8 slices; serve warm. Yield: 8 servings (serving size: 1 slice).

Note: Each serving provides 91 micrograms of folate.

CALORIES 231 (43% from fat); FAT 10.9g (sat 3.5g, mono 4.7g, poly 1.6g); PROTEIN 26.5g; CARB 7.1g; FIBER 2.6g; CHOL 70mg; IRON 2.6mg; SODIUM 377mg; CALC 91mg

DRIED CHERRY-AND-FRESH ORANGE COMPOTE

6 large oranges
2 large oranges, halved
¼ cup packed brown sugar
Dash of ground cloves
¾ cup dried tart cherries
1 tablespoon butter or stick margarine

1. Peel and section 6 oranges over a bowl, setting 3 cups sections aside. Squeeze juice from remaining sectioned oranges and orange halves to measure ⅔ cup. Discard membranes.
2. Combine juice, brown sugar, and cloves in a medium nonaluminum saucepan; bring to a boil. Add cherries; reduce heat, and simmer 5 minutes. Remove from heat, and stir in butter. Combine cherry mixture and reserved 3 cups orange sections in a bowl, and serve at room temperature. Yield: 4 servings (serving size: ¾ cup).

Note: Each serving provides 60 micrograms of folate.

CALORIES 241 (12% from fat); FAT 3.2g (sat 1.9g, mono 0.9g, poly 0.2g); PROTEIN 2.5g; CARB 55.2g; FIBER 7.5g; CHOL 8mg; IRON 1mg; SODIUM 38mg; CALC 84mg

Super Supper Sandwiches

Sandwiches now thought of as lunch fare were once the main course at American dinner tables. Let's welcome them back.

Sandwiches—usually regarded as lunch staples—are a favorite supper food.

These sandwiches are knife-and-fork foods—more substantial than their handheld lunchtime cousins. Serve these warm, rather than cold or at room temperature.

SPINACH AND GOAT CHEESE ON FOCACCIA

(pictured on page 96)

2 teaspoons olive oil
4 cups vertically sliced onion
1 tablespoon sherry vinegar
¼ teaspoon black pepper
6 cups loosely packed spinach leaves
½ cup (2 ounces) crumbled goat or feta cheese
2 (2-ounce) pieces focaccia (Italian flatbread), cut in half horizontally and toasted

1. Heat oil in a large nonstick skillet over medium-high heat. Add onion; cook 5 minutes, stirring occasionally. Continue cooking 12 minutes or until golden brown, stirring constantly. Stir in vinegar and pepper. Remove from pan. Add spinach to pan; cook 1 minute or until spinach wilts. Remove from heat.
2. Divide cheese evenly between bottom halves of focaccia. Top each half with ½ cup onion mixture, ⅓ cup spinach, and top half of a focaccia. Serve immediately. Yield: 2 servings.

CALORIES 446 (24% from fat); FAT 12.1g (sat 5.1g, mono 4.7g, poly 1g); PROTEIN 18g; CARB 68.8g; FIBER 14.6g; CHOL 26mg; IRON 6.8mg; SODIUM 835mg; CALC 385mg

SAUTÉED CHERRY TOMATOES AND TARRAGON ON ENGLISH MUFFINS

Chopped salad*

*Combine 1 cup torn Boston lettuce, ¼ cup carrot strips, ¼ cup coarsely chopped radishes, and ¼ cup coarsely chopped peeled cucumber in a large bowl. Add 2 tablespoons low-fat red wine vinaigrette; toss well. Serves 2.

SAUTÉED CHERRY TOMATOES AND TARRAGON ON ENGLISH MUFFINS

This quick little supper sandwich uses organic cherry tomatoes from Baja that can now be found most of the year in many markets.

1 teaspoon olive oil
¼ cup diced shallots
2 cups halved cherry tomatoes
¼ teaspoon freshly ground black pepper
⅛ teaspoon salt
1 teaspoon chopped fresh tarragon
3 ounces thinly sliced part-skim mozzarella cheese
2 English muffins, split and toasted

1. Heat oil in a medium nonstick skillet over medium-high heat. Add shallots, and sauté 2 minutes. Add tomatoes, pepper, and salt; sauté 2 minutes. Remove from heat; stir in tarragon.
2. Preheat broiler.
3. Divide cheese evenly among muffin halves. Place muffins on a baking sheet, and broil 1 minute or until cheese melts. Spoon ⅓ cup tomato mixture over each muffin half. Serve immediately. Yield: 2 servings (serving size: 2 muffin halves).

CALORIES 355 (28% from fat); FAT 11g (sat 5g, mono 4.4g, poly 1g); PROTEIN 17.7g; CARB 47.7g; FIBER 2.2g; CHOL 25mg; IRON 3.2mg; SODIUM 698mg; CALC 400mg

THREE-MUSHROOM SAUTÉ OVER TOAST

Serve this mushroom mixture over thick-cut slices of garlic-rubbed toast made from a loaf of crusty peasant or country bread. The addition of tomato paste gives the sauce excellent color and flavor, and a tiny amount of flour thickens the mushroom juices nicely.

  ¼   cup dried porcini mushrooms
        (about ¼ ounce)
  1   cup boiling water
  1   tablespoon olive oil
  ½   cup finely chopped onion
  1   tablespoon tomato paste
  6   cups sliced button mushrooms
        (about 1 pound)
  3   cups thinly sliced shiitake
        mushroom caps (about 7
        ounces)
  1   teaspoon all-purpose flour
  ¼   teaspoon salt
  ¼   teaspoon black pepper
  2   tablespoons chopped fresh
        parsley
  1   garlic clove, minced
  1   garlic clove, halved
  4   (1½-ounce) slices peasant or
        country bread, toasted
  ½   cup (2 ounces) shredded fontina
        or fresh Parmesan cheese

1. Combine porcini mushrooms and boiling water in a bowl; cover and let stand 30 minutes. Drain porcinis in a colander over a bowl, reserving liquid. Rinse and chop porcinis.
2. Heat oil in a large skillet over medium-high heat until hot. Add onion; sauté 5 minutes or until lightly browned. Stir in tomato paste, and sauté 30 seconds. Add porcini, button, and shiitake mushrooms, stirring to coat. Sauté 5 minutes or until mushrooms release moisture and darken, stirring once. Sprinkle mushroom mixture with flour; cook 1 minute, stirring constantly. Stir in reserved mushroom liquid; sprinkle with salt and pepper. Bring to a boil; cook 1 minute. Stir in parsley and minced garlic. Remove from heat.

3. Rub garlic halves on 1 side of each toast slice; sprinkle each slice with 2 tablespoons cheese. Top each with ¾ cup mushroom mixture. Yield: 4 servings.

CALORIES 264 (30% from fat); FAT 8.9g (sat 3.3g, mono 3.8g, poly 0.8g); PROTEIN 11.6g; CARB 36.7g; FIBER 4.1g; CHOL 17mg; IRON 3.3mg; SODIUM 406mg; CALC 105mg

CANNELLINI BEANS AND GREENS ON GARLIC TOAST

(pictured on page 94)

  3   cups water
 12   cups torn kale (about 1 bunch)
  1   teaspoon olive oil
  1½ cups finely chopped onion
  ½   teaspoon dried oregano
  1   cup diced seeded plum tomato
  ⅛   teaspoon salt
  ⅛   teaspoon dried crushed red
        pepper
  2   garlic cloves, minced
  1   (16-ounce) can cannellini beans
        or other white beans, rinsed
        and drained
  1   garlic clove, halved
  4   (1½-ounce) slices country or
        peasant bread, toasted
  ¾   cup (3 ounces) grated fresh
        Parmesan cheese, divided

1. Bring 3 cups water to a boil in a large Dutch oven; add kale. Cook 6 minutes or until tender; drain in a colander over a bowl, reserving 1 cup cooking liquid.
2. Heat oil in a large nonstick skillet over medium-high heat. Add onion and oregano; sauté 5 minutes. Add tomato, salt, crushed red pepper, and minced garlic; sauté 1 minute. Stir in kale, reserved liquid, and beans; cook 3 minutes.
3. Rub garlic halves on 1 side of each toast slice. Place toast slices, garlic sides up, on 4 plates; sprinkle each slice with 2 tablespoons cheese. Top each with 1 cup bean mixture and 1 tablespoon cheese. Yield: 4 servings.

CALORIES 472 (23% from fat); FAT 11.8g (sat 4.4g, mono 3.7g, poly 2.2g); PROTEIN 25.9g; CARB 72g; FIBER 8.5g; CHOL 15mg; IRON 7.6mg; SODIUM 889mg; CALC 630mg

ARTICHOKE, LEEK, AND PEA RAGOÛT OVER TOAST

April is one of the best months for artichokes, so try to use fresh ones in this delicate spring braise.

  1½ cups water
  ¼   cup fresh lemon juice
 16   baby artichokes (about 2½
        pounds)
  1   teaspoon vegetable oil
  2   cups thinly sliced leek (about
        2 large)
  ½   cup dry white wine
  1   cup canned vegetable broth
  2   tablespoons chopped fresh
        parsley
  1   teaspoon chopped fresh tarragon
  ¼   teaspoon black pepper
  ⅛   teaspoon salt
  2   teaspoons all-purpose flour
  1   cup frozen green peas, thawed
  ¼   cup low-fat sour cream
  1½ teaspoons Dijon mustard
  4   (1½-ounce) slices firm white
        sandwich bread (such as
        Pepperidge Farm), toasted

1. Combine water and lemon juice. Working with 1 artichoke at a time, cut off stem to within 1 inch of base; peel stem. Remove bottom leaves and tough outer leaves, leaving tender heart and bottom. Cut artichoke lengthwise into quarters. Remove fuzzy thistle from bottom with a knife. Place artichoke in lemon water. Repeat procedure with remaining artichokes. Drain.
2. Heat oil in a large nonstick skillet over medium-high heat. Add leek, and sauté 4 minutes. Add artichokes, and sauté 2 minutes. Stir in wine; cook until liquid evaporates. Add broth, parsley, tarragon, pepper, and salt; reduce heat, and simmer 2 minutes. Sprinkle with flour; stir in peas, and cook 2 minutes. Remove from heat. Combine sour cream and mustard; stir into vegetable mixture. Spoon vegetable mixture over toast. Yield: 4 servings (serving size: ¾ cup vegetable mixture and 1 toast slice).

CALORIES 280 (17% from fat); FAT 5.4g (sat 1.8g, mono 1.6g, poly 1.2g); PROTEIN 10.6g; CARB 51.3g; FIBER 9.3g; CHOL 6mg; IRON 5.1mg; SODIUM 759mg; CALC 162mg

Asparagus-and-Spinach Toast with Fontina Cheese

1 pound asparagus spears
2 teaspoons butter or stick margarine
1 cup (¼-inch) diagonally sliced green onions
⅔ cup water
⅛ teaspoon salt
4 cups chopped spinach
1 tablespoon thinly sliced fresh basil
¼ teaspoon black pepper
¼ cup (1 ounce) shredded fontina or mozzarella cheese
4 (1½-ounce) slices wheat bread, toasted

1. Snap off tough ends of asparagus. Melt butter in a large nonstick skillet over medium-high heat. Add onions; sauté 1 minute. Add asparagus, water, and salt; bring to a boil. Reduce heat, and simmer 5 minutes. Add spinach; simmer 3 minutes. Stir in basil and pepper.
2. Sprinkle 1 tablespoon cheese over each toast slice; cut each slice diagonally in half. Place 4 toast halves on each of 2 plates. Spoon 1 cup asparagus mixture over each serving. Yield: 2 servings.

CALORIES 366 (30% from fat); FAT 12.4g (sat 6g, mono 3.8g, poly 1.4g); PROTEIN 16.7g; CARB 50.8g; FIBER 7.8g; CHOL 27mg; IRON 5.7mg; SODIUM 692mg; CALC 274mg

Pucker Up, Sweetie

That notorious old sourpuss might just be the sweetest thing you've ever tasted.

Sourness brings lemons their bad rap. With a sugar content of 10% to 15%, most fruits have a sufficient supply of natural sugar to balance their acidity and cause a pleasant reaction in our mouths. Lemons, on the other hand, check in at a meager 1% sugar—not nearly enough to counter the fruit's wallop of citric acid. To change a lemon, give it some sweetness. As in a glass of lemonade, lemon and sugar taste great when combined in the right proportion.

Easy Lemon Squares

(pictured on front cover)

Crust:

¼ cup granulated sugar
3 tablespoons butter or stick margarine, softened
1 cup all-purpose flour

Topping:

3 large eggs
¾ cup granulated sugar
2 teaspoons grated lemon rind
⅓ cup fresh lemon juice
3 tablespoons all-purpose flour
½ teaspoon baking powder
⅛ teaspoon salt
2 teaspoons powdered sugar

1. Preheat oven to 350°.
2. To prepare crust, beat ¼ cup granulated sugar and butter at medium speed of a mixer until creamy. Lightly spoon 1 cup flour into a dry measuring cup; level with a knife. Gradually add 1 cup flour to sugar mixture, beating at low speed until mixture resembles fine crumbs. Gently press mixture into bottom of an 8-inch square baking pan. Bake at 350° for 15 minutes; cool on a wire rack.
3. To prepare topping, beat eggs at medium speed until foamy. Add ¾ cup granulated sugar and next 5 ingredients; beat until well-blended. Pour mixture over crust. Bake at 350° for 20 to 25 minutes. Cool on wire rack. Sift powdered sugar evenly over top. Yield: 16 servings (serving size: 1 square).

CALORIES 118 (24% from fat); FAT 3.2g (sat 1.7g, mono 1g, poly 0.3g); PROTEIN 2.2g; CARB 20.5g; FIBER 0.3g; CHOL 47mg; IRON 0.6mg; SODIUM 68mg; CALC 16mg

Lemon Ice with Crystallized Ginger

1¼ cups sugar
2¼ cups water
1 cup fresh lemon juice (about 5 large lemons)
½ teaspoon unflavored gelatin
2 tablespoons water
2 tablespoons finely chopped crystallized ginger

1. Combine sugar and 2¼ cups water in a saucepan; bring to a boil. Cook 5 minutes without stirring. Remove from heat; stir in juice.
2. Sprinkle gelatin over 2 tablespoons water in a small saucepan; let stand 1 minute. Cook over low heat, stirring until gelatin dissolves. Remove from heat; cool slightly. Stir gelatin mixture and ginger into sugar syrup.
3. Pour mixture into freezer can of an ice-cream freezer, and freeze according to manufacturer's instructions. Spoon into a freezer-safe container; cover and freeze at least 8 hours. Yield: 8 servings (serving size: ½ cup).

CALORIES 134 (0% from fat); FAT 0g; PROTEIN 0.3g; CARB 35g; FIBER 0.1g; CHOL 0mg; IRON 0.3mg; SODIUM 2mg; CALC 6mg

SECTIONING LEMONS

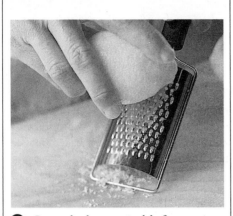

❶ *Grate the lemon rind before sectioning the fruit. Use a handheld grater or a box grater. Be careful to grate only the colored peel, not the white pith, which is bitter.*

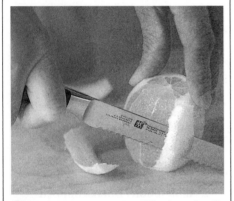

❷ *To get sections, cut off both ends of lemon. Then cut off peel (white pith and all) to expose the fruit.*

❸ *Cut between membranes to obtain the sections, removing seeds as you go. Squeeze juice from remaining membrane into a bowl.*

SERIOUSLY LEMON TART

(pictured on page 95)

Cooking spray
½ (15-ounce) package refrigerated pie dough (such as Pillsbury)
1½ cups granulated sugar
2 teaspoons grated lemon rind
1 cup lemon sections (about 4 large lemons), seeds removed
½ teaspoon salt
3 large egg whites, lightly beaten
2 large eggs, lightly beaten
12 very thin lemon slices
2 tablespoons brown sugar

1. Preheat oven to 450°.
2. Coat bottom of a 9-inch round removable-bottom tart pan with cooking spray. Press dough into bottom and up sides of pan. Line bottom of dough with a piece of foil; arrange pie weights or dried beans on foil. Bake at 450° for 5 minutes. Remove pie weights and foil. Bake an additional 5 minutes. Cool on a wire rack.
3. Reduce oven temperature to 350°.
4. Combine granulated sugar, lemon rind, lemon sections, and salt in a medium nonaluminum saucepan, and cook over medium heat 4 minutes or until sugar dissolves. Combine egg whites and eggs in a large bowl, stirring well with a whisk. Gradually add lemon mixture to egg mixture, stirring constantly with a whisk; pour into pie crust. Arrange lemon slices on custard; bake at 350° for 10 minutes. Sprinkle with brown sugar. Bake an additional 10 minutes. Remove from oven.
5. Preheat broiler.
6. Broil 1 minute or until lightly browned. Cool on wire rack 1 hour. Chill 4 hours or until set. Yield: 8 servings (serving size: 1 wedge).

CALORIES 309 (24% from fat); FAT 8.4g (sat 3.4g, mono 2.3g, poly 2.2g); PROTEIN 4g; CARB 56.4g; FIBER 0.1g; CHOL 60mg; IRON 0.5mg; SODIUM 285mg; CALC 22mg

LEMON MERINGUE PIE

You'll want to eat this pie right away since the delicate meringue will start to collapse after about a day.

Crust:

1¼ cups graham cracker crumbs (about 8 cookie sheets)
2 tablespoons sugar
1 tablespoon butter or stick margarine, melted
1 large egg white, lightly beaten
Cooking spray

Filling:

2 teaspoons grated lemon rind
½ cup fresh lemon juice (about 3 lemons)
1 (14-ounce) can fat-free sweetened condensed milk
1 (6-ounce) carton lemon fat-free yogurt (such as Yoplait)
1½ teaspoons unflavored gelatin
3 tablespoons water

Meringue:

⅔ cup sugar
¼ cup water
3 large egg whites
¼ teaspoon cream of tartar

1. Preheat oven to 325°.
2. To prepare crust, combine first 4 ingredients in a bowl; toss with a fork until moist. Press into a 9-inch pie plate coated with cooking spray. Bake at 325° for 15 minutes or until lightly browned; cool on a wire rack.
3. To prepare filling, combine lemon rind and next 3 ingredients in a medium bowl, and set aside. Sprinkle gelatin over 3 tablespoons water in a small microwave-safe bowl; let stand 1 minute. Microwave at HIGH 15 seconds, and stir until gelatin dissolves. Stir gelatin mixture thoroughly into yogurt mixture. Spoon filling into prepared crust. Press plastic wrap onto surface of filling; chill 1 hour or until almost firm.

4. To prepare meringue, combine ⅔ cup sugar and ¼ cup water in a small saucepan; bring to a boil. Cook, without stirring, until a candy thermometer registers 240°. Beat egg whites and cream of tartar at high speed of a mixer until foamy. Pour hot sugar syrup in a thin stream over egg white mixture, beating at high speed until stiff peaks form. Remove plastic wrap from filling. Spread meringue evenly over filling, sealing to edge of crust.
5. Preheat broiler.
6. Broil meringue for 1 minute or until lightly browned, and cool on wire rack. Chill until set. Yield: 9 servings (serving size: 1 wedge).

CALORIES 293 (9% from fat); FAT 2.9g (sat 1.1g, mono 0.9g, poly 0.6g); PROTEIN 6.8g; CARB 59.9g; FIBER 0.1g; CHOL 9mg; IRON 0.6mg; SODIUM 178mg; CALC 141mg

FROZEN LEMON MOUSSE WITH BLACKBERRY-RASPBERRY SAUCE

1 envelope unflavored gelatin
2 tablespoons water
3 large egg whites
1 cup sugar
¼ cup fresh lemon juice
1½ teaspoons grated lemon rind
1 teaspoon lemon extract
1 cup frozen whipped topping, thawed
¾ cup lemon fat-free yogurt (such as Yoplait)
Dash of salt
Blackberry-Raspberry Sauce
Lemon rind strips (optional)

1. Sprinkle gelatin over water in a small microwave-safe bowl; let stand 1 minute. Microwave at HIGH 15 seconds, and stir until gelatin dissolves; cool slightly.
2. Beat egg whites at high speed of a mixer until soft peaks form. Combine sugar and lemon juice in a saucepan; cook over medium heat until sugar dissolves. Increase heat to medium-high, and cook, without stirring, until a candy thermometer registers 240°. Pour hot sugar syrup in a thin stream over egg whites, beating at medium speed, then at high speed until stiff peaks form (about 5 minutes). Beat in gelatin mixture, grated lemon rind, and lemon extract. Fold in whipped topping, yogurt, and salt. Spoon ¾ cup lemon mixture into each of 8 (6-ounce) custard cups or ramekins. Cover and freeze 4 hours or up to 24 hours. Serve frozen with Blackberry-Raspberry Sauce. Garnish with lemon rind strips, if desired. Yield: 8 servings (serving size: 1 mousse and 2 tablespoons sauce).

CALORIES 198 (8% from fat); FAT 1.8g (sat 1.6g, mono 0g, poly 0g); PROTEIN 3g; CARB 41.7g; FIBER 1.1g; CHOL 1mg; IRON 0.1mg; SODIUM 68mg; CALC 33mg

Blackberry-Raspberry Sauce:

½ cup sugar
⅓ cup water
1 cup fresh or frozen blackberries
1 cup fresh or frozen raspberries
1 tablespoon fresh lemon juice

1. Combine sugar and water in a small saucepan, and bring to a boil. Cook over medium heat 1 minute, stirring until sugar dissolves. Combine sugar syrup, blackberries, raspberries, and lemon juice in a blender. Pulse mixture 3 times or until berries are chopped. Cover and chill. Yield: 1¾ cups (serving size: 2 tablespoons).
Note: Store remaining sauce in an airtight container in refrigerator. Serve over low-fat ice cream or pancakes.

CALORIES 33 (3% from fat); FAT 0.1g (sat 0g, mono 0g, poly 0.1g); PROTEIN 0.2g; CARB 9.6g; FIBER 1.1g; CHOL 0mg; IRON 0.1mg; SODIUM 0mg; CALC 5mg

LEMON CHEESECAKE WITH BLUEBERRY SAUCE

Crust:

1 cup gingersnap crumbs (about 27 cookies, finely crushed)
2 tablespoons butter or stick margarine, melted
Cooking spray

Filling:

1 cup sugar
3 tablespoons all-purpose flour
3 (8-ounce) blocks fat-free cream cheese, softened
1 (8-ounce) block ⅓-less-fat cream cheese, softened
2 large eggs
2 large egg whites
2 teaspoons grated lemon rind
2 teaspoons fresh lemon juice
1 (6-ounce) carton lemon fat-free yogurt (such as Yoplait)
Blueberry Sauce

1. Preheat oven to 300°.
2. To prepare crust, combine crumbs and butter; firmly press into bottom of a 9-inch springform pan coated with cooking spray. Bake at 300° for 15 minutes; cool on a wire rack.
3. To prepare filling, beat sugar, flour, and cheeses at medium-high speed of a mixer until smooth. Add eggs and egg whites, 1 at a time, beating after each addition. Add rind, juice, and yogurt; beat well. Pour mixture into prepared crust; bake at 300° for 1 hour and 10 minutes or until set. Turn oven off; cool cheesecake in closed oven 1 hour. Remove cheesecake from oven; cool to room temperature. Cover and chill 8 hours. Serve with Blueberry Sauce. Yield: 16 servings (serving size: 1 wedge and 1 tablespoon sauce).

CALORIES 216 (28% from fat); FAT 6.8g (sat 3.6g, mono 2.1g, poly 0.5g); PROTEIN 9.7g; CARB 28.5g; FIBER 0.5g; CHOL 53mg; IRON 0.6mg; SODIUM 357mg; CALC 161mg

Blueberry Sauce:

2 cups frozen blueberries, thawed
⅓ cup sugar
2 tablespoons fresh lemon juice
4 teaspoons cornstarch

1. Combine ingredients in a nonaluminum saucepan; bring to a boil. Cook over high heat 3 minutes or until thick, stirring constantly. Cover; chill. Yield: 1¼ cups (serving size: 1 tablespoon).

CALORIES 22 (4% from fat); FAT 0.1g (sat 0g, mono 0.1g, poly 0g); PROTEIN 0.1g; CARB 5.8g; FIBER 0.4g; CHOL 0mg; IRON 0mg; SODIUM 1mg; CALC 1mg

LEMON-CREAM CHEESE COOKIE CUPS

Dough:

½ cup sugar
¼ cup butter or stick margarine, softened
1 teaspoon vanilla extract
1 large egg
1¼ cups all-purpose flour
½ teaspoon baking powder
¼ teaspoon salt
Cooking spray

Filling:

½ cup sugar
1 teaspoon grated lemon rind
1 teaspoon lemon juice
1 large egg
1 (8-ounce) block ⅓-less-fat cream cheese

Topping:

¼ cup commercial fat-free lemon curd
¼ cup sliced almonds

1. To prepare dough, beat ½ cup sugar and butter at medium speed of a mixer until light and fluffy. Add vanilla and 1 egg; beat well. Lightly spoon flour into dry measuring cups; level with a knife. Add flour, baking powder, and salt to sugar mixture; beat at low speed until well-blended. Wrap dough in plastic wrap; freeze 15 minutes. Gently press dough into bottom and up sides of 24 miniature muffin cups coated with cooking spray.
2. Preheat oven to 350°.
3. To prepare filling, place ½ cup sugar and next 4 ingredients in a food processor; process until smooth, scraping sides of bowl occasionally. Spoon 1 tablespoon filling into each prepared muffin cup. Bake at 350° for 23 minutes or until edges are brown and filling is set. Remove cups from pans immediately; cool on a wire rack.

4. To prepare topping, spoon ½ teaspoon lemon curd onto each cookie cup. Sprinkle with almonds. Yield: 2 dozen.

CALORIES 119 (39% from fat); FAT 5.2g (sat 2.8g, mono 1.7g, poly 0.3g); PROTEIN 2.4g; CARB 16.1g; FIBER 0.3g; CHOL 31mg; IRON 0.4mg; SODIUM 98mg; CALC 19mg

LEMON-POPPY SEED ROULADE

Cooking spray
2 teaspoons cake flour
4 large egg whites
¾ cup granulated sugar, divided
4 large egg yolks
1 teaspoon grated lemon rind
1 tablespoon fresh lemon juice
1 tablespoon vegetable oil
⅔ cup sifted cake flour
1 tablespoon poppy seeds
1 teaspoon baking powder
¼ teaspoon salt
3 tablespoons powdered sugar, divided
1 cup frozen reduced-calorie whipped topping, thawed
½ cup bottled lemon curd (such as Crosse & Blackwell)

1. Preheat oven to 350°.
2. Coat a 15 x 10-inch jelly-roll pan with cooking spray; line bottom with wax paper. Coat wax paper with cooking spray; dust with 2 teaspoons flour.
3. Beat egg whites at high speed of a mixer until foamy. Gradually add ½ cup granulated sugar, 1 tablespoon at a time, beating until stiff peaks form.
4. Beat egg yolks in a large bowl at high speed of a mixer 4 minutes. Gradually add ¼ cup granulated sugar, beating until thick and pale (about 2 minutes). Beat in lemon rind, juice, and oil. Gently fold egg white mixture into egg yolk mixture. Combine ⅔ cup flour, poppy seeds, baking powder, and salt, stirring well with a whisk; gently fold into egg mixture.
5. Spoon cake batter into prepared pan. Bake at 350° for 10 minutes or until cake springs back when touched lightly in center. Loosen cake from

sides of pan, and turn out onto a dishtowel dusted with 1 tablespoon powdered sugar; carefully peel off wax paper. Sprinkle with 1 tablespoon powdered sugar; cool 1 minute. Starting at narrow end, roll up cake and towel together. Place, seam side down, on a wire rack; cool completely (about 1 hour).
6. Unroll cake carefully, removing towel. Combine whipped topping and lemon curd. Spread whipped topping mixture over cake, leaving a ½-inch margin around edges. Reroll cake, and place, seam side down, on a platter. Cover and chill 4 hours. Sift 1 tablespoon powdered sugar over cake, and cut into slices. Yield: 8 servings (serving size: 1 slice).

CALORIES 247 (22% from fat); FAT 6.1g (sat 2.2g, mono 1.6g, poly 1.6g); PROTEIN 4.4g; CARB 44.9g; FIBER 0.1g; CHOL 109mg; IRON 1.2mg; SODIUM 171mg; CALC 70mg

---

MAIN SQUEEZE

Our recipes use fresh juice, lemon rind, and lemon sections. With any form, measurement is crucial to the final balance of taste between sweet and sour. That's especially important for zest.

First, wash the lemons before removing rind. Be careful when scraping rind because the white pith underneath the skin is bitter. And don't use too much rind—that also can add bitterness.

In general, fresh lemons convert to these standard measurements:

1 medium lemon =
2 to 3 tablespoons juice

1 medium lemon =
1 teaspoon grated rind

5 to 6 lemons = 1 cup juice

MAY

Best Under the Sun

Fresh-picked strawberries are the juiciest, sweetest, and brightest.
Go get some. Now.

There's just no substitute for fresh vine-ripened strawberries. Those found at grocery stores can't compete. Because strawberries are highly perishable, any intended for the supermarket are usually picked before they're ripe. Remember, though, not to overwhelm the fresh flavor with too many ingredients. Try a mousse, a simple sweet soup, or toss the berries with greens. If you run out, get more from farms, farmers' markets, and roadside stands. But enjoy while you can: The season peaks in May.

STRAWBERRIES-AND-FETA SALAD

2 tablespoons orange juice
1 tablespoon white wine vinegar
2 teaspoons extra-virgin olive oil
¾ teaspoon sugar
6 cups gourmet salad greens
1 cup quartered strawberries
¼ cup (1 ounce) crumbled feta cheese

1. Combine first 4 ingredients in a small bowl, and stir with a whisk. Combine greens, strawberries, and cheese in a large bowl; add orange juice mixture, tossing to coat. Serve immediately. Yield: 4 servings (serving size: 1½ cups).

CALORIES 70 (53% from fat); FAT 4.1g (sat 1.4g, mono 2g, poly 0.4g); PROTEIN 2.7g; CARB 6.6g; FIBER 2.3g; CHOL 6mg; IRON 1.1mg; SODIUM 87mg; CALC 71mg

SIZE MATTERS

The taste of supermarket strawberries can suffer because commercial growers opt for large and hardy—if less flavorful—varieties. So don't let the smaller size of fresh, locally grown strawberries fool you: Ounce for ounce, those precious red gems carry more flavor than their commercial counterparts.

STRAWBERRY FOOL

A fool is an English dessert made by folding pureed fruit into whipped cream. This lighter version uses yogurt.

3 cups sliced strawberries
3 tablespoons granulated sugar
¼ cup packed light brown sugar
2 (8-ounce) cartons vanilla low-fat yogurt

1. Combine strawberries and granulated sugar in a large bowl. Cover and chill 2 hours.
2. Combine brown sugar and yogurt in a large bowl, stirring well with a whisk. Cover and chill 2 hours.
3. Gently fold strawberry mixture into yogurt mixture until swirled. Yield: 4 servings (serving size: ¾ cup).

CALORIES 219 (7% from fat); FAT 1.8g (sat 0.9g, mono 0.4g, poly 0.3g); PROTEIN 6.3g; CARB 46.4g; FIBER 2.6g; CHOL 6mg; IRON 0.8mg; SODIUM 81mg; CALC 222mg

BRANDIED STRAWBERRY JAM

This easy jam doesn't involve canning. It'll keep in the refrigerator for about two weeks.

4 cups quartered strawberries
½ cup sugar
¼ cup brandy, divided
1 teaspoon vanilla extract

1. Combine strawberries, sugar, and 3 tablespoons brandy in a heavy Dutch oven; bring to a boil. Reduce heat; simmer until reduced to 1½ cups (about 45 minutes), stirring occasionally. Remove from heat; stir in 1 tablespoon brandy and vanilla. Spoon into a bowl; cool to room temperature. Cover and chill. Yield: 1½ cups (serving size: 1 tablespoon).

CALORIES 26 (3% from fat); FAT 0.1g (sat 0g, mono 0g, poly 0.1g); PROTEIN 0.2g; CARB 6g; FIBER 0.6g; CHOL 0mg; IRON 0.1mg; SODIUM 0mg; CALC 4mg

STRAWBERRY-ORANGE MUFFINS

Serve these warm with Brandied Strawberry Jam.

1¼ cups halved strawberries
3 tablespoons butter or stick margarine, melted
2 teaspoons grated orange rind
2 large eggs
1½ cups all-purpose flour
1¼ cups sugar
1 teaspoon baking powder
½ teaspoon salt
Cooking spray
2 teaspoons sugar
Brandied Strawberry Jam (see recipe)

1. Preheat oven to 400°.
2. Combine first 4 ingredients in a blender, and process just until blended. Lightly spoon flour into dry measuring cups; level with a knife. Combine flour, 1¼ cups sugar, baking powder, and salt. Add strawberry mixture to flour mixture, stirring just until moist. Spoon batter into 12 muffin cups coated with cooking spray. Sprinkle with 2 teaspoons sugar. Bake at 400° for 20 minutes or until muffins spring back when touched lightly in center. Remove from pan immediately. Yield: 1 dozen (serving size: 1 muffin).

CALORIES 184 (20% from fat); FAT 4g (sat 2.1g, mono 1.2g, poly 0.3g); PROTEIN 2.8g; CARB 34.8g; FIBER 0.8g; CHOL 45mg; IRON 1mg; SODIUM 179mg; CALC 33mg

STRAWBERRIES ROMANOFF SUNDAES

(pictured on page 116)

- 2 cups quartered strawberries
- ¼ cup triple sec (orange-flavored liqueur)
- 3 tablespoons sugar
- 1¼ cups sliced strawberries
- 3 cups vanilla low-fat ice cream
- 2 tablespoons chopped pistachios, toasted
- Mint leaves (optional)

1. Combine first 3 ingredients in a blender, and process until smooth. Combine strawberry puree and sliced strawberries in a bowl; cover and chill.
2. Serve strawberry mixture over ice cream. Sprinkle with nuts. Garnish sundaes with mint leaves, if desired. Yield: 6 servings (serving size: ⅓ cup sauce, ½ cup ice cream, and 1 teaspoon nuts).

CALORIES 195 (23% from fat); FAT 5g (sat 2g, mono 2.1g, poly 0.6g); PROTEIN 3.8g; CARB 30.9g; FIBER 2.3g; CHOL 9mg; IRON 0.6mg; SODIUM 57mg; CALC 109mg

STRAWBERRY SOUP

- 3⅓ cups quartered strawberries
- ½ cup orange juice
- ½ cup Riesling or other slightly sweet white wine
- 2½ tablespoons sugar
- 1⅓ cups plain fat-free yogurt
- 2 teaspoons finely chopped fresh mint

1. Place first 4 ingredients in a blender; process until smooth. Pour strawberry puree into a large bowl, and add yogurt, stirring with a whisk. Cover and chill. Spoon 1 cup soup into each of 5 bowls, and sprinkle with mint. Yield: 5 servings.

CALORIES 116 (4% from fat); FAT 0.5g (sat 0.1g, mono 0.1g, poly 0.2g); PROTEIN 4.3g; CARB 21.2g; FIBER 2.4g; CHOL 1mg; IRON 0.7mg; SODIUM 48mg; CALC 139mg

SIMPLE STRAWBERRY MOUSSE

- 2 cups quartered strawberries
- 3 tablespoons sugar
- ½ cup low-fat sour cream
- 1½ cups frozen reduced-calorie whipped topping, thawed

1. Combine strawberries and sugar in a blender, and process until smooth. Combine strawberry puree and sour cream in a large bowl, stirring well with a whisk. Fold whipped topping into strawberry mixture. Spoon into 6 (6-ounce) custard cups. Cover and freeze 4 hours or until firm. Yield: 6 servings.

CALORIES 102 (41% from fat); FAT 4.7g (sat 3.6g, mono 0.7g, poly 0.2g); PROTEIN 1.4g; CARB 14.5g; FIBER 1.2g; CHOL 8mg; IRON 0.2mg; SODIUM 20mg; CALC 40mg

SPARKLING STRAWBERRY LEMONADE

- 3 cups quartered strawberries
- 1 cup cold water
- 1 tablespoon sugar
- 1 (6-ounce) can frozen lemonade concentrate, undiluted
- 2 cups sparkling water, chilled

1. Combine first 3 ingredients in a blender, and process until smooth. Combine strawberry puree and lemonade in a pitcher; stir until lemonade dissolves. Add sparkling water; pour over ice. Yield: 6 servings (serving size: 1 cup).

CALORIES 82 (3% from fat); FAT 0.3g (sat 0g, mono 0g, poly 0.2g); PROTEIN 0.5g; CARB 20.8g; FIBER 1.9g; CHOL 0mg; IRON 0.5mg; SODIUM 2mg; CALC 13mg

30 MINUTES OR LESS

They're Biting on Aisle Seven

Cooking with canned seafood makes a fast, tasty, and nutritious weeknight dinner as convenient as your can opener.

MEDITERRANEAN SALMON CAKES WITH CUCUMBER SAUCE

Preparation time: 14 minutes
Cooking time: 16 minutes

Sauce:

- ⅔ cup diced cucumber
- ⅔ cup plain low-fat yogurt
- ¼ teaspoon dried dill
- 2 garlic cloves, crushed

Salmon cakes:

- 1 (14.75-ounce) can red salmon, drained
- 1 (15-ounce) can chickpeas (garbanzo beans), drained
- 1 cup fresh breadcrumbs (about 2 [1-ounce] slices)
- ¼ cup sliced ripe olives
- ½ cup chopped fresh parsley
- 2 tablespoons lime juice
- 1 teaspoon hot sauce
- ½ teaspoon ground cumin
- ¼ teaspoon salt
- 2 large egg whites, lightly beaten
- 1 tablespoon vegetable oil, divided

1. To prepare sauce, combine cucumber, yogurt, dill, and garlic in a small bowl.
2. To prepare salmon cakes, remove bones and skin from salmon. Place chickpeas in a medium bowl; partially mash chickpeas with a fork. Stir in salmon, breadcrumbs, and olives. Combine parsley and next 5 ingredients in a small bowl; stir into salmon

Continued

mixture. Divide mixture into 12 equal portions, shaping each into a ¾-inch-thick patty.

3. Heat 1½ teaspoons oil in a large nonstick skillet over medium-high heat. Add 6 patties; cook 4 minutes. Carefully turn patties over, and cook 4 minutes or until golden. Repeat procedure with 1½ teaspoons oil and remaining patties. Serve with sauce. Yield: 6 servings (serving size: 2 salmon cakes and ¼ cup sauce).

CALORIES 243 (29% from fat); FAT 8.5g (sat 1.8g, mono 3.1g, poly 3g); PROTEIN 18g; CARB 28.2g; FIBER 2.6g; CHOL 23mg; IRON 3mg; SODIUM 399mg; CALC 221mg

CRAB SALAD WITH WHITE BEANS AND GOURMET GREENS

Preparation time: 10 minutes
Chilling time: 20 minutes

- ⅓ cup chopped yellow bell pepper
- ⅓ cup chopped red onion
- ¼ cup chopped celery
- 2 tablespoons white wine vinegar
- 1 tablespoon fresh lemon juice
- 1 tablespoon olive oil
- ¼ teaspoon salt
- ⅛ teaspoon hot sauce
- 2 (6-ounce) cans lump crabmeat, drained
- 1 (16-ounce) can cannellini beans or other white beans, rinsed and drained
- 6 cups torn gourmet salad greens

1. Combine first 10 ingredients; toss gently. Cover and chill 20 minutes. Serve over greens. Yield: 6 servings (serving size: ⅔ cup salad and 1 cup greens).

CALORIES 149 (25% from fat); FAT 4.1g (sat 0.6g, mono 2g, poly 1g); PROTEIN 12.8g; CARB 16.6g; FIBER 4.3g; CHOL 29mg; IRON 3.3mg; SODIUM 353mg; CALC 117mg

MANHATTAN CLAM CHOWDER

Preparation time: 5 minutes
Cooking time: 25 minutes

- 1 tablespoon olive oil
- 1 cup chopped onion
- 1 teaspoon bottled minced garlic (about 2 cloves)
- 2½ cups chopped peeled baking potato (about 1 pound)
- 1 cup water
- 1 teaspoon dried oregano
- ¼ teaspoon black pepper
- 2 (14.5-ounce) cans diced tomatoes, undrained
- 1 (8-ounce) bottle clam juice
- 2 (6½-ounce) cans chopped clams, undrained
- 2 tablespoons chopped fresh parsley

1. Heat oil in a large saucepan over medium-high heat. Add onion and garlic; sauté 2 minutes. Add potato and next 5 ingredients; bring to a boil. Cover and cook 15 minutes or until potato is tender. Stir in clams; cook 3 minutes. Ladle into soup bowls; sprinkle with parsley. Yield: 6 servings (serving size: 1⅓ cups).

CALORIES 143 (20% from fat); FAT 3.1g (sat 0.5g, mono 1.9g, poly 0.5g); PROTEIN 8g; CARB 21.8g; FIBER 2.6g; CHOL 21mg; IRON 4.2mg; SODIUM 660mg; CALC 92mg

TUNA MELTS

Preparation time: 15 minutes
Cooking time: 5 minutes

- ⅓ cup chopped celery
- 3 tablespoons light mayonnaise
- 2 tablespoons Dijon mustard
- 2 teaspoons lime juice
- ½ teaspoon coarsely ground black pepper
- 1 (12-ounce) can solid white tuna in water, drained
- 4 English muffins, split and toasted
- 8 (¼-inch-thick) slices tomato
- ½ cup (2 ounces) shredded reduced-fat Swiss cheese

1. Preheat broiler.
2. Combine first 6 ingredients. Spread 3 tablespoons tuna mixture onto each muffin half. Top each with 1 tomato slice and 1 tablespoon cheese. Broil 5 minutes or until cheese melts. Yield: 4 servings (serving size: 2 muffin halves).

CALORIES 368 (23% from fat); FAT 9.3g (sat 2.7g, mono 2.8g, poly 2.9g); PROTEIN 29.7g; CARB 39.8g; FIBER 0.9g; CHOL 42mg; IRON 2.8mg; SODIUM 954mg; CALC 282mg

BACON-AND-CLAM PIZZA

Preparation time: 10 minutes
Cooking time: 20 minutes

- 2 bacon slices
- 1½ cups sliced onion
- 1 teaspoon dried thyme
- ¼ teaspoon black pepper
- 1 (1-pound) Italian cheese-flavored pizza crust (such as Boboli)
- ½ cup reduced-fat Alfredo sauce (such as Contadina)
- 2 (6½-ounce) cans chopped clams, drained
- ⅓ cup (1½ ounces) preshredded fresh Parmesan cheese
- 2 tablespoons chopped fresh parsley

1. Preheat oven to 400°.
2. Cook bacon in a nonstick skillet over medium heat until crisp. Remove bacon from pan; crumble. Set aside. Add onion and thyme to bacon drippings in pan; sauté over medium-high heat 6 minutes or until lightly browned. Stir in pepper. Place crust on a baking sheet. Spread Alfredo sauce over crust; top with onion mixture, clams, bacon, and cheese. Bake at 400° for 12 minutes or until cheese melts. Sprinkle with parsley. Yield: 6 servings.

CALORIES 354 (34% from fat); FAT 13.5g (sat 5.6g, mono 5.5g, poly 1.7g); PROTEIN 19.1g; CARB 37.9g; FIBER 1.7g; CHOL 34mg; IRON 9.1mg; SODIUM 717mg; CALC 352mg

Banana Layer Cake with Lemon-Cream Cheese Frosting, page 130

Pineapple-Rum Slush,
page 123

Bell Pepper-Feta Pasta Toss, page 137

Leeks Cordon Bleu, page 135

Parmesan-Herb Crusted Tofu Sandwich, page 122

*Strawberries Romanoff
Sundae, page 111*

*Salmon on Greens with
Lime-Ginger Dressing, page 138*

Topping the Untoppable

Our annual cheese cook-off gave us big winners once again—five cheese-filled masterpieces you'll want to make faster than you can say, "Pass the mascarpone!"

Our love of cheese led us to create a special contest to find the best cheese recipes in the land from a competition featuring some of the country's top chefs. Our *Cooking Light* with Wisconsin Cheese Chef's Showcase, co-hosted by the Wisconsin Milk Marketing Board, challenged chefs to use real cheese in creating a delicious, low-fat dish easily adaptable to an average home kitchen. Each recipe must use at least one of the more than 300 varieties of Wisconsin cheese, employ readily available ingredients, and reflect *Cooking Light's* philosophy of lighter, healthier food.

CHICKEN IN MUSTARD WITH BEANS, GARLIC, AND MASCARPONE CHEESE

If you don't have shallots, use red onion. Pancetta is a lean, smoked Italian ham, but if you can't find it, use 2 ounces of bacon instead. Small, tender haricots verts are preferred, but regular green beans will work just as well. You can also use penne or fusilli in place of the pappardelle.

—Jody Adams, Rialto, Cambridge, Massachusetts

Marinated chicken:

½ cup Dijon mustard
2 tablespoons sliced shallot
1 tablespoon chopped fresh thyme
½ teaspoon cracked black pepper
2 garlic cloves, crushed
2 bay leaves
2 chicken breast halves (about 1 pound), skinned
2 chicken drumsticks (about ½ pound), skinned
2 chicken thighs (about ½ pound), skinned

Remaining ingredients:

2 ounces pancetta, cut into ¼-inch pieces
12 garlic cloves, peeled
12 shallots, peeled
¼ cup white wine vinegar
1 (16-ounce) can fat-free, less-sodium chicken broth
1 tablespoon chopped fresh thyme
1 teaspoon tomato paste
½ teaspoon dried crushed red pepper
½ cup (2 ounces) mascarpone cheese
1 pound haricots verts or tiny green beans, trimmed
1 tablespoon chopped fresh parsley
¼ teaspoon salt
⅛ teaspoon freshly ground black pepper
3 cups hot cooked pappardelle (about 6 ounces uncooked pasta)
½ cup (2 ounces) grated Asiago cheese
Thyme sprigs (optional)

1. To prepare marinated chicken, combine first 6 ingredients in a large zip-top plastic bag. Add chicken; seal and marinate in refrigerator 2 hours, turning bag occasionally. Remove chicken from bag, reserving marinade.
2. Heat a large nonstick skillet over low heat. Add pancetta; cook 5 minutes. Remove from pan; set aside. Increase heat to medium; add 12 peeled garlic cloves and 12 peeled shallots to pan. Sauté 15 minutes or until lightly browned, and add to pancetta. Set aside. Add vinegar to pan; cook 5 minutes, stirring frequently to deglaze pan. Add reserved marinade, and bring to a boil. Add chicken breasts, breast sides down, drumsticks, and thighs. Stir in pancetta mixture, broth, 1 tablespoon thyme, tomato paste, and red pepper. Cover, reduce heat, and simmer 20 minutes or until chicken breast is tender. Remove chicken breast from pan. Cook drumsticks and thighs 10 minutes. Remove chicken from pan. Cook sauce, uncovered, until slightly thick, about 10 minutes. Add mascarpone, stirring with a whisk until smooth. Remove from heat.
3. Steam haricots verts, covered, 3 minutes or until tender. Toss with parsley, salt, and ⅛ teaspoon black pepper.
4. Combine pasta and Asiago, and toss gently. Serve chicken over pasta mixture, and top with mascarpone sauce. Serve with haricots verts. Garnish with thyme sprigs, if desired. Yield: 4 servings (serving size: 3 ounces chicken, ½ cup pasta, ⅔ cup mascarpone sauce, and about ½ cup haricots verts).

CALORIES 689 (36% from fat); FAT 27.9g (sat 10.8g, mono 11.1g, poly 3.7g); PROTEIN 53.6g; CARB 27.9g; FIBER 4.4g; CHOL 191mg; IRON 5.6mg; SODIUM 1,704mg; CALC 296mg

Fontina-Stuffed Baked Salmon with Herb Jus

Use homemade chicken stock if possible for the best flavor. Remove the skin from the salmon; that's where the fishy taste is. Serve in a pasta bowl to capture the flavorful jus, or broth.

—Caprial Pence, Caprial's Bistro, Portland, Oregon

Herb jus:

½ cup dry red wine
½ cup dry sherry
¼ cup chopped shallots
2 garlic cloves, minced
1½ cups chopped fennel bulb (about 1 fennel bulb)
2 (16-ounce) cans fat-free, less-sodium chicken broth
1 teaspoon chopped fresh thyme
1 teaspoon chopped fresh basil
1 teaspoon chopped fresh rosemary
¼ teaspoon salt
¼ teaspoon black pepper

Salmon:

1 teaspoon olive oil
½ cup chopped shallots
2 garlic cloves, minced
2 cups coarsely chopped cremini mushrooms (about ½ pound)
½ cup dry sherry
1 cup (4 ounces) cubed fontina cheese
¼ cup (1 ounce) finely shredded fresh Parmesan cheese
2 teaspoons chopped fresh thyme
6 (6-ounce) skinned salmon fillets (about 1 inch thick)
Cooking spray
¼ cup dry white wine
¼ teaspoon salt
¼ teaspoon black pepper
Hazelnut-Herb Couscous
¼ cup (1 ounce) shaved fresh Parmesan cheese
2 teaspoons chopped flat-leaf parsley
Basil sprigs (optional)

1. To prepare herb jus, combine first 4 ingredients in a saucepan over high heat. Bring to a boil; cook until reduced to ¼ cup (about 8 minutes). Add fennel and broth. Bring to a boil. Reduce heat; simmer until reduced to 2 cups (about 30 minutes). Add 1 teaspoon thyme, chopped basil, and rosemary; simmer 5 minutes. Add ¼ teaspoon salt and ¼ teaspoon pepper.
2. Preheat oven to 375°.
3. To prepare salmon, heat oil in a nonstick skillet over medium-high heat. Add ½ cup shallots and 2 minced garlic cloves; sauté 1 minute. Add mushrooms; sauté 2 minutes. Add ½ cup sherry; cook 4 minutes or until most of liquid evaporates. Remove from heat; cool completely. Stir in fontina, shredded Parmesan, and 2 teaspoons thyme. Cut 1 (¾-inch-deep) diagonal slit across center of 1 fillet; cut another slit in the opposite direction to form an X. Pull back salmon to form a pocket. Repeat with remaining fillets. Stuff ⅓ cup cheese mixture into each pocket. Place fillets on a jelly-roll pan coated with cooking spray. Drizzle with white wine, and sprinkle with ¼ teaspoon salt and ¼ teaspoon pepper. Bake at 375° for 15 minutes or until fish flakes easily when tested with a fork. Serve with herb jus and Hazelnut-Herb Couscous; sprinkle with shaved Parmesan and parsley. Garnish with basil sprigs, if desired. Yield: 6 servings (serving size: 1 fillet, ⅓ cup herb jus, and ⅔ cup couscous).

CALORIES 614 (39% from fat); FAT 26.7g (sat 8g, mono 12g, poly 3.8g); PROTEIN 53.8g; CARB 37.8g; FIBER 2.2g; CHOL 139mg; IRON 3.3mg; SODIUM 1,104mg; CALC 282mg

Hazelnut-Herb Couscous:

¼ cup hazelnuts (about 1 ounce)
1 (16-ounce) can fat-free, less-sodium chicken broth
1 teaspoon chopped fresh thyme
1 teaspoon chopped fresh rosemary
1 teaspoon chopped fresh oregano
¼ teaspoon salt
⅛ teaspoon black pepper
2 garlic cloves, minced
1⅓ cups uncooked couscous

1. Preheat oven to 350°.
2. Place hazelnuts on a baking sheet. Bake at 350° for 15 minutes, stirring once. Turn nuts out onto a towel. Roll up towel, and rub off skins. Chop nuts, and set aside.
3. Bring chicken broth and next 6 ingredients to a boil in a medium saucepan; gradually stir in couscous. Remove from heat; cover couscous, and let stand 5 minutes. Fluff couscous with a fork. Stir in hazelnuts. Yield: 6 servings (serving size: ⅔ cup).

CALORIES 169 (18% from fat); FAT 3.3g (sat 0.2g, mono 2.3g, poly 0.3g); PROTEIN 6.9g; CARB 28.3g; FIBER 1.6g; CHOL 0mg; IRON 1mg; SODIUM 341mg; CALC 14mg

Smoked-Gouda Risotto with Spinach and Mushrooms

Any combination of mushrooms will work. Use cold chicken stock (even though simmering stock is typically used in risotto) to prevent splattering. Make sure there's some liquid left in the risotto; in fact, it should be pourable because the rice will absorb the liquid as it sits.

Winning recipe—Charles Dale, Renaissance Restaurant, Aspen, Colorado

Risotto:

2 cups water
2 (16-ounce) cans fat-free, less-sodium chicken broth
1 tablespoon butter
⅓ cup chopped shallots
2 cups Arborio rice or other short-grain rice
½ cup dry white wine
½ teaspoon salt
1½ cups (6 ounces) shredded smoked Gouda cheese
5 cups chopped spinach (about 5 ounces)

Mushrooms:

- 1 tablespoon olive oil
- 2 cups sliced shiitake mushroom caps (about 3½ ounces)
- 2 cups sliced button mushrooms (about ½ pound)
- 2 cups sliced cremini mushrooms (about ½ pound)
- 2 cups sliced oyster mushrooms (about 3½ ounces)
- ⅓ cup chopped shallots
- ¼ cup dry white wine
- 1½ teaspoons chopped fresh thyme
- 1½ teaspoons chopped fresh rosemary
- 1 garlic clove, minced
- ¼ teaspoon salt
- ¼ teaspoon black pepper
- ¼ cup (1 ounce) grated fresh Parmesan cheese
- Rosemary sprigs (optional)

1. To prepare risotto, combine water and broth; set aside. Melt butter in a large nonstick saucepan over medium heat. Add ⅓ cup shallots; cover and cook 2 minutes. Add rice; cook 2 minutes, uncovered, stirring constantly. Stir in ½ cup wine; cook 30 seconds or until liquid is nearly absorbed, stirring constantly. Add ½ teaspoon salt and broth mixture, ½ cup at a time, stirring constantly until each portion of broth mixture is absorbed before adding next (about 20 minutes total). Stir in Gouda; cook just until melted. Stir in spinach; cook just until spinach is wilted.

2. To prepare mushrooms, heat oil in a large nonstick skillet over medium-high heat. Add mushrooms, and sauté 5 minutes or until beginning to brown. Add ⅓ cup shallots, ¼ cup wine, thyme, chopped rosemary, and garlic, and sauté 1 minute or until wine evaporates. Sprinkle with ¼ teaspoon salt and pepper.

3. Divide risotto evenly among 6 bowls; top with mushroom mixture, and sprinkle with Parmesan. Garnish with rosemary sprigs, if desired. Yield: 6 servings (serving size: 1 cup risotto, 1 cup mushroom mixture, and 2 teaspoons Parmesan).

CALORIES 480 (27% from fat); FAT 14.4g (sat 7.5g, mono 4.9g, poly 0.9g); PROTEIN 20.4g; CARB 68.4g; FIBER 4.9g; CHOL 41mg; IRON 6.5mg; SODIUM 983mg; CALC 318mg

SEARED PORK TENDERLOIN WITH THREE CHEESE-WILD RICE SPOON GRITS AND BRAISED SWISS CHARD

You can use veal tenderloins instead of pork. You also can use Vidalia onions that have been slivered and caramelized in place of the pearl onions. And you can use brown rice instead of wild rice.

—*Kevin Cullen,* Goodfellow's, *Minneapolis, Minnesota*

Pearl onions:

- 24 pearl onions, peeled

Grits:

- 1 ear shucked corn
- ½ cup minced sweet onion
- 1 garlic clove, minced
- 1 (16-ounce) can fat-free, less-sodium chicken broth
- ⅓ cup uncooked regular grits
- ⅓ cup cooked wild rice
- ¼ cup (1 ounce) grated Pepato or Romano cheese
- ¼ cup (1 ounce) shredded Gruyère cheese
- ¼ cup (1 ounce) shredded sharp Cheddar cheese
- ¼ teaspoon Worcestershire sauce
- ¼ teaspoon ground red pepper

Swiss chard:

- ¾ cup Cabernet Sauvignon or other dry red wine
- ¾ cup fat-free, less-sodium chicken broth
- ¾ pound red Swiss chard, torn

Pork:

- 4 (4-ounce) pork tenderloin medallions
- ¼ teaspoon salt
- 1 tablespoon vegetable oil

1. Preheat oven to 350°.
2. Place pearl onions on a baking sheet. Bake at 350° for 15 minutes.
3. Prepare grill or broiler.

4. To prepare grits, place corn on a grill rack or broiler pan. Grill or broil 20 minutes or until lightly browned; turn every 5 minutes. Cool. Cut kernels from ear of corn to measure ½ cup. Set kernels aside.

5. Bring minced onion, garlic, and 1 can broth to a boil in a medium saucepan. Stir in grits; reduce heat, and simmer 5 minutes, stirring occasionally. Stir in corn, rice, cheeses, Worcestershire sauce, and pepper. Remove from heat; keep warm.

6. To prepare Swiss chard, bring wine and ¾ cup broth to a boil in a large Dutch oven. Add Swiss chard; cover and cook 2 minutes or until wilted. Drain chard in a colander over a bowl, reserving wine mixture.

7. Heat oven to 350°.

8. To prepare pork, sprinkle with salt. Heat oil in a large ovenproof skillet over medium-high heat. Add pork; cook 1 minute on each side or until browned. Place skillet in oven; roast pork at 350° for 8 minutes or until desired degree of doneness. Cut medallions in half. Place ½ cup grits on each of 4 plates; top evenly with pork, chard, and pearl onions. Spoon 2 tablespoons of reserved wine mixture around grits. Yield: 4 servings.

CALORIES 387 (31% from fat); FAT 13.3g (sat 5.7g, mono 4.3g, poly 2.4g); PROTEIN 36.5g; CARB 31.9g; FIBER 3.2g; CHOL 96mg; IRON 4.9mg; SODIUM 879mg; CALC 318mg

HOMEMADE PAPPARDELLE PASTA WITH MUSHROOMS, GREEN PEAS, AND ASPARAGUS

If you don't have time to make pasta, you can use a good commercial fresh pasta—the kind in the refrigerated section of the supermarket. Don't be tempted to use more garlic in this dish; it will overpower the other flavors. Any combination of mushrooms can be used.
—Chris Hastings, Hot and Hot Fish Club, *Birmingham, Alabama*

Pasta:

    1   teaspoon saffron threads
    ¼   cup water
    2   cups all-purpose flour,
        divided
    1   teaspoon salt
    1   tablespoon olive oil
    2   large eggs, lightly beaten

Mushroom broth:

    1   tablespoon butter
    ½   cup dried porcini mushrooms
    8   shiitake mushroom stems
    6   thyme sprigs
    1   carrot, quartered
    1   celery stalk, quartered
    1   small onion, quartered
    1   garlic clove
    1   bay leaf
    1   cup fat-free, less-sodium
        chicken broth or vegetable
        broth

Remaining ingredients:

    1   tablespoon olive oil
    1   tablespoon diced shallot
    8   large shiitake mushroom caps,
        quartered
    1   garlic clove, minced
    ½   cup (1-inch) sliced asparagus
    ½   cup fresh or frozen petite
        green peas
    1   tablespoon chopped fresh
        chives
    ½   teaspoon butter
    ½   cup (2 ounces) grated fresh
        Parmesan cheese

1. To prepare pasta, combine saffron and ¼ cup water in a saucepan. Cook over low heat 10 minutes; cool. Lightly spoon flour into dry measuring cups; level with a knife. Combine 1½ cups flour and salt in a bowl. Make a well in center of mixture; add 3 tablespoons saffron water, 1 tablespoon oil, and eggs. Stir to form a dough. Turn dough out onto a lightly floured surface; shape into a ball. Knead until smooth and elastic (about 10 to 15 minutes); add ½ cup flour, 1 tablespoon at a time, to prevent dough from sticking to hands. Dust dough lightly with flour, and wrap in plastic wrap. Chill 1 hour.
2. Divide dough in half. Working with 1 portion at a time, pass dough through smooth rollers of pasta machine on the widest setting. Continue moving width gauge to narrower settings; pass dough through rollers once at each setting, dusting with flour, if needed. Repeat procedure with remaining half of dough. Cut dough portions into 8 x 1-inch strips. Hang pasta on a wooden drying rack (no longer than 30 minutes).
3. To prepare mushroom broth, melt 1 tablespoon butter in a small saucepan over medium heat. Add porcinis and next 7 ingredients; cook 5 minutes. Add chicken broth; bring to a boil. Reduce heat to medium-low; simmer until reduced to 1¼ cups (about 25 minutes). Strain broth through a sieve into a bowl; reserve ¾ cup broth. Discard solids.
4. Cook pasta in boiling water 2 minutes or until al dente; drain.
5. Heat 1 tablespoon oil in a nonstick skillet over medium-high heat. Add shallot, mushroom caps, and minced garlic; cook 3 minutes. Add reserved ¾ cup broth; reduce heat to medium, and cook 3 minutes. Stir in asparagus, peas, chives, and ½ teaspoon butter. Add cooked pasta; toss to coat. Sprinkle with cheese. Yield: 5 servings (serving size: 1 cup pasta and about 1½ tablespoons cheese).

CALORIES 346 (34% from fat); FAT 13g (sat 4.5g, mono 6.2g, poly 1.1g); PROTEIN 13.9g; CARB 42.8g; FIBER 2.5g; CHOL 101mg; IRON 3.3mg; SODIUM 810mg; CALC 162mg

Be True to Your Tofu

Tofu's subtle flavor and tender texture merge so well with western and Asian seasonings that there's no need to think of this Japanese classic as merely a substitute for something else.

While tofu comes in many forms, two kinds are used in these recipes—the Japanese block tofu that comes packed in a water-filled plastic pouch, and the tofu that comes packaged in a small, aseptic juice container-style box. The latter, such as the Mori-Nu brand (often used in the *Cooking Light* Test Kitchens), is more convenient. It requires no refrigeration, can be stored on your shelf for months, and can be eaten when you're ready. It also comes in low-fat versions.

SOUPY NOODLES WITH SILKEN TOFU AND BOK CHOY

The broth can be made a day ahead.

Stir-Fry Broth

    1   tablespoon dark sesame oil,
        divided
    1   (12.3-ounce) package firm tofu,
        drained and cut into ½-inch
        cubes
    6   cups chopped bok choy
        (about 1 bunch)
    1   tablespoon minced peeled fresh
        ginger
    2   garlic cloves, chopped
    2½ cups hot cooked Chinese-style
        noodles (about 4 ounces
        uncooked pasta)
    1   tablespoon low-sodium soy
        sauce
    ½   teaspoon salt
    ½   cup chopped fresh cilantro
    ¼   teaspoon chili oil (optional)

1. Bring Stir-Fry Broth to a simmer in a large saucepan (do not boil). Remove

mushrooms with a slotted spoon; set aside. Keep broth warm.

2. Heat 2 teaspoons sesame oil in a large nonstick skillet over medium-high heat. Add tofu; stir-fry 5 minutes or until lightly browned. Remove from pan. Heat 1 teaspoon sesame oil in pan. Add bok choy, ginger, and garlic; stir-fry 1 minute. Add ½ cup broth and mushrooms; cook 1 minute. Stir in noodles, soy sauce, and salt. Divide vegetable mixture evenly among 8 bowls; top with tofu and remaining broth. Sprinkle with cilantro. Drizzle with chili oil, if desired. Yield: 8 servings (serving size: 1 cup).

CALORIES 254 (28% from fat); FAT 8g (sat 1.2g, mono 2.3g, poly 3.9g); PROTEIN 13.1g; CARB 36.7g; FIBER 4.2g; CHOL 0mg; IRON 7.8mg; SODIUM 737mg; CALC 218mg

Stir-Fry Broth:

    6 cups water
    1 cup sliced onion
    1 cup chopped green onions
    1 cup sliced cilantro stems
      (about 1 bunch)
    ½ cup thinly sliced carrot
    2 tablespoons low-sodium soy
      sauce
   12 dried shiitake mushrooms
    3 (½-inch) slices peeled fresh
      ginger
    2 garlic cloves, unpeeled

1. Combine all ingredients in a large saucepan. Bring to a boil; reduce heat, and simmer until reduced to 5 cups (about 30 minutes). Strain broth through a sieve into a large bowl. Reserve 4 cups broth; set mushrooms aside, discarding remaining solids. Thinly slice mushrooms; return to broth. Yield: 4 servings (serving size: 1 cup).

CALORIES 36 (3% from fat); FAT 0.1g (sat 0g, mono 0g, poly 0g); PROTEIN 1.4g; CARB 8.8g; FIBER 1.2g; CHOL 0mg; IRON 0.3mg; SODIUM 243mg; CALC 2mg

TOFU, MUSHROOMS, AND BELL PEPPERS IN SWEET-AND-SOUR SAUCE

Sauce:

    ¾ cup dry white wine
    ⅓ cup water
    2 tablespoons Dijon mustard
    2 tablespoons Worcestershire
      sauce
    2 tablespoons molasses
    1 tablespoon low-sodium soy
      sauce
    1 garlic clove, crushed

Remaining ingredients:

    3 cups broccoli florets
    4 teaspoons roasted peanut or
      vegetable oil, divided
    2 cups diced onion
   1½ cups coarsely chopped red
      bell pepper
    ⅔ cup coarsely chopped yellow
      bell pepper
    2 cups quartered button
      mushrooms
    1 cup quartered shiitake
      mushroom caps
    ¼ teaspoon freshly ground black
      pepper
    1 (12.3-ounce) package reduced-
      fat firm tofu, drained and cut
      into 1-inch cubes
    3 cups hot cooked long-grain
      brown rice
    ¼ cup chopped fresh cilantro

1. To prepare sauce, combine first 7 ingredients in a bowl.
2. Steam broccoli, covered, 5 minutes or until crisp-tender; keep warm. Heat 3 teaspoons oil in a Dutch oven over high heat. Add onion and bell peppers. Cook 8 minutes; stir occasionally. Add 1 teaspoon oil, mushrooms, and black pepper; cook 2 minutes or until lightly browned. Stir in sauce; reduce heat to medium-low. Place tofu over mushroom mixture. Cover and cook 15 minutes. Stir in broccoli. Serve with rice; sprinkle with cilantro. Yield: 6 servings

(serving size: 1 cup vegetables and ½ cup rice).

CALORIES 252 (16% from fat); FAT 4.6g (sat 0.7g, mono 1.5g, poly 1.6g); PROTEIN 9.9g; CARB 44.1g; FIBER 4.4g; CHOL 0mg; IRON 3.7mg; SODIUM 359mg; CALC 98mg

MARINATED TOFU WITH STICKY RICE AND ASPARAGUS

    2 (16-ounce) packages firm tofu,
      drained
    ½ cup hoisin sauce
    ⅓ cup sake (rice wine)
    3 tablespoons low-sodium soy
      sauce
    3 tablespoons tomato paste
    2 tablespoons water
    2 teaspoons brown sugar
    3 garlic cloves, minced
    1 tablespoon roasted peanut or
      vegetable oil, divided
    1 pound asparagus spears
      (about 24)
    3 cups hot cooked sticky rice

1. Cut each block of tofu crosswise into 6 slices. Arrange tofu slices in a single layer in a large nonstick skillet; cook over medium-high heat 5 minutes on each side or until lightly browned. Arrange tofu slices in a single layer in a shallow dish.
2. Combine hoisin sauce and next 6 ingredients in a bowl, and stir with a whisk. Reserve ½ cup hoisin mixture, and pour remaining hoisin mixture over tofu slices, turning tofu to coat. Let stand 30 minutes.
3. Heat 1½ teaspoons oil over medium-high heat in skillet; add half of tofu and marinade. Cook 2 minutes on each side or until browned. Repeat procedure with 1½ teaspoons oil and remaining tofu.
4. Snap off tough ends of asparagus. Steam asparagus, covered, 5 minutes. Place 6 asparagus spears and ¾ cup rice on each of 4 plates; arrange 3 tofu slices and 2 tablespoons reserved hoisin mixture on each plate. Yield: 4 servings.

CALORIES 480 (29% from fat); FAT 15.7g (sat 2.4g, mono 4.3g, poly 7.8g); PROTEIN 25g; CARB 64g; FIBER 6.2g; CHOL 1mg; IRON 15.1mg; SODIUM 907mg; CALC 290mg

TOFU-MUSHROOM BURGERS

You can use any kind of tofu here. For a more dense texture, use cooked brown rice or bulgur instead of breadcrumbs. Serve with mustard, horseradish, and a little mayonnaise.

- 1 (12.3-ounce) package firm tofu, cut in half lengthwise
- 1 teaspoon olive oil
- 1½ cups diced onion
- 2 teaspoons dried marjoram
- ½ teaspoon dried thyme
- 2½ cups finely chopped mushrooms
- 2 teaspoons Worcestershire sauce
- 1 tablespoon low-sodium soy sauce
- 2 large garlic cloves, minced
- 1½ cups fresh breadcrumbs (about 3 slices bread)
- ¼ cup dry-roasted cashews, finely ground
- 1½ teaspoons Dijon mustard
- ¼ teaspoon freshly ground black pepper
- 1 large egg, lightly beaten
- Cooking spray
- 6 (3-ounce) Kaiser rolls

1. Place tofu on several layers of paper towels; cover with additional towels. Let stand 1 hour; press occasionally. Place in a bowl; mash with a potato masher.
2. Heat oil in a large nonstick skillet over medium-high heat. Add onion, marjoram, and thyme; sauté 5 minutes. Add mushrooms; sauté 8 minutes. Add Worcestershire sauce, soy sauce, and garlic; sauté 1 minute. Remove from heat; spoon into a bowl. Stir in tofu, breadcrumbs, nuts, mustard, pepper, and egg. Divide into 6 equal portions; shape each into a ¾-inch-thick patty. Place pan coated with cooking spray over medium-high heat until hot. Add patties; cook 3 minutes. Carefully turn patties over; cook 3 minutes or until browned. Serve on rolls. Yield: 6 servings.

CALORIES 401 (27% from fat); FAT 12.2g (sat 2.4g, mono 4g, poly 4.5g); PROTEIN 16.2g; CARB 61g; FIBER 4.9g; CHOL 37mg; IRON 7.5mg; SODIUM 725mg; CALC 218mg

PARMESAN-HERB CRUSTED TOFU SANDWICH

(pictured on page 115)

The secret to this dish is to thinly slice the tofu, and then bread it thickly. Water-packed firm tofu works best here; the silken tofu is just too delicate.

Tofu:

- 1 (14-ounce) package firm tofu, drained
- 1 cup breadcrumbs (about 2 slices stale bread)
- ¼ cup (1 ounce) grated fresh Parmesan cheese
- 1 teaspoon dried marjoram
- ½ teaspoon dried savory
- ¼ teaspoon dried thyme
- ¼ teaspoon black pepper, divided
- ¼ cup fat-free milk
- ⅛ teaspoon salt
- 2 large egg whites, lightly beaten
- ¼ cup all-purpose flour
- Cooking spray

Remaining ingredients:

- 3 tablespoons light mayonnaise
- 1 tablespoon chopped fresh chives
- 1 teaspoon low-sodium soy sauce
- 1 small garlic clove, minced
- 4 (2-ounce) sesame buns
- 4 romaine lettuce leaves
- 12 (¼-inch-thick) slices plum tomato

1. To prepare tofu, cut crosswise into 12 slices. Place a large nonstick skillet over medium heat. Add tofu; cook 5 minutes on each side. Remove tofu from pan; cool to room temperature.
2. Combine breadcrumbs, cheese, marjoram, savory, thyme, and ⅛ teaspoon pepper.
3. Combine ⅛ teaspoon pepper, milk, salt, and egg whites. Place flour in a shallow dish; dredge 1 tofu slice in flour. Dip in milk mixture; dredge in breadcrumb mixture. Repeat procedure with remaining tofu, flour, milk mixture, and breadcrumb mixture. Place a nonstick skillet coated with cooking spray over medium heat until hot. Add tofu; sauté 3 minutes on each side.
4. Combine mayonnaise, chives, soy sauce, and garlic. Spread 1 tablespoon mayonnaise mixture evenly over cut sides of each bun. Arrange 1 lettuce leaf and 3 tomato slices over bottom half of each bun; top each with 3 tofu slices. Cover with tops of buns. Serve immediately. Yield: 4 servings.

CALORIES 459 (28% from fat); FAT 14.4g (sat 3.4g, mono 3.6g, poly 6.2g); PROTEIN 22.6g; CARB 60.7g; FIBER 4.4g; CHOL 9mg; IRON 9.8mg; SODIUM 905mg; CALC 366mg

TOFU IN SPICY RED COCONUT SAUCE

- 2 teaspoons roasted peanut or vegetable oil
- 1¼ cups sliced green onions
- 1 tablespoon minced peeled fresh ginger
- 2 large garlic cloves, minced
- 2 tablespoons mushroom-flavored or plain low-sodium soy sauce
- 1 tablespoon red curry paste
- ½ teaspoon salt
- 1 (14-ounce) can light coconut milk
- 1 (12.3-ounce) package reduced-fat firm tofu, drained and cut into ½-inch cubes
- 2 tablespoons chopped fresh basil
- 2 cups hot cooked jasmine or basmati rice

1. Heat oil in a large nonstick skillet over medium-high heat. Add green onions, ginger, and garlic; stir-fry 1 minute. Stir in soy sauce, curry paste, salt, milk, and tofu; bring to a simmer. Reduce heat to medium; cook 2 minutes. Stir in basil; serve over rice. Yield: 4 servings (serving size: ¾ cup tofu mixture and ½ cup rice).

CALORIES 258 (30% from fat); FAT 8.5g (sat 4g, mono 2.4g, poly 1.7g); PROTEIN 10.1g; CARB 34.5g; FIBER 1.8g; CHOL 0mg; IRON 3.1mg; SODIUM 727mg; CALC 81mg

Beachside Banquets

Here's a cook's easy guide to a week of sun, sand, and surf that doesn't mean leaving great meals behind.

Unless you're staying at a superdeluxe beachfront community, the local grocery store is more likely to carry dozens of brands of snack chips and pretzels than sourdough bread or imported Parmesan cheese. But we've got just the ticket to help you enjoy your beach vacation without anxiety attacks or fruitless trips to the store: an easy-to-follow cook's care package for your week at the beach.

We've created six menus so you won't have to plan any meals for your trip (although you will need to bring along some of the ingredients).

TWO-TONE ROASTED POTATOES

We like this recipe with a mixture of sweet potatoes and baking potatoes, but you can make it with just one or the other.

1 teaspoon chili powder
¾ teaspoon salt
¼ teaspoon ground cinnamon
¼ teaspoon ground red pepper
¼ teaspoon black pepper
1½ tablespoons olive oil
1 garlic clove, minced, or ½ teaspoon bottled minced garlic
3 small sweet potatoes (about 1½ pounds), each cut lengthwise into 8 wedges
3 small baking potatoes (about 1½ pounds), each cut lengthwise into 8 wedges

1. Preheat oven to 450°.
2. Combine first 7 ingredients in a large zip-top plastic bag. Add potatoes; seal and shake to coat. Place potatoes on a baking sheet. Bake at 450° for 35 minutes or until tender. Yield: 8 servings (serving size: 6 wedges).

CALORIES 206 (13% from fat); FAT 2.9g (sat 0.4g, mono 1.9g, poly 0.4g); PROTEIN 3.3g; CARB 42.5g; FIBER 4.3g; CHOL 0mg; IRON 1.8mg; SODIUM 241mg; CALC 30mg

LEMON-GARLIC SHRIMP KEBABS

48 large unpeeled shrimp (about 2 pounds)
½ cup fresh lemon juice (about 3 lemons)
½ cup dry white wine
2 tablespoons bottled minced garlic (about 12 cloves)
2 tablespoons steak sauce (such as Heinz 57)
2 teaspoons coarsely ground black pepper
Cooking spray

1. Peel shrimp, leaving tails intact. Combine lemon juice, wine, garlic, steak sauce, and pepper in a large zip-top plastic bag; seal bag, and shake to blend. Add shrimp to bag, and seal. Marinate in refrigerator 20 minutes, turning bag once.
2. Prepare grill.
3. Remove shrimp from bag, discarding marinade. Thread 8 shrimp onto each of 6 (12-inch) skewers. Place kebabs on a grill rack coated with cooking spray, and grill 2 minutes on each side or until shrimp are done. Yield: 6 servings (serving size: 1 kebab).
Note: Substitute ⅓ cup water and 2 tablespoons vinegar for wine, if desired.

CALORIES 135 (14% from fat); FAT 2.1g (sat 0.4g, mono 0.3g, poly 0.8g); PROTEIN 23.3g; CARB 3.7g; FIBER 0.2g; CHOL 172mg; IRON 2.9mg; SODIUM 201mg; CALC 67mg

PINEAPPLE-RUM SLUSH

(pictured on page 114)

3 cups pineapple juice
1 cup fresh lemon juice (about 5 large lemons)
¾ cup golden or dark rum
¾ cup water
½ cup sugar

1. Combine all ingredients in a large plastic pitcher; cover and freeze at least 4 hours or until slushy. Yield: 6 servings (serving size: 1 cup).
Note: Substitute orange juice for rum, if desired.

CALORIES 228 (0% from fat); FAT 0.1g (sat 0g, mono 0g, poly 0g); PROTEIN 0.6g; CARB 37.4g; FIBER 0.3g; CHOL 0mg; IRON 0.3mg; SODIUM 2mg; CALC 24mg

GREENS WITH CREAMY BERRY DRESSING

⅓ cup sweetened dried cranberries (such as Craisins)
¼ cup balsamic vinegar
¼ cup light mayonnaise
1 tablespoon Dijon mustard
1 tablespoon water
½ teaspoon sugar
¼ teaspoon black pepper
2 garlic cloves, crushed, or 1 teaspoon bottled minced garlic
6 cups torn romaine lettuce
1 cup seedless red grapes, halved
1 cup thinly sliced cucumber
1 cup fat-free plain croutons
½ cup thinly sliced red onion, separated into rings

1. Combine cranberries and vinegar in a small bowl. Cover and let stand 30 minutes. Add mayonnaise and next 5 ingredients; stir well with a whisk. Cover and chill.
2. Combine lettuce and next 4 ingredients in a large bowl; add dressing, tossing gently to coat. Serve immediately. Yield: 6 servings (serving size: 1½ cups).

CALORIES 115 (24% from fat); FAT 3.1g (sat 0.5g, mono 0.8g, poly 1.4g); PROTEIN 2.6g; CARB 19.6g; FIBER 1.7g; CHOL 3mg; IRON 1.1mg; SODIUM 295mg; CALC 40mg

TAKE SIX (ANY SIX)

A week at the beach should be spontaneous. Do whatever you want to do every day—and eat what strikes your fancy. These six flexible menus give you a week's worth of meal plans.

MENU 1

FRENCH-BREAD PIZZA WITH SAUSAGE, CLAMS, AND MUSHROOMS

TOSSED SALAD WITH DIJON VINAIGRETTE

Fresh fruit

MENU 2

LEMON-GARLIC SHRIMP KEBABS

TWO-TONE ROASTED POTATOES

CARAMEL MUDSLIDE

MENU 3

CREAMY PESTO RIGATONI WITH CHUNKY TOMATO VINAIGRETTE

French bread

CHERRIES WITH RUM-SUGAR CREAM

MENU 4

RUM-PEPPER STEAK SANDWICHES

Fresh corn on the cob

CHUNKY PLUM-AND-GINGER ICE CREAM

MENU 5

SUNSET CHICKEN WITH GRILLED VEGETABLE-RICE PILAF

GREENS WITH CREAMY BERRY DRESSING

Angel food cake with chocolate sauce

MENU 6

PINEAPPLE-RUM SLUSH

GRILLED TUNA WITH PAPAYA CHUTNEY

MIXED GREENS WITH DIJON VINAIGRETTE

CHERRIES WITH RUM-SUGAR CREAM

1 cup fat-free sour cream
2 tablespoons brown sugar
2 teaspoons dark rum (optional)
48 fresh cherries with stems (about 1 pound)

1. Combine first 3 ingredients; cover and chill. Serve as a dip with cherries. Yield: 6 servings (serving size: 8 teaspoons dip and 8 cherries).
Note: Substitute fresh strawberries for cherries, if desired.

CALORIES 90 (6% from fat); FAT 0.6g (sat 0.2g, mono 0.2g, poly 0.2g); PROTEIN 3.5g; CARB 16.6g; FIBER 1.5g; CHOL 0mg; IRON 0.3mg; SODIUM 28mg; CALC 12mg

DIJON VINAIGRETTE

½ cup fat-free, less-sodium chicken broth
½ cup balsamic vinegar
2 tablespoons olive oil
2 teaspoons Dijon mustard
1 teaspoon anchovy paste
¼ teaspoon black pepper
3 garlic cloves, minced, or 1½ teaspoons bottled minced garlic

1. Combine all ingredients in a jar. Cover tightly, and shake vigorously. Chill at least 1 hour.
2. Drizzle vinaigrette evenly over salad greens. Yield: 1¼ cups (serving size: 2 tablespoons).
Note: Dijon Vinaigrette will keep for a week in refrigerator.

CALORIES 29 (90% from fat); FAT 2.9g (sat 0.4g, mono 2g, poly 0.2g); PROTEIN 0.4g; CARB 0.6g; FIBER 0g; CHOL 0mg; IRON 0.1mg; SODIUM 123mg; CALC 2mg

CARAMEL MUDSLIDE

2 cups vanilla low-fat ice cream
1½ cups sliced ripe banana (about 2 bananas)
½ cup 1% low-fat milk
⅓ cup Frangelico (hazelnut-flavored liqueur) or dark rum
¼ cup plus 2 tablespoons fat-free caramel sundae syrup
2 tablespoons chopped macadamia nuts, toasted

1. Combine first 4 ingredients in a blender; process until smooth. Pour evenly into 6 glasses; gently stir 1 tablespoon syrup into each glass. Sprinkle evenly with nuts. Yield: 6 servings (serving size: ⅔ cup).
Note: Substitute 1% low-fat milk for Frangelico, if desired.

CALORIES 216 (18% from fat); FAT 4.4g (sat 1.7g, mono 2.3g, poly 0.1g); PROTEIN 2.9g; CARB 33.6g; FIBER 0.9g; CHOL 7mg; IRON 0.2mg; SODIUM 83mg; CALC 110mg

FRENCH-BREAD PIZZA WITH SAUSAGE, CLAMS, AND MUSHROOMS

Almost any kind of cheese will work in this hearty dish. Try mozzarella, Asiago, provolone, Romano, or Cheddar.

1 (4-ounce) link sweet Italian sausage
2 tablespoons all-purpose flour
1½ cups sliced mushrooms
½ cup 1% low-fat milk
½ teaspoon dried oregano
⅛ teaspoon black pepper
1 (6½-ounce) can chopped clams, undrained
¾ cup (3 ounces) grated fresh Parmesan cheese, divided
1 (16-ounce) loaf French bread, cut in half horizontally
2 tablespoons chopped fresh parsley

1. Preheat oven to 400°.
2. Remove casing from sausage. Cook sausage in a large nonstick skillet over medium heat until browned, stirring to crumble. Add flour, and cook 2 minutes, stirring frequently. Add mushrooms, milk, oregano, pepper, and clams; bring to a boil, stirring constantly. Reduce heat; simmer 5 minutes or until thick. Remove from heat. Stir in ½ cup cheese.
3. Place bread halves on a baking sheet; spread clam mixture evenly over cut sides of bread. Sprinkle with ¼ cup cheese and parsley. Bake at 400° for 12 minutes or until golden brown. Cut each half into 3 pieces. Yield: 6 servings (serving size: 1 piece).

CALORIES 363 (28% from fat); FAT 11.3g (sat 4.7g, mono 4.4g, poly 1.3g); PROTEIN 19.3g; CARB 44.8g; FIBER 2.7g; CHOL 35mg; IRON 4mg; SODIUM 1,048mg; CALC 276mg

CREAMY PESTO RIGATONI WITH CHUNKY TOMATO VINAIGRETTE

Serve this with a simple salad, using the Dijon Vinaigrette *(see recipe on previous page), and add French bread.*

4 cups diced seeded tomato (about 4 large tomatoes)
½ cup chopped red onion
3 tablespoons balsamic vinegar
1 tablespoon olive oil
1 cup fat-free, less-sodium chicken broth
¾ cup fresh basil leaves
¼ cup (1 ounce) grated fresh Parmesan cheese, divided
½ teaspoon salt
¼ teaspoon black pepper
3 garlic cloves or 1½ teaspoons bottled minced garlic
1 (8-ounce) block fat-free cream cheese, softened
6 cups hot cooked rigatoni (about ¾ pound uncooked pasta)
¼ cup pine nuts, toasted

1. Combine first 4 ingredients in a bowl, and set aside.
2. Combine broth, basil, 2 tablespoons Parmesan, salt, pepper, garlic, and cream cheese in a blender; process until smooth. Combine basil mixture and rigatoni in a Dutch oven, and cook over low heat until thoroughly heated. Spoon pasta onto each of 6 plates. Top with tomato vinaigrette, 2 tablespoons Parmesan, and pine nuts. Yield: 6 servings (serving size: 1 cup pasta, ⅔ cup tomato vinaigrette, 1 teaspoon Parmesan cheese, and 2 teaspoons pine nuts).

CALORIES 353 (21% from fat); FAT 8.2g (sat 1.8g, mono 3.5g, poly 2.2g); PROTEIN 17.8g; CARB 52.6g; FIBER 3.2g; CHOL 10mg; IRON 3.5mg; SODIUM 594mg; CALC 195mg

CHUNKY PLUM-AND-GINGER ICE CREAM

4 cups vanilla low-fat ice cream, softened
1 cup diced plums (about 3 plums)
1 tablespoon finely chopped crystallized ginger
6 gingersnaps

1. Combine first 3 ingredients in a freezer-safe container. Cover; freeze until firm. Spoon ice cream into 6 bowls; crumble 1 gingersnap over each serving. Yield: 6 servings (serving size: ⅔ cup ice cream and 1 gingersnap).

CALORIES 177 (27% from fat); FAT 5.3g (sat 2.7g, mono 1.8g, poly 0.5g); PROTEIN 4.1g; CARB 29.8g; FIBER 0.6g; CHOL 15mg; IRON 0.7mg; SODIUM 86mg; CALC 139mg

GRILLED TUNA WITH PAPAYA CHUTNEY

6 (6-ounce) tuna steaks (about ¾ inch thick)
2 tablespoons low-sodium soy sauce
3 cups diced peeled papaya or mango
½ cup golden raisins
⅓ cup cider or balsamic vinegar
¼ cup water
2 tablespoons brown sugar
½ teaspoon ground ginger
Dash of salt
Cooking spray

1. Place tuna steaks in a shallow dish. Drizzle soy sauce over both sides of fish; cover and marinate in refrigerator 30 minutes.
2. Combine papaya and next 6 ingredients in a small saucepan, and bring mixture to a boil. Cover, reduce heat, and simmer 20 minutes or until papaya is tender. Remove chutney from heat, and keep warm.
3. Prepare grill.
4. Place tuna on a grill rack coated with cooking spray, and grill 4 minutes on each side or until tuna is

Continued

WHAT TO PACK

Even if your beach house is well-stocked, take these items with you.

Handy Tools:
A favorite knife, especially for paring
Measuring spoons
Cutting board
Zip-top plastic bags

Specialty Ingredients:
Balsamic vinegar
Olive oil
Parmesan cheese
Cooking spray

medium-rare or desired degree of doneness. Serve tuna steaks with papaya chutney. Yield: 6 servings (serving size: 1 tuna steak and about ⅓ cup chutney).

CALORIES 336 (24% from fat); FAT 9.1g (sat 2.3g, mono 2.5g, poly 3.1g); PROTEIN 40.9g; CARB 22.1g; FIBER 1.8g; CHOL 65mg; IRON 2.4mg; SODIUM 201mg; CALC 38mg

RUM-PEPPER STEAK SANDWICHES

Marinade:

½ cup dark rum
2 tablespoons brown sugar
1 tablespoon coarsely ground black pepper
¼ teaspoon salt
5 garlic cloves, crushed, or 2½ teaspoons bottled minced garlic
1 (1½-pound) flank steak

Flavored mayonnaise:

½ cup fat-free or light mayonnaise
2 teaspoons prepared horseradish

Remaining ingredients:

8 (½-inch-thick) slices red onion (about 2 onions)
16 (1-ounce) slices sourdough bread
2 cups thinly sliced romaine lettuce
16 (¼-inch-thick) slices tomato (about 3 tomatoes)

1. To prepare marinade, combine first 5 ingredients in a large zip-top plastic bag. Trim fat from steak, and add steak to bag. Seal and marinate in refrigerator at least 2 hours, turning bag occasionally. Remove steak from bag, reserving marinade. Pour marinade into a microwave-safe dish. Microwave marinade at HIGH 1 minute or until mixture boils.
2. To prepare flavored mayonnaise, combine mayonnaise and horseradish, and set aside.
3. Prepare grill.

4. Place steak and red onion slices on a grill rack, and grill onions 4 minutes on each side, basting with reserved marinade. Remove onions from grill. Turn steak, and grill 8 minutes or until steak is desired degree of doneness. Remove steak from grill. Place bread slices on grill rack, and grill 2 minutes on each side or until toasted.
5. Cut steak diagonally across grain into thin slices. Spread 1 tablespoon flavored mayonnaise on one side of 8 toasted bread slices. Divide steak, onion slices, lettuce, and tomato slices evenly among 8 bread slices. Top with remaining bread slices. Yield: 8 servings (serving size: 1 sandwich).
Note: Substitute pineapple juice for rum, if desired.

CALORIES 345 (29% from fat); FAT 11g (sat 4.4g, mono 4.6g, poly 0.7g); PROTEIN 22.6g; CARB 39.2g; FIBER 2.6g; CHOL 45mg; IRON 3.8mg; SODIUM 640mg; CALC 84mg

SUNSET CHICKEN WITH GRILLED VEGETABLE-RICE PILAF

Marinade:

½ cup fresh lime juice (about 4 limes)
2 tablespoons hot sauce
3 garlic cloves, minced, or 1½ teaspoons bottled minced garlic
6 (4-ounce) skinned, boned chicken breast halves

Rice:

½ cup golden raisins
1 (16-ounce) can fat-free, less-sodium chicken broth
1 cup uncooked basmati or long-grain rice

Spice mix:

2 teaspoons chili powder
1 teaspoon ground cumin
¾ teaspoon salt
½ teaspoon black pepper

Remaining ingredients:

1 large onion, cut into 12 wedges
1 cup (1-inch) pieces red bell pepper
1 cup (1-inch) pieces green bell pepper
Cooking spray
2 tablespoons chopped cashews
2 teaspoons olive oil

1. To prepare marinade, combine first 3 ingredients in a shallow dish, and add chicken, turning to coat. Cover and chill 1 hour. Drain; discard marinade.
2. To prepare rice, bring raisins and broth to a boil in a medium saucepan. Add rice. Cover; reduce heat. Simmer 20 minutes or until liquid is absorbed. Keep warm.
3. To prepare spice mix, combine chili powder, cumin, salt, and black pepper in a small bowl. Rub 1 tablespoon spice mix over chicken. Combine remaining spice mix, onion, and bell peppers in a bowl, tossing to coat. Thread vegetables alternately onto 3 (12-inch) skewers.
4. Prepare grill.
5. Place kebabs and chicken on a grill rack coated with cooking spray; grill 7 minutes on each side or until chicken is done and vegetables are tender.
6. Remove vegetables from skewers. Combine cooked rice, vegetables, cashews, and oil in a large bowl; toss well. Serve with chicken. Yield: 6 servings (serving size: 1 chicken breast half and 1 cup pilaf).

CALORIES 348 (13% from fat); FAT 5.1g (sat 1g, mono 2.4g, poly 1g); PROTEIN 30.4g; CARB 43.6g; FIBER 2.9g; CHOL 66mg; IRON 3.7mg; SODIUM 415mg; CALC 48mg

¡Cinco de Mayo, América!

This springtime Mexican holiday has found a welcome home in the United States. And no wonder—it's friendly, fun, easy, and tastes great.

MIXED FAJITAS WITH PEPPERS AND ONIONS

1¼ pounds flank steak
1 cup fresh lime juice (about 6 limes)
⅔ cup beer
4 teaspoons chili powder
2 teaspoons ground cumin
1 teaspoon dried oregano
1 teaspoon salt
½ teaspoon black pepper
4 garlic cloves, minced
1¼ pounds skinned, boned chicken breast
Cooking spray
1 tablespoon olive oil
2 cups vertically sliced onion (about 2 large onions)
2 cups red bell pepper strips (about 2 peppers)
2 cups green bell pepper strips (about 2 peppers)
12 (10-inch) flour tortillas
1½ cups diced seeded tomato (about 1 large)
½ cup minced fresh cilantro

1. Trim fat from steak, and score a diamond pattern on both sides of steak.
2. Combine lime juice and next 7 ingredients in a small bowl. Divide marinade equally between 2 large zip-top plastic bags, adding steak to 1 bag and chicken to the other. Seal bags, and marinate in refrigerator 6 hours or overnight, turning bags occasionally. Remove steak and chicken from bags, discarding marinade.
3. Prepare grill or broiler.
4. Place steak on a grill rack or broiler pan coated with cooking spray, and cook 10 minutes on each side or until desired degree of doneness. Cut steak diagonally across grain into thin slices. Place chicken on grill rack or broiler pan coated with cooking spray; cook 6 minutes on each side or until done. Cut chicken into thin slices.
5. Heat oil in a large nonstick skillet over medium heat. Add onion and bell peppers; sauté 10 minutes or until onion mixture begins to brown.
6. Warm tortillas according to package directions.
7. Spoon steak or chicken, onion mixture, tomato, and cilantro down center of each tortilla; roll up. Yield: 12 servings (serving size: 1 tortilla, 2 ounces meat, ½ cup onion mixture, 2 tablespoons tomato, and 2 teaspoons cilantro).

CALORIES 378 (30% from fat); FAT 12.4g (sat 3.5g, mono 5.3g, poly 2.3g); PROTEIN 26.8g; CARB 38.7g; FIBER 3.3g; CHOL 57mg; IRON 4.1mg; SODIUM 444mg; CALC 97mg

PINEAPPLE-CHIPOTLE SALSA

2 teaspoons vegetable oil
3 cups diced fresh or canned pineapple tidbits
1½ cups diced onion
1 cup diced seeded tomato
2 garlic cloves, minced
½ cup pineapple juice
2 tablespoons brown sugar
2 tablespoons cider vinegar
2 drained canned chipotle chiles in adobo sauce, minced
1 tablespoon adobo sauce (from drained chipotle chiles)
½ cup chopped fresh cilantro
2 tablespoons fresh lime juice
½ teaspoon salt

1. Heat oil in a large skillet over medium-high heat. Add pineapple and onion; sauté 10 minutes or until lightly browned. Add tomato and garlic; sauté 1 minute. Stir in pineapple juice, brown sugar, vinegar, chiles, and adobo sauce. Cook 6 minutes, stirring occasionally. Stir in cilantro, fresh lime juice, and salt. Cool. Yield: 2½ cups (serving size: ¼ cup).

CALORIES 63 (19% from fat); FAT 1.3g (sat 0.2g, mono 0.3g, poly 0.6g); PROTEIN 0.8g; CARB 13.4g; FIBER 1.6g; CHOL 0mg; IRON 0.6mg; SODIUM 129mg; CALC 19mg

FLAN DE QUESO

Cream cheese gives this flan a firm texture similar to a creamy cheesecake.

¾ cup packed brown sugar
2 tablespoons water
2 tablespoons granulated sugar
1 tablespoon cornstarch
2 teaspoons vanilla extract
4 large egg whites
3 large eggs
1 (8-ounce) block ⅓-less-fat cream cheese
2 cups 1% low-fat milk
⅔ cup fat-free sweetened condensed milk
1 (5-ounce) can evaporated fat-free milk
Mint leaves (optional)

1. Preheat oven to 325°.
2. Combine brown sugar and water in a small, heavy saucepan over medium-low heat, and cook until sugar dissolves and is golden (about 5 minutes), stirring frequently. Immediately pour into 2 (8-inch) cake pans, tipping quickly until caramelized sugar coats bottoms of pans.
3. Combine granulated sugar and next 5 ingredients in a food processor or blender, and process until smooth. Pour into a large bowl. Add milks, stirring until well-blended.
4. Divide mixture evenly between prepared cake pans. Place pans in a

Continued

jelly-roll pan; add hot water to jelly-roll pan to a depth of 1 inch. Bake at 325° for 1 hour and 15 minutes or until a knife inserted in center comes out clean. Remove pans from water. Cover and chill 3 hours.

5. Loosen edges of flans with a knife or rubber spatula. Place a large plate, upside down, on top of each pan; invert onto plates. Drizzle any remaining caramelized syrup over flans. Cut each into 8 wedges. Garnish with mint leaves, if desired. Yield: 16 servings.

CALORIES 160 (26% from fat); FAT 4.6g (sat 2.6g, mono 1.4g, poly 0.2g); PROTEIN 6.1g; CARB 23.3g; FIBER 0g; CHOL 55mg; IRON 0.4mg; SODIUM 127mg; CALC 120mg

ADOBADO PORK TENDERLOIN

The Spanish term adobado *refers to a dish that has been marinated and that generally contains chiles. In this recipe, anchos (AHN-chohs), dried poblano chiles, are used to give the dish some mild heat. Serve with salsa and corn tortillas.*

  5 ancho chiles
  2 cups boiling water
  1 cup fat-free, less-sodium
      chicken broth
  2 tablespoons sugar
  3 tablespoons cider vinegar
  1 teaspoon dried oregano
  2 teaspoons olive oil
  ½ teaspoon salt
  ½ teaspoon ground cumin
  ¼ teaspoon black pepper
  ⅛ teaspoon ground cloves
  4 large garlic cloves, halved
  2 pounds pork tenderloin
Cooking spray

1. Heat a large nonstick skillet over medium-high heat until hot. Add chiles; cook 2 minutes, turning frequently. Remove from heat; cool. Discard stems and seeds. Combine roasted chiles and boiling water in a bowl; cover and let stand for 20 minutes or until soft. Drain well. Combine rehydrated chiles, broth, and next 9 ingredients in a blender; process until smooth.

Cook chile paste in skillet over medium-low heat until very thick (about 8 minutes), stirring frequently. Cool.
2. Trim fat from pork. Slice pork lengthwise, cutting to, but not through, other side. Open halves, laying flat. Place pork in a 13 x 9-inch baking dish; spread chile paste over all sides of pork. Cover and marinate in refrigerator 6 hours or overnight.
3. Prepare grill.
4. Remove pork from dish, reserving chile paste. Insert a meat thermometer into thickest part of pork. Place pork on a grill rack coated with cooking spray; cook 8 minutes on each side or until thermometer registers 160° (slightly pink), brushing frequently with reserved chile paste. Yield: 8 servings (serving size: 3 ounces pork).

CALORIES 182 (28% from fat); FAT 5.7g (sat 1.6g, mono 2.7g, poly 0.9g); PROTEIN 25.5g; CARB 6.6g; FIBER 1.1g; CHOL 79mg; IRON 1.8mg; SODIUM 278mg; CALC 20mg

WATERMELON MARGARITAS

To freeze watermelon, place diced watermelon on a baking sheet in the freezer for six hours or overnight. Store frozen cubes in a zip-top freezer bag up to two weeks.

  2 cups diced seeded watermelon,
      frozen
  ¾ cup tequila
  ⅓ cup triple sec (orange-flavored
      liqueur)
  1 tablespoon sugar
  2 tablespoons lime juice
  2 cups crushed ice
Granulated sugar (optional)
Lime slices (optional)
Orange slices (optional)

1. Place first 5 ingredients in a blender, and process until smooth. Add ice; process until smooth. If desired, serve in glasses rimmed with sugar, and garnish with lime and orange slices. Yield: 5 servings (serving size: 1 cup).

CALORIES 157 (2% from fat); FAT 0.2g (sat 0.2g, mono 0g, poly 0g); PROTEIN 0.2g; CARB 6g; FIBER 0.4g; CHOL 0mg; IRON 0.1mg; SODIUM 2mg; CALC 6mg

CRAB-STUFFED JALAPEÑOS WITH AVOCADO DUNK

You can make the avocado dunk a day in advance. To keep the color green, place avocado seed in the mixture.

Stuffed jalapeños:

  20 large jalapeño peppers
       (about 1 pound)
Cooking spray
  2 tablespoons minced red bell
      pepper
  2 tablespoons minced onion
  1 garlic clove, minced
  ¾ cup lump crabmeat, shell pieces
      removed
  1 tablespoon chopped fresh
      cilantro
  ¼ teaspoon salt
  3 large egg whites
  3 tablespoons plain fat-free
      yogurt
  1 cup dry breadcrumbs
  ¾ cup yellow cornmeal
  1 teaspoon salt
  1 teaspoon garlic powder

Avocado dunk:

  ½ cup diced peeled avocado
  ¼ cup vegetable broth
  ¼ cup fat-free sour cream
  ¼ cup chopped green onions
  2 tablespoons fresh lime juice
  2 tablespoons chopped fresh
      cilantro
  ¼ teaspoon salt
  1 garlic clove, minced

1. Preheat broiler.
2. To prepare stuffed jalapeños, place jalapeños on a foil-lined baking sheet; broil 12 minutes or until blackened, turning occasionally. Place in a zip-top plastic bag; seal. Let stand 15 minutes; peel jalapeños. Cut a lengthwise slit in each, discarding stems, seeds, and membranes.
3. Place a medium nonstick skillet coated with cooking spray over low heat until hot. Add bell pepper, onion, and 1 minced garlic clove, and cook 5 minutes or until soft. Remove from

heat; stir in crabmeat, 1 tablespoon cilantro, and ¼ teaspoon salt. Divide crab mixture evenly among jalapeños (each will be very full).

4. Preheat oven to 375°.

5. Beat egg whites in a medium bowl at high speed of a mixer until soft peaks form. Fold in yogurt.

6. Combine breadcrumbs, cornmeal, 1 teaspoon salt, and garlic powder in a small bowl. Dip each stuffed jalapeño in egg white mixture; dredge in bread crumb mixture. Place breaded jalapeños on a baking sheet coated with cooking spray. Lightly spray jalapeños with cooking spray. Bake at 375° for 15 minutes or until golden.

7. To prepare avocado dunk, place avocado and remaining 7 ingredients in a food processor or blender, and process until smooth. Yield: 10 servings (serving size: 2 stuffed jalapeños and 1½ tablespoons avocado dunk).

CALORIES 133 (15% from fat); FAT 2.2g (sat 0.4g, mono 1g, poly 0.5g); PROTEIN 7.0g; CARB 21.7g; FIBER 2.1g; CHOL 10mg; IRON 1.7mg; SODIUM 520mg; CALC 57mg

JICAMA SALAD

Sometimes referred to as a Mexican potato, jicama (HEE-kah-mah) is a sweet, nutty-flavored root vegetable with white flesh and tan-colored skin. Enjoy this crunchy vegetable, similar in texture to water chestnuts, raw or cooked.

    4 oranges
    2 cups (½-inch) julienne-cut
         peeled jicama
    1 cucumber (about ½ pound),
         peeled, halved lengthwise,
         seeded, and thinly sliced
    2 cups cubed peeled cantaloupe
    ½ cup vertically sliced red onion
    ¼ cup chopped fresh cilantro
    2 tablespoons chopped fresh mint
    ¼ cup fresh lime juice
    ½ teaspoon salt
    ½ teaspoon hot chili powder

1. Peel and section oranges over a bowl; squeeze membranes to extract juice.

Set sections aside; reserve ¼ cup orange juice. Discard membranes.

2. Place orange sections, jicama, and next 5 ingredients in a large bowl. Combine reserved orange juice, lime juice, salt, and chili powder. Pour juice mixture over jicama mixture, and toss gently. Cover and chill 2 hours. Yield: 8 servings (serving size: 1 cup).

CALORIES 70 (4% from fat); FAT 0.3g (sat 0.1g, mono 0.1g, poly 0.1g); PROTEIN 1.6g; CARB 17g; FIBER 4.2g; CHOL 0mg; IRON 0.6mg; SODIUM 156mg; CALC 45mg

SHRIMP-AND-BLACK BEAN NACHOS

Shrimp salsa:

    ¾ cup chopped fresh cilantro
    ½ cup diced red onion
    2 tablespoons fresh lime juice
    1 tablespoon minced seeded
         serrano chile
    1 tablespoon extra-virgin olive oil
    1 teaspoon Worcestershire sauce
    ½ teaspoon salt
    ¼ teaspoon black pepper
    ¾ pound medium shrimp,
         cooked, peeled, and chopped
    2 cups diced tomato
    ½ cup diced peeled avocado

Remaining ingredients:

    1 cup drained canned black beans
    ½ teaspoon ground cumin
    30 baked tortilla chips

1. To prepare shrimp salsa, combine first 9 ingredients in a large bowl; toss well. Cover and refrigerate 30 minutes. Stir in tomato and avocado.

2. Place beans and cumin in a food processor or blender, and process 30 seconds or until smooth. Spread each chip with 1 teaspoon black-bean mixture. Top with 1 tablespoon shrimp salsa. Serve immediately. Yield: 15 servings (serving size: 2 nachos).

CALORIES 83 (26% from fat); FAT 2.4g (sat 0.4g, mono 1.4g, poly 0.4g); PROTEIN 5.4g; CARB 10.7g; FIBER 1.6g; CHOL 26mg; IRON 1.2mg; SODIUM 187mg; CALC 29mg

Tuba or Not to Be

On International Tuba Day, May 1, let's lift our voices for the unsung musical masters of symphonic heavy metal.

MARINATED POTATO-AND-ARTICHOKE SALAD

Apparently someone thought we said this was International Tuber Day. We realize how this makes tubists feel, and we apologize. But this is an awfully nice salad.

    2 pounds small red potatoes,
         quartered
    2 cups (1-inch) cut green beans
         (about ½ pound)
    1 (6-ounce) bottle marinated
         artichoke hearts, undrained
    2 tablespoons chopped pitted
         kalamata olives
    2 tablespoons white wine vinegar
    2 tablespoons chopped fresh
         parsley
    ½ teaspoon salt
    ¼ teaspoon black pepper

1. Place potatoes in a saucepan; cover with water, and bring to a boil. Cook 20 minutes or until very tender. Add beans; cook 2 minutes or until beans are crisp-tender. Drain well.

2. Drain artichokes in a colander over a bowl, reserving 2 tablespoons marinade; chop artichokes. Add artichokes and olives to potato mixture.

3. Combine reserved 2 tablespoons marinade, vinegar, and remaining 3 ingredients. Drizzle dressing over salad, tossing to coat. Cover and chill. Yield: 8 servings (serving size: 1 cup).

CALORIES 136 (25% from fat); FAT 3.8g (sat 0.6g, mono 2.7g, poly 0.4g); PROTEIN 3.8g; CARB 23.4g; FIBER 2.7g; CHOL 0mg; IRON 2.2mg; SODIUM 342mg; CALC 38mg

For the Love of Cakes

Layer cakes from scratch are not only tastier than anything from a box, they're also surprisingly easy.

BANANA LAYER CAKE WITH LEMON-CREAM CHEESE FROSTING

(pictured on page 113)

Cooking spray
1 tablespoon all-purpose flour
1½ cups sugar
⅓ cup vegetable shortening
1 teaspoon vanilla extract
3 large eggs
2 cups all-purpose flour
¾ teaspoon baking soda
½ teaspoon salt
1 cup mashed ripe banana (about 2)
½ cup low-fat buttermilk
Lemon-Cream Cheese Frosting (see recipe)
1½ cups sliced ripe banana (about 2)

1. Preheat oven to 350°.
2. Coat bottoms of 2 (9-inch) round cake pans with cooking spray (do not coat sides of pans); line bottoms with wax paper. Coat wax paper with cooking spray; dust with 1 tablespoon flour.
3. Beat sugar, shortening, and vanilla at medium speed of a mixer 5 minutes. Add eggs, 1 at a time; beat well after each addition. Lightly spoon 2 cups flour into dry measuring cups; level with a knife. Combine 2 cups flour, soda, and salt, with a whisk. Combine mashed banana and buttermilk. Add flour mixture to sugar mixture alternately with buttermilk mixture, beginning and ending with flour mixture.
4. Pour batter into prepared pans. Sharply tap pans once on counter to remove air bubbles. Bake at 350° for 30 minutes or until a wooden pick inserted in center comes out clean. Cool in pans 10 minutes on a wire rack; remove from pans. Remove wax paper. Cool completely on wire rack.
5. Place 1 cake layer on a plate; spread with ½ cup Lemon-Cream Cheese Frosting. Arrange banana slices over frosting. Top with remaining cake layer. Spread remaining frosting over top and sides of cake. Chill 1 hour. Store cake loosely covered in refrigerator. Yield: 18 servings (serving size: 1 slice).

CALORIES 308 (29% from fat); FAT 9.9g (sat 4.6g, mono 3g, poly 1.3g); PROTEIN 4.4g; CARB 51.6g; FIBER 1g; CHOL 53mg; IRON 1mg; SODIUM 209mg; CALC 27mg

MOLASSES-SPICE CAKE WITH LEMON-CREAM CHEESE FROSTING

1 tablespoon all-purpose flour
1 cup sugar
⅓ cup vegetable shortening
1 teaspoon vanilla extract
3 large eggs
1¾ cups all-purpose flour
1½ teaspoons baking powder
1 teaspoon ground cinnamon
½ teaspoon salt
¼ teaspoon ground allspice
¼ teaspoon ground cloves
¾ cup 1% low-fat milk
¼ cup molasses
Lemon-Cream Cheese Frosting (see recipe)

1. Preheat oven to 350°.
2. Coat bottoms of 2 (9-inch) round cake pans with cooking spray (do not coat sides of pans); line bottoms with wax paper. Coat wax paper with cooking spray; dust with 1 tablespoon flour.
3. Beat sugar, shortening, and vanilla at medium speed of a mixer for 5 minutes. Add eggs, 1 at a time, beating well after each addition. Lightly spoon 1¾ cups flour into dry measuring cups; level with a knife. Combine 1¾ cups flour and next 5 ingredients, stirring well with a whisk. Combine milk and molasses. Add flour mixture to sugar mixture alternately with milk mixture, beginning and ending with flour mixture.
4. Pour batter into prepared pans. Sharply tap pans once on counter to remove air bubbles. Bake at 350° for 30 minutes or until a wooden pick inserted in center comes out clean. Cool in pans 10 minutes on a wire rack; remove from pans. Remove wax paper. Cool completely on wire rack.
5. Place 1 cake layer on a plate; spread with ½ cup Lemon-Cream Cheese Frosting, and top with remaining cake layer. Spread remaining frosting over top and sides of cake. Chill 1 hour. Store cake loosely covered in refrigerator. Yield: 16 servings (serving size: 1 slice).

CALORIES 304 (33% from fat); FAT 11g (sat 5.1g, mono 3.4g, poly 1.4g); PROTEIN 4.5g; CARB 47.6g; FIBER 0.4g; CHOL 60mg; IRON 1.2mg; SODIUM 226mg; CALC 71mg

LEMON-CREAM CHEESE FROSTING

Overbeating the frosting will make it runny, so be sure to beat it just until blended, and make sure the butter and cream cheese are chilled before using.

¼ cup butter or stick margarine, chilled
1 teaspoon grated lemon rind
1 teaspoon vanilla extract
1 (8-ounce) block ⅓-less-fat cream cheese, chilled
3 cups sifted powdered sugar

1. Beat first 4 ingredients at high speed of a mixer about 2 minutes or just until smooth (do not overbeat). Gradually add powdered sugar, and beat at low speed just until blended (do not overbeat). Cover and chill 2 hours. Yield: 2 cups.

CALORIES 123 (40% from fat); FAT 5.5g (sat 3.5g, mono 1.6g, poly 0.2g); PROTEIN 1.3g; CARB 17.7g; FIBER 0g; CHOL 16mg; IRON 0.1mg; SODIUM 77mg; CALC 11mg

CARAMEL-PECAN FROSTING

¼ cup butter or stick margarine
½ cup dark brown sugar
6 tablespoons evaporated fat-free
    milk
2 teaspoons vanilla extract
3 cups sifted powdered sugar
¼ cup chopped pecans

1. Melt butter in a saucepan over medium heat. Add brown sugar. Cook 3 minutes, stirring constantly with a whisk. Add milk, 1 tablespoon at a time; cook 3 minutes, stirring constantly. Cool. Stir in vanilla. Combine butter mixture and powdered sugar in a bowl; beat at high speed of a mixer until smooth. Frost cake as directed; sprinkle with pecans. Yield: 2 cups.
Note: If frosting is too thick, add 1 tablespoon evaporated fat-free milk.

CALORIES: 130 (26% from fat); FAT 3.7g (sat 1.7g, mono 1.4g, poly 0.4g); PROTEIN 0.5g; CARB 24.2g; FIBER 0.1g; CHOL 7mg; IRON 0.2mg; SODIUM 35mg; CALC 20mg

CLASSIC YELLOW LAYER CAKE WITH CARAMEL-PECAN FROSTING

1 tablespoon all-purpose flour
1⅔ cups sugar
½ cup butter or stick margarine,
    softened
1 tablespoon vanilla extract
3 large eggs
2¼ cups all-purpose flour
2¼ teaspoons baking powder
½ teaspoon salt
1¼ cups fat-free milk
Caramel-Pecan Frosting (see
    recipe)

1. Preheat oven to 350°.
2. Coat bottoms of 2 (9-inch) round cake pans with cooking spray (do not coat sides of pans); line bottoms with wax paper. Coat wax paper with cooking spray; dust with 1 tablespoon flour.
3. Beat sugar, butter, and vanilla at medium speed of a mixer until well-blended (about 5 minutes). Add eggs, 1 at a time; beat well after each addition.

❶ *Coat the bottoms of the pans with cooking spray; then line them with wax paper. Coat the wax paper with cooking spray, and dust with flour.*

❷ *Stir the flour to eliminate any lumps. Spoon it into a measuring cup, and level it with a knife. Too much flour will make the cake dry.*

❸ *When you beat the shortening and sugar together, the mixture's consistency will look like damp sand—fine-textured, but not cohesive.*

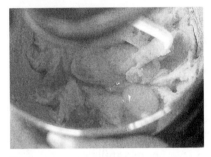

❹ *Whole eggs make a low-fat cake moist and tender. Add them one at a time to the batter, beating each one before adding the next.*

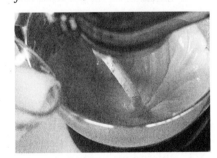

❺ *Add the flour mixture alternately with the liquid. Beat just until each component is incorporated. Over-beating can produce a tough cake.*

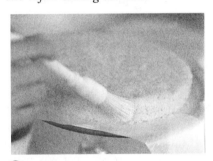

❻ *To frost the cake, brush away any loose crumbs. Place the layers on top of wax paper strips. When the cake is iced, remove the wax paper strips.*

Lightly spoon 2¼ cups flour into dry measuring cups; level with a knife. Combine 2¼ cups flour, baking powder, and salt; stir well with a whisk. Add flour mixture to sugar mixture alternately with milk, beginning and ending with flour mixture.
4. Pour batter into prepared pans. Sharply tap pans once on counter to

remove air bubbles. Bake at 350° for 30 minutes or until a wooden pick inserted in center comes out clean. Cool in pans 10 minutes on a wire rack; remove from pans. Remove wax paper. Cool completely on wire rack.
5. Place 1 cake layer on a plate; spread with ½ cup Caramel-Pecan Frosting,
Continued

and top with remaining layer. Spread remaining frosting over top and sides of cake. Store cake loosely covered in refrigerator. Yield: 18 servings (serving size: 1 slice).

CALORIES 326 (27% from fat); FAT 9.9g (sat 5.1g, mono 3.2g, poly 0.7g); PROTEIN 3.8g; CARB 56g; FIBER 0.5g; CHOL 57mg; IRON 1.1mg; SODIUM 234mg; CALC 83mg

OATMEAL LAYER CAKE WITH CARAMEL-PECAN FROSTING

These cake layers will not rise as high as those of traditional cakes.

Cooking spray
1 tablespoon all-purpose flour
1⅓ cups boiling water
1 cup quick-cooking oats
¾ cup granulated sugar
¾ cup packed dark brown sugar
⅓ cup vegetable shortening
2 teaspoons vanilla extract
3 large eggs
1½ cups all-purpose flour
1 teaspoon baking soda
1 teaspoon ground cinnamon
½ teaspoon salt
½ teaspoon ground nutmeg
½ cup low-fat buttermilk
Caramel-Pecan Frosting (page 131)

1. Preheat oven to 350°.
2. Coat bottoms of 2 (9-inch) round cake pans with cooking spray (do not coat sides of pans), and line bottoms of pans with wax paper. Coat wax paper with cooking spray, and dust with 1 tablespoon flour.
3. Combine water and oats in a medium bowl; let stand 20 minutes. Beat granulated sugar, brown sugar, shortening, and vanilla at medium speed of a mixer 5 minutes. Add eggs, 1 at a time, beating well after each addition. Add oats, beating until blended.
4. Lightly spoon 1½ cups flour into dry measuring cups; level with a knife. Combine 1½ cups flour, baking soda, cinnamon, salt, and nutmeg, stirring well with a whisk. Add flour mixture to sugar mixture alternately with buttermilk, beginning and ending with flour mixture.

5. Pour batter into prepared pans. Sharply tap pans once on counter to remove air bubbles. Bake at 350° for 35 minutes or until a wooden pick inserted in center comes out clean. Cool in pans 10 minutes on a wire rack; remove from pans. Remove wax paper. Cool completely on wire rack.
6. Place 1 cake layer on a plate; spread layer with ½ cup Caramel-Pecan Frosting, and top with remaining layer. Spread remaining frosting over top and sides of cake. Store cake loosely covered in refrigerator. Yield: 16 servings (serving size: 1 slice).

CALORIES 337 (25% from fat); FAT 9.3g (sat 3.3g, mono 3.3g, poly 1.8g); PROTEIN 4.1g; CARB 60.1g; FIBER 1g; CHOL 49mg; IRON 1.4mg; SODIUM 213mg; CALC 52mg

MALTED-MILK CHOCOLATE CAKE

Make the frosting first. Reserve a portion to ice the cake, and use the rest in the batter. To melt chocolate, microwave at HIGH 1½ minutes or until soft; stir until melted.

Cooking spray
1 tablespoon all-purpose flour
2 tablespoons butter or stick margarine, softened
2 teaspoons vanilla extract
1 (8-ounce) block ⅓-less-fat cream cheese, chilled
5 cups sifted powdered sugar
3 tablespoons hot water
3 ounces unsweetened chocolate, melted
⅓ cup vegetable shortening
3 large eggs
1¾ cups all-purpose flour
½ cup malted-milk powder
2½ teaspoons baking powder
½ teaspoon salt
⅔ cup fat-free milk
⅓ cup coarsely chopped malted-milk balls

1. Preheat oven to 350°.
2. Coat bottoms of 2 (9-inch) round cake pans with cooking spray (do not coat sides of pans); line bottoms with

wax paper. Coat wax paper with cooking spray; dust with 1 tablespoon flour.
3. Combine butter, vanilla, and cream cheese; beat at medium-high speed of a mixer 2 minutes. Gradually add sugar, beating at low speed just until smooth. Add hot water, and beat just until smooth. Add chocolate, and beat just until smooth. Reserve 1¾ cups chocolate mixture for frosting; cover and chill 2 hours. Add shortening to remaining chocolate mixture in bowl. Beat at medium speed until well-blended (about 1 minute). Add eggs, 1 at a time, beating well after each addition.
4. Lightly spoon 1¾ cups flour into dry measuring cups, level with a knife. Combine 1¾ cups flour, milk powder, baking powder, and salt, stirring well with a whisk. Add flour mixture to egg mixture alternately with milk, beginning and ending with flour mixture.
5. Pour batter into prepared pans. Sharply tap pans once on counter to remove air bubbles. Bake at 350° for 25 minutes or until a wooden pick inserted in center comes out clean. Cool in pans 10 minutes on a wire rack; remove from pans. Remove wax paper. Cool completely on wire rack.
6. Place 1 cake layer on a plate; spread with ½ cup frosting, and top with remaining cake layer. Spread remaining frosting over top and sides of cake; sprinkle top of cake with chopped malted-milk balls. Chill 1 hour. Store cake loosely covered in refrigerator. Yield: 18 servings (serving size: 1 slice).

CALORIES 325 (33% from fat); FAT 12g (sat 5.9g, mono 3.6g, poly 1.4g); PROTEIN 5.6g; CARB 50.3g; FIBER 0.5g; CHOL 50mg; IRON 1.2mg; SODIUM 261mg; CALC 100mg

HIGH-ALTITUDE ADAPTATIONS

If you're in a high altitude (above 3,500 feet), try these adjustments:
• Increase oven temperature to 375°.
• Decrease each cup of sugar by 2 tablespoons. Decrease each teaspoon of baking powder by ⅛ teaspoon.
• Increase liquid by 2 tablespoons for each cup used.
• Decrease baking time by 5 minutes.

Free Charlotte!

A vigorous defense of her family's Elegant Chocolate Charlotte lets one reader save a tradition—and a treat.

ELEGANT CHOCOLATE CHARLOTTE

—Melissa Lindquist, Grand Bay, Alabama

24 ladyfingers (2 [3-ounce] packages)
¼ cup Kahlúa (coffee-flavored liqueur)
1 (2.6-ounce) box whipped topping mix (such as Dream Whip)
1½ cups cold fat-free milk, divided
1 teaspoon vanilla extract
1¾ cups sifted powdered sugar
1 cup unsweetened cocoa
2 (8-ounce) blocks fat-free cream cheese, softened

1. Split ladyfingers in half lengthwise. Brush cut sides of ladyfinger halves with Kahlúa, and arrange, cut sides up, in bottom and up sides of a 10-inch springform pan. Cover with plastic wrap.
2. Prepare whipped topping mix according to package directions, using 1 cup cold milk and vanilla extract.
3. Combine sugar and cocoa. Beat sugar mixture and cream cheese at medium speed of a mixer until well-blended (mixture will not be completely smooth). Add ½ cup milk to cream cheese mixture; beat well. Gently fold in whipped topping. Pour mixture into prepared pan. Cover and freeze 4 hours or until firm. Yield: 12 servings.

CALORIES 220 (12% from fat); FAT 2.9g (sat 2.1g, mono 0.2g, poly 0.1g); PROTEIN 8.5g; CARB 30.6g; FIBER 0g; CHOL 28mg; IRON 1.3mg; SODIUM 254mg; CALC 156mg

BANANA-PECAN BISCOTTI

"I don't have a lot of time to cook because I'm in graduate school and doing a dietetic internship. But I can always find time to bake biscotti. This creation came about by accident when I had some overripe bananas to use up. Now it's one of my favorites."
—Amy Lundquist, Frankfort, Illinois

1¾ cups all-purpose flour
½ cup sugar
1 teaspoon baking powder
¼ teaspoon salt
⅓ cup mashed very ripe banana (about 1 banana)
1 tablespoon vegetable oil
1 teaspoon vanilla extract
1 large egg
⅓ cup chopped pecans, toasted
Cooking spray

1. Preheat oven to 350°.
2. Lightly spoon flour into dry measuring cups, and level with a knife. Combine flour, sugar, baking powder, and salt. Combine banana, oil, vanilla, and egg in a medium bowl; stir in flour mixture and pecans (dough will be sticky).
3. Turn dough out onto a lightly floured surface; shape dough into 2 (8-inch-long) rolls with floured hands. Place rolls on a baking sheet coated with cooking spray; flatten to ½-inch thickness.
4. Bake at 350° for 23 minutes. Remove rolls from baking sheet; cool 10 minutes on a wire rack. Cut each roll diagonally into 12 (½-inch) slices. Place slices, cut sides down, on baking sheet. Reduce oven temperature to 250°; bake 15 minutes. Turn cookies over; bake an additional 15 minutes (cookies will be slightly soft in center but will harden as they cool). Remove from baking sheet; cool completely on wire racks. Yield: 2 dozen (serving size: 1 biscotto).

CALORIES 72 (25% from fat); FAT 2g (sat 0.3g, mono 1g, poly 0.6g); PROTEIN 1.4g; CARB 12.2g; FIBER 0.4g; CHOL 9mg; IRON 0.5mg; SODIUM 44mg; CALC 15mg

RISOTTO WITH ASPARAGUS AND WILD MUSHROOMS

—Kim Schoenbachler-Nicks, Fairbanks, Alaska

½ ounce dried chanterelle mushrooms
8 sun-dried tomatoes, packed without oil
2 cups boiling water
2 cups (2-inch) sliced asparagus (about ¾ pound)
3 cups fat-free, less-sodium chicken broth
1½ tablespoons olive oil
⅓ cup finely chopped shallots
4 garlic cloves, minced
1 (8-ounce) package cremini mushrooms, sliced
1½ cups uncooked Arborio or other short-grain rice
½ cup dry white wine
¼ teaspoon salt
¼ teaspoon black pepper
2 tablespoons (½ ounce) grated Parmigiano-Reggiano or fresh Parmesan cheese
2 tablespoons chopped fresh parsley

1. Combine first 3 ingredients in a bowl; cover and let stand 30 minutes or until soft. Drain in a colander over a bowl, reserving 1 cup soaking liquid. Chop tomatoes; set aside chanterelles and tomatoes.
2. Steam asparagus, covered, 3 minutes or until crisp-tender; set aside.
3. Bring reserved soaking liquid and broth to a simmer in a medium saucepan (do not boil). Keep warm over low heat.
4. Heat oil in a large nonstick skillet over medium heat. Add shallots, garlic, and cremini mushrooms; sauté 6 minutes or until tender. Stir in rice; cook 1 minute. Stir in chanterelles, tomatoes, wine, salt, and pepper; cook 2 minutes or until wine is nearly absorbed. Stir in ½ cup broth mixture; cook 3 minutes or until liquid is nearly absorbed, stirring constantly. Add remaining broth mixture, ½ cup at a time, stirring

Continued

constantly until each portion of broth mixture is absorbed before adding the next portion (about 25 minutes total). Add asparagus and cheese, and cook 1 minute. Remove from heat; sprinkle with parsley. Serve immediately. Yield: 6 servings (serving size: 1 cup).

CALORIES 275 (15% from fat); FAT 4.6g (sat 1g, mono 2.8g, poly 0.5g); PROTEIN 8.4g; CARB 49.8g; FIBER 2.9g; CHOL 1mg; IRON 3.6mg; SODIUM 438mg; CALC 55mg

CHICKEN IN WHITE WINE SAUCE

"I developed this through improvisation. Slow baking produces a tasty sauce and a tender chicken breast that's wonderful and quick to prepare. I serve it with saffron- or lemon-flavored rice."
—*Charles Honaker, Fort Collins, Colorado*

  2 tablespoons all-purpose flour
  ¼ teaspoon salt
  ¼ teaspoon paprika
  ¼ teaspoon black pepper
  4 (4-ounce) skinned, boned chicken breast halves
  1 teaspoon olive oil
  ½ cup fat-free, less-sodium chicken broth
  ½ cup dry white wine
  4 teaspoons grated Parmesan cheese

1. Preheat oven to 350°.
2. Combine first 4 ingredients in a shallow dish. Dredge chicken in flour mixture.
3. Heat oil in an ovenproof skillet over medium heat. Add chicken; cook 2 minutes on each side or until browned. Add broth and wine. Bring to a boil; remove from heat. Cover and bake at 350° for 30 minutes or until chicken is done. Sprinkle with cheese. Yield: 4 servings (serving size: 1 chicken breast half and 1 teaspoon cheese).

CALORIES 160 (17% from fat); FAT 3.5g (sat 0.9g, mono 1.3g, poly 0.5g); PROTEIN 27.7g; CARB 3.5g; FIBER 0.2g; CHOL 67mg; IRON 1.2mg; SODIUM 314mg; CALC 39mg

---

MENU SUGGESTION

ASIAGO DIP WITH CROSTINI (SEE RECIPE)

PENNE WITH ITALIAN TURKEY SAUSAGE AND VEGETABLES

MIXED GREENS WITH DIJON VINAIGRETTE (PAGE 124)

ELEGANT CHOCOLATE CHARLOTTE (PAGE 133)

PENNE WITH ITALIAN TURKEY SAUSAGE AND VEGETABLES

—*Kari Barnett, Ruidoso, New Mexico*

  ½ pound hot Italian turkey sausage
  ½ cup chopped red onion
  1 garlic clove, minced
  1 cup mushrooms, quartered
  1 small red bell pepper, seeded and cut into ½-inch strips
  1 small yellow bell pepper, seeded and cut into ½-inch strips
  1 small zucchini, halved lengthwise and sliced
  1 (14.5-ounce) can diced tomatoes with basil, garlic, and oregano, undrained
  ¼ cup fat-free sour cream
  4 cups hot cooked penne (about ½ pound uncooked tube-shaped pasta)
  ¼ teaspoon black pepper

1. Remove casings from sausage. Cook sausage in a large nonstick skillet coated with cooking spray over medium-high heat until browned, stirring to crumble. Add onion and garlic; sauté 2 minutes. Add mushrooms, bell peppers, and zucchini; sauté 5 minutes or until vegetables are tender and sausage is done. Stir in tomatoes; cover and cook over medium-low heat 10 minutes. Remove from heat; stir in sour cream. Stir in pasta and black pepper. Cook over medium-low heat 3 minutes. Yield: 4 servings (serving size: 1½ cups).

CALORIES 373 (18% from fat); FAT 7.6g (sat 2g, mono 2.5g, poly 2.1g); PROTEIN 22.1g; CARB 53.4g; FIBER 4.1g; CHOL 56mg; IRON 5.1mg; SODIUM 983mg; CALC 91mg

---

LIGHTEN UP

Skinny Dip

Friends dub it "awesome," but this reader says her Asiago dip needs a leaner fit.

"I clipped the recipe from the newspaper five years ago," says Katie Langland, an Ohio native. "I know this dip has to have a million calories and a ton of fat."

Using reduced-fat versions of the mayonnaise and sour cream and cutting back on the cheese sliced the fat content nearly in half and trimmed 37 calories.

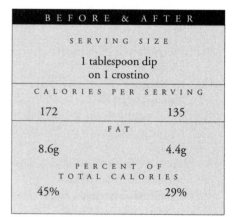

BEFORE & AFTER	
SERVING SIZE	
1 tablespoon dip on 1 crostino	
CALORIES PER SERVING	
172	135
FAT	
8.6g	4.4g
PERCENT OF TOTAL CALORIES	
45%	29%

ASIAGO DIP WITH CROSTINI

If you don't want to make crostini, use a low-fat cracker. And while this dip is best with Asiago (ah-SY-AH-go)—a firm Italian cheese with a rich, nutty flavor—you can substitute other firm, full-flavored cheeses such as Parmesan or Romano.

  1 cup light mayonnaise
  ½ cup thinly sliced green onions
  ⅓ cup (about 1½ ounces) grated Asiago or Parmesan cheese
  ¼ cup sliced mushrooms
  ¼ cup sun-dried tomato sprinkles
  1 (8-ounce) carton low-fat sour cream
  1 tablespoon (¼ ounce) grated Asiago or Parmesan cheese
  32 (½-inch-thick) slices diagonally cut French bread baguette, toasted (about 2 baguettes)

1. Preheat oven to 350°.
2. Combine first 6 ingredients in a bowl; spoon into a 1-quart casserole. Sprinkle with 1 tablespoon cheese. Bake at 350° for 30 minutes or until bubbly. Serve with toasted bread. Yield: 2 cups (serving size: 1 tablespoon dip and 1 crostino).

CALORIES 135 (29% from fat); FAT 4.4g (sat 1.3g, mono 1.4g, poly 1.4g); PROTEIN 4g; CARB 19.7g; FIBER 1.2g; CHOL 7mg; IRON 1mg; SODIUM 303mg; CALC 52mg

IN SEASON

The Peak of Leeks

The "poor man's asparagus," leeks often get overlooked. Time to see what you've been missing.

FRITTATA WITH LEEKS, SPAGHETTI, AND ZUCCHINI

1 tablespoon butter or stick margarine, divided
2 cups thinly sliced leek
1½ cups diced zucchini
⅓ cup 1% low-fat milk
2 teaspoons chopped fresh basil
¼ teaspoon salt
¼ teaspoon black pepper
4 large egg whites
3 large eggs
2 cups hot cooked spaghetti (about 4 ounces uncooked pasta)
⅓ cup (about 1½ ounces) shredded Gruyère or Swiss cheese

1. Heat 1½ teaspoons butter in a large skillet over medium heat. Add leek and zucchini; sauté 6 minutes or until leek mixture is lightly browned.
2. Combine milk and next 5 ingredients in a bowl; stir with a whisk. Stir in leek mixture and spaghetti.
3. Preheat broiler.
4. Heat 1½ teaspoons butter in skillet over low heat. Add egg mixture. Cover;

cook 10 minutes or until almost set. Top with cheese. Wrap handle of skillet with foil. Broil 5 minutes or until cheese melts. Yield: 4 servings (serving size: 1 wedge).

CALORIES 298 (34% from fat); FAT 11.3g (sat 5.3g, mono 3.6g, poly 1.2g); PROTEIN 17.1g; CARB 31.9g; FIBER 1.6g; CHOL 186mg; IRON 3mg; SODIUM 337mg; CALC 199mg

BEEF STEW WITH LEEKS AND BEER

1 tablespoon olive oil
1½ pounds sirloin tips or round steak, cut into 1-inch cubes
4 cups thinly sliced leek (about 4 large)
3½ cups quartered mushrooms (about 8 ounces)
2 cups (¼-inch-thick) sliced carrot
1 tablespoon brown sugar
1 teaspoon dried thyme
¼ teaspoon salt
¼ teaspoon black pepper
1 (14¼-ounce) can fat-free beef broth
1 (12-ounce) bottle light beer
2 tablespoons cornstarch
2 tablespoons red wine vinegar

1. Heat oil in a large Dutch oven over medium-high heat. Add half of beef; cook 5 minutes or until browned, turning occasionally. Remove from pan. Repeat procedure with remaining beef. Add leek and mushrooms to pan; sauté 3 minutes. Return beef to pan; stir in carrot and next 6 ingredients. Bring to a boil; cover, reduce heat, and simmer 2 hours or until beef is tender.
2. Combine cornstarch and vinegar in a small bowl. Add cornstarch mixture to beef mixture; bring to a boil. Cook 3 minutes, stirring constantly. Yield: 6 servings (serving size: 1⅓ cups).

CALORIES 281 (27% from fat); FAT 8.4g (sat 2.5g, mono 4.1g, poly 0.7g); PROTEIN 26.5g; CARB 20.8g; FIBER 2.6g; CHOL 69mg; IRON 5.5mg; SODIUM 196mg; CALC 70mg

LEEKS CORDON BLEU

(pictured on page 115)

4 large leeks
4 (1¼-ounce) slices reduced-fat, reduced-sodium Swiss cheese (such as Alpine Lace), cut in half lengthwise
4 (1-ounce) slices lean ham, cut in half lengthwise
2½ tablespoons all-purpose flour
¾ cup 1% low-fat milk
¾ cup fat-free, less-sodium chicken broth
2 teaspoons dry sherry
⅛ teaspoon salt
⅛ teaspoon black pepper
¼ cup breadcrumbs
2 English muffins, split and toasted

1. Remove roots, outer leaves, and tops from leeks; leave 6 inches of each leek. Cut each in half crosswise. Steam, covered, 8 minutes or until tender. Wrap each leek half in 1 piece of cheese and 1 piece of ham. Place wrapped leeks, seam sides down, in an 8-inch square baking dish.
2. Preheat oven to 450°.
3. Place flour in a small saucepan; gradually add milk, stirring with a whisk until blended. Stir in broth. Bring to a boil over medium heat; cook 6 minutes or until thick, stirring constantly with a whisk. Reduce heat; stir in sherry, salt, and pepper. Pour sauce over wrapped leeks, and sprinkle with breadcrumbs. Bake at 450° for 10 minutes or until golden. Arrange 2 wrapped leeks on each English muffin half; spoon sauce evenly over leeks. Yield: 4 servings (serving size: 1 English muffin half, 2 wrapped leeks, and ⅓ cup sauce).

CALORIES 361 (26% from fat); FAT 10.6g (sat 6g, mono 3.2g, poly 1g); PROTEIN 22.8g; CARB 44.1g; FIBER 1.7g; CHOL 40mg; IRON 4.1mg; SODIUM 841mg; CALC 488mg

LEEK-AND-POTATO GRATIN

1½ pounds Yukon gold or baking
      potatoes, cut into ¼-inch-
      thick slices
Cooking spray
1 tablespoon olive oil
4 cups thinly sliced leek
      (about 4 large)
1 garlic clove, minced
¼ teaspoon salt
Dash of black pepper
1 (14.5-ounce) can no-salt-added
      diced tomatoes, undrained
¾ cup (3 ounces) grated fresh
      Parmesan cheese
½ cup 1% low-fat milk

1. Preheat oven to 425°.
2. Arrange half of potato slices in an
11 x 7-inch baking dish coated with
cooking spray.
3. Heat oil in a large nonstick skillet
over medium-high heat. Add leek;
sauté 10 minutes or until lightly
browned. Stir in garlic, salt, and pepper. Spoon half of leek mixture over
potato slices; top with half of tomatoes
and half of cheese. Repeat layers with
remaining potatoes, leek mixture,
tomatoes, and cheese.
4. Bring milk to a boil over low heat in
a skillet; pour over potato mixture.
Cover and bake at 425° for 30 minutes
or until potatoes are tender. Uncover and
bake an additional 15 minutes or until
golden brown. Let stand 5 minutes
before serving. Yield: 6 servings.

CALORIES 265 (22% from fat); FAT 6.6g (sat 2.8g, mono 2.9g,
poly 0.5g); PROTEIN 9.8g; CARB 43.1g; FIBER 2.9g;
CHOL 10mg; IRON 3.4mg; SODIUM 367mg; CALC 269mg

BRAISED LEEKS AND MUSHROOMS

6 leeks (about 3 pounds)
1 cup fat-free beef broth
1 tablespoon tomato paste
¼ teaspoon salt
¼ teaspoon dried thyme
⅛ teaspoon black pepper
1½ teaspoons butter or stick
      margarine
2 cups quartered mushrooms
      (about 5 ounces)

1. Remove roots, outer leaves, and tops
from leeks, leaving 6 inches of each
leek. Cut each diagonally into thirds,
and then diagonally in half to form 6
triangular pieces. Rinse under cold
water; drain well.
2. Combine beef broth, tomato paste,
salt, thyme, and pepper in a bowl, and
stir with a whisk.
3. Melt butter in a large nonstick skillet over medium-high heat. Add leeks
and mushrooms, and sauté 6 minutes
or until lightly browned. Add broth
mixture. Cover, reduce heat, and simmer 15 minutes or until leeks are tender. Uncover and simmer 7 minutes or
until liquid almost evaporates, stirring
occasionally. Yield: 4 servings (serving
size: ½ cup).

CALORIES 144 (14% from fat); FAT 2.2g (sat 1g, mono 0.4g,
poly 0.5g); PROTEIN 3.8g; CARB 29.3g; FIBER 2.9g;
CHOL 4mg; IRON 4.6mg; SODIUM 204mg; CALC 115mg

PASTA WITH LEEKS AND ARTICHOKES

2 tablespoons olive oil, divided
4 cups thinly sliced leek (about
      4 large)
1 (14-ounce) can quartered
      artichoke hearts, rinsed and
      drained
1 teaspoon grated lemon rind
2 tablespoons fresh lemon juice
½ teaspoon salt
Dash of black pepper
4 cups hot cooked gemelli or
      fusilli (about 8 ounces
      uncooked short twisted
      spaghetti)
½ cup chopped fresh parsley

1. Heat 1 tablespoon oil in a large
nonstick skillet over medium-high
heat. Add sliced leek, and sauté 10
minutes or until tender. Add artichoke
hearts, and cook 1 minute.
2. Combine 1 tablespoon oil, lemon
rind, lemon juice, salt, and pepper in a
small bowl, and stir with a whisk.
3. Combine pasta, leek mixture,
lemon juice mixture, and parsley in a
large bowl; toss gently. Yield: 4 servings
(serving size: 2 cups).

CALORIES 368 (20% from fat); FAT 8.1g (sat 1.0g, mono 4.0g,
poly 1.2g); PROTEIN 11.1g; CARB 65g; FIBER 3g;
CHOL 0mg; IRON 5.5mg; SODIUM 419mg; CALC 110mg

INSIDE LEEKS

A common garden vegetable, leeks are the mildest relatives of the onion family,
and unlike onions, leeks do not form a bulb. Resembling a large green onion,
leeks have flat leaves rather than round or hollow leaves like onions.

Look for leeks that are about one inch in diameter and without blemishes or
discoloration. Before cooking, remove any damaged leaves, and wash leeks thoroughly to remove grit from under the outer leaves. If desired, split leeks in half
lengthwise to clean them. Store fresh leeks in the refrigerator up to two weeks.

Six by Six

*Here are six simple meals, each with an entrée of just six ingredients
(not counting salt, pepper, and water), that are
ready in a half-hour.*

SPICY THAI COCONUT SHRIMP

Preparation time: 20 minutes
Cooking time: 10 minutes

*To save more time, call ahead and
have the seafood market peel and
devein the shrimp for you.*

  2 cups uncooked rice
1½ tablespoons water
1½ teaspoons red curry paste (such
    as Maesri) or chile paste with
    garlic
1½ pounds medium shrimp, peeled
    and deveined
    Cooking spray
2½ cups (1-inch) sliced asparagus
    (about ¾ pound)
1½ cups sliced green onions
 ½ teaspoon salt
  1 (14-ounce) can light coconut
    milk

1. Cook rice according to package directions, omitting salt and fat. While rice is
cooking, combine water and curry paste
in a medium bowl; add shrimp, tossing
to coat. Place a large nonstick skillet
coated with cooking spray over medium-
high heat until hot. Add shrimp mixture,
and sauté 4 minutes. Add sliced asparagus and green onions; cover and cook 3
minutes or until asparagus is crisp-
tender. Stir in salt and coconut milk.

Cook 3 minutes or until thoroughly
heated, stirring occasionally. Serve over
rice. Yield: 4 servings (serving size: 1¼
cups shrimp sauce and 1 cup rice).

CALORIES 457 (16% from fat); FAT 8.1g (sat 4g, mono 1g,
poly 1.4g); PROTEIN 32.9g; CARB 57.8g; FIBER 3.9g;
CHOL 194mg; IRON 6.9mg; SODIUM 646mg; CALC 135mg

BELL PEPPER-FETA PASTA TOSS

(pictured on page 114)

Preparation time: 6 minutes
Cooking time: 15 minutes

*Draining the pasta over the bell pepper cooks the pepper strips slightly
before you toss them with the rest of
the ingredients.*

  6 ounces uncooked linguine
  1 large yellow or red bell pepper,
    seeded and cut into ⅛-inch
    strips
1¼ cups quartered cherry tomatoes
 ¾ cup finely chopped fresh parsley
 ¼ teaspoon salt
  1 (4-ounce) package crumbled
    feta cheese with basil and
    sun-dried tomatoes
  1 (2¼-ounce) can or ¼ cup
    sliced ripe olives, drained

1. Cook pasta according to package
directions, omitting salt and fat. Place
bell pepper in a colander; drain pasta
over bell pepper. Combine pasta, bell
pepper and remaining ingredients in a
large bowl; toss gently. Serve immediately. Yield: 4 servings (serving size: 1¼
cups).

CALORIES 275 (28% from fat); FAT 8.7g (sat 4.7g, mono 2.6g,
poly 0.9g); PROTEIN 10.8g; CARB 39.4g; FIBER 3.3g;
CHOL 25mg; IRON 3.8mg; SODIUM 602mg; CALC 181mg

DIJON-POTATO SALAD WITH SMOKED CHICKEN SAUSAGE

Preparation time: 10 minutes
Cooking time: 20 minutes

  6 cups diced red potato (about 2
    pounds)
  1 (12-ounce) package smoked
    chicken sausage, quartered
    lengthwise and sliced (such as
    Gerhard's)
 ½ cup finely chopped celery
 ½ cup finely chopped red onion
 ⅓ cup Dijon mustard
  1 tablespoon fresh lemon juice
 ¼ teaspoon salt
 ¼ teaspoon black pepper

1. Steam potato, covered in a
saucepan, 10 minutes or until tender.
Place potato in a medium nonstick
skillet over medium-high heat until
hot. Add sausage, and sauté 2 minutes.
Combine potato and sausage in a large
bowl. Add celery and remaining ingredients; toss well. Yield: 4 servings (serving size: 2 cups).

CALORIES 354 (31% from fat); FAT 12.1g (sat 3.1g, mono 5g,
poly 3g); PROTEIN 18.9g; CARB 43.2g; FIBER 6.3g;
CHOL 75mg; IRON 3.1mg; SODIUM 1,295mg; CALC 41mg

SALMON ON GREENS WITH LIME-GINGER DRESSING

(pictured on page 116)

Preparation time: 10 minutes
Cooking time: 12 minutes

⅔ cup fresh lime juice (about 5 limes)
½ cup honey
½ teaspoon grated peeled fresh ginger
4 (6-ounce) skinned salmon fillets (about 1 inch thick)
Cooking spray
¼ teaspoon salt
8 cups gourmet salad greens
1 cup sliced peeled mango

1. Preheat broiler.
2. Combine first 3 ingredients in a small bowl, reserving ¾ cup juice mixture for dressing. Place salmon fillets on a broiler pan coated with cooking spray. Baste fillets with remaining juice mixture. Broil 4 minutes on each side or until desired degree of doneness, basting once after turning. Sprinkle fillets with salt.
3. Divide salad greens evenly among 4 plates; arrange salmon and mango on top of greens. Drizzle with reserved dressing. Yield: 4 servings (serving size: 2 cups greens, 1 fillet, ¼ cup mango, and 3 tablespoons dressing).

CALORIES 462 (28% from fat); FAT 14.5g (sat 2.5g, mono 6.8g, poly 3.2g); PROTEIN 37.2g; CARB 48.3g; FIBER 2.5g; CHOL 111mg; IRON 2.2mg; SODIUM 243mg; CALC 60mg

ORZO WITH CHICKEN AND ASIAGO

Preparation time: 5 minutes
Cooking time: 25 minutes

1 cup water
1 (16-ounce) can fat-free, less-sodium chicken broth
12 ounces skinned, boned chicken breast, cut into bite-size pieces
1¼ cups uncooked orzo (rice-shaped pasta)
1 cup frozen green peas, thawed
½ cup (2 ounces) grated Asiago or Parmesan cheese, divided
¼ teaspoon salt
¼ teaspoon dried rosemary, basil, or oregano
⅛ teaspoon black pepper

1. Combine water and broth in a Dutch oven; bring to a boil. Add chicken and pasta; bring to a boil. Reduce heat; simmer 12 minutes, stirring occasionally. Remove from heat; stir in peas, ¼ cup cheese, salt, herbs, and pepper. Top each serving with 1 tablespoon cheese. Yield: 4 servings (serving size: 1¼ cups).

CALORIES 384 (14% from fat); FAT 5.9g (sat 2.9g, mono 1.5g, poly 0.7g); PROTEIN 34.3g; CARB 45.7g; FIBER 2.9g; CHOL 64mg; IRON 3.3mg; SODIUM 656mg; CALC 179mg

SPINACH CALZONES WITH BLUE CHEESE

Preparation time: 18 minutes
Cooking time: 12 minutes

We found that a pizza cutter works well for dividing the refrigerated dough into 4 equal portions.

1 (10-ounce) can refrigerated pizza crust
Cooking spray
4 garlic cloves, minced
4 cups spinach leaves
8 (⅛-inch-thick) slices Vidalia or other sweet onion
1⅓ cups sliced cremini or button mushrooms
¾ cup (3 ounces) crumbled blue cheese

1. Preheat oven to 425°.
2. Unroll dough onto a baking sheet coated with cooking spray; cut into 4 quarters. Pat each quarter into a 6 x 5-inch rectangle. Sprinkle garlic over rectangles. Top each rectangle with 1 cup spinach, 2 onion slices, ⅓ cup mushrooms, and 3 tablespoons cheese. Bring 2 opposite corners to center, pinching points to seal. Bring remaining 2 corners to center, pinching all points together to seal. Bake at 425° for 12 minutes or until golden. Yield: 4 servings (serving size: 1 calzone).

CALORIES 297 (28% from fat); FAT 9.1g (sat 4g, mono 3.2g, poly 1g); PROTEIN 13.4g; CARB 40.7g; FIBER 5.1g; CHOL 16mg; IRON 3.8mg; SODIUM 818mg; CALC 180mg

JUNE

The Great Flavor Caper

The only mystery to cooking with capers is why this piquant seasoning isn't used more often for new accents on familiar dishes.

Although capers have been adding their distinctively briny taste to fish and other fare since antiquity, contemporary cooks are sometimes afraid to use them. The taste of capers is bold, but use these treasures wisely, as accents instead of themes, and you'll add an instant elegance drawn from the depths of the desert.

CHICKEN PICCATA

- 4 (4-ounce) skinned, boned chicken breast halves
- ¼ cup all-purpose flour
- ¼ teaspoon salt
- ¼ teaspoon black pepper
- 2 teaspoons butter or stick margarine, divided
- 1 teaspoon olive oil
- 1½ cups dry white wine, divided
- 2 tablespoons fresh lemon juice
- 2 tablespoons capers
- ½ cup chopped fresh flat-leaf parsley
- 4 cups hot cooked linguine (about 8 ounces uncooked pasta)

1. Place each chicken breast half between 2 sheets of heavy-duty plastic wrap; flatten to ¼-inch thickness, using a meat mallet. Combine flour, salt, and pepper; dredge chicken in flour mixture.
2. Heat 1 teaspoon butter and oil in a skillet over medium-high heat. Add chicken; cook 3 minutes on each side or until browned. Add ¾ cup wine, juice, and capers to pan, scraping pan to loosen browned bits. Cook 2 minutes. Remove chicken from pan; keep warm. Stir in ¾ cup wine; cook over high heat until reduced to ½ cup (about 5 minutes). Stir in 1 teaspoon butter and parsley. Serve chicken over linguine. Drizzle with sauce. Yield: 4 servings (serving size: 1 chicken breast half, 1 cup pasta, and 2 tablespoons sauce).

CALORIES 389 (13% from fat); FAT 5.5g (sat 1.1g, mono 2.2g, poly 1.4g); PROTEIN 34.3g; CARB 48.4g; FIBER 2.8g; CHOL 66mg; IRON 4mg; SODIUM 590mg; CALC 43mg

CUBAN-STYLE BEEF AND PEPPERS

- ¼ cup raisins
- ¼ cup white rum or apple juice
- 1 pound flank steak
- 2 tablespoons olive oil
- 3 cups thinly sliced onion
- 1 cup yellow bell pepper strips
- 1 jalapeño pepper, seeded and sliced
- 4 garlic cloves, minced
- 2 tablespoons capers
- 1 teaspoon chopped fresh or ¼ teaspoon dried thyme
- 1 teaspoon ground cumin
- 6 pimento-stuffed olives, chopped
- 3 plum tomatoes, each cut into 8 wedges
- 4 cups hot cooked long-grain rice

1. Combine raisins and rum in a small bowl; let stand 30 minutes.
2. Trim fat from steak, and cut steak into thin strips.
3. Heat oil in a nonstick skillet over medium-high heat. Add onion, bell pepper, and jalapeño; sauté 10 minutes or until tender. Add steak and garlic; sauté 4 minutes or until beef is browned. Add raisin mixture, capers, thyme, cumin, olives, and tomatoes. Reduce heat; simmer 7 minutes or until steak is done, stirring occasionally. Serve over rice. Yield: 4 servings (serving size: 1 cup beef mixture and 1 cup rice).

CALORIES 562 (30% from fat); FAT 18.5g (sat 5.6g, mono 9.6g, poly 1.2g); PROTEIN 29g; CARB 69.6g; FIBER 4.3g; CHOL 57mg; IRON 5.6mg; SODIUM 466mg; CALC 67mg

PAN-SEARED SEA SCALLOPS WITH SICILIAN PESTO

This pesto uses parsley instead of basil and a Sicilian-influenced combination of capers, golden raisins, and lemon rind.

Pesto:

- ¼ cup boiling water
- ¼ cup golden raisins
- 2 tablespoons capers
- 1 cup fresh flat-leaf parsley leaves
- 1 teaspoon grated lemon rind
- ½ cup fresh lemon juice
- ¼ cup diced shallots
- 2 tablespoons chopped fresh oregano
- ¼ teaspoon freshly ground black pepper
- 2 tablespoons olive oil
- 4 cups hot cooked angel hair (8 ounces uncooked pasta)

Scallops:

- 1½ pounds sea scallops
- 1 tablespoon olive oil
- ¼ cup dry white wine
- 1 tablespoon capers

1. To prepare pesto, combine boiling water and raisins in a small bowl; let stand 30 minutes (do not drain). Combine raisin mixture, 2 tablespoons capers, and next 6 ingredients in a blender; process until smooth. Add 2 tablespoons oil; process until well-blended. Combine pesto and pasta in a large bowl; toss well. Keep warm.
2. To prepare scallops, pat dry with paper towels. Heat 1 tablespoon oil in a large nonstick skillet over medium-high heat. Add scallops; cook 3 minutes on each side or until golden brown. Remove scallops from pan, and keep warm. Add wine to pan, scraping pan to loosen browned bits. Spoon 1 cup pasta onto each of 4 plates; top evenly with scallops, and drizzle with wine mixture. Sprinkle evenly with 1 tablespoon capers. Yield: 4 servings.

CALORIES 494 (23% from fat); FAT 12.7g (sat 1.7g, mono 7.7g, poly 1.8g); PROTEIN 36.8g; CARB 58.4g; FIBER 3.7g; CHOL 56mg; IRON 4.2mg; SODIUM 790mg; CALC 97mg

BRAISED ARTICHOKES WITH CAPERS AND PARSLEY

Serve with French bread or grilled polenta.

    6 cups water
    6 tablespoons fresh lemon juice,
          divided
    4 large artichokes (about
          1 pound each)
    1 tablespoon olive oil
    ¼ cup sliced shallots
    4 garlic cloves, minced
    2 cups dry white wine
    1 tablespoon capers
    1 (16-ounce) can fat-free,
          less-sodium chicken broth
    1 cup chopped fresh parsley

1. Combine water and 2 tablespoons juice. Working with 1 artichoke at a time, cut off stem to within 1 inch of base; peel stem. Remove bottom leaves and tough outer leaves, leaving tender heart and bottom. Remove fuzzy thistle from bottom with a spoon; discard. Cut artichoke into quarters lengthwise. Place artichoke quarters in lemon water. Repeat procedure with remaining artichokes. Drain.
2. Heat oil in a large Dutch oven over medium-high heat. Add shallots; sauté 2 minutes. Add garlic; sauté 30 seconds. Add artichoke quarters. Reduce heat; cook 5 minutes, stirring frequently. Add ¼ cup lemon juice, wine, capers, and broth; bring to a boil. Cover, reduce heat, and simmer 10 minutes. Uncover and simmer 15 minutes. Stir in parsley. Yield: 4 servings (serving size: 4 artichoke quarters).

CALORIES 142 (24% from fat); FAT 3.8g (sat 0.6g, mono 2.6g, poly 0.4g); PROTEIN 6.6g; CARB 24.6g; FIBER 8.1g; CHOL 0mg; IRON 3.9mg; SODIUM 540mg; CALC 108mg

MEDITERRANEAN PASTA WITH SHRIMP AND CAPERS

    1 tablespoon olive oil
    ¾ cup (½-inch) sliced green onions
    4 garlic cloves, minced
    6 cups chopped tomato (about
          2 pounds)
    1 tablespoon tomato paste
    1 tablespoon capers
    ½ teaspoon salt
    1 pound large shrimp, peeled and
          deveined
    2 tablespoons chopped fresh or
          2 teaspoons dried oregano
    5 cups hot cooked angel hair
          (about 10 ounces uncooked
          pasta)
    5 tablespoons (1¼ ounces) finely
          crumbled feta cheese
    ¼ teaspoon freshly ground black
          pepper

1. Heat oil in a large nonstick skillet over medium-high heat. Add onions and garlic, and sauté 2 minutes. Add tomato, and cook over medium heat 7 minutes. Add tomato paste, stirring well to combine. Add capers and salt; cook 15 minutes or until mixture begins to thicken. Stir in shrimp and oregano; cook 3 minutes or until shrimp are done. Combine shrimp mixture and pasta in a large bowl, tossing gently. Sprinkle with feta cheese and pepper. Yield: 5 servings (serving size: 1 cup).

CALORIES 384 (17% from fat); FAT 7.1g (sat 1.9g, mono 2.7g, poly 1.5g); PROTEIN 24.6g; CARB 56.4g; FIBER 4.8g; CHOL 110mg; IRON 5.5mg; SODIUM 577mg; CALC 118mg

---

CHOOSING CAPERS

Look for capers in the condiment section of your supermarket. The smaller, immature buds are the most expensive, but they're the most intensely flavored. Larger capers (from raisin-size to the size of a small olive) are fine to use, too. We chose small capers while testing our recipes. Capers are flavor-assertive, and a somewhat pricey bottle will last a long time.

SEARED TUNA STEAKS WITH BALSAMIC-CAPER SAUCE

    4 (6-ounce) tuna steaks (about
          ¾ inch thick)
    ¼ cup dry breadcrumbs
    1 tablespoon commercial pesto
    1 tablespoon water
       Cooking spray
    ¼ cup balsamic vinegar
    1 tablespoon capers
    ¼ cup diced shallots
    6 cups torn spinach (about
          1 pound)
    ½ cup dry white wine
    ¼ teaspoon freshly ground
          black pepper

1. Press tuna between paper towels until barely moist. Combine breadcrumbs, pesto, and water in a small bowl, tossing well. Pat breadcrumb mixture on both sides of tuna.
2. Heat a large nonstick skillet coated with cooking spray over medium-high heat until hot. Add tuna; cook 2 minutes on each side or until medium-rare or desired degree of doneness. Remove tuna from pan; keep warm. Stir in vinegar and capers, scraping pan to loosen browned bits; cook 1 minute. Remove from heat; set aside.
3. Place a large Dutch oven coated with cooking spray over medium-high heat until hot. Add shallots, and sauté 3 minutes or until tender. Add spinach, and sauté 1 minute. Add wine and pepper; partially cover and cook for 2 minutes or until spinach wilts. Spoon 1 cup spinach on each of 4 plates; top each serving with 1 tuna steak, and drizzle with 1 tablespoon caper sauce. Yield: 4 servings (serving size: 1 tuna steak, 1 cup spinach, and 1 tablespoon sauce).

CALORIES 331 (31% from fat); FAT 11.4g (sat 3g, mono 3.7g, poly 3.3g); PROTEIN 44.7g; CARB 12.1g; FIBER 5.1g; CHOL 65mg; IRON 6.1mg; SODIUM 429mg; CALC 163mg

Home (Again) on the Range

When Waylon and Willie warned mommas not to let their babies grow up to be cowboys, they sure weren't talkin' about the food.

Real cowboy food sustained real people doing really hard work; it relied on a base of beef, biscuits, beans, and locally available vegetables. Our recipes, meanwhile, are cowboy-revival dishes that focus on local ingredients and history. They're an amalgam of western, southwestern, northern Mexican, and Native American. Perhaps not rigidly traditional, they're genuine and downright delicious.

POTATO-AND-CHEESE BISCUITS

- 1 cup (1-inch) cubed peeled Yukon gold or red potato
- 1½ cups all-purpose flour
- 2 teaspoons baking powder
- ½ teaspoon baking soda
- ¼ teaspoon salt
- 2 tablespoons chilled butter or stick margarine, cut into small pieces
- ¾ cup (3 ounces) shredded reduced-fat sharp Cheddar cheese
- ½ cup plus 1 tablespoon low-fat buttermilk
- ¼ cup minced green onions
- 1 tablespoon cold water
- 1 large egg white, lightly beaten

1. Preheat oven to 425°.
2. Cook potato in boiling water 15 minutes or until very tender. Drain well; mash potato, and cool.
3. Lightly spoon flour into dry measuring cups; level with a knife. Combine flour, baking powder, baking soda, and salt in a bowl; cut in butter with a pastry blender or 2 knives until mixture resembles coarse meal. Add mashed potato, cheese, buttermilk, and green onions; stir just until moist.
4. Turn dough out onto a floured surface, and knead lightly 5 times. Roll dough to a ¾-inch thickness, and cut with a 3-inch biscuit cutter. Place on a baking sheet. Combine water and egg white, and brush over biscuits. Bake at 425° for 20 minutes or until golden. Yield: 9 biscuits (serving size: 1 biscuit).

CALORIES 151 (29% from fat); FAT 4.8g (sat 2.8g, mono 1.3g, poly 0.3g); PROTEIN 6.3g; CARB 20.6g; FIBER 0.9g; CHOL 13mg; IRON 1.3mg; SODIUM 353mg; CALC 170mg

RANCH SALAD

- 1 cup low-fat buttermilk
- ½ cup bottled medium salsa
- 3 tablespoons light mayonnaise
- 2 tablespoons chopped fresh parsley
- 1 tablespoon lemon juice
- ½ teaspoon sugar
- ½ teaspoon dry mustard
- ¼ teaspoon salt
- 6 cups torn iceberg lettuce
- 1 cup cherry tomatoes, halved
- ¾ cup sliced radishes
- 3 tablespoons sliced green onions

1. Combine first 8 ingredients in a blender; process until smooth.
2. Combine lettuce and next 3 ingredients in a large bowl. Add 1 cup dressing; toss well. Serve immediately. Yield: 6 servings (serving size: 1 cup).
Note: Store remaining dressing in an airtight container in refrigerator up to 2 weeks.

CALORIES 42 (36% from fat); FAT 1.7g (sat 0.4g, mono 0.4g, poly 0.7g); PROTEIN 1.9g; CARB 5.5g; FIBER 1.2g; CHOL 1mg; IRON 0.6mg; SODIUM 146mg; CALC 47mg

RUBBED FLANK STEAK WITH HORSERADISH CREAM

Steak:

- 1 (1½-pound) flank steak
- ¼ cup rye or bourbon whiskey
- 2 tablespoons low-sodium soy sauce

Horseradish cream:

- ⅓ cup plain fat-free yogurt
- 2 tablespoons prepared horseradish
- 1 teaspoon Dijon mustard
- 1 large garlic clove, minced

Rub:

- 1 tablespoon sugar
- 1 tablespoon paprika
- 1 tablespoon chili powder
- 1½ teaspoons black pepper
- 1 teaspoon garlic powder
- ⅛ teaspoon salt
- Cooking spray

1. To prepare steak, trim fat from steak. Place whiskey and soy sauce in a large zip-top plastic bag. Add steak; seal and marinate in refrigerator 24 hours, turning bag occasionally.
2. To prepare horseradish cream, combine yogurt, horseradish, mustard, and minced garlic in a small bowl. Cover and chill.
3. To prepare rub, combine sugar and next 5 ingredients. Remove steak from bag; discard marinade. Rub sugar mixture over steak; chill 30 minutes.
4. Prepare grill or broiler.
5. Place steak on a grill rack or broiler pan coated with cooking spray, and cook 8 minutes on each side or until desired degree of doneness. Cut steak diagonally across grain into thin slices. Serve with horseradish cream. Yield: 6 servings (serving size: 3 ounces steak and 1 tablespoon horseradish cream).

CALORIES 232 (43% from fat); FAT 11.2g (sat 4.7g, mono 4.4g, poly 0.6g); PROTEIN 24g; CARB 6.5g; FIBER 1g; CHOL 57mg; IRON 3mg; SODIUM 276mg; CALC 43mg

SPICY BUFFALO CHILI

½ pound dried black beans
    (about 1¼ cups)
10 cups water, divided
1 dried ancho chile (about ½
    ounce)
1 tablespoon olive oil
1 pound boned buffalo steak or
    beef sirloin steak, cut into
    1-inch cubes
1 cup chopped onion
1 large garlic clove, minced
1 cup finely chopped carrot
1 cup finely chopped red bell
    pepper
½ cup finely chopped celery
1 tablespoon ground cumin
2 teaspoons dried oregano
1 teaspoon paprika
½ to 1 teaspoon dried crushed red
    pepper
1 (28-ounce) can diced tomatoes,
    undrained
1 (12-ounce) bottle dark beer
¼ cup tomato paste
2 tablespoons brown sugar
½ teaspoon salt
⅛ teaspoon black pepper

1. Sort and wash beans; place in a large Dutch oven. Cover with water to 2 inches above beans; bring to a boil, and cook 2 minutes. Remove from heat; cover and let stand 1 hour. Drain. Return beans to pan, and add 8 cups water. Bring to a boil; reduce heat, and simmer 30 minutes or until beans are tender. Drain; set aside.
2. Combine 2 cups water and ancho chile in a small saucepan, and bring to a boil. Remove from heat; cover and let stand 20 minutes or until soft. Drain and discard seeds and membranes. Chop and set aside.
3. Heat oil in a large Dutch oven over medium-high heat; add buffalo steak, browning on all sides. Add onion and garlic; sauté 3 minutes. Add carrot, bell pepper, and celery; cook 3 minutes. Stir in cumin, oregano, paprika, and crushed red pepper; cook 1 minute. Stir in ancho chile, tomatoes, and beer; bring to a boil. Cover, reduce heat, and simmer 30 minutes. Stir in beans and tomato paste; cook, covered, 15 minutes. Stir in sugar, salt, and black pepper. Yield: 8 servings (serving size: 1 cup).

Note: To mail-order buffalo steak, call D'Artagnan at 800/327-8246.

CALORIES 236 (14% from fat); FAT 3.6g (sat 0.7g, mono 1.7g, poly 0.8g); PROTEIN 19.9g; CARB 33.1g; FIBER 11.3g; CHOL 26mg; IRON 4.4mg; SODIUM 363mg; CALC 101mg

TORTILLA-CHICKEN CASSEROLE

3 ears shucked corn

Salsa:

3 cups chopped tomato (about
    3 medium tomatoes)
½ cup sliced green onions
⅓ cup minced fresh cilantro
1 tablespoon minced seeded
    jalapeño pepper
2 teaspoons lime juice
2 garlic cloves, minced
1 (8-ounce) can tomato sauce

Chicken:

3 cups water
2 teaspoons dried oregano
1 teaspoon ground cumin
¼ teaspoon salt
2 large garlic cloves, sliced
12 ounces skinned, boned chicken
    breast

Sauce:

2 tablespoons all-purpose flour
1 teaspoon chili powder
¼ teaspoon salt
¼ teaspoon ground red pepper

Remaining ingredients:

Cooking spray
12 (6-inch) corn tortillas, cut in
    half
¾ cup (3 ounces) shredded
    reduced-fat extra-sharp
    Cheddar cheese, divided
½ cup low-fat sour cream
Shredded leaf lettuce (optional)

1. Place corn on a microwave-safe plate, and cover with wax paper. Microwave at HIGH 5 minutes or just until tender. Cut kernels from ears of corn to measure 1 cup.
2. To prepare salsa, combine tomato and next 6 ingredients in a bowl; set aside.
3. To prepare chicken, combine water, oregano, cumin, ¼ teaspoon salt, and sliced garlic in a large saucepan; bring to a simmer. Add chicken; partially cover, reduce heat, and simmer 20 minutes or until done. Remove chicken from cooking liquid, reserving cooking liquid, and cool slightly. Shred chicken with 2 forks; place in a bowl. Bring cooking liquid to a boil; cook until reduced to 1½ cups (about 9 minutes). Cool; discard sliced garlic.
4. Preheat oven to 375°.
5. To prepare sauce, place flour, chili powder, ¼ teaspoon salt, and red pepper in saucepan, and gradually add cooking liquid, stirring with a whisk until blended. Cook over medium heat 4 minutes or until thick. Stir ¾ cup sauce into chicken in bowl.
6. Spread ¾ cup salsa in bottom of a 13 x 9-inch baking dish coated with cooking spray. Arrange 8 tortilla halves over salsa; top with ¾ cup salsa, half of chicken mixture, half of corn, and ¼ cup cheese. Repeat layers, ending with 8 tortilla halves. Spread remaining salsa over tortilla halves, and top with remaining sauce. Bake at 375° for 35 minutes. Sprinkle with ¼ cup cheese, and bake an additional 5 minutes or until thoroughly heated. Let casserole stand 10 minutes before serving. Top each serving with 1 tablespoon sour cream. Serve with leaf lettuce, if desired. Yield: 8 servings.

CALORIES 244 (23% from fat); FAT 6.1g (sat 2.7g, mono 1.6g, poly 1g); PROTEIN 17.9g; CARB 31.6g; FIBER 4.1g; CHOL 37mg; IRON 2.2mg; SODIUM 415mg; CALC 210mg

CHILI-ROASTED POTATOES

2 tablespoons water
2 tablespoons lemon juice
1 tablespoon olive oil
1 teaspoon Worcestershire sauce
1 teaspoon Thai chili paste (such as Dynasty)
½ teaspoon dried oregano
¼ teaspoon salt
¼ teaspoon ground cumin
¼ teaspoon ground red pepper
4 red potatoes (about 1½ pounds), each cut into 6 wedges
1 red onion, cut into 6 wedges
1 red bell pepper, seeded and cut into ½-inch strips
8 garlic cloves, peeled

1. Preheat oven to 400°.
2. Combine first 9 ingredients in a large bowl, and stir with a whisk. Add potato, onion, bell pepper, and garlic; toss well. Arrange vegetable mixture in a single layer in a shallow roasting pan; bake at 400° for 35 minutes or until potato is tender, stirring after 20 minutes. Yield: 4 servings (serving size: 1 cup).

CALORIES 189 (18% from fat); FAT 3.8g (sat 0.6g, mono 2.5g, poly 0.5g); PROTEIN 4.9g; CARB 36g; FIBER 4.3g; CHOL 0mg; IRON 2.9mg; SODIUM 206mg; CALC 48mg

SMOKY COWBOY QUESADILLAS

½ cup bottled salsa
8 (6-inch) fat-free flour tortillas
1 cup chopped smoked turkey ham (about 4 ounces)
½ cup fresh corn kernels (about 1 ear)
¼ cup chopped fresh cilantro
¾ cup (3 ounces) shredded Monterey Jack cheese with jalapeño peppers

1. Spread 2 tablespoons salsa over each of 4 tortillas; top each with ¼ cup ham, 2 tablespoons corn, 1 tablespoon cilantro, 3 tablespoons cheese, and a tortilla.

2. Place a nonstick skillet over medium heat until hot. Add 1 quesadilla; cook 2 minutes on each side or until crisp. Repeat procedure with remaining quesadillas. Cut each quesadilla into 6 wedges. Yield: 8 servings (serving size: 3 wedges).

CALORIES 154 (24% from fat); FAT 4.1g (sat 2.3g, mono 1.1g, poly 0.4g); PROTEIN 8g; CARB 21.3g; FIBER 1.4g; CHOL 8mg; IRON 1.7mg; SODIUM 598mg; CALC 132mg

PRAIRIE-FIRE BEANS

1 pound dried pinto beans (about 2 cups)
8 cups water
2 bay leaves
1 small onion, peeled
4 bacon slices, cut into ½-inch pieces
1 cup minced onion
2 garlic cloves, minced
1 (12-ounce) bottle beer
1 tablespoon dried oregano
2 to 3 teaspoons hot sauce
½ teaspoon salt
¼ teaspoon black pepper

1. Sort and wash beans; place in a large Dutch oven. Cover with water to 2 inches above beans; bring to a boil, and cook 2 minutes. Remove from heat; cover and let stand 1 hour. Drain.
2. Return beans to pan; add 8 cups water, bay leaves, and small onion. Bring to a boil; reduce heat, and simmer 1 hour or until beans are tender. Drain beans; discard bay leaves and onion.
3. Cook bacon slices in Dutch oven over medium-high heat until crisp. Remove bacon slices from pan, reserving drippings. Add minced onion and garlic to pan; sauté 5 minutes. Add beans, bacon, beer, and remaining ingredients. Bring to a boil; reduce heat, and simmer 5 minutes. Yield: 12 servings (serving size: ½ cup).

CALORIES 193 (28% from fat); FAT 5.9g (sat 2.1g, mono 2.6g, poly 0.8g); PROTEIN 9g; CARB 26.7g; FIBER 4.9g; CHOL 6mg; IRON 2.5mg; SODIUM 174mg; CALC 58mg

30 MINUTES OR LESS

Fresh Fish Fast

For naturally tender, superfast meals, the smartest solution is from the sea.

MENU SUGGESTION

MARGARITA SALMON

Angel hair pasta

Asparagus salad with feta dressing*

*Blanch 1½ pounds (2-inch) cut fresh asparagus. Combine asparagus, 6 cups torn leaf lettuce, ⅓ cup fat-free Caesar salad dressing, and 2 tablespoons crumbled feta cheese. Garnish salad with freshly ground black pepper. Serves 4.

MARGARITA SALMON

Preparation/marinating time: 20 minutes
Cooking time: 8 minutes

1 teaspoon grated lime rind
3 tablespoons fresh lime or lemon juice
1 tablespoon tequila
2 teaspoons sugar
2 teaspoons vegetable oil
½ teaspoon salt
½ teaspoon grated orange rind
1 garlic clove, crushed
4 (6-ounce) salmon fillets (about 1 inch thick)
8 ounces uncooked angel hair pasta
Lime slices (optional)

1. Combine first 8 ingredients in a large zip-top plastic bag; add fish to bag. Seal and marinate in refrigerator 20 minutes.
2. While fish is marinating, cook pasta according to package directions, omitting salt and fat. Drain and keep warm. Remove fish from bag; reserve marinade.

3. Preheat broiler.

4. Place fish on a broiler pan coated with cooking spray; broil 7 minutes or until fish flakes easily when tested with a fork, basting occasionally with reserved marinade. Serve over pasta. Garnish with lime slices, if desired. Yield: 4 servings (serving size: 1 fillet and 1 cup pasta).

CALORIES 520 (30% from fat); FAT 17.3g (sat 2.9g, mono 7.5g, poly 4.5g); PROTEIN 42.2g; CARB 45.9g; FIBER 1.4g; CHOL 111mg; IRON 0.7mg; SODIUM 381mg; CALC 23mg

CARIBBEAN CONFETTI SHRIMP

Preparation time: 16 minutes
Cooking time: 14 minutes

Buy peeled and deveined shrimp because it's a real time-saver. Start cooking the rice first, so it will be done at about the same time as the shrimp.

    2   teaspoons olive oil
    ½   cup diced onion
    ½   cup red bell pepper strips
    ½   cup green bell pepper strips
    2   garlic cloves, minced
    1   tablespoon cider vinegar
    ¼   teaspoon black pepper
    8   pimento-stuffed olives, halved
    1   (14.5-ounce) can stewed
          tomatoes, undrained
    2   bay leaves
    1   pound peeled, deveined
          medium shrimp
    1   cup frozen green peas, thawed
    2   cups hot cooked long-grain
          rice

1. Heat oil in a large nonstick skillet over medium-high heat until hot. Add onion, bell peppers, and garlic; sauté 3 minutes. Add vinegar and next 4 ingredients; bring to a boil. Cover, reduce heat to medium, and cook 5 minutes. Add shrimp; cover and cook 4 minutes. Add peas; cover and cook 1 minute. Discard bay leaves. Serve with rice. Yield: 4 servings (serving size: 1 cup shrimp mixture and ½ cup rice).

CALORIES 306 (15% from fat); FAT 5.1g (sat 0.8g, mono 2.5g, poly 1g); PROTEIN 22.9g; CARB 41.3g; FIBER 3.4g; CHOL 129mg; IRON 4.5mg; SODIUM 759mg; CALC 105mg

POTATO-CRUSTED SNAPPER

Preparation time: 5 minutes
Cooking time: 6 minutes

    ½   cup low-fat buttermilk
    ¼   teaspoon salt
    ¼   teaspoon black pepper
    2   garlic cloves, minced
    ¾   cup instant potato flakes
          (not granules)
    4   (6-ounce) red snapper or
          mahimahi fillets
    1   tablespoon butter or stick
          margarine
    4   lemon wedges

1. Combine first 4 ingredients in a shallow dish. Place potato flakes in another shallow dish. Dip fillets in buttermilk mixture; dredge in potato flakes. Melt butter in a large nonstick skillet over medium-high heat. Add fish; cook 3 minutes on each side or until golden and fish flakes easily when tested with a fork. Serve with lemon wedges. Yield: 4 servings.

CALORIES 244 (21% from fat); FAT 5.7g (sat 1.4g, mono 1.8g, poly 1.7g); PROTEIN 36.9g; CARB 9.2g; FIBER 0.4g; CHOL 63mg; IRON 0.5mg; SODIUM 316mg; CALC 101mg

PORTUGUESE-STYLE SCALLOPS

(pictured on page 151)

Preparation time: 5 minutes
Cooking time: 15 minutes

    1½ pounds sea scallops
    ½   teaspoon salt
    ¼   teaspoon black pepper
    1   tablespoon olive oil, divided
    ⅓   cup tawny port or other sweet
          red wine
    2   tablespoons fresh lemon juice
    ¼   cup chopped fresh parsley,
          divided
    5   garlic cloves, minced
    2   cups hot cooked long-grain rice

1. Sprinkle scallops with salt and pepper. Heat 1½ teaspoons oil in a 10-inch cast-iron or heavy skillet over high heat until very hot (about 3 minutes). Add half of scallops; cook 2 minutes on each side or until browned. Remove scallops from pan; keep warm. Repeat procedure with 1½ teaspoons oil and remaining scallops.

2. Combine port and lemon juice in pan, scraping pan to loosen browned bits. Add scallops, 3 tablespoons parsley, and garlic; sauté 30 seconds over high heat. Serve scallops over rice. Sprinkle with 1 tablespoon parsley. Yield: 4 servings (serving size: 5 ounces scallops and ½ cup rice).

CALORIES 241 (15% from fat); FAT 3.9g (sat 0.5g, mono 2.1g, poly 0.6g); PROTEIN 24.8g; CARB 25g; FIBER 0.6g; CHOL 45mg; IRON 1.4mg; SODIUM 456mg; CALC 52mg

CLASSICS

Purple Reign

The oddball name and intense color of the eggplant might just be there to attract attention to this versatile—berry.

Eggplant is actually a berry and is a member of the nightshade family of fruits, which also includes peppers, potatoes, and tomatoes. Eggplant is low in calories and has virtually no fat.

PARMESAN-EGGPLANT CRISPS

Chilling the coated slices before baking makes the eggplant extracrispy.

    ¼   cup fat-free mayonnaise
    1   (¾-pound) eggplant, cut
          crosswise into 24 slices
    ½   cup crushed saltine crackers
          (about 12 crackers)
    ½   cup (2 ounces) grated fresh
          Parmesan cheese
    Cooking spray

1. Spread about ½ teaspoon mayonnaise over both sides of eggplant slices, using a rubber spatula. Combine

Continued

crackers and cheese in a shallow dish; dredge eggplant in cracker mixture. Place eggplant in a single layer on a baking sheet coated with cooking spray; chill 2 hours.

2. Preheat oven to 425°.

3. Bake eggplant at 425° for 15 minutes; turn eggplant slices over, and bake an additional 5 minutes or until crisp. Yield: 4 servings (serving size: 6 slices).

CALORIES 124 (33% from fat); FAT 4.6g (sat 2.6g, mono 1.4g, poly 0.2g); PROTEIN 6.4g; CARB 14.4g; FIBER 2g; CHOL 10mg; IRON 0.5mg; SODIUM 545mg; CALC 183mg

OPEN-FACED LAMB BURGERS WITH EGGPLANT AND MUSHROOMS

1 pound lean ground lamb
2 tablespoons minced fresh or 2 teaspoons dried mint
½ teaspoon ground cumin
¼ teaspoon salt
¼ teaspoon freshly ground black pepper
2 teaspoons olive oil, divided
4 cups diced peeled eggplant (about 1 pound)
2 cups vertically sliced Vidalia or other sweet onion
2 cups thinly sliced shiitake mushroom caps (about 4 ounces)
1 tablespoon balsamic vinegar
4 (¼-inch-thick) slices tomato
2 (1½-ounce) French bread rolls, halved and toasted

1. Prepare grill.

2. Combine first 5 ingredients in a large bowl. Divide lamb mixture into 4 equal portions, shaping each into a ½-inch-thick patty. Place patties on a grill rack; grill 4 minutes on each side or until lamb is done. Keep warm.

3. Heat 1 teaspoon oil in a large non-stick skillet over medium-high heat. Add eggplant, and sauté 3 minutes. Remove from pan. Heat 1 teaspoon oil in pan; add onion, and cook 7 minutes or until golden brown, stirring frequently. Add mushrooms; cook 3 minutes. Stir in eggplant and vinegar. Remove from heat.

4. Place 1 tomato slice and 1 patty on each roll half; top each with one-fourth of eggplant mixture. Yield: 4 servings.

CALORIES 319 (34% from fat); FAT 11.9g (sat 3.5g, mono 5.8g, poly 1.1g); PROTEIN 29.7g; CARB 23.2g; FIBER 4.5g; CHOL 81mg; IRON 3.3mg; SODIUM 355mg; CALC 59mg

COUSCOUS WITH ROASTED VEGETABLES, CHICKEN SAUSAGE, AND HARISSA

This is actually best made a day ahead so the flavors can blend. For a vegetarian entrée, omit the sausage. Harissa is a fiery-hot condiment sold at Middle Eastern markets.

Vegetables:

1 small eggplant (about ¾ pound), cut into 6 wedges
2 small leeks (about ¾ pound), trimmed and each cut in half lengthwise
1 zucchini (about ½ pound), cut into 4 wedges
2 (3-ounce) chicken sausages with basil and pine nuts (such as Gerhard's)
1 Vidalia or other sweet onion, cut into 8 wedges
1 large red bell pepper, cut into 1-inch strips
1 tablespoon balsamic vinegar
1½ teaspoons olive oil
1½ tablespoons chopped fresh or 1½ teaspoons dried thyme
¼ teaspoon salt
¼ teaspoon freshly ground black pepper
5 large garlic cloves, unpeeled

Dressing:

2 tablespoons fresh lemon juice
1 tablespoon balsamic vinegar
1½ teaspoons olive oil
2 tablespoons chopped fresh or 2 teaspoons dried basil
½ teaspoon ground cumin
¼ teaspoon salt

Couscous:

1¼ cups water
¾ cup uncooked couscous
1 (15½-ounce) can chickpeas (garbanzo beans), drained
2 tablespoons commercial harissa
2 tablespoons water

1. Preheat oven to 450°.

2. To prepare vegetables, combine first 11 ingredients; toss well. Place vegetable mixture and garlic on a large foil-lined baking sheet. Bake at 450° for 20 minutes or until vegetables are browned and sausages are done. Set garlic cloves aside. Cut vegetables into 1-inch pieces. Cut sausages into ¼-inch-thick slices.

3. To prepare dressing, squeeze garlic cloves into a large bowl to extract garlic pulp. Discard skins. Mash garlic pulp with a fork. Add lemon juice and next 5 ingredients to garlic pulp, and stir well.

4. To prepare couscous, bring 1¼ cups water to a boil in a medium saucepan. Gradually stir in couscous. Remove from heat; cover and let stand 5 minutes. Fluff couscous with a fork. Combine couscous, chickpeas, dressing, vegetables, and sausage in a large bowl; toss gently.

5. Combine harissa and 2 tablespoons water in a small bowl. Spoon 2 cups couscous mixture into each of 4 serving bowls. Drizzle each serving with 1 tablespoon harissa mixture. Yield: 4 servings.

CALORIES 358 (29% from fat); FAT 11.6g (sat 2.2g, mono 5.2g, poly 3g); PROTEIN 18g; CARB 50g; FIBER 8.4g; CHOL 38mg; IRON 5.4mg; SODIUM 1,044mg; CALC 102mg

EXAMINING EGGPLANT

As is the case with many vegetables, eggplant is mostly water, with only 13 calories per ½ cup; that means negligible calories or carbohydrates to offset fat. In many of these recipes, for example, the fat content exceeds 30% of total calories. But eggplant still comes out a winner, because the actual number of fat grams per recipe is very low.

LAMB MOUSSAKA

This lamb-and-eggplant casserole is the national dish of Greece. It's great for entertaining. Serve with a Greek salad.

Lamb mixture:

1½   pounds lean ground lamb or
       beef
  2   cups chopped onion
      Cooking spray
 ½   cup dried currants or raisins
  1   teaspoon salt
 ½   teaspoon dried oregano
 ½   teaspoon ground cinnamon
 ¼   teaspoon ground nutmeg
 ¼   teaspoon black pepper
  4   (14.5-ounce) cans diced
       tomatoes, undrained
  1   large garlic clove, minced

Sauce:

  2   cups 1% low-fat milk, divided
  1   tablespoon butter or stick
       margarine
  3   large egg whites
 ¼   cup all-purpose flour
 ½   teaspoon salt

Remaining ingredients:

  2   (1¼-pound) eggplants, cut
       lengthwise into ¼-inch-thick
       slices
  1   tablespoon olive oil, divided
  1   pound peeled baking potatoes,
       cut into ¼-inch-thick slices
 ¼   cup (1 ounce) grated fresh
       Parmesan cheese, divided
      Oregano sprigs (optional)

1. To prepare lamb mixture, cook lamb in a large Dutch oven over medium-high heat until browned; stir to crumble. Remove from pan; drain. Set aside. Wipe skillet with paper towels.
2. Add onion to pan coated with cooking spray; sauté 5 minutes. Add lamb, currants, and next 7 ingredients; bring to a boil. Cook until thick (about 30 minutes).
3. Preheat broiler.

4. To prepare sauce, cook 1½ cups milk and butter in a heavy saucepan over medium-high heat to 180° or until tiny bubbles form around edge (do not boil). Remove from heat. Combine ½ cup milk, egg whites, flour, and ½ teaspoon salt in a large bowl; gradually add hot milk mixture to egg white mixture, stirring constantly with a whisk. Return milk mixture to pan, and cook until thick (about 15 minutes), stirring constantly. Remove from heat.
5. Place half of eggplant slices on a baking sheet coated with cooking spray; brush with 1½ teaspoons oil. Broil 4 minutes on each side or until browned. Repeat procedure with remaining eggplant and 1½ teaspoons oil.
6. Preheat oven to 375°.
7. Cook potato slices in boiling water 5 minutes or until crisp-tender; drain. Rinse with cold water; drain well.
8. Arrange potatoes in a 13 x 9-inch baking dish coated with cooking spray. Arrange half of eggplant slices over potatoes. Pour 4 cups lamb mixture over eggplant, and sprinkle with 1 tablespoon cheese. Arrange remaining eggplant over cheese, and top with remaining lamb mixture. Sprinkle with 1 tablespoon cheese. Spread sauce over cheese, and sprinkle with 2 tablespoons cheese. Bake at 375° for 45 minutes or until top is golden brown. Let stand 15 minutes. Garnish with oregano sprigs, if desired. Yield: 8 servings.

CALORIES 374 (28% from fat); FAT 11.7g (sat 4.3g, mono 4.9g, poly 1g); PROTEIN 28.1g; CARB 40.4g; FIBER 4.7g; CHOL 69mg; IRON 3.5mg; SODIUM 933mg; CALC 200mg

---

COLORFUL CHOICES

Among dozens of varieties—from large to small, and purple to white—the most common eggplant is the large, dark-purple American found year-round. Other types include the long, thin, pale-purple Chinese eggplant, which has a mild flavor. Look for eggplants that have smooth, shiny skin and are firm. Store them in a cool place, and use them within two days.

SESAME-EGGPLANT SALAD WITH BELL PEPPERS AND JICAMA

To toast sesame seeds, place them in a dry skillet over medium heat, and sauté until brown (about 5 minutes).

Dressing:

  1   tablespoon toasted sesame seeds
  2   tablespoons minced green
       onions
  2   tablespoons minced fresh
       cilantro
  2   tablespoons minced fresh mint
  2   tablespoons rice or white wine
       vinegar
  2   tablespoons low-sodium soy
       sauce
  2   teaspoons dark sesame oil
  1   tablespoon fresh lemon juice
  2   garlic cloves, minced

Salad:

  1   small eggplant (about 12
       ounces), quartered lengthwise
       and sliced
      Cooking spray
  3   cups (2 x ¼-inch) strips peeled
       jicama
  3   cups red and green bell pepper
       strips

1. To prepare dressing, combine first 9 ingredients in a bowl; stir with a whisk.
2. Preheat broiler.
3. To prepare salad, combine 3 tablespoons dressing and eggplant, tossing to coat. Arrange eggplant slices in a single layer on a baking sheet coated with cooking spray. Broil 4 minutes on each side. Combine remaining dressing, eggplant, jicama, and bell peppers, tossing to coat. Yield: 6 servings (serving size: 1 cup).

CALORIES 77 (33% from fat); FAT 2.8g (sat 0.4g, mono 0.9g, poly 1.2g); PROTEIN 2g; CARB 12.4g; FIBER 5.1g; CHOL 0mg; IRON 1.6mg; SODIUM 168mg; CALC 34mg

CAPONATA WITH GARLIC CROSTINI

This Sicilian appetizer will keep in the refrigerator one to two days. Bring to room temperature before serving.

Caponata:

1 tablespoon olive oil
4 cups diced eggplant (about 1 pound)
1 cup coarsely chopped Vidalia or other sweet onion
½ cup diced red bell pepper
½ cup diced yellow bell pepper
1 garlic clove, minced
1 tablespoon brown sugar
2 tablespoons fresh lemon juice
½ teaspoon salt
¼ cup golden raisins
2 tablespoons capers, drained
1 tablespoon pine nuts, toasted
2 tablespoons chopped fresh or 2 teaspoons dried basil

Crostini:

24 (½-inch-thick) slices diagonally cut French bread baguette (about 10 ounces)
1 garlic clove, halved
Olive oil-flavored cooking spray

1. Preheat oven to 375°.
2. To prepare caponata, heat oil in a large nonstick skillet over medium-high heat. Add eggplant, onion, bell peppers, and minced garlic, and sauté 5 minutes. Stir in sugar, lemon juice, and salt; cook 1 minute. Stir in raisins, capers, and pine nuts. Place eggplant mixture in a large bowl; stir in basil.
3. To prepare crostini, place bread slices on a baking sheet. Bake at 375° for 7 minutes or until toasted. Rub cut sides of garlic clove over one side of bread slices. Coat bread slices with cooking spray, and bake an additional 2 minutes. Serve caponata with crostini. Yield: 8 servings (serving size: ⅓ cup caponata and 3 crostini).

CALORIES 174 (20% from fat); FAT 3.8g (sat 0.6g, mono 2g, poly 0.8g); PROTEIN 4.9g; CARB 31.4g; FIBER 3.2g; CHOL 0mg; IRON 1.6mg; SODIUM 552mg; CALC 44mg

EGGPLANT MIXED GRILL

2 tablespoons olive oil
2 tablespoons chopped fresh parsley
2 tablespoons chopped fresh oregano
2 tablespoons chopped fresh basil
1 tablespoon balsamic vinegar
1 teaspoon kosher salt
½ teaspoon black pepper
6 garlic cloves, minced
1 red onion
18 asparagus spears (about ¾ pound)
12 cremini mushroom caps
1 (1-pound) eggplant, cut crosswise into 16 (¼-inch-thick) slices
1 red bell pepper, cut into 6 wedges
1 yellow bell pepper, cut into 6 wedges
Cooking spray

1. Combine first 8 ingredients in an extra-large zip-top plastic bag. Cut onion into 6 wedges, leaving root end intact. Add onion, asparagus, and next 4 ingredients to bag. Seal and marinate in refrigerator 2 hours, turning bag occasionally.
2. Prepare grill.
3. Remove vegetables from bag. Place vegetables on a grill rack coated with cooking spray; grill 6 minutes on each side or until tender. Yield: 6 servings.

CALORIES 100 (48% from fat); FAT 5.3g (sat 0.7g, mono 3.4g, poly 0.7g); PROTEIN 3g; CARB 12.7g; FIBER 4.1g; CHOL 0mg; IRON 1.9mg; SODIUM 202mg; CALC 29mg

AT LAST

La-Di-Da

It's not running, and it's not walking. It's sauntering. In a world too fast, this is a speed to last. In definition: "To walk with a leisurely gait." In practice: Never hurry, never wait.

MOCHA PARFAITS WITH FUDGE SAUCE

Eat this at just the right pace. Too fast is no fun and too slow it'll start to run. Strive for a sauntering savor.

½ cup coarsely chopped reduced-fat double chocolate chip cookies (about 20 bite-size cookies) (such as Snackwell's)
2 cups low-fat latte or coffee ice cream (such as Starbucks), softened
¼ cup Chocolate Fudge Sauce
¼ cup frozen fat-free whipped topping, thawed
Coffee beans (optional)

1. Place 4 (8-ounce) parfait glasses in freezer, and freeze 10 minutes. Spoon 1 tablespoon cookie crumbs into each glass; top with ¼ cup ice cream, 1 tablespoon fudge sauce, 1 tablespoon cookie crumbs, and ¼ cup ice cream. Freeze 2 hours or until firm. Top each parfait with 1 tablespoon whipped topping. Garnish with coffee beans, if desired. Serve immediately. Yield: 4 servings.

CALORIES 273 (16% from fat); FAT 4.9g (sat 2.3g, mono 1.2g, poly 1g); PROTEIN 6.4g; CARB 25.3g; FIBER 0.4g; CHOL 10mg; IRON 0.8mg; SODIUM 139mg; CALC 153mg

Chocolate Fudge Sauce:

½ cup sugar
¼ cup unsweetened cocoa
1 tablespoon cornstarch
⅓ cup water
1 teaspoon vanilla extract

1. Combine first 3 ingredients in a saucepan; stir well with a whisk. Stir in water. Bring to a boil over medium heat; cook 1 minute. Remove from heat; stir in vanilla. Spoon into an airtight container; chill. Yield: ⅔ cup (serving size: about 1 tablespoon).

CALORIES 48 (6% from fat); FAT 0.3g (sat 0.2g, mono 0g, poly 0g); PROTEIN 0.6g; CARB 10.8g; FIBER 0g; CHOL 0mg; IRON 0.3mg; SODIUM 1mg; CALC 3mg

Broccoli, Cherry Tomato, and Pasta Salad, page 166

Cantaloupe-and-Cherry Tomato Salsa, page 160

Melanie's Garden-Tomato Soup, page 159

Roasted-Vegetable Lasagna, page 160

Portuguese-Style Scallops, page 145

Italian Balsamic Chicken, page 157,
and Indian-Spiced Shrimp, page 156

Cherry Trifle with Amaretto, page 164

Coolest of the Hottest

You can't get enough fresh fruit or cool drinks in the summertime.

Juice drinks offer healthy alternatives to soft drinks and alcohol. Fresh juice tends to be low in fat, high in vitamins A and C, and a rich source of cancer-fighting antioxidants. You'll need a blender for these smoothie-type beverages inspired by Spanish juice drinks.

TROPICAL WAVE

- 1½ cups sliced ripe banana
- 1 cup cubed fresh pineapple
- 1 cup cubed peeled ripe mango
- 1 cup papaya nectar, chilled
- 2 tablespoons fresh lime juice

1. Place banana, pineapple, and mango in freezer, and freeze until firm (about 1 hour). Remove from freezer, and let stand 10 minutes. Combine fruit, nectar, and juice in a blender; process until smooth. Serve immediately. Yield: 3 servings (serving size: 1 cup).

CALORIES 184 (3% from fat); FAT 0.7g (sat 0.2g, mono 0.1g, poly 0.2g); PROTEIN 1.3g; CARB 47g; FIBER 3.2g; CHOL 0mg; IRON 0.7mg; SODIUM 2mg; CALC 15mg

WATERMELON WONDER

- 2 cups cubed seeded watermelon
- 1 cup lemon-lime soda (such as Sprite), chilled
- 2 tablespoons fresh lime juice
- ⅔ cup ice cubes

1. Place watermelon in freezer; freeze until firm (about 1 hour). Remove from freezer, and let stand 10 minutes. Combine watermelon, soda, and juice in a blender, and process until smooth. With blender on, add ice cubes, 1 at a time; process until smooth. Serve immediately. Yield: 2 servings (serving size: 1½ cups).

CALORIES 97 (6% from fat); FAT 0.7g (sat 0.1g, mono 0.2g, poly 0.2g); PROTEIN 1g; CARB 23.5g; FIBER 0.8g; CHOL 0mg; IRON 0.3mg; SODIUM 23mg; CALC 14mg

PIÑA COLADA SLUSH

- 2 cups cubed fresh pineapple
- 1½ cups pineapple juice, chilled
- ¼ cup cream of coconut (such as Coco Lopez)
- 1 cup ice cubes
- 1 cup vanilla fat-free frozen yogurt

1. Place pineapple in freezer; freeze until firm (about 1 hour). Remove from freezer; let stand 10 minutes. Combine juice and cream of coconut in a blender. With blender on, add pineapple and ice cubes, 1 at a time; process until smooth. Add yogurt; process until smooth. Serve immediately. Yield: 4 servings (serving size: 1 cup).

CALORIES 175 (29% from fat); FAT 5.6g (sat 4.6g, mono 0.3g, poly 0.2g); PROTEIN 2.6g; CARB 31.3g; FIBER 1.4g; CHOL 0mg; IRON 0.9mg; SODIUM 28mg; CALC 79mg

PASSION POTION

Substitute apricot or papaya nectar if you can't find the passionfruit nectar.

- 2 cups cubed peeled ripe mango
- 1 cup cubed pineapple
- 1½ cups orange juice, chilled
- ½ cup passionfruit nectar, chilled

1. Place mango cubes and pineapple cubes in freezer, and freeze until firm (about 1 hour). Remove from freezer; let stand 10 minutes. Combine mango, juice, and nectar in a blender, and process until smooth. With blender on, add pineapple; process until smooth. Serve immediately. Yield: 4 servings (serving size: 1 cup).

CALORIES 134 (3% from fat); FAT 0.4g (sat 0.1g, mono 0.1g, poly 0.1g); PROTEIN 1.2g; CARB 33.7g; FIBER 1.9g; CHOL 0mg; IRON 0.4mg; SODIUM 3mg; CALC 19mg

FIVE-FRUIT CRUSH

- ¾ cup sliced ripe banana
- ½ cup chopped peeled ripe mango
- 2 cups whole strawberries
- ¾ cup pineapple juice, chilled
- ½ cup orange juice, chilled
- ½ cup ice cubes

1. Place banana and mango in freezer; freeze until firm (about 1 hour). Remove from freezer; let stand 10 minutes. Combine strawberries and juices in a blender; process until smooth. With blender on, add banana, mango, and ice cubes, 1 at a time; process until smooth. Serve immediately. Yield: 4 servings (serving size: 1 cup).

CALORIES 102 (4% from fat); FAT 0.5g (sat 0.1g, mono 0.1g, poly 0.2g); PROTEIN 1.2g; CARB 25.2g; FIBER 2.8g; CHOL 0mg; IRON 0.6mg; SODIUM 2mg; CALC 25mg

KEY WEST MINTED LIMEADE

- ¼ cup sugar
- ¼ cup fresh lime juice
- 4 fresh mint leaves
- ½ cup ice cubes
- 1 cup ginger ale, chilled
- 2 lime slices
- Mint sprigs

1. Combine first 3 ingredients in a blender; process until smooth. With blender on, add ice cubes, 1 at a time; process until smooth. Stir in ginger ale. Serve over ice; garnish with lime slices and mint sprigs. Serve immediately. Yield: 2 servings (serving size: 1 cup).

CALORIES 144 (0% from fat); FAT 0g; PROTEIN 0.1g; CARB 38.3g; FIBER 0g; CHOL 0mg; IRON 0mg; SODIUM 7mg; CALC 3mg

HOW TO BLEND IN

Freeze the fruit beforehand for a thicker, slushier drink. To freeze, place the fruit in a single layer on a freezer-proof plate. Let the fruit soften at room temperature, and then drop into the blender a few chunks at a time.

The Sauce of Dreams

Whether you call it crème anglaise or just a custard sauce, this satin-smooth sauce is a classic treat that spans generations.

This classic French dessert sauce is a rich liquid custard that's traditionally used for Bavarian creams and for spooning over desserts. This sauce is made from rich milk, cream, sugar, and whole eggs or egg yolks. The creamiest custards are thickened with just the yolks. With low-fat recipes, it's tempting to use cornstarch or flour to add body while replacing fat. For these recipes, however, we used low-fat milk but kept the egg yolks because they're what makes this sauce satin-smooth.

CRÈME ANGLAISE STEP-BY-STEPS

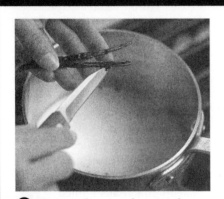

❶ *Because this is such a simple sauce, quality ingredients are key. We've opted for a vanilla bean. Cook the milk mixture 6 minutes to bring out the bean's full flavor. If all the seeds don't come out at the start, they'll be released as they steep.*

❷ *Gradually pour the hot milk mixture into the egg yolk mixture in the bowl, stirring constantly with a whisk. By doing this, you eliminate the risk of cooking the egg mixture too quickly, which could result in scrambled eggs.*

❸ *Cook over medium heat until the sauce thickens and coats the back of a spoon. Don't get impatient and turn the heat too high; the eggs could curdle.*

❹ *Immediately pour the finished sauce into a bowl. Curdling is possible as long as the sauce stays in the hot pan.*

CRÈME ANGLAISE

You can substitute 2 teaspoons vanilla extract for the bean, but the flavor will suffer. You can find vanilla beans in your supermarket's spice section.

1¾ cups 1% low-fat milk
1 (3-inch) piece vanilla bean, split lengthwise
⅓ cup sugar
4 large egg yolks

1. Pour milk into a medium saucepan. Scrape seeds from vanilla bean; add seeds and bean to milk. Cook over medium heat 6 minutes (do not boil); discard bean. Remove from heat.
2. Combine sugar and yolks in a small bowl, stirring with a whisk until blended. Gradually add milk mixture to bowl, stirring constantly with a whisk. Return mixture to pan. Cook over medium heat 6 minutes or until mixture thinly coats back of a spoon, stirring constantly with a whisk. Immediately pour mixture into a bowl. Cover and chill (mixture will thicken as it cools). Yield: 1¾ cups (serving size: ¼ cup).
Note: Store Crème Anglaise in the refrigerator up to 3 days.

CALORIES 97 (33% from fat); FAT 3.6g (sat 1.3g, mono 1.3g, poly 0.4g); PROTEIN 3.6g; CARB 12.6g; FIBER 0g; CHOL 127mg; IRON 0.4mg; SODIUM 35mg; CALC 88mg

FRUIT AMBROSIA WITH CRÈME ANGLAISE

¼ cup thawed orange juice concentrate
2 tablespoons sugar
1½ cups orange sections (about 3 oranges)
1⅓ cups sliced ripe banana (about 2 bananas)
1 cup seedless green grapes
1 cup fresh raspberries
1 cup fresh blackberries
1¼ cups Crème Anglaise, chilled (see recipe)

1. Combine orange juice concentrate and sugar in a medium bowl; add

orange sections, banana, grapes, and berries, tossing gently. Spoon ambrosia into 5 glasses; top with Crème Anglaise. Yield: 5 servings (serving size: 1 cup ambrosia and ¼ cup Crème Anglaise).

CALORIES 251 (15% from fat); FAT 4.3g (sat 1.5g, mono 1.4g, poly 0.7g); PROTEIN 5.5g; CARB 50.9g; FIBER 7g; CHOL 127mg; IRON 1mg; SODIUM 37mg; CALC 135mg

inch. Bake at 350° for 45 minutes or until a knife inserted in center comes out clean. Remove 8-inch pan from water. Serve bread pudding warm with Crème Anglaise. Yield: 10 servings.

CALORIES 319 (15% from fat); FAT 5.4g (sat 2.1g, mono 1.9g, poly 0.7g); PROTEIN 10.3g; CARB 57.5g; FIBER 1.1g; CHOL 116mg; IRON 2.1mg; SODIUM 311mg; CALC 206mg

5. Place a plate upside down on top of dish; invert onto plate. Cut into wedges. Yield: 10 servings.

CALORIES 200 (27% from fat); FAT 6g (sat 4g, mono 1g, poly 0.4g); PROTEIN 4.6g; CARB 34.9g; FIBER 0.6g; CHOL 104mg; IRON 0.4mg; SODIUM 51mg; CALC 83mg

BROWN SUGAR BREAD PUDDING WITH CRÈME ANGLAISE

1 cup dried mixed fruit, chopped
1 cup pineapple juice
¼ cup packed brown sugar
4 large egg whites
1 large egg
1¼ cups 2% reduced-fat milk
¾ cup evaporated fat-free milk
⅓ cup packed brown sugar
2 teaspoons vanilla extract
¼ teaspoon ground cinnamon
⅛ teaspoon ground nutmeg
12 (1-ounce) slices diagonally cut French bread (about 1 inch thick)
Cooking spray
4 teaspoons brown sugar
1½ teaspoons butter, cut into small pieces
1¾ cups Crème Anglaise, chilled (see recipe on previous page)

1. Preheat oven to 350°.
2. Combine first 3 ingredients in a small saucepan. Bring to a boil, and cook until reduced to 1 cup (about 8 minutes). Remove from heat.
3. Combine egg whites and egg in a medium bowl, beating with a whisk until blended. Stir in milks, ⅓ cup brown sugar, vanilla, cinnamon, and nutmeg. Arrange half of bread slices, slightly overlapping, in bottom of an 8-inch square baking pan coated with cooking spray. Spoon fruit mixture evenly over bread. Arrange remaining bread over fruit mixture. Pour egg mixture over bread. Sprinkle top with 4 teaspoons brown sugar and butter. Place pan in a 13 x 9-inch baking pan; add hot water to larger pan to a depth of 1

STRAWBERRY BAVARIAN CREAM

Cooking spray
1½ tablespoons sugar
2 cups sliced strawberries
¼ cup sugar
15 ladyfingers
¼ cup seedless strawberry jam
2 envelopes unflavored gelatin
½ cup water
2 tablespoons brandy
1¾ cups Crème Anglaise, chilled (see recipe on previous page)
1 (8-ounce) container frozen reduced-calorie whipped topping, thawed

1. Coat a 6-cup soufflé dish with cooking spray. Sprinkle with 1½ tablespoons sugar.
2. Combine strawberries and ¼ cup sugar in a bowl; mash strawberries.
3. Split ladyfingers in half lengthwise. Spread jam evenly over flat sides of ladyfingers. Arrange enough ladyfinger halves, rounded sides down, in a single layer to line bottom of prepared dish. Line sides of dish with remaining ladyfinger halves, rounded sides outward and standing upright.
4. Sprinkle gelatin over water in a bowl, and let stand 1 minute. Microwave at HIGH 1 minute or until gelatin is dissolved. Stir in brandy. Place Crème Anglaise in a bowl; stir in gelatin mixture. Place bowl in a larger bowl of ice water, stirring mixture until thick (do not allow gelatin mixture to set). Add mashed strawberries, stirring mixture until thick but not set. Stir in one-fourth of whipped topping. Gently fold in remaining whipped topping. Spoon mixture into prepared dish. Cover and chill 4 to 8 hours.

PLUM-BUTTERMILK ICE CREAM

3 cups chopped purple plums (about 6 medium)
¼ cup sugar
¼ cup honey
1 tablespoon water
½ teaspoon ground cinnamon
1¾ cups Crème Anglaise, chilled (see recipe on previous page)
1 cup low-fat buttermilk

1. Combine first 5 ingredients in a medium saucepan. Bring to a boil, partially cover, and cook 8 minutes or until tender. Mash plums. Bring to a boil; cook 2 minutes. Remove from heat; chill.
2. Combine chilled plum mixture, Crème Anglaise, and buttermilk. Pour mixture into the freezer can of an ice-cream freezer, and freeze according to manufacturer's instructions. Spoon ice cream into a freezer-safe container; cover and freeze 1 hour or until firm. Yield: 10 servings (serving size: ½ cup).

CALORIES 154 (19% from fat); FAT 3.3g (sat 1.2g, mono 1.3g, poly 0.4g); PROTEIN 3.9g; CARB 28.7g; FIBER 1.1g; CHOL 89mg; IRON 0.4mg; SODIUM 37mg; CALC 96mg

Egg-xacting Care

While many crème anglaise recipes call for a double boiler, we found it unnecessary as long as you use a pan with a thick bottom. If you have only a thin pan, decrease the heat and watch the process carefully, because your sauce will cook more quickly.

We cooked our sauce on a gas range. If your range is electric, you'll need to cook the sauce about 4 minutes longer (for a total of 10 minutes).

Party Favor

When the tortilla begat the wrap, the perfect party got even better.

Tortillas: These time-honored Mexican staples, trendily renamed "wraps" for the '90s, have been revamped with all manner of new and conveniently interchangeable stuffings. Add a good CD player, and you've got a perfectly impromptu party without all the preparation.

These lively dinner-party choices are mix 'n' match. Some recipes seem to have a natural affinity for each other, such as the Indian-Spiced Shrimp Wrap and Cucumber Raita Sauce. We offer some serving suggestions with these recipes—but it's your call. Two other notes for your party: You can make the full array of recipes for larger gatherings or downsize to a few for smaller events. And you can make all the salsas up to two days ahead.

MIX 'N' MATCH MENU

SALAD

Field Salad with Citrus Vinaigrette and Sugared Pecans

WRAPS

Indian-Spiced Shrimp Wrap

Italian Balsamic Chicken Wrap

Lamb Picadillo Wrap

SAUCES AND SALSAS

Fresh Mango Salsa

Cucumber Raita Sauce

Picnic Salsa

Antipasto Salsa

SIDES

Tuscan White Beans

Creamy Potatoes and Greens

FIELD SALAD WITH CITRUS VINAIGRETTE AND SUGARED PECANS

Cooking spray
¼ cup chopped pecans
2 teaspoons sugar
⅛ teaspoon ground red pepper
10 cups gourmet salad greens
¾ cup Citrus Vinaigrette
2 navel oranges, peeled and sectioned
¼ cup sweetened dried cranberries (such as Craisins)

1. Heat a small nonstick skillet coated with cooking spray over medium-low heat. Add pecans; cook 6 minutes or until lightly toasted, stirring frequently. Sprinkle with sugar and red pepper, and cook 1 minute, stirring constantly. Remove pecans from skillet. Cool on wax paper.
2. Combine greens, Citrus Vinaigrette, and orange sections in a large bowl; toss well. Place 1 cup greens mixture on each of 8 plates; top each serving with 1½ teaspoons pecans and 1½ teaspoons cranberries. Serve immediately. Yield: 8 servings.

CALORIES 90 (38% from fat); FAT 3.8g (sat 0.4g, mono 2.3g, poly 0.9g); PROTEIN 1.9g; CARB 13.5g; FIBER 3.1g; CHOL 0mg; IRON 0.9mg; SODIUM 72mg; CALC 41mg

---

Citrus Vinaigrette:

½ cup fresh orange juice (about 1 orange)
⅓ cup fresh grapefruit juice
2 tablespoons fresh lemon juice
1 tablespoon extra-virgin olive oil
1 tablespoon honey
1 tablespoon Dijon mustard
1 tablespoon low-sodium soy sauce
2 teaspoons minced peeled fresh ginger

1. Combine all ingredients in a blender; process until smooth. Pour into a bowl; cover and chill. Yield: 1⅓ cups (serving size: 1 tablespoon).
Note: Store in an airtight container in refrigerator up to 1 week.

CALORIES 15 (42% from fat); FAT 0.7g (sat 0.1g, mono 0.5g, poly 0.1g); PROTEIN 0.1g; CARB 2.1g; FIBER 0g; CHOL 0mg; IRON 0mg; SODIUM 44mg; CALC 1mg

---

INDIAN-SPICED SHRIMP WRAP

(pictured on page 151)

We like the Fresh Mango Salsa (see recipe) *or* Cucumber Raita Sauce (see recipe, next page) *in this wrap.*

1 tablespoon ground cumin
2 teaspoons ground coriander
2 teaspoons ground turmeric
1 teaspoon ground cardamom
½ teaspoon ground cloves
½ teaspoon black pepper
¼ teaspoon ground cinnamon
⅛ to ¼ teaspoon ground red pepper
½ teaspoon salt
2½ pounds medium shrimp, peeled and deveined
2 teaspoons vegetable oil
8 (6-inch) fat-free flour tortillas

1. Combine first 8 ingredients in a small skillet, and place over medium-high heat. Cook 2 minutes, stirring constantly; stir in salt. Cool. Combine spice mixture and shrimp in a large zip-top plastic bag. Seal and marinate in refrigerator 1 to 2 hours.

2. Heat oil in a large nonstick skillet over medium-high heat. Add shrimp mixture; sauté 7 minutes or until shrimp are done.

3. Warm tortillas according to package directions. Spoon about ½ cup shrimp mixture down center of each tortilla; roll up. Yield: 8 servings.

CALORIES 213 (14% from fat); FAT 3.3g (sat 0.6g, mono 0.8g, poly 1.3g); PROTEIN 24.1g; CARB 20.3g; FIBER 1.1g; CHOL 162mg; IRON 4.3mg; SODIUM 561mg; CALC 70mg

ITALIAN BALSAMIC CHICKEN WRAP

(pictured on page 151)

The Tuscan White Beans (page 158), Antipasto Salsa (page 158), *or* Fresh Mango Salsa (see recipe) *is terrific in this wrap.*

¼   cup minced fresh parsley
1   tablespoon dried Italian seasoning
2   tablespoons olive oil
2   tablespoons balsamic vinegar
½   teaspoon black pepper
2   garlic cloves, minced
8   (4-ounce) skinned, boned chicken breast halves
Cooking spray
8   (6-inch) fat-free flour tortillas

1. Combine first 6 ingredients in a large zip-top plastic bag. Add chicken to bag; seal and marinate in refrigerator at least 2 hours.

2. Prepare grill.

3. Remove chicken from bag; discard marinade. Place chicken on a grill rack coated with cooking spray; grill 6 minutes on each side or until done. Cool; cut chicken into ¼-inch strips.

4. Warm tortillas according to package directions. Divide chicken evenly among tortillas; roll up. Yield: 8 servings.

CALORIES 225 (13% from fat); FAT 3.2g (sat 0.6g, mono 1.6g, poly 0.5g); PROTEIN 28.5g; CARB 18.5g; FIBER 0.9g; CHOL 66mg; IRON 1.2mg; SODIUM 329mg; CALC 22mg

LAMB PICADILLO WRAP

Our Fresh Mango Salsa (see recipe) *or* Picnic Salsa (see recipe) *goes great in this wrap. If you prefer, substitute beef for lamb.*

4   pounds boned lamb shoulder
2   tablespoons finely chopped seeded jalapeño pepper
1   tablespoon dried oregano
1   tablespoon chili powder
¼   teaspoon salt
3   garlic cloves, minced
1   (6-ounce) can tomato paste
2   cups water
½   cup golden raisins
1   tablespoon unsweetened cocoa
¼   cup chopped pimento-stuffed olives
2   tablespoons minced fresh cilantro
2   tablespoons fresh lime juice
8   (6-inch) fat-free flour tortillas

1. Trim fat from lamb. Cut lamb into 3 x ¼-inch strips. Place a skillet over medium-high heat until hot. Add lamb; cook 4 minutes or until browned. Add jalapeño, oregano, chili powder, salt, and garlic, and sauté 1 minute. Stir in tomato paste, and sauté 2 minutes. Stir in water, raisins, and cocoa; bring to a boil. Reduce heat; simmer 20 minutes. Stir in olives, cilantro, and juice.

2. Warm tortillas according to package directions. Spoon about ½ cup lamb mixture down center of each tortilla; roll up. Yield: 8 servings.

CALORIES 320 (28% from fat); FAT 10g (sat 3.7g, mono 4g, poly 1g); PROTEIN 25.2g; CARB 32.6g; FIBER 2.7g; CHOL 74mg; IRON 4.2mg; SODIUM 450mg; CALC 50mg

FRESH MANGO SALSA

1½   cups chopped peeled mango
1½   cups chopped tomato
2   tablespoons minced fresh cilantro
2   tablespoons fresh lime juice
1   tablespoon finely chopped seeded jalapeño pepper
1   teaspoon minced peeled fresh ginger

1. Combine all ingredients in a bowl; cover and chill. Yield: 3 cups (serving size: ½ cup).

CALORIES 39 (7% from fat); FAT 0.3g (sat 0.1g, mono 0.1g, poly 0.1g); PROTEIN 0.7g; CARB 9.8g; FIBER 1.2g; CHOL 0mg; IRON 0.4mg; SODIUM 6mg; CALC 9mg

CUCUMBER RAITA SAUCE

Raita *(RI-tah) is a popular salad in India.*

1   (16-ounce) carton plain fat-free yogurt
1   cup chopped seeded peeled cucumber
1   cup chopped seeded tomato
½   cup minced red onion
¼   cup chopped fresh mint
1   teaspoon ground cumin
½   teaspoon salt

1. Spoon yogurt onto several layers of paper towels, and spread to ½-inch thickness. Cover with additional paper towels; let stand 10 minutes. Scrape into a bowl, using a spatula; stir in cucumber and remaining ingredients. Cover and chill 2 hours; stir before serving. Yield: 2¾ cups (serving size: ¼ cup).

CALORIES 32 (6% from fat); FAT 0.2g (sat 0.1g, mono 0.1g, poly 0g); PROTEIN 2.7g; CARB 5g; FIBER 0.4g; CHOL 1mg; IRON 0.3mg; SODIUM 140mg; CALC 88mg

PICNIC SALSA

1   cup chopped seeded watermelon
1   cup chopped cantaloupe
1   cup chopped peeled cucumber
1   cup chopped tomato
½   cup chopped green bell pepper
2   tablespoons minced seeded jalapeño pepper
2   tablespoons minced fresh parsley
2   tablespoons fresh lemon juice

1. Combine ingredients. Cover; chill. Yield: 4½ cups (serving size: ½ cup).

CALORIES 22 (12% from fat); FAT 0.3g (sat 0g, mono 0g, poly 0.1g); PROTEIN 0.7g; CARB 5g; FIBER 0.8g; CHOL 0mg; IRON 0.4mg; SODIUM 5mg; CALC 9mg

ANTIPASTO SALSA

- 1 cup diced tomato
- 1 cup diced zucchini
- ½ cup chopped drained canned artichoke hearts
- ½ cup chopped fresh basil
- ⅓ cup diced bottled roasted red bell peppers
- ¼ cup minced onion
- 2 tablespoons chopped pitted kalamata olives
- 1 tablespoon balsamic vinegar
- 2 teaspoons olive oil

1. Combine all ingredients in a medium bowl; cover and chill. Yield: 3 cups (serving size: ½ cup).

CALORIES 39 (46% from fat); FAT 2g (sat 0.3g, mono 1.4g, poly 0.3g); PROTEIN 1.3g; CARB 5.2g; FIBER 0.8g; CHOL 0mg; IRON 0.6mg; SODIUM 80mg; CALC 22mg

TUSCAN WHITE BEANS

Combine these beans with Field Salad with Citrus Vinaigrette and Sugared Pecans (page 156) on a tortilla for a lighter, vegetable-based wrap. For a completely vegetarian version, substitute 2 teaspoons olive oil for the bacon and drippings.

- 2 bacon slices
- 1 cup chopped onion
- 1 tablespoon chopped fresh or 1 teaspoon dried rosemary
- 2 (15-ounce) cans cannellini beans or other white beans, rinsed and drained
- 1 cup dry white wine
- ½ cup water
- 1 teaspoon grated lemon rind
- ½ teaspoon black pepper
- ½ cup minced fresh parsley

1. Cook bacon in a large nonstick skillet over medium-high heat until crisp. Remove bacon from pan, reserving 1 tablespoon bacon drippings in pan; crumble bacon. Add onion and rosemary to drippings in pan; sauté 2 minutes. Reduce heat to medium-low. Add beans, wine, water, rind, and pepper;

simmer 30 minutes or until thick. Stir in crumbled bacon and parsley. Yield: 7 servings (serving size: ½ cup).

CALORIES 157 (19% from fat); FAT 3.3g (sat 0.7g, mono 1.1g, poly 1.1g); PROTEIN 7.8g; CARB 25.4g; FIBER 3.6g; CHOL 1mg; IRON 2.8mg; SODIUM 183mg; CALC 57mg

---

MENU SUGGESTION

CREAMY POTATOES AND GREENS

Moroccan chicken*

Pita wedges

*Combine ½ cup chopped fresh parsley and 4 minced garlic cloves; rub over 4 (4-ounce) skinned, boned chicken breast halves. Arrange chicken in a 13 x 9-inch baking dish; add 1 (14½-ounce) can diced tomatoes, ¼ cup chopped pimento-stuffed olives, and 1 tablespoon grated lemon rind. Cover and bake at 400° for 30 minutes or until chicken is done. Slice chicken; spoon sauce evenly over chicken. Serves 4.

CREAMY POTATOES AND GREENS

- 4 cups cubed peeled baking potato
- 2 teaspoons olive oil
- 1 teaspoon minced peeled fresh ginger
- ¼ teaspoon dried crushed red pepper
- ¼ teaspoon ground turmeric
- 2 garlic cloves, minced
- 2 cups chopped spinach
- 2 tablespoons minced fresh cilantro
- ½ teaspoon salt
- 1 (8-ounce) carton plain low-fat yogurt

1. Cook potato in boiling water 8 minutes or just until tender; drain.
2. Heat oil in a large nonstick skillet over medium heat. Add ginger, red pepper, turmeric, and garlic; sauté 30 seconds. Add potato; sauté 2 minutes.

Remove from heat; stir in spinach and remaining ingredients. Serve at room temperature. Yield: 8 servings (serving size: ½ cup).

CALORIES 92 (17% from fat); FAT 1.7g (sat 0.5g, mono 1g, poly 0.2g); PROTEIN 3.5g; CARB 16.4g; FIBER 1.8g; CHOL 2mg; IRON 1.1mg; SODIUM 183mg; CALC 74mg

LIGHTEN UP

Good Morning, Glory

An Illinois reader's Morning Glory Muffin is now light enough to be a favorite any time of the day.

Name notwithstanding, the Morning Glory Muffins cooked up by Bernice and Edward Dalluege are too good to be limited to breakfast. "I've tried bran and other kinds of muffins, but I always come back to this recipe," says Bernice, a 72-year-old avid golfer and part-time sales clerk. "They're just so moist."

Alas, some of that moisture came from fat. The unglorious aftereffect of the muffins was a big, round oil slick on napkins and paper towels. By cutting down on nuts, oil, and coconut in the original recipe, we managed to slash the fat in half and knock off more than 50 calories. But we didn't sacrifice the cherished flavor or moisture, either—a little apple butter did the trick, neatly nixing the slick.

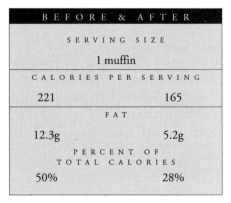

BEFORE & AFTER	
SERVING SIZE	
1 muffin	
CALORIES PER SERVING	
221	165
FAT	
12.3g	5.2g
PERCENT OF TOTAL CALORIES	
50%	28%

Apples are too delicate to be grated with a food processor, so we recommend using a stand-up grater. We left the skins on, but the result will be just as good if you peel the apples.

2½ cups all-purpose flour
1 cup packed brown sugar
2 teaspoons baking soda
2 teaspoons ground cinnamon
½ teaspoon salt
2 cups shredded carrot
1 cup shredded Rome or other
   cooking apple
¾ cup raisins
⅓ cup chopped pecans
¼ cup flaked sweetened coconut
1 (8-ounce) can crushed
   pineapple in juice, drained
⅓ cup vegetable oil
⅓ cup apple butter
2 teaspoons vanilla extract
2 large eggs
2 large egg whites
Cooking spray

1. Preheat oven to 350°.
2. Lightly spoon flour into dry measuring cups; level with a knife. Combine flour and next 4 ingredients in a large bowl. Stir in carrot and next 5 ingredients; make a well in center of mixture. Combine oil and next 4 ingredients; stir with a whisk. Add oil mixture to flour mixture, stirring just until moist.
3. Spoon batter into 24 muffin cups coated with cooking spray. Bake at 350° for 25 minutes or until muffins spring back when touched lightly in center. Remove muffins from pans immediately; cool on a wire rack. Yield: 2 dozen.
Note: You can store muffins in an airtight container and freeze up to 1 month. Wrap muffins in foil; to serve, reheat at 300°.

CALORIES 165 (28% from fat); FAT 5.2g (sat 1.1g, mono 1.8g, poly 1.9g); PROTEIN 2.6g; CARB 27.9g; FIBER 1.2g; CHOL 18mg; IRON 1.1mg; SODIUM 174mg; CALC 21mg

A Garden on Your Plate, Part II

The lush bounty of a summer garden makes your meals so delicious–and convenient–you'll never want to be without one again.

In this second of our three-part *Cooking Light* garden series, cosponsored by the Burpee seed company, we've caught up with Melanie and Buddy Colvin at the high point of any horticultural season: the bounty of the summer crop. The Colvins began reaping what they had sown in the winter (see March, page 44). But a summer crop makes all this seem as easy as, well, plucking a tomato from a vine.

MELANIE'S GARDEN-TOMATO SOUP

(pictured on page 150)

2 teaspoons olive oil
¾ cup chopped onion
1 tablespoon chopped fresh
   oregano or basil
1 teaspoon chopped fresh or
   ¼ teaspoon dried thyme
2 garlic cloves, chopped
5 cups diced tomato (about
   2 pounds)
1½ cups water
2½ tablespoons tomato paste
2 teaspoons sugar
¼ teaspoon salt
¼ teaspoon black pepper
Thinly sliced fresh basil (optional)

1. Heat oil in a large saucepan over medium heat. Add onion, oregano, thyme, and garlic; cook 4 minutes, stirring frequently. Stir in tomato and next 5 ingredients. Bring to a boil. Reduce heat; simmer 15 minutes. Place half of soup in a blender or food processor; process until smooth, and pour into a bowl. Repeat procedure with remaining soup. Serve warm or chilled. Sprinkle with fresh basil, if desired. Yield: 5 servings (serving size: 1 cup).

CALORIES 81 (29% from fat); FAT 2.6g (sat 0.4g, mono 1.4g, poly 0.5g); PROTEIN 2.3g; CARB 14.6g; FIBER 2.9g; CHOL 0mg; IRON 1.3mg; SODIUM 140mg; CALC 29mg

BARLEY SALAD WITH PESTO, TOMATO, AND ZUCCHINI

1½ cups water
1 cup uncooked quick-cooking
   barley
1½ cups fresh parsley leaves
½ cup fresh cilantro leaves
2 tablespoons pine nuts, toasted
¼ cup (1 ounce) grated fresh
   Parmesan cheese
2 tablespoons water
1 tablespoon fresh lemon juice
1 tablespoon olive oil
¾ teaspoon salt
⅛ teaspoon black pepper
1½ cups diced zucchini
1½ cups diced plum tomato
½ cup diced red onion

1. Bring 1½ cups water to a boil in a medium saucepan. Add barley; cover, reduce heat, and simmer 13 minutes. Remove from heat; let stand, covered, 5 minutes.
2. Combine parsley and cilantro in a food processor; process until minced. Add pine nuts, and process until minced. Add cheese and next 5 ingredients; process until pesto is well-blended.
3. Spoon barley into a bowl. Stir in pesto, zucchini, tomato, and onion. Yield: 6 servings (serving size: 1 cup).

CALORIES 200 (27% from fat); FAT 5.9g (sat 1.5g, mono 2.8g, poly 1.2g); PROTEIN 7.3g; CARB 32.3g; FIBER 7.1g; CHOL 3mg; IRON 2.8mg; SODIUM 389mg; CALC 105mg

CANTALOUPE-AND-CHERRY TOMATO SALSA

(pictured on page 149)

This salsa, with its unusual combination of ingredients, is great with beef, pork, quesadillas, or chips.

    2 cups diced cantaloupe
    2 cups quartered cherry tomatoes
    ¼ cup minced shallots
    ¼ cup chopped fresh oregano or
         basil
    2 tablespoons minced seeded
         jalapeño pepper
    2 teaspoons grated orange rind
    2 tablespoons orange juice
    2 tablespoons lime juice
    ¼ teaspoon salt
    ⅛ teaspoon black pepper

1. Combine all ingredients in a large bowl; toss well. Cover and refrigerate 30 minutes. Yield: 6 servings (serving size: ⅔ cup).

CALORIES 44 (10% from fat); FAT 0.5g (sat 0.1g, mono 0g, poly 0.2g); PROTEIN 1.4g; CARB 10.8g; FIBER 1.4g; CHOL 0mg; IRON 1mg; SODIUM 109mg; CALC 32mg

ROASTED-VEGETABLE LASAGNA

(pictured on page 150)

Use a sharp, potent cheese in this dish for the most flavor. Parmesan, Romano, Asiago, or sharp Cheddar will all work well in the filling. Stick to mozzarella for the top, however, because it melts and browns the best.

Vegetables:

    4 red bell peppers
    1 teaspoon olive oil
    ½ teaspoon salt
    ½ teaspoon black pepper
    6 yellow squash, halved lengthwise
         and cut into 1-inch pieces
         (about 1½ pounds)
    1 large onion, cut into 16 wedges
    4 garlic cloves, minced

Cheese mixture:

    2 cups 2% low-fat cottage cheese
    1½ cups (6 ounces) grated sharp
         provolone cheese
    ¼ cup chopped fresh basil
    1 teaspoon dried oregano

White sauce:

    3 tablespoons all-purpose flour
    1½ cups 2% reduced-fat milk
    2 tablespoons chopped fresh basil
    ¼ teaspoon black pepper
    Cooking spray
    9 cooked lasagna noodles
    2 cups spinach leaves
    ½ cup (2 ounces) shredded part-
         skim mozzarella cheese
    Fresh basil sprigs (optional)

1. Preheat broiler.
2. To prepare vegetables, cut bell peppers in half lengthwise; discard seeds and membranes. Place pepper halves, skin sides up, on a foil-lined baking sheet; flatten with hand. Broil 15 minutes or until blackened. Place in a zip-top plastic bag; seal. Let stand 15 minutes. Peel; set aside.
3. Preheat oven to 450°.
4. Combine oil, salt, ½ teaspoon black pepper, squash, and onion on a baking sheet; toss well. Bake at 450° for 20 minutes. Remove from oven; combine squash mixture and garlic in a bowl.
5. Decrease oven temperature to 375°.
6. To prepare cheese mixture, combine cottage cheese and next 3 ingredients in a bowl.
7. To prepare white sauce, place flour in a medium saucepan. Gradually add milk; stir with a whisk. Place over medium heat. Cook until thick; stir constantly. Remove from heat; stir in 2 tablespoons chopped basil and ¼ teaspoon black pepper.
8. Spread ¼ cup white sauce in a 13 x 9-inch baking dish coated with cooking spray. Arrange 3 noodles over sauce; top with 1¼ cups cheese mixture, 1 cup spinach, 4 bell pepper halves, 2 cups vegetable mixture, and ¼ cup white sauce. Repeat layers, ending with noodles. Spread

remaining white sauce over noodles. Cover and bake at 375° for 15 minutes. Uncover; sprinkle with mozzarella cheese. Bake an additional 20 minutes. Garnish with basil sprigs, if desired. Yield: 9 servings.

CALORIES 275 (30% from fat); FAT 9.1g (sat 5.2g, mono 2.6g, poly 0.6g); PROTEIN 19.3g; CARB 29.3g; FIBER 2.9g; CHOL 24mg; IRON 2.3mg; SODIUM 564mg; CALC 308mg

PASTA WITH ROASTED EGGPLANT-TOMATO SAUCE

    3 cups (1-inch) cubed peeled
         eggplant (about 12 ounces)
    Cooking spray
    1 tablespoon olive oil
    1 garlic clove, minced
    3 cups chopped tomato
         (about 1½ pounds)
    ¼ cup sliced pitted kalamata
         olives
    2 tablespoons tomato paste
    ½ teaspoon sugar
    ¼ teaspoon salt
    ¼ teaspoon black pepper
    ⅓ cup chopped fresh basil
    ⅓ cup chopped fresh oregano
    4 cups hot cooked penne
         (about 8 ounces uncooked
         tube-shaped pasta)
    ¼ cup (1 ounce) finely grated
         fresh Parmesan cheese

1. Preheat oven to 425°.
2. To prepare sauce, place eggplant in a single layer on a baking sheet coated with cooking spray; bake at 425° for 15 minutes, stirring once. Heat oil in a large nonstick skillet over medium heat. Add garlic; cook 3 minutes or until golden, stirring occasionally. Add tomato and next 5 ingredients; bring to a simmer. Reduce heat to low; cook 3 minutes or until slightly thick. Add eggplant, basil, and oregano; cook 3 minutes or until thoroughly heated.
3. Toss sauce with pasta, and sprinkle with cheese. Yield: 4 servings (serving size: 1½ cups).

CALORIES 347 (21% from fat); FAT 8.1g (sat 2.1g, mono 3.9g, poly 1.3g); PROTEIN 12.5g; CARB 58.3g; FIBER 5.9g; CHOL 5mg; IRON 4.5mg; SODIUM 358mg; CALC 154mg

Okra-Pepper Sauté

  2 teaspoons butter or stick
      margarine
  1 cup yellow bell pepper strips
  1 cup red bell pepper strips
  3 cups okra pods, cut in half
      diagonally (about ½ pound)
  2 tablespoons chopped fresh
      cilantro
  ¼ teaspoon salt
  ¼ teaspoon black pepper

1. Heat butter in a large nonstick skillet over medium heat. Add bell peppers; sauté 4 minutes. Add okra; cover, reduce heat, and cook 15 minutes or until okra is tender. Stir in cilantro, salt, and black pepper. Yield: 4 servings (serving size: ¾ cup).

CALORIES 52 (38% from fat); FAT 2.2g (sat 1.3g, mono 0.6g, poly 0.2g); PROTEIN 1.6g; CARB 7.2g; FIBER 1.4g; CHOL 5mg; IRON 1.2mg; SODIUM 173mg; CALC 53mg

Chicken Salad with Green Beans and Toasted Walnuts

Serve this herbed main-dish salad with pita bread to reduce the overall calories from fat to less than 30 percent.

  4 cups (1-inch) cut green beans
      (about 1 pound)
  2 cups chopped ready-to-eat
      roasted skinned, boned
      chicken breasts (about
      2 breasts)
  ¼ cup chopped fresh parsley
  2 tablespoons chopped walnuts,
      toasted
  1 tablespoon chopped fresh mint
  2 tablespoons white wine vinegar
  2 teaspoons olive oil
  ¼ teaspoon salt
  ¼ teaspoon black pepper

1. Steam beans, covered, 6 minutes or until crisp-tender. Drain.
2. Combine beans, chicken, parsley, nuts, and mint in a large bowl. Combine vinegar, oil, salt, and pepper

in a small bowl; stir well with a whisk. Pour over bean mixture; stir well. Yield: 4 servings (serving size: 1½ cups).

CALORIES 146 (36% from fat); FAT 5.9g (sat 1g, mono 2.6g, poly 2g); PROTEIN 16.1g; CARB 8.6g; FIBER 2.8g; CHOL 35mg; IRON 1.5mg; SODIUM 446mg; CALC 59mg

Ratatouille Stew with Sausage and Chickpeas

  1 teaspoon olive oil
  1 cup finely chopped onion
  6 ounces smoked turkey sausage
      or kielbasa, halved lengthwise
      and cut into ½-inch slices
      (about 1 cup)
  ½ cup diced yellow bell pepper
  ½ cup diced green bell pepper
  4 cups (¾-inch) cubed tomato
      (about 1½ pounds)
  2 cups diced zucchini
  2 cups diced peeled eggplant
      (about 1 pound)
  1⅓ cups fat-free, less-sodium
      chicken broth
  2 tablespoons tomato paste
  ½ teaspoon black pepper
  ¼ teaspoon salt
  1 garlic clove, minced
  1 (15-ounce) can chickpeas, rinsed
      and drained
  ½ cup chopped fresh parsley
  1 tablespoon chopped fresh thyme

1. Heat oil in a Dutch oven over medium-high heat. Add onion, sausage, and bell peppers; sauté 5 minutes. Add tomato and next 8 ingredients; bring to a boil. Cover, reduce heat, and simmer 35 minutes. Uncover; simmer 20 minutes. Stir in parsley and thyme. Yield: 4 servings (serving size: 2 cups).

CALORIES 294 (24% from fat); FAT 7.8g (sat 2.4g, mono 2.6g, poly 2g); PROTEIN 17.4g; CARB 43g; FIBER 8g; CHOL 22mg; IRON 9.8mg; SODIUM 930mg; CALC 100mg

Grandma's Awesome Best

When a teenage track enthusiast's grandmother fires up the oven, great banana bread is only a sprint away.

Banana-Oatmeal Bread

"My grandmother, Theresa Leary, bakes the most awesome low-fat goodies."
—Amber Yudchitz, Stevens Point, Wisconsin

  1 cup packed brown sugar
  7 tablespoons vegetable oil
  2 large egg whites
  1 large egg
  1⅓ cups mashed ripe banana
      (about 2 large)
  1 cup regular oats
  ½ cup fat-free milk
  2 cups all-purpose flour
  1 tablespoon baking powder
  ½ teaspoon baking soda
  ½ teaspoon salt
  ½ teaspoon ground cinnamon
      Cooking spray

1. Preheat oven to 350°.
2. Combine first 4 ingredients in a large bowl; beat well at medium speed of a mixer. Combine banana, oats, and milk; add to sugar mixture, beating well. Lightly spoon flour into dry measuring cups; level with a knife. Combine flour, baking powder, baking soda, salt, and cinnamon; stir with a whisk. Add to sugar mixture, beating just until moist. Spoon batter into a 9 x 5-inch loaf pan coated with cooking spray. Bake at 350° for 1 hour and 10 minutes or until a wooden pick inserted in center comes out clean. Cool in pan 10 minutes on a wire rack; remove from pan. Cool completely on wire rack. Yield: 18 servings.

CALORIES 185 (30% from fat); FAT 6.1g (sat 1.2g, mono 1.8g, poly 2.8g); PROTEIN 3.3g; CARB 30.1g; FIBER 1.3g; CHOL 12mg; IRON 1.3mg; SODIUM 200mg; CALC 72mg

WATERMELON SORBET

—Charlotte Bryant, Greensburg, Kentucky

- 4 cups cubed seeded watermelon
- ¼ cup sugar
- 2 tablespoons fresh lime juice

1. Place all ingredients in a food processor or blender, and process until smooth. Pour mixture into the freezer can of an ice-cream freezer, and freeze according to manufacturer's instructions. Spoon sorbet into a freezer-safe container; cover and freeze 1 hour or until firm. Yield: 4 servings (serving size: ½ cup).

CALORIES 102 (6% from fat); FAT 0.7g (sat 0.4g, mono 0.1g, poly 0g); PROTEIN 1g; CARB 24.7g; FIBER 0.9g; CHOL 0mg; IRON 0.3mg; SODIUM 3mg; CALC 14mg

GRILLED ORANGE-AND-BOURBON SALMON

—Charlene Schubert, Alpharetta, Georgia

- ¼ cup bourbon
- ¼ cup fresh orange juice
- ¼ cup low-sodium soy sauce
- ¼ cup packed brown sugar
- ¼ cup chopped green onions
- 3 tablespoons chopped fresh chives
- 2 tablespoons fresh lemon juice
- 2 garlic cloves, chopped
- 4 (6-ounce) salmon fillets (about 1 inch thick)
- Cooking spray

1. Combine first 8 ingredients in a large zip-top plastic bag, and add salmon to bag. Seal and marinate in refrigerator 1½ hours, turning bag occasionally.
2. Prepare grill or broiler.
3. Remove salmon from bag, reserving marinade. Place salmon on a grill rack or broiler pan coated with cooking spray. Cook 6 minutes on each side or until fish flakes easily when tested with a fork, basting frequently with reserved marinade. Yield: 4 servings.

CALORIES 365 (35% from fat); FAT 14.1g (sat 2.5g, mono 6.8g, poly 3.1g); PROTEIN 36g; CARB 18g; FIBER 0.3g; CHOL 111mg; IRON 1.4mg; SODIUM 575mg; CALC 34mg

CREAMY FRENCH POTATO SALAD

—Sue-Marie Smith, Louisville, Colorado

- 6 cups (1-inch) cubed peeled baking potato (about 2½ pounds)
- ½ cup low-fat sour cream
- ⅓ cup light mayonnaise
- ¼ cup fat-free French dressing
- ½ teaspoon salt
- ⅛ teaspoon black pepper
- ⅛ teaspoon celery seeds
- 1 cup chopped celery
- 1 cup diced onion
- ¼ cup diced red bell pepper
- 2 hard-cooked large eggs, chopped

1. Place potato in a large saucepan, and cover with water; bring to a boil. Reduce heat, and simmer 15 minutes or until almost tender; drain well.
2. Combine sour cream and next 5 ingredients in a large bowl; stir in potato, chopped celery, and remaining ingredients. Cover and chill at least 1 hour. Yield: 14 servings (serving size: ½ cup).

CALORIES 117 (28% from fat); FAT 3.6g (sat 1g, mono 0.9g, poly 1.3g); PROTEIN 3.2g; CARB 17.9g; FIBER 1.4g; CHOL 40mg; IRON 0.8mg; SODIUM 220mg; CALC 37mg

EATING SMART

Three Little Nutrients

Vitamin E, magnesium, and zinc: the only nutrients the American diet doesn't get enough of. But should.

Zinc abounds in red meat and shellfish. Magnesium, which gives the chlorophyll molecule its signature green color, is plentiful in green vegetables as well as nuts, legumes, whole grains, and bananas. Vitamin E is a staple in many delectable nuts, seeds, oils, and wheat germ.

OYSTERS ROCKEFELLER STRATA WITH ARTICHOKES

Each serving contains 28 milligrams of zinc or roughly double the recommended dietary requirement.

- 4 bacon slices, cut into small pieces
- 1½ cups chopped fennel bulb (about 2 bulbs)
- ½ cup chopped red onion
- 1 (8-ounce) container Standard oysters, undrained
- 1½ cups chopped smoked ham (about 6 ounces)
- ¾ cup chopped fresh parsley
- 1 (14-ounce) can artichoke hearts, drained and chopped
- 1 cup part-skim ricotta cheese
- ¼ teaspoon ground nutmeg
- ¼ teaspoon ground red pepper
- 5 large eggs
- 3¼ cups 1% low-fat milk
- 1 (10-ounce) package frozen chopped spinach, thawed, drained, and squeezed dry
- 1 (16-ounce) loaf sourdough bread baguette, cut into ½-inch slices and toasted
- Cooking spray
- 2 tablespoons (½ ounce) grated fresh Parmesan cheese
- 2 teaspoons paprika

1. Cook bacon in a Dutch oven over medium heat until crisp. Add fennel and onion to pan; sauté 8 minutes or until soft. Remove bacon mixture from pan. Add undrained oysters to pan; cook 3 minutes or until edges of oysters begin to curl. Remove oysters from pan; discard cooking liquid. Chop oysters; add to bacon mixture. Stir in ham, parsley, and artichokes.
2. Combine ricotta, nutmeg, red pepper, and 1 egg in a bowl; stir with a whisk until well-blended. Add 4 eggs; stir well. Stir in milk and spinach.
3. Arrange half of toast in a single layer in a 13 x 9-inch baking dish coated with cooking spray. Spoon half of oyster mixture evenly over bread. Pour half of milk mixture over oyster mixture; repeat layers. Sprinkle with

Parmesan and paprika. Cover; refrigerate 8 hours or overnight.

4. Preheat oven to 350°.

5. Uncover and bake at 350° for 45 minutes or until set. Yield: 8 servings.

Note: Fresh shucked oysters, which are often packaged in pop-top containers, are available in three sizes: Select, Standard, and Stewing. Standard are average size.

CALORIES 385 (29% from fat); FAT 12.4g (sat 5g, mono 4.5g, poly 1.4g); PROTEIN 26.7g; CARB 42.6g; FIBER 2.6g; CHOL 181mg; IRON 6.3mg; SODIUM 1,018mg; CALC 395mg; ZINC 27.7mg

HAPPY ENDINGS

Spring's Coolest and Creamiest

There's a lightness to everyone's step this time of year—should dessert be an exception?

TIRAMISU WITH A CITRUS TWIST

You can use a blender to process the cheese mixture, but it won't be quite as smooth.

 ⅓ cup sugar
 2 tablespoons cognac
 1 (8-ounce) block fat-free cream cheese
 1 (3.5-ounce) carton mascarpone cheese
 1½ cups hot water
 5 teaspoons instant espresso or 3 tablespoons instant coffee granules
 24 ladyfingers (2 [3-ounce] packages)
 1 cup orange sections (about 3 oranges), chopped
 1 teaspoon unsweetened cocoa
 Candied Orange Rind

1. Place first 4 ingredients in a food processor, and process until smooth.

2. Combine hot water and espresso granules in a medium bowl. Split ladyfingers in half lengthwise. Quickly dip 12 ladyfinger halves, flat sides down, into espresso, and place, dipped sides down, in bottom of a 9 x 5-inch baking dish or 1½-quart baking dish. Dip 12 more ladyfinger halves, flat sides down, into espresso; arrange, dipped sides down, on top of first layer. Spread half of cheese mixture evenly over ladyfinger halves; top with ½ cup orange sections. Repeat layers.

3. Cover with plastic wrap, and refrigerate 8 hours or overnight. Sprinkle with cocoa. Top each serving with about 1½ teaspoons Candied Orange Rind. Yield: 9 servings.

CALORIES 179 (30% from fat); FAT 6g (sat 2.9g, mono 2.1g, poly 0.4g); PROTEIN 4.8g; CARB 30.9g; FIBER 1.5g; CHOL 41mg; IRON 0.1mg; SODIUM 182mg; CALC 110mg

Candied Orange Rind:

It's crucial to stir the mixture every 30 seconds or it will burn.

 1 medium orange
 ¼ cup sugar, divided
 1 tablespoon water

1. Carefully remove rind from orange, using a vegetable peeler, making sure not to get any white pith. Cut rind into 1 x ¼-inch-thick strips; set aside.

2. Combine 2 tablespoons sugar and water in a 2-cup glass measure. Microwave at HIGH 1 minute, and stir in orange rind. Microwave at HIGH 2 minutes, stirring every 30 seconds. Add 2 tablespoons sugar; toss well. Spread rind in a single layer on wax paper; let stand at room temperature until dry. Store in an airtight container. Yield: ¼ cup (serving size: about 1½ teaspoons).

CALORIES 64 (0% from fat); FAT 0g; PROTEIN 0.3g; CARB 16.3g; FIBER 1.4g; CHOL 0mg; IRON 0mg; SODIUM 0mg; CALC 13mg

FROZEN COFFEE-FUDGE PIE

Crust:

 1 cup packaged chocolate cookie crumbs (such as Oreo)
 1 tablespoon butter or stick margarine, melted
 1 large egg white, lightly beaten
 Cooking spray

Filling:

 2 teaspoons instant coffee granules
 1 tablespoon boiling water
 ¾ cup fat-free hot fudge topping (such as Smucker's), divided
 4 cups low-fat coffee ice cream (such as Starbucks Low Fat Latte)
 9 chocolate-covered coffee beans (optional)

1. Preheat oven to 350°.

2. To prepare crust, combine first 3 ingredients, and toss with a fork until moist. Press in bottom and up sides of a 9-inch pie plate coated with cooking spray. Bake at 350° for 8 minutes. Cool on a wire rack. Place crust in freezer.

3. To prepare filling, place a large bowl in freezer. Combine coffee granules and boiling water in a small bowl; stir until coffee dissolves. Add 3 tablespoons fudge topping; stir well.

4. Spoon ice cream into chilled bowl, and stir in fudge topping mixture. Spoon ice cream mixture into chilled crust; freeze 30 minutes. Cover with plastic wrap; freeze 4 hours or until set. Place pie in refrigerator 20 minutes to soften before serving. Serve pie with 9 tablespoons fudge topping, and garnish with coffee beans, if desired. Yield: 9 servings (serving size: 1 wedge and 1 tablespoon fudge topping).

CALORIES 306 (22% from fat); FAT 7.6g (sat 3g, mono 2.9g, poly 1.2g); PROTEIN 7.1g; CARB 56.4g; FIBER 0.7g; CHOL 12mg; IRON 1.3mg; SODIUM 225mg; CALC 161mg

PINEAPPLE-COCONUT CREAM PIE

Crust:

1½ cups reduced-calorie vanilla
   wafer crumbs (about 40
   cookies)
 2 tablespoons butter or stick
   margarine, melted
 1 large egg white, lightly beaten
Cooking spray

Filling:

½ cup sugar
¼ cup cornstarch
 1 large egg, lightly beaten
1½ cups 1% low-fat milk
 1 (15¼-ounce) can crushed
   pineapple in juice, drained
¼ cup flaked sweetened coconut
½ teaspoon grated peeled fresh
   ginger
1½ cups frozen reduced-calorie
   whipped topping, thawed
 1 tablespoon flaked sweetened
   coconut, toasted

1. Preheat oven to 350°.
2. To prepare crust, combine first 3 ingredients; toss with a fork until moist. Press in bottom and up sides of a 9-inch pie plate coated with cooking spray. Bake at 350° for 8 minutes. Cool on a wire rack.
3. To prepare filling, combine sugar, cornstarch, and egg in a medium bowl, stirring well with a whisk. Heat milk over medium-high heat in a heavy saucepan to 180° or until tiny bubbles form around edge (do not boil). Gradually add hot milk to sugar mixture, stirring constantly with a whisk. Return milk mixture to pan. Cook over medium heat until thick and bubbly (about 3 minutes), stirring constantly. Reduce heat to low, and cook 2 minutes, stirring constantly. Remove from heat; stir in pineapple, ¼ cup coconut, and ginger. Place pan in a large ice-filled bowl for 15 minutes or until milk mixture is chilled; stir occasionally.
4. Remove pan from ice. Fold in whipped topping, and spoon mixture into prepared crust. Sprinkle with toasted coconut. Cover with plastic wrap. Chill 2 hours. Yield: 8 servings (serving size: 1 wedge).

CALORIES 261 (29% from fat); FAT 8.3g (sat 5.3g, mono 1.8g, poly 0.6g); PROTEIN 4g; CARB 43.2g; FIBER 0.9g; CHOL 37mg; IRON 0.8mg; SODIUM 152mg; CALC 87mg

CHERRY TRIFLE WITH AMARETTO

(pictured on page 152)

You can make this a day ahead and keep chilled until ready to serve. Ladyfingers are light, delicate sponge cakes shaped as their name implies.

½ cup sugar
¼ teaspoon salt
 2 large eggs
 2 large egg yolks
1½ cups 1% low-fat milk
¾ cup low-fat sour cream
 2 teaspoons vanilla extract
¼ cup orange juice
 2 tablespoons amaretto (almond-
   flavored liqueur)
15 ladyfingers
 1 (20-ounce) can light cherry pie
   filling

1. Combine first 4 ingredients in a small bowl; stir well with a whisk. Set aside.
2. Heat milk over medium-high heat in a heavy saucepan to 180° or until tiny bubbles form around edge (do not boil). Remove from heat. Gradually add hot milk to sugar mixture, stirring constantly with a whisk. Return milk mixture to pan, and cook over medium-low heat until thick (about 8 minutes), stirring constantly. Remove from heat. Place pan in a large ice-filled bowl for 25 minutes or until milk mixture comes to room temperature, stirring occasionally. Stir in sour cream and vanilla.
3. Combine orange juice and amaretto. Split ladyfingers in half lengthwise.

Arrange 10 ladyfinger halves, flat sides up, in a single layer in bottom of a 2-quart soufflé dish. Brush 2 tablespoons orange juice mixture over ladyfingers in dish. Spread about 1 cup pie filling evenly over ladyfingers. Spread about 1 cup custard mixture over pie filling. Brush 10 ladyfinger halves with 2 tablespoons orange juice mixture, and line dish with ladyfinger halves rounded sides outward and standing upright. Arrange 10 ladyfinger halves over custard mixture, and brush with remaining orange juice mixture. Spread remaining pie filling over ladyfingers. Spread remaining custard mixture over pie filling. Cover and chill at least 8 hours. Yield: 6 servings.

CALORIES 269 (29% from fat); FAT 8.6g (sat 3.9g, mono 2.8g, poly 0.7g); PROTEIN 6.5g; CARB 44.9g; FIBER 0g; CHOL 185mg; IRON 0.8mg; SODIUM 177mg; CALC 130mg

KEY LIME PIE

 2 large eggs
 2 large egg whites
½ cup Key lime juice (such as
   Nellie and Joe's Famous Key
   West Lime Juice)
 1 teaspoon grated lime rind
 1 (14-ounce) can fat-free
   sweetened condensed milk
 1 (6-ounce) reduced-fat graham
   cracker crust
1½ cups frozen reduced-calorie
   whipped topping, thawed

1. Preheat oven to 350°.
2. Beat eggs and egg whites at medium speed of a mixer until well-blended. Gradually add juice, rind, and milk to egg mixture, beating until well-blended. Spoon mixture into crust, and bake at 350° for 20 minutes or until almost set (center will not be firm but will set up as it chills). Cool pie on a wire rack. Cover loosely, and chill 4 hours. Spread whipped topping evenly over filling. Yield: 8 servings (serving size: 1 wedge).

CALORIES 288 (18% from fat); FAT 5.9g (sat 3g, mono 1.5g, poly 1.1g); PROTEIN 7.6g; CARB 49.2g; FIBER 0.8g; CHOL 56mg; IRON 0.6mg; SODIUM 198mg; CALC 141mg

Smart Salads

In the transitional month of June, no two salads need to look—or taste—alike.

NAPA CABBAGE-AND-TOFU SALAD WITH ORANGE-GINGER VINAIGRETTE

This salad would also work well on cellophane noodles if you're looking for a more substantial main dish. Or you could add a glass of wine and a dessert of fresh fruit for a light meal.

Vinaigrette:

   2 teaspoons grated orange rind
   3 tablespoons fresh orange juice
   1 tablespoon mirin (sweet rice wine) or slightly sweet white wine (such as Riesling)
   1 tablespoon chopped fresh cilantro
   1 teaspoon minced peeled fresh ginger
   2 teaspoons rice vinegar
   1½ teaspoons dark sesame oil
   1 teaspoon low-sodium soy sauce
   ¼ teaspoon salt

Salad:

   4 cups water
   1 (2-inch) slice peeled fresh ginger
   2 cups broccoli florets
   4 cups thinly sliced napa (Chinese) cabbage
   ¼ cup thinly sliced green onions
  10 snow peas, trimmed and cut lengthwise into thin strips
   1 (12.3-ounce) package reduced-fat firm tofu, drained and cut into ½-inch cubes
   2 teaspoons sesame seeds, toasted
   ¼ teaspoon salt
   ¼ teaspoon black pepper

1. To prepare vinaigrette, combine first 9 ingredients in a small bowl; stir well with a whisk, and set aside.
2. To prepare salad, bring water and ginger slice to a simmer in a large saucepan; add broccoli. Cook 1 minute. Add cabbage, green onions, and snow peas; cook 30 seconds. Drain and rinse with cold water; drain well. Place cabbage mixture on several layers of paper towels, and cover with additional paper towels. Let stand 5 minutes, pressing down occasionally. Combine cabbage mixture, tofu, sesame seeds, ¼ teaspoon salt, and pepper in a large bowl. Add vinaigrette, tossing to coat. Yield: 2 servings (serving size: 2½ cups).

CALORIES 204 (29% from fat); FAT 6.6g (sat 0.8g, mono 2g, poly 2.4g); PROTEIN 19.2g; CARB 18.3g; FIBER 5.8g; CHOL 0mg; IRON 5.3mg; SODIUM 918mg; CALC 348mg

QUINOA SALAD WITH APRICOTS AND PISTACHIOS

A tiny grain with a texture lighter than rice, quinoa (KEEN-wah) is often dubbed "supergrain" because it's rich in many nutrients, particularly protein. If apricots are in season where you live, substitute fresh—about 6, coarsely chopped—for dried.

Salad:

   3 cups water
   1 cup uncooked quinoa
   ½ teaspoon salt
   4 cups thinly sliced romaine lettuce
   ⅓ cup dried apricots (about 10), quartered
   ⅓ cup golden raisins
   ¼ cup shelled dry-roasted pistachios
   ¼ cup thinly sliced green onions
   ¼ cup chopped fresh parsley
   ¼ cup chopped fresh cilantro
   2 tablespoons finely chopped fresh mint
   ¼ teaspoon black pepper

Vinaigrette:

   ½ teaspoon grated lime rind
   3 tablespoons fresh lime juice
   2 tablespoons mirin (sweet rice wine) or slightly sweet white wine (such as Riesling)
   1 tablespoon olive oil
   ½ to 1 teaspoon minced seeded jalapeño pepper
   ¼ teaspoon salt
   ¼ teaspoon ground cumin
   ¼ teaspoon ground coriander
   ¼ teaspoon paprika

1. To prepare salad, combine water, quinoa, and ½ teaspoon salt in a large saucepan. Bring to a boil; reduce heat, and simmer 15 minutes. Drain quinoa mixture through a sieve over a bowl, reserving 3 tablespoons cooking liquid. Combine quinoa mixture, lettuce, and next 8 ingredients in a large bowl; set aside.
2. To prepare vinaigrette, combine reserved 3 tablespoons cooking liquid, lime rind, and remaining 8 ingredients in a bowl, stirring well with a whisk. Pour vinaigrette over quinoa mixture, and toss well. Yield: 4 servings (serving size: 1¾ cups).

CALORIES 365 (29% from fat); FAT 11.8g (sat 1.5g, mono 6.9g, poly 2.2g); PROTEIN 10.4g; CARB 57.7g; FIBER 10.6g; CHOL 0mg; IRON 7.2mg; SODIUM 481mg; CALC 96mg

BEET-AND-LENTIL SALAD ON CABBAGE SLAW

Beets may seem wintry, but in fact they're likely to be freshest in summer. Look for golden beets or Chioggia beets (a variety with red and white concentric circles) to add cheery color to this salad. But red beets work fine, too.

Pickled onion:

   ¾ cup finely chopped red onion
   ½ cup red wine vinegar

Continued

Dressing:

- 2 tablespoons olive oil
- 2 tablespoons red wine vinegar
- 1 tablespoon balsamic vinegar
- 1 teaspoon Worcestershire sauce
- 1 teaspoon prepared mustard
- ¼ teaspoon prepared horseradish
- ¼ teaspoon salt
- ⅛ teaspoon black pepper
- 1 garlic clove, minced

Salad:

- 2 pounds small golden, Chioggia, or red beets
- 1 cup dried green or brown lentils
- ¼ cup finely diced carrot
- 2 garlic cloves, peeled
- 1 bay leaf
- ⅓ cup chopped fresh parsley
- 2 tablespoons capers
- ⅛ teaspoon salt
- ⅛ teaspoon black pepper

Slaw:

- 7 cups thinly sliced green cabbage
- 1 tablespoon red wine vinegar
- ⅛ teaspoon salt
- Chopped fresh parsley (optional)

1. To prepare pickled onion, combine onion and ½ cup vinegar in a bowl. Let stand 30 minutes; drain.
2. To prepare dressing, combine oil and next 8 ingredients in a bowl, stirring with a whisk.
3. To prepare salad, leave root and 1 inch stem on beets; scrub with a brush. Place in a medium saucepan; cover with water. Bring to a boil; cover, reduce heat, and simmer 20 minutes or until tender. Drain and rinse with cold water. Drain; cool. Trim off beet roots; rub off skins. Cut beets into ½-inch cubes; place in a large bowl. Set aside. Place lentils, carrot, 2 garlic cloves, and bay leaf in a large saucepan; cover with water to 2 inches above lentils. Bring to a boil; cover, reduce heat, and simmer 20 minutes or until tender. Drain well. Discard garlic cloves and bay leaf. Add lentil mixture, pickled onion, dressing, ⅓ cup

parsley, capers, ⅛ teaspoon salt, and ⅛ teaspoon pepper to beets. Set aside.
4. To prepare slaw, toss cabbage with 1 tablespoon red wine vinegar and ⅛ teaspoon salt. Divide slaw evenly among 4 plates; top with salad. Garnish with chopped parsley, if desired. Yield: 4 servings (serving size: 1¾ cups slaw and about 1 cup salad).

CALORIES 340 (21% from fat); FAT 7.9g (sat 1.1g, mono 5.2g, poly 1g); PROTEIN 18.2g; CARB 53.6g; FIBER 10.6g; CHOL 0mg; IRON 6.7mg; SODIUM 801mg; CALC 124mg

SPRING NOODLE SALAD WITH GINGER-PEANUT VINAIGRETTE

Salad:

- ½ cup boiling water
- 1 (½-ounce) package dried shiitake mushrooms
- 6 ounces uncooked spaghettini or angel hair pasta
- 2 cups (3-inch) julienne-cut carrot (about 8 ounces)
- 2 cups (1-inch) diagonally sliced asparagus
- ½ pound snow peas, trimmed and cut lengthwise into thin strips

Vinaigrette:

- ½ cup cilantro leaves
- ¼ cup coarsely chopped fresh basil
- 2 tablespoons balsamic vinegar
- 1½ tablespoons low-sodium soy sauce
- 1 tablespoon minced peeled fresh ginger
- 1 tablespoon mirin (sweet rice wine) or slightly sweet white wine (such as Riesling)
- 1 tablespoon roasted peanut oil or vegetable oil
- ½ teaspoon salt
- 2 garlic cloves, minced
- 1 jalapeño pepper, halved and seeded

Remaining ingredients:

- 1 cup diagonally sliced green onions
- ¼ cup coarsely chopped dry-roasted peanuts, divided
- ½ cup alfalfa sprouts

1. To prepare salad, combine ½ cup boiling water and mushrooms in a bowl; cover and let stand 30 minutes. Drain mushrooms in a colander over a bowl, reserving 2 tablespoons soaking liquid. Discard mushroom stems, and thinly slice mushroom caps. Cook spaghettini in boiling water 2 minutes, omitting salt and fat. Add carrot; cook 1 minute. Add asparagus; cook 1 minute. Add snow peas; cook 1 minute. Drain well. Add mushrooms to salad; toss well.
2. To prepare vinaigrette, place 2 tablespoons reserved mushroom soaking liquid, cilantro, and next 9 ingredients in a food processor; process until smooth.
3. Combine salad, vinaigrette, onions, and 2 tablespoons peanuts in a large bowl; toss well. Arrange 1¼ cups salad mixture on each of 4 plates. Top each serving with 2 tablespoons sprouts; sprinkle each with 1½ teaspoons peanuts. Yield: 4 servings.

CALORIES 344 (24% from fat); FAT 9.1g (sat 1.4g, mono 3.9g, poly 3g); PROTEIN 13.6g; CARB 54.5g; FIBER 8.4g; CHOL 0mg; IRON 5.3mg; SODIUM 512mg; CALC 115mg

BROCCOLI, CHERRY TOMATO, AND PASTA SALAD

(pictured on page 149)

Herb mixture:

- ½ cup fresh flat-leaf parsley leaves
- ⅓ cup fresh basil leaves
- 1 tablespoon chopped fresh dill
- 1 teaspoon grated lemon rind
- 12 mint leaves
- 1 garlic clove, peeled

Dressing:

- 2 garlic cloves, peeled
- ⅓ cup 2% low-fat cottage cheese
- ¼ cup low-fat buttermilk
- 1 tablespoon fresh lemon juice
- 1 tablespoon red wine vinegar
- 1 tablespoon balsamic vinegar
- 1 tablespoon extra-virgin olive oil
- Dash of black pepper
- ½ cup (2 ounces) crumbled feta cheese

Salad:

- 7 cups small broccoli florets
- 2½ cups sliced mushrooms
- 2 cups cherry tomatoes, halved
- 2 cups cooked medium seashell or rotini pasta (about 4 ounces uncooked pasta)
- ½ cup minced shallots
- 2 tablespoons capers
- ¼ teaspoon black pepper
- 1 (14-ounce) can artichoke hearts, rinsed, drained, and halved

1. To prepare herb mixture, combine first 6 ingredients on a cutting board; finely chop, and reserve 3 tablespoons. Set remaining herb mixture aside.
2. To prepare dressing, place reserved 3 tablespoons herb mixture in a food processor. Drop 2 garlic cloves through food chute with food processor on; process until minced. Add cottage cheese and next 6 ingredients to food processor; process until smooth. Stir in feta.
3. To prepare salad, steam broccoli, covered, 5 minutes or until crisp-tender. Cool. Combine remaining herb mixture, broccoli, and remaining 7 ingredients in a large bowl. Pour dressing over salad; toss well. Yield: 4 servings (serving size: 2½ cups).

CALORIES 327 (24% from fat); FAT 8.8g (sat 3g, mono 3.4g, poly 0.9g); PROTEIN 18.4g; CARB 50g; FIBER 7g; CHOL 14mg; IRON 4.3mg; SODIUM 768mg; CALC 248mg

Mango Gonna Get Ya

Irrepressibly sunny and sensuous, the globe-hopping tropical mango is dancing its big-flavor beat into the heartland of America.

SPINACH SALAD WITH SCALLOPS, MANGO, AND SUGARED MACADAMIAS

- 2 tablespoons sugar
- 3 tablespoons water, divided
- ¼ cup macadamia nuts or pecans
- Cooking spray
- 1½ cups diced peeled mango (about 1 large), divided
- ¼ cup fresh lime juice
- ½ teaspoon grated peeled fresh ginger
- ⅛ teaspoon salt
- ½ teaspoon poppy seeds
- 1 pound sea scallops
- ¼ teaspoon salt
- ⅛ teaspoon black pepper
- 1 teaspoon vegetable oil
- 8 cups packaged spinach
- 1 cup vertically sliced red onion

1. Preheat oven to 350°.
2. Combine sugar and 1 tablespoon water in a saucepan; bring to a boil. Remove from heat; stir in nuts. Spread nut mixture on a baking sheet coated with cooking spray. Bake at 350° for 10 minutes. Immediately scrape onto a sheet of foil coated with cooking spray. Spread evenly; cool completely. Lightly chop; set aside.
3. Combine 2 tablespoons water, ½ cup mango, juice, ginger, and ⅛ teaspoon salt in a blender or food processor; process until smooth. Stir in poppy seeds; set dressing aside.
4. Sprinkle scallops with ¼ teaspoon salt and pepper. Heat oil in a grill pan or nonstick skillet over medium-high heat. Add scallops; sauté 2 minutes on each side. Remove from pan.
5. Arrange 2 cups spinach on each of 4 plates. Top evenly with scallops, 1 cup mango, and ¼ cup onion. Drizzle each serving with 3 tablespoons dressing; sprinkle with 1 tablespoon nut mixture. Yield: 4 servings.

CALORIES 278 (30% from fat); FAT 9.3g (sat 1.4g, mono 5.5g, poly 1.3g); PROTEIN 23.6g; CARB 28.5g; FIBER 6.1g; CHOL 37mg; IRON 3.7mg; SODIUM 494mg; CALC 161mg

CHICKEN WITH CURRIED MANGO SAUCE

- 4 (4-ounce) skinned, boned chicken breast halves
- ½ teaspoon salt, divided
- 1 tablespoon vegetable oil, divided
- 1 cup chopped onion
- ½ cup chopped red bell pepper
- 2 teaspoons grated peeled fresh ginger
- 1 teaspoon curry powder
- ½ teaspoon ground coriander
- 2 garlic cloves, crushed
- 1¼ cups fat-free, less-sodium chicken broth
- 1½ teaspoons cornstarch
- 1⅓ cups cubed peeled mango (about 1 large)
- 2 cups hot cooked basmati rice
- ¼ cup thinly sliced green onions

1. Sprinkle chicken with ¼ teaspoon salt. Heat 1 teaspoon oil in a large nonstick skillet over medium-high heat. Add chicken; cook 3 minutes on each side or until done. Remove from pan; keep warm.
2. Heat 2 teaspoons oil in pan over medium-high heat. Add chopped onion and bell pepper; sauté 5 minutes, stirring occasionally. Add ¼ teaspoon salt, ginger, curry, coriander, and garlic, and sauté 30 seconds. Combine broth and cornstarch, and add to pan. Bring to a boil, and cook 1 minute, stirring constantly. Remove from heat. Stir in mango.

Continued

3. Spoon rice onto 4 plates, and top with chicken. Spoon sauce over chicken, and sprinkle with green onions. Yield: 4 servings (serving size: 1 chicken breast half, ¾ cup mango sauce, and ½ cup rice).

CALORIES 335 (14% from fat); FAT 5.3g (sat 1.1g, mono 1.5g, poly 2.1g); PROTEIN 30.4g; CARB 41.5g; FIBER 2.8g; CHOL 66mg; IRON 2.4mg; SODIUM 522mg; CALC 49mg

MANGO UPSIDE-DOWN CAKE

    1   tablespoon butter or stick
        margarine, melted
    ¼   cup packed dark brown sugar
    2   tablespoons chopped
        crystallized ginger
    1   cup sliced peeled mango (about
        1 medium)
    ⅔   cup granulated sugar
    5   tablespoons butter or stick
        margarine, softened
    ½   cup egg substitute or 3 large
        egg whites
    1½ teaspoons vanilla extract
    1⅓ cups all-purpose flour
    2   teaspoons baking powder
    ½   teaspoon ground cinnamon
    ¼   teaspoon salt
    ¾   cup fat-free milk
        Frozen fat-free whipped topping
        (optional)

1. Preheat oven to 350°.
2. Coat bottom of a 9-inch round cake pan with 1 tablespoon melted butter. Sprinkle with brown sugar and ginger. Arrange mango slices spokelike over brown sugar mixture; set aside.
3. Beat granulated sugar and 5 tablespoons butter at medium speed of a mixer until well-blended. Add egg substitute and vanilla, beating until well-blended. Lightly spoon flour into dry measuring cups; level with a knife. Combine flour, baking powder, cinnamon, and salt. Add flour mixture to sugar mixture alternately with milk, beginning and ending with flour mixture; mix after each addition. Pour batter into prepared pan.
4. Bake at 350° for 40 minutes. Cool in pan 5 minutes on a wire rack.

Loosen cake from sides of pan. Place a plate upside down on top of cake. Invert onto plate. Garnish with whipped topping, if desired. Yield: 8 servings.

CALORIES 271 (30% from fat); FAT 8.9g (sat 5.4g, mono 2.5g, poly 0.4g); PROTEIN 4.2g; CARB 44.1g; FIBER 0.9g; CHOL 24mg; IRON 1.8mg; SODIUM 276mg; CALC 86mg

COCONUT-RICE SALAD WITH MANGO AND SHRIMP

    5¾ cups water, divided
    1   pound medium shrimp, peeled
        and deveined
    ¾   cup light coconut milk
    1¼ cups uncooked long-grain rice
    ¼   teaspoon salt
    2   cups cubed peeled ripe mango
        (about 2 large)
    1   cup diced seeded peeled
        cucumber
    ¼   cup chopped fresh cilantro
    ¼   cup thinly sliced green onions
    ¼   cup fresh lime juice
    3   tablespoons chopped fresh mint
    2   tablespoons minced seeded
        jalapeño pepper
    ½   teaspoon salt

1. Bring 4 cups water to a boil in a large saucepan. Add shrimp; cook 1½ minutes or until done. Drain and rinse with cold water. Cover and chill.
2. Combine 1¾ cups water and coconut milk in pan, and bring to a boil. Add rice and ¼ teaspoon salt; cover, reduce heat, and simmer 20 minutes or until liquid is absorbed. Remove from heat, and fluff with a fork. Spoon rice mixture into a large bowl; cool.
3. Add shrimp, mango, and remaining ingredients to rice mixture, tossing well. Cover and chill. Yield: 4 servings (serving size: 2 cups).

CALORIES 396 (10% from fat); FAT 4.4g (sat 2g, mono 0.8g, poly 1g); PROTEIN 22.4g; CARB 65.8g; FIBER 2.6g; CHOL 130mg; IRON 5mg; SODIUM 574mg; CALC 86mg

MANGO FREEZE

    4   cups peeled ripe mango, cut
        into 1-inch pieces (about 4
        large)
    ¾   cup powdered sugar
    ½   cup mashed ripe banana
    1   tablespoon fresh lime juice
    1   (8-ounce) carton vanilla low-fat
        yogurt

1. Place mango pieces on a baking sheet lined with plastic wrap; freeze at least 4 hours. Remove from freezer; let stand 10 minutes.
2. Place mango pieces in a food processor or blender; process until smooth, scraping sides of bowl occasionally. Add sugar, banana, and lime juice. With food processor on, slowly spoon yogurt through food chute; process until smooth, scraping sides of bowl once. Spoon mixture into a freezer-safe container; cover and freeze 3 hours or until firm. Yield: 10 servings (serving size: ½ cup).
Note: Let Mango Freeze soften a little before serving.

CALORIES 108 (4% from fat); FAT 0.5g (sat 0.2g, mono 0.2g, poly 0.1g); PROTEIN 1.6g; CARB 26.1g; FIBER 1.3g; CHOL 1mg; IRON 0.1mg; SODIUM 17mg; CALC 46mg

CUTTING MANGOES

With a sharp knife, slice the fruit lengthwise on each side of the flat pit. Score each half in square cross-sections. Turn inside out, and cut the chunks from the skin.

JULY · AUGUST

Mediterranean Weeknights

You can't bring the entire Mediterranean home, but with these easy adaptations of six favorites, you'll think you almost did.

You can easily make a Mediterranean weeknight meal match the country of your choice with specific flavor groupings. Our recipes are accompanied by taste boxes to let you know which ingredients you'll need for each country as you "tour" the six regions—almonds in Spain, for example, or cumin in Morocco. All the cuisines use at least some of the same ingredients, though.

TASTE OF SPAIN	
Almonds	Paprika
Garlic	Roasted bell
Manchego cheese	peppers
Olives	Saffron
Orange zest	Sherry vinegar

TASTE OF TURKEY			
Bay leaf	Cumin	Hazelnuts	Oregano
Black pepper	Dill	Lentils	Paprika
Coriander	Figs	Mint	Yogurt

TURKISH LAMB, FIG, AND MINT KEBABS

Serve this with a side of bulgur tossed with a little olive oil and feta cheese. Beef or pork also will taste great in place of the lamb.

  2 pounds lean boned leg of lamb
  3 tablespoons chopped fresh or
     1 tablespoon dried mint
  2 teaspoons olive oil
  1 teaspoon ground cumin
  ½ teaspoon salt
  ½ teaspoon ground cinnamon
  ½ teaspoon paprika
  ¼ teaspoon ground nutmeg
  ¼ teaspoon black pepper
  3 garlic cloves, minced
  1 cup boiling water
 24 dried figs
  2 red onions
     Cooking spray

1. Trim fat from lamb. Cut lamb into 48 (1-inch) pieces; set aside.
2. Combine mint and next 8 ingredients in a large zip-top plastic bag. Add lamb; seal and marinate in refrigerator 20 minutes, turning bag occasionally. Remove lamb from bag, and discard marinade.
3. Combine boiling water and figs in a large bowl; cover and let stand 10 minutes or until soft. Drain well; cut in half. Cut each onion into 6 wedges; cut each wedge in half crosswise (for a total of 24 pieces).
4. Thread 4 lamb pieces, 2 figs, and 2 onion pieces alternately onto each of 12 (10-inch) skewers.
5. Prepare grill or broiler.
6. Place kebabs on a grill rack or broiler pan coated with cooking spray; cook 4 minutes on each side or until desired degree of doneness. Yield: 6 servings (serving size: 2 kebabs).

CALORIES 441 (23% from fat); FAT 11.3g (sat 3.4g, mono 4.6g, poly 1.1g); PROTEIN 35g; CARB 53.4g; FIBER 10.1g; CHOL 101mg; IRON 4.4mg; SODIUM 185mg; CALC 131mg

SPANISH SHERRIED SHRIMP

(pictured on page 185)

Serve with long-grain rice tossed with garlic and almonds.

  1   tablespoon all-purpose flour
  2¼   teaspoons chopped fresh or
       ¾ teaspoon dried thyme
  ½   teaspoon salt, divided
  ¼   teaspoon black pepper
  1   pound medium shrimp, peeled
       and deveined
  1   tablespoon olive oil
  1½   cups chopped onion
  1½   cups chopped red or green bell
       pepper
  3   garlic cloves, minced
  ⅓   cup medium dry sherry
  1   (14.5-ounce) can no-salt-added
       whole tomatoes, undrained
       and chopped
  2   teaspoons sherry vinegar or
       white wine vinegar

1. Combine flour, thyme, ¼ teaspoon salt, and black pepper in a large zip-top plastic bag. Add shrimp; seal and shake well. Heat oil in a large nonstick skillet over medium-high heat. Add shrimp, and sauté 3 minutes. Remove shrimp from pan. Add onion, bell pepper, and garlic to pan; sauté 2 minutes. Add sherry; cook 1 minute. Add ¼ teaspoon salt and tomatoes; cook 4 minutes. Stir in shrimp and vinegar. Yield: 4 servings (serving size: 1¼ cups).

CALORIES 196 (24% from fat); FAT 5.3g (sat 0.8g, mono 2.7g, poly 1g); PROTEIN 19.7g; CARB 17.2g; FIBER 2.2g; CHOL 129mg; IRON 3.9mg; SODIUM 453mg; CALC 106mg

TASTE OF ITALY

Balsamic vinegar	Garlic
Cannellini beans	Lemon
Capers	Parmesan cheese
Dried basil	Pine nuts

TASTE OF MOROCCO

Chickpeas	Ground ginger
Cilantro	Honey
Cinnamon	Lemon
Cumin	Orange
Dried fruit	Paprika
Garlic	Saffron

TASTE OF FRANCE

Dried basil	Niçoise olives
Dried tarragon	Parsley
Herbes de	Tarragon vinegar
Provence	White wine

ITALIAN BEAN SALAD WITH ESCAROLE

(pictured on page 187)

Escarole is a bitter green similar to curly endive. If you can't find it, substitute 6 cups curly endive and 6 cups romaine lettuce in this main-dish salad.

Salad:

 2 cups diced tomato
 2 (19-ounce) cans cannellini beans or other white beans, rinsed and drained
12 cups torn escarole
1½ cups thinly sliced fennel bulb (about 1 bulb)
 ¾ cup thinly sliced red onion
 ¼ cup (1 ounce) grated fresh Parmesan cheese
 1 cup thinly sliced fresh basil
 2 teaspoons grated lemon rind
 3 tablespoons fresh lemon juice
 1 teaspoon fennel seeds

Vinaigrette:

 2 tablespoons extra-virgin olive oil
 2 tablespoons balsamic vinegar
 1 teaspoon fennel seeds
 1 teaspoon honey
 ⅛ teaspoon black pepper

1. To prepare salad, combine first 10 ingredients in a bowl; cover and chill 30 minutes.
2. To prepare vinaigrette, combine oil and next 4 ingredients in a small bowl, stirring with a whisk. Add to salad; toss well. Yield: 6 servings (serving size: about 2½ cups).

CALORIES 290 (28% from fat); FAT 9.1g (sat 1.8g, mono 4.4g, poly 1.9g); PROTEIN 14.4g; CARB 41.8g; FIBER 5.9g; CHOL 3mg; IRON 5.1mg; SODIUM 330mg; CALC 212mg

MOROCCAN TURKEY BURGERS

Serve these with couscous tossed with chopped fresh spinach. We used the ground turkey that's a combination of light and dark meat. You can use ground turkey breast, but the burgers won't be as moist.

 1 cup chopped onion
 ⅓ cup ketchup
 ¼ cup pitted green olives, chopped
 ¼ cup dried currants or raisins
 1 teaspoon grated lemon rind
 1 teaspoon cumin seeds
 ¼ teaspoon ground cinnamon
 ⅛ teaspoon black pepper
 1 pound ground turkey
 4 curly leaf lettuce leaves
 4 (¼-inch-thick) slices tomato
 4 (2-ounce) Kaiser rolls or hamburger buns, toasted

1. Combine first 9 ingredients in a bowl. Divide turkey mixture into 4 equal portions, shaping each into a 1-inch-thick patty. Place a large non-stick skillet over medium heat until hot. Add patties; cook 6 minutes on each side or until no longer pink. Arrange lettuce leaves and tomato slices over bottom halves of rolls; top with patties and remaining halves of rolls. Yield: 4 servings (serving size: 1 burger).

CALORIES 403 (29% from fat); FAT 13.1g (sat 4.1g, mono 5.7g, poly 2.6g); PROTEIN 26g; CARB 44.2g; FIBER 2.7g; CHOL 96mg; IRON 3.9mg; SODIUM 711mg; CALC 117mg

PROVENÇALE GRILLED TUNA

Serve with steamed red potatoes tossed with olive oil and Parmesan cheese. Herbes de Provence is a blend of dried herbs commonly used in southern France. It usually contains basil, fennel, lavender, marjoram, rosemary, and sage.

1½ cups chopped seeded tomato (about 1½ pounds)
 ¾ cup chopped fresh parsley
 ¼ cup chopped pitted niçoise olives
 1 tablespoon white wine vinegar
 ¼ teaspoon dried tarragon
 ¼ teaspoon salt
 2 garlic cloves, minced
 4 (6-ounce) tuna steaks (about ¾ inch thick)
1½ teaspoons dried herbes de Provence
 ¼ teaspoon salt
Cooking spray
Chive sprigs (optional)

1. Combine first 7 ingredients in a medium bowl. Cover and chill 20 minutes.
2. Prepare grill.
3. Sprinkle fish with herbes de Provence and ¼ teaspoon salt. Place fish on a grill rack coated with cooking spray; cook 3 minutes on each side or until fish is medium-rare or desired degree of doneness. Serve fish with tomato mixture. Garnish with chives, if desired. Yield: 4 servings (serving size: 1 tuna steak and ½ cup tomato mixture).

CALORIES 278 (31% from fat); FAT 9.7g (sat 2.4g, mono 3.1g, poly 3.1g); PROTEIN 40.8g; CARB 5g; FIBER 1.6g; CHOL 65mg; IRON 3.2mg; SODIUM 447mg; CALC 31mg

GREEK CHICKEN WITH CAPERS AND RAISINS IN FETA SAUCE

- 4 (4-ounce) skinned, boned chicken breast halves
- 2 tablespoons all-purpose flour
- 1 teaspoon dried oregano
- 1 tablespoon olive oil
- 1 cup thinly sliced onion
- 3 garlic cloves, minced
- 1½ cups fat-free, less-sodium chicken broth
- ⅓ cup golden raisins
- 2 tablespoons lemon juice
- 2 tablespoons capers
- ¼ cup (1 ounce) crumbled feta cheese
- 4 thin lemon slices

1. Place each chicken breast half between 2 sheets of heavy-duty plastic wrap; flatten to ¼-inch thickness, using a meat mallet or rolling pin. Combine flour and oregano in a shallow dish; dredge chicken in flour mixture.
2. Heat oil in a large nonstick skillet over medium-high heat. Add chicken; cook 5 minutes on each side. Remove chicken from pan; keep warm. Add onion and garlic to pan; sauté 2 minutes. Stir in broth, raisins, and lemon juice; cook 3 minutes, scraping pan to loosen browned bits. Return chicken to pan. Cover, reduce heat, and simmer 10 minutes or until chicken is done. Remove chicken from pan; keep warm. Add capers and cheese to pan, stirring with a whisk; top each chicken breast with ¼ cup sauce and 1 lemon slice. Yield: 4 servings.

CALORIES 256 (23% from fat); FAT 6.5g (sat 1.9g, mono 3.2g, poly 0.7g); PROTEIN 30g; CARB 19g; FIBER 1.3g; CHOL 72mg; IRON 1.6mg; SODIUM 671mg; CALC 71mg

Cool Coffee Desserts

Nothing works better as the perfect counterpunch to sweet summertime treats.

We crave sweets that both tantalize and refresh, but they can also become cloying, leaving us longing for something to clean a sugar-coated palate. The deep flavor of coffee, with both acidic and bitter components, is the perfect dessert-making solution. It's a great team player on the light side, too—coffee heightens the flavor of rich ingredients such as cream and nuts.

WHITE RUSSIAN TIRAMISU

This creamy tiramisu uses double-strength brewed coffee and mascarpone cheese—a soft triple cream cheese that comes in small tubs. Use regular cream cheese in its place, if you prefer.

- ½ cup ground coffee beans
- 1¾ cups cold water
- ¼ cup Kahlúa (coffee-flavored liqueur), divided
- ½ cup (3½ ounces) mascarpone cheese
- 1 (8-ounce) block fat-free cream cheese, softened
- ⅓ cup packed brown sugar
- ¼ cup granulated sugar
- 24 ladyfingers (2 [3-ounce] packages)
- 2 teaspoons unsweetened cocoa

1. Assemble drip coffee maker according to manufacturer's directions. Place ground coffee in coffee filter or filter basket. Add cold water to coffee maker, and brew to make 1½ cups. Combine brewed coffee and 2 tablespoons Kahlúa in a shallow dish, and cool.
2. Combine cheeses in a large bowl. Beat at high speed of a mixer until smooth. Add sugars and 2 tablespoons Kahlúa, and beat until well-blended.
3. Split ladyfingers in half lengthwise.
4. Quickly dip 24 ladyfinger halves, flat sides down, into coffee mixture; place, dipped sides down, in bottom of an 8-inch square baking dish, slightly overlapping ladyfinger halves. Spread half of cheese mixture over ladyfingers; sprinkle with 1 teaspoon cocoa.

Repeat procedure with remaining ladyfinger halves, coffee mixture, cheese mixture, and 1 teaspoon cocoa.
5. Place 1 wooden pick in each corner and 1 in center of tiramisu (to prevent plastic wrap from sticking to cheese mixture); cover with plastic wrap. Chill 2 hours. Yield: 12 servings.

CALORIES 134 (30% from fat); FAT 4.5g (sat 2.2g, mono 1.5g, poly 0.4g); PROTEIN 3.3g; CARB 21.7g; FIBER 0g; CHOL 31mg; IRON 0.3mg; SODIUM 139mg; CALC 77mg

INSTANT TRIPLE-COFFEE ICE CREAM

Here's a quick way to make rich-tasting coffee ice cream. We've used three kinds of coffee flavoring for a deep, complex taste.

- ¼ cup Kahlúa (coffee-flavored liqueur)
- 2 teaspoons instant espresso or 4 teaspoons instant coffee granules
- 4 cups vanilla low-fat ice cream, softened
- 2 teaspoons ground coffee beans

1. Place a large bowl in freezer 10 minutes. Combine liqueur and espresso in a microwave-safe bowl; microwave at HIGH 30 seconds. Stir until granules dissolve. Combine liqueur mixture, ice cream, and ground coffee in chilled bowl. Cover and freeze at least 3 hours or until firm. Yield: 6 servings (serving size: ½ cup).

Note: To soften ice cream in microwave, microwave on HIGH 10 seconds or until soft.

CALORIES 156 (22% from fat); FAT 3.8g (sat 2.3g, mono 1.1g, poly 0.2g); PROTEIN 3.4g; CARB 23.1g; FIBER 0g; CHOL 12mg; IRON 0.1mg; SODIUM 75mg; CALC 123mg

COFFEE-HAZELNUT BISCOTTI

These biscotti are used to complete the Coffee-Hazelnut Parfaits (see recipe), but they're also delicious on their own.

2   tablespoons Frangelico
    (hazelnut-flavored liqueur)
2   tablespoons unsweetened cocoa
1   teaspoon instant espresso or
    2 teaspoons instant coffee
    granules
1   teaspoon vegetable oil
2   large egg whites
1   large egg
1⅓   cups all-purpose flour
½   cup whole-wheat flour
½   cup granulated sugar
½   cup packed brown sugar
½   cup coarsely chopped toasted
    hazelnuts, divided
1   teaspoon baking soda
⅛   teaspoon salt
2   teaspoons ground coffee beans
    Cooking spray

1. Preheat oven to 300°.
2. Place liqueur in a small bowl. Microwave at HIGH 10 seconds. Stir in cocoa and espresso until smooth. Add oil, egg whites, and egg, stirring with a whisk until blended.
3. Lightly spoon flours into dry measuring cups; level with a knife. Place flours, sugars, 2 tablespoons hazelnuts, baking soda, and salt in a food processor; process until hazelnuts are ground. Add ground coffee; pulse 2 times or until blended. With processor on, slowly add liqueur mixture through food chute; process until dough forms a ball. Add 6 tablespoons hazelnuts; pulse 5 times or until blended (dough will be sticky). Turn dough out onto a floured surface; knead lightly 4 or 5 times. Divide into 3 equal portions, shaping each portion into a 10-inch-long roll. Place rolls 3 inches apart on a large baking sheet coated with cooking spray. Bake at 300° for 28 minutes. Remove rolls from baking sheet; cool 10 minutes on a wire rack.
4. Cut each roll diagonally into 20 (½-inch) slices. Place slices, cut sides down, on baking sheets. Bake at 300° for 20 minutes. Turn cookies over; bake an additional 10 minutes (cookies will be soft in center but will harden as they cool). Remove from baking sheets; cool completely on wire racks. Yield: 5 dozen (serving size: 1 biscotto).
Note: To toast hazelnuts, place on a baking sheet, and bake at 350° for 15 minutes, stirring once. Turn nuts out onto a towel. Roll up towel, and rub off skins. Chop nuts.

CALORIES 38 (24% from fat); FAT 1g (sat 0.1g, mono 0.6g, poly 0.1g); PROTEIN 0.8g; CARB 6.9g; FIBER 0.2g; CHOL 4mg; IRON 0.3mg; SODIUM 30mg; CALC 5mg

COFFEE-HAZELNUT PARFAITS

Instant Triple-Coffee Ice Cream
    (see recipe on previous page)
¼   cup Kahlúa-Fudge Sauce
    (page 174)
8   Coffee-Hazelnut Biscotti (see
    recipe), coarsely chopped

1. Place ¼ cup Instant Triple-Coffee Ice Cream in each of 6 parfait glasses. Top each with 1 teaspoon Kahlúa-Fudge Sauce. Sprinkle with half of chopped Coffee-Hazelnut Biscotti. Repeat layers. Yield: 6 servings.

CALORIES 242 (21% from fat); FAT 5.6g (sat 2.8g, mono 2g, poly 0.3g); PROTEIN 5.4g; CARB 38.8g; FIBER 0.3g; CHOL 19mg; IRON 0.7mg; SODIUM 125mg; CALC 155mg

CHOOSING YOUR COFFEE

To get the richest coffee flavor, we used instant espresso and freshly ground beans. Medium-grind beans, about the size used for automatic-drip coffee, are the best. One tablespoon beans yields about 2 teaspoons ground coffee.

MOCHA-ALMOND PIE

Crust:

15   reduced-fat cream-filled
    chocolate sandwich cookies
    (such as Reduced Fat Oreos)
1   tablespoon hot water
1   teaspoon unsweetened cocoa
½   teaspoon instant espresso or
    1 teaspoon instant coffee
    granules
    Cooking spray

Filling:

1½   teaspoons unflavored gelatin
2   tablespoons water
1   tablespoon instant espresso or
    2 tablespoons instant coffee
    granules
3   tablespoons sugar
2   tablespoons unsweetened cocoa
1   cup evaporated low-fat milk
2   large egg yolks, lightly beaten
⅛   teaspoon almond extract
1¼   cups frozen reduced-calorie
    whipped topping, thawed
1   tablespoon sliced almonds,
    toasted

1. To prepare crust, place cookies in a food processor; process until crumbly. Add hot water, 1 teaspoon cocoa, and ½ teaspoon espresso; pulse 5 times or just until moist. Press in bottom and up sides of a 9-inch pie plate coated with cooking spray; set aside.
2. To prepare filling, sprinkle gelatin over 2 tablespoons water in a small saucepan; let stand 1 minute. Cook over low heat, stirring until gelatin dissolves (about 3 minutes). Remove from heat; stir in 1 tablespoon espresso, and set aside. Combine sugar and 2 tablespoons cocoa in a small saucepan over low heat. Gradually add milk; cook until smooth (about 6 minutes), stirring frequently with a whisk. Gradually add hot milk mixture to egg yolks, stirring constantly with a whisk. Return egg mixture to pan. Cook over medium heat until thick (about 4 minutes),

Continued

stirring constantly. Remove from heat. Stir in gelatin mixture. Place pan in a large ice-filled bowl until filling cools to room temperature (about 15 minutes), stirring occasionally. Stir in almond extract. Spoon filling mixture into a large bowl; chill 30 minutes. Fold in whipped topping. Spoon filling into prepared crust. Chill 8 hours. Sprinkle with almonds. Yield: 8 servings (serving size: 1 wedge).

CALORIES 178 (30% from fat); FAT 6g (sat 2.9g, mono 0.9g, poly 1.2g); PROTEIN 5.5g; CARB 27g; FIBER 0.7g; CHOL 60mg; IRON 1.7mg; SODIUM 165mg; CALC 99mg

KAHLÚA-FUDGE SAUCE

1   (14-ounce) can low-fat
      sweetened condensed milk
½   cup boiling water
6   tablespoons unsweetened
      cocoa
1   teaspoon instant espresso or
      2 teaspoons instant coffee
      granules
3   tablespoons Kahlúa (coffee-
      flavored liqueur)

1. Place milk in a small saucepan; cook 5 minutes over low heat. Combine water, cocoa, and espresso in a small bowl, stirring until granules dissolve. Stir cocoa mixture into milk; cook 5 minutes, stirring frequently. Stir in liqueur; cook 1 minute. Remove from heat. Serve warm or chilled. Yield: 1¾ cups (serving size: 1 tablespoon).

CALORIES 52 (12% from fat); FAT 0.7g (sat 0.5g, mono 0.2g, poly 0g); PROTEIN 1.4g; CARB 9.7g; FIBER 0g; CHOL 2mg; IRON 0.2mg; SODIUM 15mg; CALC 38mg

A WORD ON ALCOHOL

We use small amounts of flavored liqueurs in most of these desserts to intensify their coffee taste because there are no good nonalcoholic substitutes. In recipes that involve cooking, the alcohol and its calories evaporate.

LATTE FLAN

¾   cup sugar, divided
¼   cup water
Cooking spray
3   cups 2% reduced-fat milk
2   tablespoons instant espresso or
      ¼ cup instant coffee granules
3   tablespoons Kahlúa (coffee-
      flavored liqueur)
2   large eggs
2   large egg whites

1. Preheat oven to 350°.
2. Combine ½ cup sugar and water in a heavy saucepan; cook over medium-high heat until sugar dissolves, stirring frequently. Continue cooking 10 minutes or until golden; stir constantly. Immediately pour into 6 (6-ounce) custard cups coated with cooking spray, tipping quickly until caramelized sugar coats bottom of cups.
3. Combine milk and espresso in a medium saucepan over medium heat; cook 5 minutes or until espresso dissolves (do not boil). Remove from heat; stir in ¼ cup sugar and Kahlúa.
4. Combine eggs and egg whites in a large bowl; stir well with a whisk. Gradually add hot milk mixture to egg mixture, stirring constantly. Divide mixture evenly among prepared custard cups. Place cups in a 13 x 9-inch baking pan; add hot water to pan to a depth of 1 inch. Bake at 350° for 50 minutes or until a knife inserted in center comes out clean. Remove cups from pan; cool completely on a wire rack. Cover and chill at least 8 hours.
5. Loosen edges of custards with a knife or rubber spatula. Place a dessert plate, upside down, on top of each cup, and invert custards onto plates. Drizzle any remaining caramelized syrup over custards. Yield: 6 servings.

CALORIES 210 (18% from fat); FAT 4.2g (sat 2g, mono 1.4g, poly 0.3g); PROTEIN 7.6g; CARB 36g; FIBER 0g; CHOL 83mg; IRON 0.4mg; SODIUM 102mg; CALC 161mg

CAPPUCCINO GRANITA

This Sicilian dessert classic starts with double-strength brewed coffee (dark roast is best) to heighten the coffee flavor when the mixture is frozen.

½   cup ground coffee beans
1¾ cups water
⅓   cup sugar
⅓   cup water
1   teaspoon vanilla extract
¼   teaspoon ground cinnamon
½   cup 1% low-fat milk
Mint sprigs (optional)

1. Assemble drip coffee maker according to manufacturer's directions. Place ground coffee in coffee filter or filter basket. Add 1¾ cups water to coffee maker, and brew; set coffee aside.
2. Combine sugar and ⅓ cup water in a small saucepan. Bring to a boil, and cook 1 minute or until sugar dissolves. Stir in vanilla and cinnamon. Remove from heat, and stir in brewed coffee and milk.
3. Cool coffee mixture completely; pour into an 8-inch square baking dish. Cover and freeze at least 8 hours or until firm. Remove coffee mixture from freezer; scrape entire mixture with a fork until fluffy. Spoon into a freezer-safe container; cover and freeze up to 1 month. Garnish with mint sprigs, if desired. Yield: 6 servings (serving size: ⅔ cup).

CALORIES 56 (3% from fat); FAT 0.2g (sat 0.1g, mono 0.1g, poly 0g); PROTEIN 0.7g; CARB 12.3g; FIBER 0g; CHOL 1mg; IRON 0.1mg; SODIUM 10mg; CALC 26mg

Veggie Express

These speedy vegetarian main dishes are hearty enough to satisfy any meat-lover's soul—and appetite.

POTATO GNOCCHI WITH SPINACH AND YELLOW SQUASH

Preparation time: 19 minutes
Cooking time: 7 minutes

Look for gnocchi (Italian dumplings) in the pasta section of your supermarket.

- 1 (1-pound) package vacuum-packed potato gnocchi (such as Ferrara)
- 1 tablespoon olive oil
- 1 yellow squash, quartered lengthwise and thinly sliced
- 1½ teaspoons bottled minced garlic
- 1 (10-ounce) package fresh spinach, torn
- ¼ cup fat-free milk
- ¼ teaspoon freshly ground black pepper
- ⅛ teaspoon salt
- ½ cup (2 ounces) shredded smoked Gouda cheese or grated sharp provolone cheese

1. Cook gnocchi according to package directions.
2. While gnocchi cook, heat oil in a large skillet over medium heat. Add squash; sauté 4 minutes or until crisp-tender. Add garlic; sauté 1 minute. Add spinach; cover and cook 2 minutes or just until spinach wilts. Reduce heat to low; stir in milk, pepper, and salt. Add gnocchi and cheese; stir gently. Serve immediately. Yield: 4 servings (serving size: 1 cup).

CALORIES 234 (29% from fat); FAT 7.7g (sat 3g, mono 3.6g, poly 0.5g); PROTEIN 10.8g; CARB 44.5g; FIBER 5.7g; CHOL 16mg; IRON 3.7mg; SODIUM 655mg; CALC 203mg

POLENTA WITH CORN AND GREEN CHILES

Preparation time: 10 minutes
Cooking time: 20 minutes

Polenta:

- 1¼ cups yellow cornmeal
- 2 garlic cloves, crushed
- 4 cups fat-free milk
- ¼ cup (1 ounce) preshredded fresh Parmesan cheese
- 1 tablespoon butter or stick margarine

Vegetables:

- 2 teaspoons olive oil
- ⅔ cup diced red bell pepper
- 1 (14.5-ounce) can diced tomatoes, undrained
- 1½ cups frozen whole-kernel corn, thawed
- ¼ cup chopped fresh cilantro
- ¼ teaspoon freshly ground black pepper
- 1 (4.5-ounce) can chopped green chiles

1. To prepare polenta, combine cornmeal and garlic in a large saucepan. Gradually add milk, stirring constantly with a whisk. Bring to a boil; reduce heat to medium, and cook 8 minutes, stirring frequently. Stir in cheese and butter.
2. To prepare vegetables, heat oil in a large nonstick skillet over medium heat. Add bell pepper and tomatoes; cook 8 minutes or until bell pepper is tender. Stir in corn and next 3 ingredients; cook 2 minutes. Serve with polenta. Yield: 4 servings (serving size: 1 cup polenta and ¾ cup vegetables).

CALORIES 403 (19% from fat); FAT 8.7g (sat 3.8g, mono 3.5g, poly 1g); PROTEIN 17.9g; CARB 65.6g; FIBER 5.4g; CHOL 17mg; IRON 3.5mg; SODIUM 778mg; CALC 430mg

BRAISED TOFU AND VEGETABLES IN TOMATO SAUCE

Preparation time: 10 minutes
Cooking time: 19 minutes

- 12 ounces medium egg noodles
- 2 tablespoons vegetable oil, divided
- 1 pound firm tofu, drained and cubed
- 2½ cups thinly sliced fennel bulb (about 1 small bulb)
- 1 zucchini, quartered lengthwise and thinly sliced (about 1½ cups)
- 2 tablespoons red wine vinegar
- ¼ teaspoon dried basil
- ¼ teaspoon dried oregano
- ¼ teaspoon freshly ground black pepper
- 2 (14.5-ounce) cans diced tomatoes with onions and garlic, undrained

1. Cook noodles according to package directions, omitting salt and fat.
2. Heat 1 tablespoon oil in a large nonstick skillet over medium-high heat. Add tofu, and cook 10 minutes or until golden brown, stirring frequently. Remove tofu with a slotted spoon. Heat 1 tablespoon oil in pan. Add fennel and zucchini; cook 4 minutes or until tender, stirring frequently. Stir in tofu, vinegar, basil, oregano, pepper, and tomatoes. Reduce heat; simmer until thick (about 5 minutes). Serve with noodles. Yield: 6 servings (serving size: 1 cup tofu mixture and 1 cup noodles).

CALORIES 377 (27% from fat); FAT 11.3g (sat 2g, mono 3g, poly 5.2g); PROTEIN 17.8g; CARB 54.2g; FIBER 3.7g; CHOL 54mg; IRON 10mg; SODIUM 733mg; CALC 165mg

Artichoke-Spinach Pizza

Preparation time: 15 minutes
Cooking time: 13 minutes

  1 cup part-skim ricotta cheese
  ¼ cup thinly sliced green onions
  ¼ teaspoon bottled minced garlic
  ¼ teaspoon dried oregano
  ⅛ teaspoon black pepper
  1 (10-ounce) package frozen chopped spinach, thawed and drained
  1 (1-pound) Italian cheese-flavored pizza crust (such as Boboli)
  1 (14-ounce) can quartered artichoke hearts, drained
  ⅔ cup (2½ ounces) grated sharp provolone or shredded part-skim mozzarella cheese

1. Preheat oven to 450°.
2. Combine first 5 ingredients. Stir in spinach. Place crust on a baking sheet. Spread spinach mixture over crust, leaving a ½-inch border; top with artichokes and cheese.
3. Bake at 450° for 13 minutes. Yield: 8 servings (serving size: 1 slice).

CALORIES 249 (29% from fat); FAT 8g (sat 4.1g, mono 2.8g, poly 0.8g); PROTEIN 13.9g; CARB 54.9g; FIBER 1.5g; CHOL 16mg; IRON 2.8mg; SODIUM 492mg; CALC 357mg

Italian Portobello Sandwiches

Preparation time: 10 minutes
Cooking time: 7 minutes

  1 teaspoon olive oil
  2 cups sliced portobello mushroom caps
  2 (¼-inch-thick) slices red onion, separated into rings
  ¼ cup fat-free mayonnaise
  2 tablespoons chopped fresh basil
  ¼ teaspoon ground black pepper
  4 (1½-ounce) slices sourdough bread
  ⅔ cup bottled roasted red bell peppers
  2 (1-ounce) slices provolone cheese

1. Heat oil in a large nonstick skillet over medium heat. Add mushrooms and onion; cover and cook 7 minutes or until onion is tender, stirring occasionally. Remove from heat; cool.
2. Combine mayonnaise, basil, and black pepper. Spread 1 tablespoon mayonnaise mixture on each bread slice; layer each of 2 slices with ⅓ cup bell peppers, ½ cup mushroom mixture, and 1 slice of cheese. Top with remaining bread slices. Cut each sandwich in half. Yield: 2 servings (serving size: 1 sandwich).

CALORIES 412 (27% from fat); FAT 12.3g (sat 5.3g, mono 3.8g, poly 0.8g); PROTEIN 18.3g; CARB 60.1g; FIBER 2.6g; CHOL 20mg; IRON 5.9mg; SODIUM 1,117mg; CALC 320mg

Garlicky Stewed White Beans with Mixed Peppers

Preparation time: 6 minutes
Cooking time: 20 minutes

  1 tablespoon olive oil
  1 cup chopped green bell pepper
  1 cup chopped yellow or red bell pepper
  1 tablespoon bottled minced garlic (about 4 cloves)
  ⅛ teaspoon crushed red pepper
  ½ cup water
  ¼ teaspoon dried rubbed sage
  2 (15-ounce) cans cannellini beans or other white beans, rinsed and drained
  1 (14.5-ounce) can diced tomatoes, undrained
  ¼ teaspoon coarsely ground black pepper

1. Heat oil in a large skillet over medium-high heat. Add bell peppers, and cook 5 minutes or until tender, stirring frequently. Add garlic and crushed red pepper; cook 1 minute, stirring constantly. Stir in water, sage, beans, and tomatoes; bring to a boil. Reduce heat; simmer 10 minutes or until thick, stirring occasionally. Sprinkle with black pepper. Yield: 4 servings (serving size: 1 cup).

CALORIES 307 (22% from fat); FAT 7.5g (sat 1g, mono 3.4g, poly 2.2g); PROTEIN 14.4g; CARB 49g; FIBER 7g; CHOL 0mg; IRON 5.7mg; SODIUM 456mg; CALC 111mg

LIGHTEN UP

Chile Down Under

Australian readers send a plea for our recipe-rescue service.

Living in their new hometown of Canberra, Australia, Alison Kibler and family get their Tex-Mex fix with their favorite recipe—Green-Chile Bake.

But the five eggs and three cups of Monterey Jack cheese packed into the recipe worried her. We trimmed the excess—nearly 200 calories and about two-thirds of the fat—by replacing the eggs with an egg substitute and cutting the amount of cheese in half.

Green-Chile Bake

(pictured on page 186)

We've sprinkled a mixture of Monterey Jack and manchego *(mahn-CHAY-goh)—a flavorful Spanish cheese—over the top of this casserole. Because canning mellows the heat of green chiles, this casserole isn't as hot as you might expect.*

  2 tablespoons butter or stick margarine
  1½ cups chopped onion
  2 garlic cloves, minced
  ¼ teaspoon ground cumin
  ⅛ teaspoon salt
  3 cups cooked long-grain rice
  1¼ cups egg substitute
  1 (14.5-ounce) can Mexican-style stewed tomatoes with jalapeño peppers and spices, undrained
  1 (8-ounce) can no-salt-added tomato sauce
  1 cup (4 ounces) shredded reduced-fat Monterey Jack cheese
  ½ cup (2 ounces) shredded manchego cheese
  3 (4-ounce) cans whole green chiles, drained and cut into strips
  Oregano sprigs (optional)

1. Preheat oven to 375°.
2. Melt butter in a medium nonstick skillet over medium-high heat. Add onion and garlic, and sauté 5 minutes. Remove from heat, and stir in cumin and salt. Combine onion mixture, rice, and egg substitute in a bowl. Combine tomatoes and tomato sauce in a bowl. Combine cheeses in a small bowl. Spread 1¼ cups tomato mixture in bottom of a 13 x 9-inch baking dish, and top with 1½ cups rice mixture. Arrange half of chiles on top of rice mixture, and sprinkle with half of cheese mixture. Repeat procedure with remaining tomato mixture, rice mixture, and chiles. Bake, uncovered, at 375° for 30 minutes. Sprinkle with remaining cheese mixture, and bake an additional 5 minutes or until cheese is melted. Garnish with oregano sprigs, if desired. Yield: 6 servings.

CALORIES 315 (27% from fat); FAT 9.5g (sat 5.6g, mono 3g, poly 0.3g); PROTEIN 17.1g; CARB 39.3g; FIBER 1.6g; CHOL 29mg; IRON 2.4mg; SODIUM 576mg; CALC 288mg

BEFORE & AFTER	
SERVING SIZE	
1 slice	
CALORIES PER SERVING	
506	315
FAT	
26.8g	9.5g
PERCENT OF TOTAL CALORIES	
48%	27%
CHOLESTEROL	
239mg	29mg

The Buzz

Moist, spreadable, and abundant, honey adds more than sweetness to your cooking.

Why is it that while everyone can enjoy this sweet substance, it's often overlooked as a cooking ingredient? After all, honey adds a rich, unique flavor to foods. And although honey has no nutritional advantages over sugar, it does add moistness to baked goods, it spreads easier as a glaze on fish and meats, and it dissolves in liquids like vinaigrettes.

Because honey is produced in so many places and in such different strengths and flavors, it's important to choose the best blend. The general rule states the lighter the color, the milder the flavor. We chose mild-flavored honeys such as alfalfa and clover. If you prefer, use a stronger variety such as buckwheat.

HONEY-ROASTED ONIONS

Use these golden-colored onions as a side dish for meat loaf, pork, or chicken.

 2 large Vidalias or other sweet onions (about 1¼ pounds)
 1 tablespoon water
 ¼ cup honey
 1 tablespoon stick margarine or butter, melted
 1 teaspoon paprika
 ½ teaspoon salt
 ½ teaspoon curry powder
 ⅛ to ¼ teaspoon ground red pepper

1. Preheat oven to 350°.
2. Peel onions, and cut in half crosswise. Place onions, cut sides down, in an 8-inch square baking dish; drizzle with water. Cover with foil; bake at 350° for 30 minutes.
3. Combine honey and next 5 ingredients. Turn onions over; brush half of honey mixture over onions. Bake, uncovered, an additional 30 minutes or until tender, basting with remaining honey mixture after 15 minutes. Yield: 4 servings.

CALORIES 126 (22% from fat); FAT 3.1g (sat 0.6g, mono 1.3g, poly 1g); PROTEIN 1.2g; CARB 25.6g; FIBER 1.8g; CHOL 0mg; IRON 0.5mg; SODIUM 330mg; CALC 22mg

HONEY-JALAPEÑO CORN BREAD

 1 cup all-purpose flour
 1 cup yellow cornmeal
 1 tablespoon baking powder
 1 teaspoon baking soda
 ½ teaspoon salt
 ¾ cup low-fat buttermilk
 ½ cup honey
 2 tablespoons butter or stick margarine, melted
 2 jalapeño peppers, seeded and minced
 1 large egg, lightly beaten
Cooking spray

1. Preheat oven to 425°.
2. Lightly spoon flour into a dry measuring cup; level with a knife. Combine flour, cornmeal, baking powder, baking soda, and salt in a large bowl; make a well in center of mixture. Combine buttermilk, honey, butter, peppers, and egg in a bowl; add to flour mixture. Stir just until moist. Spoon batter into an 8-inch square baking pan coated with cooking spray. Bake at 425° for 18 minutes or until a wooden pick inserted in center comes out clean. Yield: 12 servings.

CALORIES 156 (17% from fat); FAT 2.9g (sat 0.7g, mono 1.1g, poly 0.8g); PROTEIN 3.3g; CARB 29.8g; FIBER 0.9g; CHOL 18mg; IRON 1.2mg; SODIUM 239mg; CALC 93mg

HONEY-GLAZED SALMON

2 tablespoons minced shallots
1 tablespoon chopped fresh or
   1 teaspoon dried thyme
3 tablespoons honey
1 tablespoon Dijon mustard
½ teaspoon salt
¼ teaspoon ground red pepper
4 (6-ounce) salmon fillets (about
   1 inch thick)
Cooking spray
Thyme sprigs (optional)

1. Prepare grill or broiler.
2. Combine first 6 ingredients in a small bowl. Brush honey mixture over skinless side of fish. Place fish on a grill rack or broiler pan coated with cooking spray, and cook 6 minutes on each side or until fish flakes easily when tested with a fork. Garnish with thyme sprigs, if desired. Yield: 4 servings.

CALORIES 334 (39% from fat); FAT 14.4g (sat 2.5g, mono 6.8g, poly 3.1g); PROTEIN 35.1g; CARB 14.4g; FIBER 0.1g; CHOL 111mg; IRON 0.9mg; SODIUM 490mg; CALC 15mg

HONEY-PECAN CINNAMON ROLLS

1 (1-pound) loaf frozen white
   bread dough
2 tablespoons granulated sugar
2 teaspoons ground cinnamon
Butter-flavored cooking spray
⅓ cup honey
⅓ cup packed brown sugar
¼ cup chopped pecans, toasted

1. Thaw dough in refrigerator 12 hours; remove from package, cover, and bring to room temperature (about 1 hour).
2. Combine granulated sugar and cinnamon. Roll dough into a 16 x 12-inch rectangle on a lightly floured surface; coat with cooking spray, and sprinkle with sugar mixture. Coat dough again with cooking spray. Roll dough tightly, starting with a short edge, pressing to eliminate air pockets; pinch seam and ends to seal. Cut dough crosswise into 12 (1-inch-thick) slices.

Place honey in a small microwave-safe bowl; microwave at HIGH 20 seconds. Pour honey into a 9-inch round cake pan, tilting pan so honey covers bottom; sprinkle with brown sugar and pecans. Place rolls, cut sides down, in pan. Cover and let rise in a warm place (85°), free from drafts, 45 minutes or until doubled in size.
3. Preheat oven to 350°.
4. Bake at 350° for 20 minutes or until golden brown. Invert rolls immediately onto a plate; cool 5 minutes. Yield: 1 dozen (serving size: 1 roll).

CALORIES 226 (15% from fat); FAT 3.7g (sat 0.6g, mono 1.7g, poly 1.1g); PROTEIN 5.3g; CARB 43.8g; FIBER 0.3g; CHOL 0mg; IRON 1.6mg; SODIUM 297mg; CALC 45mg

COOKING CLASS

Hot & Saucy Skillets

Sensational sauces start with those tasty tidbits left in the skillet.

The brown, crunchy bits left behind in a skillet after cooking meat can become the foundation of a highly flavored sauce to complement your entrée.

The classic technique, known as *deglazing*, starts with searing something quickly in oil in a hot skillet. Heat oil in the skillet at least two minutes. When you add the meat, you should hear a loud sizzle or pop. That means the temperature is sufficient to develop a caramelized brown crust that also retains juices. Pieces of that crispy, seared shell are what stick to your skillet when you remove the meat. While the skillet is still hot, pour in wine, apple juice, or other compatible liquid. Scrape the meaty bits loose. The liquid will cook away, intensifying the flavors.

Deglazing is one of the few techniques that calls for a skillet without a nonstick surface. Only a hot skillet that allows for sticking will sear meat with a tasty crust during sautéing and capture those tidbits that add flavor during deglazing.

BEEF TENDERLOINS WITH FRENCH ONION SAUCE

2 teaspoons butter or stick
   margarine, divided
2 cups thinly sliced onion
3 cups cremini or button
   mushroom caps, halved
   (about ½ pound)
⅔ cup water
1 (10½-ounce) can beef
   consommé
1 teaspoon dried thyme
¼ teaspoon salt
¼ teaspoon coarsely ground black
   pepper
⅛ teaspoon garlic powder
4 (4-ounce) beef tenderloin steaks
   (1 inch thick)
½ cup dry red wine
4 (1-ounce) slices French bread
   (about 1 inch thick), toasted

1. Melt 1 teaspoon butter in a large skillet over medium-high heat. Add onion and mushrooms; sauté 5 minutes, stirring frequently. Stir in water and consommé, scraping pan to loosen browned bits. Bring to a boil; cover and cook 10 minutes. Remove onion mixture from pan.
2. Combine thyme, salt, pepper, and garlic powder. Rub thyme mixture over steaks. Melt 1 teaspoon butter in pan over medium-high heat. Add steaks; cook 3 minutes on each side or until browned. Remove steaks from pan; keep warm.
3. Add wine to pan, scraping pan to loosen browned bits. Stir in onion mixture; bring to a boil, and cook 1 minute. Return steaks to pan; simmer 1 minute.
4. Place 1 toast slice in each of 4 shallow serving bowls, and top each slice with a steak. Spoon onion mixture evenly over steaks. Serve immediately. Yield: 4 servings (serving size: 1 piece toast, 1 steak, and ½ cup sauce).

CALORIES 326 (29% from fat); FAT 10.6g (sat 4.4g, mono 3.8g, poly 0.8g); PROTEIN 31.5g; CARB 25.4g; FIBER 2.8g; CHOL 75mg; IRON 5.7mg; SODIUM 808mg; CALC 60mg

CURRIED CHICKEN WITH PLUMS AND GINGER

If you don't have crystallized or candied ginger, you can substitute 1 tablespoon minced fresh ginger and 1 teaspoon sugar. Serve with couscous or saffron rice tossed with chopped fresh spinach.

    2   tablespoons all-purpose flour
    1   teaspoon curry powder
    1   teaspoon poultry seasoning
    ¼   teaspoon salt
    ¼   teaspoon black pepper
    6   skinned, boned chicken thighs,
          each cut into 3 pieces
    1   teaspoon vegetable oil
    1   cup (1-inch) sliced green
          onions (about 4)
    6   red plums, quartered (about
          1½ pounds)
    ¾   cup dry white wine, divided
    2   tablespoons minced crystallized
          ginger

1. Combine first 5 ingredients in a zip-top plastic bag, and add chicken. Seal and shake to coat. Remove chicken from bag, shaking off excess flour.
2. Heat oil in a large skillet over medium-high heat. Add chicken, and cook 3 minutes on each side or until lightly browned. Remove chicken from pan; keep warm.
3. Add onions to pan, and sauté 2 minutes. Add onions to chicken, and keep warm. Add plums and ¼ cup wine to pan, scraping pan to loosen browned bits; cook 4 minutes or until plums are browned. Add ½ cup wine and ginger to pan; bring to a boil. Add chicken mixture to pan, and bring to a boil. Reduce heat, and simmer 5 minutes or until chicken is done. Yield: 4 servings (serving size: about 4 chicken pieces and 6 plum wedges).

CALORIES 270 (25% from fat); FAT 7.5g (sat 1.7g, mono 2.5g, poly 2.1g); PROTEIN 29.7g; CARB 21.2g; FIBER 2.5g; CHOL 118mg; IRON 3.1mg; SODIUM 278mg; CALC 53mg

STEP-BY-STEPS FOR CURRIED CHICKEN WITH PLUMS AND GINGER

❶ *Combine the coating mixture and chicken in a zip-top plastic bag, and shake. Vary the flavors by changing the spices you use to coat the meat. Here, poultry seasoning and curry powder spice up chicken thighs.*

❷ *Heat oil in skillet at least 2 minutes, until the skillet is hot. It's ready if water droplets dance on the surface. It's best to use a skillet without a nonstick surface.*

❸ *Sauté chicken until very brown, at least 3 minutes on each side. Tongs are the best tool for turning the pieces.*

❹ *Deglaze the skillet with part of the wine and the plums, scraping up the browned bits. As with all such sauces, for rich flavor, bring the liquid to a boil so it reduces.*

❺ *Return chicken mixture to pan with the sauce to finish cooking.*

Sesame-Crusted Pork with Apricot-Tea Glaze

To prepare the peppercorns and cumin seeds, place them in a zip-top bag and crush with a rolling pin or meat mallet.

- ½ cup boiling water
- 1 regular-size tea bag
- 1 tablespoon sesame seeds
- 1 teaspoon black peppercorns, crushed
- ½ teaspoon cumin seeds, crushed
- 4 (4-ounce) boned center-cut loin pork chops (about ½ inch thick)
- 1 teaspoon olive oil
- 2 tablespoons red wine vinegar
- 1 tablespoon low-sodium soy sauce
- ¼ cup apricot preserves
- ¼ teaspoon salt
- ¼ teaspoon black pepper
- 2 cups hot cooked couscous

1. Combine boiling water and tea bag in a medium bowl; cover and steep 5 minutes. Discard tea bag.
2. Combine sesame seeds, peppercorns, and cumin seeds in a small bowl. Coat 1 side of each pork chop with sesame-seed mixture.
3. Heat oil in a large skillet over medium-high heat until hot. Add chops, coated sides down, to skillet. Cook 4 minutes on each side or until done. Set aside, and keep warm.
4. Add tea, vinegar, and soy sauce to pan, scraping pan to loosen browned bits. Boil tea mixture 2 minutes. Reduce heat to low, and add apricot preserves, salt, and pepper, stirring until well-blended. Return chops to pan; cover and simmer 1 minute or until thoroughly heated. Serve over couscous. Yield: 4 servings (serving size: 1 chop, 1 tablespoon glaze, and ½ cup couscous).

CALORIES 352 (27% from fat); FAT 10.7g (sat 3.1g, mono 5g, poly 1.5g); PROTEIN 29.3g; CARB 34.5g; FIBER 1.5g; CHOL 71mg; IRON 2.3mg; SODIUM 354mg; CALC 38mg

Sicilian Veal Cutlets

Flattening the veal increases its diameter, so you'll need to brown the pieces in two batches. To make sure your garlic doesn't burn in the hot skillet, cook it for no more than 30 seconds, until slightly brown, before adding the wine.

- 8 (1½-ounce) veal leg cutlets
- 2 tablespoons all-purpose flour
- ½ teaspoon black pepper
- 2 teaspoons vegetable oil, divided
- 1 garlic clove, minced
- 1 cup dry white wine
- 1½ cups chopped seeded plum tomato (about 4)
- 6 pitted Greek or kalamata olives, chopped
- 1 (6-ounce) jar marinated artichoke hearts, drained and chopped
- 2 cups hot cooked angel hair (about 4 ounces uncooked pasta)

Thyme sprigs (optional)

1. Trim fat from veal. Place each piece between 2 sheets of heavy-duty plastic wrap; flatten to ⅛-inch thickness, using a meat mallet or rolling pin. Combine flour and pepper. Dredge veal in flour mixture; shake off excess flour.
2. Heat 1 teaspoon oil in a skillet over high heat until hot. Add half of cutlets to skillet. Cook 2 minutes on each side or until browned. Remove from pan. Repeat with 1 teaspoon oil and remaining veal.
3. Add garlic to pan; sauté 30 seconds. Add wine, scraping pan to loosen browned bits. Reduce heat to medium-high; boil wine mixture 3 minutes. Return veal to pan. Add tomato, olives, and artichokes; cover and simmer 1 minute or until thoroughly heated. Serve immediately with pasta. Garnish with thyme, if desired. Yield: 4 servings (serving size: 2 pieces veal, ½ cup artichoke mixture, and ½ cup pasta).

CALORIES 293 (25% from fat); FAT 8.2g (sat 1.6g, mono 2.3g, poly 2.1g); PROTEIN 23g; CARB 32g; FIBER 1.8g; CHOL 68mg; IRON 3.1mg; SODIUM 316mg; CALC 49mg

Pan-Seared Sausage with Sweet-and-Sour Onions and Mashed Potatoes

- 1 (12-ounce) package chicken-apple sausage (such as Gerhard's), cut diagonally into ½-inch pieces
- 1½ cups (2-inch) julienne-cut carrot
- 1 cup thinly sliced red onion
- 1½ cups apple juice
- 2 tablespoons balsamic vinegar
- 1 teaspoon fennel seeds, crushed
- ¼ teaspoon salt
- ¼ teaspoon black pepper
- ¼ teaspoon crushed red pepper

Mashed Potatoes

1. Heat a skillet over medium-high heat until hot. Add sausage; cook 2 minutes on each side or until browned. Remove from pan; keep warm.
2. Add carrot and onion; sauté 5 minutes. Remove with a slotted spoon; keep warm. Add juice and next 5 ingredients; cook 3 minutes, stirring frequently to deglaze pan. Return sausage and carrot mixture to pan; cover and simmer 2 minutes. Serve over Mashed Potatoes. Yield: 4 servings (serving size: 1 cup sausage mixture and 1 cup Mashed Potatoes).

CALORIES 356 (26% from fat); FAT 10.1g (sat 3.3g, mono 3.6g, poly 3.6g); PROTEIN 17.3g; CARB 52.1g; FIBER 7g; CHOL 70mg; IRON 2.9mg; SODIUM 981mg; CALC 132mg

Mashed Potatoes:

- 4 cups cubed peeled baking potato (about 1½ pounds)
- ¾ cup 1% low-fat milk
- 2 tablespoons grated Parmesan cheese
- ½ teaspoon salt
- ⅛ teaspoon black pepper

1. Place potato in a medium saucepan; add water to cover. Bring to a boil; cover, reduce heat, and simmer 25 minutes or until tender. Drain. Return potato to pan. Add milk and remaining ingredients; mash with a potato masher. Yield: 4 servings (serving size: 1 cup).

CALORIES 149 (8% from fat); FAT 1.4g (sat 0.8g, mono 0.4g, poly 0.1g); PROTEIN 5.6g; CARB 29.3g; FIBER 2.4g; CHOL 4mg; IRON 1.2mg; SODIUM 371mg; CALC 102mg

Respect Your Local Parsley

If you're using parsley only as a garnish, take a tip from great cultures around the world and work its peppery flavor into the center of your cooking.

Parsley—available year-round—holds great powers. Its slightly peppery taste and deep-green color won't overpower other foods, even when used in generous amounts, but just a dash can lend panache to the simplest dish. Other cultures have known this for centuries. In Spain, where the herb allegedly promises prosperity and a fresh sprig is present at the openings of new businesses, parsley in cooking is as common as olive oil. Italians use parsley to make vibrant and assertive sauces and stuffings. In northern Africa and the Middle East, seasoning grains and vegetables with parsley is as old as cooking itself.

PARSLEY-STUFFED ROAST LAMB

1½ cups chopped fresh parsley
½ cup dried currants
¼ cup pine nuts, toasted
1 teaspoon anchovy paste
2 garlic cloves, minced
½ teaspoon salt, divided
½ teaspoon black pepper, divided
2¼ pounds boned leg of lamb

1. Preheat oven to 400°.
2. Combine first 5 ingredients; add ¼ teaspoon salt and ¼ teaspoon pepper.
3. Unroll roast; trim fat. Spread parsley mixture into folds of roast. Reroll roast; secure at 1-inch intervals with heavy string. Sprinkle with ¼ teaspoon salt and ¼ teaspoon pepper. Place roast on a broiler pan; insert meat thermometer into thickest portion of roast. Bake at 400° for 55 minutes or until thermometer registers 145° (medium-rare) to 160° (medium). Let roast stand 10 minutes before slicing. Yield: 8 servings (serving size: 4 ounces lamb and stuffing).

CALORIES 221 (39% from fat); FAT 9.6g (sat 2.8g, mono 3.9g, poly 1.5g); PROTEIN 26.2g; CARB 7.9g; FIBER 0.8g; CHOL 76mg; IRON 3.3mg; SODIUM 300mg; CALC 34mg

PARSLIED MUSSELS AND LINGUINE

1 cup coarsely chopped fresh parsley
¾ cup coarsely chopped onion
¼ cup dry vermouth
24 mussels (about 1½ pounds), scrubbed and debearded
1½ cups diced seeded tomato
⅔ cup minced fresh parsley, divided
¼ cup water
3 garlic cloves, minced
4 cups hot cooked linguine (about 8 ounces uncooked pasta)
½ teaspoon salt
¼ teaspoon black pepper
½ cup (2 ounces) grated fresh Parmesan cheese

1. Combine first 4 ingredients in a medium-size, heavy saucepan. Cover and cook over medium-high heat 5 minutes or until mussels open; discard any unopened shells. Strain mixture through a colander into a bowl, reserving cooking liquid. Set mussels aside, and keep warm. Discard remaining solids.

2. Combine reserved cooking liquid, tomato, ⅓ cup minced parsley, water, and garlic in a small saucepan, and bring to a simmer. Cover and cook 7 minutes over medium heat. Add ⅓ cup minced parsley, linguine, salt, and pepper; toss well. Spoon 1 cup pasta mixture onto each of 4 plates; top each serving with 6 mussels and 2 tablespoons cheese. Yield: 4 servings.

CALORIES 333 (16% from fat); FAT 6g (sat 2.7g, mono 1.5g, poly 0.9g); PROTEIN 19.3g; CARB 49.8g; FIBER 2.6g; CHOL 24mg; IRON 5.3mg; SODIUM 679mg; CALC 214mg

ROASTED POTATOES WITH PARSLEY PESTO

6 cups (1-inch) cubed potato (about 2½ pounds)
Cooking spray

Parsley pesto:

4 cups fresh parsley leaves
1 cup chopped peeled cucumber
½ cup trimmed arugula
½ cup fresh basil leaves
½ cup fresh mint leaves
½ cup torn romaine lettuce
2 tablespoons extra-virgin olive oil
2 tablespoons red wine vinegar
½ teaspoon salt
¼ teaspoon dried crushed red pepper
2 garlic cloves, peeled

1. Preheat oven to 425°.
2. Place potato on a jelly-roll pan coated with cooking spray, and bake at 425° for 40 minutes or until tender, stirring occasionally. Place potato in a large bowl.
3. To prepare parsley pesto, place parsley and next 10 ingredients in a food processor; process until smooth, scraping sides of processor bowl occasionally. Add to potato in bowl, and toss well to coat. Yield: 5 servings (serving size: 1 cup).

CALORIES 216 (25% from fat); FAT 6.1g (sat 0.9g, mono 4.1g, poly 0.6g); PROTEIN 5.6g; CARB 37g; FIBER 5.3g; CHOL 0mg; IRON 4.5mg; SODIUM 274mg; CALC 94mg

TABBOULEH

This tabbouleh has a crunchier texture than most because it calls for uncooked bulgur, which softens over time as it absorbs the marinade. Belgian endive leaves make great scoopers.

- 4 cups fresh parsley sprigs
- ¼ cup fresh mint leaves
- 2 cups diced seeded cucumber
- 2 cups diced seeded tomato
- 1 cup uncooked bulgur or cracked wheat
- ¾ cup diced onion
- ⅓ cup fresh lemon juice
- 2 tablespoons extra-virgin olive oil
- ½ teaspoon salt
- 1 garlic clove, minced

1. Place parsley and mint in a food processor; process until finely minced. Combine parsley mixture, cucumber, and remaining ingredients in a large bowl; toss well. Cover and marinate in refrigerator at least 4 hours. Yield: 6 servings (serving size: 1 cup).

CALORIES 164 (30% from fat); FAT 5.4g (sat 0.8g, mono 3.5g, poly 0.7g); PROTEIN 5.2g; CARB 27.3g; FIBER 7.5g; CHOL 0mg; IRON 3.5mg; SODIUM 229mg; CALC 79mg

THE TWO PARSLEYS

Parsley comes in more than 30 varieties, but you'll generally encounter two types: curly-leaf parsley and flat-leaf or Italian parsley.

The curly-leaf variety makes an attractive garnish; the more assertive flat-leaf parsley is better for cooking. Either type can be used in these recipes.

FISH IN PARSLEY-WINE SAUCE

- 2 cups fresh parsley leaves
- 2 garlic cloves, peeled
- 1 tablespoon olive oil, divided
- ¼ teaspoon salt, divided
- ¼ teaspoon black pepper, divided
- 1⅓ cups diced onion
- 1 garlic clove, minced
- 1 cup minced fresh parsley
- ¾ cup dry white wine
- 4 (6-ounce) orange roughy or other firm white fish fillets

1. Place parsley leaves and 2 garlic cloves in a food processor; process until well-blended. Place mixture in a bowl; stir in 2 teaspoons oil, ⅛ teaspoon salt, and ⅛ teaspoon pepper. Set parsley sauce aside.
2. Heat 1 teaspoon oil in a large skillet over medium heat. Add onion and minced garlic; cook 5 minutes. Stir in minced parsley and wine, and cook 3 minutes. Arrange fillets over parsley mixture in pan; sprinkle with ⅛ teaspoon salt and ⅛ teaspoon pepper. Cook 6 minutes or until fish flakes easily when tested with a fork. Remove fish from pan; keep warm. Add parsley sauce to pan; cook 1 minute or until thoroughly heated. Spoon sauce evenly over fish. Yield: 4 servings (serving size: 1 fillet and ¼ cup sauce).

CALORIES 191 (24% from fat); FAT 5g (sat 0.6g, mono 3.5g, poly 0.4g); PROTEIN 27.2g; CARB 9.2g; FIBER 3.1g; CHOL 34mg; IRON 3.5mg; SODIUM 284mg; CALC 82mg

PARSLEY BISCUITS

- 1½ cups all-purpose flour
- 1 teaspoon baking powder
- ½ teaspoon salt
- 3 tablespoons chilled butter or stick margarine, cut into small pieces
- ¾ cup minced fresh parsley
- ⅓ cup 1% low-fat milk
- ⅓ cup plain low-fat yogurt
- Cooking spray
- 2 teaspoons 1% low-fat milk

1. Preheat oven to 400°.
2. Lightly spoon flour into dry measuring cups; level with a knife. Combine flour, baking powder, and salt in a bowl; cut in butter with a pastry blender or 2 knives until mixture resembles coarse meal. Combine parsley, ⅓ cup milk, and yogurt, stirring with a whisk. Add to flour mixture; stir just until moist.
3. Turn dough out onto a floured surface; knead lightly 3 times. Pat dough to a ¾-inch thickness; cut with a 2-inch biscuit cutter. Place on a baking sheet coated with cooking spray; brush with 2 teaspoons milk. Bake at 400° for 18 minutes or until lightly browned. Yield: 8 biscuits (serving size: 1 biscuit).

CALORIES 134 (33% from fat); FAT 4.9g (sat 2.9g, mono 1.4g, poly 0.3g); PROTEIN 3.5g; CARB 19.5g; FIBER 0.8g; CHOL 12mg; IRON 1.4mg; SODIUM 267mg; CALC 75mg

INSPIRED VEGETARIAN

Pizza Is As Flatbread Does

Borrowing a tasty idea from Spain, these flatbreads will remind you of pizza, so it's OK if you still want to call them that.

The inspiration for these flatbreads comes from Spain, especially Catalonia, where bakeries sell sweet or savory flatbreads known by the nickname *coca* (plural, *coques*).

These flatbreads don't pretend to be coques, but using the long, oval shape of that popular Spanish dish frees our expectations of just another pizza.

The toppings—corn, zucchini, radicchio—are different than pizza. So is a reduced reliance on cheese. A little cheese does help hold some vegetables on the dough. Use ricotta, Parmesan, a smoky Cheddar, or mozzarella.

The breads are made from a yeasted dough that includes cornmeal soaked in water while the yeast is proofing; this adds texture and flavor to the base. A little olive oil is traditionally added to the dough for tenderness and flavor.

FLATBREAD DOUGH

1 cup boiling water
⅓ cup yellow cornmeal
1 package dry yeast (about
    2¼ teaspoons)
¼ cup warm water (100° to 110°)
2 cups all-purpose flour
½ teaspoon salt
2 teaspoons olive oil
Cooking spray
1 tablespoon yellow cornmeal

1. Combine boiling water and ⅓ cup cornmeal in a bowl; let stand 20 minutes, stirring occasionally. Dissolve yeast in warm water in a bowl; let stand 5 minutes. Spoon flour into dry measuring cups, and level with a knife. Combine cornmeal mixture, flour, and salt in a food processor, and pulse 4 times. With processor on, slowly add yeast mixture and oil through food chute; process until dough forms a ball. Process 1 additional minute. (To prepare dough by hand, combine cornmeal mixture, flour, and salt in a bowl; stir until well-blended. Add yeast mixture and oil, stirring well.) Turn dough out onto a floured surface, and knead lightly 4 or 5 times (dough will feel tacky).
2. Place dough in a bowl coated with cooking spray, turning to coat top. Cover; let rise in a warm place (85°), free from drafts, 1 hour or until doubled in size. (Press two fingers into dough. If indentation remains, dough has risen enough.)
3. Punch dough down; cover and let rest 5 minutes. Divide dough into 4 equal portions, shaping each into a ball (cover remaining dough while working to prevent it from drying).
4. Roll each ball into a 10 x 6-inch oval. Dust 2 baking sheets evenly with 1 tablespoon cornmeal. Place 2 ovals on each baking sheet. Add toppings; according to recipe directions. Yield: 4 servings (serving size: 1 flatbread).
Note: If you use whole-grain cornmeal, which contains hull and germ of dried corn kernel, increase flour to 2¼ cups.

CALORIES 304 (10% from fat); FAT 3.3g (sat 0.4g, mono 1.8g, poly 0.5g); PROTEIN 8.3g; CARB 59g; FIBER 2.9g; CHOL 0mg; IRON 3.8mg; SODIUM 295mg; CALC 11mg

ZUCCHINI, WALNUT, AND BLUE CHEESE FLATBREADS

Flatbread Dough (see recipe)
Olive oil-flavored cooking spray
5 cups thinly sliced zucchini
    (about 4 zucchini)
½ teaspoon salt
¼ teaspoon black pepper
½ cup thinly sliced green
    onions
¼ cup chopped walnuts
⅔ cup part-skim ricotta cheese
½ cup (2 ounces) crumbled blue
    cheese
2 tablespoons chopped fresh or
    2 teaspoons dried oregano

1. Prepare Flatbread Dough; let rise, and shape into 4 ovals on baking sheets as directed. Cover and set aside.
2. Preheat oven to 475°.
3. Place a large nonstick skillet coated with cooking spray over medium-high heat. Add zucchini, salt, and pepper; sauté 8 minutes. Add onions and walnuts; sauté 1 minute.
4. Combine ricotta cheese and blue cheese in a small bowl.
5. Divide half of zucchini mixture evenly among 4 flatbread dough ovals; dot evenly with cheese mixture. Top with remaining zucchini mixture and oregano. Bake at 475° for 15 minutes. Yield: 4 servings (serving size: 1 flatbread).

CALORIES 489 (29% from fat); FAT 15.6g (sat 5.5g, mono 4.9g, poly 3.8g); PROTEIN 20.1g; CARB 68.5g; FIBER 4.6g; CHOL 23mg; IRON 5.4mg; SODIUM 844mg; CALC 248mg

ROASTED PEPPER, CORN, AND MUSHROOM FLATBREADS

Flatbread Dough (see recipe)
2 large red bell peppers
2 tablespoons chopped fresh sage
1 teaspoon olive oil
1½ cups sliced mushrooms
¼ teaspoon salt
1 cup fresh corn kernels
⅓ cup coarsely chopped ripe olives
¼ teaspoon black pepper
1 cup (4 ounces) crumbled goat
    cheese

1. Prepare Flatbread Dough; let rise, and shape into 4 ovals on baking sheets as directed. Cover and set aside.
2. Preheat broiler.
3. Cut bell peppers in half lengthwise; discard seeds and membranes. Place pepper halves, skin sides up, on a foil-lined baking sheet; flatten with hand. Broil 10 minutes or until blackened. Place in a zip-top plastic bag; seal. Let stand 10 minutes. Peel and cut into thin strips.
4. Preheat oven to 475°.
5. Heat sage and oil in a medium nonstick skillet over medium-high heat. Add mushrooms and salt; sauté 2 minutes. Add roasted bell peppers and corn; sauté 5 minutes. Remove from heat; stir in olives and black pepper.
6. Divide corn mixture among 4 flatbread ovals; sprinkle evenly with cheese. Bake at 475° for 15 minutes or until cheese begins to melt. Yield: 4 servings (serving size: 1 flatbread).

CALORIES 449 (25% from fat); FAT 12.4g (sat 5.2g, mono 5g, poly 1.4g); PROTEIN 14.5g; CARB 71g; FIBER 5.3g; CHOL 25mg; IRON 5.3mg; SODIUM 863mg; CALC 171mg

MUSHROOM, ONION, AND CHERRY TOMATO FLATBREADS

Flatbread Dough (see recipe)
Cooking spray
2 cups thinly sliced onion,
    separated into rings
6 cups sliced mushrooms
2 teaspoons chopped fresh or
    ½ teaspoon dried thyme
½ teaspoon salt, divided
½ teaspoon freshly ground black
    pepper
2 garlic cloves, minced
1⅓ cups quartered cherry tomatoes
½ cup (2 ounces) grated fresh
    Parmesan cheese

1. Prepare Flatbread Dough; let rise, and shape into 4 ovals on baking sheets as directed. Cover dough, and set aside.
2. Preheat oven to 475°.
3. Place a large nonstick skillet coated with cooking spray over medium-high

Continued

heat until hot. Add onion; sauté 4 minutes or until lightly browned. Add mushrooms; sprinkle with thyme and ¼ teaspoon salt. Sauté 6 minutes or until tender. Remove from heat; stir in pepper and garlic.

4. Divide mushroom mixture evenly among 4 flatbread dough ovals; sprinkle ¼ teaspoon salt over mushroom mixture. Arrange ⅓ cup tomato over each flatbread, and top each with 2 tablespoons cheese. Bake at 475° for 12 minutes or until cheese is melted. Yield: 4 servings (serving size: 1 flatbread).

CALORIES 425 (17% from fat); FAT 7.9g (sat 2.9g, mono 2.9g, poly 0.9g); PROTEIN 16.8g; CARB 72.8g; FIBER 6.1g; CHOL 10mg; IRON 5.8mg; SODIUM 973mg; CALC 205mg

SEARED RADICCHIO-AND-PORTOBELLO FLATBREADS

Truffle oil—which has a pungent, earthy flavor—is potent, so a little goes a long way. If you prefer, use olive oil; it works just as well.

Flatbread Dough (page 183)
2 teaspoons olive oil
3 cups (¾-inch-thick) sliced portobello mushrooms (about 2 large mushrooms)
½ teaspoon salt, divided
4 cups thinly sliced radicchio (about 8 ounces)
⅓ cup (about 2 ounces) diced fresh mozzarella cheese
½ teaspoon black pepper
1 teaspoon truffle or olive oil
¼ cup (1 ounce) grated fresh Parmesan cheese
¼ cup chopped fresh parsley

1. Prepare Flatbread Dough; let rise and shape into 4 ovals on baking sheets as directed. Cover and set aside.
2. Preheat oven to 475°.
3. Heat 2 teaspoons oil in a medium nonstick skillet over medium-high heat. Add mushrooms; sprinkle with ¼ teaspoon salt. Sauté 3 minutes. Remove mushrooms from pan. Add radicchio to pan, and sprinkle with ¼

teaspoon salt. Cook until wilted (about 2 minutes), stirring frequently. Combine mushrooms and radicchio; cool slightly. Stir in mozzarella and pepper. Divide mushroom mixture evenly among 4 flatbread dough ovals. Bake at 475° for 12 minutes or until browned. Drizzle each flatbread with ¼ teaspoon truffle oil; sprinkle each with 1 tablespoon Parmesan and 1 tablespoon parsley. Yield: 4 servings (serving size: 1 flatbread).

CALORIES 429 (25% from fat); FAT 12g (sat 4g, mono 5.8g, poly 1.1g); PROTEIN 15.5g; CARB 64.8g; FIBER 4.3g; CHOL 16mg; IRON 5.1mg; SODIUM 771mg; CALC 189mg

CORN, PATTYPAN SQUASH, AND CHEDDAR FLATBREADS

Pattypan is a small, round variety of summer squash with a scalloped edge.

Flatbread Dough (page 183)
Cooking spray
2 cups fresh corn kernels (about 4 ears)
2 cups sliced pattypan or yellow squash (about 8 ounces)
2 tablespoons chopped seeded jalapeño pepper
½ teaspoon salt, divided
⅓ cup thinly sliced green onions
¼ teaspoon white pepper
⅓ cup chopped fresh cilantro, divided
1½ cups (6 ounces) shredded sharp Cheddar cheese

1. Prepare Flatbread Dough; let rise, and shape into 4 ovals on baking sheets as directed. Cover and set aside.
2. Preheat oven to 475°.
3. Heat a nonstick skillet coated with cooking spray over medium-high heat. Add corn, squash, jalapeño, and ¼ teaspoon salt. Cook 3 minutes, stirring frequently. Add onions; cook 1 minute, stirring constantly. Remove from heat; sprinkle with ¼ teaspoon salt and white pepper. Stir in 3 tablespoons cilantro. Divide vegetable mixture and cheese evenly among 4 flatbread dough ovals. Bake at 475° for 12 minutes or

until crust is browned. Sprinkle with remaining cilantro. Yield: 4 servings (serving size: 1 flatbread).

CALORIES 563 (30% from fat); FAT 18.7g (sat 9.6g, mono 6.1g, poly 1.5g); PROTEIN 22.5g; CARB 78.4g; FIBER 7g; CHOL 45mg; IRON 5.2mg; SODIUM 869mg; CALC 347mg

TOMATO, BASIL, AND PARMESAN FLATBREADS

(pictured on page 185)

Flatbread Dough (page 183)
2 yellow tomatoes, cut in half and thinly sliced crosswise (about 8 ounces)
3 cups thinly sliced plum tomato (about 8 ounces)
½ cup minced fresh basil
4 teaspoons olive oil
¼ teaspoon salt
⅛ teaspoon black pepper
4 garlic cloves, minced
1 cup (4 ounces) grated fresh Parmesan cheese

1. Prepare Flatbread Dough; let rise, and shape into 4 ovals on baking sheets as directed. Cover and set aside.
2. Preheat oven to 475°.
3. Divide tomatoes evenly among 4 flatbread dough ovals. Bake at 475° for 13 minutes. Combine basil and next 4 ingredients in a small bowl; spread evenly over tomatoes. Sprinkle evenly with cheese. Bake at 475° for 2 minutes or until cheese is melted. Yield: 4 servings (serving size: 1 flatbread).

CALORIES 497 (29% from fat); FAT 15.8g (sat 5.8g, mono 7.4g, poly 1.4g); PROTEIN 20.2g; CARB 69.1g; FIBER 4.8g; CHOL 19mg; IRON 4.9mg; SODIUM 911mg; CALC 370mg

Spanish Sherried Shrimp,
page 170

Tomato, Basil, and Parmesan
Flatbreads, page 184

Maple Fruit Crisps, page 201

Green-Chile Bake, page 176

Italian Bean Salad with Escarole, page 171

*French Toast-Peach Cobbler,
page 194*

*Grilled Teriyaki Pork Chops
with Summery Peach Salsa,
page 199*

Fast Food Fakeout

These lower fat, less-salty variations of your kids' favorite junk foods are so good you'll have to put a drive-through lane in your kitchen.

Kids (and a lot of adults, too) love ooey, gooey, cheesy, sugary, salty foods. So why not give them what they want—sort of. We've created kid-friendly recipes for nachos, pizza, and cookies that will rival, and even beat, the lure of fatty snacks and fast food. The knockoffs are so similar to the regular versions in taste and appearance that kids (and maybe some adults, too) won't be able to tell the difference.

CORN DOGS

¼ cup toasted wheat germ, divided
2 tablespoons seasoned breadcrumbs
1 (11.5-ounce) can refrigerated corn bread twists
1 tablespoon all-purpose flour
8 teaspoons prepared mustard
1 (14-ounce) package fat-free turkey-and-beef hot dogs
2 large egg whites lightly beaten

1. Preheat oven to 375°.
2. Combine 2 tablespoons wheat germ and breadcrumbs in a shallow dish. Set aside.
3. Unroll dough. Working with 2 dough portions at a time, pinch perforations to seal. Roll dough into a 6 x 3-inch rectangle on a surface sprinkled with 2 tablespoons wheat germ and flour. Spread 1 teaspoon mustard over rectangle. Place 1 hot dog on rectangle. Wrap dough around hot dog; pinch ends to seal. Repeat procedure with remaining dough, mustard, and hot dogs.
4. Dip each corn dog in egg white; dredge in breadcrumb mixture. Place corn dogs on a baking sheet. Bake at 375° for 25 minutes or until golden brown. Yield: 8 servings (serving size: 1 corn dog).

CALORIES 211 (28% from fat); FAT 6.6g (sat 1.6g, mono 2.6g, poly 2.3g); PROTEIN 11.3g; CARB 25.3g; FIBER 0.6g; CHOL 15mg; IRON 1.9mg; SODIUM 949mg; CALC 8mg

OVEN "FRIED" CHICKEN FINGERS WITH HONEY-MUSTARD DIPPING SAUCE

Sauce:

¼ cup honey
¼ cup spicy brown mustard

Chicken:

1½ pounds chicken breast tenders (about 16 pieces)
½ cup low-fat buttermilk
½ cup coarsely crushed cornflakes
¼ cup seasoned breadcrumbs
1 tablespoon instant minced onion
1 teaspoon paprika
¼ teaspoon dried thyme
¼ teaspoon black pepper
1 tablespoon vegetable oil

1. To prepare sauce, combine honey and mustard in a small bowl; cover and chill.
2. Preheat oven to 400°.
3. To prepare chicken, combine chicken and buttermilk in a shallow dish; cover and chill 15 minutes. Drain chicken, discarding liquid.
4. Combine cornflakes and next 5 ingredients in a large zip-top plastic bag; add 4 chicken pieces to bag. Seal and shake to coat. Repeat procedure with remaining chicken. Spread oil evenly in a jelly-roll pan, and arrange chicken in a single layer in pan. Bake at 400° for 4 minutes on each side or until done. Serve with sauce. Yield: 8 servings (serving size: 2 chicken tenders and 1 tablespoon sauce).

CALORIES 185 (18% from fat); FAT 3.7g (sat 0.8g, mono 1.2g, poly 1.2g); PROTEIN 21.6g; CARB 16g; FIBER 0.3g; CHOL 49mg; IRON 1.3mg; SODIUM 306mg; CALC 46mg

PEANUT BUTTER-AND-JELLY COOKIES

Natural peanut butter (made from ground peanuts with no added sugar) is the best choice for these thumbprint-style cookies; it adds a strong peanut flavor and helps the cookies hold their shape better during baking.

½ cup packed brown sugar
¼ cup natural creamy peanut butter (such as Smucker's)
¼ cup dark corn syrup
3 tablespoons butter or stick margarine, softened
1 large egg
2 teaspoons vanilla extract
1⅓ cups all-purpose flour
2 tablespoons cornstarch
½ teaspoon baking powder
¼ teaspoon baking soda
¼ teaspoon salt
¼ cup granulated sugar
Cooking spray
¼ cup grape or other flavored jelly or jam

1. Beat first 4 ingredients at medium speed of a mixer until well-blended. Add egg; beat well. Beat in vanilla. Lightly spoon flour into dry measuring cups; level with a knife. Combine flour and next 4 ingredients, stirring well with a whisk. Add flour mixture to brown sugar mixture; beat well. Cover; freeze 30 minutes or until firm.
2. Preheat oven to 375°.
3. Shape dough into 24 balls; roll in granulated sugar. Place 1 inch apart on baking sheets coated with cooking spray. Press thumb into center of each cookie, leaving an indentation. Spoon about ½ teaspoon jelly into center of each cookie. Bake at 375° for 12 minutes or until lightly browned. Cool 2 minutes on pans. Remove from pans, and cool completely on wire racks. Yield: 2 dozen (serving size: 1 cookie).

CALORIES 105 (27% from fat); FAT 3.1g (sat 1.1g, mono 1.2g, poly 0.6g); PROTEIN 1.6g; CARB 18g; FIBER 0.4g; CHOL 13mg; IRON 0.5mg; SODIUM 82mg; CALC 12mg

LOADED NACHOS

- 8 ounces ground round
- ½ cup chopped bottled roasted red bell peppers
- 1 teaspoon chili powder
- ½ teaspoon dried oregano
- ¼ teaspoon salt
- 1 (14.5-ounce) can no-salt-added diced tomatoes, undrained
- 1 garlic clove, crushed
- Cooking spray
- 1 (16-ounce) can fat-free refried beans with mild chiles
- ¼ cup minced fresh cilantro, divided
- ¼ cup chopped green onions, divided
- 27 baked tortilla chips (about 3 ounces)
- 1 cup (4 ounces) shredded Monterey Jack cheese
- 3 tablespoons low-fat sour cream
- 27 pickled jalapeño pepper slices (optional)

1. Preheat oven to 375°.
2. Cook meat in a large nonstick skillet over medium-high heat until browned, stirring to crumble. Stir in bell peppers and next 5 ingredients; cook for 8 minutes or until thick, stirring occasionally. Remove from pan.
3. Place pan coated with cooking spray over medium heat until hot. Add beans, 2 tablespoons cilantro, and 2 tablespoons green onions; cook 2 minutes or until thoroughly heated. Place chips on a large ovenproof serving platter; spread warm bean mixture evenly over chips. Spoon meat mixture over bean mixture; top with cheese. Bake at 375° for 9 minutes or until cheese melts. Remove from oven; top with sour cream, 2 tablespoons cilantro, and 2 tablespoons onions. Top with jalapeño pepper slices, if desired. Serve immediately. Yield: 9 servings (serving size: 3 loaded chips).

CALORIES 183 (30% from fat); FAT 6.2g (sat 3.2g, mono 2g, poly 0.4g); PROTEIN 37.3g; CARB 19.2g; FIBER 2.9g; CHOL 26mg; IRON 2.3mg; SODIUM 449mg; CALC 152mg

PEPPERONI PIZZA

You can use refrigerated pizza crust dough in place of the homemade crust, but it will add about 2 grams of fat to each serving.

Crust:

- 1½ cups all-purpose flour, divided
- 1 teaspoon sugar
- 1 package quick-rise yeast
- ½ cup warm water (100° to 110°)
- ¼ teaspoon salt
- Cooking spray

Sauce:

- 2 garlic cloves, minced
- 1 teaspoon dried oregano
- ¼ teaspoon salt
- ⅛ teaspoon crushed red pepper
- 1 (8-ounce) can no-salt-added tomato sauce
- 1 tablespoon minced fresh parsley

Remaining ingredients:

- 2 teaspoons cornmeal
- 16 slices turkey pepperoni (such as Hormel)
- 1½ cups (6 ounces) preshredded part-skim mozzarella cheese
- 2 tablespoons grated Parmesan cheese

1. To prepare crust, lightly spoon flour into dry measuring cups, and level with a knife. Dissolve sugar and yeast in warm water in a large bowl, and let stand 5 minutes. Add 1¼ cups flour and ¼ teaspoon salt; stir until a soft dough forms. Turn dough out onto a lightly floured surface. Knead until smooth and elastic (about 10 minutes), and add enough of remaining flour, 1 tablespoon at a time, to prevent dough from sticking to hands (dough will feel tacky).
2. Place dough in a large bowl coated with cooking spray, turning to coat top. Cover and let rise in a warm place (85°), free from drafts, 30 minutes or until doubled in size. (Press two fingers into dough. If indentation remains, dough has risen enough.)
3. To prepare sauce, place a small saucepan coated with cooking spray over medium heat until hot. Add garlic, and sauté 1 minute. Add oregano, ¼ teaspoon salt, red pepper, and tomato sauce; reduce heat, and simmer 20 minutes, stirring occasionally. Stir in parsley, and keep warm.
4. Preheat oven to 450°.
5. Punch dough down; cover and let rest 5 minutes. Roll dough into a 12-inch circle on a floured surface. Place dough on a 12-inch pizza pan or baking sheet coated with cooking spray and sprinkled with cornmeal. Crimp edges of dough with fingers to form a rim. Cover and let rise 10 minutes.
6. Spread sauce over pizza crust, leaving a ½-inch border; top with pepperoni. Sprinkle with cheeses. Bake at 450° for 10 minutes or until crust is puffy and lightly browned. Remove pizza to cutting board; cut into 6 slices. Yield: 6 servings (serving size: 1 slice).

CALORIES 234 (24% from fat); FAT 6.3g (sat 3.6g, mono 1.7g, poly 0.5g); PROTEIN 13.4g; CARB 30.2g; FIBER 1.3g; CHOL 24mg; IRON 2.1mg; SODIUM 461mg; CALC 223mg

AT LAST

Here, Leezard, Leezard

July 4th might mean fireworks and speeches in your town, but Lovington, New Mexico, makes tracks for the World's Greatest Lizard Race.

This celebration isn't about racing lizards. Fashionably inclined local merchants dress up in reptile regalia, and the art-minded show off chalk drawings of lizards small as skinks or large as iguanas. Prizes and trophies are awarded. What food is compatible with such a fête? This is the Southwest, of course, so there has to be nachos.

WORLD'S GREATEST CHICKEN NACHOS

This spicy picadillo mixture uses chicken, instead of traditional beef. Serve with chopped cilantro, shredded lettuce, sliced radish, and low-fat sour cream.

Chicken picadillo:

½ teaspoon vegetable oil
8 ounces ground chicken or turkey
½ teaspoon ground cumin
½ teaspoon dried oregano
½ teaspoon salt
2 jalapeño peppers, seeded and finely chopped
1 teaspoon all-purpose flour
1 teaspoon chili powder
3 tablespoons raisins
1 tablespoon cider vinegar
2 teaspoons sugar
1 (14.5-ounce) can diced tomatoes, drained
1 (16-ounce) can pink beans (such as Goya) or other small beans, drained

Nachos:

40 baked tortilla chips
½ cup bottled salsa
½ cup (2 ounces) shredded sharp Cheddar cheese

1. Preheat oven to 450°.
2. To prepare chicken picadillo, heat oil in a large nonstick skillet over medium-high heat. Add chicken, cumin, oregano, salt, and jalapeños; cook until chicken is browned, stirring to crumble. Stir in flour and chili powder; cook 1 minute. Add raisins, vinegar, sugar, and tomatoes; cook 3 minutes, stirring frequently. Add beans; cook until thoroughly heated.
3. To prepare nachos, arrange chips on a large baking sheet. Spoon chicken picadillo and salsa evenly over chips; sprinkle with cheese. Bake at 450° for 5 minutes or until cheese is melted. Yield: 8 servings (serving size: 5 nachos).

CALORIES 208 (26% from fat); FAT 6g (sat 2.5g, mono 1.9g, poly 1.3g); PROTEIN 11.6g; CARB 28g; FIBER 3.6g; CHOL 31mg; IRON 1.9mg; SODIUM 545mg; CALC 123mg

Thai Salad Days

For a delicious light meal, nothing hits the spot like these naturally low-fat favorites from the streets and cafés of Thailand.

SEARED SCALLOPS AND FRESH-ORANGE SALAD

We liked watercress and endive in this salad, but most combinations of pungent greens will work.

Shallots:

2 tablespoons vegetable oil
⅓ cup sliced shallots

Salad:

3 cups trimmed watercress (about 3 bunches)
3 cups coarsely chopped curly endive
1 cup orange sections (about 3 oranges)
½ cup diced peeled avocado (about 1 small)
1½ pounds sea scallops
¼ teaspoon salt
1 teaspoon vegetable oil

Dressing:

½ cup fresh lemon juice (about 2 lemons)
2 tablespoons brown sugar
1½ tablespoons Thai fish sauce
1 tablespoon minced seeded Thai, hot red, or serrano chile
2 garlic cloves, crushed
⅓ cup chopped fresh mint

1. To prepare shallots, heat 2 tablespoons oil in a small saucepan over medium-high heat. Add shallots, and cook 2 minutes or until crispy, stirring constantly. Remove shallots from pan with a slotted spoon; drain and cool.
2. To prepare salad, arrange watercress and endive on a serving platter. Top with orange sections and avocado. Sprinkle scallops with salt. Heat 1

teaspoon oil in a nonstick skillet over medium-high heat. Add scallops, and cook 4 minutes, turning once. Spoon scallops over greens mixture.
3. To prepare dressing, combine lemon juice and next 4 ingredients in a bowl; stir well with a whisk. Heat dressing in a small saucepan over medium heat 1 minute; pour over salad. Sprinkle with mint and shallots. Yield: 4 servings.

CALORIES 292 (27% from fat); FAT 8.9g (sat 1.5g, mono 3.2g, poly 3.1g); PROTEIN 31.4g; CARB 22.7g; FIBER 3.4g; CHOL 56mg; IRON 1.4mg; SODIUM 933mg; CALC 126mg

GRILLED THAI CHICKEN SALAD WITH MANGO AND GINGER

(pictured on page 2)

Dressing:

¼ cup fresh lemon juice
2 to 3 tablespoons Thai fish sauce
2 tablespoons brown sugar
2 tablespoons minced seeded Thai, hot red, or serrano chiles

Salad:

12 ounces skinned, boned chicken breast
Cooking spray
2 cups sliced peeled mango (about 2 mangoes)
⅔ cup thinly sliced shallots
¼ cup matchstick-cut peeled fresh ginger
4 cups mixed salad greens
⅔ cup torn mint leaves

1. To prepare dressing, combine first 4 ingredients in a bowl, and stir well with a whisk. Set dressing aside.

Continued

2. Prepare grill or broiler.

3. To prepare salad, combine 1 tablespoon dressing and chicken, and toss to coat. Place chicken on a grill rack or broiler pan coated with cooking spray; cook 6 minutes on each side or until chicken is done. Cut chicken diagonally across grain into thin slices. Combine chicken, mango, shallots, and ginger. Toss with remaining dressing. Divide salad greens evenly among 3 plates. Top salad greens with chicken salad; sprinkle with mint. Yield: 3 servings (serving size: 1 cup chicken salad, 1⅓ cups salad greens, and about 3 tablespoons mint).

CALORIES 282 (7% from fat); FAT 2.2g (sat 0.5g, mono 0.5g, poly 0.5g); PROTEIN 30.2g; CARB 6.1g; FIBER 3.4g; CHOL 66mg; IRON 2.4mg; SODIUM 1,390mg; CALC 76mg

VEGETABLE CRUDITÉ ROLLS WITH SPICY THAI DIPPING SAUCE

In the Thai manner, the vegetables are rolled up in lettuce leaves and dunked in the sauce.

- ¼ cup fresh lemon juice
- 2 tablespoons Thai fish sauce
- ¼ teaspoon black pepper
- 5 large portobello mushroom caps (about 2 pounds)
- Cooking spray
- ½ pound green beans, trimmed
- 6 romaine lettuce leaves
- 6 radicchio leaves
- 1 large red bell pepper, seeded and cut into ½-inch strips
- 1 (15-ounce) can whole baby corn, drained
- ½ cup chopped basil leaves
- Spicy Thai Dipping Sauce

1. Prepare grill or broiler.
2. Combine first 4 ingredients in a large zip-top plastic bag, and seal. Marinate mushroom mixture 15 minutes, turning bag occasionally. Remove mushrooms from bag; discard marinade. Place mushrooms on a grill rack or broiler pan coated with cooking spray; cook 3 minutes on each side.

Cut mushrooms into ½-inch-wide slices, and set aside.
3. Steam green beans, covered, 5 minutes or until tender.
4. Arrange romaine and radicchio leaves on a large platter. Divide mushrooms, green beans, bell pepper, and corn evenly among lettuce leaves. Sprinkle with basil. Roll up leaves, and serve with Spicy Thai Dipping Sauce. Yield: 6 servings (serving size: 2 lettuce rolls and 2 tablespoons sauce).

CALORIES 127 (9% from fat); FAT 1.2g (sat 0.2g, mono 0.1g, poly 0.5g); PROTEIN 6.8g; CARB 27.3g; FIBER 3.8g; CHOL 0mg; IRON 2.9mg; SODIUM 1,252mg; CALC 43mg

Spicy Thai Dipping Sauce:

- ½ cup fresh lemon juice (about 2 lemons)
- ¼ cup Thai fish sauce
- 1 tablespoon brown sugar
- 2 Thai, hot red, or serrano chiles, seeded and thinly sliced
- 1 small garlic clove, minced

1. Combine all ingredients in a bowl; let stand 10 minutes. Yield: ¾ cup (serving size: 2 tablespoons).

CALORIES 21 (0% from fat); FAT 0g; PROTEIN 1g; CARB 4.5g; FIBER 0.1g; CHOL 0mg; IRON 0.1mg; SODIUM 1,084mg; CALC 4mg

TURKEY SALAD WITH TOASTED RICE POWDER AND LEMON GRASS

We liked the crunch of the ground rice powder, but you can omit it, if desired. The rice itself should be coarsely ground to remain crunchy, not sandy.

Toasted rice powder:

- 3 tablespoons uncooked sticky rice or short-grain rice

Dressing:

- ⅓ cup fresh lemon juice
- 3 tablespoons Thai fish sauce
- 1½ teaspoons brown sugar
- ½ teaspoon ground red pepper

Salad:

- 2 teaspoons vegetable oil
- 1 pound ground turkey
- ⅓ cup thinly sliced green onions
- ¼ cup thinly sliced peeled fresh lemon grass
- ¼ cup chopped fresh mint
- ¼ cup chopped fresh cilantro
- 6 Boston lettuce leaves

1. To prepare toasted rice powder, sauté rice 3 minutes in a medium skillet over medium-high heat, stirring constantly. Remove from heat; cool. Place rice in a spice or coffee grinder; pulse 5 times or just until coarsely ground.
2. To prepare dressing, combine juice, fish sauce, brown sugar, and red pepper in a bowl; stir well with a whisk.
3. To prepare salad, heat oil in pan over medium heat. Add turkey; cook 2 minutes or until browned, stirring to crumble. Remove turkey from pan with a slotted spoon. Combine turkey, dressing, onions, lemon grass, mint, and cilantro in a bowl; toss gently. Spoon ⅔ cup turkey mixture onto each lettuce leaf. Sprinkle evenly with rice powder. Yield: 6 servings.

CALORIES 154 (27% from fat); FAT 4.6g (sat 1.2g, mono 1.8g, poly 1.0g); PROTEIN 18.2g; CARB 9.4g; FIBER 0.8g; CHOL 44mg; IRON 1.8mg; SODIUM 696mg; CALC 32mg

FIERY THAI BEEF SALAD

Dressing:

- ⅓ cup fresh lime juice
- ¼ cup chopped fresh cilantro
- 2 tablespoons brown sugar
- 1 tablespoon water
- 1 tablespoon Thai fish sauce
- 5 garlic cloves, minced
- 2 Thai, hot red, or serrano chiles, seeded and minced

Salad:

- 1 (1-pound) flank steak
- ¼ teaspoon salt
- ⅛ teaspoon black pepper
- Cooking spray
- 6 cups torn romaine lettuce
- 1¾ cups quartered cherry tomatoes
- 1 cup thinly sliced red onion, separated into rings
- ¼ cup coarsely chopped fresh mint
- 2 tablespoons sliced peeled fresh lemon grass

1. To prepare dressing, combine first 7 ingredients in a bowl; stir well with a whisk.
2. Prepare grill or broiler.
3. Sprinkle both sides of steak with salt and pepper. Place steak on a grill rack or broiler pan coated with cooking spray, and cook 6 minutes on each side or until desired degree of doneness. Let stand 10 minutes. Cut steak diagonally across grain into thin slices; cut each slice into 2-inch pieces.
4. Combine steak, lettuce, and next 4 ingredients in a large bowl; add dressing, tossing to coat. Yield: 4 servings (serving size: 2 cups).

CALORIES 265 (38% from fat); FAT 11.3g (sat 4.7g, mono 4.3g, poly 0.6g); PROTEIN 25.5g; CARB 16g; FIBER 3g; CHOL 57mg; IRON 4.1mg; SODIUM 572mg; CALC 65mg

GRILLED-EGGPLANT SALAD WITH CILANTRO-CHILE DRESSING

Grilled vegetables work best. If you like, you can make this dish ahead and serve it cold.

Dressing:

- ¼ cup fresh lime juice
- 2 tablespoons chopped fresh cilantro
- 1 tablespoon brown sugar
- 1 tablespoon Thai fish sauce
- 1 tablespoon minced seeded Thai, hot red, or serrano chile
- 2 garlic cloves, minced

Salad:

- 12 cherry tomatoes, quartered
- 12 (½-inch-thick) slices eggplant (about 2 pounds)
- ¼ teaspoon salt, divided
- Cooking spray
- 6 (½-inch-thick) slices red onion
- ¼ cup torn mint leaves
- ¼ cup torn basil leaves

1. To prepare dressing, combine first 6 ingredients in a bowl; stir well with a whisk.
2. Prepare grill or broiler.
3. To prepare salad, combine tomatoes and dressing, and set aside. Sprinkle eggplant with ⅛ teaspoon salt. Place eggplant on a grill rack or broiler pan coated with cooking spray; cook 5 minutes on each side or until eggplant is done. Remove eggplant from grill rack or pan; set aside. Sprinkle onion with ⅛ teaspoon salt. Place onion on grill rack or broiler pan coated with cooking spray; cook 5 minutes on each side or until onion is tender.
4. Arrange eggplant and onion slices on 6 plates. Top with tomato mixture; sprinkle with mint and basil. Yield: 6 servings (serving size: 2 eggplant slices, 1 onion slice, and about ¼ cup tomato mixture).

CALORIES 77 (6% from fat); FAT 0.5g (sat 0.1g, mono 0.1g, poly 0.1g); PROTEIN 2.9g; CARB 18.2g; FIBER 3.6g; CHOL 0mg; IRON 1.2mg; SODIUM 326mg; CALC 75mg

THE THAI PANTRY

Here are key ingredients you'll need to make these classic Thai salads.

Chiles: Look for small, very hot red chiles, sometimes labeled Thai chiles. Serrano chiles are a good substitute; we used them in many of these recipes.

Thai fish sauce: A spicy condiment made from water, anchovies, and salt. Like soy sauce, it's extremely high in sodium, so use sparingly.

Fresh lemons and limes: These salads need the punch of fresh juice. Don't be tempted to use bottled.

Get Thee to an Orchard

In the peak of peach season, it's unimaginable to miss the flavor and aroma of this juiciest of fruits.

Take just one bite of a peach and summer announces its arrival on your tongue. Peaches are the true culinary harbingers of the season, the sweet bounty of summer.

GRILLED PEACH HALVES WITH SAVORY GINGER GLAZE

This is a great side dish served with pork or roasted chicken.

- 6 peaches
- 3 tablespoons brown sugar
- 2 tablespoons minced shallots
- 2 tablespoons low-sodium soy sauce
- 1 tablespoon minced peeled fresh ginger
- 1 tablespoon hoisin sauce
- 1 teaspoon grated orange rind
- 2 tablespoons orange juice
- Cooking spray

1. Cut an X on bottom of each peach, carefully cutting just through skin. Fill a large Dutch oven with water; bring to a boil. Immerse peaches 20 seconds; remove with a slotted spoon, and plunge into ice water. Slip skins off peaches, using a paring knife (skin will be very loose). Cut peaches in half; remove pits.
2. Prepare grill.
3. Combine sugar and next 6 ingredients. Brush cut sides of peaches with

Continued

There's nothing like a fresh peach, but the fuzzy skin can be annoying, especially in cooking. All of these recipes call for peeled peaches. We think the easiest way is by blanching. First, cut an X in the bottom of each peach, carefully cutting just through the skin.

❶ *Heat a large pot of water to boiling, and add the peaches. Cook 20 seconds to 1 minute—the riper they are, the less time they need.*

❷ *Remove the peaches from the water with a slotted spoon. Place them in a sink filled with ice water.*

❸ *Use a paring knife or your fingers to remove the skins, which should slip right off. (Only Poached Peach Cups with Red Wine Sorbet [see recipe] calls for a slight variation of this peeling method.)*

ginger mixture. Place peaches, cut sides down, on a grill rack coated with cooking spray; cook 10 minutes or until tender, turning and basting once with ginger mixture. Yield: 6 servings (serving size: 2 peach halves).

CALORIES 80 (3% from fat); FAT 0.3g (sat 0g, mono 0g, poly 0.1g); PROTEIN 1g; CARB 19.5g; FIBER 2.4g; CHOL 0mg; IRON 0.3mg; SODIUM 176mg; CALC 13mg

FRENCH TOAST-PEACH COBBLER

(pictured on page 188)

The sturdier the bread, the better for this simple dessert. Turbinado sugar crystals have a coarse texture and add a nice crunch to the topping, but you can use granulated sugar instead.

```
12  large ripe peaches
⅓  cup all-purpose flour
 1  cup granulated sugar, divided
Cooking spray
 1  teaspoon grated orange rind
⅓  cup fresh orange juice
¼  cup butter or stick margarine,
      melted
¼  teaspoon ground cinnamon
 3  large egg whites
 8  (1.5-ounce) slices hearty white
      bread (such as Pepperidge
      Farm)
 2  tablespoons turbinado sugar or
      granulated sugar
```

1. Cut an X on bottom of each peach, carefully cutting just through skin. Fill a large Dutch oven with water, and bring to a boil. Immerse peaches 20 seconds; remove with a slotted spoon, and plunge into ice water. Slip skins off peaches, using a paring knife (skin will be very loose). Cut peaches in half; remove pits. Slice peaches to yield 12 cups.
2. Lightly spoon flour into a dry measuring cup, and level with a knife. Combine peaches, flour, and ¾ cup granulated sugar in a 13 x 9-inch baking dish coated with cooking spray,

and let stand 30 minutes, stirring occasionally.
3. Preheat oven to 350°.
4. Combine ¼ cup granulated sugar, orange rind, orange juice, butter, cinnamon, and egg whites in a shallow bowl, stirring with a whisk. Trim crusts from bread; cut each slice into 2 triangles. Dip bread triangles in orange juice mixture; arrange on top of peach mixture. Sprinkle turbinado sugar over bread. Bake at 350° for 45 minutes or until golden. Yield: 10 servings.

CALORIES 289 (17% from fat); FAT 5.6g (sat 3g, mono 1.7g, poly 0.4g); PROTEIN 4.5g; CARB 58.5g; FIBER 4.6g; CHOL 13mg; IRON 1mg; SODIUM 162mg; CALC 35mg

POACHED PEACH CUPS WITH RED WINE SORBET

Because the peaches are poached in a wine syrup that's then made into a sorbet, use slightly underripe, firm peaches. Very ripe peaches may get too soft to keep their shape and hold the sorbet.

```
1¼  cups sugar
 ½  cup water
  1  (1.5-liter) bottle fruity red wine
       (such as Beaujolais)
  4  large peaches
  1  (3-inch) lemon rind strip
  3  tablespoons fresh lemon juice
  6  whole allspice
```

1. Combine first 3 ingredients in a large saucepan; bring to a boil. Cover and cook 5 minutes. Add peaches, rind, juice, and allspice; reduce heat, and simmer, uncovered, 10 minutes or until peaches are tender. Remove peaches with a slotted spoon, reserving wine mixture; plunge peaches into ice water. Slip skins off peaches, using a paring knife. Cut peaches in half, and remove pits. Place peaches in a large shallow dish; cover and chill.
2. Strain wine mixture through a sieve lined with cheesecloth into a bowl, and discard solids. Cover and chill. Pour wine mixture into the freezer can of an ice-cream freezer, and freeze according to manufacturer's instructions. Spoon

mixture into a freezer-safe container; cover and freeze.

3. Spoon sorbet into peach halves. Serve immediately. Yield: 8 servings (serving size: 1 peach half and ½ cup sorbet).

CALORIES 169 (1% from fat); FAT 0.1g (sat 0g, mono 0g, poly 0g); PROTEIN 1g; CARB 43.6g; FIBER 1.7g; CHOL 0mg; IRON 0.8mg; SODIUM 15mg; CALC 19mg

ROASTED CHICKEN, RED ONIONS, AND PEACHES

4 large peaches
1 tablespoon sugar
8 chicken thighs (about 2 pounds), skinned
2 large red onions, each cut into 8 wedges
½ teaspoon salt
¼ teaspoon black pepper
1 teaspoon vegetable oil
2 tablespoons balsamic vinegar
2 tablespoons molasses
1 teaspoon dried thyme
¼ teaspoon dried crushed red pepper
4 cups hot cooked couscous

1. Cut an X on bottom of each peach, carefully cutting just through skin. Fill a large Dutch oven with water; bring to a boil. Immerse peaches 20 seconds; remove with a slotted spoon, and plunge into ice water. Slip skins off peaches, using a paring knife (skin will be very loose). Cut peaches in half; remove pits.
2. Preheat oven to 425°.
3. Place peaches in a large bowl; sprinkle with sugar. Cover and chill.
4. Combine chicken and onions in a 13 x 9-inch baking dish; sprinkle with salt and black pepper. Drizzle with oil; toss chicken gently to coat. Bake at 425° for 30 minutes.
5. Combine vinegar, molasses, thyme, and crushed red pepper; drizzle over chicken, turning to coat. Bake chicken an additional 20 minutes. Add peaches to chicken mixture in dish, basting with cooking liquid. Bake an additional 10 minutes or until chicken is done.

Place 1 cup couscous on each of 4 plates, and top with 2 chicken thighs, 4 red onion wedges, and 2 peach halves. Spoon sauce over each serving. Yield: 4 servings.

CALORIES 472 (14% from fat); FAT 7.3g (sat 1.7g, mono 2.1g, poly 2.3g); PROTEIN 35.3g; CARB 67.5g; FIBER 5.4g; CHOL 113mg; IRON 3.8mg; SODIUM 422mg; CALC 61mg

PEACHES WITH MINT-ALMOND PESTO AND BRIE

Serve this as a special first course during the summer.

4 peaches
1 cup fresh mint leaves
¼ cup sugar
2 tablespoons balsamic vinegar
⅛ teaspoon black pepper
2 tablespoons chopped almonds, toasted
8 cups gourmet salad greens
1 (4½-ounce) round Brie cheese, cut into 8 wedges
8 (1-ounce) slices French bread

1. Cut an X on bottom of each peach, carefully cutting just through skin. Fill a Dutch oven with water; bring to a boil. Immerse peaches 20 seconds; remove with a slotted spoon, and plunge into ice water. Slip skins off peaches, using a paring knife (skin will be very loose). Cut peaches in half; remove pits.
2. Combine mint and sugar in a blender or food processor; process until chopped. Add vinegar and pepper; process until well-blended. Pour mint mixture into a large bowl, and add almonds and peach halves. Cover and chill 4 hours. Remove peaches with a slotted spoon, reserving marinade.
3. Arrange salad greens on 8 plates, and top each serving with a peach half and a cheese wedge. Drizzle with marinade. Serve with French bread. Yield: 8 servings (serving size: 1 peach half, 1 cup salad greens, ½ ounce Brie, and 1 slice bread).

CALORIES 202 (27% from fat); FAT 6g (sat 3.1g, mono 1.6g, poly 1.1g); PROTEIN 7.1g; CARB 30g; FIBER 3.3g; CHOL 11mg; IRON 1.6mg; SODIUM 279mg; CALC 108mg

PEACH CAKE

3 cups coarsely chopped peeled peaches (about 1 pound)
½ cup sugar, divided
2 teaspoons fresh lemon juice
1 tablespoon butter or stick margarine, softened
1 teaspoon vanilla extract
¼ teaspoon almond extract
1 large egg, lightly beaten
1 cup all-purpose flour
1 teaspoon baking powder
½ teaspoon grated lemon rind
¼ teaspoon salt
⅓ cup 2% reduced-fat milk
Cooking spray
4 teaspoons sliced almonds, toasted
2 cups vanilla low-fat frozen yogurt

1. Preheat oven to 375°.
2. Combine chopped peaches, ¼ cup sugar, and lemon juice. Set aside. Beat ¼ cup sugar and butter at medium speed of a mixer until well-blended. Add vanilla extract, almond extract, and egg; beat well.
3. Lightly spoon flour into a dry measuring cup, and level with a knife. Combine flour, baking powder, lemon rind, and salt. Add flour mixture to butter mixture alternately with milk, beginning and ending with flour mixture; mix after each addition. Spoon cake batter into an 8-inch square baking dish coated with cooking spray. Spoon peach mixture over batter. Sprinkle with almonds. Bake at 375° for 40 minutes or until golden brown. Serve warm with frozen yogurt. Yield: 6 servings (serving size: 1 cake piece and ⅓ cup yogurt).

CALORIES 266 (16% from fat); FAT 4.7g (sat 2.3g, mono 1.2g, poly 0.7g); PROTEIN 5.8g; CARB 51.2g; FIBER 2.1g; CHOL 48mg; IRON 1.3mg; SODIUM 234mg; CALC 125mg

California Grillin'

A California college student shares her favorite grilled fish dish.

GRILLED MAHIMAHI SKEWERS WITH PINEAPPLE-MANDARIN SAUCE

"I spend most of my time camping outdoors. While everyone else is cooking hot dogs, I'm making fajitas or grilling an herb-crusted fish. I serve this dish over cooked rice."

—*Robin Monahan,*
Fountain Valley, California

- ½ cup chopped onion
- ⅓ cup honey
- ½ cup dry red wine
- 2 tablespoons balsamic vinegar
- 2 tablespoons pineapple juice
- 1 tablespoon low-sodium soy sauce
- 1 tablespoon mirin (sweet rice wine) or slightly sweet white wine (such as Riesling)
- 2 cups diced fresh pineapple
- 1½ pounds mahimahi steaks, cut into 24 (1-inch) pieces
- 24 (1-inch) cubes fresh pineapple
- 24 (1-inch) pieces green bell pepper
- 1 tablespoon chopped fresh or 1 teaspoon dried rubbed sage
- ¼ teaspoon salt
- ¼ teaspoon black pepper
- Cooking spray
- Chopped fresh chives (optional)

1. Combine chopped onion and honey in a medium nonstick skillet, and place over medium heat. Cook 12 minutes or until golden brown, stirring occasionally. Add red wine and next 4 ingredients; cook 10 minutes. Stir in diced pineapple, and cook 5 minutes. Keep warm.

2. Prepare grill.

3. Thread 3 mahimahi pieces, 3 pineapple cubes, and 3 bell pepper pieces alternately onto each of 8 (12-inch) skewers. Sprinkle kebabs with sage, salt, and black pepper. Place kebabs on a grill rack coated with cooking spray; grill kebabs 15 minutes or until fish is done, turning every 5 minutes. Serve with pineapple sauce. Sprinkle with chives, if desired. Yield: 4 servings (serving size: 2 kebabs and ½ cup pineapple sauce).

CALORIES 392 (18% from fat); FAT 7.8g (sat 2g, mono 2.7g, poly 1.9g); PROTEIN 35.1g; CARB 47.7g; FIBER 2.7g; CHOL 66mg; IRON 2.8mg; SODIUM 427mg; CALC 34mg

SEARED TOFU-AND-SOBA NOODLE SALAD

—*Laura Mleko, Arlington Heights, Illinois*

- 2 (12.3-ounce) packages reduced-fat firm tofu, drained
- ¼ cup rice vinegar
- ¼ cup low-sodium soy sauce
- 2 tablespoons sugar
- 1 tablespoon sesame oil
- 2 teaspoons grated peeled fresh ginger
- ½ teaspoon salt
- ¼ teaspoon black pepper
- 1 tablespoon olive oil
- 6 cups chopped romaine lettuce
- 4 cups cooked soba (about 8 ounces uncooked buckwheat noodles)
- ½ cup chopped green onions

1. Cut each block of tofu in half lengthwise. Place tofu slices on several layers of paper towels; cover with additional paper towels. Let stand 30 minutes, pressing down occasionally.

2. Combine vinegar and next 6 ingredients in a jar; cover tightly, and shake vigorously. Set aside.

3. Heat oil in a large nonstick skillet over medium-high heat. Add tofu slices; cook 5 minutes on each side or until lightly browned. Cut each tofu slice in half lengthwise. Arrange lettuce on a platter; top with noodles, tofu slices, and onions. Drizzle with dressing. Yield: 4 servings (serving size: 1½ cups lettuce, 1 cup noodles, 2 tofu slices, 2 tablespoons onions, and 3 tablespoons dressing).

CALORIES 398 (22% from fat); FAT 9.7g (sat 1.5g, mono 4.5g, poly 3.1g); PROTEIN 22.3g; CARB 52.8g; FIBER 1.8g; CHOL 0mg; IRON 4mg; SODIUM 961mg; CALC 117mg

QUICK-AND-ZESTY REFRIED BEAN DIP

—*Kristi Nilles, Newport Beach, California*

- ¼ cup chopped red onion
- 2 tablespoons bottled salsa
- 1 tablespoon fresh lime juice
- 1 teaspoon hot sauce
- 1 (16-ounce) can fat-free refried beans
- ¼ cup chopped fresh cilantro
- ¼ cup (1 ounce) shredded sharp Cheddar cheese

1. Combine first 5 ingredients in a small saucepan; cook over medium-low heat 5 minutes or until thoroughly heated. Add chopped cilantro and cheese, stirring mixture until cheese melts. Serve warm. Yield: 1¾ cups (serving size: 1 tablespoon).

CALORIES 18 (15% from fat); FAT 0.3g (sat 0.2g, mono 0.1g, poly 0g); PROTEIN 1.1g; CARB 2.6g; FIBER 0.8g; CHOL 1mg; IRON 0.3mg; SODIUM 73mg; CALC 14mg

TOFFEE DIP WITH APPLES

—*Sue Martin, Birmingham, Alabama*

- ¾ cup packed brown sugar
- ½ cup powdered sugar
- 1 teaspoon vanilla extract
- 1 (8-ounce) block ⅓-less-fat cream cheese, softened
- ¾ cup toffee bits (such as Skor) (about 4 ounces)
- 1 cup pineapple juice
- 6 Red Delicious apples, each cored and cut into 8 wedges
- 6 Granny Smith apples, each cored and cut into 8 wedges

1. Combine first 4 ingredients in a bowl; beat at medium speed of a mixer until smooth. Add toffee bits, and mix well. Cover and chill.

2. Combine juice and apples in a bowl; toss well. Drain apples; serve with dip. Yield: 2 cups (serving size: 1 tablespoon dip and 3 apple wedges).

CALORIES 92 (28% from fat); FAT 2.9g (sat 1.8g, mono 0.8g, poly 0.2g); PROTEIN 0.8g; CARB 16.9g; FIBER 1.4g; CHOL 8mg; IRON 0.2mg; SODIUM 51mg; CALC 13mg

HAPPY HEART MACARONI

"I was reading your magazine and noticed several different articles talking about foods that are healthy for the heart. I decided to create a recipe that included all of them. I make this often for myself and my friends."
—Sylvia Nolan, North Palm Springs, California

1 tablespoon olive oil
2 garlic cloves, crushed
1 cup chopped tomato
2 tablespoons chopped fresh or 2 teaspoons dried parsley
1 tablespoon chopped fresh or 1 teaspoon dried basil
2 teaspoons honey
¼ teaspoon salt
⅛ teaspoon black pepper
2 cups cooked elbow macaroni (about 4 ounces uncooked)
½ cup canned black beans, rinsed and drained
2 cups chopped fresh spinach

1. Heat oil in a large nonstick skillet over medium heat until hot. Add garlic; sauté 1 minute. Add tomato and next 5 ingredients, and sauté 3 minutes. Add macaroni, beans, and spinach; cook 1 minute or until thoroughly heated. Yield: 2 servings (serving size: 1½ cups).

CALORIES 364 (21% from fat); FAT 8.5g (sat 1.2g, mono 5.2g, poly 1.3g); PROTEIN 12.9g; CARB 61.5g; FIBER 7.6g; CHOL 0mg; IRON 5.1mg; SODIUM 466mg; CALC 95mg

MENU SUGGESTION

GREEK CHICKEN SALAD

Stuffed zucchini *

*Cut 4 medium zucchini in half lengthwise; scoop out pulp, and coarsely chop. Sauté pulp, ½ cup chopped onion, and 2 teaspoons minced garlic until tender. Add 1 cup chopped seeded tomato; cook 3 minutes. Stir in ½ cup seasoned breadcrumbs. Stuff shells; sprinkle with ¼ cup grated Parmesan cheese. Cut each half into 3 pieces; bake at 350° for 15 minutes. Serves 8.

GREEK CHICKEN SALAD

"My brother's wife makes a heavier version of this recipe for family get-togethers. I thought it would be easy to lighten. It turned out fantastic."
—Billy Kutulas, Atlanta, Georgia

3 cups chopped cooked chicken breast (about 12 ounces)
1 cup diced seeded peeled cucumber
½ cup (2 ounces) crumbled feta cheese
¼ cup chopped fresh parsley
2 tablespoons sliced pitted kalamata olives
¾ cup plain fat-free yogurt
½ cup light mayonnaise
1 tablespoon dried oregano
3 garlic cloves, minced
4 (6-inch) pitas, each cut in half
8 Boston lettuce leaves

1. Combine first 5 ingredients in a large bowl. Combine yogurt, mayonnaise, oregano, and garlic in a small bowl. Pour over chicken mixture; toss well. Cover and chill 2 hours.

2. Line each pita half with a lettuce leaf, and fill with ½ cup chicken salad. Yield: 8 servings.

CALORIES 234 (30% from fat); FAT 7.8g (sat 2.3g, mono 2.3g, poly 2.8g); PROTEIN 18.8g; CARB 21.4g; FIBER 1.2g; CHOL 48mg; IRON 1.9mg; SODIUM 420mg; CALC 131mg

THE PERFECT CHEESECAKE

"I love cheesecake, so I've experimented with lots of low-fat recipes. And my wife, Edna, has graciously become my chief tester. When she tried this experimentation, she said, 'Don't you dare change it.' I didn't."
—Sidney Meadow, Danbury, Connecticut

1 (32-ounce) carton plain fat-free yogurt
½ cup graham cracker crumbs (about 6 cookie squares)
Cooking spray
⅓ cup all-purpose flour
1 cup sugar
2 teaspoons vanilla extract
1 tablespoon grated lemon rind
⅓ cup fat-free sour cream
2 (8-ounce) blocks ⅓-less-fat cream cheese, softened
1 (8-ounce) carton egg substitute

1. Place a colander in a 2-quart glass measure or a medium bowl. Line colander with four layers of cheesecloth, allowing cheesecloth to extend over outside edges. Spoon yogurt into colander. Cover loosely with plastic wrap, and refrigerate 12 hours. Spoon yogurt cheese into a bowl, and discard liquid.

2. Firmly press crumbs in bottom and up sides of a 9-inch springform pan coated with cooking spray.

3. Preheat oven to 350°.

4. Lightly spoon flour into a dry measuring cup, and level with a knife. Combine drained yogurt, flour, sugar, and next 4 ingredients in a large bowl; beat at medium speed of a mixer until blended. Slowly add egg substitute, and beat until combined. Pour cheese mixture into prepared crust. Place in a large shallow baking pan, and add hot water to pan to a depth of 1 inch. Bake at 350° for 1 hour and 10 minutes. Remove sides from pan, and cool to room temperature. Cover and chill at least 8 hours. Yield: 12 servings (serving size: 1 slice).

CALORIES 263 (32% from fat); FAT 9.4g (sat 5.7g, mono 2.7g, poly 0.4g); PROTEIN 12.7g; CARB 30g; FIBER 0.1g; CHOL 29mg; IRON 0.8mg; SODIUM 264mg; CALC 224mg

Spicy Ginger Chicken with Peanuts

"I like bold flavors. So when a friend gave me this recipe, I changed it a lot—increased the ginger and garlic, added more red peppers, changed the oil. As my friend says, once you make this, it's going to be your favorite."
—Rick Glisson, Schertz, Texas

    3 tablespoons low-sodium soy
         sauce, divided
    1 tablespoon dry white wine
    1 pound skinned, boned chicken
         breast, cut into bite-size pieces
   ¼ cup water
    1 tablespoon sugar
    1 tablespoon white vinegar
    1 teaspoon cornstarch
    1 tablespoon vegetable oil
    4 dried red chile peppers, seeded
   ½ cup sliced green onions
    1 tablespoon minced peeled fresh
         ginger
    4 garlic cloves, minced
   ¼ cup unsalted, dry-roasted peanuts
   1½ cups hot cooked basmati rice

1. Combine 1 tablespoon soy sauce, wine, and chicken in a zip-top plastic bag; seal. Marinate in refrigerator at least 1 hour, turning occasionally.
2. Combine 2 tablespoons soy sauce, water, sugar, vinegar, and cornstarch in a small bowl.
3. Heat oil in a wok or large nonstick skillet over medium-high heat until hot. Add chile peppers; stir-fry 1 minute. Add chicken mixture; stir-fry 3 minutes. Add green onions, ginger, and garlic; stir-fry 1 minute. Add cornstarch mixture and peanuts; bring to a boil, and cook 1 minute, stirring constantly. Serve chicken mixture over rice. Yield: 3 servings (serving size: ⅔ cup chicken mixture and ½ cup rice).

CALORIES 434 (26% from fat); FAT 12.6g (sat 2.2g, mono 4.8g, poly 4.5g); PROTEIN 41.8g; CARB 37.7g; FIBER 2.3g; CHOL 88mg; IRON 3mg; SODIUM 588mg; CALC 63mg

Vermont's Roadside Riches

If you go looking for fresh summer food in the right places, such as the back roads of Vermont, you can find great meals and good friends.

Food is socializing by other means. The growing, the selling, the cooking, the eating. We know that intrinsically, but it's easy to forget. Our editors went looking for fresh summer produce in the Vermont countryside, and discovered that food is a basic source of pleasure, not just sustenance. The highlight was a visit to a roadside open-air market full of people, dogs, bicycles, sunshine, and all manner of communal commerce: fresh vegetables of just about every kind, homemade yeast breads, maple syrup, handfuls of garlic, fresh egg rolls, just-picked blackberries—and a terrific meal.

MENU SUGGESTION

*Barbecued flank steak**

CHILI-ROASTED CORN
ON THE COB

Jasmine rice

*Marinate 1 (1½-pound) flank steak, ⅓ cup sherry, ⅓ cup low-sodium soy sauce, ¼ cup packed brown sugar, 2 teaspoons dark sesame oil, ½ teaspoon crushed red pepper, and 3 minced garlic cloves in a zip-top plastic bag 2 to 8 hours. Grill steak 8 minutes on each side, basting frequently with marinade. Serves 6.

Chili-Roasted Corn on the Cob

    6 ears corn with husks
    2 teaspoons chili powder
   ½ teaspoon salt
   ½ teaspoon ground cumin
    1 tablespoon butter or stick
         margarine, melted

1. Place corn with husks in cold water; soak 30 minutes. Combine chili powder, salt, cumin, and butter in a bowl. Pull husks back; scrub silks from corn.
2. Brush chili powder mixture over corn. Wrap husks around corn.
3. Prepare grill or broiler.

4. Place corn on a grill rack or broiler pan; cook 20 minutes or until corn is lightly browned, turning every 5 minutes. Yield: 6 servings (serving size: 1 ear of corn).

CALORIES 101 (27% from fat); FAT 3g (sat 1.4g, mono 0.9g, poly 0.6g); PROTEIN 2.6g; CARB 19.4g; FIBER 3.1g; CHOL 5mg; IRON 0.7mg; SODIUM 236mg; CALC 6mg

Summer-Berry Compote

    2 cups fresh blueberries
   ½ cup packed brown sugar
    2 tablespoons champagne or
         white wine vinegar
   ½ teaspoon grated lemon rind
    2 tablespoons fresh lemon juice
   1½ cups fresh raspberries
   1½ cups fresh blackberries
    2 peaches, each peeled and cut
         into 6 wedges

1. Combine first 5 ingredients in a medium nonaluminum saucepan; bring to a boil. Cover, reduce heat, and simmer 20 minutes. Cool to room temperature.
2. Spoon about ¼ cup blueberry mixture into each of 6 shallow bowls, and top each serving with ¼ cup raspberries, ¼ cup blackberries, and 2 peach wedges. Yield: 6 servings.

CALORIES 146 (3% from fat); FAT 0.5g (sat 0g, mono 0.1g, poly 0.3g); PROTEIN 1.1g; CARB 36.9g; FIBER 6g; CHOL 0mg; IRON 0.9mg; SODIUM 11mg; CALC 39mg

CREAMY ROASTED-TOMATO SOUP WITH BASIL CROSTINI

4   large tomatoes, cored, cut in
    half crosswise, and seeded
    (about 2 pounds)
1   tablespoon olive oil, divided
1   cup chopped carrot
¾   cup chopped shallots (about 5
    shallots)
1   (16-ounce) can fat-free,
    less-sodium chicken broth
1   cup 2% reduced-fat milk
¼   teaspoon salt
¼   teaspoon freshly ground black
    pepper
Basil Crostini

1. Preheat oven to 425°.
2. Place tomato halves, cut sides down,
in a jelly-roll pan, and drizzle with 2
teaspoons oil. Bake at 425° for 35 minutes or until tender and slightly
charred. Remove tomatoes from oven;
cool. Discard skins from tomato halves.
3. Heat 1 teaspoon oil in a Dutch oven
over medium-high heat. Add carrot
and shallots; sauté 8 minutes. Stir in
broth. Partially cover, reduce heat, and
simmer 20 minutes or until carrot is
tender. Add tomato halves. Place half
of tomato mixture in a blender; process
until smooth. Pour pureed mixture
into a large bowl, and repeat procedure
with remaining tomato mixture.
Return pureed tomato mixture to pan.

Stir in milk, salt, and pepper, and cook
over low heat 5 minutes or until thoroughly heated. Serve with Basil
Crostini. Yield: 5 servings (serving size:
1 cup soup and 2 crostini).

CALORIES 268 (22% from fat); FAT 6.5g (sat 1.8g, mono 3.2g,
poly 0.9g); PROTEIN 10.5g; CARB 43g; FIBER 4.2g;
CHOL 6mg; IRON 2.5mg; SODIUM 709mg; CALC 156mg

Basil Crostini:

10 (¼-inch-thick) slices French
    bread baguette
1   garlic clove, halved
2   tablespoons (½ ounce) grated
    fresh Parmesan cheese
1   tablespoon chopped fresh basil

1. Preheat broiler.
2. Place bread slices on a baking sheet,
and broil 15 seconds or until toasted.
Rub bread with cut sides of garlic.
Sprinkle with cheese and basil. Broil 20
seconds or until cheese melts. Yield: 5
servings (serving size: 2 crostini).

CALORIES 149 (13% from fat); FAT 2.2g (sat 0.8g, mono 0.8g,
poly 0.4g); PROTEIN 5.5g; CARB 26.3g; FIBER 1.5g;
CHOL 2mg; IRON 1.3mg; SODIUM 350mg; CALC 73mg

VERMONT-CHEDDAR SPOON BREAD

Cooking spray
½   cup plus 2 teaspoons cornmeal,
    divided
1½ cups fat-free milk
¼   teaspoon salt
⅛   teaspoon black pepper
1   large egg yolk, lightly beaten
2   large egg whites
½   cup (2 ounces) shredded
    Vermont sharp Cheddar
    cheese

1. Preheat oven to 375°.
2. Coat a 1-quart soufflé dish with
cooking spray; sprinkle with 2 teaspoons cornmeal, and set aside.
3. Combine ½ cup cornmeal, milk,
salt, and pepper in a medium saucepan,
and cook over medium heat 5 minutes
or until thick, stirring constantly.
Remove from heat.

4. Gradually stir ½ cup hot cornmeal
mixture into egg yolk; add to remaining cornmeal mixture, stirring constantly. Pour into a large bowl; cool
completely.
5. Beat egg whites at high speed of a
mixer until stiff peaks form. Gently
fold egg whites and cheese into cornmeal mixture. Spoon batter into prepared dish. Bake at 375° for 1 hour or
until puffy and browned. Serve immediately. Yield: 4 servings (serving size:
1 cup).

CALORIES 183 (32% from fat); FAT 6.6g (sat 3.6g, mono 2g,
poly 0.5g); PROTEIN 10.6g; CARB 19.4g; FIBER 1g;
CHOL 71mg; IRON 1.1mg; SODIUM 311mg; CALC 223mg

GRILLED TERIYAKI PORK CHOPS WITH SUMMERY PEACH SALSA

(pictured on page 188)

4   (6-ounce) center-cut pork
    chops (about ¾ inch thick)
¼   cup low-sodium soy sauce
3   tablespoons minced shallots
2   tablespoons dry white wine
2   tablespoons fresh lime juice
1   tablespoon minced peeled fresh
    ginger
1½ teaspoons brown sugar
2   garlic cloves, minced
Summery Peach Salsa

1. Trim fat from pork. Combine pork
and next 7 ingredients in a large zip-
top plastic bag. Seal and marinate in
refrigerator 4 hours, turning bag occasionally. Remove pork from bag,
reserving marinade.
2. Prepare grill.
3. Place pork on a grill rack coated
with cooking spray; cook 7 minutes on
each side or until done, basting frequently with reserved marinade. Serve
with Summery Peach Salsa. Yield: 4
servings (serving size: 1 pork chop and
½ cup salsa).

CALORIES 315 (36% from fat); FAT 12.5g (sat 4.2g, mono 5.5g,
poly 1.5g); PROTEIN 28.4g; CARB 21.5g; FIBER 1.7g;
CHOL 84mg; IRON 1.9mg; SODIUM 552mg; CALC 29mg

Continued

Summery Peach Salsa:

- 1 cup diced peach
- ½ cup diced plum
- ¼ cup minced shallots
- 3 tablespoons orange juice
- 2 tablespoons minced fresh parsley
- 1 teaspoon grated lime rind
- 2 tablespoons fresh lime juice
- 1½ tablespoons chopped seeded jalapeño pepper
- 1 tablespoon minced fresh mint
- 1 tablespoon honey
- 1 teaspoon minced peeled fresh ginger

1. Combine all ingredients in a bowl. Cover and chill. Yield: 2 cups (serving size: ½ cup).

CALORIES 65 (3% from fat); FAT 0.2g (sat 0g, mono 0.1g, poly 0.1g); PROTEIN 1g; CARB 16.5g; FIBER 1.6g; CHOL 0mg; IRON 0.4mg; SODIUM 3mg; CALC 13mg

ROASTED GREEN BEANS

Wax beans (pale-yellow cousins of green beans) are abundant in the summer. You can substitute any herb for the basil.

- 1¼ pounds green or wax beans, trimmed
- 2 tablespoons slivered almonds
- 1 tablespoon lemon juice
- 2 teaspoons olive oil
- ½ teaspoon salt
- ¼ teaspoon garlic powder
- ¼ teaspoon dried basil
- ¼ teaspoon freshly ground black pepper

1. Preheat oven to 450°.
2. Combine all ingredients in a jelly-roll pan, tossing well. Bake at 450° for 10 minutes or until beans are tender and browned, stirring occasionally. Yield: 4 servings (serving size: 1 cup).

CALORIES 83 (43% from fat); FAT 4g (sat 0.5g, mono 2.7g, poly 0.6g); PROTEIN 3.2g; CARB 11.3g; FIBER 3.4g; CHOL 0mg; IRON 1.6mg; SODIUM 302mg; CALC 63mg

GRILLED EGGPLANT, TOMATO, PROVOLONE, AND SUN-DRIED TOMATO-PESTO SANDWICH

You'll have leftover pesto, which is great with pasta or as a dip.

- ½ teaspoon dried basil
- ¼ teaspoon dried oregano
- ¼ teaspoon salt
- ⅛ teaspoon black pepper
- 8 (¼-inch-thick) slices eggplant (about 1½ pounds)
- 4 (½-inch-thick) slices yellow tomato (about 10 ounces)
- 4 (½-inch-thick) slices red tomato (about 10 ounces)
- Cooking spray
- 8 (1½-ounce) slices French bread
- ½ cup Sun-Dried Tomato Pesto
- 2 (1½-ounce) slices provolone cheese, each cut in half
- 1 cup gourmet salad greens

1. Prepare grill or broiler.
2. Combine first 4 ingredients in a small bowl. Sprinkle evenly over eggplant and tomato slices.
3. Place eggplant on a grill rack or broiler pan coated with cooking spray; cook 5 minutes on each side or until eggplant is tender and browned. Place tomato on grill rack or broiler pan coated with cooking spray, and cook 2 minutes on each side or until tomato is done. Place bread on grill rack or broiler pan coated with cooking spray; cook 1 minute on each side or until bread is lightly toasted.
4. Spread 1 tablespoon Sun-Dried Tomato Pesto on each bread slice, and place ½ slice of cheese on each of 4 bread slices. Arrange greens, eggplant, and tomato evenly over cheese, and top with 4 bread slices. Yield: 4 servings.

CALORIES 442 (27% from fat); FAT 13.2g (sat 4.9g, mono 4.7g, poly 2.3g); PROTEIN 17.7g; CARB 67.4g; FIBER 9.7g; CHOL 15mg; IRON 4.4mg; SODIUM 986mg; CALC 267mg

Sun-Dried Tomato Pesto:

- ½ cup sun-dried tomatoes, packed without oil
- ¾ cup boiling water
- 1 cup chopped seeded plum tomato
- ½ cup basil leaves
- 2 tablespoons pine nuts
- 1 tablespoon olive oil
- ⅛ teaspoon black pepper
- 4 garlic cloves

1. Combine sun-dried tomatoes and boiling water in a bowl, and let stand 4 minutes. Drain tomatoes, and chop.
2. Combine drained chopped tomatoes, plum tomato, and remaining ingredients in a blender or food processor, and process 20 seconds or until a paste forms. Yield: 1 cup (serving size: 2 tablespoons).
Note: Store pesto in refrigerator in an airtight container.

CALORIES 28 (64% from fat); FAT 2g (sat 0.3g, mono 1g, poly 0.6g); PROTEIN 0.8g; CARB 2.7g; FIBER 0.5g; CHOL 0mg; IRON 0.4mg; SODIUM 58mg; CALC 7mg

ROASTED-VEGETABLE PASTA SALAD WITH GRILLED CHICKEN

Vegetables:

- 1½ cups (3 x ½-inch) julienne-cut yellow squash
- 1¼ cups (3 x ½-inch) julienne-cut carrot
- 1 cup vertically sliced onion
- 1 cup (3 x ½-inch) julienne-cut zucchini
- 1 cup (3 x ½-inch) julienne-cut red bell pepper
- 1 tablespoon olive oil

Chicken:

- 4 (4-ounce) skinned, boned chicken breast halves
- ½ teaspoon dried basil
- ½ teaspoon dried oregano
- Cooking spray

Vinaigrette:

¼ cup balsamic vinegar
¼ cup fresh lemon juice
1 tablespoon olive oil
1½ teaspoons Dijon mustard
1 teaspoon salt
¼ teaspoon black pepper
1 garlic clove, crushed

Remaining ingredients:

8 cups cooked ziti (about 6 cups uncooked short tube-shaped pasta)
2 tablespoons chopped fresh basil
16 cherry tomatoes, halved

1. Preheat oven to 450°.
2. To prepare vegetables, combine first 6 ingredients in a roasting pan; toss gently to coat. Bake at 450° for 20 minutes.
3. To prepare chicken, sprinkle chicken with dried basil and oregano.
4. Prepare grill.
5. Place chicken on a grill rack coated with cooking spray; cook 4 minutes on each side or until chicken is done. Cool; cut into ¼-inch-wide strips.
6. To prepare vinaigrette, combine vinegar and next 6 ingredients; stir with a whisk.
7. Combine roasted vegetables, chicken, vinaigrette, pasta, fresh basil, and tomatoes in a large bowl; toss gently to coat. Yield: 6 servings (serving size: 2 cups).

CALORIES 422 (15% from fat); FAT 7.2g (sat 1.2g, mono 4.3g, poly 1.3g); PROTEIN 27.7g; CARB 61.1g; FIBER 5.5g; CHOL 44mg; IRON 4.1mg; SODIUM 494mg; CALC 52mg

MAPLE FRUIT CRISPS

(pictured on page 186)

½ cup all-purpose flour
½ cup regular oats
⅓ cup packed brown sugar
1 teaspoon baking powder
½ teaspoon ground cinnamon
¼ teaspoon ground nutmeg
2 tablespoons slivered almonds
1 large egg
2½ cups fresh blackberries or blueberries
⅓ cup maple syrup
4 nectarines, each peeled and cut into 8 wedges
1½ cups vanilla low-fat frozen yogurt

1. Preheat oven to 350°.
2. Lightly spoon flour into a dry measuring cup; level with a knife. Place flour and next 5 ingredients in a food processor; pulse 2 times or until blended. Add almonds; pulse 3 times or until chopped. Add egg; pulse 5 times or until mixture resembles coarse meal.
3. Combine blackberries, maple syrup, and nectarines in a bowl; toss to coat. Divide fruit mixture evenly among 6 (10-ounce) ramekins or custard cups; crumble oat mixture evenly over fruit mixture. Bake at 350° for 35 minutes or until bubbly. Serve with frozen yogurt. Yield: 6 servings (serving size: 1 ramekin and ¼ cup frozen yogurt).
Note: You can make this recipe in a 1½-quart casserole and bake it 35 minutes.

CALORIES 289 (12% from fat); FAT 3.9g (sat 1g, mono 1.3g, poly 1.1g); PROTEIN 5.8g; CARB 61.2g; FIBER 6.4g; CHOL 40mg; IRON 2.1mg; SODIUM 111mg; CALC 141mg

FOR TWO

Doubles, Anyone?

Bringing a partner to the cooking of that special meal makes the entire evening more fun.

You can get an extra pair of helping hands in the kitchen from your guest. Joining forces will pay off in both bonding and dining. You'll be able to take on a more elaborate meal than either of you might try on your own, you'll share in the give-and-take of cooking tasks, and you'll cut your cleanup time in half.

And this menu combines the best of both worlds: The more upscale and out-of-the-ordinary ingredients that require additional time, such as the salad and scallops, are offset by components such as the couscous and dessert, which are simple. Making the Eggplant Caviar ahead saves even more time.

PARTY MENU FOR TWO

EGGPLANT CAVIAR
WITH PITA WEDGES

GRILLED SCALLOP-AND-FIG
KEBABS

CURRIED COUSCOUS

WATERCRESS SALAD WITH
BLUE CHEESE AND
PRALINE

PEACH CANTALOUPE TOSS

About 988 calories and 17 grams of fat
(15% calories from fat) per serving

Eggplant Caviar with Pita Wedges

Make this dish the day before. It'll give you something to munch on as you prepare the rest of the menu. Store any leftover caviar in an airtight container in the refrigerator up to three days.

 1 (1-pound) eggplant, cut crosswise into ½-inch-thick slices
Cooking spray
 1 teaspoon dark sesame oil
 ¼ cup coarsely chopped walnuts
 ¼ teaspoon dried oregano
 2 garlic cloves
 ½ cup fresh parsley sprigs
 1 teaspoon grated lemon rind
 1 tablespoon fresh lemon juice
 ½ teaspoon salt
 ¼ teaspoon ground red pepper
Chopped fresh parsley (optional)
 5 (7-inch) pitas, each cut into 8 wedges and toasted

1. Preheat oven to 500°.
2. Arrange eggplant in a single layer on a baking sheet coated with cooking spray; lightly coat both sides of eggplant with cooking spray. Bake at 500° for 15 minutes, turning after 8 minutes.
3. Heat oil in a skillet over medium-high heat. Add walnuts, oregano, and garlic; sauté 2 minutes. Drop walnut mixture through food chute of a food processor with food processor on, and process until minced. Drop parsley sprigs through food chute with food processor on, and process until minced. Add eggplant, lemon rind, lemon juice, salt, and red pepper, and process until smooth. Spoon eggplant mixture into a bowl, and sprinkle with chopped parsley, if desired. Serve with pita wedges. Yield: 10 servings (serving size: about 2 tablespoons caviar and 4 pita wedges).

CALORIES 160 (17% from fat); FAT 3g (sat 0.3g, mono 0.6g, poly 1.6g); PROTEIN 5.4g; CARB 28.3g; FIBER 2.3g; CHOL 0mg; IRON 1.6mg; SODIUM 360mg; CALC 49mg

Grilled Scallop-and-Fig Kebabs

You can make the marinade a day ahead or assign that task to your guest while you prepare the couscous. The Curried Couscous (see recipe) doesn't need to be served hot, but the kebabs do, so grill them last.

 3 tablespoons orange marmalade
 ¼ cup chopped green onions
 2 tablespoons low-sodium soy sauce
 ½ teaspoon ground red pepper
 1 large garlic clove, chopped
16 sea scallops (about 12 ounces)
 8 dried figs (about 5 ounces)
 2 lemons, quartered
 1 teaspoon olive oil

1. Combine first 5 ingredients in a zip-top plastic bag; seal and shake vigorously. Add scallops; seal and marinate in refrigerator 20 minutes. Remove scallops from bag, reserving marinade. Thread 4 scallops, 2 figs, and 2 lemon quarters alternately onto each of 4 (12-inch) skewers.
2. Preheat grill.
3. Coat a grill rack with oil. Place kebabs on grill rack; cook 6 minutes or until scallops are done, turning and basting with reserved marinade. Yield: 2 servings (serving size: 2 kebabs).

CALORIES 451 (9% from fat); FAT 4.5g (sat 0.6g, mono 1.9g, poly 1.1g); PROTEIN 32g; CARB 76.2g; FIBER 9.7g; CHOL 56mg; IRON 2.8mg; SODIUM 785mg; CALC 176mg

Curried Couscous

 1 teaspoon butter or stick margarine
 ¼ teaspoon curry powder
 ⅛ teaspoon ground allspice
1⅓ cups fat-free, less-sodium chicken broth
 ⅔ cup uncooked couscous

1. Melt butter in a medium saucepan over medium heat. Add curry and allspice; cook 1 minute, stirring constantly. Add broth, and bring to a boil. Stir in couscous. Remove from heat; cover and let stand 5 minutes. Fluff with a fork. Yield: 2 servings (serving size: 1 cup).

CALORIES 201 (11% from fat); FAT 2.4g (sat 1.2g, mono 0.6g, poly 0.1g); PROTEIN 8.3g; CARB 36.4g; FIBER 1.9g; CHOL 5mg; IRON 1mg; SODIUM 344mg; CALC 3mg

Watercress Salad with Blue Cheese and Praline

You can either make the praline a couple of days ahead or have your partner make it while you're preparing the salad dressing. Get these components ready while the scallops are marinating, and then toss before serving.

Dressing:

 1 tablespoon water
1½ teaspoons fresh lemon juice
 1 teaspoon Dijon mustard
 ½ teaspoon extra-virgin olive oil
 ⅛ teaspoon black pepper
Dash of salt
Dash of dried tarragon
 1 small garlic clove, minced

Praline:

 ¼ cup sugar
 2 tablespoons chopped walnuts
Cooking spray

Salad:

 1 cup trimmed watercress
 1 cup Boston lettuce leaves
 1 tablespoon (¼ ounce) crumbled blue cheese or feta cheese

1. To prepare dressing, combine first 8 ingredients; stir well with a whisk.
2. To prepare praline, place sugar in a small skillet over medium heat, and cook until sugar dissolves, stirring to dissolve sugar evenly. Stir in chopped walnuts, and cook over low heat 30 seconds or until golden. Remove from heat. Rapidly spread mixture onto foil coated with cooking spray. Cool completely; break into small pieces.

3. To prepare salad, combine watercress, lettuce, and blue cheese in a bowl; add dressing and praline, tossing well. Serve immediately. Yield: 2 servings (serving size: 1½ cups).

CALORIES 180 (34% from fat); FAT 6.8g (sat 1.1g, mono 2.1g, poly 3.1g); PROTEIN 3.6g; CARB 28g; FIBER 1.4g; CHOL 3mg; IRON 0.7mg; SODIUM 280mg; CALC 58mg

PEACH-CANTALOUPE TOSS

Our menu should leave you satisfied, but if you still want dessert, make this dish ahead and serve chilled.

1¼ cups sliced peeled peaches (about 2 peaches)
  1 cup cantaloupe balls (about ½ cantaloupe)
  ¼ cup sugar
  1 tablespoon fresh lemon juice
  ¼ teaspoon salt

1. Combine all ingredients. Cover and chill 1½ hours. Yield: 2 servings (serving size: 1 cup).

CALORIES 172 (2% from fat); FAT 0.3g (sat 0.1g, mono 0g, poly 0.1g); PROTEIN 1.5g; CARB 44.1g; FIBER 2.8g; CHOL 0mg; IRON 0.3mg; SODIUM 300mg; CALC 15mg

DINNER TONIGHT

One if by Land, Two if by Sea

When you put marinades and fish together, you have fast and great-tasting dishes to bring everyone running to your weeknight dinner table.

By nature, fish and shellfish are fork-tender, so they need only to bathe in a marinade long enough to pick up flavor. That's usually about 15 to 30 minutes. Another four to 12 minutes on a grill rack or broiler pan, and you have something delicious.

LEMON-DILL POLLOCK

Pollock (POL-uhk) is a delicate-flavored, firm white fish that's a cousin to cod. Pollock is used to make the imitation shellfish called surimi.

  ⅓ cup minced fresh dill
  ¼ cup fresh lemon juice
  1 tablespoon olive oil
  4 teaspoons Dijon mustard
  ¼ teaspoon salt
  ¼ teaspoon sugar
  ¼ teaspoon black pepper
  1 garlic clove, minced
  4 (6-ounce) pollock or other firm white fish fillets
Cooking spray

1. Combine first 9 ingredients in a large zip-top plastic bag; seal and marinate in refrigerator 20 minutes. Remove fish from bag; discard marinade.
2. Prepare grill or broiler.
3. Place fish on a grill rack or broiler pan coated with cooking spray. Cook 4 minutes on each side or until fish flakes easily when tested with a fork. Yield: 4 servings.

CALORIES 180 (19% from fat); FAT 3.7g (sat 0.5g, mono 1.5g, poly 1g); PROTEIN 33.2g; CARB 1.4g; FIBER 0.1g; CHOL 121mg; IRON 1.1mg; SODIUM 292mg; CALC 114mg

CURRIED PEANUT SHRIMP

  ⅓ cup orange marmalade
  ¼ cup orange juice
  2 tablespoons reduced-fat creamy peanut butter
  1 tablespoon Dijon mustard
1½ teaspoons curry powder
  1 teaspoon vegetable oil
  ½ teaspoon salt
  ¼ teaspoon crushed red pepper
  ¼ teaspoon chile sauce with garlic
32 large shrimp, peeled and deveined (about 1 pound)
Cooking spray

1. Combine first 9 ingredients in a blender, and process until smooth. Reserve ¼ cup marmalade mixture. Place remaining marmalade mixture in a large zip-top plastic bag, and add shrimp. Seal and shake to coat. Marinate in refrigerator 30 minutes.
2. Prepare grill or broiler.
3. Remove shrimp from bag, reserving marinade. Thread shrimp onto 4 (12-inch) skewers. Place kebabs on a grill rack or broiler pan coated with cooking spray; cook 3 minutes on each side or until shrimp are done, basting frequently with reserved marinade. Spoon reserved ¼ cup marmalade mixture over shrimp. Yield: 4 servings (serving size: 8 shrimp).

CALORIES 228 (24% from fat); FAT 6.2g (sat 1g, mono 2.1g, poly 2g); PROTEIN 19.6g; CARB 24.6g; FIBER 0.3g; CHOL 129mg; IRON 2.5mg; SODIUM 626mg; CALC 60mg

MUSTARD-MAPLE SALMON

  3 tablespoons Dijon mustard
  3 tablespoons maple syrup
  1 tablespoon balsamic vinegar
  ¼ teaspoon salt
  ⅛ teaspoon freshly ground black pepper
  4 (6-ounce) salmon fillets (about 1 inch thick)
Cooking spray

1. Combine first 5 ingredients in a large zip-top plastic bag; add salmon. Seal and marinate in refrigerator 20 minutes.
2. Prepare grill or broiler.
3. Remove salmon from bag, reserving marinade. Place salmon on a grill rack or broiler pan coated with cooking spray, and cook 6 minutes on each side or until fish flakes easily when tested with a fork; baste salmon occasionally with reserved marinade. Yield: 4 servings.

CALORIES 329 (41% from fat); FAT 14.9g (sat 2.5g, mono 7.1g, poly 3.2g); PROTEIN 34.8g; CARB 10.8g; FIBER 0g; CHOL 111mg; IRON 0.9mg; SODIUM 566mg; CALC 19mg

KOREAN-STYLE STRIPED BASS

Striped bass is a mild, firm fish from the Atlantic Coast. It's also sold in fish markets as striper, greenhead, or squidhound. Striped bass cooks best under the broiler because the fillets are usually cut thin and fall apart easily.

    ¼   cup low-sodium soy sauce
    1   tablespoon brown sugar
    1   tablespoon dry sherry
    1   tablespoon rice vinegar
    2   teaspoons grated peeled fresh
          ginger
    1   teaspoon sesame seeds, toasted
    1   teaspoon dark sesame oil
    ½   teaspoon chile paste with garlic
    1   garlic clove, minced
    4   (6-ounce) striped bass fillets
        Cooking spray

1. Combine first 10 ingredients in a large zip-top plastic bag. Seal and marinate in refrigerator 20 minutes. Remove fish from bag; discard marinade.
2. Preheat broiler.
3. Place fillets on a broiler pan coated with cooking spray. Broil 4 minutes or until fish flakes easily when tested with a fork. Yield: 4 servings.

CALORIES 213 (30% from fat); FAT 7.2g (sat 1.4g, mono 2.7g, poly 2.1g); PROTEIN 32.6g; CARB 2.2g; FIBER 0g; CHOL 116mg; IRON 2.8mg; SODIUM 366mg; CALC 143mg

SASSY BARBECUED SHRIMP

    32 large shrimp, peeled and
          deveined (about 1 pound)
    ½   cup chopped green onions
    ½   cup ketchup
    ¼   cup molasses
    2   tablespoons water
    2   tablespoons low-sodium soy
          sauce
    2   teaspoons dark sesame oil
    2   teaspoons chile paste
    2   garlic cloves, minced
        Cooking spray

1. Combine first 9 ingredients in a large zip-top plastic bag. Seal and shake to coat. Marinate in refrigerator 15 minutes.
2. Prepare grill or broiler.
3. Remove shrimp from bag, reserving marinade. Thread 4 shrimp onto each of 8 (12-inch) skewers. Place kebabs on a grill rack or broiler pan coated with cooking spray. Cook 3 minutes on each side or until shrimp are done; baste frequently with reserved marinade. Yield: 4 servings (serving size: 8 shrimp).

CALORIES 218 (17% from fat); FAT 4.2g (sat 0.6g, mono 1.1g, poly 1.6g); PROTEIN 19.1g; CARB 26.5g; FIBER 0.9g; CHOL 129mg; IRON 3.8mg; SODIUM 791mg; CALC 108mg

CAESAR MAHIMAHI

    ¼   cup plain fat-free yogurt
    2   tablespoons grated Parmesan
          cheese
    2   tablespoons fresh lemon juice
    2   tablespoons low-fat buttermilk
    1   tablespoon Dijon mustard
    2   teaspoons Worcestershire sauce
    2   teaspoons anchovy paste
    ¼   teaspoon black pepper
    6   garlic cloves, crushed
    4   (6-ounce) mahimahi or other
          firm white fish fillets
        Cooking spray

1. Combine first 9 ingredients, and stir well with a whisk. Pour yogurt mixture into a large zip-top plastic bag, and add fish to bag. Seal and marinate in refrigerator 20 minutes.
2. Prepare grill or broiler.
3. Remove fish from bag, reserving marinade. Place fish on a grill rack or broiler pan coated with cooking spray, and cook 3 minutes on each side or until fish flakes easily when tested with a fork, basting frequently with reserved marinade. Yield: 4 servings.

CALORIES 193 (14% from fat); FAT 3g (sat 0.8g, mono 0.4g, poly 0.3g); PROTEIN 34.7g; CARB 4.7g; FIBER 0.1g; CHOL 127mg; IRON 2.1mg; SODIUM 728mg; CALC 84mg

CARIBBEAN MANGO TILAPIA

Tilapia (teh-LAH-pee-uh) is a farm-raised white fish with a delicate texture and sweet flavor.

    4   serrano chiles, seeded
    3   garlic cloves, peeled
    2   large shallots, peeled
    2   cups chopped peeled mango
    ⅓   cup cider vinegar
    ¼   cup fresh orange juice
    1   tablespoon chopped fresh or
          1 teaspoon dried thyme
    2   teaspoons olive oil
    ¼   teaspoon salt
    4   (6-ounce) tilapia fillets
        Cooking spray

1. Combine first 3 ingredients in a food processor, and process until minced. Add mango and next 5 ingredients; process until smooth. Place mango mixture and fish in a zip-top plastic bag; seal and marinate in refrigerator 20 minutes. Remove fish from bag, reserving marinade. Pour reserved marinade into a small saucepan, and bring to a boil. Reduce heat, and simmer 5 minutes. Remove from heat.
2. Prepare grill or broiler.
3. Place fish on a grill rack or broiler pan coated with cooking spray. Cook 4 minutes on each side or until fish flakes easily when tested with a fork. Serve with mango sauce. Yield: 4 servings (serving size: 1 fillet and ¼ cup mango sauce).

CALORIES 263 (23% from fat); FAT 6.8g (sat 0.8g, mono 3.3g, poly 2g); PROTEIN 32.7g; CARB 19.3g; FIBER 1.6g; CHOL 75mg; IRON 0.5mg; SODIUM 239mg; CALC 21mg

SEPTEMBER

You Go, Grill

The American passion for grilling is, apparently, eternal. With good reason.

Grilling is the ultimate high-flavor, low-fat cooking method. It intensifies the flavor of foods without relying on extra fat.

GRILLED SALMON WITH EAST-WEST SPICE RUB AND ORANGE-SOY GLAZE

(pictured on page 222)

Leave the skin on the salmon while you grill it. The skin protects the flesh from the heat, allowing it to cook on one side.

Spice mixture:

    1   tablespoon sugar
    1½ teaspoons five-spice powder
    1½ teaspoons ground coriander
    1½ teaspoons black pepper
    ½   teaspoon salt

Glaze:

    3   (3 x ½-inch) orange rind strips
    ½   cup fresh orange juice
    ½   cup low-sodium soy sauce
    ⅓   cup honey
    2   tablespoons minced green onions
    1   tablespoon minced peeled fresh
        ginger
    1½ teaspoons dark sesame oil
    4   garlic cloves, minced
    1   (3-inch) cinnamon stick

Remaining ingredients:

    8   (6-ounce) salmon fillets (about
        2 inches thick)
    Cooking spray
    ¼   cup thinly sliced green onions
    1   tablespoon sesame seeds, toasted

1. To prepare spice mixture, combine first 5 ingredients in a small bowl.
2. To prepare glaze, combine rind and next 8 ingredients in a saucepan. Bring to a boil. Reduce heat, and simmer 10 minutes. Strain through a sieve; discard solids.
3. Prepare grill.
4. Rub fillets with spice mixture. Cover; refrigerate 10 minutes. Place, skin sides down, on a grill rack coated with cooking spray. Grill, covered, 16 minutes or until fish flakes easily when tested with a fork, basting occasionally with glaze. Remove skin; discard. Arrange fillets on a platter; sprinkle with sliced onions and sesame seeds. Yield: 8 servings (serving size: 1 fillet).

CALORIES 357 (39% from fat); FAT 15.5g (sat 2.7g, mono 7.3g, poly 3.7g); PROTEIN 36.1g; CARB 17g; FIBER 0.3g; CHOL 111mg; IRON 1.5mg; SODIUM 716mg; CALC 32mg

GRILLED VEGETABLES WITH RANCH DRESSING

(pictured on page 227)

    2   red bell peppers, seeded
    2   yellow bell peppers, seeded
    1   small eggplant, cut in half
        lengthwise (about 1 pound)
    16 asparagus spears (about 1 pound)
    1   medium zucchini or yellow
        squash, cut in half lengthwise
    8   plum tomatoes
    2   tablespoons olive oil
    ½   teaspoon black pepper
    ¼   teaspoon salt
    Cooking spray
    Ranch Dressing

1. Prepare grill.
2. Brush first 6 ingredients with oil; sprinkle evenly with black pepper and salt. Place bell peppers on a grill rack coated with cooking spray; grill 5 minutes. Add eggplant; grill 5 minutes. Add asparagus; grill 5 minutes. Add zucchini; grill 5 minutes. Add tomatoes; grill 5 minutes. Remove vegetables from grill. Cut each bell pepper into quarters; cut each eggplant half and zucchini half into 4 equal pieces. Serve vegetables with Ranch Dressing. Yield: 8 servings (serving size: 2 bell pepper quarters, 1 eggplant piece, 2 asparagus spears, 1 zucchini piece, 1 tomato, and 2 tablespoons dressing).

CALORIES 105 (39% from fat); FAT 4.6g (sat 0.8g, mono 2.7g, poly 0.6g); PROTEIN 4.6g; CARB 13.9g; FIBER 3.5g; CHOL 0mg; IRON 1.6mg; SODIUM 181mg; CALC 57mg

Ranch Dressing:

    ¾   cup low-fat buttermilk
    ¼   cup fat-free sour cream
    ½   teaspoon dry mustard
    ½   teaspoon dried oregano
    ½   teaspoon dried basil
    ¼   teaspoon salt
    ¼   teaspoon dried dill
    ¼   teaspoon black pepper
    1   garlic clove, minced

1. Combine all ingredients in a bowl; stir well with a whisk. Cover and chill. Yield: 1 cup (serving size: 2 tablespoons).

CALORIES 18 (20% from fat); FAT 0.4g (sat 0.3g, mono 0.1g, poly 0g); PROTEIN 1.4g; CARB 1.9g; FIBER 0.1g; CHOL 0mg; IRON 0.1mg; SODIUM 90mg; CALC 33mg

ADOBO-MARINATED PORK TENDERLOIN WITH GRILLED PINEAPPLE SALSA

    1   cup fresh lime juice (about
        8 limes)
    2   teaspoons black pepper
    2   teaspoons dried oregano
    2   teaspoons ground cumin
    1½ teaspoons salt
    6   garlic cloves, crushed
    2   pounds pork tenderloin
    1½ teaspoons olive oil
    Cooking spray
    ¼   cup coarsely chopped fresh
        cilantro
    2   tablespoons finely chopped
        green onions
    Grilled Pineapple Salsa

1. Combine first 6 ingredients in a 2-quart baking dish. Trim fat from pork. Place pork in dish, turning to coat; cover and marinate in refrigerator 1 hour, turning pork occasionally.
2. Prepare grill.
3. Remove pork from dish; discard marinade. Brush pork with oil. Insert a meat thermometer into thickest portion of pork. Place on a grill rack coated with cooking spray; grill 25 minutes or until thermometer registers 160° (slightly pink). Cut into ¼-inch-thick slices. Sprinkle with cilantro and green onions. Serve with Grilled Pineapple Salsa. Yield: 8 servings (serving size: 3 ounces pork and ⅓ cup salsa).

CALORIES 194 (26% from fat); FAT 5.6g (sat 1.6g, mono 2.6g, poly 0.7g); PROTEIN 25.5g; CARB 10.5g; FIBER 1.5g; CHOL 79mg; IRON 2.8mg; SODIUM 306mg; CALC 42mg

Grilled Pineapple Salsa:

    5 (1-inch) slices fresh pineapple
       (about 4½ pounds)
    1 red bell pepper
    1 yellow bell pepper
       Cooking spray
    ½ cup finely chopped red onion
    ½ cup chopped fresh cilantro
    3 tablespoons fresh lime juice
    1 tablespoon brown sugar
 1½ teaspoons minced crystallized
       ginger
    2 jalapeño peppers, seeded and
       minced
    1 drained canned chipotle chile in
       adobo sauce, minced

1. Preheat grill.
2. Place first 3 ingredients on a grill rack coated with cooking spray; grill 3 minutes on each side. Discard stems and seeds from bell peppers; dice pineapple and bell peppers. Combine pineapple, bell pepper, onion, and remaining ingredients; toss gently. Yield: 3 cups (serving size: ⅓ cup).

CALORIES 36 (10% from fat); FAT 0.4g (sat 0g, mono 0.1g, poly 0.1g); PROTEIN 0.6g; CARB 8.7g; FIBER 1.1g; CHOL 0mg; IRON 0.7mg; SODIUM 11mg; CALC 13mg

NEW ORLEANS-STYLE BARBECUED SHRIMP WITH CANE-SYRUP GLAZE

Serve these kebabs with the Grilled Garlic-and-Herb Grits (see recipe). *It's a nice change of pace from rice.*

   48 extra-large shrimp, peeled and
       deveined (about 3 pounds)
    1 cup water
    ½ cup sliced green onions
    ½ cup golden cane syrup (such as
       Lyle's Golden Syrup)
    2 tablespoons butter or stick
       margarine
    1 tablespoon hot sauce
    1 tablespoon Worcestershire sauce
    2 teaspoons paprika
    2 teaspoons dried thyme
    2 teaspoons dried oregano
    1 to 2 teaspoons ground red
       pepper
    ½ teaspoon salt
    ½ teaspoon black pepper
    6 garlic cloves, minced
    2 bay leaves
       Cooking spray

1. Peel shrimp, reserving shells; cover and chill shrimp. Combine reserved shrimp shells and water in a medium saucepan. Bring to a boil; reduce heat, and simmer 10 minutes, stirring occasionally. Strain broth through a sieve into a large bowl; discard shells.
2. Combine reserved broth, onions, and next 12 ingredients in a large saucepan. Bring to a boil; reduce heat, and simmer 10 minutes. Cool to room temperature. Combine shrimp and syrup mixture in a dish; cover and marinate in refrigerator 1 hour.
3. Prepare grill.
4. Remove shrimp from dish, reserving marinade. Place reserved marinade in a small saucepan; bring to a boil. Cook 1 minute; remove from heat.
5. Thread 6 shrimp onto each of 8 (12-inch) skewers. Place kebabs on a grill rack coated with cooking spray, and grill 6 minutes, turning once. Serve with reserved marinade, if desired. Yield: 8 servings (serving size: 1 kebab).

Note: Substitute dark cane syrup (such as Steen's) for golden cane syrup.

CALORIES 225 (22% from fat); FAT 5.4g (sat 2.3g, mono 1.2g, poly 1.1g); PROTEIN 26.5g; CARB 16.9g; FIBER 0.5g; CHOL 202mg; IRON 4.3mg; SODIUM 398mg; CALC 106mg

GRILLED GARLIC-AND-HERB GRITS

Taste this Southern classic prepared on the grill, and you'll understand why it's been such a longtime favorite.

    4 cups water
    1 teaspoon hot sauce
    ½ teaspoon salt
    ½ teaspoon freshly ground
       black pepper
    1 (16-ounce) can fat-free,
       less-sodium chicken broth
    2 garlic cloves, minced
    2 cups uncooked quick-cooking
       grits
    ½ cup (2 ounces) grated fresh
       Parmesan cheese
    3 tablespoons chopped fresh parsley
       Cooking spray

1. Bring first 6 ingredients to a boil in a medium saucepan; gradually add grits, stirring constantly. Reduce heat to low; cover and cook 5 minutes or until thick, stirring occasionally. Remove from heat; stir in cheese and parsley. Spoon grits into a 13 x 9-inch baking dish coated with cooking spray, spreading evenly. Press plastic wrap onto surface of grits, and chill 4 hours. Remove plastic wrap.
2. Invert grits onto a cutting board; cut in half lengthwise; make 3 crosswise cuts in each strip to form 8 rectangles. Cut each rectangle diagonally into 2 triangles.
3. Prepare grill.
4. Place triangles on a grill rack coated with cooking spray; grill 6 minutes on each side or until lightly browned and thoroughly heated. Yield: 8 servings (serving size: 2 triangles).

CALORIES 171 (12% from fat); FAT 2.2g (sat 1.2g, mono 0.6g, poly 0.2g); PROTEIN 6.8g; CARB 30.8g; FIBER 2g; CHOL 5mg; IRON 1.6mg; SODIUM 386mg; CALC 89mg

Dessert Is the Best Revenge

Don't get mad, get sweet.

"Living well is the best revenge," wrote F. Scott Fitzgerald. No one really knows what "living well" means anyway. But we do know what tickles our palates, knits the raveled sleeve of care, and clangs our trolleys: dessert.

This is all the revenge you will ever need. Are you listening, world? Eat dessert. Forget plotting and payback. Dessert is the balm to the bad, the silver in the lining. It's the bomb.

CAPPUCCINO CHEESECAKE WITH FUDGE SAUCE

(pictured on page 221)

1½ cups reduced-fat chocolate wafer crumbs (about 50 cookies)
3 tablespoons butter or stick margarine, melted
2 tablespoons sugar
Cooking spray
1 cup sugar
3 tablespoons all-purpose flour
2 (8-ounce) blocks fat-free cream cheese
2 (8-ounce) blocks ⅓-less-fat cream cheese
2 large eggs
2 large egg whites
2 tablespoons instant espresso or ¼ cup instant coffee granules
1 teaspoon vanilla extract
½ teaspoon ground cinnamon
1½ cups fat-free hot fudge topping, divided

1. Preheat oven to 325°.
2. Combine first 3 ingredients in a small bowl; firmly press mixture into bottom of a 9-inch springform pan coated with cooking spray. Bake at 325° for 10 minutes; cool on a wire rack.
3. Preheat oven to 450°.
4. Place 1 cup sugar, flour, and cheeses in a large bowl; beat at medium speed of a mixer until smooth. Add eggs and egg whites, 1 at a time, beating well after each addition. Add espresso, vanilla, and cinnamon; beat well. Pour cheese mixture into prepared crust; spoon 4 mounds of fudge topping (2 tablespoons each) onto cheese mixture; swirl mixtures together, using a knife. Bake at 450° for 10 minutes. Reduce oven temperature to 250° (do not remove cheesecake from oven); bake an additional 1 hour or until almost set. Remove cheesecake from oven, and cool to room temperature. Cover and chill at least 8 hours.
5. Drizzle 1 tablespoon fudge topping onto each of 16 plates; top each with 1 cheesecake wedge. Yield: 16 servings.

CALORIES 313 (30% from fat); FAT 10.3g (sat 5.9g, mono 3g, poly 0.7g); PROTEIN 9.9g; CARB 44.1g; FIBER 1.1g; CHOL 60mg; IRON 0.7mg; SODIUM 468mg; CALC 130mg

COCONUT-PEACH COBBLER WITH BOURBON-PECAN ICE CREAM

(pictured on page 1)

To peel the peaches, blanch them in boiling water 1 minute; then plunge into cold water. The skins should slip off easily.

Ice cream:

4 cups vanilla low-fat ice cream, softened
¼ cup bourbon
¼ cup chopped pecans, toasted

Crust:

2 cups all-purpose flour
3 tablespoons granulated sugar
1 tablespoon baking powder
¼ teaspoon salt
½ cup flaked sweetened coconut, toasted
6 tablespoons chilled butter or stick margarine, cut into small pieces
½ cup evaporated fat-free milk
2 large egg yolks

Filling:

11 cups sliced peeled peaches (about 4 pounds)
1 cup packed brown sugar
6 tablespoons all-purpose flour
¼ teaspoon ground nutmeg
Dash of salt
Cooking spray
1 tablespoon granulated sugar

1. To prepare ice cream, combine first 3 ingredients in a bowl; cover and freeze at least 3 hours.
2. To prepare crust, lightly spoon 2 cups flour into dry measuring cups, and level with a knife. Combine 2 cups flour, 3 tablespoons granulated sugar, baking powder, and ¼ teaspoon salt in a food processor, and pulse 2 times or until blended. Add coconut and butter, and pulse 10 times or until mixture resembles coarse meal. Combine milk and egg yolks. Remove 1 tablespoon milk mixture; set aside. With processor on, slowly pour remaining milk mixture through food chute; pulse 5 times or just until blended. Press mixture gently into a 6-inch square on heavy-duty plastic wrap; cover with additional plastic wrap. Chill at least 30 minutes. Roll dough, still covered, into a 14 x 10-inch rectangle.
3. Preheat oven to 350°.
4. To prepare filling, combine peaches and next 4 ingredients in a large bowl; spoon into a 13 x 9-inch baking dish coated with cooking spray. Remove 1 sheet of plastic wrap from dough; place dough on peach mixture, pressing to edge of dish. Remove remaining sheet

of plastic wrap; brush dough with reserved milk mixture. Cut 6 (2-inch) slits in dough; sprinkle with 1 tablespoon granulated sugar. Bake at 350° for 35 minutes or until golden. Let stand 30 minutes on a wire rack. Serve with ice cream. Yield: 16 servings (serving size: 1 piece cobbler and ¼ cup ice cream).

CALORIES 310 (26% from fat); FAT 9g (sat 4.8g, mono 2.8g, poly 0.8g); PROTEIN 5.1g; CARB 52.9g; FIBER 3.1g; CHOL 44mg; IRON 1.5mg; SODIUM 242mg; CALC 145mg

EASY LEMON ICE CREAM WITH GINGERSNAP COOKIES

(pictured on page 222)

    4 cups vanilla low-fat ice cream, softened
    1 tablespoon grated lemon rind
    ⅓ cup fresh lemon juice
    16 Gingersnap Cookies

1. Combine ice cream, lemon rind, and lemon juice; cover and freeze until firm. Serve with Gingersnap Cookies. Yield: 8 servings (serving size: ½ cup ice cream and 2 cookies).

(Totals include Gingersnap Cookies) CALORIES 184 (31% from fat); FAT 6.4g (sat 3.9g, mono 2g, poly 0.3g); PROTEIN 3.4g; CARB 30g; FIBER 0.3g; CHOL 19mg; IRON 0.9mg; SODIUM 140mg; CALC 116mg

Gingersnap Cookies:

To make the dough easier to handle, freeze it before slicing the cookies.

    1¼ cups all-purpose flour
    ½ teaspoon baking soda
    ⅛ teaspoon salt
    2 tablespoons dark molasses
    1 tablespoon cold strongly brewed coffee
    ½ cup sugar
    6 tablespoons butter or stick margarine, softened
    2 tablespoons finely chopped crystallized ginger
    ½ teaspoon ground cinnamon
    ¼ teaspoon ground cloves
    2 tablespoons sugar

1. Lightly spoon flour into dry measuring cups; level with a knife. Combine flour, baking soda, and salt in a bowl; set aside. Combine molasses and coffee in a small bowl; set aside.
2. Beat ½ cup sugar and butter at medium speed of a mixer until light and fluffy. Add ginger, cinnamon, and cloves; beat well. Add flour mixture and molasses mixture; beat at low speed until well-blended.
3. Gently press dough into a ball; wrap in plastic wrap, and freeze 15 minutes. Shape dough into a 7-inch roll; flatten to 1-inch thickness. Wrap in plastic wrap; freeze 8 hours or overnight.
4. Preheat oven to 350°.
5. Cover 2 baking sheets with parchment paper; secure to baking sheets. Cut dough into 40 (⅛-inch-thick) slices; place ½ inch apart on prepared baking sheets. Sprinkle with 2 tablespoons sugar. Bake at 350° for 10 minutes (cookies will be slightly soft in center, but will harden as they cool). Remove from baking sheets; cool completely on wire racks. Yield: 40 cookies (serving size: 1 cookie).
Note: Store remaining gingersnaps in an airtight container.

CALORIES 45 (36% from fat); FAT 1.8g (sat 1.1g, mono 0.6g, poly 0.1g); PROTEIN 0.4g; CARB 7g; FIBER 0.1g; CHOL 5mg; IRON 0.4mg; SODIUM 42mg; CALC 11mg

WHITE CHOCOLATE-CRANBERRY BLONDIES

    1 cup packed brown sugar
    6 tablespoons butter or stick margarine, softened
    1 large egg
    2 teaspoons vanilla extract
    1¼ cups all-purpose flour
    ½ teaspoon baking powder
    ⅛ teaspoon salt
    1 cup dried cranberries
    ⅓ cup vanilla-flavored milk chips
    Cooking spray

1. Preheat oven to 350°.
2. Beat sugar and butter at medium speed of a mixer until well-blended (about 2 minutes). Add egg and vanilla, beating well. Lightly spoon flour into dry measuring cups, and level with a knife. Combine flour, baking powder, and salt, stirring well with a whisk. Add flour mixture to sugar mixture; beat at low speed just until blended. Stir in cranberries and chips. Spread batter evenly in an 8-inch square baking pan coated with cooking spray. Bake at 350° for 33 minutes or until a wooden pick inserted in center comes out clean. Cool in pan on a wire rack. Cut into 16 squares. Yield: 16 servings (serving size: 1 square).

CALORIES 178 (30% from fat); FAT 5.9g (sat 3.5g, mono 1.8g, poly 0.3g); PROTEIN 2g; CARB 30.3g; FIBER 0.6g; CHOL 26mg; IRON 1.1mg; SODIUM 90mg; CALC 32mg

HONEYED APPLE TORTE

(pictured on page 228)

As this buttery cake bakes, the apples sink into it as though they've been swallowed. Choose medium-size apples for the best presentation. Rome, Winesap, and Newton Pippin will work, too.

    ⅓ cup honey
    2 tablespoons fresh lemon juice
    3 Granny Smith apples, peeled and each cut into 8 wedges (about 1¼ pounds)
    ¾ cup granulated sugar
    6 tablespoons butter or stick margarine, softened
    ¼ cup packed brown sugar
    1 teaspoon vanilla extract
    2 large eggs
    1 teaspoon grated lemon rind
    1 cup all-purpose flour
    1 teaspoon baking powder
    ¼ teaspoon salt
    Cooking spray
    1 tablespoon granulated sugar
    ½ teaspoon ground cinnamon

1. Preheat oven to 350°.
2. Combine honey and lemon juice in a large nonstick skillet; bring to a simmer over medium heat. Add apples; cook 14 minutes or until almost

Continued

tender, stirring frequently. Remove from heat; set aside.

3. Beat ¾ cup granulated sugar, butter, brown sugar, and vanilla at medium speed of a mixer until well-blended (about 4 minutes). Add eggs, 1 at a time, beating well after each addition. Beat in lemon rind. Lightly spoon flour into a dry measuring cup, and level with a knife. Combine flour, baking powder, and salt, stirring well with a whisk. Gradually add flour mixture to sugar mixture, beating at low speed until blended. Pour batter into a 9-inch springform pan coated with cooking spray.

4. Remove apples from skillet with a slotted spoon; discard remaining liquid. Arrange apple slices spokelike on top of batter, pressing slices gently into batter. Combine 1 tablespoon granulated sugar and cinnamon; sprinkle evenly over apples. Bake at 350° for 1 hour or until cake springs back when touched lightly in center. Cool in pan on a wire rack. Cut into wedges using a serrated knife. Yield: 10 servings (serving size: 1 wedge).

CALORIES 272 (27% from fat); FAT 8.3g (sat 4.6g, mono 2.4g, poly 0.5g); PROTEIN 2.7g; CARB 48.7g; FIBER 1.4g; CHOL 63mg; IRON 1mg; SODIUM 194mg; CALC 46mg

---

WHITE CHOCOLATE-ALMOND MERINGUE TORTE WITH RASPBERRIES

    4 large egg whites
    ¼ teaspoon salt
    ¼ teaspoon cream of tartar
    1 cup sugar
    ⅓ cup ground toasted blanched
       almonds
    ½ cup vanilla-flavored milk chips
    4 cups fresh raspberries
    2 tablespoons amaretto (almond-
       flavored liqueur)
    2 cups frozen reduced-calorie
       whipped topping, thawed

1. Preheat oven to 250°.
2. Cover a large baking sheet with parchment paper. Draw 2 (8-inch) circles on paper. Turn paper over, and secure with masking tape. Beat egg whites, salt, and cream of tartar at high speed of a mixer until foamy. Gradually add sugar, 1 tablespoon at a time, beating until stiff peaks form. Fold in toasted almonds. Spread half of mixture into each circle on prepared baking sheet, using back of a spoon. Bake at 250° for 1 hour or until meringues are crisp. Sprinkle each meringue with half of milk chips. Return meringues to oven; turn oven off, and let stand 5 minutes. Spread softened chips with a spatula. Cool and carefully remove meringues from paper.
3. Combine raspberries and amaretto in a bowl.
4. Place 1 meringue on a serving platter; spread 1 cup whipped topping over top. Arrange half of raspberry mixture over whipped topping. Top with remaining meringue; spread 1 cup whipped topping over top. Arrange remaining raspberry mixture over whipped topping. Serve immediately. Yield: 8 servings (serving size: 1 wedge).

CALORIES 270 (29% from fat); FAT 8.7g (sat 4.4g, mono 3g, poly 0.9g); PROTEIN 4.6g; CARB 44.6g; FIBER 4.8g; CHOL 2mg; IRON 0.8mg; SODIUM 121mg; CALC 63mg

---

CHOCOLATE-BANANA PUDDING WITH TOFFEE BARS

    ⅔ cup all-purpose flour
    ¾ cup sugar
    ½ teaspoon salt
    3 cups 1% low-fat milk
    4 large egg yolks
    1 ounce semisweet chocolate
    2 teaspoons vanilla extract
    2 cups frozen reduced-calorie
       whipped topping, thawed
    3 (1.4-ounce) English toffee candy
       bars (such as Heath), divided
       and chopped
   30 reduced-fat chocolate wafers
       (such as Nilla)
    3 cups sliced ripe banana

1. Lightly spoon flour into dry measuring cups, and level with a knife. Combine flour, sugar, and salt in a medium saucepan; gradually add milk and egg yolks, stirring well with a whisk. Cook over medium heat until thick (about 10 minutes), stirring constantly. Add chocolate; stir until melted. Remove from heat; stir in vanilla. Set aside.
2. Combine whipped topping and 2 chopped candy bars.
3. Arrange 15 wafers in bottom of a 2-quart baking or soufflé dish; top with 1½ cups banana slices. Spoon half of custard over banana; top with half of candy bar mixture. Repeat layers. Top with 1 chopped candy bar. Cover and chill at least 2 hours. Yield: 12 servings.

CALORIES 284 (28% from fat); FAT 8.7g (sat 5.3g, mono 1.8g, poly 1g); PROTEIN 5.6g; CARB 46.9g; FIBER 1.4g; CHOL 80mg; IRON 1.1mg; SODIUM 204mg; CALC 111mg

---

LIGHTEN UP

Eyes on the Pie

An orchard-fresh entry bowled over judges with its taste—and its decadence. Our lighter version fixes the fat but sacrifices none of the flavor.

At the Culinary Institute of America's All-American Apple Pie Academic Scholarship Contest, Meri Jo Leach's sweet-tart entry won her a $25,000 scholarship toward her bachelor's degree at the CIA's Hyde Park, New York, campus—one of the most esteemed culinary schools.

But her contest-winning pie boasted close to 400 calories and more than 20 grams of fat per slice. Most of the fat, as you might have guessed, was in the crust.

Cutting back on the butter and vegetable shortening, as well as using fat-free milk instead of heavy cream to brush over the crust, allowed us at *Cooking Light* to keep Meri Jo's basic formula intact while dropping fat grams into the single digits and slicing off more than 100 calories.

BLUE-RIBBON APPLE PIE

The judges liked this pie because of the variety of apples used. The apples ranged in flavor from sweet to tart and in texture from tender to crisp.

Crust:

  2 cups all-purpose flour
  ½ teaspoon salt
  ¼ cup chilled butter or stick
      margarine, cut into small pieces
  ¼ cup vegetable shortening
  ½ teaspoon cider vinegar
  5 to 7 tablespoons ice water

Filling:

  2 cups thinly sliced peeled Granny Smith or other tart apple such as Newton Pippin, or Crispin (about 1 pound)
  2 cups thinly sliced peeled Braeburn or other all-purpose apple such as Empire (about 1 pound)
  1 cup thinly sliced peeled Rome or other firm baking apple such as Baldwin or Winesap (about ½ pound)
  1 cup thinly sliced peeled McIntosh or other tender apple such as Gravenstein or Jonathan (about ½ pound)
  1 tablespoon fresh lemon juice
  ½ cup granulated sugar
  ¼ cup packed brown sugar
  3 tablespoons all-purpose flour
  ¾ teaspoon ground cinnamon
  ¼ teaspoon salt
Cooking spray
  2 teaspoons fat-free milk
  1 tablespoon granulated sugar

1. To prepare crust, lightly spoon 2 cups flour into dry measuring cups; level with a knife. Combine 2 cups flour and ½ teaspoon salt in a bowl; cut in butter and shortening with a pastry blender or 2 knives until mixture resembles coarse meal. Add vinegar, and sprinkle with ice water, 1 tablespoon at a time; toss with a fork until moist and crumbly. Divide dough in half. Gently press each dough half into a 4-inch circle on heavy-duty plastic wrap, and cover with additional plastic wrap. Roll one half of dough, still covered, into a 12-inch circle; chill. Roll other half of dough, still covered, into an 11-inch circle; chill.
2. Preheat oven to 450°.
3. To prepare filling, combine apples and lemon juice in a large bowl. Combine ½ cup granulated sugar, brown sugar, 3 tablespoons flour, cinnamon, and ¼ teaspoon salt. Sprinkle over apple mixture, tossing well to combine.
4. Remove 1 sheet of plastic wrap from 12-inch circle; fit dough into a 9-inch pie plate coated with cooking spray, allowing dough to extend over edge of plate. Remove top sheet of plastic wrap. Spoon apple mixture into crust. Remove 1 sheet of plastic wrap from 11-inch circle, and place dough on top of apple mixture. Remove top sheet of plastic wrap. Press edges of dough together; fold edges under, and flute. Cut 6 (1-inch) slits in pastry, using a sharp knife. Brush top and edges of pie with milk; sprinkle with 1 tablespoon granulated sugar. Place pie on a baking sheet; bake at 450° for 15 minutes. Reduce oven temperature to 375° (do not remove pie from oven). Bake an additional 45 minutes or until golden (shield crust with foil if it gets too brown). Cool on a wire rack. Yield: 10 servings (serving size: 1 wedge).

CALORIES 282 (30% from fat); FAT 9.4g (sat 4g, mono 2.8g, poly 1.6g); PROTEIN 3g; CARB 47.6g; FIBER 2g; CHOL 13mg; IRON 1.5mg; SODIUM 226mg; CALC 16mg

BEFORE & AFTER	
SERVING SIZE	
1 wedge	
CALORIES	
397	282
FAT	
20.8g	9.4g
PERCENT OF TOTAL CALORIES	
47%	30%
CHOLESTEROL	
44mg	13mg

AT LAST

Keep on Cluckin'

GOLDEN NUGGETS

We used English muffins for sturdy, substantial crumbs, but you can substitute firm, hearty bread.

  ½ cup low-fat buttermilk
  1 tablespoon fresh lemon juice
  1 teaspoon dried Italian seasoning
  ½ teaspoon salt
  ¼ teaspoon ground red pepper
  ¼ teaspoon black pepper
  1 pound skinned, boned chicken breast, cut into ½-inch strips
  2 cups fresh English muffin breadcrumbs (about 2 muffins)
  ⅓ cup grated Parmesan cheese
Cooking spray

1. Combine first 6 ingredients in a zip-top plastic bag. Add chicken to bag; seal. Marinate in refrigerator 30 minutes, turning occasionally.
2. Preheat oven to 375°.
3. Combine breadcrumbs and cheese in a bowl. Remove chicken from bag, and arrange on a sheet of wax paper. Sprinkle chicken evenly with 1 cup breadcrumb mixture. Turn chicken, and sprinkle with remaining breadcrumb mixture. Arrange chicken strips on a baking sheet coated with cooking spray. Bake at 375° for 30 minutes or until golden brown. Yield: 4 servings (serving size: about 4 chicken strips).

CALORIES 262 (16% from fat); FAT 4.8g (sat 2.2g, mono 1.4g, poly 0.6g); PROTEIN 32.8g; CARB 19.9g; FIBER 0.2g; CHOL 71mg; IRON 2.3mg; SODIUM 674mg; CALC 207mg

Stock Your Pot

Your favorite comfort foods get even better with this homemade chicken stock.

Chicken stock is the foundation of soups, stews, sauces, and favorites such as potpies or chili.

CHICKEN STOCK

The vinegar lends a kick to the stock, but you can omit it, if desired. A 3½-pound chicken will yield about 4 cups of cooked chicken.

  1   (3½-pound) chicken (broiler-fryer)
  1   tablespoon black peppercorns
  1   teaspoon salt
 10   parsley sprigs
  6   garlic cloves, sliced
  3   bay leaves
  2   carrots, cut into 2-inch-thick pieces
  1   onion, unpeeled and quartered
  8   cups water
  1   tablespoon cider vinegar (optional)

1. Combine first 8 ingredients in a large Dutch oven; add water. Bring to a boil over medium heat. Reduce heat; simmer, uncovered, 40 minutes or until chicken is done. Remove chicken from cooking liquid; cool. Remove meat from bones, and reserve meat for use in following recipes. Return bones to the cooking liquid; stir in vinegar, if desired. Partially cover, and simmer 1 hour.
2. Strain stock through a sieve into a large bowl, and discard solids. Cover and chill stock 8 hours. Skim solidified fat from surface of stock, and discard. Yield: 6 cups stock (serving size: 1 cup). *Note:* Reserved meat from chicken will keep 3 days in an airtight container in refrigerator or 3 months in freezer.

CALORIES 35 (33% from fat); FAT 1.3g (sat 0.4g, mono 0.5g, poly 0,3g); PROTEIN 5.4g; CARB 0.1g; FIBER 0g; CHOL 16mg; IRON 0.2mg; SODIUM 405mg; CALC 3mg

STEP-BY-STEPS TO CHICKEN STOCK

Our recipe for Chicken Stock (see recipe) *is adaptable for your convenience. The only caveat is to avoid using vegetables and herbs with strong flavors such as rutabagas, turnips, and ginger; they'll overpower the taste of the stock.*

❶ *Combine all ingredients except the water in a large Dutch oven or stockpot—one that will accommodate at least 4 quarts.*

❷ *Add water to stockpot, and bring to a boil over medium heat.*

❸ *Once it comes to a boil, reduce heat to a simmer. You're at the right temperature when bubbles barely break the surface. This will keep the chicken tender; boiling will toughen it.*

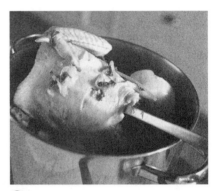

❹ *After about 40 minutes, lift the chicken out of the stock using a long metal spoon inserted in the cavity. Let the chicken cool; remove the meat from the bones. Discard the skin. Return the bones to the stock; simmer 1 hour.*

❺ *Strain the stock through a sieve into a large bowl; discard the solids.*

❻ *After the stock has chilled 8 hours, remove the fat with a spoon.*

CHICKEN TETRAZZINI WITH BROCCOLI

We prefer sharp provolone in this dish, but any strong cheese, such as Asiago, Gruyère, Swiss, or Parmesan, will do.

- 4 cups broccoli florets (about 2 bunches)
- 12 ounces uncooked spaghetti
- 2 tablespoons butter or stick margarine
- 3 cups sliced mushrooms (about 8 ounces)
- 1 teaspoon dried oregano
- 1 teaspoon dried basil
- 2 garlic cloves, crushed
- ½ cup all-purpose flour
- 3 cups Chicken Stock (see recipe on previous page)
- 1 cup 2% reduced-fat milk
- ¾ cup (3 ounces) shredded sharp provolone or grated fresh Parmesan cheese
- 2 tablespoons dry sherry
- ¾ teaspoon salt
- ⅛ teaspoon black pepper
- 4 cups chopped cooked chicken
- Cooking spray
- ¼ cup dry breadcrumbs

1. Cook broccoli in boiling water 5 minutes or until tender; remove broccoli with a slotted spoon, and drain. Return water to a boil; add spaghetti. Cook pasta according to package directions, omitting salt and fat; drain.
2. Preheat oven to 450°.
3. Melt butter in a large nonstick skillet over medium-high heat. Add mushrooms, oregano, basil, and garlic; sauté 4 minutes. Lightly spoon flour into a dry measuring cup; level with a knife. Stir flour into mushroom mixture. Gradually add Chicken Stock and milk; stir well with a whisk. Bring to a boil, and cook 5 minutes or until thick, stirring occasionally. Add cheese, sherry, salt, and pepper; stir well. Remove from heat, and stir in chicken.
4. Arrange 3 cups spaghetti in a 13 x 9-inch baking dish coated with cooking spray. Top with 2 cups broccoli and half of chicken mixture. Repeat layers. Sprinkle with breadcrumbs. Bake at 450° for 15 minutes or until golden brown. Yield: 8 servings.

CALORIES 422 (26% from fat); FAT 12.3g (sat 5.5g, mono 3.7g, poly 1.8g); PROTEIN 30.8g; CARB 46.2g; FIBER 3.1g; CHOL 74mg; IRON 3.9mg; SODIUM 604mg; CALC 175mg

CHICKEN-AND-SPINACH MANICOTTI

Filling:

- 1 teaspoon olive oil
- 1 cup finely chopped onion
- 1 large garlic clove, minced
- 2½ cups finely chopped cooked chicken
- ¾ cup finely chopped smoked ham (about ¼ pound)
- ½ cup (2 ounces) grated fresh Parmesan cheese
- ½ teaspoon dried basil
- ¼ teaspoon black pepper
- ⅛ teaspoon ground nutmeg
- 2 large egg whites
- 1 (10-ounce) package frozen chopped spinach, thawed, drained, and squeezed dry

Sauce:

- 3 cups Chicken Stock (see recipe on previous page)
- ¼ teaspoon salt
- ⅛ teaspoon ground nutmeg
- ⅛ teaspoon black pepper
- ⅛ teaspoon ground red pepper
- ½ cup all-purpose flour
- 1 cup 2% reduced-fat milk
- ½ cup (2 ounces) grated fresh Parmesan cheese
- 12 cooked manicotti
- Cooking spray

1. Preheat oven to 375°.
2. To prepare filling, heat oil in a medium nonstick skillet over medium heat. Add onion; sauté 5 minutes. Add garlic; sauté 30 seconds. Combine onion mixture, chicken, and next 7 ingredients in a medium bowl.
3. To prepare sauce, combine stock and next 4 ingredients in a medium saucepan; bring to a boil. Lightly spoon flour into a dry measuring cup; level with a knife. Place flour in a small bowl; gradually add milk, stirring with a whisk until blended. Add to pan; bring to a boil. Cook 2 minutes or until thick, stirring constantly with a whisk. Stir 1 cup sauce into chicken mixture in bowl. Add ½ cup cheese to sauce in pan, stirring until smooth.
4. Spoon chicken mixture into cooked manicotti (about ⅓ cup per manicotti). Arrange stuffed manicotti in a 13 x 9-inch baking dish coated with cooking spray. Pour cheese sauce over manicotti. Bake at 375° for 45 minutes or until browned and bubbly. Yield: 6 servings (serving size: 2 manicotti with sauce).

CALORIES 460 (26% from fat); FAT 13.2g (sat 5.5g, mono 4.4g, poly 1.9g); PROTEIN 39.7g; CARB 43.8g; FIBER 3.2g; CHOL 83mg; IRON 4.2mg; SODIUM 998mg; CALC 356mg

CHICKEN À LA KING

- 1 teaspoon butter or stick margarine
- 3 cups sliced mushrooms (about 8 ounces)
- ½ cup finely chopped green bell pepper
- ¼ cup minced green onions
- ⅓ cup all-purpose flour
- 1 cup 2% reduced-fat milk
- 1 cup Chicken Stock (see recipe on previous page)
- 3 tablespoons dry sherry
- 2 tablespoons ⅓-less-fat cream cheese
- 2 cups chopped cooked chicken
- ½ cup chopped bottled roasted red bell peppers
- ½ teaspoon salt
- ⅛ teaspoon ground nutmeg
- 8 (1-ounce) slices white bread, each toasted and sliced in half diagonally
- 2 tablespoons chopped fresh parsley

1. Melt butter in a large nonstick skillet over medium-high heat. Add mushrooms; sauté 3 minutes. Add green bell pepper and onions, and

Continued

sauté 2 minutes. Lightly spoon flour into a dry measuring cup; level with a knife. Stir flour into mushroom mixture; cook 1 minute, stirring constantly. Combine milk, Chicken Stock, and sherry. Gradually add milk mixture to pan, stirring with a whisk until blended. Bring to a boil over medium heat; cook 3 minutes or until thick, stirring constantly. Add cream cheese, stirring until smooth. Stir in chicken, red bell peppers, salt, and nutmeg; cook 1 minute. Remove from heat. Arrange 4 toast pieces on each of 4 plates; spoon 1 cup chicken mixture over toast on each plate. Sprinkle evenly with parsley. Yield: 4 servings.

CALORIES 390 (25% from fat); FAT 10.9g (sat 4.2g, mono 3.7g, poly 1.8g); PROTEIN 27.8g; CARB 44.6g; FIBER 3g; CHOL 68mg; IRON 4.2mg; SODIUM 879mg; CALC 167mg

CHOCK-FULL CHICKEN NOODLE SOUP

Only one pot is needed to make this hearty soup.

½ teaspoon olive oil
1 cup chopped onion
1 teaspoon dried oregano
1 garlic clove, minced
6 cups Chicken Stock (page 212), divided
2 cups diced peeled baking potato
1 cup chopped celery
1 cup (¼-inch-thick) sliced carrot
3 cups chopped cooked chicken
2 cups chopped spinach
1 teaspoon salt
3 ounces uncooked medium egg noodles (about 1½ cups)
2 tablespoons all-purpose flour
¼ teaspoon black pepper

1. Heat oil in a Dutch oven over medium-high heat. Add onion, and sauté 3 minutes. Add oregano and garlic, and sauté 30 seconds. Add 5¾ cups Chicken Stock and potato. Bring to a boil; reduce heat, and simmer 15 minutes or until potato is tender. Mash potato in stock mixture. Add celery and carrot; bring to a boil, reduce heat, and simmer 5 minutes. Add chicken, spinach, and salt; bring to a boil. Reduce heat; simmer 3 minutes. Add noodles. Bring to a boil; cook 5 minutes.
2. Combine ¼ cup stock and flour in a small bowl; stir well with a whisk. Stir flour mixture into soup; simmer 3 minutes. Stir in pepper. Yield: 5 servings (serving size: about 2 cups).

CALORIES 332 (22% from fat); FAT 8.1g (sat 2.2g, mono 3g, poly 1.9g); PROTEIN 31.6g; CARB 32.7g; FIBER 4.2g; CHOL 96mg; IRON 3.5mg; SODIUM 1,068mg; CALC 75mg

RED CHICKEN CHILI

A big dose of chili powder makes this dish spicy—and the chicken red.

2 teaspoons olive oil
3 cups chopped onion
¼ cup chili powder
1½ teaspoons dried oregano
1½ teaspoons ground cumin
¾ teaspoon salt
2 garlic cloves, minced
3 cups Chicken Stock (page 212)
1 (16-ounce) can kidney beans, drained
1 (15-ounce) can black beans, drained
1 (14.5-ounce) can whole tomatoes, undrained and chopped
3 cups diced cooked chicken
½ cup (2 ounces) shredded reduced-fat extra-sharp Cheddar cheese
½ cup low-fat sour cream

1. Heat oil in a large Dutch oven over medium-high heat. Add onion; sauté 5 minutes. Add chili powder and next 4 ingredients; sauté 30 seconds. Add Chicken Stock, beans, and tomatoes; bring to a boil. Reduce heat to medium-low; simmer 30 minutes. Stir in chicken; simmer 15 minutes. Serve with cheese and sour cream. Yield: 8 servings (serving size: 1 cup chili, 1 tablespoon cheese, and 1 tablespoon sour cream).

CALORIES 280 (30% from fat); FAT 9.2g (sat 3.3g, mono 3.3g, poly 1.6g); PROTEIN 24.5g; CARB 26.6g; FIBER 5.4g; CHOL 54mg; IRON 3.6mg; SODIUM 743mg; CALC 150mg

OLD-FASHIONED CHICKEN POTPIE

Homemade stock adds a depth of flavor to this comfort classic.

Crust:

1 cup all-purpose flour, divided
3 tablespoons ice water
1 teaspoon cider vinegar
¼ teaspoon salt
¼ cup vegetable shortening

Filling:

3 cups Chicken Stock (page 212), divided
2⅓ cups cubed red potato (about 1 pound)
1 cup (¼-inch-thick) sliced carrot
2 teaspoons butter or stick margarine
½ cup chopped shallots or onions
½ cup all-purpose flour
2 cups diced cooked chicken
1 cup frozen petite green peas
¾ teaspoon salt
¼ teaspoon dried thyme
Dash of black pepper
Cooking spray
2 teaspoons 1% low-fat milk

1. To prepare crust, lightly spoon 1 cup flour into dry measuring cups; level with a knife. Combine ¼ cup flour, ice water, and vinegar in a small bowl. Combine ¾ cup flour and ¼ teaspoon salt in a large bowl; cut in shortening with a pastry blender or 2 knives until mixture resembles coarse meal. Add vinegar mixture; stir just until moist. Gently press mixture into a 5-inch circle on heavy-duty plastic wrap; cover with additional plastic wrap. Chill 15 minutes. Roll dough, still covered, into a 13 x 10-inch oval. Place dough in freezer 5 minutes or until plastic wrap can be easily removed.
2. Preheat oven to 400°.
3. To prepare filling, bring 2½ cups Chicken Stock to a boil in a medium saucepan. Add potato and carrot; cook 2 minutes. Drain mixture in a colander over a bowl, reserving cooking liquid.

4. Melt butter in a large nonstick skillet over medium heat. Add shallots; cook 3 minutes. Lightly spoon ½ cup flour into a dry measuring cup; level with a knife. Combine ½ cup flour and ½ cup Chicken Stock; stir with a whisk. Add to skillet. Stir in potato mixture, reserved cooking liquid, chicken, peas, ¾ teaspoon salt, thyme, and pepper. Cook 10 minutes. Remove from heat; cool slightly. Spoon chicken mixture into a 1½-quart casserole dish coated with cooking spray. Remove 1 sheet of plastic wrap from dough. Place dough on top of chicken mixture, pressing to edge of dish. Remove top sheet of plastic wrap. Cut 5 slits in crust to allow steam to escape. Gently brush crust with milk. Bake at 400° for 45 minutes or until golden. Let stand 10 minutes. Yield: 6 servings.

CALORIES 366 (30% from fat); FAT 12.4g (sat 3.6g, mono 4g, poly 3.1g); PROTEIN 20.2g; CARB 42.5g; FIBER 2.8g; CHOL 46mg; IRON 3.5mg; SODIUM 698mg; CALC 40mg

NO TIME TO CHILL

Chilling the stock overnight makes degreasing a cinch because the fat solidifies on top. But you can also proceed with a recipe right after making the stock. One of our favorite methods to collect the fat involves a **fat-separator cup.** The cup is made of inexpensive plastic or glass with a spout at the base. When you pour out the stock, the fat floating on top stays behind.

Good to the Last Harvest, Part III

It's time to plant root vegetables and greens to perk up your cooking well into winter.

In their third seasonal planting of a collaborative gardening project that's sponsored by *Cooking Light* and the Burpee seed company (see March [page 44] and June [page 159] for the first two seasons), Buddy and Melanie Colvin are laying in seeds and plants for a hardy crop of vegetables, beginning with early lettuce.

The Colvins also dote on collards and kale, cabbage and Swiss chard. "In the fall and winter, we eat greens three to four times a week," says Melanie. "When you eat them young and fresh from the garden, they're really tender and tasty—even delicate—especially when compared to those leathery bunches of greens sold in the grocery stores. All these fresh ones need is a quick sauté in olive oil, with maybe a little garlic and a squeeze of lemon juice."

In fact, she says, although the fall garden may seem more subdued in appearance than those of spring and summer, it provides some of the most vivid flavors of the year.

BROWN SUGAR-BUTTERNUT PIE

Crust:

22 gingersnaps (about 5.5 ounces)
1 tablespoon granulated sugar
1 tablespoon butter or stick margarine, melted
Cooking spray

Filling:

2 tablespoons water
3 cups cubed peeled butternut squash (about 1 small)
¾ cup evaporated fat-free milk
⅔ cup packed brown sugar
1½ teaspoons ground cinnamon
¾ teaspoon ground ginger
¼ teaspoon salt
¼ teaspoon ground nutmeg
⅛ teaspoon ground cloves
2 large eggs
½ cup frozen reduced-fat whipped topping, thawed

1. Preheat oven to 375°.
2. To prepare crust, place cookies in a food processor, and process until finely ground (to yield about 1 cup). Add granulated sugar and butter, and pulse 8 times or until combined. Press crumb mixture into bottom and up sides of a 9-inch pie plate coated with cooking spray. Bake at 375° for 6 minutes; cool on a wire rack.
3. To prepare filling, place water and squash in a microwave-safe dish. Cover with wax paper; microwave at HIGH 12 minutes or until very tender, stirring after 6 minutes. Drain and mash.
4. Combine squash, milk, and next 7 ingredients in a medium saucepan. Cook over medium heat until thick (about 8 minutes), stirring constantly with a whisk. Pour mixture into prepared crust. Bake at 375° for 20 minutes or until set; cool on a wire rack. Top each serving with 1 tablespoon whipped topping. Yield: 8 servings.

CALORIES 238 (24% from fat); FAT 6.4g (sat 2.6g, mono 2.2g, poly 1g); PROTEIN 5.2g; CARB 41.6g; FIBER 0.8g; CHOL 67mg; IRON 2mg; SODIUM 167mg; CALC 156mg

BEETS WITH DILLED CUCUMBER SALSA

1   cup finely chopped cucumber
2   tablespoons minced fresh dill
1   tablespoon chopped red onion
2   tablespoons plain low-fat yogurt
1   tablespoon red wine vinegar
¼   teaspoon coarsely ground black pepper
⅛   teaspoon salt
1½ pounds beets (about 3)
4   lettuce leaves

1. Combine first 7 ingredients in a small bowl; stir well. Cover and chill.
2. Leave root and 1 inch of stem on beets; scrub with a brush. Place in a medium saucepan; cover with water. Bring to a boil; cover, reduce heat, and simmer 45 minutes or until tender. Drain and rinse with cold water. Drain and cool. Trim off beet roots; rub off skins. Cut beets into ¼-inch slices.
3. Arrange beet slices on 4 lettuce-lined plates; top each serving with ¼ cup salsa. Yield: 4 servings.

CALORIES 63 (6% from fat); FAT 0.4g (sat 0.1g, mono 0.1g, poly 0.1g); PROTEIN 2.8g; CARB 13.2g; FIBER 1.5g; CHOL 0mg; IRON 1.4mg; SODIUM 171mg; CALC 50mg

BRUSSELS SPROUTS AND CARROTS WITH ALMONDS

If your Brussels sprouts are really big, you may want to cut them into six wedges.

1   tablespoon butter or stick margarine
1½ cups julienne-cut carrot
3   cups trimmed Brussels sprouts, quartered (about ¾ pound)
2   tablespoons minced fresh parsley
1   tablespoon sliced almonds, toasted
1   teaspoon brown sugar
¼   teaspoon salt
⅛   teaspoon black pepper

1. Melt butter in a large nonstick skillet over medium-high heat. Add carrot; sauté 4 minutes. Reduce heat to medium. Add Brussels sprouts; sauté 5 minutes or until crisp-tender. Add parsley and remaining ingredients; cook 30 seconds or until sugar melts, stirring constantly. Yield: 4 servings (serving size: ¾ cup).

CALORIES 84 (42% from fat); FAT 3.9g (sat 1.9g, mono 1.4g, poly 0.4g); PROTEIN 3g; CARB 11.3g; FIBER 4.4g; CHOL 8mg; IRON 1.3mg; SODIUM 208mg; CALC 47mg

CREAM OF CARROT, POTATO, AND TURNIP SOUP

1   tablespoon butter or stick margarine
2½ cups sliced carrot (about 1 pound)
1½ cups (½-inch) cubed peeled turnip (about ½ pound)
¾   cup chopped celery
2½ cups (½-inch) cubed peeled red potato (about 1 pound)
1½ cups water
¼   teaspoon salt
⅛   teaspoon black pepper
2   (16-ounce) cans fat-free, less-sodium chicken broth
1   tablespoon finely chopped fresh or 1 teaspoon dried rubbed sage

1. Melt butter in a large saucepan over medium-high heat. Add carrot, turnip, and celery; sauté 10 minutes. Add potato, water, salt, pepper, and chicken broth; cover and bring to a boil. Reduce heat, and simmer 20 minutes or until vegetables are tender. Stir in sage.
2. Place half of soup in a blender; process until smooth. Pour pureed soup into a large bowl. Repeat procedure with remaining soup. Return soup to pan; cook until thoroughly heated. Yield: 6 servings (serving size: 1½ cups).

CALORIES 111 (17% from fat); FAT 2.1g (sat 1.2g, mono 0.6g, poly 0.2g); PROTEIN 4.2g; CARB 19.2g; FIBER 3.3g; CHOL 5mg; IRON 0.9mg; SODIUM 492mg; CALC 35mg

HARVEST MINESTRONE

1   tablespoon olive oil
1   cup chopped onion
1   cup (¼-inch-thick) diagonally sliced carrot
¾   cup thinly sliced celery
3   cups diced tomato
2   cups diced peeled butternut squash (about 1 small)
2   cups water
½   teaspoon salt
¼   teaspoon black pepper
2   (16-ounce) cans fat-free, less-sodium chicken broth
1   (16-ounce) can cannellini beans or other white beans, rinsed and drained
2   garlic cloves, minced
2   cups small broccoli or cauliflower florets
2   cups thinly sliced green cabbage
2   cups thinly sliced collard greens (about ½ bunch) or kale or spinach
½   cup uncooked small seashell pasta or elbow macaroni
2   tablespoons finely chopped fresh or 2 teaspoons dried rubbed sage
2   teaspoons finely chopped fresh or ¾ teaspoon dried thyme

1. Heat oil in a large Dutch oven over medium heat until hot. Add onion, carrot, and celery, and sauté 6 minutes or until onion is tender. Add tomato and next 7 ingredients, and bring to a boil. Cover, reduce heat, and simmer 20 minutes or until vegetables are tender. Stir in broccoli, cabbage, greens, and pasta; cover and cook 5 minutes or until pasta is done. Stir in sage and thyme. Yield: 8 servings (serving size: 1½ cups).

CALORIES 173 (17% from fat); FAT 3.2g (sat 0.4g, mono 1.5g, poly 0.8g); PROTEIN 8.2g; CARB 30.2g; FIBER 5.2g; CHOL 0mg; IRON 2.6mg; SODIUM 499mg; CALC 102mg

---

MENU SUGGESTION

CITRUS CURRIED COUSCOUS WITH BRUSSELS SPROUTS

Mediterranean turkey burgers*

*Combine 1 pound ground turkey, ⅔ cup dry breadcrumbs, ⅓ cup mango chutney, 2 cups chopped fresh spinach, and 2 minced garlic cloves. Divide into 4 patties; broil 7 minutes on each side or until done. Combine ¼ cup light mayonnaise and 1 tablespoon chutney. Serve patties on toasted English muffin halves; top with mayonnaise-chutney mixture. Serves 4.

CITRUS CURRIED COUSCOUS WITH BRUSSELS SPROUTS

Dressing:

¼ cup fat-free, less-sodium chicken broth
¼ cup fresh orange juice
¼ cup lemon juice
1 tablespoon olive oil
2 teaspoons curry powder
¼ teaspoon salt
⅛ teaspoon black pepper

Remaining ingredients:

4 cups trimmed Brussels sprouts (about 1 pound)
1½ cups water
1 cup uncooked couscous
⅓ cup finely shredded carrot
¼ cup golden raisins
3 tablespoons pine nuts, toasted

1. To prepare dressing, combine first 7 ingredients; stir well with a whisk.
2. Steam Brussels sprouts, covered, 8 minutes or until tender. Drain and dice Brussels sprouts.
3. Bring 1½ cups water to a boil in a medium saucepan; gradually stir in couscous. Remove from heat; cover and let stand 5 minutes. Fluff with a fork. Add Brussels sprouts, couscous, carrot, raisins, and pine nuts to dressing; toss well. Yield: 5 servings (serving size: 1 cup).

CALORIES 227 (25% from fat); FAT 6.4g (sat 0.9g, mono 3.2g, poly 1.6g); PROTEIN 8.3g; CARB 38.7g; FIBER 5.2g; CHOL 0mg; IRON 2.6mg; SODIUM 174mg; CALC 44mg

---

BUTTERNUT-BEEF CHILI

(pictured on page 223)

1 pound ground round
1 cup chopped onion
1 cup chopped green bell pepper
3 cups chopped tomato
3 cups chopped peeled butternut squash (about 1 small)
3 cups water
2 tablespoons tomato paste
1½ teaspoons dried oregano
1½ teaspoons ground cumin
1½ teaspoons chili powder
½ teaspoon salt
1 (16-ounce) can kidney beans, drained
2 garlic cloves, minced
½ cup small pitted ripe olives
2 to 3 tablespoons minced seeded jalapeño pepper
6 tablespoons thinly sliced green onions
2 tablespoons chopped fresh cilantro

1. Combine first 3 ingredients in a Dutch oven, and cook over medium-high heat until beef is browned, stirring to crumble. Drain well; return beef mixture to pan. Stir in tomato and next 9 ingredients; bring to a boil. Reduce heat, and simmer 20 minutes or until squash is tender, stirring occasionally. Stir in olives and jalapeño; cook 5 minutes. Ladle chili into soup bowls, and top each serving with 1 tablespoon green onions and 1 teaspoon cilantro. Yield: 6 servings (serving size: 1½ cups).

CALORIES 262 (23% from fat); FAT 6.8g (sat 2g, mono 3g, poly 0.9g); PROTEIN 22.9g; CARB 30.1g; FIBER 5.6g; CHOL 46mg; IRON 5.3mg; SODIUM 444mg; CALC 94mg

---

GROWING YOUR FALL GARDEN

Fall Planting: Set out transplants of cole crops such as collards, kale, and Brussels sprouts, as well as cool-season greens, including spinach, mustard greens, and Swiss chard. Plant root crops such as carrots, turnips, and beets from seed. Lay out sets of onions and leeks, which are easy to grow. Be sure to water new transplants regularly until the winter rains set in.

Fall Harvesting: Harvest baby fall greens early, enjoying their tangy flavor in winter salads. Lettuce, Swiss chard, spinach, and mustard greens will turn to mush when the thermometer dips. Use a cold frame or fabric row cover to protect them from early frosts.

Fall Herbs: Fall and winter are satisfying seasons in the herb garden. Before first frost, harvest the last of summer herbs. Freeze basil as pesto, dry excess herbs, or use them to flavor vinegars or make salt-free herbal seasoning mixes. Then enjoy the evergreen, perennial herbs, which add color and structure to the garden in winter. These include rosemary, sage, thyme, oregano, winter savory, lavender, and mint.

Making the Most of Where You Live

A quest for fresh, healthy ingredients in your hometown can be the start of something wonderful for your cooking—and for your life.

If you care enough to look for them, the resources you need to fully enjoy cooking are usually all around you. Making good food important enough in your life to seek it out makes what you find that much more precious. Here are some tips to help your search:

Find the fair. When you go, head to the agricultural tent where local gardeners boast their prowess.

Explore and ask around. If you pass an apple orchard while driving, stop and ask the grower when the apples are sold and if there are any other orchards nearby.

Seek ethnic markets. If your supermarket doesn't offer the ethnic foods you like, keep your eyes open for Mexican, Indian, Asian, or Middle Eastern markets.

Frequent your farmers' market. These are almost always the greatest sources of the freshest and best local food.

GOLDEN CORN CHOWDER WITH ROASTED CHILES

(pictured on page 224)

Jalapeño peppers vary in size and hotness, so you may want to use fewer. Poblanos or Anaheim chiles are milder and can be substituted for jalapeño peppers.

- 4 to 6 jalapeño peppers
- 3 cups cubed peeled Yukon gold or red potato (about 1 pound)
- 2 tablespoons butter or stick margarine
- 1 cup chopped onion
- ⅔ cup diced orange or yellow bell pepper
- 3 tablespoons chopped celery
- 3 cups fresh corn kernels (about 4 ears)
- 3 cups 1% low-fat milk
- 2 cups chopped seeded yellow tomato (about 1 pound)
- ¾ teaspoon salt
- ¼ teaspoon white pepper
- 6 tablespoons (1½ ounces) shredded reduced-fat Monterey Jack cheese
- 2 tablespoons chopped fresh cilantro

1. Preheat broiler.
2. Place jalapeño peppers on a foil-lined baking sheet; broil 10 minutes or until blackened, turning occasionally. Place jalapeño peppers in a small zip-top plastic bag, and seal. Let stand 15 minutes. Peel peppers; cut in half lengthwise, discarding seeds and membranes. Finely chop jalapeño peppers; set aside.
3. Place potato in a medium saucepan, and cover with water; bring to a boil. Reduce heat, and simmer 15 minutes or until tender. Drain; partially mash potato with a potato masher.
4. Melt butter in a Dutch oven over medium heat. Add onion, bell pepper, and celery; cook 10 minutes, stirring frequently. Add jalapeño peppers, potato, corn, milk, tomato, salt, and white pepper; cook until thick (about 30 minutes), stirring occasionally. Ladle soup into 6 bowls, and sprinkle with cheese and cilantro. Yield: 6 servings (serving size: 1⅓ cups soup, 1 tablespoon cheese, and 1 teaspoon cilantro).

CALORIES 265 (26% from fat); FAT 7.8g (sat 4.2g, mono 2.3g, poly 0.8g); PROTEIN 11.4g; CARB 41.5g; FIBER 5.4g; CHOL 20mg; IRON 1.8mg; SODIUM 466mg; CALC 230mg

FIGS WITH RICOTTA, HONEY, AND WALNUTS

- 15 fresh figs, trimmed
- ½ cup whole-milk ricotta cheese
- ⅓ cup honey
- ⅓ cup chopped walnuts

1. Cut each fig into 4 wedges, cutting to, but not through, base of fig. Spread wedges apart slightly; place 3 figs on each of 5 dessert plates. Spoon about 1½ teaspoons cheese into each fig; spoon about 1 tablespoon honey evenly around each serving, and sprinkle each with about 1 tablespoon walnuts. Yield: 5 servings.
Note: Substitute dried figs for fresh.

CALORIES 273 (27% from fat); FAT 8.3g (sat 2.4g, mono 2g, poly 3.4g); PROTEIN 6g; CARB 49.9g; FIBER 6.1g; CHOL 13mg; IRON 1mg; SODIUM 23mg; CALC 110mg

MÉLANGE OF KALE, POTATOES, AND TOMATOES WITH PARMESAN

(pictured on page 225)

- 1 pound kale
- 8 cups water
- 2 cups (¼-inch-thick) slices Yukon gold or red potato (about 1¼ pounds)
- 1 tablespoon olive oil
- ¼ teaspoon dried crushed red pepper
- 3 garlic cloves, minced
- 2½ cups chopped seeded tomato
- 1 tablespoon fresh lemon juice
- ½ teaspoon salt
- ¼ teaspoon black pepper
- 2 teaspoons olive oil
- ¼ cup (1 ounce) shaved fresh Parmesan cheese

1. Remove stems from kale. Wash and pat dry; coarsely chop enough kale to measure 9 cups.
2. Bring water to a boil in a Dutch oven. Add potato; cook 5 minutes or until almost tender. Add kale; cook 2 minutes or until vegetables are tender. Drain potato mixture in a colander

over a bowl, reserving ½ cup cooking liquid.

3. Heat 1 tablespoon oil in a large skillet over medium heat. Add red pepper and garlic; sauté 30 seconds. Add potato mixture, reserved ½ cup cooking liquid, tomato, lemon juice, salt, and black pepper; stir gently. Cook 5 minutes or until thoroughly heated, stirring occasionally. Spoon 1½ cups potato mixture onto each of 4 plates. Drizzle each serving with ½ teaspoon oil. Arrange 1 tablespoon cheese over each serving. Yield: 4 servings.

CALORIES 288 (28% from fat); FAT 9.1g (sat 2.2g, mono 4.8g, poly 1.3g); PROTEIN 11.8g; CARB 45.7g; FIBER 6.2g; CHOL 5mg; IRON 5.1mg; SODIUM 493mg; CALC 320mg

STEAMED SEA BASS ON SPINACH WITH LEMON SAUCE

(pictured on page 228)

If Meyer lemons are unavailable, substitute one tangerine and half a regular lemon.

  1 Meyer lemon
  1 lime
  ¼ cup minced shallots
  2 teaspoons butter
  2 teaspoons olive oil
  ½ teaspoon salt, divided
  2 teaspoons chopped fresh dill
  4 (6-ounce) sea bass or other firm white fish fillets (about 1½ inches thick)
  ¼ teaspoon black pepper, divided
  2 cups water
  1 (10-ounce) package fresh spinach

1. Remove rind from lemon, using a vegetable peeler (avoid white pith of rind), reserving lemon rind.
2. Peel and section lemon and lime over a large bowl; squeeze membranes to extract juice, reserving 3 tablespoons juice. Discard membranes.
3. Combine sections, reserved 3 tablespoons juice, shallots, butter, oil, and ⅛ teaspoon salt in a small saucepan; bring to a boil. Remove from heat; stir in dill.

4. Sprinkle fillets with ¼ teaspoon salt and ⅛ teaspoon pepper. Arrange fillets in a steamer basket. Combine reserved lemon rind and water in a Dutch oven; place steamer basket in pan, and bring water to a boil. Steam fillets, covered, 12 minutes or until fish flakes easily when tested with a fork.
5. Place spinach in a large nonstick skillet over medium-high heat; sauté 3 minutes or until wilted. Sprinkle spinach with ⅛ teaspoon salt and ⅛ teaspoon pepper. Place ½ cup spinach on each of 4 plates; top each portion with 1 fillet and about 3 tablespoons lemon sauce. Yield: 4 servings.

CALORIES 246 (29% from fat); FAT 8g (sat 2.4g, mono 3g, poly 1.7g); PROTEIN 34.5g; CARB 11.7g; FIBER 3.6g; CHOL 75mg; IRON 3.1mg; SODIUM 489mg; CALC 124mg

POTAGE OF TURNIPS, LEEKS, AND POTATOES

Potage (poh-TAZH) is a French term to describe a dish that's midway in texture between a broth and a thick soup.

  1½ tablespoons butter
  6 cups (½-inch) cubed Yukon gold or red potato (about 2 pounds)
  3 cups (½-inch) cubed peeled turnip (about 1¼ pounds)
  2 cups chopped leek (about 2 large)
  4½ cups water, divided
  1½ teaspoons salt
  5 thyme sprigs
  2 tablespoons chopped fresh parsley
  2 teaspoons chopped fresh thyme
  ½ teaspoon black pepper
  10 cups coarsely chopped turnip greens (about ½ pound)
  ½ cup (2 ounces) grated Gruyère cheese

1. Melt butter in a Dutch oven over medium heat. Add potato, turnip, leek, and ½ cup water. Cover and cook 10 minutes, stirring occasionally. Add 4 cups water, salt, and thyme sprigs; bring to a boil. Reduce heat; simmer, uncovered, 25 minutes. Discard thyme sprigs. Stir in parsley, chopped thyme, and pepper.

2. Cook turnip greens in boiling water in a saucepan 5 minutes; drain well. Stir into potato mixture. Ladle soup into serving bowls; sprinkle with cheese. Yield: 7 servings (serving size: 1½ cups soup and about 1 tablespoon cheese).

CALORIES 207 (24% from fat); FAT 5.6g (sat 3.2g, mono 1.6g, poly 0.5g); PROTEIN 7.4g; CARB 33.9g; FIBER 5.7g; CHOL 16mg; IRON 3.5mg; SODIUM 639mg; CALC 286mg

ENLIGHTENED TRAVELER

Where the Wild Things Are

Watchable wildlife programs let you bag an assortment of visual prey in out-of-the-way spots all over America.

A national program makes wildlife-watching more accessible. The National Watchable Wildlife Program is a partnership of government agencies, public parks, conservation organizations, and private businesses, working to form a coast-to-coast network of wildlife-viewing sites.

BANANA-PECAN PANCAKES

These pancakes are served at the Thornrose House bed-and-breakfast in Staunton, Virginia, near one of many wildlife-viewing sites.

  1 cup all-purpose flour
  ½ cup yellow cornmeal
  ¼ cup oat bran
  ½ teaspoon baking soda
  ¼ teaspoon salt
  1½ cups low-fat buttermilk
  ⅓ cup mashed ripe banana
  2 tablespoons reduced-calorie stick margarine, melted
  2 teaspoons honey
  1 large egg, lightly beaten
  ¼ cup chopped pecans, toasted
  Cooking spray
  6 tablespoons maple syrup

Continued

1. Lightly spoon flour into a dry measuring cup; level with a knife. Combine flour, cornmeal, and next 3 ingredients in a large bowl. Combine buttermilk and next 4 ingredients; add to flour mixture, stirring until smooth. Fold in pecans.
2. Spoon about ¼ cup batter onto a hot nonstick griddle or nonstick skillet coated with cooking spray. Turn pancakes when tops are covered with bubbles and edges look cooked. Serve with syrup. Yield: 12 (4-inch) pancakes (serving size: 2 pancakes and 1 tablespoon syrup).

CALORIES 149 (26% from fat); FAT 4.3g (sat 0.9g, mono 1.9g, poly 1g); PROTEIN 3.8g; CARB 24.5g; FIBER 1.1g; CHOL 18mg; IRON 1.1mg; SODIUM 142mg; CALC 51mg

From the Editor

Still galloping around the globe, Graham Kerr is back on the air with new ways to make cooking—and living—fun.

Cooking Light Editor-at-Large Graham Kerr has been luring people into their kitchens for more than 45 years, always with the promise of fun.

Graham's new television show, *The Gathering Place,* will explore "how to live creatively within reason at the end of an unreasonable age," he says. Home base for the show is Toronto's Arcadian Court, a splendid room that for 105 years has hosted fine dining at The Hudson Bay Co.

The studio audience sits at small tables sampling recipes Graham developed after exploring nearly 40 countries around the world.

Read on for just two examples of the kinds of dishes viewers can expect to see.

MOUSSAKA

The addition of bulgur (cracked wheat) gives this dish an interesting texture.

18 (¼-inch-thick) slices peeled eggplant (about 1¼ pounds)
Cooking spray
1 teaspoon olive oil
1 cup chopped onion
3 garlic cloves, minced
¾ pound lean ground lamb
3 tablespoons tomato paste
2 cups dry red wine or nonalcoholic red wine
¼ cup uncooked bulgur or cracked wheat
1 teaspoon dried oregano
½ teaspoon salt
¼ teaspoon black pepper
⅛ teaspoon ground cinnamon
1¼ cups 1% low-fat milk
2 tablespoons cornstarch
⅛ teaspoon ground nutmeg
2 tablespoons egg substitute
6 tablespoons (1½ ounces) grated fresh Parmesan cheese

1. Prepare broiler.
2. Arrange eggplant slices in a single layer on a baking sheet coated with cooking spray. Broil 3 inches from heat 5 minutes or until lightly browned.
3. Preheat oven to 350°.
4. Heat oil in a nonstick skillet over medium-high heat. Add onion; sauté 3 minutes. Add garlic; sauté 1 minute. Add lamb; cook 5 minutes or until lamb is browned, stirring to crumble. Add tomato paste; cook 2 minutes. Stir in wine and next 5 ingredients; bring to a boil, and cook 5 minutes or until thick. Set aside.
5. Combine milk, cornstarch, and nutmeg in a small saucepan. Bring to a boil; reduce heat, and simmer 1 minute. Remove from heat; add egg substitute, stirring with a whisk.
6. Arrange 6 eggplant slices in bottom of an 11 x 7-inch baking dish coated with cooking spray, and top with 1 cup of meat mixture. Sprinkle with 1½ tablespoons cheese. Repeat procedure twice with remaining eggplant, remaining meat mixture, and 3 tablespoons cheese. Pour milk mixture over layers, and sprinkle with 1½ tablespoons cheese. Bake at 350° for 25 minutes or until sauce is set.
7. Preheat broiler. Broil moussaka 5 minutes or until browned. Yield: 6 servings (serving size: 1 piece).

CALORIES 218 (29% from fat); FAT 7g (sat 2.9g, mono 2.6g, poly 1.2g); PROTEIN 19g; CARB 20.6g; FIBER 4.3g; CHOL 44mg; IRON 2.4mg; SODIUM 395mg; CALC 185mg

GREEK ISLANDS BREAD PUDDING

4 (6-inch) whole-wheat pitas, each cut into 6 wedges
6 tablespoons dried currants or raisins
1½ cups 1% low-fat milk
1 (12-ounce) can evaporated fat-free milk
6 tablespoons honey, divided
2 tablespoons orange rind strips
2 teaspoons dried rosemary
1½ cups egg substitute
1 teaspoon vanilla extract
¼ teaspoon ground cinnamon
2 tablespoons sliced almonds

1. Preheat oven to 350°.
2. Arrange 8 pita wedges in a deep 9-inch round cake pan or 2-quart soufflé dish; sprinkle with 2 tablespoons currants. Repeat layers twice, ending with currants.
3. Combine milks, ¼ cup honey, orange rind, and rosemary in a medium saucepan. Cook over medium heat 10 minutes. Strain milk mixture through a sieve into a large bowl; discard solids. Add egg substitute, vanilla, and cinnamon to milk mixture; stir with a whisk. Pour over pita layers; cover and chill 30 minutes. Drizzle with 1 tablespoon honey; sprinkle with almonds. Bake at 350° 50 minutes or until a knife inserted in center comes out clean. Drizzle with 1 tablespoon honey. Cool on a wire rack. Yield: 6 servings (serving size: 1 wedge).

CALORIES 277 (8% from fat); FAT 2.6g (sat 0.7g, mono 1.1g, poly 0.4g); PROTEIN 14.5g; CARB 48.7g; FIBER 3g; CHOL 5mg; IRON 2.6mg; SODIUM 190mg; CALC 299mg

Cappuccino Cheesecake with Fudge Sauce, page 208

Easy Lemon Ice Cream with Gingersnap Cookies, page 209

Grilled Salmon with East-West Spice Rub and Orange-Soy Glaze, page 206

Butternut-Beef Chili,
page 217

Garlicky Roasted-Potato Salad,
page 230

*Golden Corn Chowder with
Roasted Chiles, page 218*

Mélange of Kale, Potatoes, and Tomatoes with Parmesan, page 218

Cheese-and-Pepperoni Bread, page 229

Grilled-Vegetable Sandwich with Romesco Sauce, page 237

Pasta with Asparagus and Creamy Lemon Sauce, page 232

Grilled Vegetables with
Ranch Dressing , page 206

Steamed Sea Bass on Spinach with Lemon Sauce, page 219

Honeyed Apple Torte, page 209

Better Than 10 Mothers

If garlic isn't enough to send you, and your cooking, into eternal bliss, what is?

Let's face it, there are two kinds of people on this earth: those who love garlic and those who don't. How could garlic lovers not be passionate about this lily root? Studies continue to show the nutritional and healthful effects of garlic.

You also have to wonder at garlic's amazing versatility. Europeans tend to cook garlic quickly: They typically mince it finely and add it to hot oil a minute before the sautéing process is halted with a liquid. In Asia, garlic is allowed to brown, producing a taste that blends naturally with items such as ginger, soy, and sharp spices. Either way, garlic becomes the star of whatever it touches. It's delicious, adaptable, capable of leading you into an appreciation of a variety of world cuisines, and good for you to boot.

CHEESE-AND-PEPPERONI BREAD

(pictured on page 225)

- 1 package dry yeast (about 2¼ teaspoons)
- 2 tablespoons sugar
- 1¼ cups warm water (100° to 110°)
- 1 tablespoon butter or stick margarine, melted
- 3 cups bread or all-purpose flour, divided
- 1 cup shredded reduced-fat sharp Cheddar cheese
- ¾ cup chopped turkey pepperoni (about 3 ounces)
- 1 teaspoon dry mustard
- ½ teaspoon salt
- ⅛ teaspoon ground red pepper
- 2 garlic cloves, minced
- Cooking spray

1. Dissolve yeast and sugar in warm water in a large bowl; let stand 5 minutes. Stir in butter. Lightly spoon flour into dry measuring cups; level with a knife. Add 2½ cups flour, cheese, and next 5 ingredients to yeast mixture; stir until blended. Turn dough out onto a floured surface. Knead until smooth and elastic (about 10 minutes); add enough remaining flour, 1 tablespoon at a time, to prevent dough from sticking to hands (dough will feel tacky).

2. Place dough in a small bowl coated with cooking spray, turning to coat top. Cover and let rise in a warm place (85°), free from drafts, until doubled in size. Punch dough down; let rest 5 minutes. Roll into a 14 x 7-inch rectangle on a floured surface. Roll up rectangle tightly, starting with a short edge, pressing firmly to eliminate air pockets; pinch seam and ends to seal. Place roll, seam side down, in a 9 x 5-inch loaf pan coated with cooking spray. Cover and let rise 1 hour and 30 minutes or until doubled in size.

3. Preheat oven to 350°.

4. Uncover dough. Bake at 350° for 45 minutes or until browned on bottom and loaf sounds hollow when tapped. Remove from pan; cool on a wire rack. Yield: 1 (2-pound) loaf, 14 servings.

Bread machine variation: Lightly spoon flour into dry measuring cups; level with a knife. It's unnecessary to heat water to 100° to 110°. Follow manufacturer's instructions for placing flour, yeast, sugar, water, butter, mustard, salt, and red pepper into bread pan. Select fruit or sweet bake cycle; start bread machine. At beep for second kneading, add cheese, pepperoni, and garlic; close lid. Continue with bread machine program.

CALORIES 165 (21% from fat); FAT 3.8g (sat 1.8g, mono 1.1g, poly 0.4g); PROTEIN 8.1g; CARB 23.8g; FIBER 0.2g; CHOL 16mg; IRON 1.6mg; SODIUM 269mg; CALC 78mg

SHERRY-ORANGE ROAST LAMB

- 1 (5-pound) boned leg of lamb
- 5 garlic cloves, halved
- 1 cup orange juice
- ½ cup cream sherry or orange juice
- 1 teaspoon chopped fresh or ½ teaspoon dried rosemary
- ½ teaspoon salt
- ½ teaspoon black pepper
- 6 garlic cloves, minced
- 1 bay leaf
- ½ teaspoon salt
- 4 navel oranges, quartered
- 1 teaspoon cornstarch
- 1 teaspoon chopped fresh parsley

1. Unroll roast, and trim fat. Reroll roast; secure at 2-inch intervals with heavy string. Make 10 (½-inch-deep) slits in surface of roast; stuff garlic halves into slits.

2. Combine juice and next 6 ingredients in a large zip-top plastic bag. Add lamb; seal and marinate in refrigerator 8 to 24 hours.

3. Preheat oven to 450°.

4. Remove lamb from bag, reserving marinade; discard bay leaf. Place roast on a broiler pan, and insert a meat thermometer into thickest portion of roast. Sprinkle roast with ½ teaspoon salt. Bake roast at 450° for 20 minutes, basting once with ¼ cup reserved marinade. Reduce oven temperature to 400° (do not remove lamb from oven); add quartered oranges, and bake 1 hour or until thermometer registers 145° (medium-rare) to 160° (medium). Let roast stand 10 minutes before slicing. Combine pan drippings, remaining marinade, and cornstarch in a small saucepan; bring to a boil, and cook 1 minute. Stir in parsley. Serve sauce with lamb. Yield: 16 servings (serving size: 3 ounces lamb, 1 orange quarter, and 1½ tablespoons sauce).

CALORIES 200 (30% from fat); FAT 6.6g (sat 2.4g, mono 2.9g, poly 0.5g); PROTEIN 24.7g; CARB 7.2g; FIBER 1.6g; CHOL 76mg; IRON 2mg; SODIUM 206mg; CALC 27mg

Catalan Chicken Ragoût

When explorers brought back chocolate from the New World, it was used in savory dishes and desserts.

- 3 tablespoons chopped fresh parsley
- 2 tablespoons sliced almonds, toasted
- ¼ teaspoon salt
- 4 garlic cloves, peeled
- 1 (1-ounce) slice Italian bread, toasted
- ½ ounce semisweet chocolate, chopped
- 1 teaspoon olive oil
- 8 (4-ounce) chicken thighs, skinned
- 1¼ cups chopped onion
- 1¼ cups chopped red bell pepper
- 1 cup fat-free, less-sodium chicken broth
- 1 (14.5-ounce) can diced tomatoes, undrained
- 2 tablespoons chopped pitted green olives
- 2 tablespoons sherry vinegar or red wine vinegar

1. Combine first 6 ingredients in a food processor; process until finely chopped. Set aside.
2. Heat oil in a large nonstick skillet over medium-high heat. Add chicken; sauté 8 minutes on each side or until browned. Remove from pan. Add onion to pan; reduce heat to medium. Sauté 20 minutes or until browned; stir occasionally. Add bell pepper; sauté 5 minutes. Add chicken, broth, and tomatoes; bring to a boil. Reduce heat; simmer 15 minutes. Add parsley mixture, and cook 5 minutes. Stir in olives and vinegar; cook 3 minutes. Yield: 4 servings (serving size: 2 chicken thighs and about ¾ cup sauce).

CALORIES 294 (30% from fat); FAT 9.8g (sat 2.5g, mono 4.1g, poly 2g); PROTEIN 30.2g; CARB 19.9g; FIBER 3g; CHOL 109mg; IRON 3.4mg; SODIUM 679mg; CALC 78mg

Rosemary-Garlic Flank Steak with Red Onion-Garlic Marmalade

- 1½ pounds flank steak
- ½ cup dry red wine
- 1 teaspoon chopped fresh or ½ teaspoon dried rosemary
- 1 teaspoon olive oil
- ½ teaspoon coarsely ground black pepper
- ¼ teaspoon salt
- 4 garlic cloves, minced
- Cooking spray
- Red Onion-Garlic Marmalade
- Lavender sprigs (optional)

1. Trim fat from steak. Combine wine and next 5 ingredients in large zip-top plastic bag. Add steak to bag; seal. Marinate in refrigerator 2 hours, turning occasionally.
2. Prepare grill.
3. Remove steak from bag; discard marinade. Place steak on a grill rack coated with cooking spray; grill 8 minutes on each side or until desired degree of doneness. Place on a platter; cover with foil. Let stand 5 minutes. Cut diagonally across grain into thin slices. Serve with Red Onion-Garlic Marmalade. Garnish with lavender sprigs, if desired. Yield: 6 servings (serving size: 3 ounces steak and ⅓ cup marmalade).

(Totals include Red Onion-Garlic Marmalade) CALORIES 300 (46% from fat); FAT 15.3g (sat 5.9g, mono 6.2g, poly 1.4g); PROTEIN 23.5g; CARB 18.8g; FIBER 2.4g; CHOL 60mg; IRON 2.9mg; SODIUM 284mg; CALC 46mg

Red Onion-Garlic Marmalade:

- 8 cups vertically sliced red onion (about 2½ pounds)
- ¼ cup red wine vinegar
- 1 tablespoon vegetable oil
- 1½ cups dry red wine
- 1 tablespoon dried herbes de Provence or thyme
- 2 tablespoons brown sugar
- ½ teaspoon salt
- ¼ teaspoon black pepper
- 8 garlic cloves, halved

1. Combine onion and vinegar in a large bowl; toss well.
2. Heat oil in a Dutch oven over medium-high heat. Add onion mixture. Cook 5 minutes; stir occasionally. Stir in wine and remaining ingredients; bring to a boil. Reduce heat. Simmer until liquid almost evaporates (about 1½ hours); stir occasionally. Increase heat to high. Cook 3 minutes; stir constantly. Yield: 2 cups (serving size: ⅓ cup).
Note: Most of the alcohol evaporates when heated, but you can substitute a nonalcoholic red wine.

CALORIES 121 (23% from fat); FAT 3.1g (sat 0.6g, mono 0.9g, poly 1.4g); PROTEIN 2.6g; CARB 22.5g; FIBER 3.5g; CHOL 0mg; IRON 0.9mg; SODIUM 248mg; CALC 56mg

Garlicky Roasted-Potato Salad

(pictured on page 223)

- 3 pounds medium-size red potatoes, quartered
- 1 tablespoon vegetable oil
- 1 tablespoon stone-ground mustard
- 2 teaspoons coriander seeds, crushed
- 6 garlic cloves, halved
- ½ cup chopped fresh parsley
- ½ cup plain low-fat yogurt
- ⅓ cup thinly sliced green onions
- ¾ teaspoon salt
- ¼ teaspoon black pepper
- Green onion (optional)

1. Preheat oven to 400°.
2. Combine first 5 ingredients, tossing to coat. Place in a shallow roasting pan. Bake at 400° for 30 minutes or until tender, stirring occasionally. Cool to room temperature.
3. Combine parsley and next 4 ingredients in a large bowl. Add cooled potato mixture, and toss gently. Serve salad at room temperature or chilled. Garnish with green onion, if desired. Yield: 8 servings (serving size: 1 cup).

CALORIES 159 (13% from fat); FAT 2.3g (sat 0.5g, mono 0.6g, poly 0.9g); PROTEIN 5g; CARB 30.9g; FIBER 3.5g; CHOL 1mg; IRON 2.7mg; SODIUM 270mg; CALC 66mg

Grouper with Charmoula

Charmoula is a Moroccan herb paste used primarily as a marinade for fish.

½ cup chopped fresh cilantro
½ cup chopped fresh parsley
3 garlic cloves, peeled
¼ cup fresh lemon juice
1 tablespoon olive oil
¾ teaspoon ground cumin
¼ teaspoon salt
¼ teaspoon ground red pepper
¼ teaspoon paprika
⅛ teaspoon ground cinnamon
4 (6-ounce) grouper (1 inch thick)
Cooking spray
4 cups hot cooked couscous

1. Combine first 3 ingredients in a food processor; process until chopped. Add juice and next 6 ingredients; process until smooth. Arrange fish in a single layer in a shallow dish; spread cilantro mixture evenly over both sides of fish. Cover and marinate in refrigerator 30 minutes. Remove fish from dish; discard marinade.
2. Preheat broiler.
3. Place fish on a broiler pan coated with cooking spray; broil 7 minutes or until fish flakes easily. Serve with couscous. Yield: 4 servings (serving size: 1 fillet and 1 cup couscous).

CALORIES 371 (10% from fat); FAT 4.3g (sat 0.7g, mono 1.7g, poly 0.9g); PROTEIN 40.3g; CARB 41.7g; FIBER 2.4g; CHOL 63mg; IRON 3.3mg; SODIUM 171mg; CALC 62mg

Herb-Garlic Chicken

6 (6-ounce) skinned chicken breast halves
½ teaspoon salt
¼ teaspoon black pepper
2 teaspoons vegetable oil, divided
40 garlic cloves, peeled (about 5 whole garlic heads)
1 cup dry white wine or fat-free, less-sodium chicken broth
1 cup fat-free, less-sodium chicken broth
½ teaspoon dried herbes de Provence or thyme

1. Sprinkle chicken with salt and pepper. Heat 1 teaspoon oil in a Dutch oven over medium-high heat. Add half of chicken; cook 3 minutes on each side or until browned. Remove from pan. Repeat procedure with 1 teaspoon oil and remaining chicken. Add garlic to pan; cook 4 minutes or until lightly browned, stirring frequently. Add wine, broth, and herbes de Provence, scraping pan to loosen browned bits. Return chicken to pan; cover, reduce heat, and simmer 30 minutes or until chicken is tender. Yield: 6 servings (serving size: 1 chicken breast half and ⅓ cup sauce).

CALORIES 275 (21% from fat); FAT 6.5g (sat 1.7g, mono 2.2g, poly 1.8g); PROTEIN 44.4g; CARB 7.4g; FIBER 0.3g; CHOL 116mg; IRON 1.9mg; SODIUM 383mg; CALC 61mg

30 MINUTES OR LESS

Tossing 'n' Turning

For a new twist on pasta, throw in an egg. The creamy result will make you glad you did.

Egg coats pasta in a creamy, rich dressing; pasta cooks egg. That combination provides protein and carbohydrates—and also forms the perfect backdrop for any number of ingredients.

Fettuccine with Spinach and Prosciutto

Preparation time: 14 minutes
Cooking time: 16 minutes

8 ounces uncooked fettuccine
1 tablespoon olive oil
1 small garlic clove, minced
2 ounces thinly sliced prosciutto, chopped
1 (10-ounce) package fresh spinach
1 large egg
½ cup (2 ounces) grated fresh Parmesan cheese, divided
⅛ teaspoon black pepper

1. Cook pasta according to package directions, omitting salt and fat. Drain pasta in a colander over a bowl, reserving ½ cup cooking liquid.
2. While pasta cooks, heat oil in a large nonstick skillet over medium-high heat. Add garlic; sauté 15 seconds. Add prosciutto and spinach; sauté 3 minutes or until spinach wilts.
3. Combine reserved ½ cup cooking liquid and egg in a bowl; stir well with a whisk. Add pasta and egg mixture to pan; stir well. Cook over low heat 4 minutes or until egg mixture is slightly thick, stirring constantly (do not boil). Stir in ¼ cup cheese and pepper. Spoon 1 cup pasta mixture onto each of 4 plates; top each serving with 1 tablespoon cheese. Serve immediately. Yield: 4 servings.

CALORIES 344 (28% from fat); FAT 10.8g (sat 3.8g, mono 4.8g, poly 1.2g); PROTEIN 18.7g; CARB 43.1g; FIBER 5.1g; CHOL 73mg; IRON 4.4mg; SODIUM 514mg; CALC 257mg

Linguine with Parmesan-Clam Sauce

Preparation time: 8 minutes
Cooking time: 20 minutes

8 ounces uncooked linguine
1 tablespoon olive oil
½ cup chopped onion
½ teaspoon dried thyme
¼ teaspoon crushed red pepper
1 garlic clove, minced
2 (6-ounce) cans chopped clams, undrained
½ cup 2% reduced-fat milk
1 large egg
½ cup (2 ounces) grated fresh Parmesan cheese
⅓ cup chopped fresh parsley

1. Cook pasta according to package directions, omitting salt and fat; drain.
2. While pasta cooks, heat oil in a large skillet over medium heat. Add onion, thyme, red pepper, and garlic; cook until onion is golden brown (about 6 minutes). Stir in undrained clams; bring to a boil. Add pasta to pan.

Continued

Combine milk and egg in a small bowl; stir well with a whisk. Add milk mixture to pan; stir well. Cook over low heat 5 minutes or until milk mixture is thick, stirring constantly (do not boil). Sprinkle mixture with cheese and parsley. Serve immediately. Yield: 4 servings (serving size: 1 cup).

CALORIES 386 (24% from fat); FAT 10.4g (sat 3.3g, mono 4.3g, poly 1g); PROTEIN 22.1g; CARB 49.3g; FIBER 2g; CHOL 95mg; IRON 6.5mg; SODIUM 751mg; CALC 284mg

PENNE WITH ROASTED EGGPLANT, CHICKPEAS, AND FETA

Preparation time: 9 minutes
Cooking time: 21 minutes

    5 cups (1-inch) cubed peeled
       eggplant (about 1½ pounds)
 1½ tablespoons olive oil
    8 ounces uncooked penne
       (tube-shaped pasta)
    ½ teaspoon dried oregano
    1 (15-ounce) can chickpeas
       (garbanzo beans), rinsed and
       drained
    1 (14.5-ounce) can stewed
       tomatoes, undrained
    1 large egg
    ½ cup (2 ounces) crumbled feta
       cheese
    ¼ teaspoon salt
    ¼ teaspoon black pepper

1. Preheat oven to 500°.
2. Combine eggplant and oil in a jelly-roll pan. Bake at 500° for 12 minutes, stirring once.
3. While eggplant bakes, cook pasta according to package directions, omitting salt and fat. Drain pasta in a colander over a bowl, reserving ½ cup cooking liquid.
4. Combine oregano, chickpeas, and tomatoes in a large skillet over medium heat; cook 4 minutes. Stir in eggplant and pasta. Combine reserved ½ cup cooking liquid and egg in a small bowl; stir well with a whisk. Add egg mixture to pan; stir well. Cook over low heat 5 minutes or until egg mixture is slightly

thick, stirring constantly (do not boil). Stir in feta, salt, and pepper. Serve immediately. Yield: 5 servings (serving size: 1½ cups).

CALORIES 388 (23% from fat); FAT 10g (sat 2.9g, mono 4.3g, poly 1.6g); PROTEIN 15.4g; CARB 60.6g; FIBER 5.5g; CHOL 54mg; IRON 3.6mg; SODIUM 586mg; CALC 132mg

SEASHELL PASTA WITH GINGERED SCALLOPS AND SNOW PEAS

Preparation time: 10 minutes
Cooking time: 20 minutes

    8 ounces uncooked small seashell
       pasta (about 2 cups)
    ¾ pound snow peas, trimmed and
       cut in half
    1 tablespoon olive oil
    ¾ cup chopped onion
    2 teaspoons minced peeled fresh
       ginger
    1 pound bay scallops
    3 tablespoons dry white wine
    ¾ cup fat-free milk
    1 large egg
    ½ cup thinly sliced fresh basil
    ½ teaspoon salt
    ¼ teaspoon black pepper

1. Cook pasta in boiling water 5 minutes. Add snow peas; cook 2 minutes or until tender. Drain.
2. While pasta cooks, heat oil in a large skillet over medium heat. Add onion; sauté 4 minutes or until tender. Add ginger; sauté 1 minute. Add scallops and wine; cook 3 minutes or until scallops are almost done.
3. Combine milk and egg in a small bowl; stir well with a whisk. Add pasta mixture and milk mixture to pan; stir well. Cook over low heat 5 minutes or until milk mixture is slightly thick, stirring constantly (do not boil). Stir in basil, salt, and pepper. Serve immediately. Yield: 5 servings (serving size: 1½ cups).

CALORIES 341 (14% from fat); FAT 5.4g (sat 0.9g, mono 2.6g, poly 1g); PROTEIN 25.8g; CARB 45.7g; FIBER 3.4g; CHOL 75mg; IRON 3.7mg; SODIUM 420mg; CALC 123mg

PASTA WITH ASPARAGUS AND CREAMY LEMON SAUCE

(pictured on page 226)

Preparation time: 8 minutes
Cooking time: 20 minutes

    8 ounces uncooked angel hair
       pasta
 2½ cups (1-inch) sliced asparagus
       (about 1 pound)
    1 tablespoon butter or stick
       margarine
    ½ cup chopped green onions
 1½ teaspoons grated lemon rind
    3 tablespoons fresh lemon juice
    ¾ cup fat-free milk
    2 large eggs
    1 tablespoon chopped fresh or
       1 teaspoon dried dill
    ¼ teaspoon salt
    ⅛ teaspoon ground nutmeg

1. Cook pasta in boiling water 4 minutes. Add asparagus; cook 2 minutes or until tender. Drain.
2. While pasta cooks, melt butter in a large skillet over medium heat. Add onions and rind; sauté 1 minute. Add juice; cook 1 minute or until liquid almost evaporates.
3. Combine milk and eggs in a small bowl; stir well with a whisk. Add pasta mixture and milk mixture to pan; stir well. Cook over low heat 3 minutes or until milk mixture is slightly thick, stirring constantly (do not boil). Stir in dill, salt, and nutmeg. Serve immediately. Yield: 4 servings (serving size: 1½ cups).

CALORIES 318 (19% from fat); FAT 6.7g (sat 2.8g, mono 2g, poly 0.9g); PROTEIN 14.3g; CARB 50.9g; FIBER 3.5g; CHOL 119mg; IRON 3.6mg; SODIUM 241mg; CALC 114mg

INSTANT GRATIFICATION

It's important that you serve all these dishes immediately—otherwise, the creamy texture may turn gummy. Reheat any leftovers in the microwave.

Where Have All the Cupcakes Gone?

If you miss these sweet treats of memory, now's the perfect time to bring them back from the glory days.

A cupcake is cozy, intimate, and complete. And it's all yours to savor. So why have bakeries displaced them with monster muffins? Why are cupcakes, and even their recipes, so difficult to find?

As these recipes prove, making cupcakes is easy—the batter takes only minutes to prepare. And you can make cupcakes just about whenever you like, so a tray can always be ready for you, your kids, or your friends.

BANANA CUPCAKES WITH CREAM CHEESE FROSTING

For the best frosting, make sure the cream cheese is chilled. If the frosting is too thin, place it in the refrigerator for 30 minutes or until spreadable. Store frosted cupcakes in the refrigerator.

Cupcakes:

    ¾ cup granulated sugar,
          divided
    ½ cup mashed ripe banana
    ¼ cup butter or stick margarine,
          softened
    1 teaspoon vanilla extract
    2 large eggs
    1 cup all-purpose flour
    ½ teaspoon baking soda
    ¼ teaspoon salt
    ¼ teaspoon ground nutmeg
    ¼ cup plain fat-free yogurt

Frosting:

    1¾ cups sifted powdered sugar
    ½ cup (4 ounces) ⅓-less-fat cream
          cheese, chilled
    ½ teaspoon vanilla extract
    2 tablespoons finely chopped
          walnuts, toasted

1. Preheat oven to 350°.
2. To prepare cupcakes, combine ¼ cup granulated sugar and banana; set aside. Beat ½ cup granulated sugar, butter, and 1 teaspoon vanilla at medium speed of a mixer until well-blended (about 3 minutes). Add eggs, 1 at a time, beating well after each addition. Add banana mixture to sugar mixture, beating well. Lightly spoon flour into a dry measuring cup; level with a knife. Combine flour, baking soda, salt, and nutmeg in a bowl, stirring well with a whisk. Add flour mixture to sugar mixture alternately with yogurt, beginning and ending with flour mixture; mix after each addition.
3. Spoon batter into 12 muffin cups lined with paper liners. Bake at 350° for 25 minutes or until a wooden pick inserted in center comes out clean. Cool in pan 10 minutes on a wire rack; remove from pan. Cool completely on wire rack.
4. To prepare frosting, beat powdered sugar, cream cheese, and ½ teaspoon vanilla at medium speed of a mixer just until blended (do not overbeat). Spread frosting over cupcakes, and sprinkle with toasted walnuts. Yield: 1 dozen (serving size: 1 cupcake).

CALORIES 247 (28% from fat); FAT 7.8g (sat 4.2g, mono 2.3g, poly 0.9g); PROTEIN 3.8g; CARB 41g; FIBER 0.6g; CHOL 54mg; IRON 0.7mg; SODIUM 193mg; CALC 25mg

Cupcakes:

    ¾ cup granulated sugar
    5 tablespoons butter or stick
          margarine, softened
    1 teaspoon vanilla extract
    2 large eggs
    1 cup all-purpose flour
    ¼ cup unsweetened cocoa
    ½ teaspoon baking soda
    ¼ teaspoon salt
    ½ cup fat-free milk

Frosting:

    1 tablespoon butter or stick
          margarine
    ¼ cup granulated sugar
    3 tablespoons fat-free milk
    1 ounce unsweetened chocolate,
          chopped
    1¾ cups sifted powdered sugar
    1 teaspoon vanilla extract

1. Preheat oven to 350°.
2. To prepare cupcakes, beat first 3 ingredients at medium speed of a mixer until well-blended (about 3 minutes). Add eggs, 1 at a time, beating well after each addition. Lightly spoon flour into a dry measuring cup, and level with a knife. Combine flour, cocoa, baking soda, and salt, stirring well with a whisk. Add flour mixture to sugar mixture alternately with ½ cup milk, beginning and ending with flour mixture; mix after each addition.
3. Spoon batter into 12 muffin cups lined with paper liners. Bake at 350° for 22 minutes or until cupcakes spring back easily when touched lightly in center. Cool in pan 10 minutes on a wire rack, and remove from pan. Cool completely on wire rack.
4. To prepare frosting, melt 1 tablespoon butter in a small, heavy saucepan over low heat. Add ¼ cup granulated sugar, 3 tablespoons milk, and chopped chocolate, and cook 3 minutes, stirring constantly. Remove from heat, and cool. Stir in powdered

Continued

sugar and 1 teaspoon vanilla. Spread frosting over cupcakes. Yield: 1 dozen (serving size: 1 cupcake).

CALORIES 261 (28% from fat); FAT 8.2g (sat 4.8g, mono 2.4g, poly 0.4g); PROTEIN 3.5g; CARB 44.5g; FIBER 0.3g; CHOL 53mg; IRON 1.1mg; SODIUM 180mg; CALC 32mg

PEANUT BUTTER CUPCAKES

Cupcakes:

⅔ cup packed brown sugar
¼ cup creamy peanut butter
3 tablespoons butter or stick margarine, softened
1 teaspoon vanilla extract
1 large egg
1 large egg white
1¼ cups all-purpose flour
1¼ teaspoons baking powder
¼ teaspoon salt
¼ cup 1% low-fat milk

Frosting:

1 tablespoon butter or stick margarine
¼ cup granulated sugar
2 tablespoons creamy peanut butter
¼ cup 1% low-fat milk
1¾ cups sifted powdered sugar
1 teaspoon vanilla extract

1. Preheat oven to 350°.
2. To prepare cupcakes, beat first 4 ingredients at medium speed of a mixer until well-blended (about 5 minutes). Add egg and egg white, 1 at a time, beating well after each addition. Lightly spoon flour into dry measuring cups, and level with a knife. Combine flour, baking powder, and salt in a bowl, stirring well with a whisk. Add flour mixture to sugar mixture alternately with ¼ cup milk, beginning and ending with flour mixture; mix after each addition.
3. Spoon batter into 12 muffin cups lined with paper liners. Bake at 350° for 20 minutes or until a wooden pick inserted in center comes out clean.

Cool in pan 10 minutes on a wire rack; remove from pan. Cool completely on wire rack.
4. To prepare frosting, melt 1 tablespoon butter in a small saucepan over medium-high heat. Add granulated sugar and 2 tablespoons peanut butter; cook 2 minutes, stirring constantly. Gradually add ¼ cup milk, stirring until frosting is smooth. Remove from heat, and cool completely. Gradually add powdered sugar and 1 teaspoon vanilla, beating just until blended (do not overbeat). Spread frosting over cupcakes. Yield: 1 dozen (serving size: 1 cupcake).

CALORIES 276 (28% from fat); FAT 8.6g (sat 3.3g, mono 3.3g, poly 1.5g); PROTEIN 5.1g; CARB 45.8g; FIBER 0.8g; CHOL 29mg; IRON 1.1mg; SODIUM 202mg; CALC 69mg

DOUBLE-MAPLE CUPCAKES

Cupcakes:

½ cup granulated sugar
5 tablespoons butter or stick margarine, softened
1 teaspoon vanilla extract
½ teaspoon imitation maple flavoring
2 large eggs
1¼ cups all-purpose flour
1¼ teaspoons baking powder
¼ teaspoon salt
¼ cup 1% low-fat milk
¼ cup maple syrup

Frosting:

3 tablespoons maple syrup
2 tablespoons butter or stick margarine, softened
½ teaspoon vanilla extract
½ teaspoon imitation maple flavoring
⅛ teaspoon salt
1¾ cups sifted powdered sugar

1. Preheat oven to 350°.
2. To prepare cupcakes, beat first 4 ingredients at medium speed of a mixer until well-blended (about 5 minutes).

Add eggs, 1 at a time, beating well after each addition. Lightly spoon flour into dry measuring cups; level with a knife. Combine flour, baking powder, and ¼ teaspoon salt in a bowl, stirring well with a whisk. Combine milk and ¼ cup maple syrup. Add flour mixture to sugar mixture alternately with milk mixture, beginning and ending with flour mixture; mix after each addition.
3. Spoon batter into 12 muffin cups lined with paper liners. Bake at 350° for 20 minutes or until a wooden pick inserted in center comes out clean. Cool in pan 10 minutes on a wire rack; remove from pan. Cool completely on wire rack.
4. To prepare frosting, beat 3 tablespoons maple syrup and next 4 ingredients at medium speed of a mixer 1 minute. Gradually add powdered sugar, beating just until blended (do not overbeat). Spread frosting over cupcakes. Yield: 1 dozen (serving size: 1 cupcake).

CALORIES 255 (28% from fat); FAT 7.8g (sat 4.5g, mono 2.3g, poly 0.4g); PROTEIN 2.7g; CARB 43.9g; FIBER 0.4g; CHOL 55mg; IRON 1mg; SODIUM 207mg; CALC 50mg

---

FOR A CAKE INSTEAD OF CUPCAKES

To make these cupcake recipes as a cake, bake in a 9-inch square baking pan or round cake pan. Spoon the batter into a pan coated with cooking spray. Bake at 350° for 25 minutes or until a wooden pick inserted in center comes out clean. Cool cake in pan on a wire rack; frost top. Serves 12. Nutritional information per serving is the same as for one cupcake.

Win Your 5 O'Clock Challenge

Winners from our recipe contest can help you win your 5 o'clock challenge.

Editor-at-Large Graham Kerr crowned a winner in the $16,000 *Cooking Light*/Healthy Choice 5 O'Clock Challenge recipe contest.

The rules challenged *Cooking Light's* readers to create light, quick-and-easy recipes that featured at least one product from contest cosponsor Healthy Choice.

BUTTERNUT-AND-SPINACH LASAGNA

This $10,000 grand prize winning recipe from Teresa Lloro of Montclair, California, earned honors for blending squash's sweetness with bitter spinach.

Vegetable filling:

2   teaspoons olive oil
3   cups chopped leek (about 4)
1   tablespoon chopped fresh or
     1 teaspoon dried rubbed sage
3   garlic cloves, minced
5   cups (½-inch) cubed peeled
     butternut squash
½   cup dry white wine
½   cup water
¼   teaspoon black pepper
1   (10-ounce) package frozen
     chopped spinach, thawed,
     drained, and squeezed dry

Sauce:

3   tablespoons all-purpose flour
2½ cups 1% low-fat milk
¼   cup (2 ounces) block-style Healthy
     Choice Fat-free Cream Cheese or
     any fat-free cream cheese
¼   teaspoon ground nutmeg
⅛   teaspoon black pepper

Remaining ingredients:

1¼ cups (5 ounces) Healthy Choice
     Garlic Lovers Cheese Shreds or
     shredded part-skim mozzarella
     cheese
¾   cup (3 ounces) shredded sharp
     provolone cheese
Cooking spray
12 cooked lasagna noodles
Sage sprigs (optional)

1. Preheat oven to 400°.
2. To prepare vegetable filling, heat oil in a large nonstick skillet over medium heat. Add leek, chopped sage, and garlic; sauté 5 minutes. Add squash, wine, and water; cover and cook 20 minutes or until squash is tender, stirring occasionally. Stir in ¼ teaspoon pepper and spinach.
3. To prepare sauce, place flour in a large saucepan, and gradually add milk, stirring with a whisk until blended. Place over medium heat, and cook until thick (about 10 minutes), stirring constantly. Remove from heat; add cream cheese, nutmeg, and ⅛ teaspoon pepper, stirring with a whisk.
4. Combine cheese shreds and provolone cheese. Spread ½ cup sauce in bottom of a 13 x 9-inch baking dish coated with cooking spray. Arrange 3 noodles over sauce; top with 2 cups vegetable filling, ½ cup cheese mixture, and ½ cup sauce. Repeat layers, ending with noodles. Spread remaining sauce over noodles. Cover and bake at 400° for 30 minutes. Uncover and sprinkle with ½ cup cheese mixture; bake an additional 10 minutes. Let stand 10 minutes before serving. Garnish with sage sprigs, if desired. Yield: 8 servings.

CALORIES 364 (17% from fat); FAT 6.8g (sat 3.3g, mono 2.1g, poly 0.8g); PROTEIN 19.8g; CARB 57.1g; FIBER 5.5g; CHOL 15mg; IRON 4mg; SODIUM 386mg; CALC 359mg

AFRICAN CHICKEN-PEANUT SOUP

In this $4,000 first-runner-up entry, Julie DeMatteo of Clementon, New Jersey, gives a traditional African dish some American appeal.

Cooking spray
1½ cups cubed peeled sweet potato
½   cup chopped onion
½   cup diced red bell pepper
2   garlic cloves, minced
1   jalapeño pepper, seeded and
     minced
2   cups chopped cooked chicken
     breast (about 8 ounces)
1   cup bottled salsa
½   teaspoon ground cumin
2   (16-ounce) cans fat-free,
     less-sodium chicken broth
2   (15-ounce) cans Healthy Choice
     Chicken with Rice Soup or any
     less-sodium chicken-and-rice
     soup, undiluted
1   (15-ounce) can black beans,
     drained
⅓   cup creamy peanut butter

1. Place a large Dutch oven coated with cooking spray over medium-high heat until hot. Add sweet potato, onion, bell pepper, garlic, and jalapeño; sauté 5 minutes. Stir in chicken and next 5 ingredients; bring to a boil. Reduce heat; simmer 10 minutes. Add peanut butter, stirring with a whisk; cook 2 minutes. Yield: 11 servings (serving size: 1 cup).

CALORIES 188 (28% from fat); FAT 5.9g (sat 1.3g, mono 2.4g, poly 1.6g); PROTEIN 15.2g; CARB 19.3g; FIBER 3.4g; CHOL 21mg; IRON 1.4mg; SODIUM 556mg; CALC 35mg

ROASTED MEDITERRANEAN CHICKEN

The $2,000 second runner-up recipe from Karen M. Arena of Englishtown, New Jersey, relies on a lower fat Alfredo sauce for extra flavor.

1¼ cups Healthy Choice Four
    Cheese Alfredo Sauce or any
    refrigerated commercial light
    Alfredo sauce
 4 teaspoons fresh lemon juice
 1 tablespoon olive oil
 ½ teaspoon black pepper
 ¼ teaspoon salt
 5 garlic cloves, crushed
 4 (4-ounce) skinned, boned
    chicken breast halves
Cooking spray
 8 small red potatoes (about 1
    pound)
 8 plum tomatoes, quartered
 1 (14-ounce) can artichoke hearts,
    drained
10 garlic cloves, peeled
 1 tablespoon chopped fresh or 1
    teaspoon dried rosemary
12 large pitted ripe olives,
    quartered
Rosemary sprigs (optional)

1. Preheat oven to 450°.
2. Combine first 6 ingredients. Arrange chicken in a 13 x 9-inch baking dish coated with cooking spray. Brush ¾ cup sauce mixture over chicken. Arrange potatoes, tomatoes, artichokes, and 10 garlic cloves around chicken. Brush vegetables with ⅓ cup sauce mixture. Sprinkle with chopped rosemary and olives. Bake at 450° for 20 minutes. Brush chicken and vegetables with remaining sauce mixture; bake an additional 25 minutes or until potatoes are tender. Garnish with rosemary sprigs, if desired. Yield: 4 servings (serving size: 1 chicken breast half and 1½ cups vegetables).

CALORIES 387 (25% from fat); FAT 10.8g (sat 2.5g, mono 5.1g, poly 2.3g); PROTEIN 35.2g; CARB 40.5g; FIBER 4.3g; CHOL 71mg; IRON 4.5mg; SODIUM 1,077mg; CALC 288mg

Power to the Peppers

Grab the freshest bell peppers you can find for some of the season's tastiest and most versatile meals.

If your cooking repertoire hasn't discovered the powerful flavors and versatility of fresh bell peppers, summer to early fall is the time of year to add to your mastery two exceptional types of dishes: braised peppers and a pepper-based romesco sauce. These dishes can go anywhere and never lose their style or impact.

BRAISED BELL PEPPERS

Serve these peppers as a side dish or use them in other recipes. The aniseed adds a subtle sweetness to the peppers. For a more robust flavor, try using 2½ teaspoons of finely chopped fresh rosemary in place of the anise, and omit the basil.

Olive oil-flavored cooking spray
 4 cups red bell pepper strips
    (about 1¼ pounds)
 4 cups yellow bell pepper strips
    (about 1¼ pounds)
2½ cups vertically sliced onion
 ½ teaspoon salt
 ¼ teaspoon aniseed, crushed
    (optional)
 2 garlic cloves, minced
 2 cups water
 2 tablespoons tomato paste
 1 tablespoon chopped fresh
    basil
 1 tablespoon red wine vinegar
 ¼ teaspoon black pepper

1. Place a large nonstick skillet coated with cooking spray over medium-high heat. Add bell peppers, onion, salt, aniseed, and garlic; sauté 15 minutes, stirring occasionally. Stir in water and tomato paste. Bring mixture to a boil; reduce heat, and simmer 30 minutes or until bell peppers are soft. Stir in basil, vinegar, and black pepper. Yield: 4 cups (serving size: ½ cup).
Note: Store leftover bell peppers up to 4 days in the refrigerator.

CALORIES 45 (12% from fat); FAT 0.6g (sat 0.1g, mono 0.1g, poly 0.3g); PROTEIN 1.5g; CARB 9.6g; FIBER 2.5g; CHOL 0mg; IRON 1.5mg; SODIUM 153mg; CALC 17mg

ROMESCO SAUCE

There are several versions of this famous sauce; this one is thick and smooth. A high percentage of its calories come from fat, but think of it more as a condiment—a little goes a long way. It does wonders for tying together the elements of a vegetable stew and can easily replace mayonnaise on a grilled vegetable sandwich.

 1 large red bell pepper
 ⅓ cup blanched almonds (about
    1½ ounces)
 1 teaspoon paprika
 ½ teaspoon salt
 ¼ teaspoon ground red pepper
 4 plum tomatoes, quartered and
    seeded
 2 (1-inch-thick) slices Italian
    bread, toasted (about 2 ounces)
 3 garlic cloves, peeled
 ¼ cup extra-virgin olive oil
 2 tablespoons sherry vinegar or
    white wine vinegar

1. Preheat broiler.
2. Cut bell pepper in half lengthwise; discard seeds and membranes. Place pepper halves, skin sides up, on a foil-lined baking sheet; flatten with hand. Broil 15 minutes or until blackened. Place in a zip-top plastic bag; seal. Let stand 15 minutes; peel.
3. Combine bell pepper, almonds, and next 6 ingredients in a food processor; process until minced. Add oil and vinegar; process until smooth. Yield: 2 cups (serving size: 1 tablespoon).

CALORIES 35 (67% from fat); FAT 2.6g (sat 0.3g, mono 1.8g, poly 0.4g); PROTEIN 0.7g; CARB 2.4g; FIBER 0.5g; CHOL 0mg; IRON 0.3mg; SODIUM 54mg; CALC 6mg

GRILLED-VEGETABLE SANDWICH WITH ROMESCO SAUCE

(pictured on page 226)

Country or peasant breads have a dense texture that's perfect for grilled vegetable sandwiches. But French or Italian bread makes a fine substitute.

- 1 (¾-pound) eggplant
- 1 small zucchini
- 2 (¼-inch-thick) slices onion
- 1 red bell pepper, halved and seeded
- 1 yellow bell pepper, halved and seeded
- Olive oil-flavored cooking spray
- ¼ teaspoon salt
- ¼ teaspoon black pepper
- 2 tablespoons Romesco Sauce (see recipe on previous page)
- 4 (1-inch-thick) slices diagonally cut country or peasant bread, toasted (about 4 ounces)

1. Prepare grill or broiler.
2. Cut eggplant lengthwise into 4 (½-inch-thick) slices. Cut zucchini lengthwise into 4 (¼-inch-thick) slices. Reserve remaining eggplant and zucchini for another use. Coat both sides of eggplant, zucchini, onion, and bell peppers with cooking spray.
3. Place vegetables on grill rack or broiler pan coated with cooking spray; cook 5 minutes on each side or until tender. Remove from grill or broiler; sprinkle with salt and black pepper. Spread 1½ teaspoons Romesco Sauce over each bread slice; layer each of 2 slices with 2 eggplant slices, 2 zucchini slices, 1 onion slice, half of red bell pepper, and half of yellow bell pepper. Place remaining bread slices on top of sandwiches. Cut each sandwich in half; secure with wooden picks. Yield: 2 servings (serving size: 1 sandwich).

CALORIES 261 (19% from fat); FAT 5.4g (sat 0.8g, mono 2.5g, poly 1.1g); PROTEIN 8.4g; CARB 46.5g; FIBER 6.3g; CHOL 0mg; IRON 3.3mg; SODIUM 729mg; CALC 75mg

SUMMER VEGETABLE-AND-CHICKPEA STEW WITH ROMESCO

For an easy variation, steam spinach leaves or wedges of savoy cabbage and add them to the plate.

- 1 tablespoon olive oil
- 2 cups chopped onion
- 2 cups cubed peeled red potato (about 1 pound)
- 1 cup (¾-inch-thick) sliced carrot
- ¾ teaspoon salt
- ½ teaspoon chopped fresh or ¼ teaspoon dried thyme
- ⅛ teaspoon saffron threads
- 4 cups cauliflower florets (about 1 pound)
- 4 cups diced seeded tomato (about 4 large tomatoes)
- 3 cups water
- 2 cups Braised Bell Peppers, undrained (see recipe on previous page)
- ¼ cup dry sherry
- 1 teaspoon paprika
- 1 (15-ounce) can chickpeas (garbanzo beans), rinsed and drained
- 3 tablespoons chopped fresh flat-leaf parsley
- ¼ teaspoon black pepper
- 6 tablespoons Romesco Sauce (see recipe on previous page)

1. Heat oil in a large Dutch oven over medium-high heat. Add onion and next 5 ingredients; cover and cook 10 minutes, stirring frequently. Add cauliflower and next 6 ingredients; bring to a boil. Reduce heat, and simmer, uncovered, 15 minutes or until cauliflower is tender. Stir in parsley and black pepper. Top each serving with 1 tablespoon Romesco Sauce. Yield: 6 servings (serving size: 2 cups stew and 1 tablespoon Romesco Sauce).
Note: Substitute 1 cup yellow bell pepper strips and 1 cup red bell pepper strips for Braised Bell Peppers. Add to Dutch oven; cook with onion mixture.

CALORIES 276 (23% from fat); FAT 7.2g (sat 1.1g, mono 3.9g, poly 1.6g); PROTEIN 10.2g; CARB 47.4g; FIBER 9.4g; CHOL 0mg; IRON 4.3mg; SODIUM 588mg; CALC 86mg

PASTA WITH BRAISED BELL PEPPERS, CAPERS, AND OLIVES

Asiago cheese works well with the strong flavors in this dish; so do capers and lemon zest. Serve pasta hot or at room temperature.

- 4 cups Braised Bell Peppers, undrained (see recipe on previous page)
- 4 cups hot cooked penne (about 8 ounces uncooked tube-shaped pasta)
- ¾ cup (3 ounces) grated aged Asiago or Parmesan cheese
- ¼ cup chopped fresh flat-leaf parsley
- ¼ cup chopped pitted kalamata olives
- 3 tablespoons chopped fresh basil
- 2 tablespoons capers
- 1 tablespoon grated lemon rind
- 1 tablespoon extra-virgin olive oil
- ¼ teaspoon black pepper
- ⅛ teaspoon salt
- Dash of crushed red pepper

1. Combine all ingredients in a large bowl; toss well to coat. Yield: 5 servings (serving size: 2 cups).

CALORIES 340 (26% from fat); FAT 9.8g (sat 3.7g, mono 4.1g, poly 1.2g); PROTEIN 14g; CARB 51.1g; FIBER 5.4g; CHOL 18mg; IRON 4.7mg; SODIUM 840mg; CALC 232mg

SMOKY-SOFT POLENTA WITH BRAISED BELL PEPPERS

- 1 cup yellow cornmeal
- ½ teaspoon salt
- 4 cups water
- 1 cup (4 ounces) shredded smoked mozzarella, gouda, or other smoked cheese
- ¼ teaspoon black pepper
- 4 cups Braised Bell Peppers, undrained (see recipe on previous page)
- 1 tablespoon chopped fresh parsley

1. Place cornmeal and salt in a large saucepan. Gradually add water, stirring

Continued

constantly with a whisk. Bring to a boil; reduce heat to medium, and cook 20 minutes, stirring frequently. Remove from heat; stir in cheese and black pepper. Serve polenta with Braised Bell Peppers. Sprinkle with parsley. Yield: 4 servings (serving size: 1 cup polenta and 1 cup peppers).

CALORIES 296 (24% from fat); FAT 8g (sat 4g, mono 2.1g, poly 1g); PROTEIN 11.5g; CARB 46.7g; FIBER 6.8g; CHOL 22mg; IRON 4.6mg; SODIUM 707mg; CALC 185mg

Most Valuable Trifle Award

An Atlanta Braves baseball executive hits a grand slam with her favorite dessert.

CHOCOLATE-BANANA TRIFLE

"This trifle is one of my very favorites to serve at dinner parties. It's beautiful, and the taste is so satisfying that my guests are always surprised that it's low in fat."

—*Cara Maglione, Smyrna, Georgia*

⅔ cup sugar
⅔ cup evaporated fat-free milk
3 tablespoons unsweetened cocoa
1 tablespoon cornstarch
¼ cup Kahlúa (coffee-flavored liqueur)
1 (16-ounce) angel food cake, cut into 1-inch cubes
2 (1.4-ounce) English toffee candy bars (such as Skor or Heath bars), chopped and divided
3 cups fat-free milk
3 (3.4-ounce) packages vanilla instant pudding mix (*not* sugar-free)
2 cups sliced banana
1 (12-ounce) container frozen reduced-calorie whipped topping, thawed

1. Combine first 4 ingredients in a medium saucepan; bring to a boil. Cook until sugar dissolves and mixture is thick (about 3 minutes), stirring frequently. Remove from heat; stir in Kahlúa. Cool.
2. Combine chocolate mixture and cake in a large bowl. Reserve 1 tablespoon chopped candy bar; set aside. Stir remaining chopped candy into cake mixture.
3. Beat 3 cups milk and pudding mix at medium speed of a mixer until well-blended. Stir into cake mixture. Cover; chill 15 minutes.
4. Spoon half of cake mixture into a trifle dish or bowl. Arrange 1 cup bananas evenly over cake mixture; top with half of whipped topping. Repeat layers; end with whipped topping. Sprinkle with reserved 1 tablespoon chopped candy bar. Chill 1 hour. Yield: 16 servings (serving size: 1 cup).

CALORIES 306 (14% from fat); FAT 4.7g (sat 3.9g, mono 0.6g, poly 0.2g); PROTEIN 5.5g; CARB 60g; FIBER 0.5g; CHOL 4mg; IRON 0.4mg; SODIUM 473mg; CALC 134mg

LINGUINE WITH ROASTED GREEN TOMATOES

"I grow my own tomatoes and love the green ones fried, but I know I shouldn't eat fried foods. I created this recipe as a replacement, and now I make it whenever I can."

—*Mari G. Chandler, Anniston, Alabama*

6 green tomatoes, cut into ½-inch-thick slices (about 3 pounds)
Olive oil-flavored cooking spray
1 cup fresh breadcrumbs
¾ cup (3 ounces) grated fresh Parmesan cheese, divided
3 tablespoons chopped fresh parsley
¼ teaspoon salt
¼ teaspoon black pepper
3 garlic cloves, crushed
8 cups hot cooked linguine (about 1 pound uncooked pasta)
¾ cup fat-free Caesar dressing

1. Preheat oven to 425°.
2. Place tomato slices on a baking sheet coated with cooking spray. Combine breadcrumbs, ¼ cup cheese, parsley, salt, pepper, and garlic. Sprinkle breadcrumb mixture evenly over tomato slices. Bake at 425° for 20 minutes or until tender.
3. Combine pasta, ½ cup cheese, and dressing; toss well. Place 1⅓ cups pasta mixture on each of 6 plates; divide tomatoes evenly over pasta. Yield: 6 servings.

CALORIES 413 (12% from fat); FAT 5.6g (sat 2.6g, mono 1.4g, poly 0.8g); PROTEIN 16.2g; CARB 75.3g; FIBER 4.6g; CHOL 10mg; IRON 3.8mg; SODIUM 884mg; CALC 211mg

JIM'S CHILI-CHICKEN SOUP

"My boyfriend, Jim, and I created this soup to include most of the major food groups."

—*Meg Wood, Seattle, Washington*

1 teaspoon olive oil
½ cup chopped onion
3 garlic cloves, minced
1 (14.5-ounce) can no-salt-added diced tomatoes, undrained
1½ cups shredded cooked chicken breast (about ½ pound)
¼ cup taco sauce
1 teaspoon dried oregano
½ teaspoon black pepper
¼ teaspoon crushed red pepper
3 (16-ounce) cans fat-free, less-sodium chicken broth
1 (15½-ounce) can chickpeas (garbanzo beans), drained
1 (4.5-ounce) can chopped green chiles
1 cup cooked long-grain rice

1. Heat oil in a large saucepan over medium-high heat. Add onion and garlic; sauté 3 minutes. Add tomatoes; cook over low heat 5 minutes. Stir in chicken and next 7 ingredients; bring to a boil. Reduce heat; simmer 10 minutes. Stir in rice. Yield: 8 servings (serving size: 1 cup).

CALORIES 187 (13% from fat); FAT 2.6g (sat 0.5g, mono 1g, poly 0.7g); PROTEIN 15.6g; CARB 24.5g; FIBER 1.9g; CHOL 24mg; IRON 2mg; SODIUM 693mg; CALC 51mg

MACARONI-AND-CHEESE CASSEROLE

"I combined several different macaroni-and-cheese recipes to make this lighter version of an old favorite. People don't even know it's low fat. Even my young cousins think it tastes great."
—Sallie C. Johnson, Vienna, Virginia

8 ounces uncooked medium elbow macaroni
2 tablespoons cornstarch
2 cups fat-free milk
1 cup (4 ounces) shredded reduced-fat sharp Cheddar cheese, divided
1 (10-ounce) package frozen chopped spinach, thawed and drained
2 teaspoons Worcestershire sauce
½ teaspoon salt
¼ teaspoon black pepper
3 drops of hot pepper sauce
Cooking spray

1. Preheat oven to 350°.
2. Cook pasta according to package directions, omitting salt and fat.
3. Combine cornstarch and milk in a medium, heavy saucepan over medium heat; stir with a whisk. Bring to a boil. Cook 1 minute. Stir in ½ cup cheese and spinach. Reduce heat to low; cook until cheese melts. Stir in ½ cup cheese; remove from heat. Stir in Worcestershire sauce, salt, pepper, and pepper sauce. Combine cheese mixture and pasta; spoon into a 2-quart baking dish coated with cooking spray. Bake at 350° for 10 minutes. Yield: 5 servings (serving size: 1 cup).

CALORIES 300 (16% from fat); FAT 5.4g (sat 2.8g, mono 1.3g, poly 0.5g); PROTEIN 17.5g; CARB 45.3g; FIBER 2.8g; CHOL 17mg; IRON 3.1mg; SODIUM 523mg; CALC 395mg

MEXICAN LASAGNA

"I recently became a vegetarian, and this is one dish that my husband—who still eats meat—and I both adore."
—Joy Lillemoen Boser, East Bethel, Minnesota

2 cups frozen whole-kernel corn, thawed
⅓ cup sliced green onions
2 teaspoons ground cumin
2 teaspoons dried oregano
1 (15-ounce) can black beans, rinsed and drained
1 (14.5-ounce) can diced tomatoes with basil, garlic, and oregano
1 (4.5-ounce) can chopped green chiles
4 (6-inch) corn tortillas
Cooking spray
1½ cups (6 ounces) preshredded reduced-fat four-cheese Mexican blend (such as Sargento) or reduced-fat Monterey Jack cheese
6 tablespoons plain low-fat yogurt

1. Preheat oven to 400°.
2. Combine first 7 ingredients in a bowl. Place 2 tortillas in an 11 x 7-inch baking dish coated with cooking spray. Spoon half of corn mixture over tortillas. Top with ¾ cup cheese. Repeat layers; end with cheese. Bake at 400° for 15 minutes. Let stand 2 minutes. Top each serving with 1 tablespoon yogurt. Yield: 6 servings.

CALORIES 260 (21% from fat); FAT 6.2g (sat 3.4g, mono 1.7g, poly 0.7g); PROTEIN 16.8g; CARB 39.3g; FIBER 5g; CHOL 11mg; IRON 3.3mg; SODIUM 958mg; CALC 338mg

Time Warp: Slow Is Fast

Nothing about a slow cooker will slow you down. This time-saver turns a few minutes of morning preparation into a flavor-packed dinner.

On a harried weeknight, there's nothing better than a dinner that takes eight hours to cook—if you're using a slow cooker. In the morning, put the ingredients of your choice into the pot, plug it in, and go do whatever you want. All day long, your dish will simmer on low heat. When you return to your kitchen in the evening, your dinner will be fully cooked.

Though most popular for cooking chilis and stews, slow cookers also can be used for dishes that are usually prepared in a pan or skillet, such as chicken Provençale and barbecued beef. The slow cooker intensifies flavor with persistent, gentle heat, giving those few minutes of before-work prep time a payoff in taste that would seem to have required hours in the kitchen.

PROVENÇALE CHICKEN SUPPER

Use bone-in chicken breasts for this French country dish.

4 (6-ounce) skinned chicken breast halves
2 teaspoons dried basil
⅛ teaspoon salt
⅛ teaspoon black pepper
1 cup diced yellow bell pepper
1 (16-ounce) can cannellini beans or other white beans, rinsed and drained
1 (14½-ounce) can pasta-style tomatoes, undrained

1. Place chicken in an electric slow cooker; sprinkle with basil, salt, and
Continued

black pepper. Add bell pepper, beans, and tomatoes. Cover with lid; cook on low-heat setting 8 hours. Yield: 4 servings (serving size: 1 chicken breast half and 1 cup bean mixture).

CALORIES 296 (10% from fat); FAT 3.4g (sat 0.6g, mono 0.8g, poly 1.3g); PROTEIN 34g; CARB 32.5g; FIBER 5.1g; CHOL 66mg; IRON 4mg; SODIUM 785mg; CALC 81mg

THAI-STYLE PORK STEW

Peanut butter melds with classic Asian flavors to lend this one-dish meal a Thai flair. Lime makes a perfect accent.

Stew:

- 2 **pounds boned pork loin, cut into 4 pieces**
- 2 **cups (1 x ¼-inch) julienne-cut red bell pepper**
- ¼ **cup teriyaki sauce**
- 2 **tablespoons rice or white wine vinegar**
- 1 **teaspoon crushed red pepper**
- 2 **garlic cloves, minced**
- ¼ **cup creamy peanut butter**

Remaining ingredients:

- 6 **cups hot cooked basmati rice**
- ½ **cup chopped green onions**
- 2 **tablespoons chopped dry-roasted peanuts**
- 8 **lime wedges**

1. To prepare stew, trim fat from pork; discard fat. Place pork, bell pepper, and next 4 ingredients in an electric slow cooker. Cover with lid, and cook on low-heat setting 8 hours. Remove pork from slow cooker, and coarsely chop. Add peanut butter to liquid in slow cooker; stir well. Stir in pork.
2. Combine stew and rice in a large bowl. Top each serving with onions and peanuts; serve with lime wedges. Yield: 8 servings (serving size: 1 cup stew, 1 tablespoon green onions, about ½ teaspoon peanuts, and 1 lime wedge).

CALORIES 412 (30% from fat); FAT 13.6g (sat 3.6g, mono 6.2g, poly 2.5g); PROTEIN 28.9g; CARB 42.3g; FIBER 2.1g; CHOL 64mg; IRON 2.9mg; SODIUM 425mg; CALC 37mg

CHUNKY SAUSAGE-AND-HOMINY CHILI

Chili:

- 1¼ **cups bottled salsa**
- 1 **cup (1-inch) pieces red bell pepper**
- 1 **cup (1-inch) pieces yellow bell pepper**
- 1 **tablespoon chili powder**
- 1 **(15.5-ounce) can white hominy or whole-kernel corn, drained**
- 1 **(12-ounce) package chicken sausages with habanero chiles and tequila (such as Gerhard's), cut into ½-inch pieces**

Remaining ingredients:

- 2 **cups hot cooked long-grain rice**
- ¼ **cup crushed baked tortilla chips**
- ¼ **cup chopped fresh cilantro**
- ¼ **cup chopped green onions**
- ¼ **cup fat-free sour cream**

1. To prepare chili, combine first 6 ingredients in an electric slow cooker. Cover with lid; cook on low-heat setting 8 hours.
2. Spoon ½ cup rice into each of 4 bowls; top each serving with 1 cup chili, 1 tablespoon crushed chips, 1 tablespoon cilantro, 1 tablespoon green onions, and 1 tablespoon sour cream. Yield: 4 servings.
Note: You can substitute smoked turkey sausage for chicken sausage.

CALORIES 412 (23% from fat); FAT 10.6g (sat 2.7g, mono 3.8g, poly 3.2g); PROTEIN 18.1g; CARB 63.1g; FIBER 9.6g; CHOL 66mg; IRON 4mg; SODIUM 1,111mg; CALC 85mg

BARBECUED-BEEF SANDWICHES

- 2 **pounds boned chuck roast**
- 2 **cups vertically sliced onion**
- 1 **cup bottled barbecue sauce**
- 1 **tablespoon cornstarch**
- 1 **tablespoon water**
- 6 **(2-ounce) Kaiser rolls or hamburger buns, toasted**

1. Trim fat from beef, and cut into 1-inch cubes. Place beef in an electric slow cooker; stir in onion and barbecue sauce. Cover with lid; cook on low-heat setting 8 hours.
2. Remove beef and onions from slow cooker with a slotted spoon. Shred beef with 2 forks. Combine cornstarch and water; add to barbecue sauce mixture in slow cooker, stirring well. Cover with lid; cook on high-heat setting 1 minute. Return shredded beef to slow cooker; cover and cook 10 minutes. Serve on rolls. Yield: 6 servings (serving size: 1 cup beef mixture and 1 roll).
Note: You can freeze barbecued beef mixture in an airtight container up to 3 months.

CALORIES 410 (27% from fat); FAT 12.2g (sat 4g, mono 4.5g, poly 2.1g); PROTEIN 34.1g; CARB 38.4g; FIBER 2.5g; CHOL 86mg; IRON 5.5mg; SODIUM 715mg; CALC 102mg

CHICKEN AND CARROTS WITH WINE SAUCE

Hours of cooking mellow the garlic. Serve French bread to sop up the sauce.

- 2 **cups diagonally sliced carrot (about 8 ounces)**
- 8 **chicken thighs (about 2 pounds), skinned**
- 12 **garlic cloves, peeled**
- ½ **cup dry white wine**
- 1 **teaspoon dried thyme**
- ½ **teaspoon salt**
- ¼ **teaspoon black pepper**

1. Combine carrot, chicken, and garlic in an electric slow cooker, and add wine. Sprinkle with thyme, salt, and black pepper. Cover with lid; cook on low-heat setting 8 hours.
2. Remove carrot, chicken, and garlic with a slotted spoon, reserving cooking liquid. Place ⅓ cup carrot, 3 garlic cloves, and 2 chicken thighs in each of 4 shallow bowls. Spoon 2 tablespoons of reserved cooking liquid over each serving. Yield: 4 servings.

CALORIES 243 (25% from fat); FAT 6.8g (sat 1.7g, mono 2.1g, poly 1.7g); PROTEIN 34.6g; CARB 9.4g; FIBER 2g; CHOL 141mg; IRON 2.8mg; SODIUM 463mg; CALC 58mg

OCTOBER

Perfection from the Past

One of the oldest of foods, grains continue to sustain humanity. So is it any surprise that our fate may be tied to their future?

It's almost astonishing to realize how much we owe to grain. It's so much a part of America that we even evoke it in one of our most popular patriotic songs. But beyond "amber waves of grain" are tables filled with bread and pasta. And it's not just about wheat: Rice, corn, and increasing amounts of oats are also deeply imbedded in our culture as well as our fortunate tummies.

As we look ahead toward a new millennium, we find new validation for ancient foodstuffs. It's not just the Incas' quinoa linking us to the dietary wisdom of the ancients, it's also flaxseed from Europe, which adds heart-healthy omega-3 fatty acids and fiber to our diet; oat bran, which assists in lowering serum-cholesterol levels; and brown rice, no longer limited to obscure health-food restaurants and communes.

measuring cups, and level with a knife. Combine flour, flaxseed meal, ¼ cup flaxseeds, baking powder, baking soda, and salt, and gradually add to sugar mixture, beating until well-blended. Stir in chopped dates. Spoon batter into an 8 x 4-inch loaf pan coated with cooking spray. Bake at 350° for 55 minutes or until a wooden pick inserted in center comes out clean. Cool 10 minutes in pan on a wire rack, and remove from pan. Cool completely on wire rack. Yield: 16 servings (serving size: 1 slice).

CALORIES 129 (30% from fat); FAT 4.3g (sat 0.9g, mono 1.3g, poly 1.8g); PROTEIN 2.2g; CARB 21g; FIBER 0.9g; CHOL 28mg; IRON 0.7mg; SODIUM 137mg; CALC 16mg

RIZ AUX GOMBOS

This dish from Guadeloupe is a Caribbean cousin of Limpin' Susan, a dish from the South Carolina Low Country. Serve it with fish, chicken, or pork.

       2 teaspoons olive oil
       2 cups thinly sliced okra
          (about ½ pound)
       3 cups water
    1½ cups uncooked long-grain rice
       ¼ cup minced green onions
       2 tablespoons minced fresh
          parsley
       1 teaspoon minced fresh or
          ¼ teaspoon dried thyme
       1 teaspoon minced seeded
          habanero pepper or 2
          teaspoons minced seeded
          jalapeño pepper
       ½ teaspoon salt
       2 garlic cloves, minced

1. Heat oil in a large saucepan over medium-high heat. Add okra; sauté 4 minutes. Add water and remaining ingredients; bring to a boil. Reduce heat; simmer 15 minutes or until rice is done. Yield: 10 servings (serving size: ½ cup).

CALORIES 119 (8% from fat); FAT 1.1g (sat 0.2g, mono 0.7g, poly 0.1g); PROTEIN 2.5g; CARB 24.2g; FIBER 0.7g; CHOL 0mg; IRON 1.5mg; SODIUM 121mg; CALC 28mg

BANANA-DATE FLAXSEED BREAD

Flaxseed has long been popular with European bakers because of its robust, nutty flavor. But new studies suggest that this powerhouse whole grain contains fibers and fat that may play a role in warding off heart disease and certain types of cancer. Find flaxseeds at health-food stores and some supermarkets. Store in an airtight container in your refrigerator or freezer.

       ½ cup flaxseeds
       ⅔ cup mashed ripe banana
       ½ cup sugar
       ¼ cup vegetable oil
       2 large eggs
    1½ cups all-purpose flour
       ¼ cup flaxseeds
       ½ teaspoon baking powder
       ½ teaspoon baking soda
       ½ teaspoon salt
       ½ cup whole pitted dates, chopped
          Cooking spray

1. Place ½ cup flaxseeds in a blender, and process until ground to measure ¾ cup flaxseed meal. Set aside.
2. Preheat oven to 350°.
3. Beat banana, sugar, oil, and eggs at medium speed of a mixer until well-blended. Lightly spoon flour into dry

ROASTED CORN-AND-PEPPER SALSA

This salsa is a flavorful accompaniment with grilled beef or chicken.

       1 small red bell pepper, cut in half
          and seeded
       1 small green bell pepper, cut in
          half and seeded
       3 ears shucked corn
       2 teaspoons olive oil, divided
       ½ teaspoon salt, divided
          Cooking spray
       ⅛ teaspoon grated orange rind
       1 tablespoon fresh orange juice
       1 tablespoon fresh lemon juice
       1 tablespoon diced onion
       1 teaspoon minced seeded
          jalapeño pepper
       ¼ teaspoon freshly ground black
          pepper
       1 garlic clove, minced

1. Prepare grill.
2. Brush bell peppers and corn with 1 teaspoon oil, and sprinkle with ¼ teaspoon salt. Place bell peppers and corn on grill rack coated with cooking spray. Grill bell peppers 5 minutes or until crisp-tender, turning occasionally. Remove bell peppers from grill. Grill corn 10 minutes or until lightly browned, turning occasionally. Cool slightly. Dice bell peppers. Cut kernels

from ears of corn; discard cobs. Combine bell peppers, corn, 1 teaspoon oil, ¼ teaspoon salt, orange rind, and remaining ingredients in a bowl, and toss well. Serve at room temperature. Yield: 2½ cups (serving size: ¼ cup).

CALORIES 39 (30% from fat); FAT 1.3g (sat 0.2g, mono 0.4g, poly 0.6g); PROTEIN 0.9g; CARB 7g; FIBER 1.1g; CHOL 0mg; IRON 0.3mg; SODIUM 122mg; CALC 3mg

QUINOA TABBOULEH

A staple in the diet of the ancient Incas, quinoa (KEEN-wah) is well on its way to being dubbed supergrain of the millennium. High in fiber and a high-quality protein similar to that found in meat, this grain cooks up like rice and has a mild flavor similar to couscous. Quinoa is available in health-food stores and many supermarkets.

 1¾ cups water
  1 cup uncooked quinoa
  ½ cup coarsely chopped seeded tomato
  ½ cup chopped fresh mint or parsley
  ¼ cup raisins
  ¼ cup chopped cucumber
  ¼ cup fresh lemon juice
  2 tablespoons chopped green onions
  1 tablespoon extra-virgin olive oil
  2 teaspoons minced fresh onion
  ½ teaspoon salt
  ¼ teaspoon freshly ground black pepper

1. Combine water and quinoa in a medium saucepan; bring to a boil. Cover, reduce heat, and simmer 20 minutes or until liquid is absorbed. Remove from heat; fluff with a fork. Stir in tomato and remaining ingredients. Cover; let stand 1 hour. Serve chilled or at room temperature. Yield: 5 servings (serving size: 1 cup).

CALORIES 182 (24% from fat); FAT 4.8g (sat 0.6g, mono 2.5g, poly 1.1g); PROTEIN 5g; CARB 31.6g; FIBER 5.3g; CHOL 0mg; IRON 3.5mg; SODIUM 259mg; CALC 31mg

CALAS

This rice fritter originated in western Africa and comes in many versions. It was extremely popular in antebellum New Orleans. This one is a lightened version of a recipe found in one of the city's oldest cookbooks, 1885's The Creole Cookery Book, *published by the Christian Women's Exchange. In it, the dish is titled "Callers."*

 1½ cups cooked long-grain rice
  ¼ cup warm water
 1½ teaspoons baking powder
  ½ teaspoon salt
  ½ teaspoon grated whole nutmeg
 1¼ cups all-purpose flour
  3 large eggs, lightly beaten
  2 tablespoons vegetable oil
  1 tablespoon powdered sugar

1. Place rice in a medium bowl. Drizzle warm water over rice; mash rice with a fork until almost smooth. Stir in baking powder, salt, and nutmeg. Lightly spoon flour into dry measuring cups; level with a knife. Gradually add flour and eggs to rice mixture, stirring with a whisk until well-blended.
2. Heat oil in a large skillet over medium heat. Drop rice mixture by level tablespoons into pan. Cook 4 minutes on each side or until golden. Remove fritters from pan with a slotted spoon. Pat dry with paper towels. Sprinkle with powdered sugar. Serve immediately. Yield: 2½ dozen (serving size: 3 fritters).

CALORIES 142 (29% from fat); FAT 4.5g (sat 1g, mono 1.4g, poly 1.6g); PROTEIN 4.2g; CARB 20.6g; FIBER 0.6g; CHOL 66mg; IRON 1.3mg; SODIUM 210mg; CALC 54mg

DROP BISCUITS

The dough for these biscuits is dropped into muffin tins instead of onto a baking sheet, but the final shape of the biscuits is still free-form like traditional drop biscuits.

  2 cups all-purpose flour
  1 tablespoon baking powder
  1 teaspoon sugar
  ½ teaspoon salt
  ¼ cup chilled butter or stick margarine, cut into small pieces
  1 cup fat-free milk
Cooking spray

1. Preheat oven to 450°.
2. Lightly spoon flour into dry measuring cups; level with a knife. Combine flour, baking powder, sugar, and salt in a bowl; cut in butter with a pastry blender or 2 knives until mixture resembles coarse meal. Add milk; stir just until moist.
3. Spoon batter into 12 muffin cups coated with cooking spray. Bake at 450° for 12 minutes or until golden. Remove biscuits from pan immediately, and place on a wire rack. Yield: 1 dozen (serving size: 1 biscuit).

CALORIES 119 (31% from fat); FAT 4.1g (sat 2.5g, mono 1.1g, poly 0.2g); PROTEIN 2.9g; CARB 17.6g; FIBER 0.6g; CHOL 11mg; IRON 1.1mg; SODIUM 270mg; CALC 97mg

Come on Back

The wholesome roots of vegetarian cooking are freshening up the future.

Vegetarian dishes from 30 years ago are making a fresh appearance—only this time they've gone mainstream. You don't have to be a vegetarian anymore to know the value of eating unprocessed foods packed with important nutrients. Everyone is looking to food as not only a source of pleasure, but as the foundation of our good health. Brown rice, tofu, sea vegetables, legumes—everyone is eating them, not just vegetarians.

WHEAT BERRY SOUP WITH WHITE BEANS AND ROSEMARY

This soup sounds like the ultimate health-food dish from the '70s, but today this hearty main-dish soup graces the tables of many fine Italian restaurants. Start this soup early in the day, or the night before because the beans and wheat berries (unprocessed kernels of wheat) require long soaking and cooking times.

Soup:

1½ cups dried navy beans (about ¾ pound)
1¼ cups uncooked wheat berries
1 teaspoon salt, divided
1 tablespoon olive oil
2 cups diced onion
1 cup diced celery
½ cup diced carrot
1 tablespoon chopped fresh or 1 teaspoon dried rosemary
3 garlic cloves, crushed
8 cups water
4 parsley sprigs
2 thyme sprigs
1 bay leaf
¼ teaspoon black pepper
1 (14.5-ounce) can diced tomatoes, undrained

Garnish:

½ cup chopped fresh parsley
⅓ cup (1½ ounces) grated fresh Parmesan cheese
1 tablespoon chopped fresh or 1 teaspoon dried rosemary
¼ teaspoon black pepper
1 garlic clove, chopped

1. To prepare soup, sort and wash beans; place in a large bowl. Cover with water to 2 inches above beans; cover and let stand 8 hours or overnight. Drain.
2. Place wheat berries in a medium bowl; cover with water to 2 inches above wheat berries. Cover and let stand 8 hours or overnight. Drain. Place wheat berries in a large saucepan. Cover with water to 2 inches above wheat berries. Bring to a boil; reduce heat, and simmer 25 minutes. Stir in ½ teaspoon salt; cook 20 minutes or until tender. Drain.
3. While wheat berries are cooking, heat oil in a Dutch oven over medium heat. Add onion, celery, carrot, 1 tablespoon fresh rosemary, and 3 crushed garlic cloves; cook 12 minutes, stirring occasionally. Stir in beans, 8 cups water, parsley sprigs, thyme sprigs, and bay leaf. Partially cover, and cook 1½ hours or until beans are tender. Discard bay leaf, parsley, and thyme. Stir in wheat berries, ½ teaspoon salt, ¼ teaspoon pepper, and tomatoes; cook 5 minutes or until thoroughly heated.
4. To prepare garnish, combine chopped parsley and remaining 4 ingredients. Ladle soup into bowls; sprinkle each serving with about 2 tablespoons garnish. Yield: 6 servings (serving size: 1½ cups).
Note: Wheat berries are available in most health-food stores and many larger supermarkets.

CALORIES 399 (13% from fat); FAT 5.7g (sat 1.7g, mono 2.5g, poly 0.8g); PROTEIN 22.9g; CARB 69.9g; FIBER 9.4g; CHOL 5mg; IRON 5.9mg; SODIUM 649mg; CALC 222mg

To gain an extra measure of flavor, steep the milk with onion and herbs before making the sauce. Smoked Gouda works great for the second cheese.

2 (1-ounce) slices white bread
2 cups 2% reduced-fat milk, divided
½ cup thinly sliced onion
1 teaspoon black peppercorns
4 parsley sprigs
2 thyme sprigs
1 bay leaf
1 garlic clove, minced
4 teaspoons all-purpose flour
½ teaspoon prepared mustard
¼ teaspoon salt
⅛ teaspoon ground red pepper
4 cups hot cooked elbow macaroni (about 8 ounces uncooked)
1½ cups (6 ounces) shredded reduced-fat sharp Cheddar cheese
⅓ cup (1½ ounces) shredded smoked Gouda or Gouda cheese
Cooking spray

1. Place bread in a food processor; pulse 10 times or until coarse crumbs form to measure ⅔ cup. Set aside.
2. Combine 1½ cups milk, onion, and next 5 ingredients in a saucepan; bring to a boil over medium heat. Remove from heat; cover and let stand 30 minutes. Strain milk mixture through a sieve into a large bowl; discard solids.
3. Preheat oven to 350°.
4. Place flour in a small bowl; gradually add remaining ½ cup milk, stirring with a whisk until blended. Add flour mixture, mustard, salt, and red pepper to milk mixture, stirring well with a whisk. Stir in macaroni and cheeses; spoon into an 8-inch square baking dish coated with cooking spray. Top with breadcrumbs. Bake at 350° for 25 minutes or until lightly browned. Yield: 5 servings (serving size: 1½ cups).

CALORIES 360 (30% from fat); FAT 11.8g (sat 6.6g, mono 3.2g, poly 0.7g); PROTEIN 21.2g; CARB 43.3g; FIBER 1.9g; CHOL 40mg; IRON 2mg; SODIUM 522mg; CALC 496mg

SPICY CARROT SALAD

Grated carrot salads have been around a long time, but this one is made with cooked sliced carrots, warm spices, and accents of feta cheese and olives.

4   cups (½-inch-thick) sliced carrot
1   teaspoon grated lemon rind
1   tablespoon fresh lemon juice
1   teaspoon paprika
1   teaspoon extra-virgin olive oil
½   teaspoon ground cumin
¼   teaspoon salt
¼   teaspoon black pepper
⅛   teaspoon ground red pepper
1   large garlic clove, minced
¼   cup (1 ounce) crumbled feta
      cheese
2   tablespoons chopped pitted
      kalamata olives (about 6)
2   tablespoons coarsely chopped
      fresh flat-leaf parsley
4   cups torn spinach

1. Cook carrot in boiling water 4 minutes or until crisp-tender; drain and rinse with cold water.
2. Combine rind and next 8 ingredients in a large bowl. Add carrot, feta, olives, and parsley; stir well to coat. Place 1 cup spinach on each of 4 plates; top with 1 cup carrot salad. Yield: 4 servings.

CALORIES 98 (33% from fat); FAT 3.6g (sat 1.4g, mono 1.5g, poly 0.4g); PROTEIN 4g; CARB 14.9g; FIBER 6.2g; CHOL 6mg; IRON 2.7mg; SODIUM 341mg; CALC 132mg

GARDEN POTATOES AND ROOT VEGETABLES WITH GREENS

This is one of the easiest side dishes to make—and to vary. You can substitute turnip, rutabaga, parsley root, or any other root vegetable for the celeriac.

3   cups cubed peeled Yukon gold
      or red potato (about 1½
      pounds)
1½ cups diced peeled celeriac
      (celery root), turnip, or other
      root vegetable (about ½
      pound)
½   teaspoon salt, divided
4   cups coarsely chopped Swiss
      chard (about 1 pound)
½   cup chopped green onions
2   tablespoons butter or stick
      margarine
¼   teaspoon freshly ground black
      pepper

1. Place potato and celeriac in a Dutch oven; cover with water. Bring to a boil. Stir in ¼ teaspoon salt; cook 20 minutes. Add Swiss chard; cook 10 minutes or until tender. Drain well; place potato mixture in a large bowl. Partially mash potatoes with a potato masher; stir in ¼ teaspoon salt, onions, butter, and pepper. Yield: 8 servings (serving size: ½ cup).

CALORIES 98 (28% from fat); FAT 3.1g (sat 1.8g, mono 0.9g, poly 0.2g); PROTEIN 2.3g; CARB 16.6g; FIBER 1.8g; CHOL 8mg; IRON 1.2mg; SODIUM 249mg; CALC 32mg

SAUTÉED CARROTS WITH SEAWEED, GINGER, AND TOFU

The deep-black color and unique flavor of arame seaweed *make it an attractive accent for carrots and spicy fresh ginger. Adding the tofu and serving it with brown rice make a complete meal.*

1   cup dried arame or other
      shredded seaweed (about
      1 ounce)
1   pound firm or extrafirm tofu,
      drained and cut into ½-inch
      slices
1   tablespoon dark sesame oil,
      divided
1½ cups julienne-cut carrot (about
      1 pound)
⅓   cup thinly sliced green onions
1   tablespoon minced peeled fresh
      ginger
¼   teaspoon salt
2   tablespoons low-sodium soy
      sauce
4   cups hot cooked long-grain
      brown rice
1   tablespoon sesame seeds, toasted

1. Cover arame with water; let stand 15 minutes. Drain.
2. Brush tofu slices with 1 teaspoon oil. Heat a large nonstick skillet over medium-high heat. Add tofu, and cook until liquid from tofu evaporates (about 3 minutes). Remove tofu from pan. Cool and cut into ¼-inch pieces; set aside.
3. Heat 2 teaspoons oil in pan over medium-high heat. Add carrot, onions, and ginger; cook 4 minutes or until carrot is golden brown, stirring frequently. Stir in arame and salt; cook 3 minutes or until arame is tender. Stir in tofu and soy sauce. Cook 5 minutes or until thoroughly heated. Serve with rice. Sprinkle with sesame seeds. Yield: 4 servings (serving size: 1 cup tofu mixture and 1 cup rice).
Note: Seaweed is sold at health-food stores and Asian supermarkets.

CALORIES 393 (27% from fat); FAT 11.8g (sat 1.8g, mono 3.6g, poly 5.6g); PROTEIN 17.3g; CARB 53g; FIBER 8.9g; CHOL 0mg; IRON 8.7mg; SODIUM 877mg; CALC 232mg

SOY FOR THE CENTURIES

Only recently has the soybean gained stature in American kitchens. Researchers are discovering that soybeans contain powerful compounds that may help to prevent heart disease, osteoporosis, and cancer.

Studies confirm that diets rich in soy protein can lower both total and LDL, or "bad," cholesterol by an average of 9% to 13%.

Other studies, though preliminary, demonstrate that 40 grams of soy protein a day—about the amount in a cup of firm tofu—were enough to strengthen bones and so might help reduce the risk of osteoporosis.

Researchers believe that plant hormones called *isoflavones* provide the bulk of soy's goodness. Tapping into these disease-fighting powerhouses should be easy because an ever-growing array of soy products—soynut butter, soy milk yogurt, soy cheese—is now crowding supermarket shelves.

PASTA WITH ASPARAGUS AND MUSHROOMS

For a tasty touch, drizzle a few drops of truffle oil over the dish.

- ¼ cup chopped fresh parsley
- 2 teaspoons chopped fresh basil
- 2 garlic cloves, minced
- 4 teaspoons butter or stick margarine
- ⅓ cup diced shallots
- 6 cups sliced cremini mushrooms
- ½ teaspoon salt
- ½ cup dry white wine
- 8 ounces uncooked pappardelle (wide ribbon pasta) or fettuccine
- 2 cups (2-inch) sliced asparagus (about 1 pound)
- ½ cup (2 ounces) grated fresh Parmesan cheese, divided
- ¼ teaspoon freshly ground black pepper

1. Combine first 3 ingredients, and set aside.
2. Melt butter in a large nonstick skillet over medium-high heat. Add shallots; sauté 1 minute. Add mushrooms and salt; sauté 5 minutes. Stir in wine; cook 1 minute. Reduce heat to low. Add 2 tablespoons parsley mixture; sauté 2 minutes. Keep warm.
3. Bring water to a boil in a large Dutch oven. Add pasta; cook 6½ minutes. Add asparagus; cook 1½ minutes or until asparagus is crisp-tender. Drain pasta mixture in a colander over a bowl, reserving ½ cup cooking liquid. Combine reserved cooking liquid, pasta mixture, mushroom mixture, and ¼ cup cheese. Arrange 2 cups pasta mixture on each of 4 plates. Sprinkle evenly with remaining parsley mixture, ¼ cup cheese, and pepper. Yield: 4 servings.

CALORIES 357 (23% from fat); FAT 9g (sat 5g, mono 2.3g, poly 0.9g); PROTEIN 16.7g; CARB 54.2g; FIBER 4.4g; CHOL 20mg; IRON 4.8mg; SODIUM 575mg; CALC 215mg

BROWN RICE AND SAUTÉED VEGETABLES

This is a dish designed for leftovers and improvisation based on the odds and ends in your refrigerator. You can substitute other crunchy vegetables such as parsnips and fennel for the carrot and bell pepper.

- 1 tablespoon vegetable oil
- 2 cups chopped onion
- 1½ teaspoons dried basil
- 1 cup diced red bell pepper
- 1 cup thinly sliced carrot
- 4 cups torn spinach
- 1 cup chopped mushrooms
- ¼ teaspoon salt
- 3 garlic cloves, minced
- 2 tablespoons low-sodium soy sauce
- ¼ teaspoon black pepper
- 3 cups hot cooked long-grain brown rice

1. Heat oil in a large nonstick skillet over medium-high heat. Add onion and basil; sauté 2 minutes. Add bell pepper and carrot; sauté 4 minutes. Add spinach, mushrooms, salt, and garlic; sauté 3 minutes or until spinach wilts. Stir in soy sauce and black pepper. Remove from heat; serve over rice. Yield: 4 servings (serving size: ¾ cup vegetables and ¾ cup rice).

CALORIES 271 (18% from fat); FAT 5.4g (sat 1g, mono 1.5g, poly 2.4g); PROTEIN 7.9g; CARB 50.2g; FIBER 8.1g; CHOL 0mg; IRON 3.5mg; SODIUM 454mg; CALC 112mg

LIGHTEN UP

Taking Care of Tradition

We breathed new life into the treasured recipes of three Bayville, New York, families by trimming fat while retaining old-world flavors.

On Thursday nights, the Pierno clan of Bayville gathers for dinner at the home of parents Tom and Patricia. "I'm on my feet all day, so I like to make something simple with ingredients I have on hand," says Patricia Pierno. Pasta with Creamy Pancetta-and-Pea Sauce was once the perfect solution. But times have changed. "We all love fattening things," Patricia explains. "We just don't eat that way anymore." So the recipe had to be filed away. We reworked the base for the creamy sauce with 1% milk, light cream cheese, and a little flour for thickening. Also less cheese, less oil, and a little less pancetta. In the end, we eliminated two-thirds of the fat (almost 30 grams) and stripped away 118 unnecessary calories.

BEFORE & AFTER	
SERVING SIZE	
1⅓ cups Fusilli with Creamy Pancetta-and-Pea Sauce	
CALORIES	
528	410
FAT	
43.1g	13.7g
PERCENT OF TOTAL CALORIES	
73%	30%

Fusilli with Creamy Pancetta-and-Pea Sauce

Pancetta *(pan-CHEH-tuh), a type of Italian bacon cured with salt and spices but not smoked, adds a distinctive flavor. Substitute American-style bacon if you can't find it.*

Cooking spray
¼ cup chopped pancetta or bacon (about 1 ounce)
1 teaspoon olive oil
1 cup diced onion
1 garlic clove, minced
2 tablespoons all-purpose flour
2 cups 1% low-fat milk
¼ cup (2 ounces) ⅓-less-fat cream cheese
2½ cups frozen green peas, thawed
1¼ cups (5 ounces) grated fresh Parmesan cheese, divided
⅓ cup chopped fresh basil
¼ teaspoon salt
¼ teaspoon black pepper
5 cups hot cooked fusilli (about 4 cups uncooked short twisted spaghetti)

1. Heat a nonstick skillet coated with cooking spray over medium heat. Add pancetta; cook 1 minute or until browned. Place pancetta in a large bowl. Heat oil in pan. Add onion and garlic; sauté 7 minutes. Add onion mixture to pancetta. Place flour in pan. Gradually add milk; stir with a whisk until blended. Cook over medium heat until thick (about 5 minutes); stir constantly. Add cream cheese; stir until cheese melts. Stir in peas, 1 cup Parmesan, basil, salt, and pepper. Add cheese sauce and pasta to pancetta mixture; toss well. Sprinkle with remaining ¼ cup Parmesan. Yield: 6 servings (serving size: 1⅓ cups).

CALORIES 410 (30% from fat); FAT 13.7g (sat 7.1g, mono 4.6g, poly 1g); PROTEIN 21.6g; CARB 49.5g; FIBER 5.1g; CHOL 30mg; IRON 3mg; SODIUM 656mg; CALC 419mg

Chicken Cacciatore, Sicilian Style

(pictured on page 264)

—Mary LaCava Caputo

2 tablespoons olive oil, divided
4 (6-ounce) skinned chicken breast halves
4 chicken thighs (about 1 pound), skinned
4 chicken drumsticks (about 1 pound), skinned
2 cups chopped onion
4 garlic cloves, minced
1 cup chopped celery
½ cup chopped fresh basil
½ cup chopped fresh flat-leaf parsley
½ cup red wine vinegar
¼ cup sliced green olives
¼ cup capers
1 tablespoon sugar
Dash of ground red pepper
1 (28-ounce) can Italian-style tomatoes, undrained and chopped
2 bay leaves
8 cups hot cooked macaroni or cavatappi (about 12 ounces uncooked spiral-shaped pasta)
Parsley sprigs (optional)

1. Heat 1½ teaspoons oil in a large nonstick skillet over medium-high heat until hot. Add chicken breasts to pan, and sauté 1 to 2 minutes on each side or until chicken is lightly browned. Remove chicken breasts from pan. Add 1½ teaspoons oil and remaining chicken, and sauté 1 to 2 minutes on each side or until chicken is lightly browned. Remove chicken from pan.
2. Heat 1 tablespoon oil in pan. Add onion and garlic, and sauté 5 minutes. Add celery, and sauté 5 minutes. Add basil and next 8 ingredients. Return chicken to pan, and bring to a boil. Cover, reduce heat, and simmer 20 minutes. Uncover and simmer 25 minutes or until chicken is tender. Discard bay leaves. Serve with pasta, and garnish with parsley sprigs, if desired. Yield: 8 servings (serving size: 1 chicken breast half or 1 thigh and 1 drumstick, ½ cup sauce, and 1 cup pasta).

CALORIES 406 (18% from fat); FAT 8.3g (sat 1.6g, mono 3.9g, poly 1.6g); PROTEIN 37.9g; CARB 43.6g; FIBER 3g; CHOL 99mg; IRON 4mg; SODIUM 663mg; CALC 79mg

Quick Taco Salad

—Rosemary Clarke

12 ounces ground round
2 cups chopped yellow, red, or green bell pepper
2 cups bottled salsa
¼ cup chopped fresh cilantro
4 cups coarsely chopped romaine lettuce
2 cups chopped plum tomato
1 cup (4 ounces) shredded reduced-fat sharp Cheddar cheese
1 cup crumbled baked tortilla chips (about 12 chips)
¼ cup chopped green onions

Continued

1. Cook beef and bell pepper in a large nonstick skillet over medium-high heat until beef is browned; stir to crumble. Add salsa; bring to a boil. Stir in cilantro; keep warm.

2. Place 1 cup lettuce on each of 4 plates; top each with 1 cup meat mixture. Sprinkle each serving with ½ cup tomato, ¼ cup cheese, ¼ cup chips, and 1 tablespoon onions. Yield: 4 servings.

CALORIES 332 (30% from fat); FAT 11.1g (sat 4.8g, mono 3.5g, poly 0.9g); PROTEIN 32g; CARB 28.5g; FIBER 6.3g; CHOL 68mg; IRON 5.6mg; SODIUM 908mg; CALC 348mg

---

30 MINUTES OR LESS

Keeping the Classics Quick

Modern-convenience shortcuts to traditional dishes easily bridge the centuries.

If your schedule doesn't allow for dalliance in the kitchen, turn to super-convenient products and timesaving kitchenware. Presliced mushrooms, preshredded cheese, and canned tomatoes can give you all the flavor you need without tying up valuable evening hours.

Add some technology to your preparation—use a microwave or pressure cooker, for instance—and you can save even more time. We think a lot about how things will get better, or faster, in the future. With these dishes, the future is now.

INSTANT BLACK BEAN SOUP

Preparation time: 3 minutes
Cooking time: 17 minutes

2 (15-ounce) cans no-salt-added black beans, undrained
½ cup bottled salsa
1 tablespoon chili powder
1 (16-ounce) can fat-free, less-sodium chicken broth
½ cup (2 ounces) shredded reduced-fat sharp Cheddar cheese
5 tablespoons low-fat sour cream
5 tablespoons minced green onions
2½ tablespoons chopped fresh cilantro

1. Place beans and liquid in a medium saucepan; partially mash beans with a potato masher. Place over high heat; stir in salsa, chili powder, and broth. Bring to a boil. Ladle soup into bowls; top with cheese, sour cream, onions, and cilantro. Yield: 5 servings (serving size: 1 cup soup, about 1½ tablespoons cheese, 1 tablespoon sour cream, 1 tablespoon green onions, and 1½ teaspoons cilantro).

CALORIES 212 (21% from fat); FAT 4.9g (sat 2.6g, mono 1.2g, poly 0.5g); PROTEIN 14.7g; CARB 28.7g; FIBER 5.4g; CHOL 13mg; IRON 2.9mg; SODIUM 411mg; CALC 163mg

BISTRO FILLETS OF SOLE

Preparation time: 6 minutes
Cooking time: 24 minutes

8 (3-ounce) sole or orange roughy fillets
½ cup dry vermouth
1 teaspoon capers
1 (8-ounce) bottle clam juice
1 large egg yolk
2 tablespoons light mayonnaise
1 tablespoon 1% low-fat milk
⅛ teaspoon ground red pepper
½ cup minced fresh parsley
8 (¼-inch-thick) slices diagonally cut French bread baguette, toasted

1. Arrange fish in a single layer in a 10-inch skillet; add vermouth, capers, and clam juice. Bring to a simmer; cover and simmer over medium-low heat 10 minutes or until fish flakes easily when tested with a fork. Remove fish from pan, and keep warm; reserve cooking liquid. Bring cooking liquid to a boil; cook until reduced by half (about 9 minutes). Gradually add hot liquid to egg yolk in a bowl, stirring constantly with a whisk. Return egg mixture to pan. Add mayonnaise, milk, and red pepper; cook over medium heat 1 minute, stirring constantly. Stir in parsley. Spoon 3 tablespoons sauce onto each of 4 plates; top each portion with 2 fillets and 2 toast slices. Yield: 4 servings.

CALORIES 203 (23% from fat); FAT 5.1g (sat 0.9g, mono 2.1g, poly 1.3g); PROTEIN 27.7g; CARB 9.9g; FIBER 0.8g; CHOL 93mg; IRON 1.5mg; SODIUM 437mg; CALC 41mg

CHEESE-AND-BEAN ENCHILADAS

Preparation time: 12 minutes
Cooking time: 12 minutes

You can make these enchiladas without the beans, too. Either way, they're terrific.

1 (10-ounce) bag frozen chopped onion
1 (16-ounce) can fat-free refried beans with mild green chiles (such as Taco Bell)
2 cups (8 ounces) preshredded reduced-fat Mexican blend or Cheddar cheese, divided
12 (6-inch) corn tortillas
1 (19-ounce) can enchilada sauce
2 tablespoons low-fat sour cream
2 tablespoons chopped ripe olives
6 tablespoons minced fresh cilantro

1. Preheat oven to 400°.

2. Place onion in a sieve; rinse with hot water. Drain well. Combine onion and beans in a microwave-safe bowl. Microwave at HIGH 3 minutes or until heated. Stir in 1½ cups cheese.

3. Stack tortillas; wrap stack in damp paper towels, and microwave at HIGH 1 minute or until soft. Pour half of enchilada sauce in a 13 x 9-inch baking dish; dip both sides of each tortilla into sauce. Spoon about ¼ cup bean mixture down center of each tortilla; roll up. Arrange tortillas in baking dish; top with remaining sauce and ½ cup cheese. Bake at 400° for 8 minutes or until thoroughly heated. Top each serving with sour cream, olives, and cilantro. Yield: 6 servings (serving size: 2 enchiladas, 1 teaspoon sour cream, 1 teaspoon olives, and 1 tablespoon cilantro).

CALORIES 328 (27% from fat); FAT 9.8g (sat 5.3g, mono 2.7g, poly 1.5g); PROTEIN 18.4g; CARB 45g; FIBER 6.7g; CHOL 15mg; IRON 2.7mg; SODIUM 987mg; CALC 400mg

RAPID RISOTTO

Preparation time: 4 minutes
Cooking time: 14 minutes
Standing time: 5 minutes

 1 tablespoon olive oil
 1 cup uncooked Arborio rice or
    other short-grain rice
 ½ cup frozen chopped onion
 ½ cup dry white wine
 1 (16-ounce) can fat-free,
    less-sodium chicken broth
 1 cup finely chopped plum
    tomatoes (about ¼ pound)
 2 tablespoons dried parsley
 ½ teaspoon freshly ground black
    pepper
 3 ounces chopped prosciutto
    (about ¾ cup)
 ¼ cup (1 ounce) preshredded fresh
    Parmesan cheese
 Parsley sprigs (optional)

1. Heat oil in a 6-quart pressure cooker over medium heat until hot. Add rice and onion, and sauté 1 minute. Stir in wine and broth. Close lid securely, and bring to high pressure over high heat (about 4 minutes). Adjust heat to medium or level needed to maintain high pressure, and cook 3 minutes. Remove from heat, and let stand 5 minutes. Place pressure cooker under cold running water. Remove lid, and stir in tomatoes, dried parsley, pepper, and prosciutto. Cook, uncovered, over medium-high heat 3 minutes, stirring constantly. Stir in cheese. Garnish with parsley sprigs, if desired. Yield: 4 servings (serving size: 1 cup).

CALORIES 306 (22% from fat); FAT 7.6g (sat 2.4g, mono 4.1g, poly 0.8g); PROTEIN 13g; CARB 45.1g; FIBER 1.7g; CHOL 17mg; IRON 3.3mg; SODIUM 683mg; CALC 98mg

HUNTER'S CHICKEN

Preparation time: 7 minutes
Cooking time: 12 minutes

 1 (9-ounce) package fresh
    linguine, uncooked
12 chicken breast tenders (about
    1 pound)
 2 tablespoons Italian-seasoned
    breadcrumbs
 1 tablespoon olive oil
 2 tablespoons chopped
    pimento-stuffed olives
 ½ teaspoon dried Italian seasoning
 ¼ teaspoon salt
 ⅛ teaspoon black pepper
 2 (14½-ounce) cans Italian-style
    stewed tomatoes, undrained
 ¼ cup (1 ounce) preshredded
    part-skim mozzarella cheese

1. Cook pasta according to package directions. Drain well; keep warm.
2. While pasta cooks, dredge chicken in breadcrumbs. Heat oil in a large nonstick skillet over medium-high heat; add chicken. Cook 3 minutes on each side or until browned. Stir in olives and next 4 ingredients. Cook 5 minutes or until chicken is done. Serve over linguine, and top with cheese. Yield: 4 servings (serving size: ¾ cup linguine, about ¾ cup chicken with sauce, and 1 tablespoon cheese).

CALORIES 432 (18% from fat); FAT 8.6g (sat 2.4g, mono 3.7g, poly 1.4g); PROTEIN 38.1g; CARB 50.4g; FIBER 2.5g; CHOL 138mg; IRON 3.7mg; SODIUM 930mg; CALC 153mg

BURGUNDY BEEF

Preparation time: 15 minutes
Cooking time: 15 minutes

To make this delicious dish, we started with a ready-to-eat pot roast, which you can find in your grocer's meat case. Package weights will vary.

 1 (12-ounce) package uncooked
    medium egg noodles
 1 (2¼ to 2½-pound) package
    refrigerated fully cooked beef
    pot roast with gravy (such as
    Burnett and Son)
 ¾ cup dry red wine
 ½ teaspoon dried oregano
 ¼ teaspoon cracked black pepper
 2 cups frozen pearl onions
 1 (8-ounce) package presliced
    mushrooms
 ¼ cup water
 1 tablespoon cornstarch

1. Cook noodles according to package directions. Drain well; keep warm.
2. While noodles cook, remove beef from package, reserving gravy. Cut beef into thin slices. Combine reserved gravy, wine, and next 4 ingredients in a large nonstick skillet; bring to a boil. Reduce heat to medium; cook 5 minutes. Stir in beef, and cook 2 minutes. Combine water and cornstarch in a small bowl. Add cornstarch mixture to beef mixture; bring to a boil. Cook 1 minute, stirring constantly. Serve over noodles. Yield: 8 servings (serving size: 1 cup beef mixture and 1 cup noodles).

CALORIES 394 (19% from fat); FAT 8.3g (sat 2.9g, mono 3.6g, poly 0.8g); PROTEIN 38.1g; CARB 41.9g; FIBER 1.9g; CHOL 120mg; IRON 5.3mg; SODIUM 457mg; CALC 38mg

What Goes Around Comes Around

Of all the New World foods, none has had more influence on international cuisines than the juicy tomato.

Europeans first tasted the tomato in the 16th century when the conquistadors reached Mexico and Central America. Soon, the juicy little discovery made its way back to Europe where it found favor first in the Mediterranean countries of Spain and Italy. From there, the tomato spread, trailing a scent as heady as the rich soil in which the plant prospers.

But with passion came a price. As the demand for tomatoes mounted, growers worked to increase yield. Diversity of shape, taste, and color were sacrificed in favor of ease of harvest, hardiness, and transportability. By the 1950s, commercial growers brought genetically manipulated hybrids to market.

It wasn't long before a few folks began casting wistful glances back to the tomatoes of our past. Contrary to what we think of today as the archetypal tomato—red, squat, stolid, and the size of a balled fist—tomatoes of yesteryear were of many different shapes and colors.

While hybrid varieties still dominate the home-garden market, heirloom tomatoes are now popping up in backyards across the country. The demand for heirlooms has increased so much that Burpee Seeds, for example, recently issued a separate catalog featuring only heirloom vegetables. What's old is new again.

FRESH-TOMATO LASAGNA

Sauce:

- 4½ cups chopped onion (about 3)
- 2 garlic cloves, minced
- 6 cups chopped seeded peeled tomato (about 3½ pounds)
- 1 cup chopped fresh parsley
- 2 teaspoons dried oregano
- ½ teaspoon salt
- ½ teaspoon dried thyme
- ½ teaspoon dried marjoram
- ½ teaspoon black pepper
- 2 (6-ounce) cans Italian-style tomato paste

Filling:

- ½ teaspoon dried basil
- 1 (15-ounce) carton fat-free ricotta cheese
- 1 (12.3-ounce) package reduced-fat firm tofu, drained

Remaining ingredients:

- Cooking spray
- 12 cooked lasagna noodles
- 2 cups (8 ounces) shredded sharp provolone cheese
- ½ cup (2 ounces) grated fresh Romano or Parmesan cheese

1. To prepare sauce, heat a Dutch oven over medium-high heat until hot. Add onion and garlic; cover and cook 5 minutes, stirring occasionally. Add tomato and next 7 ingredients. Bring to a boil; cover, reduce heat, and simmer 45 minutes, stirring occasionally.
2. Preheat oven to 350°.
3. To prepare filling, combine basil, ricotta, and tofu in a bowl; mash ricotta mixture with a potato masher.
4. Spread 2 cups sauce in a 13 x 9-inch baking dish coated with cooking spray. Arrange 3 noodles over sauce; top with 1 cup filling, ½ cup provolone cheese, 2 tablespoons Romano, and 1½ cups sauce. Repeat layers twice, ending with noodles. Spread remaining sauce over noodles. Sprinkle with ½ cup provolone cheese and 2 tablespoons Romano. Bake at 350° for 45 minutes. Let stand 10 minutes before serving. Yield: 8 servings.

CALORIES 391 (26% from fat); FAT 11.1g (sat 6.3g, mono 2.9g, poly 1g); PROTEIN 27.7g; CARB 49.5g; FIBER 4.4g; CHOL 33mg; IRON 4.2mg; SODIUM 886mg; CALC 476mg

TUSCAN FRESH-TOMATO SAUCE

Salting and draining the tomatoes first intensifies the flavor of the sauce. Use it as a topping for bruschetta, toss it with pasta, or use it as a sauce for fish, poultry, or meat.

- 4 cups diced peeled plum tomatoes (about 2 pounds)
- ½ teaspoon salt
- 1 tablespoon extra-virgin olive oil
- ¼ to ½ teaspoon freshly ground black pepper
- ¼ teaspoon crushed red pepper
- 3 garlic cloves, crushed
- ½ cup chopped fresh basil
- 2 tablespoons chopped fresh parsley

1. Place tomato in a colander; sprinkle with salt. Drain 1 hour.
2. Combine olive oil, peppers, and garlic in a large bowl. Stir in tomato, basil, and parsley. Yield: 3 cups (serving size: ½ cup).

CALORIES 49 (50% from fat); FAT 2.7g (sat 0.4g, mono 1.7g, poly 0.4g); PROTEIN 1.3g; CARB 6.4g; FIBER 1.4g; CHOL 0mg; IRON 0.7mg; SODIUM 207mg; CALC 17mg

Smoked Tomato-and-Tomatillo Salsa

You can actually "smoke" without using an outdoor grill with the simple technique we've used here. This unusual and versatile salsa is great with tortilla chips, as a filling for a wrap, or as a topping for any grilled meat.

¾ pound tomatillos (about 7 large)
½ cup hickory wood chips
2 cups halved cherry tomatoes (about ¾ pound)
¼ cup chopped fresh cilantro
2 tablespoons chopped shallots
1 tablespoon fresh lemon juice
½ teaspoon salt
½ teaspoon dried oregano
¼ teaspoon freshly ground black pepper
1 jalapeño pepper, halved and seeded
1 garlic clove, peeled

1. Discard husks and stems from tomatillos, and cut each in half. Set aside. Line a Dutch oven with foil, and add hickory chips. Heat chips, covered, over medium-high heat 10 minutes or until chips begin to smoke. Arrange tomatillos and tomatoes in a vegetable steamer. Place steamer in foil-lined pan. Cover and smoke 10 minutes. Remove tomatillo mixture from pan, and cool to room temperature.
2. Place tomatillo mixture, cilantro, and remaining ingredients in a food processor. Process until finely chopped. Yield: 3 cups (serving size: ¼ cup).
Note: Store in an airtight container in refrigerator up to 1 week; serve with a slotted spoon.

CALORIES 16 (17% from fat); FAT 0.3g (sat 0g, mono 0g, poly 0.1g); PROTEIN 0.7g; CARB 3.5g; FIBER 0.7g; CHOL 0mg; IRON 0.4mg; SODIUM 105mg; CALC 9mg

---

> **MENU SUGGESTION**
>
> CHEDDAR, BACON, AND TOMATO STRATA
>
> *Fruit with pineapple-yogurt dressing ***
>
> *Combine 1 cup lemon low-fat yogurt, 2 tablespoons thawed pineapple juice concentrate, 2 tablespoons light sour cream, and a dash of nutmeg. Spoon over fresh fruit such as cantaloupe, kiwifruit, and raspberries. Serves 8.

Cheddar, Bacon, and Tomato Strata

3 bacon slices
1 cup vertically sliced onion
2 garlic cloves, minced
2 cups fat-free milk
¼ cup thinly sliced fresh basil
¼ teaspoon salt
¼ teaspoon dried thyme
¼ teaspoon black pepper
3 large eggs
3 large egg whites
8 cups cubed Italian bread (about 14 ounces)
Cooking spray
2 cups (8 ounces) shredded reduced-fat sharp Cheddar cheese, divided
3 large tomatoes, each seeded and cut into 4 (½-inch-thick) slices

1. Cook bacon in a large nonstick skillet over medium heat until crisp. Remove bacon from pan, and crumble. Add onion to drippings in pan; sauté 4 minutes. Add garlic, and sauté 1 minute. Remove from heat; combine onion mixture and bacon.
2. Combine milk and next 6 ingredients; stir well with a whisk. Arrange 4 cups bread cubes in a 13 x 9-inch baking dish coated with cooking spray; top with ⅔ cup cheese, half of onion mixture, and 6 tomato slices. Pour half of milk mixture over tomatoes. Top with 4 cups bread cubes, ⅔ cup cheese, remaining onion mixture, 6 tomato slices, and remaining milk mixture.

Cover and chill at least 1 hour or up to 24 hours.
3. Preheat oven to 325°.
4. Bake, uncovered, at 325° for 55 minutes. Sprinkle with ⅔ cup cheese; bake an additional 5 minutes or until cheese melts. Let stand 5 minutes before serving. Yield: 8 servings.

CALORIES 316 (28% from fat); FAT 9.8g (sat 4.8g, mono 3.3g, poly 0.8g); PROTEIN 19.6g; CARB 37g; FIBER 2.3g; CHOL 106mg; IRON 1.9mg; SODIUM 670mg; CALC 356mg

---

Fresh-Tomato Soup au Gratin

Soup:

1 teaspoon butter or stick margarine
¼ cup finely chopped onion
5 cups chopped seeded tomato (about 2¾ pounds)
2 cups 1% low-fat milk
½ teaspoon salt
Dash of black pepper

Croutons:

1 garlic clove, cut in half
2 (1-ounce) slices diagonally cut French bread (about 1 inch thick)
½ cup (2 ounces) shredded reduced-fat Monterey Jack or reduced-fat, reduced-sodium Swiss cheese (such as Alpine Lace)

1. To prepare soup, melt butter in a large saucepan over medium heat. Add onion; sauté 3 minutes. Add tomato; cook, covered, over medium heat 10 minutes. Uncover; cook until mixture is reduced to 2 cups (about 25 minutes), stirring occasionally.
2. Place tomato mixture in a blender, and process until smooth. Combine tomato mixture, milk, salt, and pepper in pan; cook over medium-low heat 2 minutes or until heated.
3. Preheat broiler.

Continued

4. To prepare croutons, rub cut sides of garlic over both sides of each bread slice; place bread on a baking sheet. Broil 30 seconds on each side or until toasted. Cut each slice in half crosswise. Place 1 cup soup in each of 4 ovenproof bowls; top each serving with 1 crouton and 2 tablespoons cheese. Broil 2 minutes or until cheese melts. Yield: 4 servings.

CALORIES 193 (28% from fat); FAT 6.1g (sat 3.2g, mono 2g, poly 0.6g); PROTEIN 11.5g; CARB 25g; FIBER 3.1g; CHOL 17mg; IRON 1.5mg; SODIUM 561mg; CALC 289mg

PANZANELLA SALAD WITH PARSLEY

Panzanella *(pahn-zah-NEHL-uh)* is an Italian bread salad. This version is based on the traditional combination of tomatoes, olive oil, vinegar, and seasonings. Fresh ingredients are key in making this recipe work.

2½ cups (½-inch) cubed French bread (about 3 [1-ounce] slices)
2 cups (½-inch) cubed tomato
¼ cup sliced shallots
2 teaspoons extra-virgin olive oil
2 teaspoons balsamic vinegar
¼ teaspoon salt
½ cup chopped fresh parsley

1. Preheat oven to 325°.
2. Place bread on a jelly-roll pan. Bake at 325° for 10 minutes or until lightly browned.
3. Combine tomato, shallots, oil, vinegar, and salt in a large bowl. Cover and let stand at room temperature 2 hours. Stir in bread cubes and parsley. Serve immediately. Yield: 4 servings (serving size: 1 cup).

CALORIES 71 (28% from fat); FAT 2.2g (sat 0.3g, mono 1.3g, poly 0.3g); PROTEIN 2.1g; CARB 11.6g; FIBER 1.4g; CHOL 0mg; IRON 1mg; SODIUM 193mg; CALC 23mg

BREADED BROILED TOMATOES

This familiar side dish that dates back to the 19th century is still a popular companion to all types of meat. You can substitute any fresh herb for cilantro—try oregano with beef, rosemary with lamb, or tarragon with chicken. We've updated this recipe with a surprise: We used buttermilk in place of melted butter.

1 (1-ounce) slice white bread
4 large tomatoes (about 2½ pounds)
½ cup low-fat buttermilk
½ cup (2 ounces) grated fresh Romano or Parmesan cheese
1 teaspoon freshly ground black pepper
1 large egg white, lightly beaten
Cooking spray
8 teaspoons chopped fresh cilantro

1. Preheat oven to 400°.
2. Place bread in a food processor, and process until finely ground to measure ½ cup. Set aside.
3. Core tomatoes; cut each tomato in half crosswise. Push seeds out of tomato halves with thumbs. Spoon 1 tablespoon buttermilk into each tomato half. Combine breadcrumbs, cheese, pepper, and egg white in a small bowl. Divide breadcrumb mixture evenly among tomato halves. Place tomato halves on a baking sheet coated with cooking spray. Bake at 400° for 17 minutes.
4. Preheat broiler.
5. Broil tomato halves 2 minutes or until lightly browned. Sprinkle each tomato half with 1 teaspoon cilantro. Yield: 8 servings (serving size: 1 tomato half).

CALORIES 72 (35% from fat); FAT 2.8g (sat 1.5g, mono 0.7g, poly 0.2g); PROTEIN 4.6g; CARB 9.1g; FIBER 1.5g; CHOL 7mg; IRON 0.8mg; SODIUM 126mg; CALC 106mg

MARINATED TOMATO-AND-"SMOKED" MOZZARELLA SALAD

The components of this salad are similar to the traditional Caprice salad consisting of tomatoes, mozzarella, and fresh basil. Here the marinade takes on an Asian flair with rice vinegar, ginger, and Chinese five-spice powder.

2 cups water
1½ teaspoons barbecue smoked seasoning (such as Hickory Liquid Smoke)
1 cup (4 ounces) cubed fresh mozzarella cheese
3 tablespoons rice vinegar
1 teaspoon vegetable oil
1 tablespoon honey
½ teaspoon grated peeled fresh ginger
¼ teaspoon salt
¼ teaspoon freshly ground black pepper
⅛ teaspoon five-spice powder
1 garlic clove, minced
1½ cups coarsely chopped tomato (about ½ pound)
1½ cups coarsely chopped yellow tomato (about ½ pound)
5 cups (1-inch) cubed French bread (about 8 [1-ounce] slices)

1. Combine water and smoked seasoning in a zip-top plastic bag, and add mozzarella. Seal and marinate in refrigerator 2 hours. Remove cheese from bag; discard marinade.
2. Combine vinegar and next 7 ingredients in a large zip-top plastic bag, and add tomato. Seal and marinate in refrigerator 2 hours. Drain tomato mixture, reserving marinade.
3. Preheat oven to 400°.
4. Place bread cubes in a single layer on a jelly-roll pan. Bake at 400° for 10 minutes or until toasted.
5. Combine cheese, tomato, reserved tomato marinade, and croutons in a large bowl. Serve immediately. Yield: 7 servings (serving size: 1 cup).

CALORIES 167 (29% from fat); FAT 5.4g (sat 2.5g, mono 1.7g, poly 0.8g); PROTEIN 6.7g; CARB 23.4g; FIBER 1.9g; CHOL 13mg; IRON 1.2mg; SODIUM 349mg; CALC 113mg

Back to Basics —Way Back

If you're a fan of the modern baked tortilla chip, you're going to love 2,000-year-old Mexican tostadas.

Many regard the advent of the baked tortilla chip as one of the great inventions of this century. The truth is, toasted tortillas and tortilla chips were probably being served in pre-Columbian America. Today tostadas are fried and function like little pedestals on which other foods are piled. Tostadas are outrageously good, but very high in fatty calories. So why not go back to the original recipe and toast them instead of frying them?

TOMATILLO PUREE

Tomatillos, or Mexican green tomatoes, are small and green, with a thin, papery husk that should be removed before cooking.

1¼ pounds tomatillos (about
       12 large)
8   cups water
3   tablespoons chopped fresh
       cilantro
¼   teaspoon salt

1. Discard husks and stems from tomatillos. Bring water to a boil in a Dutch oven. Add tomatillos; cover and remove from heat. Let stand 5 minutes or until tender; drain. Place tomatillos in a blender; process until smooth. Stir in cilantro and salt. Cover and chill. Yield: 2½ cups (serving size: ½ cup).
Note: Substitute 4 (11-ounce) cans tomatillos if you can't find fresh. Drain canned tomatillos, and puree with cilantro. Omit salt; canned tomatillos contain added sodium.

CALORIES 28 (23% from fat); FAT 0.7g (sat 0.1g, mono 0.1g, poly 0.3g); PROTEIN 1.4g; CARB 5.9g; FIBER 1.3g; CHOL 0mg; IRON 0.7mg; SODIUM 133mg; CALC 18mg

DRIED-CHILE PUREE

This is an intense chile sauce traditional to Mexico. We've relied on two dried chiles that are easy to find: the pasilla, *which is long, dark brown, and mild; and the* ancho, *which is heart shaped, dark brown, and mild. You can use only one, if it's all you can find, but the combination of the two results in a more balanced flavor.*

2   pasilla chiles
1   ancho chile
4   cups boiling water

1. Remove stems and seeds from chiles. Combine chiles and boiling water in a large bowl; cover and let stand 30 minutes or until soft. Drain chiles in a colander over a bowl, reserving 2 tablespoons soaking liquid. Combine chiles and reserved soaking liquid in a blender, and process until smooth. Cover and chill. Yield: ¼ cup (serving size: 1 tablespoon).

CALORIES 24 (26% from fat); FAT 0.7g (sat 0.2g, mono 0.2g, poly 0.3g); PROTEIN 1g; CARB 4.5g; FIBER 2g; CHOL 0mg; IRON 0.6mg; SODIUM 28mg; CALC 10mg

MONTE ALBÁN GUACAMOLE

This is how the guacamole at Monte Albán, Mexico might have tasted. For historical fidelity, we have omitted the garlic and citrus juice because these ingredients were introduced by the Spanish. Fortunately, the tartness of the Tomatillo Puree *(see recipe) makes up for the lack of lemon juice. Spread on the Shrimp-and-Guacamole Tostadas (page 254), or serve as a dip with baked tortilla chips.*

1   cup Tomatillo Puree (see recipe)
1   teaspoon minced seeded serrano
       chile
½   teaspoon salt
6   peeled ripe avocados, seeded
       (about 2 pounds)

1. Combine Tomatillo Puree, serrano chile, salt, and avocados in a bowl, and mash mixture to desired consistency.

Cover and chill. Yield: 3⅓ cups (serving size: ⅓ cup).

CALORIES 113 (83% from fat); FAT 10.4g (sat 1.6g, mono 6.4g, poly 1.4g); PROTEIN 1.6g; CARB 6.1g; FIBER 3.6g; CHOL 0mg; IRON 0.8mg; SODIUM 150mg; CALC 11mg

BUILDING A BETTER TOSTADA

A tostada is a crisp, flat corn tortilla piled with toppings. Sounds easy, but the challenge in making tostadas is finding the right balance between crunchiness and flexibility.

❶ *Cook a tortilla too long, and it will shatter when you bite into it, the toppings cascading down your shirt. Underbake it, and a tortilla has the texture of wet cardboard.*

❷ *The secret is to bake the tortillas until they're crisp yet pliable—about 7 minutes, depending on your oven.*

❸ *Make the first layer of ingredients a wet one, such as refried beans, mashed squash, or guacamole. That will keep the tortillas slightly moist, while also holding the next layer of toppings in place. Serve immediately.*

SQUASH-AND-MUSHROOM TOSTADAS

(pictured on page 263)

Any combination of dried mushrooms will work here. We used a prepackaged mix that contains shiitake, wood ear, and porcini. To save time, substitute 1⅓ cups canned pumpkin for the cooked, mashed squash.

- 1 cup mixed dried mushrooms
- 1 cup boiling water
- ¾ cup Tomatillo Puree (page 253)
- 1 tablespoon Dried-Chile Puree (page 253)
- 2 poblano chiles
- 1 butternut squash, halved lengthwise (about 1¾ pounds)
- 3 tablespoons pine nuts, toasted and divided
- 1 tablespoon honey
- ½ teaspoon salt
- 6 (6-inch) corn tortillas

1. Combine mushrooms and boiling water in a bowl; cover and let stand for 1 hour. Drain. Slice mushroom caps; discard stems. Combine mushrooms, Tomatillo Puree, and Dried-Chile Puree in a small nonstick skillet; bring to a boil over medium-high heat. Reduce heat; simmer 5 minutes or until thick. Keep warm.
2. Preheat broiler.
3. Place chiles on a foil-lined baking sheet; broil 10 minutes or until blackened, turning occasionally. Place in a zip-top plastic bag; seal. Let stand 15 minutes. Peel chiles; cut in half lengthwise. Discard seeds and membranes. Cut each chile into 6 strips, and set aside.
4. Preheat oven to 350°.
5. Place squash halves, cut sides down, on a baking sheet; bake at 350° for 45 minutes or until tender. Cool; discard seeds, and scoop out squash pulp. Combine squash pulp, 2 tablespoons pine nuts, honey, and salt in a microwave-safe bowl.
6. Place tortillas directly on middle rack in oven. Bake at 350° for 7 minutes (tortillas should be slightly pliable).

7. Microwave squash mixture at HIGH 30 seconds or until hot. Spread ¼ cup squash mixture over each tortilla; top each with ¼ cup mushroom mixture. Arrange 2 chile strips over mushroom mixture on each tostada, and sprinkle each with ½ teaspoon pine nuts. Yield: 6 servings.

CALORIES 179 (27% from fat); FAT 5.4g (sat 0.8g, mono 1.8g, poly 2.2g); PROTEIN 4.4g; CARB 34.1g; FIBER 4.3g; CHOL 0mg; IRON 1.6mg; SODIUM 284mg; CALC 98mg

SHRIMP-AND-GUACAMOLE TOSTADAS

(pictured on page 262)

- 30 medium shrimp, peeled and deveined (about 1 pound)
- 2 tablespoons chili powder
- ½ teaspoon salt
- Cooking spray
- 6 (6-inch) corn tortillas
- ⅔ cup Monte Albán Guacamole (page 253)
- ¼ cup chopped green onions

1. Prepare grill or broiler.
2. Thread 5 shrimp onto each of 6 (12-inch) skewers. Combine chili powder and salt; sprinkle both sides of shrimp with chili powder mixture. Place shrimp in a shallow baking dish; cover and marinate in refrigerator 15 minutes. Place kebabs on a grill rack or broiler pan coated with cooking spray; cook 2 minutes on each side or until shrimp are done.
3. Preheat oven to 350°.
4. Place tortillas directly on middle rack in oven. Bake at 350° for 7 minutes (tortillas should be slightly pliable). Top each tortilla with about 2 tablespoons Monte Albán Guacamole and 5 shrimp. Sprinkle evenly with green onions. Yield: 6 servings.

CALORIES 161 (30% from fat); FAT 5.4g (sat 0.9g, mono 2.4g, poly 1.3g); PROTEIN 13.8g; CARB 15.7g; FIBER 3.4g; CHOL 86mg; IRON 2.4mg; SODIUM 393mg; CALC 87mg

BLACK BEAN-AND-CHICKEN TOSTADAS

Quail and turkey were the pre-Columbian favorites. For convenience, we've substituted chicken, even though it was introduced later by the Spanish.

- 1 tablespoon chili powder
- ½ teaspoon salt
- 4 (4-ounce) skinned, boned chicken breast halves
- Cooking spray
- 6 (6-inch) corn tortillas
- 1 (15-ounce) can black beans, drained
- 1 tablespoon Dried-Chile Puree (page 253)
- ¾ cup Tomatillo Puree (page 253)
- ⅓ cup chopped green onions

1. Prepare grill or broiler.
2. Combine chili powder and salt; rub over both sides of chicken. Place chicken on a grill rack or broiler pan coated with cooking spray; cook 5 minutes on each side or until done. Cool slightly, and coarsely chop.
3. Preheat oven to 350°.
4. Place tortillas directly on middle rack in oven. Bake at 350° for 7 minutes (tortillas should be slightly pliable). Mash beans in a microwave-safe bowl to desired consistency; stir in Dried-Chile Puree. Microwave at HIGH 30 seconds or until hot. Divide bean mixture evenly among tortillas; top with chicken. Spoon 2 tablespoons Tomatillo Puree over chicken on each tostada; sprinkle each with about 1 tablespoon onions. Yield: 6 servings.

CALORIES 215 (10% from fat); FAT 2.5g (sat 0.5g, mono 0.5g, poly 0.8g); PROTEIN 23.6g; CARB 25.6g; FIBER 4.4g; CHOL 44mg; IRON 2.4mg; SODIUM 458mg; CALC 77mg

An Enduring Appetite

From the dawn of humankind to the birth of a new millennium, the search for and enjoyment of meat has been a constant. Today, its presence still defines a meal, and its flavors are what we crave.

Meat is so much a part of the American diet that many people consider meals "real" only if they include meat or poultry.

Pigs were the first animals to become a staple in the New World. By 1627, hogs were "innumerable" in Jamestown, Virginia, and by the end of the century, the average American farming family had four or five pigs.

Cattle took a bit longer to become established. As the East Coast grew crowded, people moved west not only in search of gold but also for land to raise meat and crops. Before the United States turned 100, rail hubs in cities like Kansas City had become terminals for the huge cattle drives that began in Texas and ultimately involved millions of heads of cattle.

Chicken, which used to be harder to raise in significant quantities than pork and beef, was a relatively slow starter in the United States. But chicken-farming operations have become far more efficient, creating a product that's inexpensive, relatively low in fat, cooks quickly and easily, and is generally perceived as healthful. In 1992, chicken surpassed beef as the most widely eaten meat in the country.

Lean meat is one of the most nutrient-dense foods, containing all the essential amino acids (those that our bodies are incapable of synthesizing from other foods) and a slew of micronutrients in one package. Even if the emphasis has shifted from red meat to white, the taste remains. And will endure.

STIR-FRIED PORK WITH BROCCOLI AND CASHEWS

Lean pork tenderloin allows liberal use of cashews and a splash of sesame oil.

Cooking spray
4 cups vertically sliced sweet onion
2 cups small broccoli florets
1 (1-pound) pork tenderloin, cut into thin slices
¼ teaspoon crushed red pepper
½ cup chopped green onions
1 tablespoon sugar
1 tablespoon minced peeled fresh ginger
3 garlic cloves, minced
½ cup fat-free, less-sodium chicken broth
3 tablespoons low-sodium soy sauce
½ cup chopped dry-roasted cashews
2 teaspoons dark sesame oil
2 cups hot cooked long-grain rice

1. Place a large nonstick skillet coated with cooking spray over medium-high heat. Add sweet onion; cook 8 minutes, stirring occasionally. Remove sweet onion from pan; place in a bowl. Recoat pan with cooking spray. Add broccoli; stir-fry 3 minutes. Add broccoli to sweet onion. Recoat pan with cooking spray. Add pork and red pepper; stir-fry 4 minutes or until pork loses its pink color. Reduce heat. Stir in green onions, sugar, ginger, and garlic; cook 30 seconds, stirring constantly. Stir in onion mixture, chicken broth, soy sauce, and cashews; cook 1 minute. Drizzle with sesame oil. Serve with rice. Yield: 4 servings (serving size: 1¼ cups stir-fry and ½ cup rice).

CALORIES 441 (28% from fat); FAT 13.5g (sat 2.9g, mono 6.8g, poly 2.8g); PROTEIN 32.5g; CARB 48.7g; FIBER 5.4g; CHOL 74mg; IRON 4.5mg; SODIUM 606mg; CALC 86mg

PORK WITH APPLES AND ONIONS

This quintessential New England fall dish is light, due in part to today's leaner pork. The apples and onions turn into an almost chunky applesauce.

6 (6-ounce) center-cut pork chops (about ¾ inch thick)
1 teaspoon salt
½ teaspoon black pepper
Cooking spray
1 tablespoon olive oil
2 large onions, each cut into 8 wedges
⅔ cup Sauvignon Blanc or other dry white wine
4 Granny Smith apples, peeled and each cut into 6 wedges (about 1½ pounds)
1 tablespoon fresh lemon juice
Chopped fresh parsley (optional)

1. Sprinkle both sides of chops with salt and pepper. Place a Dutch oven coated with cooking spray over medium-high heat until hot. Add 3 chops; cook 4 minutes on each side or until lightly browned. Remove chops from pan. Repeat procedure with remaining chops. Remove chops from pan; set aside.
2. Heat oil in pan. Add onion; cook 8 minutes or until golden brown, stirring occasionally. Add wine; cook 1 minute. Return chops to pan, nestling them into onion mixture. Reduce heat to medium-low. Cover and cook 15 minutes. Add apple to pan. Cover and cook 25 minutes or until chops are tender. Remove chops from pan; keep chops warm. Increase heat, and bring apple mixture to a boil; cook 10 minutes or until liquid almost evaporates. Stir in lemon juice. Serve chops with apple mixture. Sprinkle with parsley, if desired. Yield: 6 servings (serving size: 1 pork chop and ¾ cup apple mixture).

CALORIES 324 (35% from fat); FAT 12.7g (sat 3.8g, mono 6.2g, poly 1.4g); PROTEIN 31.7g; CARB 20.3g; FIBER 3.8g; CHOL 88mg; IRON 1.7mg; SODIUM 488mg; CALC 32mg

MOROCCAN-STYLE CHICKEN THIGHS

*Chicken thighs are quite popular now
because they're more flavorful than the
white meat and they stand up to bolder
spices. If you can find boned thighs, all
the easier. Serve with couscous.*

  2 teaspoons ground cumin
  1 teaspoon ground cardamom
  ½ teaspoon salt
  ½ teaspoon ground cinnamon
  ¼ teaspoon ground red pepper
  ¼ teaspoon black pepper
  8 chicken thighs (about
     2 pounds), skinned
  1 tablespoon olive oil
  1 (15-ounce) can chickpeas
     (garbanzo beans), drained
  1 (14.5-ounce) can no-salt-added
     diced tomatoes, drained
  2 cups (¼-inch) sliced zucchini
  ½ cup fat-free, less-sodium chicken
     broth
  1 tablespoon fresh lemon juice
  Cilantro sprigs (optional)

1. Combine first 6 ingredients in a
small bowl; rub chicken with cumin
mixture. Heat oil in a large nonstick
skillet over medium-high heat. Add
chicken, and sauté 3 minutes on each
side. Add chickpeas and tomatoes;
cook 5 minutes. Add zucchini and
broth; bring to a boil. Cover, reduce
heat, and simmer 10 minutes. Stir in
lemon juice. Garnish with cilantro,
if desired. Yield: 4 servings (serving
size: 2 chicken thighs and ½ cup
chickpea mixture).

CALORIES 338 (29% from fat); FAT 10.8g (sat 2.1g, mono 4.7g,
poly 2.5g); PROTEIN 34.9g; CARB 25.9g; FIBER 3.1g;
CHOL 113mg; IRON 4.8mg; SODIUM 625mg; CALC 95mg

POLPETTE AND ORZO IN BROTH

*Spaghetti and meatballs (polpette)
were a midcentury hit, but these
lighter, truly Italian staples are lovely
en brodo, or in broth. Serve with some
crusty bread and a green salad.*

  3 (16-ounce) cans fat-free,
     less-sodium chicken broth
  1 (1-ounce) slice Italian bread
  ½ cup 1% low-fat milk
  1 pound ground sirloin
  ½ cup minced fresh onion
  ½ cup (2 ounces) grated fresh
     Parmesan cheese, divided
  ¼ cup chopped fresh parsley
  ¼ teaspoon salt
  ¼ teaspoon black pepper
  1 cup shredded carrot
  2 cups hot cooked orzo (about 1
     cup uncooked rice-shaped pasta)
  ¼ cup plus 2 tablespoons chopped
     fresh parsley

1. Bring broth to a simmer in a Dutch
oven (do not boil). Keep warm over
low heat.
2. Soak bread in milk 5 minutes, and
squeeze moisture from bread. Discard
milk. Combine bread, beef, minced
onion, ¼ cup cheese, ¼ cup parsley,
salt, and pepper in a bowl. Shape mixture into 24 (1½-inch) meatballs. Add
meatballs and carrot to broth, and
bring to a boil. Reduce heat, and simmer 8 minutes. Stir in orzo, and cook 2
minutes. Sprinkle with ¼ cup cheese
and ¼ cup plus 2 tablespoons parsley.
Yield: 6 servings (serving size: 4 meatballs, 1 cup broth, 2 teaspoons cheese,
and 1 tablespoon parsley).

CALORIES 337 (19% from fat); FAT 7.2g (sat 3.2g, mono 2.5g,
poly 0.5g); PROTEIN 28.9g; CARB 36.6g; FIBER 2.1g;
CHOL 53mg; IRON 4.1mg; SODIUM 823mg; CALC 165mg

ROAST STRIP LOIN OF BEEF WITH ROAST VEGETABLES

*Kosher salt is coarser than table salt,
but you can use table salt if you prefer.*

Vegetables:

  2 cups (1-inch-thick) sliced carrot
  3 cups peeled sweet potato, cut into
     1-inch pieces (about 1 pound)
  2 cups trimmed Brussels sprouts,
     halved (about 12 ounces)
  1 large onion, cut into 8 wedges
  2 teaspoons vegetable oil
  ¼ teaspoon kosher salt
  ⅛ teaspoon black pepper

Roast:

  2 teaspoons chopped fresh or
     ½ teaspoon dried rosemary
  ½ teaspoon kosher salt
  ¼ teaspoon coarsely ground black
     pepper
  2 garlic cloves, minced
  1 (3-pound) boned beef strip loin
     roast
  Cooking spray

Glaze:

  3 tablespoons stone-ground or
     country-style Dijon mustard
  2 tablespoons honey

1. Preheat oven to 400°.
2. To prepare vegetables, place carrot
in a microwave-safe bowl, and microwave at HIGH 2 minutes. Combine carrot, sweet potato, and next 5
ingredients; toss well to coat. Set aside.
3. To prepare roast, combine rosemary,
½ teaspoon kosher salt, coarsely
ground black pepper, and garlic. Trim
fat from roast, and rub top of roast
with rosemary mixture. Place roast on
a broiler pan coated with cooking
spray. Insert a meat thermometer into
thickest part of roast. Arrange vegetables around roast. Bake at 400° for 1
hour or until thermometer registers
145° (medium-rare) to 160° (medium).
Place roast on a platter; cover with foil.
Let stand 15 minutes.

4. To prepare glaze, combine mustard and honey. Drizzle over vegetables; toss gently. Bake at 400° for 10 minutes. Yield: 6 servings (serving size: 3 ounces beef and about 1 cup vegetables).

CALORIES 289 (31% from fat); FAT 9.8g (sat 3.6g, mono 3.8g, poly 1.7g); PROTEIN 19.5g; CARB 32.1g; FIBER 5.1g; CHOL 76mg; IRON 3.3mg; SODIUM 614mg; CALC 53mg

CHICKEN IN A POT

This dish couples old-fashioned cooking with a modern penchant for lighter fare. You'll have 3 cups of chicken stock left over. Pour it into jars three-fourths full, and freeze up to three months.

    10 black peppercorns
     4 whole allspice
     4 thyme sprigs
     1 bay leaf
    10 small red potatoes (about
          1 pound)
     5 carrots, cut into 1-inch-thick
          pieces (about ¾ pound)
     2 leeks, trimmed and each cut
          into 3 pieces
     2 onions, quartered
     3 (16-ounce) cans fat-free,
          less-sodium chicken broth
          or 6 cups water
     1 (3-pound) chicken
     ½ teaspoon salt
     ¼ teaspoon black pepper
    1½ tablespoons butter or stick
          margarine
     2 tablespoons all-purpose flour
     ½ cup 2% reduced-fat milk
    Minced fresh chives (optional)

1. Place first 4 ingredients on a double layer of cheesecloth. Gather edges of cheesecloth together, and tie securely. Place cheesecloth bag, potatoes, and next 7 ingredients in a large Dutch oven or stockpot over medium-high heat. Bring to a boil; reduce heat, and simmer, uncovered, 25 minutes. Turn chicken over, and cook 20 minutes or until vegetables are tender and chicken is done.
2. Remove chicken and vegetables with a slotted spoon, and keep warm.

Discard cheesecloth bag. Return broth mixture to a boil, and cook until reduced to 4 cups (about 15 minutes). Remove from heat. Reserve 3 cups broth mixture for another use.
3. Melt butter in a saucepan over medium heat. Stir in flour; reduce heat, and cook 1 minute. Add 1 cup broth, and stir with a whisk. Stir in milk. Cook until thick (about 8 minutes), stirring frequently.
4. Remove meat from bones; discard bones and skin. Chop chicken. Arrange vegetables on a platter, and top with chicken. Spoon sauce over chicken and vegetables. Sprinkle with chives, if desired. Yield: 5 servings.

CALORIES 401 (25% from fat); FAT 11.1g (sat 4.4g, mono 3.6g, poly 1.9g); PROTEIN 35.2g; CARB 39.1g; FIBER 5.7g; CHOL 92mg; IRON 4mg; SODIUM 979mg; CALC 118mg

PAN-BROILED FILLETS

     ¼ teaspoon kosher salt
     4 (4-ounce) beef tenderloin steaks
          (1 inch thick)
     4 garlic cloves, minced
     1 cup medium dry sherry
     1 tablespoon low-sodium soy sauce
     ¼ teaspoon black pepper
     1 tablespoon butter or stick
          margarine
     1 tablespoon grated peeled fresh
          ginger (optional)

1. Sprinkle salt in a large cast-iron skillet over medium-high heat. Add steaks; sauté 2 minutes on each side. Remove from pan. Add garlic to pan; sauté 30 seconds. Add sherry; boil 30 seconds, scraping pan to loosen browned bits. Return steaks to pan; cook 2 minutes. Add soy sauce and pepper. Remove steaks to serving plates. Remove pan from heat; stir butter into sherry mixture until blended. Spoon sauce evenly over steaks. Top each steak with ¾ teaspoon ginger, if desired. Yield: 4 servings (serving size: 1 steak and about 1 tablespoon sauce).

CALORIES 211 (44% from fat); FAT 10.3g (sat 4.8g, mono 3.7g, poly 0.5g); PROTEIN 24.1g; CARB 3.7g; FIBER 0.1g; CHOL 78mg; IRON 3.4mg; SODIUM 290mg; CALC 19mg

HAPPY ENDINGS

Eternal Verities

You thought you'd evolve out of your sweet tooth? Better take some of these classic desserts and snacks into the next few eons.

LEMON-POPPY SEED POUND CAKE

    Cooking spray
     1 teaspoon all-purpose flour
     1 cup granulated sugar
     ⅓ cup butter or stick margarine,
          softened
     2 large egg whites
     1 large egg
     1 tablespoon grated lemon rind
     1 teaspoon vanilla extract
    1⅔ cups all-purpose flour
     2 tablespoons poppy seeds
     1 teaspoon baking powder
     ¼ teaspoon baking soda
     ⅛ teaspoon salt
     ¾ cup low-fat buttermilk
     ⅔ cup powdered sugar
     4 teaspoons lemon juice

1. Preheat oven to 350°.
2. Coat an 8 x 4-inch loaf pan with cooking spray; dust with 1 teaspoon flour. Set aside.
3. Beat granulated sugar and butter at medium speed of a mixer until well-blended (about 4 minutes). Add egg whites and egg, 1 at a time, beating well after each addition. Beat in lemon rind and vanilla. Lightly spoon 1⅔ cups flour into dry measuring cups; level with a knife. Combine 1⅔ cups flour and next 4 ingredients, stirring well with a whisk. Add flour mixture to sugar mixture alternately with buttermilk, beginning and ending with flour mixture. Pour batter into prepared pan; bake at 350° for 1 hour or until a wooden pick inserted in center comes

Continued

out clean. Cool in pan 10 minutes on a wire rack; remove from pan. Poke holes in top of cake using a skewer. Combine powdered sugar and lemon juice in a small bowl; brush over warm cake. Cool completely. Yield: 12 servings (serving size: 1 slice).

CALORIES 226 (27% from fat); FAT 6.7g (sat 3.6g, mono 1.8g, poly 0.8g); PROTEIN 3.8g; CARB 38.2g; FIBER 0.6g; CHOL 32mg; IRON 1.1mg; SODIUM 166mg; CALC 70mg

RICOTTA CHEESECAKE

Crust:

1½ cups all-purpose flour
3 tablespoons sugar
1½ teaspoons grated lemon rind
½ teaspoon baking powder
⅛ teaspoon salt
3 tablespoons chilled butter or stick margarine, cut into small pieces
3 tablespoons ice water
1 large egg, lightly beaten

Filling:

1 (15-ounce) carton fat-free ricotta cheese
1 (8-ounce) block ⅓-less-fat cream cheese
¼ cup all-purpose flour
¾ cup sugar
½ cup plain fat-free yogurt
2 teaspoons lemon rind
1½ teaspoons vanilla extract
2 large eggs
2 large egg whites
Cooking spray
3 tablespoons golden raisins

1. To prepare crust, lightly spoon 1½ cups flour into dry measuring cups; level with a knife. Combine 1½ cups flour, 3 tablespoons sugar, and next 3 ingredients in a bowl; cut in butter with a pastry blender or 2 knives until mixture resembles coarse meal. Add ice water and 1 egg; toss with a fork until moist. Gently press mixture into a 4-inch circle on heavy-duty plastic wrap;

cover with additional plastic wrap. Roll dough, still covered, into an 11-inch circle; chill 10 minutes.
2. To prepare filling, place cheeses in a bowl, and beat at medium speed of a mixer until smooth. Lightly spoon ¼ cup flour into a dry measuring cup, and level with a knife. Add ¼ cup flour and next 6 ingredients to cheese mixture; beat until smooth.
3. Preheat oven to 325°.
4. Remove 1 sheet of plastic wrap from dough. Fit dough into a 9-inch springform pan coated with cooking spray. Remove top sheet of plastic wrap. Press dough against bottom and sides of pan. Pour filling into crust. Sprinkle with raisins. Bake at 325° for 1 hour and 20 minutes or until filling is set. Loosen cake from sides of pan using a narrow metal spatula; cool on a wire rack. Yield: 10 servings (serving size: 1 wedge).

CALORIES 316 (30% from fat); FAT 10.6g (sat 6g, mono 3.2g, poly 0.6g); PROTEIN 13.9g; CARB 42.9g; FIBER 0.7g; CHOL 98mg; IRON 1.4mg; SODIUM 241mg; CALC 140mg

PEAR-ALMOND CRUMBLE

½ cup all-purpose flour
½ cup packed brown sugar
¼ cup chilled butter or stick margarine, cut into small pieces
2 tablespoons chopped almonds, toasted
7 cups cubed peeled Anjou, Bartlett, or Bosc pear (about 3 pounds)
1 tablespoon fresh lemon juice
2 cups vanilla fat-free frozen yogurt
¼ cup fat-free caramel sundae syrup

1. Preheat oven to 375°.
2. Lightly spoon flour into a dry measuring cup; level with a knife. Combine flour and sugar in a medium bowl; cut in butter with a pastry blender or 2 knives until mixture resembles coarse meal. Stir in almonds.
3. Combine pear and lemon juice in a bowl. Spoon into an 8-inch square

baking dish; sprinkle with crumb mixture. Bake at 375° for 50 minutes or until golden brown. Spoon pear mixture into 8 bowls; top each serving with ¼ cup frozen yogurt and 1½ teaspoons syrup. Yield: 8 servings.

CALORIES 288 (23% from fat); FAT 7.2g (sat 3.7g, mono 2.3g, poly 0.5g); PROTEIN 3.2g; CARB 56.2g; FIBER 3.8g; CHOL 16mg; IRON 1.1mg; SODIUM 108mg; CALC 90mg

CARROT CUPCAKES WITH COCONUT-CREAM CHEESE FROSTING

Cupcakes:

⅔ cup granulated sugar
3 tablespoons vegetable oil
1 teaspoon vanilla extract
1 large egg
1 cup finely shredded carrot
1 (8-ounce) can crushed pineapple in juice, well-drained
1 cup all-purpose flour
1 teaspoon baking powder
¾ teaspoon ground cinnamon
¼ teaspoon baking soda
⅛ teaspoon salt
⅛ teaspoon ground nutmeg
¼ cup raisins

Frosting:

¼ cup (2 ounces) ⅓-less-fat cream cheese, chilled
1 tablespoon butter or stick margarine, softened
⅛ teaspoon imitation coconut flavor (optional)
1⅓ cups powdered sugar
3 tablespoons flaked sweetened coconut

1. Preheat oven to 350°.
2. To prepare cupcakes, beat first 4 ingredients at medium speed of a mixer until well-blended. Add carrot and pineapple; beat well. Lightly spoon flour into a dry measuring cup; level with a knife. Combine flour, baking powder, and next 4 ingredients, stirring well with a whisk. Add flour mixture

to sugar mixture; beat well. Stir in raisins.

3. Spoon batter into 12 muffin cups lined with paper liners. Bake at 350° for 20 minutes or until a wooden pick inserted in center comes out clean. Cool in pan 5 minutes on a wire rack; remove from pan. Cool on wire rack.

4. To prepare frosting, beat cream cheese, butter, and coconut flavor at medium speed of a mixer just until blended. Gradually add powdered sugar (do not overbeat). Spread frosting over cupcakes; sprinkle with coconut. Store, covered, in refrigerator. Yield: 1 dozen (serving size: 1 cupcake).

CALORIES 220 (27% from fat); FAT 6.6g (sat 2.5g, mono 1.8g, poly 1.9g); PROTEIN 2.4g; CARB 38.7g; FIBER 0.9g; CHOL 25mg; IRON 0.8mg; SODIUM 133mg; CALC 38mg

My Life in Chocolate

The No. 1 food craving among the women of the world, chocolate isn't likely to lose its ranking anytime soon.

Worshiped by Mayan Indians, sung of gloriously in Mozart's *Cosi Fan Tutte*, chocolate has always been a seducer of appetites. Still is. According to the Chocolate Manufacturers Association, Americans eat 12.1 pounds of the cocoa-based godsend per year. Apiece. And we're only 11th in world standings. The British are tops, gobbling 30 pounds each.

Emperor Montezuma of Mexico, believing chocolate was an aphrodisiac, reportedly consumed his chocolate drink before entering his harem. And during World War II, the U.S. government rationed pocket chocolate bars to soldiers to tide them over when food was scarce. Today, the U.S. Army rations include three 4-ounce chocolate bars.

OATMEAL-RAISIN COOKIES

(pictured on page 262)

½ cup granulated sugar
½ cup packed brown sugar
⅓ cup butter or stick margarine, softened
1 teaspoon vanilla extract
⅛ teaspoon salt
1 large egg
1 cup all-purpose flour
1 cup regular oats
½ cup raisins
Cooking spray

1. Preheat oven to 350°.
2. Beat first 6 ingredients at medium speed of a mixer until light and fluffy. Lightly spoon flour into a dry measuring cup, and level with a knife. Add flour and oats to egg mixture; beat until blended. Stir in raisins. Drop by level tablespoons 2 inches apart onto baking sheets coated with cooking spray. Bake at 350° for 15 minutes or until golden brown. Cool on pan 3 minutes. Remove cookies from pan; cool on wire racks. Yield: 2 dozen (serving size: 1 cookie).

CALORIES 101 (28% from fat); FAT 3.1g (sat 1.7g, mono 0.9g, poly 0.2g); PROTEIN 1.5g; CARB 17.3g; FIBER 0.6g; CHOL 16mg; IRON 0.6mg; SODIUM 43mg; CALC 10mg

CHOCOLATE-CHIP MERINGUE COOKIES

3 large egg whites
¼ teaspoon cream of tartar
¼ teaspoon salt
1 cup sugar
3 tablespoons unsweetened cocoa
3 tablespoons semisweet chocolate minichips

1. Preheat oven to 300°.
2. Beat egg whites, cream of tartar, and salt at high speed of a mixer until soft peaks form. Add sugar, 1 tablespoon at a time, beating until stiff peaks form. Sift cocoa over egg white mixture; fold in. Fold in minichips.
3. Cover a baking sheet with parchment paper; secure to baking sheet with masking tape. Drop batter by level tablespoons onto prepared baking sheet. Bake at 300° for 40 minutes or until crisp. Cool on pan on a wire rack. Remove cookies from pan. Repeat procedure with remaining batter, reusing parchment paper. Store in an airtight container. Yield: 4 dozen (serving size: 1 cookie).

CALORIES 22 (12% from fat); FAT 0.3g (sat 0.2g, mono 0.1g, poly 0g); PROTEIN 0.3g; CARB 4.7g; FIBER 0g; CHOL 0mg; IRON 0.1mg; SODIUM 16mg; CALC 1mg

MOCHA-FUDGE PUDDING CAKE

You basically have a pudding layer underneath the cakey part—so be sure you don't mistake it for being underdone.

¾ cup sugar
2 tablespoons butter or stick margarine, softened
½ cup 1% low-fat milk
1 tablespoon Kahlúa (coffee-flavored liqueur) or cold brewed coffee or water
1 cup all-purpose flour
½ cup unsweetened cocoa, divided
1½ teaspoons baking powder
⅛ teaspoon salt
Cooking spray
⅔ cup sugar
2 teaspoons instant coffee granules
1¼ cups boiling water
2¼ cups vanilla fat-free ice cream

1. Preheat oven to 350°.
2. Combine ¾ cup sugar and butter in a bowl; beat at medium speed of a mixer 3 minutes. Add milk and

Continued

liqueur; beat well. Lightly spoon flour into a dry measuring cup; level with a knife. Combine flour, ¼ cup cocoa, baking powder, and salt in a bowl; gradually add to sugar mixture, beating until well-blended. Spoon batter into an 8-inch square baking pan coated with cooking spray.

3. Combine remaining ¼ cup cocoa, ⅔ cup sugar, and coffee granules in a small bowl; sprinkle over batter. Pour boiling water over batter (do not stir). Bake at 350° for 30 minutes or until cake springs back when touched lightly in center (a wooden pick will not test clean when inserted in center). Serve warm with ice cream. Yield: 9 servings (serving size: 1 [3-inch] square and ¼ cup ice cream).

CALORIES 274 (12% from fat); FAT 3.6g (sat 2.1g, mono 1g, poly 0.2g); PROTEIN 4.9g; CARB 55.4g; FIBER 0.7g; CHOL 8mg; IRON 1.6mg; SODIUM 182mg; CALC 123mg

MINT-FUDGE TART

Crust:

32 reduced-fat chocolate wafer cookies, finely crushed
2 tablespoons butter or stick margarine, melted
1 large egg white

Filling:

⅓ cup unsweetened cocoa
1 (14-ounce) can fat-free sweetened condensed milk
½ cup (4 ounces) ⅓-less-fat cream cheese, softened
¼ cup fat-free chocolate sundae syrup (such as Smucker's)
1 teaspoon vanilla extract
¼ teaspoon mint extract
2 large eggs

Topping:

8 crème de menthe chocolaty mint thins (such as Andes)
1½ cups frozen reduced-calorie whipped topping, thawed

1. Preheat oven to 350°.
2. To prepare crust, combine first 3 ingredients in a bowl, and toss with a fork until moist. Firmly press mixture in bottom of a 9-inch springform pan.
3. To prepare filling, beat cocoa and milk at medium speed of a mixer until blended. Add cream cheese; beat well. Add syrup, extracts, and eggs; beat just until smooth. Pour mixture into prepared crust. Bake at 350° for 35 minutes or until set. (Do not overbake.) Cool completely on a wire rack. Cover and chill 4 hours.
4. To prepare topping, shave long edge of mint thins using a vegetable peeler. Spread whipped topping over tart; sprinkle with shaved mint thins. Yield: 10 servings (serving size: 1 wedge).

CALORIES 301 (30% from fat); FAT 9.9g (sat 5.1g, mono 2g, poly 0.7g); PROTEIN 7.8g; CARB 44.5g; FIBER 0.1g; CHOL 63mg; IRON 1mg; SODIUM 185mg; CALC 131mg

CHOCOLATE-TRUFFLE SOUFFLÉS

(pictured on page 261)

Crème de cacao is a dark chocolate-flavored liqueur. But any fruit, nut, or coffee-flavored liqueur will work. If you prefer to leave out the liqueur, replace it with an equal amount of chocolate syrup.

Cooking spray
2 tablespoons granulated sugar
1 cup 1% low-fat milk
¾ cup powdered sugar
½ cup unsweetened cocoa
2 tablespoons all-purpose flour
¼ teaspoon salt
1 ounce semisweet chocolate, chopped
3 tablespoons crème de cacao (chocolate-flavored liqueur) or chocolate syrup
2 large egg yolks
4 large egg whites
¼ teaspoon cream of tartar
⅓ cup powdered sugar
1 tablespoon powdered sugar

1. Coat 8 (6-ounce) ramekins with cooking spray; sprinkle with granulated sugar. Place on a baking sheet; set aside.
2. Combine milk, ¾ cup powdered sugar, cocoa, flour, and salt in a medium, heavy saucepan, and cook 5 minutes over medium heat, stirring constantly with a whisk until mixture thickens and comes to a boil. Remove from heat; add chocolate, stirring until melted. Stir in liqueur. Gradually add chocolate mixture to egg yolks in a bowl, stirring well. Return mixture to pan. Cook 1 minute over medium heat, stirring constantly. Spoon mixture into a large bowl; cool to room temperature, stirring occasionally.
3. Preheat oven to 375°.
4. Beat egg whites and cream of tartar at high speed of a mixer until foamy. Add ⅓ cup powdered sugar, 1 tablespoon at a time, beating until stiff peaks form. Gently stir one-fourth of egg white mixture into chocolate mixture; gently fold in remaining egg white mixture. Spoon batter evenly into prepared ramekins. Bake at 375° for 23 minutes or until puffy and set. Sprinkle soufflés with 1 tablespoon powdered sugar. Serve immediately. Yield: 8 servings.

CALORIES 172 (19% from fat); FAT 3.6g (sat 1.8g, mono 1.2g, poly 0.3g); PROTEIN 5.4g; CARB 30.3g; FIBER 0.1g; CHOL 56mg; IRON 1.3mg; SODIUM 120mg; CALC 55mg

*Chocolate-Truffle Soufflé,
page 260*

Curried Mussel Pilaf, page 268

Oatmeal-Raisin Cookies,
page 259

Shrimp-and-Guacamole Tostadas,
page 254

Portobello-Layered Mashed Potatoes, page 265

Squash-and-Mushroom Tostadas, page 254

Cheddar-Potato Bread,
page 265

Chicken Cacciatore, Sicilian Style,
page 247

Spudnik

What is it with potatoes, the second most-consumed food in America? Just taste, versatility, nutrition—oh yeah, and a cushy job with NASA.

Interest in America's favorite vegetable is on the rise. Literally. In 1995, the potato soared into space on the space shuttle *Columbia*. The potato was the first food ever to be grown in zero gravity. Why all the interest from the National Aeronautics and Space Administration? Same as for you and me: Potatoes are tasty, easy to prepare, and full of nutrients, including potassium, complex carbohydrates, iron, and vitamins such as C, niacin, thiamine, and B6.

The potato is the second most-consumed food in the United States, trailing only milk products. The average American eats 120 pounds of potatoes a year, almost 365 per person, or one a day. Potatoes can grow in more than a dozen climates, and do in 130 countries, from the ocean's edge in Sri Lanka to mountain slopes 13,000 feet above sea level near Lima, Peru, home of the International Potato Center. The center sees potatoes as an underused resource capable of nourishing increasing numbers of the world's poor.

CHEDDAR-POTATO BREAD

(pictured on page 264)

This sensational bread is even better toasted the next day. The shredded cheese blends into the dough, but the diced pieces create yummy pockets of melted cheese. Because some of the cheese is kneaded into the dough, this bread is not ideal for bread machine preparation.

  2 cups (1-inch) cubed peeled baking potato (about ¾ pound)
  1 package dry yeast (about 2¼ teaspoons)
  1 teaspoon sugar
3½ cups bread flour, divided
  ¾ cup (3 ounces) shredded sharp Cheddar cheese
  1 tablespoon olive oil
1½ teaspoons salt
  1 teaspoon dry mustard
  ¼ teaspoon ground red pepper
Cooking spray
  ½ cup (2 ounces) diced sharp Cheddar cheese

1. Cook potato in boiling water 10 minutes or until very tender. Drain potato in a colander over a bowl, reserving 1 cup cooking liquid. Mash potato with a fork until smooth. Cool cooking liquid to 100° to 110°. Dissolve yeast and sugar in cooled cooking liquid in a large bowl; let stand 5 minutes. Lightly spoon flour into dry measuring cups; level with a knife. Add 2½ cups flour, mashed potato, shredded cheese, oil, salt, mustard, and pepper to yeast mixture; stir until well-blended.
2. Turn dough out onto a floured surface. Knead until smooth and elastic (about 10 minutes); add ½ cup flour, 1 tablespoon at a time, to prevent dough from sticking to hands (dough will feel tacky).
3. Place dough in a large bowl coated with cooking spray, turning to coat top. Cover dough, and let rise in a warm place (85°), free from drafts, 45 minutes or until doubled in size. (Press two fingers into dough. If indentation remains, dough has risen enough.) Punch dough down; sprinkle with diced cheese. Knead dough until cheese is well-blended (about 5 minutes), and add enough of remaining flour, 1 tablespoon at a time, to prevent dough from sticking to hands. Roll dough into a 14 x 7-inch rectangle on a lightly floured surface. Roll up rectangle tightly, starting with a short edge, pressing firmly to eliminate air pockets, and pinch seam and ends to seal. Place roll, seam side down, in a 9 x 5-inch loaf pan coated with cooking spray. Cover and let rise 40 minutes or until doubled in size.
4. Preheat oven to 375°.
5. Uncover dough. Bake at 375° for 55 minutes or until loaf is browned on top and sounds hollow when tapped. Remove from pan; cool on a wire rack. Yield: 1 loaf, 16 servings per loaf (serving size: 1 slice).

CALORIES 175 (23% from fat); FAT 4.4g (sat 2.1g, mono 1.5g, poly 0.4g); PROTEIN 6.4g; CARB 26.9g; FIBER 0.5g; CHOL 9mg; IRON 1.5mg; SODIUM 203mg; CALC 70mg

PORTOBELLO-LAYERED MASHED POTATOES

(pictured on page 263)

Yukon gold potatoes are moist and make excellent mashed potatoes, but baking potatoes will work, too. For better flavor, cook the potatoes before peeling.

  3 pounds Yukon gold potatoes
  ¾ cup low-fat buttermilk
  1 teaspoon salt, divided
  ¼ teaspoon ground nutmeg
  ¼ teaspoon black pepper, divided
1½ tablespoons butter or stick margarine
  ¼ cup minced fresh onion
  2 garlic cloves, minced
3½ cups finely chopped portobello mushroom caps (about 1 pound)
  ⅓ cup chopped fresh or 2 tablespoons dried basil
Cooking spray
  ¼ cup (1 ounce) grated fresh Parmesan cheese
  ½ teaspoon paprika
  ½ teaspoon olive oil

1. Place potatoes in a saucepan, and cover with water; bring to a boil. Reduce heat, and simmer 30 minutes or until tender; drain, reserving ½ cup

Continued

cooking liquid. Cool and peel potatoes; mash. Add reserved cooking liquid, buttermilk, ¾ teaspoon salt, nutmeg, and ⅛ teaspoon pepper, and beat at medium speed of a mixer until smooth.

2. Melt butter in a medium nonstick skillet over medium-high heat. Add onion and garlic; sauté 2 minutes. Add mushrooms; cook 2 minutes without stirring. Cook until liquid almost evaporates (about 4 minutes), stirring frequently. Remove from heat, and stir in remaining ¼ teaspoon salt, ⅛ teaspoon pepper, and basil.

3. Preheat oven to 375°.

4. Spread one-third of potato mixture in an 8-inch square baking dish or 2-quart casserole coated with cooking spray. Spread half of mushroom mixture over potato mixture; repeat layers, ending with potato mixture. Sprinkle with cheese and paprika; drizzle with oil. Bake at 375° for 25 minutes. Yield: 8 servings (serving size: about 1 cup).

CALORIES 223 (17% from fat); FAT 4.3g (sat 2.3g, mono 1.2g, poly 0.3g); PROTEIN 6.7g; CARB 39.9g; FIBER 3.3g; CHOL 8mg; IRON 1.4mg; SODIUM 394mg; CALC 88mg

CURRIED POTATO GRATIN

4 cups thinly sliced red potato (about 3 pounds)
2½ cups 1% low-fat milk
⅓ cup all-purpose flour
2 teaspoons butter or stick margarine
¼ cup sliced green onions
1 tablespoon curry powder
1 garlic clove, crushed
½ cup plain low-fat yogurt
½ cup tomato sauce
½ teaspoon salt
Cooking spray
¼ cup (1 ounce) grated fresh Parmesan cheese

1. Place potato in a large saucepan; cover with water. Bring to a boil; cook 15 minutes or until tender. Drain and cool.

2. Preheat oven to 425°.

3. Combine milk and flour in a small bowl; stir with a whisk. Melt butter in a medium saucepan over medium heat. Add onions, curry powder, and garlic. Cook 1 minute. Stir in milk mixture, and cook until thick (about 1 minute), stirring frequently. Remove from heat. Stir in yogurt, tomato sauce, and salt. Arrange 2 cups potato in an 11 x 7-inch baking dish coated with cooking spray. Spoon half of sauce over potato. Repeat layers with remaining potato and sauce. Sprinkle with cheese. Bake at 425° for 30 minutes or until golden brown. Let stand 10 minutes. Yield: 8 servings (serving size: ½ cup).

CALORIES 218 (14% from fat); FAT 3.3g (sat 1.9g, mono 0.9g, poly 0.2g); PROTEIN 9.2g; CARB 38.9g; FIBER 3.8g; CHOL 9mg; IRON 2.9mg; SODIUM 368mg; CALC 196mg

JAMAICAN JERK CHICKEN HASH

Jerk chicken, a traditional dish of the Caribbean, almost always contains hot peppers, thyme, and allspice. Our version is milder, but full of flavor.

¼ cup chopped green onions
2 tablespoons chopped peeled fresh ginger
1 tablespoon chopped jalapeño pepper
1 tablespoon fresh lime juice
1 tablespoon dark rum
1 tablespoon molasses
1 teaspoon ground allspice
½ teaspoon salt
½ teaspoon dried thyme
2 garlic cloves, crushed
8 skinned, boned chicken thighs (about 1½ pounds)
3 cups (½-inch) cubed peeled baking potato (about 1 pound)
2 teaspoons vegetable oil
⅔ cup evaporated low-fat milk
¼ teaspoon salt
Chopped fresh parsley (optional)

1. Combine first 10 ingredients in a blender, and process until smooth. Combine green onion mixture and chicken in a large zip-top plastic bag;

seal and marinate in refrigerator 24 hours, turning bag occasionally.

2. Place potato in a saucepan, and cover with water; bring to a boil. Reduce heat, and simmer 15 minutes or until tender; drain. Cool.

3. Heat oil in a large nonstick skillet over medium heat. Add chicken and marinade; cook 5 minutes on each side or until done. Remove chicken from pan; chop. Add chicken, potato, milk, and ¼ teaspoon salt to pan; cook 5 minutes or until thoroughly heated, stirring occasionally. Garnish with parsley, if desired. Yield: 4 servings (serving size: 1 cup).

CALORIES 368 (24% from fat); FAT 9.8g (sat 2.4g, mono 3g, poly 3g); PROTEIN 38.9g; CARB 30.1g; FIBER 2.2g; CHOL 148mg; IRON 3.3mg; SODIUM 644mg; CALC 158mg

BAKED BASQUE POTATOES

Bell peppers and sherry vinegar give these potatoes their distinctive flavor. Either long white or russet potatoes will work in this recipe.

6 cups (1-inch) cubed peeled potato (about 2 pounds)
1 (16-ounce) can fat-free, less-sodium chicken broth
4 teaspoons olive oil, divided
2 cups coarsely chopped onion
2 cups coarsely chopped green bell pepper
½ cup coarsely chopped red bell pepper
½ teaspoon salt
2 garlic cloves, minced
2 tablespoons paprika
3 tablespoons sherry vinegar or red wine vinegar
1 tablespoon chopped fresh or 1 teaspoon dried tarragon
Cooking spray
¼ cup dry breadcrumbs
¼ cup (1 ounce) grated fresh Parmesan cheese

1. Preheat oven to 400°.

2. Combine potato and chicken broth in a large saucepan; bring to a boil. Cover, reduce heat, and simmer 12

minutes. Drain potato through a sieve into a large bowl, reserving 1 cup cooking liquid.

3. Heat 2 teaspoons oil in a large non-stick skillet over medium heat. Add onion, bell peppers, salt, and garlic; sauté 2 minutes. Stir in ¼ cup reserved cooking liquid and paprika; cover and cook 8 minutes or until peppers are tender. Stir in potato, ¾ cup reserved cooking liquid, vinegar, and tarragon; bring to a boil, stirring to coat. Spoon potato mixture into a 2-quart casserole coated with cooking spray. Combine breadcrumbs and cheese, and sprinkle over potato mixture. Drizzle bread-crumb mixture with 2 teaspoons oil. Bake at 400° for 25 minutes or until golden brown. Yield: 6 servings (serving size: about 1 cup).

CALORIES 240 (20% from fat); FAT 5.4g (sat 1.4g, mono 2.8g, poly 0.8g); PROTEIN 7.9g; CARB 40.3g; FIBER 5g; CHOL 3mg; IRON 3mg; SODIUM 527mg; CALC 101mg

RUM-SWEET POTATO FLAN

The orange-fleshed sweet potato is part of the morning glory family and not officially related to potatoes, but we couldn't resist turning to it here for a terrific dessert.

    3   cups (1-inch) cubed peeled
        sweet potato (about 1 pound)
    1   cup sugar, divided
    Cooking spray
    3   tablespoons dark rum
    2   teaspoons vanilla extract
    1   teaspoon butter, melted
    ½   teaspoon ground cinnamon
    ⅛   teaspoon salt
    4   large eggs
    1   (12-ounce) can evaporated
        low-fat milk

1. Preheat oven to 300°.
2. Cook sweet potato in boiling water 10 minutes or until tender, and drain. Mash sweet potato with a fork until smooth.
3. Place ½ cup sugar in a heavy saucepan. Cook over medium heat until sugar dissolves, stirring

frequently. Continue cooking 5 minutes or until golden, stirring constantly. Immediately pour into an 8-inch round cake pan coated with cooking spray, tipping pan quickly until caramelized sugar coats bottom of pan.
4. Place sweet potato, ½ cup sugar, rum, and remaining 6 ingredients in a large bowl, stirring well with a whisk. Pour sweet potato mixture into prepared pan. Place pan in a 13 x 9-inch baking dish; add hot water to dish to a depth of 1 inch. Bake at 300° for 1½ hours or until a knife inserted in center comes out clean. Remove pan from dish; cool pan completely on a wire rack. Cover and chill at least 3 hours.
5. Loosen edge of flan with a knife or rubber spatula. Place a dessert plate, upside down, on top of pan; invert flan onto plate. Drizzle any remaining caramelized syrup over flan. Yield: 8 servings (serving size: 1 wedge).

CALORIES 241 (15% from fat); FAT 4.1g (sat 1.4g, mono 1.4g, poly 0.7g); PROTEIN 7.2g; CARB 43.8g; FIBER 1.7g; CHOL 119mg; IRON 0.8mg; SODIUM 135mg; CALC 148mg

AT LAST

Y2K? Why, Indeed?

Get over it. This country wasn't founded by people who were afraid of computers.

Earlier this century, before there were roads or even decent bridges, people built houses and either created jobs or found hard work picking asparagus or harvesting oysters. They made lives—and history. So did the native peoples and immigrants all across this land in previous centuries.

And maybe we, their descendants, will continue to do so in the future—unless, of course, everything goes to hoo-ha in a handbasket because our hallowed computers won't turn over the number 2000 this New Year's Eve at midnight.

    4   baking potatoes (about 6
        ounces each)
    4   teaspoons olive oil
    1   teaspoon dried basil
    1   teaspoon kosher salt
    ½   teaspoon dried oregano
    ¼   teaspoon black pepper
    ½   cup chopped onion
    1   tablespoon minced garlic

1. Prepare grill.
2. Cut 1 potato lengthwise into quarters; place on a 12-inch square of foil. Brush cut sides of potato with 1 teaspoon oil. Sprinkle with ¼ teaspoon basil, ¼ teaspoon salt, ⅛ teaspoon oregano, and a dash of pepper. Top with 2 tablespoons onion and ¾ teaspoon garlic. Reassemble potato; tightly wrap potato in foil. Repeat procedure with remaining potatoes and ingredients. Nestle potatoes in coals or on briquettes; grill 1 hour or until tender, turning every 15 minutes. Yield: 4 servings (serving size: 1 potato).
Note: To prepare potatoes in a conventional oven, preheat oven to 475°. Place foil-wrapped potatoes on bottom rack in oven. Bake at 475° for 1 hour or until tender.

CALORIES 237 (18% from fat); FAT 4.7g (sat 0.7g, mono 3.3g, poly 0.5g); PROTEIN 4.2g; CARB 45.6g; FIBER 3.6g; CHOL 0mg; IRON 2.6mg; SODIUM 600mg; CALC 34mg

Reclaiming a Lost Abundance

More than sustenance, fish is history, culture, and commerce—from the codfish wars that led to the settlement of North America to the complex fish farms of today.

The wild-fish harvest is diminishing at an alarming rate. Many experts blame overfishing; others, pollution; yet others, the global warming of the seas.

But not all is gloom and doom. Throughout the world, entrepreneurs are farming fish. Only a few years ago, catfish and salmon were the most widely available fish, but today many other species are being successfully farmed.

Changes in American diets account for the efforts to preserve fish. Fish taste delicious, as well as provide protein that's low in saturated fat. Fatty fish—such as bluefish, salmon, and mackerel—are rich in omega-3, a fatty acid that helps inhibit the formation of clots in the blood and is said to lower cholesterol levels.

The new farm-raised fish and shellfish may have different flavors and textures than their wild counterparts. The oils in fresh herbs or bold seasonings, such as jalapeño peppers or hot pepper flakes, will perk up the taste of fish.

MAHIMAHI WITH ASPARAGUS AND CASHEWS

You can substitute any firm-fleshed, nonoily fillets such as monkfish, tilapia, cod, or grouper.

- 1 tablespoon vegetable oil
- ⅔ cup vertically sliced onion
- 1½ tablespoons minced peeled fresh ginger
- 1 tablespoon grated orange rind
- 8 garlic cloves, minced
- 4 (6-ounce) mahimahi fillets
- 1 tablespoon grated lemon rind
- 1 tablespoon fresh lemon juice
- 1 tablespoon low-sodium soy sauce
- 1 teaspoon sherry vinegar or white wine vinegar
- 1 teaspoon honey
- ½ teaspoon dark sesame oil
- ¼ teaspoon salt
- 4 cups (1-inch) sliced asparagus (about 1¼ pounds)
- ¼ cup coarsely chopped dry-roasted cashews
- 2 tablespoons chopped fresh cilantro
- 2 cups hot cooked brown rice
- Orange rind strips (optional)

1. Heat vegetable oil in a large non-stick skillet over medium-high heat. Add onion; sauté 1 minute. Add ginger, grated orange rind, and garlic; sauté 1 minute. Add fish; cook 3 minutes on each side or until lightly browned, stirring onion mixture in pan constantly to prevent burning. Sprinkle fish with lemon rind and juice.

2. Combine soy sauce, vinegar, honey, sesame oil, and salt in a medium bowl; add asparagus and cashews, tossing well to coat. Add asparagus mixture to pan; cook 4 minutes or until fish flakes easily when tested with a fork. Sprinkle with cilantro; serve over rice. Garnish with orange rind strips, if desired. Yield: 4 servings (serving size: 5 ounces fish, ¾ cup asparagus mixture, and ½ cup rice).

CALORIES 380 (28% from fat); FAT 11.7g (sat 2.4g, mono 5.2g, poly 4.1g); PROTEIN 32.5g; CARB 39g; FIBER 5.6g; CHOL 43mg; IRON 3mg; SODIUM 371mg; CALC 78mg

CURRIED MUSSEL PILAF

(pictured on page 261)

Find curry paste in East Indian and Asian markets or the gourmet section of the supermarket. It's a blend of clarified butter, curry powder, vinegar, and other seasonings, and is often used instead of curry powder.

- 1½ cups water
- 2¼ pounds mussels, scrubbed and debearded
- 2 tablespoons fresh lime juice
- 2 teaspoons olive oil
- 3 garlic cloves, minced
- 1 to 2 tablespoons red curry paste
- 5 cups hot cooked long-grain rice
- 1 cup frozen green peas, thawed
- ½ cup sliced celery
- ¼ cup thinly sliced green onions
- ¼ cup chopped, drained, sliced water chestnuts
- 3 tablespoons light coconut milk
- 2 tablespoons chopped dry-roasted peanuts
- 2 tablespoons minced fresh basil
- ¼ teaspoon salt
- ¼ teaspoon hot pepper sauce
- ⅛ teaspoon black pepper
- Lime wedges (optional)

1. Bring water to a boil in a large Dutch oven. Add mussels; cover and cook 3 minutes or until shells open. Remove from heat, and discard any unopened shells. Cool mussels. Remove meat from shells, and discard shells. Combine meat and lime juice in a bowl; set aside.

2. Heat oil in a large nonstick skillet over medium heat. Add garlic; sauté 1 minute. Stir in curry paste, and sauté 1 minute. Stir in rice and next 5 ingredients; cook 2 minutes or until thoroughly heated. Stir in peanuts, basil, salt, pepper sauce, and black pepper. Place 1½ cups rice mixture on each of 4 plates; top each serving with ½ cup mussels. Garnish with lime wedges, if desired. Yield: 4 servings.

CALORIES 408 (13% from fat); FAT 6g (sat 1.3g, mono 3g, poly 0.8g); PROTEIN 12.7g; CARB 74.6g; FIBER 4.1g; CHOL 9mg; IRON 4.9mg; SODIUM 495mg; CALC 68mg

ULTIMATE CRAB DIP

Serve this dip with crackers or toasted French bread.

- 2 (8-ounce) blocks fat-free cream cheese
- ¼ cup low-fat plain yogurt
- 1 tablespoon prepared horseradish
- ½ teaspoon Worcestershire sauce
- ¼ teaspoon ground red pepper
- ¼ teaspoon hot sauce
- 1 tablespoon finely chopped green onions
- ½ cup chopped water chestnuts
- 1 pound lump crabmeat, shell pieces removed

1. Beat cream cheese at high speed of a mixer until smooth. Add yogurt, horseradish, Worcestershire sauce, pepper, and hot sauce; beat well. Stir in green onions, water chestnuts, and crabmeat. Yield: 4 cups (serving size: ¼ cup).

CALORIES 15 (6% from fat); FAT 0.4g (sat 0g, mono 0g, poly 0.1g); PROTEIN 10g; CARB 2g; FIBER 1.2g; CHOL 32mg; IRON 0.4mg; SODIUM 256mg; CALC 116mg

OYSTER-AND-SCALLOP STEW

The consistency of this stew is light and delicate, more like a broth than a chowder.

- 2 teaspoons butter or stick margarine
- 2 cups (¾-inch) cubed peeled baking potato (about 8 ounces)
- ¾ cup thinly sliced green onions
- ⅓ cup diced celery
- 1 jalapeño pepper, seeded and finely chopped
- 2 (1-pound) containers Standard oysters, undrained
- 1 pound sea scallops, quartered
- 1 cup frozen whole-kernel corn, thawed
- 1 cup 2% reduced-fat milk
- ½ cup diced seeded peeled tomato
- ¼ teaspoon salt
- ⅛ teaspoon black pepper

1. Melt butter in a large Dutch oven over medium heat. Add potato, onions, celery, and jalapeño pepper; cover and cook 2 minutes. Increase heat to medium-high; add oysters and scallops, and cook 5 minutes, stirring frequently. Stir in corn, milk, and tomato; bring to a boil. Cover, reduce heat, and simmer 10 minutes or until potato is tender. Sprinkle with salt and black pepper. Yield: 6 servings (serving size: 1⅓ cups).
Note: Substitute bay scallops for quartered sea scallops, if desired.

CALORIES 266 (23% from fat); FAT 6.7g (sat 2.4g, mono 1.1g, poly 1.6g); PROTEIN 26.8g; CARB 24.3g; FIBER 1.9g; CHOL 115mg; IRON 11.1mg; SODIUM 434mg; CALC 153mg

CRAB CAKES

- 1 pound lump crabmeat, shell pieces removed
- ½ cup crushed saltine crackers (about 12 crackers)
- ⅓ cup chopped fresh parsley
- ⅓ cup chopped bottled roasted red bell peppers
- 2 tablespoons plain low-fat yogurt
- 1 tablespoon water
- 1 tablespoon fresh lime juice
- ¼ teaspoon hot sauce
- ¼ teaspoon salt
- 1 large egg white, lightly beaten
- 1 tablespoon vegetable oil, divided

1. Combine all ingredients except oil in a large bowl. Divide crab mixture into 6 equal portions, shaping each into a 1-inch-thick patty. Heat 1½ teaspoons oil in a large nonstick skillet over medium-high heat. Add 3 patties; cook 4 minutes. Carefully turn patties over; cook 3 minutes or until golden. Repeat procedure with remaining 1½ teaspoons oil and remaining patties. Yield: 6 servings.

CALORIES 137 (30% from fat); FAT 4.6g (sat 0.9g, mono 1.4g, poly 1.7g); PROTEIN 16.9g; CARB 6.2g; FIBER 0.4g; CHOL 76mg; IRON 1.3mg; SODIUM 457mg; CALC 106mg

LINGUINE WITH CLAM SAUCE

Quahogs, the term Native Americans gave to hard-shelled clams, are now farm raised. Unlike many clam sauces for pasta that go heavy on the olive oil, this one teems with flavor from the reduced clam stock and vegetables.

- 1 tablespoon olive oil
- 1 cup chopped Vidalia or other sweet onion
- 4 garlic cloves, minced
- 2 cups chopped seeded plum tomato
- 1 tablespoon chopped fresh parsley
- ¼ teaspoon crushed red pepper
- 2 tablespoons water
- 36 littleneck or quahog clams
- ⅛ teaspoon salt
- 4 cups hot cooked linguine (about 8 ounces uncooked pasta)

1. Heat oil in a medium nonstick skillet over medium-high heat. Add onion and garlic; sauté 2 minutes. Add tomato, parsley, and red pepper; cook 3 minutes, and set aside.
2. Add water and clams to a large Dutch oven over medium-high heat; cover and cook 4 minutes or until shells open. Remove clams from pan, and reserve ¾ cup cooking liquid. Discard any unopened shells. Cool clams. Remove meat from shells. Place cooking liquid in pan over medium-high heat until reduced to ½ cup (about 5 minutes). Add clams, cooking liquid, and salt to tomato mixture. Serve clam sauce over pasta. Yield: 4 servings (serving size: 1 cup pasta and ½ cup sauce).

CALORIES 312 (15% from fat); FAT 5.1g (sat 0.7g, mono 2.7g, poly 0.9g); PROTEIN 14.2g; CARB 52.4g; FIBER 3.3g; CHOL 14mg; IRON 8.8mg; SODIUM 111mg; CALC 50mg

EASY BAKED FISH FILLETS

Haddock or cod is a good substitute for grouper. Adjust the baking time depending on the thickness of the fish.

1½   pounds grouper or other white fish fillets
   Cooking spray
 1   tablespoon fresh lime juice
 1   tablespoon light mayonnaise
 ⅛   teaspoon onion powder
 ⅛   teaspoon black pepper
 ½   cup fresh breadcrumbs
1½   tablespoons butter or stick margarine, melted
 2   tablespoons chopped fresh parsley

1. Preheat oven to 425°.
2. Place fish in an 11 x 7-inch baking dish coated with cooking spray. Combine lime juice, mayonnaise, onion powder, and pepper in a small bowl, and spread over fish. Sprinkle with breadcrumbs; drizzle with butter. Bake at 425° for 20 minutes or until fish flakes easily when tested with a fork. Sprinkle with parsley. Yield: 4 servings (serving size: 5 ounces fish).

CALORIES 223 (30% from fat); FAT 7.5g (sat 2.7g, mono 2g, poly 1.3g); PROTEIN 33.6g; CARB 5.3g; FIBER 0.2g; CHOL 84mg; IRON 1.8mg; SODIUM 223mg; CALC 56mg

BAKED SALMON WITH A GREEN ONION GARNISH

 1   (8-ounce) carton plain low-fat yogurt
 ½   cup diced seeded peeled cucumber
 1   tablespoon chopped fresh dill
 2   teaspoons prepared horseradish
 2   teaspoons stone-ground mustard
 1   teaspoon honey
 1   (2-pound) salmon fillet (about 2 inches thick)
   Cooking spray
 1   teaspoon dark sesame oil
 ½   teaspoon low-sodium soy sauce
 8   green onion tops, split lengthwise

1. Spoon yogurt onto several layers of heavy-duty paper towels; spread to ½-inch thickness. Cover with additional paper towels, and let stand 5 minutes. Scrape into a bowl using a rubber spatula. Combine yogurt, cucumber, and next 4 ingredients; cover and refrigerate.
2. Preheat oven to 425°.
3. Place fillet on a jelly-roll pan coated with cooking spray. Brush fillet with oil and soy sauce. Bring water to a boil in a medium saucepan; add onion strips. Cook 10 seconds or until limp. Drain. Arrange onion strips over fillet. Bake at 425° for 20 minutes or until fillet flakes easily when tested with a fork. Serve with yogurt sauce. Yield: 5 servings (serving size: about 5 ounces salmon and about 2 tablespoons yogurt sauce).

CALORIES 348 (44% from fat); FAT 16.9g (sat 3.2g, mono 7.8g, poly 3.7g); PROTEIN 40.2g; CARB 6.7g; FIBER 0.7g; CHOL 121mg; IRON 1.3mg; SODIUM 179mg; CALC 116mg

SHRIMP WITH PEPPERS

The peppers and onion simmer in a flavorful orange sauce; serve it over couscous or rice to catch every drop.

 1   tablespoon olive oil
1½   pounds large shrimp, peeled and deveined
2½   cups red bell pepper strips
 1   cup vertically sliced Walla Walla or other sweet onion
 ⅔   cup fresh orange juice (about 2 oranges)
 1   tablespoon water
 1   teaspoon cornstarch
 3   tablespoons chopped fresh basil
 2   tablespoons jalapeño jelly
 1   tablespoon fresh lime juice
 ½   teaspoon hoisin sauce
 ½   teaspoon salt
 ⅛   teaspoon freshly ground black pepper

1. Heat oil in a large nonstick skillet over medium-high heat. Add shrimp; sauté 3 minutes or until shrimp are done. Remove shrimp from pan with a slotted spoon; keep warm.

2. Add bell pepper and onion to pan; sauté 2 minutes over medium-high heat. Add orange juice; reduce heat, and simmer 3 minutes. Combine water and cornstarch in a small bowl. Add cornstarch mixture, basil, jelly, and lime juice to pan; bring to a boil. Cook 4 minutes, stirring occasionally. Add hoisin sauce; cook 1 minute. Stir in shrimp, salt, and black pepper. Yield: 4 servings (serving size: 1 cup).

CALORIES 242 (22% from fat); FAT 6g (sat 0.9g, mono 2.8g, poly 1.3g); PROTEIN 27.2g; CARB 19.5g; FIBER 1.7g; CHOL 194mg; IRON 4mg; SODIUM 499mg; CALC 85mg

SHELLFISH GUMBO

By toasting the flour in the oven, you can avoid the tediousness of standing over a cooktop browning the flour in the fat to make a roux.

 ½   cup all-purpose flour
 2   tablespoons vegetable oil
1½   cups chopped onion
 ½   cup chopped celery
 4   cups frozen cut okra
1½   cups chopped seeded peeled tomato
 ⅓   cup chopped smoked ham (about 2 ounces)
 3   (16-ounce) cans fat-free, less-sodium chicken broth
 2   garlic cloves, minced
 1   pound medium shrimp, peeled and deveined
 8   ounces lump crabmeat, shell pieces removed
 1   (8-ounce) container Standard oysters, drained
 ½   teaspoon hot sauce

1. Preheat oven to 350°.
2. Lightly spoon flour into a dry measuring cup; level with a knife. Place flour in a 9-inch pie plate; bake at 350° for 45 minutes or until light brown. Cool on a wire rack.
3. Heat oil in a large Dutch oven over medium-high heat. Stir in 3 tablespoons toasted flour, and reserve remaining flour for another use. Add onion and celery, and sauté 2 minutes.

Add okra, tomato, ham, and broth; bring to a boil. Reduce heat, and simmer 45 minutes. Stir in garlic. Bring to a boil, and add shrimp, crabmeat, and oysters. Cook 2 minutes or until shrimp are done and edges of oysters curl. Stir in hot sauce. Yield: 6 servings (serving size: 1½ cups).

CALORIES 272 (26% from fat); FAT 8g (sat 1.6g, mono 1.8g, poly 3.3g); PROTEIN 29.7g; CARB 20.4g; FIBER 2.6g; CHOL 145mg; IRON 5.1mg; SODIUM 859mg; CALC 200mg

IN SEASON

Appleseed II: The Return

Bayville's newest seedling stems from the original journey of Johnny Appleseed. Can an apple spice cake be far behind?

When Bayville, New York, residents planted a young Rambo apple seedling in front of their elementary school in April, 1999, the village joined a historic—and futuristic—movement to repopulate America with trees from the most famous botanical missionary of them all. Taken from cuttings of the last known surviving apple tree planted 150 years ago by John Chapman, also known as Johnny Appleseed, more than 10,000 young trees are literally keeping the legend growing across the United States. Rambo—whose summer fruit is large, green, firm, and tart—is just one among the more than 7,000 varieties of apples available today worldwide. No other fruit comes close to the apple for appeal and versatility. Nor does any other food make you think more of home and hearth. And now, history.

DRIED CHERRY-AND-APPLE CHUTNEY

Serve at room temperature with pork or beef.

  4 cups diced Rome or Granny Smith apple
2½ cups dried tart cherries (about ¾ pound)
  1 cup diced onion
1½ cups orange juice
  1 cup red wine vinegar
  ½ cup maple syrup
  1 tablespoon dried mint
  ½ teaspoon salt
  ½ teaspoon white pepper

1. Combine all ingredients in a large saucepan. Bring to a boil. Reduce heat, and cook, uncovered, 1 hour and 15 minutes, stirring occasionally. Remove from heat; cool. Refrigerate in airtight containers up to 2 weeks. Yield: 5 cups (serving size: ¼ cup).

CALORIES 100 (4% from fat); FAT 0.2g (sat 0g, mono 0g, poly 0.1g); PROTEIN 0.9g; CARB 26.2g; FIBER 1.8g; CHOL 1mg; IRON 1mg; SODIUM 62mg; CALC 19mg

GOLDEN SPICED FRUIT

  ½ cup golden raisins
  ½ cup Riesling or other slightly sweet white wine
  ⅓ cup sugar
1½ teaspoons grated peeled fresh ginger
  1 (1-inch) julienne-cut lemon rind strip
  1 (3-inch) cinnamon stick
1½ cups (1-inch) cubed fresh pineapple
1½ cups chopped peeled Golden Delicious apple (about 2 apples)
  2 teaspoons cornstarch
  2 teaspoons water

1. Combine first 6 ingredients in a large saucepan over medium-high heat; add pineapple and apple. Bring to a boil; reduce heat, and simmer 10 minutes or until apple is soft. Remove from heat. Cover and let stand 15 minutes. Remove lemon rind and cinnamon stick. Return fruit mixture to a simmer. Combine cornstarch and water; stir into fruit mixture. Cook until slightly thick (about 4 minutes). Yield: 2 cups (serving size: ¼ cup).

CALORIES 93 (2% from fat); FAT 0.2g (sat 0g, mono 0g, poly 0.1g); PROTEIN 0.5g; CARB 24g; FIBER 1.2g; CHOL 1mg; IRON 0.4mg; SODIUM 3mg; CALC 10mg

NUTTY APPLE SPICE CAKE WITH QUICK BUTTERSCOTCH SAUCE

It's not necessary to peel the apples in this very moist cake. The sugar produces a wonderful, crunchy top on the cake that's best eaten the day it's made.

Cake:

  2 cups sugar
  ½ cup vegetable oil
  3 large eggs
  2 cups all-purpose flour
  2 teaspoons ground cinnamon
  1 teaspoon baking soda
  ¼ teaspoon salt
  ¼ teaspoon ground nutmeg
  3 cups diced Granny Smith apple (about ¾ pound)
  ½ cup chopped walnuts or pecans, toasted
Cooking spray

Sauce:

  ⅓ cup golden raisins
  ¼ cup dark rum or apple juice
  1 (12.25-ounce) bottle fat-free butterscotch topping (such as Smucker's)

1. Preheat oven to 350°.
2. To prepare cake, beat sugar, oil, and eggs at medium speed of a mixer until well-blended. Lightly spoon flour into dry measuring cups; level with a knife. Combine flour, cinnamon, and next 3 ingredients in a small bowl. Add flour mixture to sugar mixture, beating just until blended. Fold in apple and walnuts.

Continued

3. Pour batter into a 13 x 9-inch baking pan coated with cooking spray. Bake at 350° for 55 minutes or until a wooden pick inserted in center comes out clean. Run a knife around outside edge; cool.

4. To prepare sauce, combine raisins and rum in a microwave-safe bowl; let stand 5 minutes. Stir in butterscotch topping; microwave at HIGH 45 seconds or until hot. Serve cake with sauce. Yield: 16 servings (serving size: 1 cake piece and 1½ tablespoons sauce).

Note: Cake will keep for several days in an airtight container, but crunchy top will soften.

CALORIES 324 (29% from fat); FAT 10.3g (sat 1.7g, mono 2.9g, poly 5g); PROTEIN 4.3g; CARB 57.6g; FIBER 1.6g; CHOL 41mg; IRON 1.2mg; SODIUM 170mg; CALC 23mg

APPLE-MASCARPONE PARFAITS

Mascarpone is a soft triple-cream cheese, similar in texture to cream cheese. You can substitute regular cream cheese, but the parfaits won't be as flavorful.

 1 tablespoon butter or stick margarine
 4 cups diced peeled Granny Smith apple (about 1½ pounds)
 ½ cup packed brown sugar
 2 tablespoons fresh lime juice
 2 tablespoons water
 ½ teaspoon ground ginger
 ⅛ teaspoon salt
 2 cups 2% low-fat cottage cheese
 ¼ cup (2 ounces) mascarpone cheese
 ⅓ cup granulated sugar
 1 teaspoon vanilla extract

1. Melt butter in a large nonstick skillet over medium-high heat. Add apple and next 5 ingredients, and cook 12 minutes or until liquid is almost absorbed. Remove from heat.

2. Place cottage cheese in a food processor, and process until smooth (about 2 minutes). Add mascarpone, granulated sugar, and vanilla; process until smooth. Spoon 2 tablespoons cheese mixture into each of 6 parfait glasses, and top each with 2 tablespoons apple mixture. Repeat layers in each glass with 3 tablespoons cheese mixture and 2 tablespoons apple mixture, ending with 3 tablespoons cheese mixture. Cover and chill at least 4 hours. Yield: 6 servings.

CALORIES 265 (20% from fat); FAT 5.8g (sat 3.3g, mono 1.8g, poly 0.3g); PROTEIN 10.8g; CARB 43.5g; FIBER 1.4g; CHOL 15mg; IRON 0.6mg; SODIUM 390mg; CALC 82mg

APPLE BROWN BETTY

This classic recipe came from the need to use stale bread and whatever fruit happened to be around—usually apples.

 4 (1-ounce) slices bread
 3 tablespoons butter or stick margarine, melted
 ⅓ cup granulated sugar
 ⅓ cup packed brown sugar
 1 teaspoon ground cinnamon
 ⅛ teaspoon salt
 ⅛ teaspoon ground allspice
 6 cups sliced peeled Granny Smith apple (about 2 pounds)
 ½ cup apple cider
 1 teaspoon grated lemon rind
 2 tablespoons fresh lemon juice
 1 teaspoon vanilla extract
 4 cups vanilla low-fat ice cream

1. Preheat oven to 350°.

2. Place bread in a food processor or blender; process until finely ground to measure 2 cups. Combine breadcrumbs and butter; set aside. Combine sugars and next 3 ingredients in a large bowl. Stir in apple and next 4 ingredients. Spoon 3 cups apple mixture into an 8-inch square baking dish. Sprinkle with 1 cup breadcrumb mixture. Top with remaining apple and breadcrumb mixtures. Bake at 350° for 1 hour and 15 minutes or until bubbly. Cool on a wire rack. Spoon into 8 serving bowls; top each with ½ cup ice cream. Yield: 8 servings.

CALORIES 284 (25% from fat); FAT 7.8g (sat 4.6g, mono 2.3g, poly 0.4g); PROTEIN 3.6g; CARB 55.8g; FIBER 1.9g; CHOL 21mg; IRON 0.8mg; SODIUM 200mg; CALC 121mg

CREAMY APPLE-AMARETTO RICE PUDDING

These apples are cooked down to a sauce that's then stirred into the rice pudding. Arborio rice, used for risotto, provides the creamy texture here.

 3 McIntosh, Jonathan, or Winesap apples, peeled and cut into quarters (about 1 pound)
 ¼ cup apple cider
 5 cups 2% reduced-fat milk
 ¾ cup sugar
 ⅛ teaspoon salt
 ¾ cup uncooked Arborio rice or other short-grain rice
 ⅛ teaspoon ground nutmeg
 2 tablespoons amaretto
 1 teaspoon vanilla extract
 2 large eggs

1. Combine apple and cider in a medium, heavy saucepan. Bring to a boil, stirring frequently. Cover, reduce heat to medium, and cook 20 minutes or until apple is very soft. Spoon apple mixture into a small bowl; cool.

2. Combine milk, sugar, and salt in pan; bring to a simmer. Add rice and nutmeg; stir well. Reduce heat, and simmer 40 minutes or until rice is tender, stirring occasionally. Combine apple mixture, amaretto, vanilla, and eggs in a blender or food processor; process until smooth. Stir egg mixture into rice mixture; cook until thick (about 5 minutes), stirring constantly (do not boil). Spoon rice mixture into a large bowl; cover and chill 8 hours. Yield: 8 servings (serving size: ¾ cup).

CALORIES 276 (15% from fat); FAT 4.5g (sat 2.1g, mono 1.3g, poly 0.4g); PROTEIN 8g; CARB 51.3g; FIBER 1.2g; CHOL 68mg; IRON 1.1mg; SODIUM 129mg; CALC 196mg

The Kitchen Two-Step

If you're cooking for two, these recipes are just for you—and your dinner mate.

MEDITERRANEAN TUNA CAKES WITH CITRUS MAYONNAISE

Fresh tuna makes all the difference in this recipe and is worth the expense. Pulse it about 5 times in the food processor to finely chop.

Mayonnaise:

- 2 tablespoons fat-free mayonnaise
- 1 tablespoon fat-free milk
- ½ teaspoon grated lime rind
- 1 tablespoon fresh lime juice
- ⅛ teaspoon ground cumin

Tuna cakes:

- ¾ pound tuna steaks, finely chopped
- ¾ cup finely chopped red bell pepper
- 1 tablespoon chopped fresh or 1 teaspoon dried mint
- 1 tablespoon chopped fresh cilantro
- 1 tablespoon dry breadcrumbs
- 1 tablespoon finely chopped onion
- 1 tablespoon fat-free mayonnaise
- 1 teaspoon lemon juice
- ⅛ teaspoon salt
- 2 tablespoons dry breadcrumbs
- 1 teaspoon olive oil
- Cooking spray

1. To prepare mayonnaise, combine first 5 ingredients in a small bowl. Cover and chill.
2. To prepare tuna cakes, combine tuna and next 8 ingredients in a bowl; stir until well-blended. Divide tuna mixture into 4 equal portions; shape each into a ½-inch-thick patty. Dredge patties in 2 tablespoons breadcrumbs.
3. Heat oil in a nonstick skillet coated with cooking spray over medium-high heat until hot. Add patties, and cook 3 minutes on each side or until browned. Serve with mayonnaise. Yield: 2 servings (serving size: 2 tuna cakes and 2 tablespoons mayonnaise).

CALORIES 345 (31% from fat); FAT 11.7g (sat 2.6g, mono 4.2g, poly 3.3g); PROTEIN 41.8g; CARB 16.2g; FIBER 1.3g; CHOL 65mg; IRON 3.3mg; SODIUM 582mg; CALC 41mg

CURRIED SALMON WITH TOMATO JAM

Salmon:

- 1 tablespoon all-purpose flour
- 2 teaspoons curry powder
- ½ teaspoon dried basil
- ¼ teaspoon salt
- 2 (6-ounce) skinned salmon fillets (about 1 inch thick)
- 1 teaspoon vegetable oil
- Cooking spray

Tomato jam:

- 2½ cups diced tomato
- ½ cup chopped onion
- 2 teaspoons minced peeled fresh ginger
- ¼ cup dried currants
- 1 tablespoon cider vinegar
- 1½ cups hot cooked basmati rice

1. To prepare salmon, combine first 4 ingredients in a shallow dish. Dredge salmon in flour mixture. Reserve remaining flour mixture for tomato jam.
2. Heat oil in a large nonstick skillet coated with cooking spray over medium-high heat. Add salmon; cook 4 minutes on each side or until fish is golden and flakes easily when tested with a fork. Remove from pan; keep warm.
3. To prepare tomato jam, place pan over medium-high heat. Add tomato, onion, and ginger; sauté 1 minute. Stir in reserved flour mixture, currants, and vinegar; bring to a boil. Cook until reduced to 1 cup (about 10 minutes). Spoon ¾ cup rice onto each of 2 plates; top each serving with 1 salmon fillet and ¼ cup tomato jam. Yield: 2 servings.

Note: Store remaining tomato jam in refrigerator up to 3 days.

CALORIES 545 (29% from fat); FAT 17.7g (sat 2.9g, mono 7.6g, poly 4.4g); PROTEIN 40.1g; CARB 54.9g; FIBER 3.3g; CHOL 111mg; IRON 3.8mg; SODIUM 393mg; CALC 60mg

FETA CHICKEN AND VEGETABLES

- 1 tablespoon all-purpose flour
- ½ teaspoon dried marjoram or thyme
- ¼ teaspoon black pepper
- ⅛ teaspoon salt
- 2 (4-ounce) skinned, boned chicken breast halves
- 1 teaspoon olive oil
- Cooking spray
- ⅔ cup red bell pepper strips
- ½ cup vertically sliced red onion
- ⅓ cup fat-free, less-sodium chicken broth
- 1 teaspoon white wine vinegar
- ¼ cup (1 ounce) crumbled feta cheese, divided
- Oregano sprigs (optional)

1. Combine first 4 ingredients in a shallow dish. Dredge chicken in flour mixture. Heat oil in a nonstick skillet coated with cooking spray over medium-high heat. Add chicken, and cook 4 minutes on each side or until browned. Remove chicken from pan; keep warm. Add bell pepper, onion, broth, and vinegar to pan; cook 5 minutes or until vegetables are soft, stirring frequently. Spoon bell pepper mixture into a bowl; stir in 2 tablespoons cheese. Return chicken to pan, and sprinkle with 2 tablespoons cheese. Cover; cook over low heat 2 minutes or until cheese melts. Divide vegetable mixture evenly between 2 plates, and top each serving with a chicken breast half. Garnish with oregano sprigs, if desired. Yield: 2 servings.

CALORIES 234 (28% from fat); FAT 7.3g (sat 2.8g, mono 2.7g, poly 0.7g); PROTEIN 29.8g; CARB 8.2g; FIBER 1.3g; CHOL 78mg; IRON 1.8mg; SODIUM 461mg; CALC 95mg

MARINATED TOFU-AND-
EGGPLANT SANDWICHES

Marinade:

2 tablespoons water
1 tablespoon low-sodium soy
   sauce
1 tablespoon seasoned rice
   vinegar
2 teaspoons minced peeled fresh
   ginger
2 teaspoons honey
2 garlic cloves, minced

Remaining ingredients:

4 (½-inch-thick) slices peeled
   eggplant (about ¼ pound)
2 (½-inch-thick) slices firm tofu
   (about ¼ pound)
2 large fresh shiitake mushroom
   caps
Cooking spray
2 tablespoons light mayonnaise
2 teaspoons to 1 tablespoon
   prepared horseradish
2 English muffins, split and
   toasted

1. Preheat broiler.
2. To prepare marinade, combine first
6 ingredients in large shallow baking
dish. Cut 2 slits into top of each eggplant slice. Add eggplant slices, tofu
slices, and mushrooms to marinade.

Let stand 6 minutes, turning after 3
minutes. Arrange eggplant, tofu, and
mushrooms on a broiler pan coated
with cooking spray. Broil 6 minutes on
each side. Pour marinade over eggplant, tofu, and mushrooms.
3. Combine mayonnaise and horseradish in a small bowl. Spread mayonnaise
mixture evenly over muffin halves. Top
bottom half of each muffin with 1 eggplant slice, 1 tofu slice, 1 mushroom, 1
eggplant slice, and muffin top. Yield: 2
sandwiches (serving size: 1 sandwich).

CALORIES 317 (25% from fat); FAT 8.7g (sat 1.5g, mono 1.8g,
poly 4.1g); PROTEIN 12g; CARB 49.7g; FIBER 2.8g;
CHOL 5mg; IRON 5.7mg; SODIUM 712mg; CALC 184mg

COQ AU VIN

2 tablespoons plus 1 teaspoon
   all-purpose flour
½ teaspoon minced fresh or
   ¼ teaspoon dried thyme
½ pound skinned, boned chicken
   breast, cut diagonally into
   1-inch-wide strips
2 bacon slices
1¼ cups thinly sliced carrot
1 cup frozen pearl onions, thawed
1 cup sliced mushrooms
¾ cup dry red wine
½ cup fat-free, less-sodium
   chicken broth
1½ teaspoons tomato paste
¼ teaspoon salt
1 cup hot cooked wide egg
   noodles

1. Combine flour and thyme in a shallow bowl. Dredge chicken in flour mixture; reserve remaining flour mixture.
2. Cook bacon in a large nonstick skillet over medium heat until crisp. Remove bacon from pan; chop. Add
chicken to bacon drippings in pan;
cook 3 minutes on each side or until
lightly browned. Remove chicken from
pan; keep warm. Add reserved flour
mixture, chopped bacon, carrot,
onions, and mushrooms to pan; sauté
2 minutes. Add wine, broth, tomato
paste, and salt; cook 5 minutes or until
vegetables are tender. Return chicken

to pan; cook 5 minutes or until
chicken is done. Serve over noodles.
Yield: 2 servings (serving size: 2 cups
chicken mixture and ½ cup noodles).

CALORIES 395 (17% from fat); FAT 7.3g (sat 2.3g, mono 2.7g,
poly 1.3g); PROTEIN 35g; CARB 47g; FIBER 5.5g;
CHOL 97mg; IRON 4.2mg; SODIUM 588mg; CALC 90mg

ASIAN PORK-AND-
NOODLE SOUP

*Save time by cooking the pork while
the broth mixture simmers.*

2 cups water
½ cup drained, sliced water
   chestnuts
¼ cup thinly sliced fresh shiitake
   mushroom caps
1 teaspoon minced peeled fresh
   ginger
1 teaspoon low-sodium soy sauce
2 green onions, cut into 2-inch
   pieces
2 garlic cloves, thinly sliced
1 (14¼-ounce) can low-salt
   beef broth
1 (3-inch) cinnamon stick
6 ounces pork tenderloin
⅛ teaspoon black pepper
Cooking spray
2 ounces uncooked soba
   (buckwheat noodles), broken
   in half
1 tablespoon rice vinegar
½ teaspoon dark sesame oil

1. Bring first 9 ingredients to a boil in
a large saucepan; reduce heat, and
simmer 30 minutes.
2. Preheat broiler.
3. Sprinkle pork with pepper; place on
a broiler pan coated with cooking
spray. Broil 7 minutes on each side or
until done. Cool slightly; cut pork into
strips.
4. Bring broth mixture to a boil; add
soba noodles. Cook 6 minutes or until
tender. Stir in pork, vinegar, and oil.
Yield: 2 servings (serving size: 2 cups).

CALORIES 277 (17% from fat); FAT 5.2g (sat 1.2g, mono 1.8g,
poly 0.9g); PROTEIN 23.4g; CARB 29.8g; FIBER 1g;
CHOL 59mg; IRON 2.7mg; SODIUM 137mg; CALC 39mg

NOVEMBER

America's Favorite Pies

It's prime pie season, and we've got the perfect prizes to power your personal celebration.

Pies are the most sensible of all foods. They come in their own packaging and are frequently as good cold as hot. You can put anything in a pie—meats to sweets—once you've made the crust, and that's pretty much what people have done over the ages.

But at the holidays there's just one kind of pie on your mind: the one for dessert.

level with a knife. Combine ¼ cup flour and ¼ cup brown sugar in a bowl; cut in 2 tablespoons butter with a pastry blender or 2 knives until mixture resembles coarse meal.

7. Drizzle syrup over apple mixture; sprinkle topping over syrup. Bake at 375° for 30 minutes or until apple is tender. Cool on a wire rack. Yield: 10 servings (serving size: 1 wedge).

CALORIES 277 (27% from fat); FAT 8.4g (sat 4.2g, mono 2.4g, poly 1g); PROTEIN 2.1g; CARB 50.1g; FIBER 2.4g; CHOL 16mg; IRON 1.3mg; SODIUM 109mg; CALC 33mg

CARAMEL-APPLE CRUMB PIE

In this variation on the classic apple pie theme, caramel syrup is drizzled over the apples and then topped with a crunchy streusel.

Crust:

- 1 cup all-purpose flour
- ⅛ teaspoon salt
- 2 tablespoons chilled butter or stick margarine, cut into small pieces
- 2 tablespoons vegetable shortening
- 3 tablespoons plus ½ teaspoon ice water
- 1 teaspoon cider vinegar
- Butter-flavored cooking spray

Filling:

- 1 tablespoon butter or stick margarine
- ½ cup packed brown sugar
- ¾ teaspoon ground cinnamon
- 9 cups sliced peeled Granny Smith apple (about 2¾ pounds)
- 3 tablespoons all-purpose flour
- 2 teaspoons lemon juice

Topping:

- ¼ cup all-purpose flour
- ¼ cup packed brown sugar
- 2 tablespoons chilled butter or stick margarine, cut into small pieces
- ¼ cup fat-free caramel sundae syrup

1. Preheat oven to 375°.
2. To prepare crust, lightly spoon 1 cup flour into a dry measuring cup; level with a knife. Combine 1 cup flour and salt in a bowl; cut in 2 tablespoons butter and shortening with a pastry blender or 2 knives until mixture resembles coarse meal. Sprinkle surface with ice water, 1 tablespoon at a time; add vinegar. Toss with a fork until moist and crumbly (do not form a ball).
3. Press mixture gently into a 4-inch circle on heavy-duty plastic wrap; cover with additional plastic wrap. Roll dough, still covered, into a 12-inch circle. Freeze 10 minutes or until plastic wrap can be easily removed.
4. Remove 1 sheet of plastic wrap; fit dough into a 9-inch pie plate coated with cooking spray. Remove top sheet of plastic wrap. Fold edges under; flute. Line bottom of dough with a piece of foil; arrange pie weights (or dried beans) on foil. Bake at 375° for 15 minutes or until edge is lightly browned. Remove pie weights and foil; cool on a wire rack.
5. To prepare filling, melt 1 tablespoon butter in a large nonstick skillet over medium-high heat. Combine ½ cup brown sugar and cinnamon. Add sugar mixture and apple to skillet; cook 5 minutes, stirring occasionally. Remove from heat; stir in 3 tablespoons flour and lemon juice. Spoon into prepared crust.
6. To prepare topping, lightly spoon ¼ cup flour into a dry measuring cup;

PUMPKIN-MAPLE PIE

We've made our pumpkin pie even richer by adding maple syrup.

Crust:

- 1 cup all-purpose flour
- 2 tablespoons sugar
- ⅛ teaspoon salt
- ¼ cup chilled butter or stick margarine, cut into small pieces
- 3½ tablespoons ice water
- Cooking spray

Filling:

- ½ cup sugar
- ⅓ cup maple syrup
- 1 teaspoon ground ginger
- 1 teaspoon ground cinnamon
- ¼ teaspoon ground nutmeg
- 2 large eggs
- 1 cup evaporated fat-free milk
- 1 (15-ounce) can pumpkin

1. To prepare crust, lightly spoon 1 cup flour into a dry measuring cup; level with a knife. Combine 1 cup flour, 2 tablespoons sugar, and salt in a bowl; cut in butter with a pastry blender or 2 knives until mixture resembles coarse meal. Sprinkle surface with ice water, 1 tablespoon at a time; toss with a fork until moist and crumbly (do not form a ball).
2. Press mixture gently into a 4-inch circle on heavy-duty plastic wrap; cover

dough with additional plastic wrap. Roll dough, still covered, into a 12-inch circle. Freeze 10 minutes or until plastic wrap can be easily removed.

3. Remove 1 sheet of plastic wrap; fit dough into a 9-inch pie plate coated with cooking spray. Remove top sheet of plastic wrap. Fold edges under; flute.

4. Preheat oven to 425°.

5. To prepare filling, beat ½ cup sugar and next 5 ingredients at medium speed of a mixer until well-blended. Add milk and pumpkin; beat well. Pour into prepared crust. Bake at 425° for 10 minutes. Reduce oven temperature to 350° (do not remove pie from oven); bake an additional 50 minutes or until set. Cool on a wire rack. Yield: 8 servings (serving size: 1 wedge).

CALORIES 267 (25% from fat); FAT 7.5g (sat 4.1g, mono 2.2g, poly 0.5g); PROTEIN 6.3g; CARB 44.5g; FIBER 2.6g; CHOL 72mg; IRON 2mg; SODIUM 152mg; CALC 129mg

LEMON-BUTTERMILK CHESS PIE

Chess pie is a Southern favorite.

Crust:

    1   cup all-purpose flour
    2   tablespoons sugar
    ⅛   teaspoon salt
    ¼   cup chilled butter or stick
        margarine, cut into small
        pieces
    3½ tablespoons ice water
        Cooking spray

Filling:

    1   cup sugar
    2   tablespoons all-purpose flour
    2   teaspoons lemon rind
    2   tablespoons fresh lemon juice
    1   teaspoon vanilla extract
    2   large eggs
    2   large egg whites
    1   cup low-fat buttermilk

1. Preheat oven to 425°.

2. To prepare crust, lightly spoon 1 cup flour into a dry measuring cup; level with a knife. Combine 1 cup flour, 2 tablespoons sugar, and salt in a bowl; cut in butter with a pastry blender or 2 knives until mixture resembles coarse meal. Sprinkle surface with ice water, 1 tablespoon at a time; toss with a fork until moist and crumbly (do not form a ball).

3. Press mixture gently into a 4-inch circle on heavy-duty plastic wrap; cover dough with additional plastic wrap. Roll dough, still covered, into a 12-inch circle. Freeze 10 minutes or until plastic wrap can be easily removed.

4. Remove 1 sheet of plastic wrap; fit dough into a 9-inch pie plate coated with cooking spray. Remove top sheet of plastic wrap. Fold edges under; flute. Line dough with a piece of foil; arrange pie weights (or dried beans) on foil. Bake at 425° for 10 minutes or until edge is lightly browned. Remove pie weights and foil; reduce oven temperature to 350°. Bake crust an additional 5 minutes; cool on a wire rack.

5. To prepare filling, combine 1 cup sugar and next 6 ingredients in a bowl; stir with a whisk until well-blended. Gradually stir in buttermilk. Pour into prepared crust. Bake at 350° for 40 minutes or until set, shielding crust with foil after 30 minutes, if necessary. Cool on a wire rack. Yield: 8 servings (serving size: 1 wedge).

CALORIES 265 (26% from fat); FAT 7.8g (sat 4.3g, mono 2.3g, poly 0.5g); PROTEIN 5.5g; CARB 43.7g; FIBER 0.5g; CHOL 71mg; IRON 1mg; SODIUM 141mg; CALC 50mg

CHOCOLATE-CREAM PIE

Doesn't sound like a pie to serve at Thanksgiving? Set it out, and watch it go.

Crust:

    40 graham crackers (10 full cracker
        sheets)
    2   tablespoons sugar
    2   tablespoons butter or stick
        margarine, melted
    1   large egg white
        Cooking spray

Filling:

    2   cups fat-free milk, divided
    ⅔   cup sugar
    ⅓   cup unsweetened cocoa
    3   tablespoons cornstarch
    ⅛   teaspoon salt
    1   large egg
    2   ounces semisweet chocolate,
        chopped
    1   teaspoon vanilla extract
    1½ cups frozen reduced-calorie
        whipped topping, thawed
    ¾   teaspoon grated semisweet
        chocolate

1. Preheat oven to 350°.

2. To prepare crust, place crackers in a food processor; process until crumbly. Add 2 tablespoons sugar, butter, and egg white; pulse 6 times or just until moist. Press crumb mixture into a 9-inch pie plate coated with cooking spray. Bake at 350° for 8 minutes; cool on a wire rack 15 minutes.

3. To prepare filling, combine ½ cup milk, ⅔ cup sugar, and next 4 ingredients in a bowl, stirring with a whisk.

4. Heat remaining 1½ cups milk in a heavy saucepan over medium-high heat to 180° or until tiny bubbles form around edge (do not boil). Remove from heat. Gradually add hot milk to sugar mixture, stirring constantly with a whisk. Return milk mixture to pan. Add chopped chocolate; cook over medium heat until thick and bubbly (about 5 minutes), stirring constantly. Reduce heat to low; cook 2 minutes, stirring constantly. Remove from heat; stir in vanilla. Pour into prepared crust; cover surface of filling with plastic wrap. Chill 3 hours or until cold. Remove plastic wrap; spread whipped topping evenly over filling. Sprinkle with grated chocolate. Yield: 10 servings (serving size: 1 wedge).

Note: If you want to serve this with a dessert wine, try Paul Thomas "Razz," nonvintage Washington State. It's made from raspberries, which go well with chocolate.

CALORIES 242 (30% from fat); FAT 8g (sat 4.6g, mono 2.1g, poly 0.8g); PROTEIN 5g; CARB 38.5g; FIBER 0.1g; CHOL 30mg; IRON 1.4mg; SODIUM 189mg; CALC 83mg

CLASSIC PECAN PIE

(pictured on page 299)

We kept the fat in this piecrust to a minimum, resulting in a biscuitlike crust.

Crust:

  1 cup all-purpose flour
  2 tablespoons granulated sugar
  ½ teaspoon baking powder
  ¼ teaspoon salt
  ¼ cup fat-free milk
  1 tablespoon butter or stick
     margarine, melted
Cooking spray

Filling:

  1 large egg
  4 large egg whites
  1 cup light or dark-colored corn
     syrup
  ⅔ cup packed dark brown sugar
  ¼ teaspoon salt
  1 cup pecan halves
  1 teaspoon vanilla extract

1. To prepare crust, lightly spoon 1 cup flour into a dry measuring cup; level with a knife. Combine 1 cup flour, granulated sugar, baking powder, and ¼ teaspoon salt. Add milk and butter; toss with a fork until moist.
2. Press mixture gently into a 4-inch circle on heavy-duty plastic wrap; cover dough with additional plastic wrap. Roll dough, still covered, into an 11-inch circle. Freeze 10 minutes or until plastic wrap can be easily removed.
3. Remove 1 sheet of plastic wrap; fit dough into a 9-inch pie plate coated with cooking spray. Remove top sheet of plastic wrap. Fold edges under; flute.
4. Preheat oven to 350°.
5. To prepare filling, beat egg and next 4 ingredients at medium speed of a mixer until well-blended. Stir in pecan halves and vanilla. Pour mixture into prepared crust. Bake at 350° for 20 minutes; then cover with foil. Bake an additional 20 minutes or until a knife inserted 1 inch from edge comes out clean. Do not overbake. Cool pie on a wire rack. Yield: 10 servings (serving size: 1 wedge).

CALORIES 288 (29% from fat); FAT 9.2g (sat 1.5g, mono 5.1g, poly 2g); PROTEIN 4.3g; CARB 48.1g; FIBER 1g; CHOL 25mg; IRON 1.1mg; SODIUM 253mg; CALC 52mg

SHOOFLY PIE

Thought to be of Pennsylvania Dutch origin, this type of shoofly pie is a dark, rich, very sweet molasses pie.

  2   cups all-purpose flour, divided
  ½   teaspoon salt, divided
  ¼   cup vegetable shortening
  3½ tablespoons ice water
      Cooking spray
  ½   cup packed brown sugar
  3   tablespoons vegetable shortening
  1   cup boiling water
  1   teaspoon baking soda
  1   cup molasses

1. Lightly spoon flour into dry measuring cups; level with a knife. Combine 1 cup flour and ¼ teaspoon salt in a bowl; cut in ¼ cup shortening with a pastry blender or 2 knives until mixture resembles coarse meal. Sprinkle surface with ice water, 1 tablespoon at a time; toss with a fork until moist and crumbly (do not form a ball).
2. Press mixture gently into a 4-inch circle on heavy-duty plastic wrap; cover dough with additional plastic wrap. Roll dough, still covered, into a 12-inch circle. Freeze 10 minutes or until plastic wrap can be easily removed.
3. Remove 1 sheet of plastic wrap; fit dough into a 9-inch pie plate coated with cooking spray. Remove top sheet of plastic wrap. Fold edges under; flute.
4. Preheat oven to 350°.
5. Combine remaining 1 cup flour, ¼ teaspoon salt, and brown sugar in a bowl; cut in 3 tablespoons shortening with a pastry blender or 2 knives until mixture resembles coarse meal. Combine boiling water and baking soda; stir in molasses. Pour molasses mixture into prepared crust; sprinkle flour mixture over molasses mixture. Place pie on a baking sheet; bake at 350° for 40 minutes or until set. Cool on a wire rack. Yield: 10 servings (serving size: 1 wedge).

CALORIES 284 (25% from fat); FAT 7.8g (sat 1.9g, mono 2.5g, poly 2.3g); PROTEIN 2.6g; CARB 51.8g; FIBER 0.7g; CHOL 0mg; IRON 2.9mg; SODIUM 260mg; CALC 79mg

30 MINUTES OR LESS

Noodles East

For a delicious, nutritious dinner in minutes, forget takeout—go for the pasta.

Because of their increasing popularity, several different Asian pastas are available in mainstream grocery stores and in Asian markets. You'll find remarkably thin *cellophane noodles* formed from the starch of mung beans, hearty brown *soba noodles* made with buckwheat flour, or delicate white *rice sticks* fashioned from rice flour.

CHINESE PORK WITH EGGPLANT AND RICE STICKS

Preparation time: 20 minutes
Cooking time: 10 minutes

  3 ounces uncooked rice sticks
     (rice-flour noodles) or 4 ounces
     angel hair or vermicelli
  ½ pound boneless pork loin roast
  ¼ teaspoon salt
  ½ teaspoon cracked black pepper
  ¼ teaspoon ground red pepper
  2 teaspoons vegetable oil, divided
  4 cups (½-inch) cubed peeled
     eggplant (about 8 ounces)
  2 cups finely chopped onion
  1 teaspoon bottled minced garlic
  ¼ teaspoon crushed red pepper
  ¼ cup fat-free, less-sodium
     chicken broth
  2 tablespoons rice vinegar
  1 tablespoon brown sugar
  1 tablespoon ketchup
  1 teaspoon low-sodium soy sauce
  2 tablespoons sesame seeds
  1 cup coarsely chopped fresh
     cilantro

1. Cook rice sticks according to package directions; drain and keep warm.
2. Trim fat from pork; cut into ½-inch pieces. Combine salt, cracked pepper, and ground red pepper. Sprinkle pork with pepper mixture.
3. Heat 1 teaspoon oil in a large nonstick skillet over medium-high heat. Add eggplant, and stir-fry 2 minutes. Remove from pan. Heat remaining 1 teaspoon oil in pan. Add pork, and stir-fry 2 minutes. Add onion; stir-fry 3 minutes. Add garlic and crushed red pepper, and stir-fry 1 minute. Add broth, vinegar, sugar, ketchup, and soy sauce; bring to a boil, and cook 2 minutes. Return eggplant to pan, and cook until thoroughly heated. Sprinkle with sesame seeds and cilantro. Serve over rice sticks. Yield: 4 servings (serving size: 1 cup stir-fry mixture and ½ cup rice sticks).

CALORIES 294 (29% from fat); FAT 9.5g (sat 2.2g, mono 3.6g, poly 2.7g); PROTEIN 17.1g; CARB 37.1g; FIBER 5.3g; CHOL 35mg; IRON 3mg; SODIUM 317mg; CALC 101mg

STIR-FRIED SHRIMP AND ONIONS OVER NOODLES

Preparation time: 9 minutes
Cooking time: 21 minutes

To save some time, buy your shrimp already peeled and deveined.

  3 ounces uncooked cellophane
      noodles (bean threads) or 4
      ounces uncooked vermicelli
1½ teaspoons sugar, divided
  1 teaspoon whiskey (optional)
  ½ teaspoon low-sodium soy sauce
  ¾ pound peeled and deveined
      large shrimp
  2 teaspoons vegetable oil, divided
  2 onions, sliced and separated into
      rings (about ¾ pound)
  ¼ cup fat-free, less-sodium
      chicken broth
  2 tablespoons ketchup, divided
  ¼ cup minced green onions

1. Prepare noodles according to package directions; set aside.

2. Combine ½ teaspoon sugar, whiskey, and soy sauce in a bowl, and add shrimp. Cover and refrigerate.
3. Heat 1 teaspoon oil in a large nonstick skillet over medium-high heat. Add sliced onion, and cook 5 minutes or until lightly browned. Stir in remaining 1 teaspoon sugar, broth, and 1 tablespoon ketchup, and cook 2 minutes. Remove onion mixture from pan; keep warm.
4. Heat 1 teaspoon oil in pan. Add shrimp mixture and green onions, and cook 3 minutes, stirring constantly. Stir in 1 tablespoon ketchup. Cook 1 minute or until shrimp are done. Stir in onion mixture. Serve over noodles. Yield: 3 servings (serving size: 1 cup stir-fry and ⅔ cup noodles).

CALORIES 327 (13% from fat); FAT 4.7g (sat 0.9g, mono 1.1g, poly 2.1g); PROTEIN 19g; CARB 52.3g; FIBER 2.8g; CHOL 129mg; IRON 2.4mg; SODIUM 317mg; CALC 77mg

SOBA WITH MARINATED BEEF AND TOMATOES

Preparation time: 3 minutes
Marinating time: 10 minutes
Cooking time: 17 minutes

  1 (1-pound) flank steak
  1 teaspoon cornstarch
  2 teaspoons vegetable oil, divided
  1 teaspoon water
  1 teaspoon whiskey (optional)
  ½ teaspoon low-sodium soy sauce
  ¼ teaspoon salt
10 ounces uncooked soba
      (buckwheat noodles) or
      vermicelli
  ½ cup (1-inch) sliced green onions
  ½ cup fat-free, less-sodium
      chicken broth
  ½ teaspoon sugar
  4 plum tomatoes, quartered
  1 teaspoon oyster sauce
  1 garlic clove, crushed

1. Trim fat from steak, and cut steak diagonally across grain into thin slices. Combine cornstarch, 1 teaspoon oil, water, whiskey, if desired, soy sauce, and salt in a large zip-top plastic bag.

Add steak; seal and toss well to coat. Marinate in refrigerator 10 minutes.
2. While steak is marinating, cook noodles according to package directions. Drain noodles, and keep warm. Remove steak from bag, discarding marinade. Heat remaining 1 teaspoon oil in a large nonstick skillet over medium-high heat. Add green onions, and sauté 30 seconds. Add steak, and cook 4 minutes or until steak loses its pink color. Remove steak from pan, and keep warm. Add broth, sugar, and tomato to pan, and stir well. Cover, reduce heat, and cook 3 minutes or until thick. Stir in steak, oyster sauce, and garlic, and cook 4 minutes or until thoroughly heated. Combine beef mixture and noodles in a large bowl, and toss well. Yield: 4 servings (serving size: 1½ cups).

CALORIES 483 (23% from fat); FAT 12.6g (sat 5g, mono 4.8g, poly 1.2g); PROTEIN 32.4g; CARB 54.8g; FIBER 2.2g; CHOL 57mg; IRON 4mg; SODIUM 828mg; CALC 44mg

CURRIED COCONUT CHICKEN OVER NOODLES

Preparation time: 10 minutes
Cooking time: 15 minutes

2½ cups uncooked Chinese egg
      noodles or angel hair or
      vermicelli
  2 teaspoons vegetable oil, divided
  1 cup thinly sliced onion
  2 cups fresh basil leaves
  1 garlic clove, crushed
  2 teaspoons curry powder
  ½ teaspoon salt
  ⅛ teaspoon ground red pepper
  ½ pound skinned, boned chicken
      breast, cut into 1-inch pieces
  ¾ cup light coconut milk

1. Prepare noodles according to package directions, omitting salt; drain noodles, and keep warm.
2. Heat 1 teaspoon oil in a large nonstick skillet over medium-high heat until hot. Add onion; stir-fry 1 minute. Add basil; stir-fry 2 minutes. Remove from pan; keep warm.

Continued

3. Heat remaining 1 teaspoon oil in skillet over medium-high heat. Add garlic; stir-fry 30 seconds. Add curry powder, salt, and red pepper; stir-fry 10 seconds. Add chicken, and stir-fry 3 minutes. Stir in milk; reduce heat to medium, and cook 2 minutes or until chicken is done. Stir in basil mixture, and toss well. Serve over noodles. Yield: 2 servings (serving size: 1 cup chicken with sauce and 1 cup noodles).

CALORIES 475 (26% from fat); FAT 13.5g (sat 4.7g, mono 3.6g, poly 3.9g); PROTEIN 35.9g; CARB 51.4g; FIBER 5.3g; CHOL 119mg; IRON 4.7mg; SODIUM 709mg; CALC 122mg

STIR-FRIED CHICKEN WITH VEGETABLES AND LO MEIN NOODLES

(pictured on page 298)

Preparation time: 15 minutes
Cooking time: 15 minutes

¾ cup fat-free, less-sodium chicken broth
2 tablespoons bourbon or water
1 tablespoon oyster sauce
2 teaspoons sugar
2 teaspoons low-sodium soy sauce
½ teaspoon salt
1 pound skinned, boned chicken breast, cut into ½-inch-wide strips
10 ounces uncooked wide lo mein noodles or fettuccine
2 teaspoons vegetable oil, divided
1 cup small broccoli florets
½ cup diagonally sliced carrot
½ cup (1-inch) sliced green onions
1 (8-ounce) package cremini mushrooms, quartered
1 (8-ounce) package frozen sugar snap peas, thawed

1. Combine first 6 ingredients in a small bowl. Combine ¼ cup broth mixture and chicken in a bowl. Reserve remaining broth mixture.
2. Prepare noodles according to package directions, omitting salt; drain noodles, and keep warm.

3. Heat 1 teaspoon oil in a large non-stick skillet until hot. Add chicken mixture; stir-fry 5 minutes or until done. Remove from pan; keep warm. Heat remaining 1 teaspoon oil in pan until hot. Add broccoli and remaining 4 ingredients; stir-fry 5 minutes or until crisp-tender. Return chicken to pan, and add reserved broth mixture; cover and cook over medium heat 2 minutes or until thoroughly heated. Serve over noodles. Yield: 5 servings (serving size: 1 cup stir-fry and 1 cup noodles).

CALORIES 381 (10% from fat); FAT 4.2g (sat 0.8g, mono 0.9g, poly 1.7g); PROTEIN 31.8g; CARB 53g; FIBER 4.3g; CHOL 53mg; IRON 4.7mg; SODIUM 525mg; CALC 62mg

COOKING CLASS

Tough Love

Braising turns even the toughest cuts of meat into melt-in-your-mouth dinners.

Some of the best cuts of meat are tough, but when they're steeped in moist heat or *braised*, their very nature is transformed.

APPLE ORCHARD POT ROAST

1 (3-pound) boneless beef bottom round roast
2 teaspoons vegetable oil
1½ cups apple juice
1 cup dry white wine
½ cup orange juice
½ teaspoon salt
6 garlic cloves, peeled
6 whole cloves
2 (1 x 3-inch) orange rind strips
1 (3-inch) cinnamon stick
8 turnips (about 1 pound), peeled
6 carrots (about ¾ pound), peeled and cut into thirds
4 parsnips (about ¾ pound), peeled and cut into thirds
2 peeled baking potatoes (about 1 pound), halved and quartered
1 peeled sweet potato (about 1 pound), halved and quartered

1. Preheat oven to 300°.
2. Trim fat from roast. Heat oil in a Dutch oven over medium-high heat until hot. Add roast; cook 5 minutes, browning on all sides. Add apple juice, wine, and orange juice; scrape pan to loosen browned bits. Add salt and next 4 ingredients. Bring to a boil; remove from heat. Cover; bake at 300° for 1 hour.
3. Turn roast over. Add vegetables; cover and bake 2 additional hours. Increase oven temperature to 400° (do not remove roast from oven). Bake, uncovered, 20 minutes or until very tender. Remove roast and vegetables from pan. Cover roast with foil; let stand 10 minutes before slicing. Strain cooking liquid through a sieve; discard solids. Serve with roast and vegetables. Yield: 8 servings (serving size: 3 ounces beef, about 1 cup vegetable mixture, and ¼ cup gravy).

CALORIES 335 (18% from fat); FAT 6.7g (sat 2.1g, mono 2.5g, poly 0.9g); PROTEIN 32.2g; CARB 36g; FIBER 4.9g; CHOL 73mg; IRON 5.1mg; SODIUM 274mg; CALC 70mg

BRAISED PORK LOIN WITH PORT AND PRUNES

(pictured on page 297)

Spice rub:

1½ teaspoons black pepper
1 teaspoon salt
1 teaspoon dry mustard
1 teaspoon dried rubbed sage
½ teaspoon dried thyme

Remaining ingredients:

1 (3¼-pound) boneless pork loin roast
1 tablespoon olive oil
2 cups sliced onion
1 cup finely chopped leek
1 cup finely chopped carrot
1 cup port or other sweet red wine
¾ cup fat-free, less-sodium chicken broth
1 cup pitted prunes (about 20 prunes)
2 bay leaves

1. Preheat oven to 325°.
2. To prepare spice rub, combine first 5 ingredients. Trim fat from pork; rub surface of roast with spice rub. Secure at 2-inch intervals with heavy string.
3. Heat oil in a large Dutch oven over medium-high heat. Add pork; cook 8 minutes, browning on all sides. Remove from pan. Add onion, leek, and carrot to pan; cover, reduce heat, and cook 5 minutes, stirring frequently. Stir in port and broth, scraping pan to loosen browned bits. Return pork to pan; add prunes and bay leaves. Bring to a boil. Cover and bake at 325° for 1½ hours or until pork is tender; discard bay leaves.
4. Place pork on a platter; cover with foil. Remove 6 prunes with a slotted spoon. Place prunes in a food processor or blender; process until smooth. Stir pureed prunes into port mixture. Serve sauce with pork. Yield: 8 servings (serving size: about 3 ounces pork and ½ cup sauce).

CALORIES 361 (37% from fat); FAT 14.8g (sat 4.7g, mono 7.2g, poly 1.6g); PROTEIN 36.9g; CARB 19.8g; FIBER 2.8g; CHOL 102mg; IRON 2.7mg; SODIUM 458mg; CALC 48mg

LAMB SHANKS WITH FENNEL AND WHITE BEANS

Because the meat is removed from the bones, try to find large, meaty lamb shanks. To complete the menu, just add a green salad. Gremolata, a mixture of parsley, lemon, and garlic, is the traditional garnish for osso buco (an Italian dish of veal shanks). We've added fennel fronds because fennel is used in the dish.

Fennel gremolata:

- 2 tablespoons minced fennel fronds
- 2 tablespoons minced fresh flat-leaf parsley
- 1 tablespoon grated lemon rind
- 1 garlic clove, minced

Beans:

- ¾ cup dried navy beans or other small white beans
- 2 (1½-pound) lamb shanks
- 1 teaspoon chopped fresh or ¼ teaspoon dried rosemary
- ½ teaspoon salt
- ½ teaspoon black pepper
- 2 teaspoons olive oil
- 1 cup chopped fennel bulb
- ½ cup thinly sliced carrot
- ½ teaspoon fennel seeds, crushed
- 3 garlic cloves, minced
- 2 leeks, trimmed, quartered lengthwise, and sliced
- 1½ cups fat-free, less-sodium chicken broth
- ½ cup dry white wine
- 1 tablespoon chopped fennel fronds
- 3 sprigs fresh thyme
- 2 plum tomatoes, peeled, seeded, and chopped (about ¼ pound)
- ⅛ teaspoon salt
- ⅛ teaspoon black pepper

1. To prepare fennel gremolata, combine first 4 ingredients in a small bowl, and set aside.
2. To prepare beans, sort and wash dried beans; place in a large Dutch oven. Cover with water to 2 inches above beans; bring to a boil, and cook 2 minutes. Remove from heat; cover and let stand 1 hour. Drain beans.
3. Trim fat from lamb. Combine rosemary, ½ teaspoon salt, and ½ teaspoon pepper. Rub surface of lamb with rosemary mixture. Heat oil in a Dutch oven over medium-high heat. Add lamb; cook 10 minutes, browning on all sides. Remove from pan. Add fennel bulb, carrot, fennel seeds, 3 garlic cloves, and leeks to pan; cover, reduce heat, and cook 10 minutes, stirring frequently to loosen browned bits. Stir in broth and wine, scraping pan to loosen browned bits. Return lamb to pan; add beans, 1 tablespoon fennel fronds, thyme, and tomato. Bring to a boil. Cover; reduce heat. Simmer 1 hour and 15 minutes or until lamb is tender; discard thyme. Remove lamb from pan; cover and keep warm.

4. Simmer bean mixture, uncovered, 10 minutes. Sprinkle bean mixture with ⅛ teaspoon salt and ⅛ teaspoon pepper. Remove lamb from bones. Divide lamb among 4 shallow bowls, and serve with bean mixture and fennel gremolata. Yield: 4 servings (serving size: 3 ounces lamb, 1 cup bean mixture, and 1 tablespoon gremolata).

CALORIES 562 (23% from fat); FAT 14.5g (sat 4.5g, mono 6.3g, poly 1.6g); PROTEIN 67.7g; CARB 39.2g; FIBER 5.7g; CHOL 172mg; IRON 10.1mg; SODIUM 742mg; CALC 164mg

THAI BRAISED BEEF WITH COCONUT MILK AND GINGER

- 1 (2½-pound) boneless chuck roast
- 1 teaspoon salt
- 2 teaspoons ground coriander
- 1 teaspoon ground cardamom
- 1 teaspoon ground cumin
- 1 teaspoon ground red pepper
- 1 teaspoon ground turmeric
- 1 teaspoon freshly ground black pepper
- 2 teaspoons vegetable oil, divided
- 3 cups chopped onion
- 1 cup diced carrot
- 2 tablespoons minced peeled fresh ginger
- 4 garlic cloves, minced
- 1 (16-ounce) can fat-free, less-sodium chicken broth
- 1½ cups light coconut milk
- 2 tablespoons sliced peeled fresh lemon grass or 1 tablespoon thinly sliced lime rind
- 3 bay leaves
- 6 cups hot cooked Chinese-style egg noodles (about 12 ounces uncooked)
- 1 cup chopped fresh cilantro

1. Trim fat from beef. Cut beef into 2-inch pieces. Combine salt and next 6 ingredients in a small bowl. Sprinkle 2 tablespoons of spice mixture over beef, and toss to coat; reserve remaining spice mixture.
2. Preheat oven to 325°.

Continued

3. Heat 1 teaspoon oil in a large Dutch oven over medium-high heat. Add beef; cook 5 minutes, browning on all sides. Remove from pan. Heat remaining 1 teaspoon oil in pan. Add onion, carrot, ginger, and garlic; sauté 8 minutes or until tender. Stir in broth, scraping pan to loosen browned bits. Return beef to pan. Add remaining spice mixture, coconut milk, lemon grass, and bay leaves. Bring to a boil. Cover and bake at 325° for 2 hours. Remove beef from pan using a slotted spoon; shred with 2 forks, set aside, and keep warm. Bring vegetable mixture to a boil over medium-high heat. Cook 10 minutes or until slightly thick. Discard bay leaves. Serve beef and vegetable mixture over noodles. Sprinkle with cilantro. Yield: 6 servings (serving size: 3 ounces beef, ¾ cup vegetable mixture, and 1 cup noodles).
Note: You can find light coconut milk in the Asian or Mexican section of most supermarkets. If yours does not carry it, ask your grocer to order it for you. For more information on availability, see Web site www.atasteofthai.com.

CALORIES 554 (29% from fat); FAT 18g (sat 7g, mono 6.4g, poly 2.4g); PROTEIN 40.5g; CARB 54.9g; FIBER 4.5g; CHOL 145mg; IRON 8.3mg; SODIUM 905mg; CALC 81mg

SPANISH-STYLE BRAISED BEEF

This recipe calls for eye-of-round roast, but bottom round works, too, as long as it's at least an inch thick. The almond pesto, stirred in at the end, gives the sauce body and a rich finish. This dish makes a lot of sauce, which is great over mashed potatoes.

Almond pesto:

⅓ cup slivered almonds, toasted
3 tablespoons chopped fresh parsley
1 tablespoon beef broth
2 garlic cloves, peeled
1 hard-cooked large egg yolk

Spice rub:

2 teaspoons dried marjoram
2 teaspoons paprika
1 teaspoon freshly ground black pepper
¼ teaspoon salt

Remaining ingredients:

1 (2½-pound) beef eye-of-round roast
1 tablespoon olive oil
1 cup dry sherry
2 cups thinly sliced onion
1 (14.5-ounce) can diced tomatoes, drained
1 cup beef broth
1 (12-ounce) bottle roasted red bell peppers, drained and cut into ½-inch strips
¼ teaspoon salt
¼ teaspoon freshly ground black pepper
4 cups hot cooked long-grain rice

1. To prepare almond pesto, combine first 5 ingredients in a food processor; process until blended and a paste forms. Cover and refrigerate.
2. Preheat oven to 350°.
3. To prepare spice rub, combine marjoram, paprika, 1 teaspoon black pepper, and ¼ teaspoon salt. Trim fat from beef; rub surface of beef with spice rub.
4. Heat oil in a Dutch oven over medium-high heat. Add beef; cook 5 minutes, browning on all sides. Remove from pan. Stir in sherry, scraping pan to loosen browned bits. Return beef to pan. Add onion, tomatoes, 1 cup broth, and pepper strips. Cover. Bake at 350° for 3 hours or until meat shreds easily with a fork. Remove beef from pan. Cut beef into 2-inch pieces. Add pesto to pan, stirring until blended. Place pan over medium heat; cook 10 minutes. Stir in ¼ teaspoon salt and ¼ teaspoon black pepper. Serve beef and sauce mixture over rice. Yield: 6 servings (serving size: about 3 ounces beef, ¾ cup sauce, and ⅔ cup rice).

CALORIES 519 (24% from fat); FAT 14.1g (sat 3.6g, mono 6.9g, poly 1.3g); PROTEIN 50.7g; CARB 44.9g; FIBER 3.1g; CHOL 144mg; IRON 6.7mg; SODIUM 818mg; CALC 71mg

CHINESE RED COOKED PORK

Soy sauce and red wine give this dish its color. Star anise is a star-shaped pod native to China. It adds a sweet, licorice flavor to the dish, but can be omitted. Serve pork with steamed broccoli, bok choy, or asparagus.

2 pounds boneless pork loin roast
½ cup dry red wine, divided
2 tablespoons sugar
1 cup chopped onion
2 tablespoons minced peeled fresh ginger
4 garlic cloves, minced
½ cup low-sodium soy sauce
7 whole green onions
6 star anise (optional)
1 cup water
3 cups hot cooked long-grain rice
3 tablespoons chopped green onions

1. Trim fat from pork. Cut pork into 2-inch pieces.
2. Combine ¼ cup wine and sugar in a large Dutch oven. Cook over medium-high heat until sugar melts and mixture thickens. Add pork, chopped onion, ginger, and garlic, and cook 5 minutes, browning pork on all sides. Add ¼ cup wine, soy sauce, whole green onions, and star anise, if desired. Bring mixture to a boil; reduce heat, and simmer 10 minutes, stirring occasionally. Stir in water; cover and simmer 1 hour and 15 minutes or until pork shreds easily with a fork. Spoon over rice, and sprinkle with chopped green onions. Yield: 6 servings (serving size: 1 cup pork mixture, ½ cup rice, and 1½ teaspoons chopped green onions).

CALORIES 383 (26% from fat); FAT 11g (sat 3.7g, mono 4.9g, poly 1.2g); PROTEIN 33.3g; CARB 36g; FIBER 1.6g; CHOL 85mg; IRON 3.1mg; SODIUM 741mg; CALC 52mg

Braising *turns even the toughest meats into tender, delicious dishes—as long as meats are exposed long enough to low heat. But because different cuts can vary dramatically in their tenderness, cooking times may not always be the same—or correspond exactly to the time recommended in the recipes. So keep an eye on the timer, but also have a fork ready.*

❶ *Before the meat is browned, coat it with a spice rub for extra flavor. Using a Dutch oven, heat the oil over medium-high heat. Add the meat to the pan and brown on all sides. This step creates a caramelized crust and leaves browned bits in the pan that are incorporated into the sauce. Do not overcrowd the pot; this will prevent browning. If necessary, prepare the meat in batches.*

❷ *Remove the meat from the pan, and set aside. Add the vegetables, and stir them with a metal or wooden spatula, scraping up the browned bits from the bottom of the pan.*

❸ *Add the liquid, stirring and scraping any remaining browned bits still stuck to the pan. Bring to a boil, and return the meat to the pan. Cover with a lid, and cook according to the recipe. For most braised dishes, the liquid should be no more than 1 to 2 inches deep and come about halfway up the meat.*

❹ *After the allotted time, check the meat with a fork for tenderness. If the meat shreds easily, it's ready. If it's still firm, continue to cook, checking periodically, until the meat is tender.*

MOROCCAN BRAISED VEAL SHANKS

This Moroccan version of the classic Italian dish osso buco *has a more exotic, spicy flavor. It's also good served over orzo. Substitute any kind of winter squash or sweet potato for the butternut squash.*

Spice rub:

- 2 teaspoons chili powder
- 1 teaspoon ground turmeric
- 1 teaspoon salt
- 1 teaspoon dried marjoram
- 1 teaspoon ground cumin
- 1 teaspoon black pepper

Remaining ingredients:

- 4 (16-ounce) veal shanks
- 1 tablespoon olive oil
- 3 cups chopped onion
- ¾ cup chopped celery
- ¾ cup diced carrot
- 2 tablespoons chopped garlic cloves
- 2 teaspoons minced peeled fresh ginger
- 1 teaspoon ground turmeric
- 1 tablespoon paprika
- 1 teaspoon ground coriander
- 3 cups fat-free, less-sodium chicken broth
- 1 cup dry white wine
- 3 tablespoons fresh lemon juice
- 2 tablespoons tomato paste
- 3 cups (½-inch) cubed peeled butternut squash or sweet potato
- 4 carrots, cut into 1-inch-thick pieces (about 8 ounces)
- 1 cup drained canned chickpeas (garbanzo beans)
- 4 cups hot cooked couscous
- 4 teaspoons chopped fresh mint (optional)

1. Preheat oven to 350°.
2. To prepare spice rub, combine first 6 ingredients in a small bowl. Trim fat from veal; rub surface of veal with spice rub.

Continued

3. Heat oil in a large Dutch oven or large heavy stockpot over medium-high heat. Add veal; cook 3 minutes on each side. Remove from pan. Add onion, celery, diced carrot, garlic, and ginger to pan; cover, reduce heat, and cook 10 minutes, stirring frequently. Stir in 1 teaspoon turmeric, paprika, and coriander. Add broth, wine, juice, and tomato paste, scraping pan to loosen browned bits. Return veal to pan; bring to a boil. Cover and bake at 350° for 45 minutes. Turn shanks; add squash, carrot pieces, and chickpeas. Cover and bake an additional 45 minutes or until veal shreds easily with a fork. Remove veal from pan, and remove meat from bones. Serve veal and vegetable mixture over couscous. Garnish with mint, if desired. Yield: 6 servings (serving size: about 3 ounces veal, 1⅓ cups vegetable mixture, and ⅔ cup couscous).

CALORIES 455 (15% from fat); FAT 7.4g (sat 1.7g, mono 3.2g, poly 1.4g); PROTEIN 38.4g; CARB 61g; FIBER 7.9g; CHOL 97mg; IRON 4.8mg; SODIUM 811mg; CALC 112mg

---

BEST CUTS FOR BRAISING

Tough cuts of meat work best for braising because they tend to have plenty of hard-worked muscle, along with a substance known as *collagen*. Over low heat, collagen melts into a flavorful, natural thickener that helps make rich sauces. Tender meats, on the other hand, tend to dry out in slow cooking. So for braising, look for cuts from lower legs, shoulders, necks, breasts, and rib cages. For example:

Beef: Chuck (bone in or boneless), bottom round, rump roast, round steak, and eye of round.

Pork: Boston butt (pork shoulder butt), picnic shoulder, blade end of the loin, ham hocks, pork neck, leg, and shank.

Lamb: Shanks, shoulder (roast, chops, or stew meat), neck, leg of lamb, and sirloin.

Veal: Cuts from the shoulder, breast, and shank.

Guiltless Getaway

A trend toward healthier menus and abundant activities means your next escape to a cozy bed-and-breakfast inn will leave you happier and more refreshed than ever before.

Over the past several decades, the nation's top bed-and-breakfast inns, much like many resorts and spas, have begun moving toward lighter foods and more fitness-oriented activities as a way to accommodate the changing desires of their clients. We visited the Mast Farm Inn—a lovingly restored, 1880s farm-and-rooming house in North Carolina's High Country. There, Executive Chef Scott Haulman has been working for years to perfect a style of cooking he calls New Southern—a lighter, quasi-nouvelle approach to traditional High Country and Carolina coastal staples. Haulman called his approach "stealth health"—food that tastes so good you can't entirely believe that it's good for you.

APPLE-ORANGE SPICE CAKE

Use a tube pan or an angel food cake pan, a round pan with deep sides and a hollow center.

Cake:

Cooking spray
1   tablespoon all-purpose flour
4   large eggs
1¾ cups sugar
3   cups all-purpose flour
1   tablespoon baking powder
½   teaspoon salt
½   teaspoon ground cinnamon
¼   teaspoon ground allspice
¼   teaspoon ground nutmeg
1   teaspoon grated orange rind
½   cup fresh orange juice (about 3 oranges)
½   cup vegetable oil
1   teaspoon vanilla extract
3   cups thinly sliced Granny Smith or other tart apple (about ¾ pound)
2   teaspoons sugar
¼   teaspoon ground cinnamon

Glaze:

¼   cup sugar
2   tablespoons low-fat buttermilk
¼   teaspoon baking soda

1. Preheat oven to 375°.
2. To prepare cake, coat a 10-inch tube pan with cooking spray; dust with 1 tablespoon flour.
3. Beat eggs in a large bowl at medium speed of a mixer until foamy; gradually add 1¾ cups sugar, beating well. Lightly spoon 3 cups flour into dry measuring cups; level with a knife. Combine 3 cups flour, baking powder, and next 4 ingredients, stirring well with a whisk. Combine rind, juice, oil, and vanilla. Add flour mixture to egg mixture alternately with juice mixture, beginning and ending with flour mixture. Combine apple, 2 teaspoons sugar, and ¼ teaspoon cinnamon.
4. Pour half of batter into prepared pan. Arrange half of apple mixture over batter, overlapping slices slightly. Repeat procedure. Bake at 375° for 1 hour or until a wooden pick inserted in center comes out clean. Cool in pan on a wire rack 20 minutes. Carefully remove cake from pan.
5. To prepare glaze, combine ¼ cup sugar, buttermilk, and soda in a saucepan. Cook over medium heat 2 minutes or until foamy, stirring constantly. Drizzle glaze over warm cake. Cool completely on rack. Yield: 18 servings.

CALORIES 253 (27% from fat); FAT 7.6g (sat 1.5g, mono 2.3g, poly 3.2g); PROTEIN 3.8g; CARB 43g; FIBER 1.1g; CHOL 49mg; IRON 1.3mg; SODIUM 180mg; CALC 60mg

FRITTATA WITH BLACK BEANS AND SALSA

Salsa:

- 1 cup diced tomato
- ⅓ cup chopped fresh cilantro
- 1½ tablespoons fresh lime juice
- 1 garlic clove, minced
- 1 jalapeño pepper, seeded and minced
- Dash of salt

Frittata:

- 2 teaspoons vegetable oil
- ¼ cup chopped green onions
- 3 ounces baked tortilla chips (about 3 cups), coarsely crushed
- 4 large egg whites, lightly beaten
- 3 large eggs, lightly beaten
- 1 (15-ounce) can black beans, drained
- ½ teaspoon ground cumin
- ½ cup (2 ounces) shredded reduced-fat Monterey Jack cheese with jalapeño peppers

1. To prepare salsa, combine first 6 ingredients in a bowl. Cover and marinate in refrigerator 30 minutes.
2. Preheat broiler.
3. To prepare frittata, heat oil in a large nonstick skillet over medium heat. Add green onions and chips; sauté 2 minutes. Remove from heat. Combine egg whites, eggs, and beans;

pour into skillet. Sprinkle with cumin. Wrap handle of skillet with foil; place skillet in oven. Broil 2½ minutes or until center is set. Sprinkle with cheese. Broil 20 seconds or until cheese melts. Cut into wedges; serve with salsa. Yield: 4 servings (serving size: 1 wedge and ¼ cup salsa).

CALORIES 320 (29% from fat); FAT 10.3g (sat 3.4g, mono 3.5g, poly 2.3g); PROTEIN 20.4g; CARB 38.1g; FIBER 5.2g; CHOL 175mg; IRON 3.1mg; SODIUM 597mg; CALC 201mg

SAVORY HIGH COUNTRY DUCK BREAST

You can find frozen duck breasts in the meat case of most supermarkets.

Roasted vegetables:

- 4 cups (1-inch) cubed peeled sweet potato
- 1 cup (½-inch) sliced parsnip
- 2 teaspoons vegetable oil
- ¼ teaspoon salt
- ¼ teaspoon garlic powder
- ¼ teaspoon dried thyme
- 8 garlic cloves, peeled
- 1 large onion, cut into ½-inch-thick wedges (about 14 ounces)

Duck:

- 4 (6-ounce) boned duck breast halves
- ¼ teaspoon salt
- ¼ teaspoon dried thyme
- ¼ teaspoon coarsely ground black pepper
- 1 teaspoon vegetable oil

Remaining ingredients:

- 2 cups hot cooked brown basmati rice
- Apple Chutney

1. Preheat oven to 400°.
2. To prepare roasted vegetables, combine first 8 ingredients in a large roasting pan; toss well to coat. Bake at 400° for 35 minutes or until parsnip is tender.

3. To prepare duck, remove skin. Sprinkle duck breasts with ¼ teaspoon salt, ¼ teaspoon thyme, and pepper. Heat 1 teaspoon oil in a large nonstick skillet over medium-high heat. Add duck; sauté 2 minutes on each side. Wrap handle of skillet with foil; place skillet in oven. Bake at 400° for 5 minutes. Remove from oven. Cut each breast half lengthwise into thin strips. Arrange strips around rice. Serve with roasted vegetables and Apple Chutney. Yield: 4 servings (serving size: 5 ounces duck, 1½ cups roasted vegetables, ½ cup rice, and ¼ cup chutney).

(Totals include Apple Chutney) CALORIES 582 (24% from fat); FAT 15.4g (sat 4.7g, mono 4.8g, poly 3.9g); PROTEIN 26.8g; CARB 85.1g; FIBER 9.5g; CHOL 76mg; IRON 4.5mg; SODIUM 382mg; CALC 108mg

Apple Chutney:

- 1 tablespoon vegetable oil
- 2 cups chopped onion
- ½ teaspoon whole cloves
- ¼ teaspoon ground cinnamon
- ¼ teaspoon ground cumin
- ⅛ teaspoon ground cardamom
- ⅛ teaspoon ground turmeric
- ⅛ teaspoon ground red pepper
- 5 cups diced Braeburn or Gala apple (about 1½ pounds)
- ½ cup fresh cranberries
- ½ cup packed brown sugar
- ¼ cup cider vinegar
- 1 teaspoon minced peeled fresh ginger

1. Heat oil in a saucepan. Add onion and next 6 ingredients; sauté 5 minutes. Add apple and remaining ingredients; cook 15 minutes, stirring frequently. Discard cloves. Serve warm. Yield: 4 cups (serving size: ¼ cup).
Note: Store leftover chutney in an airtight container in the refrigerator up to 2 weeks.

CALORIES 64 (14% from fat); FAT 1g (sat 0.2g, mono 0.3g, poly 0.5g); PROTEIN 0.3g; CARB 14.5g; FIBER 1.4g; CHOL 0mg; IRON 0.3mg; SODIUM 4mg; CALC 14mg

SWEET POTATO-CORN BREAD FRITTERS

Self-rising flour and self-rising cornmeal contain baking powder and salt. Substitute the same amount of all-purpose flour and regular cornmeal, adding 2 teaspoons baking powder and ½ teaspoon salt.

2½   cups self-rising flour
 1   cup self-rising yellow cornmeal
 1   cup diced peeled cooked sweet potato
 ¼   teaspoon apple-pie spice
 2   cups low-fat buttermilk
 3   large eggs
 8   teaspoons vegetable oil
10   tablespoons molasses

1. Lightly spoon flour into dry measuring cups; level with a knife. Combine flour, cornmeal, potato, and spice in a large bowl. Combine buttermilk and eggs; add to flour mixture, stirring until smooth.
2. Heat 2 teaspoons oil in a large nonstick skillet over medium heat. Spoon 2 tablespoons batter per fritter into hot pan; cook 3 minutes on each side or until golden brown. Repeat with remaining oil and batter. Serve fritters with molasses. Yield: 10 servings (serving size: 3 fritters and 1 tablespoon molasses).

CALORIES 294 (20% from fat); FAT 6.4g (sat 1.5g, mono 1.9g, poly 2.3g); PROTEIN 7.8g; CARB 51.4g; FIBER 0.4g; CHOL 68mg; IRON 3.5mg; SODIUM 629mg; CALC 259mg

MAST FARM INN SHRIMP AND GRITS

 1   pound large shrimp (about 20 shrimp)
Cooking spray
 2   teaspoons Cajun seasoning (such as Paul Prudhomme's Seafood Magic)
Appalachian Hiking Grits
 1   cup Rosemary-Tomato Sauce

1. Peel shrimp. Starting at tail end, butterfly each shrimp, cutting to, but not through, top of shrimp.
2. Heat a nonstick skillet coated with cooking spray over medium-high heat. Add shrimp and seasoning; sauté 3 minutes or until shrimp are done. Spoon ½ cup Appalachian Hiking Grits onto each of 4 plates; top each serving with 5 shrimp. Spoon ¼ cup Rosemary-Tomato Sauce around shrimp on each plate. Yield: 4 servings.

(Totals include Appalachian Hiking Grits and Rosemary-Tomato Sauce) CALORIES 234 (27% from fat); FAT 7g (sat 3.1g, mono 1.9g, poly 0.9g); PROTEIN 21.6g; CARB 21g; FIBER 2.1g; CHOL 142mg; IRON 3.3mg; SODIUM 615mg; CALC 108mg

Appalachian Hiking Grits:

 2   cups water
 ¼   teaspoon salt
 ¼   teaspoon garlic powder
 ⅛   teaspoon dry mustard
 ⅛   teaspoon paprika
 ½   cup uncooked regular grits
 ¼   cup (1 ounce) shredded sharp Cheddar cheese
 2   teaspoons butter or stick margarine

1. Bring first 5 ingredients to a boil. Stir in grits; cover, reduce heat, and simmer 20 minutes, stirring occasionally. Stir in cheese and butter. Yield: 4 servings (serving size: ½ cup).

CALORIES 114 (35% from fat); FAT 4.4g (sat 2.7g, mono 1.2g, poly 0.1g); PROTEIN 3.5g; CARB 15.2g; FIBER 1g; CHOL 13mg; IRON 0.8mg; SODIUM 211mg; CALC 52mg

Rosemary-Tomato Sauce:

You can substitute canned, diced tomatoes for the fresh, if desired.

 2   teaspoons olive oil
 1   cup diced onion
1½   cups diced red bell pepper
 1   tablespoon chopped fresh or 1 teaspoon dried rosemary
 4   cups coarsely chopped peeled tomato
 ½   cup dry white wine
 ¼   teaspoon salt
 8   garlic cloves, minced

1. Heat oil in a large saucepan over medium-high heat. Add onion; sauté 3 minutes. Add bell pepper and rosemary; sauté 1 minute. Stir in tomato, wine, salt, and garlic; bring to a boil. Reduce heat, and simmer 30 minutes. Yield: 3½ cups (serving size: ¼ cup).
Note: Store leftover sauce in an airtight container in the refrigerator up to 1 week or freeze up to 3 months.

CALORIES 28 (29% from fat); FAT 0.9g (sat 0.1g, mono 0.5g, poly 0.2g); PROTEIN 0.8g; CARB 5g; FIBER 1.1g; CHOL 0mg; IRON 0.5mg; SODIUM 48mg; CALC 11mg

HEALTHY B&B'S

To find a B&B or an inn committed to delicious but healthful food and fitness options, try these tips.

Previsit at a bookstore. *America's Favorite Inns, B&Bs & Small Hotels,* by Sandra W. Soule (St. Martin, 1997) is based on the comments of actual guests. *The Innkeepers' Register* (Independent Innkeepers' Association, 800/344-5244) lists inns committed to quality food.

Check credentials. Membership in the Professional Association of Innkeepers International (Web site: www.paii.org) usually is a tip-off that the inn really takes quality food seriously.

Search the Web. Type in the name of the B&B that you're interested in or "bed-and-breakfast inns" on your favorite search engine for options, usually listed by region or state.

Stay—Just a Little Bit Longer

Thanksgiving starts with the big meal, but that doesn't mean the rest of the long weekend has to be a food fizzle for you or your guests.

When Thanksgiving Day is over, and your house is filled with friends and relatives staying over until Sunday, the question that looms large is "What to provide?" Thankfully, the answer is simple: *brunch*.

The key is to keep your brunch menu light yet hearty enough to satisfy, unique but easy to prepare in advance. We've put together two menus with some options for side dishes.

> ### MAKE-AHEAD BRUNCH MENU 1
>
> SPARKLING CITRUS PUNCH
>
> OVERNIGHT ARTICHOKE-AND-HAM STRATA
>
> BLACK-EYED PEA HUMMUS
>
> SPINACH-AND-MIXED GREENS SALAD OR APPLE-AND-PEAR SLAW
>
> CRANBERRY-ORANGE TRIFLE
>
> **about 849 calories (16% from fat) and 14.8g fat per menu serving**

SPARKLING CITRUS PUNCH

Make-ahead tip: Combine the fruit juices a day in advance. Then add sparkling water or champagne just before serving.

- ¾ cup apricot nectar, chilled
- ¾ cup pink grapefruit juice cocktail, chilled
- 1 (12-ounce) can orange-tangerine juice concentrate, thawed and undiluted
- 3 cups sparkling water or champagne, chilled

1. Combine first 3 ingredients in a pitcher; chill. Add sparkling water; serve immediately over ice. Yield: 2 quarts (serving size: ¾ cup).

CALORIES 114 (0% from fat); FAT 0g; PROTEIN 0.3g; CARB 26.5g; FIBER 0.2g; CHOL 0mg; IRON 0.1mg; SODIUM 4mg; CALC 264mg

OVERNIGHT ARTICHOKE-AND-HAM STRATA

Make-ahead tip: Prepare strata a day ahead; cover and chill 8 hours or overnight. In the morning, uncover the strata and bake it straight out of the refrigerator in a preheated oven.

- 3 English muffins, split and quartered
- Cooking spray
- 1 tablespoon butter or stick margarine, melted
- 1 cup chopped lean ham (about 4 ounces)
- ½ cup (2 ounces) grated fresh Parmesan cheese
- 2 tablespoons chopped fresh chives
- 1 (14-ounce) can artichoke hearts, drained and chopped
- 3 large garlic cloves, minced
- ⅛ teaspoon ground nutmeg
- 1 (12-ounce) can evaporated fat-free milk
- 3 large eggs
- 3 large egg whites

1. Arrange muffin pieces, crust sides down, in an 8-inch square baking dish coated with cooking spray; drizzle with butter. Arrange ham and next 4 ingredients over muffin pieces.
2. Combine nutmeg and remaining 3 ingredients in a bowl; stir well with a whisk. Pour over muffin mixture. Cover; chill 8 hours or overnight.
3. Preheat oven to 375°.
4. Uncover strata; bake at 375° for 50 minutes or until set. Let stand 10 minutes. Yield: 6 servings.

CALORIES 280 (29% from fat); FAT 8.9g (sat 4.1g, mono 3.1g, poly 0.8g); PROTEIN 20.4g; CARB 29.8g; FIBER 0.1g; CHOL 133mg; IRON 2.3mg; SODIUM 819mg; CALC 367mg

BLACK-EYED PEA HUMMUS

Make-ahead tip: Make hummus up to two days in advance; just cover and chill.

- 3 garlic cloves, peeled
- ½ cup fresh lemon juice (about 2 lemons)
- ⅓ cup tahini (sesame-seed paste)
- 1 teaspoon ground cumin
- ½ teaspoon salt
- ½ teaspoon paprika
- 2 (15.8-ounce) cans black-eyed peas, drained
- 14 (6-inch) pitas, quartered
- Fresh chives (optional)

1. Drop garlic through chute of a food processor with processor on; process 3 seconds or until garlic is minced. Add lemon juice and next 5 ingredients; process until smooth, scraping sides of bowl occasionally. Serve with pita wedges. Garnish with fresh chives, if desired. Yield: 3½ cups (serving size: 2 tablespoons dip and 2 pita wedges).

CALORIES 121 (15% from fat); FAT 2g (sat 0.3g, mono 0.6g, poly 0.9g); PROTEIN 4.7g; CARB 21.2g; FIBER 1.3g; CHOL 0mg; IRON 1.4mg; SODIUM 263mg; CALC 45mg

SPINACH-AND-MIXED GREENS SALAD

Make-ahead tip: Prepare dressing and salad greens a day ahead. Cover and chill separately.

Dressing:

1½ tablespoons extra-virgin olive
      oil
1 tablespoon water
1 tablespoon balsamic vinegar
2 teaspoons Dijon mustard
¼ teaspoon salt
¼ teaspoon black pepper
2 tablespoons thinly sliced green
     onions

Greens:

6 cups torn spinach
4 cups gourmet salad greens
2 tablespoons fresh tarragon
     leaves or 2 teaspoons dried
     tarragon

1. To prepare dressing, combine first 6 ingredients in a large bowl; stir well with a whisk. Stir in green onions.
2. To prepare greens, combine spinach, salad greens, and tarragon in a large bowl; add dressing, and toss well. Serve salad immediately. Yield: 8 servings (servings size: 1 cup).

CALORIES 39 (65% from fat); FAT 2.8g (sat 0.4g, mono 1.9g, poly 0.3g); PROTEIN 1.7g; CARB 2.5g; FIBER 2.2g; CHOL 0mg; IRON 1.6mg; SODIUM 146mg; CALC 55mg

APPLE-AND-PEAR SLAW

Make-ahead tip: Make the dressing up to one week in advance; cover and chill. Slice the fruit; toss it with the coleslaw mix and dressing in the morning.

¼ cup cider vinegar
1 tablespoon brown sugar
2 teaspoons poppy seeds
½ teaspoon salt
¼ teaspoon black pepper
2 cups thinly sliced Granny Smith
     apple (about 1 large apple)
2 cups thinly sliced pear (about
     1 large pear)
1 (12-ounce) package cabbage-
     and-carrot coleslaw

1. Combine first 5 ingredients in a small bowl; set aside.
2. Combine apple, pear, and coleslaw in a large bowl; stir in dressing. Chill up to 2 hours. Yield: 6 servings (serving size: 1 cup).

CALORIES 82 (10% from fat); FAT 0.9g (sat 0.1g, mono 0.1g, poly 0.4g); PROTEIN 1.1g; CARB 19.7g; FIBER 3.8g; CHOL 0mg; IRON 0.7mg; SODIUM 208mg; CALC 50mg

CRANBERRY-ORANGE TRIFLE

Make-ahead tip: Prepare the cranberry sauce and custard up to three days in advance; cover and chill separately. Then assemble the trifle the day before, and store in the refrigerator.

Cranberry sauce:

1 (12-ounce) bag fresh cranberries
1½ teaspoons grated orange rind
1¼ cups fresh orange juice (about
      6 oranges)
½ cup sugar
½ cup water

Custard:

1¾ cups 2% reduced-fat milk,
      divided
1 large egg
⅓ cup sugar
3 tablespoons cornstarch
¼ teaspoon salt
1 teaspoon vanilla extract

Remaining ingredients:

4 large navel oranges (about
     2 pounds)
36 ladyfingers (3 [3-ounce]
      packages)
½ cup reduced-calorie frozen
     whipped topping (optional)
8 teaspoons toasted sliced
     almonds (optional)

1. To prepare cranberry sauce, combine first 5 ingredients in a medium saucepan, and bring to a boil. Reduce heat, and simmer 30 minutes, stirring occasionally. Press cranberry mixture through a sieve over a bowl, reserving 1⅔ cups cranberry puree; discard solids. Cover and chill.
2. To prepare custard, combine ¼ cup milk and egg in a small bowl, and stir well with a whisk. Place ⅓ cup sugar, cornstarch, and salt in a medium saucepan, and gradually add 1½ cups milk, stirring well with a whisk. Bring to a boil over medium heat, and cook 1 minute, stirring constantly. Gradually stir about one-fourth of hot milk mixture into egg mixture; add to remaining hot milk mixture, stirring constantly. Cook over medium heat 3 minutes or until mixture is thick, stirring constantly. Remove from heat, and stir in vanilla. Pour custard into a bowl, and cover surface with plastic wrap. Chill.
3. Peel oranges, removing white pithy part. Cut each orange in half lengthwise. Cut each half crosswise into thin slices; set aside.
4. Split ladyfingers; tear each half into thirds. Line bottom of a 3-quart straight-sided glass bowl or trifle bowl with half of ladyfinger pieces. Spoon 1 cup custard over ladyfingers. Spoon half of cranberry sauce over custard.

Arrange half of orange slices over cranberry sauce and around side of bowl. Repeat layers, ending with orange slices. Cover and chill 8 hours. If desired, top each serving with 1 tablespoon whipped topping and 1 teaspoon almonds. Yield: 8 servings (serving size: 1 cup).

CALORIES 277 (16% from fat); FAT 4.9g (sat 1.3g, mono 1.9g, poly 0.7g); PROTEIN 4.5g; CARB 66.9g; FIBER 4.3g; CHOL 77mg; IRON 0.5mg; SODIUM 131mg; CALC 119mg

---

GREEN BEANS NIÇOISE

Make-ahead tip: Prepare the green beans and tomato mixture a day in advance; cover and chill separately. Toss before serving.

   2 pounds green beans, trimmed
1⅓ cups chopped plum tomato
       (about ¾ pound)
   ½ cup minced shallots
   ¼ cup water
   2 tablespoons chopped ripe olives
   2 tablespoons red wine vinegar
   1 tablespoon olive oil
   2 teaspoons Dijon mustard
   ½ teaspoon salt

1. Place beans into a large saucepan of boiling water; cook 5 minutes. Drain and plunge beans into ice water; drain.
2. Combine tomato and remaining 7 ingredients; pour over beans, and toss to coat. Yield: 8 servings (serving size: 1 cup).

CALORIES 68 (29% from fat); FAT 2.2g (sat 0.3g, mono 1.4g, poly 0.3g); PROTEIN 2.6g; CARB 11.5g; FIBER 2.8g; CHOL 0mg; IRON 1.5mg; SODIUM 213mg; CALC 49mg

---

APRICOT SCONES

Make-ahead tip: Prepare scones a day ahead; cool on a wire rack. Wrap in foil; reheat at 350° for 25 minutes.

2½ cups all-purpose flour
   ½ cup sugar
   2 teaspoons baking powder
   ½ teaspoon baking soda
   ¼ teaspoon salt
   ¼ cup chilled butter or stick
       margarine, cut into small
       pieces
   ½ cup finely chopped dried
       apricots
   ½ cup low-fat buttermilk
   2 large eggs
Cooking spray
   2 teaspoons sugar
   ½ teaspoon ground cinnamon

1. Preheat oven to 400°.
2. Lightly spoon flour into dry measuring cups; level with a knife. Combine flour, ½ cup sugar, and next 3 ingredients; cut in butter with a pastry blender or 2 knives until mixture resembles coarse meal. Stir in apricots. Combine buttermilk and eggs, stirring well with a whisk. Add to flour mixture, stirring just until moist (dough will be sticky).
3. Turn dough out onto a lightly floured surface; knead lightly 4 times. Pat dough into a 9-inch circle on a baking sheet coated with cooking spray. Cut dough into 12 wedges, cutting into, but not through, dough. Combine 2 teaspoons sugar and cinnamon, and sprinkle over dough. Bake at 400° for 20 minutes or until golden. Serve warm. Yield: 1 dozen (serving size: 1 scone).

CALORIES 196 (24% from fat); FAT 5.2g (sat 2.8g, mono 1.5g, poly 0.4g); PROTEIN 4.4g; CARB 33.7g; FIBER 1.3g; CHOL 47mg; IRON 1.8mg; SODIUM 239mg; CALC 71mg

---

LIGHTEN UP

Sibling Revelries

A reader's fabulous carrot cake gets lightened, and still pleases the crowd—her large family.

Tonia Bailey has been baking since she was "old enough to read a recipe," but in her youth, she had little to show for her work. The cakes, pies, and cookies she made disappeared even before they'd cooled. Ten eager siblings were the reason.

The family's favorite dessert is rich, decadent carrot cake, crowned with butter and cream cheese icing. "Growing up, I'd make this cake so often, I had the recipe memorized," says the Ventura, California, mother of three.

These days the avid cyclist, swimmer, and water-skier usually eats lighter foods, but she hasn't forgotten this beloved recipe. Though she and her numerous brothers and sisters are not as active—or quite as slender—as they used to be, no one wants to give up their carrot cake.

So we subtracted more than 200 calories and nearly 20 grams of fat.

BEFORE & AFTER	
SERVING SIZE	
1 slice	
CALORIES	
512	304
FAT	
29g	9.5g
PERCENT OF TOTAL CALORIES	
51%	28%
CHOLESTEROL	
77mg	33mg

Continued

CARROT CAKE

To give our cake moistness and more flavor, we used apple butter—a thick, dark-brown spread made of apples, sugar, and spices. You can find it with jams and jellies in your grocery store.

    2 cups all-purpose flour
    ½ cup granulated sugar
    ½ cup packed brown sugar
    2 teaspoons baking soda
    2 teaspoons ground cinnamon
    1 teaspoon salt
    ½ cup apple butter
    ½ cup vegetable oil
    1 tablespoon vanilla extract
    2 large eggs
    2 large egg whites
    3 cups shredded carrot
       Cooking spray
       Cream Cheese Frosting

1. Preheat oven to 350°.
2. Lightly spoon flour into dry measuring cups; level with a knife. Combine flour, granulated sugar, and next 4 ingredients; make a well in center of mixture. Combine apple butter and next 4 ingredients in a large bowl; stir well with a whisk. Add apple butter mixture to flour mixture, stirring just until moist. Fold in carrot.
3. Pour batter into 2 (8-inch) round cake pans coated with cooking spray. Bake at 350° for 35 minutes or until a wooden pick inserted in center comes out clean. Cool in pans 10 minutes on a wire rack; remove from pans. Cool completely on wire rack.
4. Place 1 cake layer on a plate; spread with ⅔ cup frosting, and top with remaining cake layer. Spread remaining frosting over top and sides of cake. Store cake loosely covered in refrigerator. Yield: 18 servings (serving size: 1 slice).

(Totals include Cream Cheese Frosting) CALORIES 304 (28% from fat); FAT 9.5g (sat 2.9g, mono 2.8g, poly 3.2g); PROTEIN 3.6g; CARB 51.6g; FIBER 1g; CHOL 33mg; IRON 1.1mg; SODIUM 357mg; CALC 38mg

Cream Cheese Frosting:

    ½ cup (4 ounces) block-style
       fat-free cream cheese, chilled
    ¼ cup butter or stick margarine,
       softened
    1 teaspoon grated lemon rind
    1 teaspoon vanilla extract
   3½ cups sifted powdered sugar

1. Beat first 4 ingredients at medium speed of a mixer until smooth. Gradually add sugar to butter mixture; beat at low speed just until blended (do not overbeat). Yield: 2 cups (serving size: 1 tablespoon).

CALORIES 67 (20% from fat); FAT 1.5g (sat 0.9g, mono 0.4g, poly 0.1g); PROTEIN 0.5g; CARB 13.2g; FIBER 0g; CHOL 5mg; IRON 0mg; SODIUM 36mg; CALC 11mg

BAKING

Legends of the Loaves

The aroma of our fresh-baked holiday breads carries more than sensory pleasure—it also bears the story of our many national heritages.

During the holidays, we celebrate by decorating our homes with festive ornaments and preparing elaborate meals for friends and family. Our aprons dusty with flour, many of us knead away at secret family recipes to create cherished holiday breads.

They're recipes that our grandmothers brought with them from the old country. Danish mothers, for instance, preserve tradition by inviting their children to take part in *julebagning,* or Christmas baking. In Italy and in Italian homes the world over, the age-old belief endures that sharing a fruit-filled *panettone* will summon prosperity in the coming year.

In this season of celebration, these bread favorites not only resonate with a delicious nostalgia—but also keep your silhouette from shifting south into an equatorial bulge.

CHRISTOPSOMO (GREEK CHRISTMAS BREAD)

Around the holidays, this rich, buttery egg bread is typically decorated with long ropes of dough shaped in the form of an early Christian cross, hence the name "Christ's Bread." Though mahleb, *a spice made from ground black cherry pits, is often used for flavoring, we've substituted the easier-to-find aniseed.*

    1 package dry yeast (about 2¼
       teaspoons)
    1 tablespoon sugar
    ½ cup warm water (100° to 110°)
    6 tablespoons butter or stick
       margarine, softened
    2 large eggs
   3½ cups all-purpose flour, divided
    ⅓ cup sugar
    2 tablespoons nonfat dry milk
    2 teaspoons aniseed, crushed
    ½ teaspoon salt
       Cooking spray
    1 large egg white, lightly beaten
    8 candied cherries

1. Dissolve yeast and 1 tablespoon sugar in warm water in a large bowl; let stand 5 minutes. Add butter and eggs; beat at medium speed of a mixer until smooth. Lightly spoon flour into dry measuring cups, and level with a knife. Combine 3 cups flour, ⅓ cup sugar, dry milk, aniseed, and salt; add to yeast mixture, beating well. Turn dough out onto a lightly floured surface. Knead until smooth and elastic (about 10 minutes); add enough remaining flour, 1 tablespoon at a time, to prevent dough from sticking to hands.
2. Place dough in a large bowl coated with cooking spray, turning to coat top. Cover and let rise in a warm place (85°), free from drafts, about 1½ hours. Dough will not double in size. (Press two fingers into dough. If indentation remains, dough has risen enough.)
3. Punch dough down; let rest 5 minutes. Pinch 2 (1½-inch) balls off dough; cover and set aside. Shape

remaining dough into an 8-inch round; place on a baking sheet coated with cooking spray. Brush with egg white. Shape each dough ball into an 8-inch-long rope; cut a 2-inch slash into each end of ropes. Place 1 rope across middle of dough; brush middle of rope with egg white. Place other rope across middle of rope, forming a cross. Curl slashed ends together to form a circle at end of each rope; place a cherry in middle of each circle. Arrange 4 cherries around center of cross. Cover and let rise 1 hour.

4. Preheat oven to 350°.

5. Uncover dough. Bake at 350° for 35 minutes or until loaf sounds hollow when tapped. Remove loaf from pan, and cool on a wire rack. Yield: 16 servings (serving size: 1 wedge).

Note: If you don't have time to decorate this bread, skip step 3. Punch dough down; let rest. Shape dough into an 8-inch round. Cover and let rise 1 hour. Bake as directed.

CALORIES 185 (26% from fat); FAT 5.3g (sat 1.1g, mono 2.2g, poly 1.6g); PROTEIN 4.5g; CARB 29.8g; FIBER 1g; CHOL 28mg; IRON 1.6mg; SODIUM 140mg; CALC 24mg

FREEZER FRIENDLY

All of these festive holiday sweet breads can be made in advance and frozen.

For best results, be meticulous about packaging. Wrap unglazed loaves tightly in a double thickness of plastic wrap or foil. Or slice your loaf, wrap it, and then place it in a large zip-top plastic freezer bag.

Whole loaves will keep six to nine months at the recommended 0°; bread slices will keep up to four months. (If your freezer is warmer, you'll need to cut down on these storage times.)

To thaw, keep bread wrapped tightly and let stand at room temperature. Or pull out individual slices from freezer and pop them directly into the toaster. Drizzle with glaze (if the recipe calls for one) prior to serving.

JULEKAGE (DANISH CHRISTMAS FRUIT LOAF)

Typically baked with candied citrus rind and either spiced apples or dried fruit (our choice), this rich Scandinavian sweet bread is then crowned with a sweet, snowy-white glaze.

Dough:

4¼ cups all-purpose flour, divided
3 tablespoons granulated sugar, divided
⅓ cup chopped almonds
⅓ cup raisins
¼ cup nonfat dry milk
2 tablespoons chopped candied citron
2 tablespoons chopped candied lemon peel
2 tablespoons chopped candied orange peel
1 teaspoon salt
1 teaspoon grated lemon rind
½ teaspoon ground cardamom
1 package dry yeast (about 2¼ teaspoons)
½ cup warm water (100° to 110°)
6 tablespoons butter or stick margarine, softened
1 teaspoon vanilla extract
2 large eggs, lightly beaten
Cooking spray
1 tablespoon fat-free milk
⅛ teaspoon salt
1 large egg
1 tablespoon turbinado or granulated sugar

Glaze:

½ cup sifted powdered sugar
2 teaspoons water
¼ teaspoon almond extract

1. To prepare dough, lightly spoon flour into dry measuring cups, and level with a knife. Combine 4 cups flour, 2 tablespoons granulated sugar, almonds, and next 8 ingredients in a large bowl.

2. Dissolve 1 tablespoon granulated sugar and yeast in warm water in a large bowl; let stand 5 minutes. Stir in butter, vanilla, and 2 beaten eggs until well-blended. Gradually add flour mixture; stir to combine. Turn dough out onto a lightly floured surface. Knead until smooth and elastic (about 8 minutes); add enough remaining flour, 1 tablespoon at a time, to prevent dough from sticking to hands.

3. Place dough in a large bowl coated with cooking spray, turning to coat top. Cover and let rise in a warm place (85°), free from drafts, 1 hour and 45 minutes. Dough will not double in size. (Press two fingers into dough. If indentation remains, dough has risen enough.)

4. Punch dough down; let rest 5 minutes. Roll into an 11 x 9-inch rectangle on a lightly floured surface. Roll up rectangle tightly, starting with a short edge, pressing firmly to eliminate air pockets; pinch seam and ends to seal. Place, seam side down, in a 9 x 5-inch loaf pan coated with cooking spray. Cover and let rise 1½ hours.

5. Preheat oven to 375°.

6. Uncover dough. Combine fat-free milk, ⅛ teaspoon salt, and 1 egg; brush lightly over loaf. Sprinkle with turbinado sugar. Bake at 375° for 45 minutes or until loaf sounds hollow when tapped. Remove from pan; cool on a wire rack.

7. To prepare glaze, combine powdered sugar, 2 teaspoons water, and almond extract in a small bowl. Drizzle over loaf. Yield: 1 loaf, 16 servings (serving size: 1 slice).

CALORIES 234 (26% from fat); FAT 6.7g (sat 1.3g, mono 3g, poly 1.8g); PROTEIN 5.9g; CARB 37.6g; FIBER 1.4g; CHOL 42mg; IRON 1.9mg; SODIUM 249mg; CALC 47mg

STOLLE DE NOËL
(CHRISTMAS STOLLEN)

Our version of this 14th-century German holiday bread contains a lot less butter, but is chock-full of dried fruits and has the same characteristic firm, dry texture of the original.

Marinated fruit:

- ¼ cup kirsch (cherry brandy) or apple juice
- 3 tablespoons candied lemon peel
- 3 tablespoons candied orange peel
- 3 tablespoons candied citron
- 3 tablespoons dried currants
- 3 tablespoons golden raisins

Dough:

- 1 package dry yeast (about 2¼ teaspoons)
- ¼ teaspoon granulated sugar
- ¼ cup warm water (100° to 110°)
- 3½ cups all-purpose flour, divided
- ½ cup fat-free milk
- ¼ cup granulated sugar
- ¼ cup butter or stick margarine, melted
- 1 teaspoon salt
- 1 large egg
- ½ cup coarsely chopped almonds
- Cooking spray

Glaze:

- 1 tablespoon butter or stick margarine, softened
- 2 tablespoons powdered sugar

1. To prepare marinated fruit, combine first 6 ingredients in a small bowl, and let stand 1 hour. Drain mixture in a sieve over a bowl, reserving brandy and fruit mixture separately.
2. To prepare dough, dissolve yeast and ¼ teaspoon granulated sugar in warm water in a large bowl; let stand 5 minutes. Lightly spoon flour into dry measuring cups; level with a knife. Add 1½ cups flour, reserved brandy, milk, ¼ cup granulated sugar, ¼ cup butter, salt, and egg to yeast mixture; beat at medium speed of a mixer until mixture is smooth. Stir in marinated fruit, 1½ cups flour, and almonds. Turn dough out onto a lightly floured surface. Knead until smooth and elastic (about 8 minutes); add enough remaining flour, 1 tablespoon at a time, to prevent dough from sticking to hands.
3. Place dough in a bowl coated with cooking spray; turn to coat top. Cover; let rise in a warm place (85°), free from drafts, about 2 hours. Dough will not double in size. (Press two fingers into dough. If indentation remains, dough has risen enough.)
4. Punch dough down; let rest 5 minutes. Roll into a 13 x 8-inch oval on a lightly floured surface. Place on a baking sheet coated with cooking spray; fold dough over lengthwise, leaving a 3-inch border. Cover dough, and let rise 1 hour.
5. Preheat oven to 350°.
6. Uncover dough, and bake at 350° for 25 minutes or until browned and loaf sounds hollow when tapped; cool. Brush with 1 tablespoon butter; sprinkle with powdered sugar. Yield: 16 servings (serving size: 1 slice).

CALORIES 218 (24% from fat); FAT 5.8g (sat 1g, mono 2.7g, poly 1.6g); PROTEIN 4.4g; CARB 33.2g; FIBER 1.4g; CHOL 14mg; IRON 1.6mg; SODIUM 213mg; CALC 32mg

PANETTONE
(ITALIAN CHRISTMAS BREAD)

This Italian fruitcake-style yeast bread is typically baked into a tall, cylindrical shape (empty coffee cans work great as baking pans). While its origins are sketchy, one legend holds that in the late 1400s, a young Milanese nobleman fell in love with the daughter of a baker named Toni and created "Pan de Toni" to impress his love's father.

Marinated fruit:

- ⅓ cup golden raisins
- ⅓ cup chopped dried apricots
- ⅓ cup dried tart cherries
- ¼ cup triple sec (orange-flavored liqueur) or orange juice

Dough:

- 1 package dry yeast (about 2¼ teaspoons)
- ¼ teaspoon granulated sugar
- ¼ cup warm water (100° to 110°)
- 3¾ cups all-purpose flour, divided
- 6 tablespoons butter or stick margarine, melted
- ¼ cup fat-free milk
- ¼ cup granulated sugar
- ½ teaspoon salt
- 1 large egg
- 1 large egg yolk
- 2 tablespoons pine nuts
- Cooking spray
- 1 teaspoon butter or stick margarine, melted
- 2 teaspoons turbinado or granulated sugar

1. To prepare marinated fruit, combine first 4 ingredients in a small bowl; let stand 1 hour. Drain fruit in a sieve over a bowl, reserving fruit and 2 teaspoons liqueur separately.
2. To prepare dough, dissolve yeast and ¼ teaspoon granulated sugar in warm water in a small bowl; let stand 5 minutes. Lightly spoon flour into dry measuring cups; level with a knife. Combine ½ cup flour, 6 tablespoons butter, and next 5 ingredients in a large bowl; beat at medium speed of a mixer 1 minute or until smooth. Add yeast mixture and ½ cup flour; beat 1 minute. Stir in marinated fruit, 2½ cups flour, and pine nuts. Turn dough out onto a lightly floured surface. Knead until smooth and elastic (about 8 minutes); add enough remaining flour, 1 tablespoon at a time, to prevent dough from sticking to hands.
3. Place dough in a large bowl coated with cooking spray, turning to coat top. Cover and let rise in a warm place (85°), free from drafts, about 1½ hours. Dough will not double in size. (Press two fingers into dough. If indentation remains, dough has risen enough.)
4. Punch dough down; let rest 5 minutes. Divide in half, shaping each portion into a ball. Place balls into 2 (13-ounce) coffee cans coated with

cooking spray. Cover dough, and let rise 1 hour.

5. Preheat oven to 375°.

6. Uncover dough. Place coffee cans on bottom rack in oven, and bake at 375° for 30 minutes or until browned and loaf sounds hollow when tapped. Remove bread from cans, and cool on a wire rack. Combine reserved 2 teaspoons liqueur and 1 teaspoon butter; brush over loaves. Sprinkle evenly with turbinado sugar. Yield: 2 loaves, 8 servings per loaf (serving size: 1 slice).

CALORIES 211 (28% from fat); FAT 6.6g (sat 1.3g, mono 2.7g, poly 2.1g); PROTEIN 4.5g; CARB 33.8g; FIBER 1.4g; CHOL 27mg; IRON 1.9mg; SODIUM 137mg; CALC 19mg

Pretty with Pink

A former banker turned cook colors her veggies too tasty to pass up.

CRANBERRY-AND-SWEET POTATO BAKE

"The combination of fuchsia and orange is beautiful, and the sweetness of the potatoes offsets the tart cranberries."

—*Kristen Muller, Long Island, New York*

2 (15-ounce) cans sweet potatoes, drained
1 (8-ounce) can crushed pineapple in juice, drained
2 tablespoons butter or stick margarine, melted
¼ teaspoon salt
⅛ teaspoon ground nutmeg
Dash of black pepper
1 large egg
1 (16-ounce) can whole-berry cranberry sauce, divided
Cooking spray

1. Preheat oven to 350°.

2. Combine sweet potatoes and pineapple in a large bowl; mash with a potato masher. Stir in butter, salt, nutmeg, pepper, and egg. Swirl in 1 cup cranberry sauce. Spoon ⅓ cup sweet potato mixture into each of 8 (4-ounce) ramekins coated with cooking spray. Top each with 1 tablespoon cranberry sauce. Bake at 350° for 40 minutes. Yield: 8 servings.

Note: Substitute a 1-quart casserole for ramekins. Bake at 350° for 40 minutes.

CALORIES 212 (17% from fat); FAT 3.9g (sat 2g, mono 1.1g, poly 0.4g); PROTEIN 2.6g; CARB 43.2g; FIBER 1.7g; CHOL 35mg; IRON 1.3mg; SODIUM 186mg; CALC 32mg

BROCCOLI, CHEESE, AND RICE CASSEROLE

"A friend served this dish at dinner. I loved it but forgot to get the recipe, so I created my own light version. I can put it together quickly, and it's easy to make ahead and pop in the oven before dinner. Another plus is that kids love it."

—*Ellen Brown, Ridgefield, Connecticut*

1 cup uncooked instant rice
½ cup chopped onion
¼ cup fat-free milk
4 ounces light processed cheese, cubed (such as Velveeta Light)
2 tablespoons butter or stick margarine, softened
2 (10-ounce) packages frozen chopped broccoli, thawed and drained
1 (10¾-ounce) can condensed reduced-fat, reduced-sodium cream of mushroom soup, undiluted

1. Preheat oven to 350°.

2. Combine all ingredients in a large bowl, and spoon into a 2-quart casserole. Bake at 350° for 45 minutes. Yield: 8 servings (serving size: ½ cup).

CALORIES 137 (29% from fat); FAT 4.4g (sat 1.7g, mono 1.4g, poly 0.9g); PROTEIN 6.6g; CARB 19.2g; FIBER 2.2g; CHOL 8mg; IRON 1.1mg; SODIUM 410mg; CALC 160mg

PLANTATION BEANS AND CABBAGE

"I got this recipe from a friend more than 20 years ago and have been making it ever since, with one adjustment. I cut back on the amount of bacon to lower the fat. I love the sweet-and-sour flavor of this dish, and it even tastes great cold."

—*Barbara Pollack, Mohegan Lake, New York*

2 bacon slices
1 cup finely chopped onion
2 (16-ounce) packages frozen French-style green beans, thawed
1 cup water
¼ teaspoon salt
¼ teaspoon black pepper
2 cups very thinly sliced green cabbage
6 tablespoons sugar
¼ cup cider vinegar

1. Cook bacon in a Dutch oven over medium-high heat until crisp. Remove bacon from pan, reserving 1 tablespoon bacon drippings in pan; crumble bacon, and set aside. Add onion to pan; cook over medium heat 2 minutes. Add green beans, and cook 2 minutes. Stir in water, salt, and pepper. Bring to a boil; cover, reduce heat, and simmer 5 minutes. Stir in cabbage; cover and simmer 5 minutes. Combine sugar and vinegar, stirring until sugar dissolves. Add sugar mixture to pan; cook, uncovered, 1 minute. Sprinkle with bacon. Yield: 8 servings (serving size: 1 cup).

CALORIES 98 (13% from fat); FAT 1.4g (sat 0.5g, mono 0.5g, poly 0.3g); PROTEIN 2.6g; CARB 21.2g; FIBER 4g; CHOL 1mg; IRON 1.2mg; SODIUM 93mg; CALC 61mg

IRISH MASHED POTATOES

"I created this recipe after tasting the best mashed potatoes I had ever had, in Dublin, Ireland. The secret ingredients were cabbage and cream. I substituted low-fat cream cheese and fat-free sour cream for the cream with great results. If I have leftover cabbage, I freeze it to have on hand for this recipe."

—Norma Ramsdell, North Port, Florida

- 3 pounds peeled Yukon gold or red potatoes, halved
- 2½ cups coarsely chopped cabbage
- 6 garlic cloves, peeled
- 1 chicken-flavored bouillon cube
- ½ cup (4 ounces) ⅓-less-fat cream cheese
- ¼ cup fat-free milk
- ¼ cup fat-free sour cream
- ½ teaspoon kosher salt
- ¼ teaspoon black pepper
- Cooking spray

1. Preheat oven to 350°.
2. Combine first 4 ingredients in a large stockpot; cover with water. Bring to a boil; cover, reduce heat, and simmer 30 minutes. Drain.
3. Return potato mixture to pan. Add cream cheese and next 4 ingredients; mash with a potato masher. Spoon potato mixture into a 1½-quart casserole coated with cooking spray. Cover and bake at 350° for 45 minutes or until thoroughly heated. Yield: 6 servings (serving size: 1 cup).
Note: You can make this a day ahead; just cool, cover, and refrigerate. Reheat in oven or microwave.

CALORIES 264 (17% from fat); FAT 5g (sat 2.9g, mono 1.3g, poly 0.2g); PROTEIN 7.5g; CARB 47.2g; FIBER 3.7g; CHOL 15mg; IRON 1mg; SODIUM 352mg; CALC 56mg

ORANGE-GLAZED CARROTS

"This is one of my favorite side-dish recipes because it's so easy to prepare. I include orange extract to give the carrots a hint of citrus."
—Mary Jane Snyder, Owings Mills, Maryland

- 2 tablespoons butter or stick margarine
- ⅓ cup honey
- 2 tablespoons minced fresh parsley
- ½ teaspoon salt
- ¼ teaspoon black pepper
- ¼ teaspoon imitation orange extract
- Dash of dried thyme
- 1½ pounds baby carrots

1. Preheat oven to 375°.
2. Place butter in a small microwave-safe bowl; microwave at HIGH 20 seconds or until melted. Stir in honey and next 5 ingredients.
3. Place carrots in a 1-quart casserole, and pour honey mixture over carrots. Cover and bake at 375° for 1 hour or until tender. Yield: 5 servings (serving size: ½ cup).

CALORIES 169 (26% from fat); FAT 4.9g (sat 2.9g, mono 1.4g, poly 0.3g); PROTEIN 1.5g; CARB 32.6g; FIBER 4.4g; CHOL 12mg; IRON 0.9mg; SODIUM 331mg; CALC 42mg

CLASSICS

Trompe l'Ewe

A smart reworking of the traditional Irish shepherd's pie creates a new vegetarian classic.

Michael Foley, whose accolades include a 1984 James Beard award and a 1990 Golden Plate award from the White House, decided that his Printer's Row Restaurant in Chicago would offer tasty and imaginative vegetarian fare. In his Shepherdless Pie, Michael replaced the usual lamb or ground beef with chopped Granny Smith apples and raclette cheese. (Raclette is similar to Gruyère cheese in texture and flavor.) The tart apples blend well with the pungent raclette.

SHEPHERDLESS PIE

Look for the semifirm raclette in supermarkets' specialty cheese sections. Or substitute Gruyère for raclette.

- 1½ cups diced peeled celeriac (celery root)
- 2 large peeled baking potatoes, chopped (about 1½ pounds)
- ½ cup 1% low-fat milk
- 1⅓ cups chopped peeled Granny Smith apple
- 1½ tablespoons butter, divided
- 1 teaspoon salt
- 1½ cups finely chopped onion
- 1 cup finely chopped carrot
- ½ cup finely chopped celery
- 1 cup finely chopped peeled turnip (about ½ pound)
- 3½ cups sliced mushrooms
- 3 tablespoons chopped fresh parsley
- 1 teaspoon ground savory
- 1 teaspoon chopped fresh or ¼ teaspoon dried thyme
- 1 tablespoon all-purpose flour
- ½ cup apple juice
- ¾ cup (about 3 ounces) grated raclette or Gruyère cheese
- 1 (10-ounce) bag fresh spinach
- Cooking spray
- 2 tablespoons dry breadcrumbs

1. Preheat oven to 350°.
2. Place celeriac and potato in a saucepan; cover with water, and bring to a boil. Reduce heat; simmer 12 minutes or until potato is tender. Drain.
3. Bring milk to a boil in a small saucepan over medium heat; add apple. Reduce heat, and simmer 7 minutes.
4. Place potato mixture, apple mixture, 1½ teaspoons butter, and salt in a food processor; process until smooth.
5. Melt 1 tablespoon butter in a large nonstick skillet over medium-high heat. Add onion, carrot, and celery; sauté 5 minutes. Add turnip; cook 3 minutes. Add mushrooms, parsley, savory, and thyme; cook 2 minutes or until vegetables are tender and liquid almost evaporates. Sprinkle with flour; stir in flour well, and cook 2 minutes. Stir in apple juice; cook 2 minutes. Cool to room temperature. Stir in cheese.

6. Steam spinach, covered, 5 minutes. Drain and coarsely chop.

7. Coat 6 (12-ounce) soufflé dishes with cooking spray. Spoon ½ cup potato mixture into each dish. Top each with ⅓ cup spinach; top spinach with ⅔ cup onion mixture. Spoon remaining potato mixture evenly into dishes. Sprinkle evenly with breadcrumbs. Bake at 350° for 30 minutes. Yield: 6 servings.

CALORIES 259 (30% from fat); FAT 8.7g (sat 4.8g, mono 2.4g, poly 0.7g); PROTEIN 10.7g; CARB 37.8g; FIBER 7g; CHOL 24mg; IRON 3.5mg; SODIUM 612mg; CALC 280mg

IN SEASON

Sinfully Good Seeds

Behind its tough exterior lies the pomegranate's treasure: hundreds of pretty seeds bursting with tangy flavor.

The pomegranate's tough, bitter flesh surrounds hundreds of delicious, ruby-hued kernels, which have an unusual sweet-sour taste, a high potassium content, and moderate amounts of vitamin C.

POMEGRANATE JUICE

Be sure to use a nonreactive saucepan, such as one with a nonstick coating. Aluminum will react with the acid in the seeds, giving the juice a slightly metallic or off taste.

  3 **cups pomegranate seeds (about 4 large pomegranates)**
  2 **cups water**

1. Place seeds in a heavy-duty, zip-top plastic bag; seal, pressing as much air as possible out of bag. Gently mash seeds with a rolling pin or bottom of a bottle. Place mashed seeds, juice, and water in a medium nonreactive saucepan, and bring to a boil. Cook 10 minutes.

Strain mixture through a sieve into a bowl; discard solids. Store in refrigerator or proceed with recipe as directed. Yield: 2 cups (serving size: ½ cup).

CALORIES 52 (3% from fat); FAT 0.2g (sat 0g, mono 0g, poly 0.1g); PROTEIN 0.7g; CARB 13.1g; FIBER 0.2g; CHOL 0mg; IRON 0.2mg; SODIUM 2mg; CALC 2mg

POMEGRANATE SYRUP

This sweet-tart syrup is delicious brushed on chicken, lamb, or pork. It can also be drizzled over pancakes or ice cream. The syrup is used in a few of the following recipes. You can find bottles of commercial pomegranate syrup in Middle Eastern markets—labeled "pomegranate concentrated juice."

  2 **cups Pomegranate Juice (see recipe)**
1¼ **cups sugar**
  1 **(2 x 1-inch) strip orange rind**

1. Combine all ingredients in a medium nonreactive saucepan. Bring to a boil; reduce heat to medium, and cook until reduced to 1½ cups (about 15 minutes). Discard rind. Yield: 1½ cups (serving size: 2 tablespoons).
Note: Pomegranate Syrup can be kept in refrigerator up to 2 weeks.

CALORIES 98 (1% from fat); FAT 0.1g (sat 0g, mono 0g, poly 0g); PROTEIN 0.2g; CARB 25.2g; FIBER 0.1g; CHOL 0mg; IRON 0.1mg; SODIUM 1mg; CALC 1mg

AMOROUS DUO

  3 **tablespoons Pomegranate Syrup (see recipe)**
  2 **tablespoons amaretto (almond-flavored liqueur)**
  1 **cup vanilla low-fat frozen yogurt**
  ½ **cup crushed ice**

1. Place all ingredients in a blender, and process until smooth. Yield: 2 servings (serving size: ¾ cup).

CALORIES 214 (13% from fat); FAT 3g (sat 1.8g, mono 0.8g, poly 0.1g); PROTEIN 2.7g; CARB 38.3g; FIBER 0.1g; CHOL 9mg; IRON 0.2mg; SODIUM 57mg; CALC 93mg

STEP-BY-STEP: SEEDING AND JUICING A POMEGRANATE

When seeding and juicing pomegranates, wear gloves and an old shirt; the fruit produces a red juice that will stain. One good-size fruit will yield about ¾ cup seeds or ½ cup juice.

For seeds:

❶ *With gloves on, cut pomegranate in half crosswise (like you cut an orange).*

❷ *With the cut sides away from you and your thumbs on the crown end, break each half in half.*

❸ *The pomegranate is now in quarters with the seeds protruding. Coax seeds out from the base with thumbs, being careful not to break seeds. Remove and discard white membrane.*

For juice:

❹ *The best way to juice the seeds is to place them in a plastic bag and crush them with a rolling pin.*

❺ *Place the seeds, juice, and water in a saucepan and bring to a boil. Cook 10 minutes; strain and refrigerate.*

POMEGRANATE PASSION

You'll need to plan ahead if you're going to make this rich, custardlike dessert. First, double the recipe for the Pomegranate Juice *(page 295);* you need some to make the Pomegranate Syrup *(page 295).* Also, the desserts have to chill at least 4 hours to allow the gelatin to set.

     1   envelope unflavored gelatin
     ¾   cup Pomegranate Juice (page
           295)
     ½   cup sugar
     ½   cup boiling water
   1½   cups vanilla low-fat ice cream,
           softened
     1   tablespoon lime juice
     1   (8-ounce) carton low-fat sour
           cream
     ½   cup Pomegranate Syrup (page
           295)
     ¼   cup pomegranate seeds

1. Sprinkle gelatin over Pomegranate Juice in a large bowl; let stand 2 minutes. Add sugar and boiling water, and stir until sugar dissolves. Add ice cream, lime juice, and sour cream; stir well with a whisk. Pour into 8 (6-ounce) custard cups or ramekins; chill 4 hours or until firm.
2. Spoon 1 tablespoon Pomegranate Syrup into each of 8 shallow bowls. Loosen edges of custards with a knife or rubber spatula; invert custards into bowls. Sprinkle evenly with seeds. Yield: 8 servings.

CALORIES 187 (22% from fat); FAT 4.6g (sat 2.8g, mono 1.3g, poly 0.2g); PROTEIN 2.8g; CARB 35.4g; FIBER 0.1g; CHOL 14mg; IRON 0.2mg; SODIUM 35mg; CALC 65mg

CRAB-AND-POMEGRANATE APPETIZER

     4   ounces lump crabmeat, drained
           and shell pieces removed
     ½   (2-pound) cantaloupe, peeled,
           seeded, and cut lengthwise
           into 12 slices
     1   tablespoon fresh lime juice
     ½   cup pomegranate seeds

1. Arrange crabmeat in center of a serving platter, and arrange cantaloupe around crabmeat. Sprinkle lime juice over crabmeat and cantaloupe. Top with pomegranate seeds. Yield: 4 servings (serving size: 3 cantaloupe slices, 1 ounce crabmeat, and 2 tablespoons seeds).

CALORIES 65 (10% from fat); FAT 0.7g (sat 0.1g, mono 0.1g, poly 0.3g); PROTEIN 6.5g; CARB 9g; FIBER 0.5g; CHOL 28mg; IRON 0.5mg; SODIUM 85mg; CALC 37mg

KIDNEY BEAN, CORN, AND POMEGRANATE SALAD

(pictured on page 297)

This unusual combination turns out to be one of our favorite salads; serve as a side to pork or chicken. The leftovers are great rolled up in tortillas with sliced avocado.

     1   (16-ounce) can dark red kidney
           beans, drained
     1   (15.25-ounce) can whole-
           kernel corn, drained
     ½   cup pomegranate seeds (about
           1 pomegranate)
     2   tablespoons chopped fresh
           cilantro
     2   tablespoons chopped fresh parsley
     ⅓   cup bottled olive oil vinaigrette

1. Arrange beans on one side of a serving platter. Arrange corn on other side of platter. Sprinkle seeds, cilantro, and parsley over beans and corn. Drizzle vinaigrette over salad. Yield: 4 servings (serving size: ¾ cup).

CALORIES 215 (18% from fat); FAT 4.3g (sat 0.5g, mono 1.8g, poly 1.8g); PROTEIN 8.5g; CARB 40.7g; FIBER 3.3g; CHOL 0mg; IRON 2.6mg; SODIUM 563mg; CALC 29mg

BLACK CAT

     1   cup cranberry juice cocktail,
           chilled
     ¾   cup cola, chilled
     ¼   cup Pomegranate Syrup (page
           295)

1. Combine all ingredients in a pitcher just before serving. Pour mixture over ice. Yield: 2 servings (serving size: 1 cup).

CALORIES 211 (1% from fat); FAT 0.2g (sat 0g, mono 0.1g, poly 0g); PROTEIN 0.3g; CARB 54.1g; FIBER 0.1g; CHOL 0mg; IRON 0.4mg; SODIUM 10mg; CALC 8mg

POMEGRANATE POUND CAKE

     ¾   cup sugar
     6   tablespoons butter or stick
           margarine
     2   large eggs
     1   large egg white
     ¾   cup low-fat buttermilk
     2   teaspoons grated lime rind
     2   teaspoons vanilla extract
     ½   teaspoon baking soda
   2½   cups all-purpose flour
     ¼   teaspoon salt
     ¾   cup pomegranate seeds
           (about 1 large pomegranate)
   Cooking spray

1. Preheat oven to 350°.
2. Beat sugar and butter at medium-high speed of a mixer until well-blended (about 7 minutes). Add eggs and egg white, 1 at a time, beating well after each addition. Combine buttermilk, rind, vanilla, and baking soda. Lightly spoon flour into dry measuring cups; level with a knife. Combine flour and salt, stirring well with a whisk. Add flour mixture to sugar mixture alternately with buttermilk mixture, beginning and ending with flour mixture. Fold in pomegranate seeds.
3. Spoon batter into an 8 x 4-inch loaf pan coated with cooking spray. Bake at 350° for 1 hour or until a wooden pick inserted in center comes out clean. Cool in pan 10 minutes on a wire rack; remove from pan. Cool completely on wire rack. Yield: 12 servings (serving size: 1 slice).

CALORIES 223 (29% from fat); FAT 7.2g (sat 4g, mono 2.1g, poly 0.5g); PROTEIN 4.7g; CARB 34.5g; FIBER 0.7g; CHOL 52mg; IRON 1.4mg; SODIUM 184mg; CALC 30mg

*Kidney Bean, Corn, and
Pomegranate Salad, page 296*

*Braised Pork Loin with Port
and Prunes with mashed
potatoes, page 280*

Stir-Fried Chicken with Vegetables and Lo Mein Noodles, page 280

Maple-Glazed Sweet Potatoes, page 303

Classic Pecan Pie, page 278

Spirited Cranberry-Apricot Sauce,
page 302

Lemon-Sage Turkey, page 301

Thanksgiving Countdown

It's all in the timing: For the perfect holiday turkey dinner, try this day-by-day, step-by-step cooking guide.

Thanksgiving is the best time to be a cook. Everyone's hungry, looking forward to one of the year's favorite meals: the ideal moment to show off your prowess.

That's why we've come up with this day-by-day, step-by-step countdown (page 302) to help you pull off your showpiece meal with confidence. Following our easy and well-paced plan will give you a memorable classic for your most special audience—the people who share your table. The production doesn't stop there—tips on what to do with the leftovers start on page 304.

HOLIDAY MENU FOR SIX

LEMON-SAGE TURKEY WITH
WILD-MUSHROOM GRAVY

SPIRITED CRANBERRY-APRICOT SAUCE

ROASTED MASHED POTATOES WITH LEEKS

SAUSAGE-AND-HERB DRESSING

MAPLE-GLAZED SWEET POTATOES

GREEN BEANS AND PAN-ROASTED RED ONIONS

PARSNIP, TURNIP, AND RUTABAGA GRATIN

CORNMEAL CLOVERLEAF ROLLS

LEMON-SAGE TURKEY WITH WILD-MUSHROOM GRAVY

(pictured on page 300)

Remember to reserve the drippings from the bottom of the pan to make the gravy.

    3 tablespoons grated lemon rind
    ¼ cup fresh lemon juice
    3 tablespoons dried thyme
    2 tablespoons dried rubbed sage
    1 tablespoon cracked black pepper
    1 teaspoon salt
    1 (12-pound) fresh or frozen
       turkey, thawed
    2 (16-ounce) cans fat-free,
       less-sodium chicken broth
Cooking spray
Wild-Mushroom Gravy (see recipe)

1. Combine first 6 ingredients; set aside.
2. Remove and discard giblets from turkey, reserving neck for gravy. Rinse turkey with cold water; pat dry. Trim excess fat. Starting at neck cavity, loosen skin from breast and drumsticks by inserting fingers, gently pushing between skin and meat. Lift wing tips up and over back; tuck under turkey. Rub spice mixture under loosened skin and rub into body cavity.
3. Preheat oven to 350°.
4. Pour 1 can of broth into a shallow roasting pan. Place turkey, breast side up, on a rack coated with cooking spray. Place rack in roasting pan. Insert meat thermometer into meaty part of thigh, making sure not to touch bone. Bake at 350° for 1½ hours. Carefully pour remaining can of broth into pan. Bake an additional 1½ hours or until thermometer registers 180°. Remove turkey from oven; reserve pan drippings to make gravy. Cover turkey loosely with foil; let stand 15 to 20 minutes. Discard skin. Serve with Wild-Mushroom Gravy. Yield: 12 servings (serving size: 6 ounces turkey and ¼ cup gravy).

(Totals include Wild-Mushroom Gravy) CALORIES 308 (20% from fat); FAT 6.7g (sat 2.1g, mono 1.9g, poly 1.8g); PROTEIN 53.4g; CARB 5.8g; FIBER 0.7g; CHOL 147mg; IRON 4.9mg; SODIUM 460mg; CALC 62mg

---

WILD-MUSHROOM GRAVY

If your pan doesn't yield enough drippings, add water or chicken broth.

Pan drippings
    2 cups water
    ¾ cup thinly sliced shallots
    ½ cup thinly sliced carrot
    1 turkey neck
    1 cup sliced button mushrooms
    1 cup thinly sliced shiitake
       mushroom caps (about 3½
       ounces)
    5 tablespoons all-purpose flour
    1 teaspoon red currant jelly
    ¼ teaspoon black pepper

1. Place a large zip-top plastic bag inside a 4-cup measure. Pour drippings from turkey roasting pan into bag; let stand 10 minutes (fat will rise to top). Seal bag; carefully snip off 1 bottom corner of bag. Drain drippings to measure 2 cups, stopping before fat layer reaches opening. Reserve 2 tablespoons fat in bag; set aside.
2. Combine water, shallots, carrot, and turkey neck in a medium saucepan; bring to a boil. Cover, reduce heat, and simmer 30 minutes. Strain cooking liquid though a sieve over a bowl, reserving ¾ cup cooking liquid. Discard solids, reserving turkey neck. Remove meat from neck; chop. Add meat and reserved ¾ cup cooking liquid to defatted 2 cups drippings in 4-cup measure.

Continued

3. Heat reserved 2 tablespoons fat in a saucepan over medium heat. Add mushrooms; sauté 2 minutes. Add flour; cook 1 minute. Gradually add cooking liquid mixture; cook 10 minutes or until slightly thick, stirring occasionally. Remove from heat; stir in jelly and pepper. Yield: 3 cups (serving size: ¼ cup).

CALORIES 43 (52% from fat); FAT 2.5g (sat 0.7g, mono 1g, poly 0.6g); PROTEIN 1.6g; CARB 3.5g; FIBER 0.3g; CHOL 5mg; IRON 0.4mg; SODIUM 4mg; CALC 3mg

SPIRITED CRANBERRY-APRICOT SAUCE

(pictured on page 300)

½ cup thinly sliced dried apricots (about 3 ounces)
¼ cup sherry or orange juice
¾ cup water
⅔ cup sugar
¼ cup honey
1 (12-ounce) package fresh or frozen cranberries

1. Combine apricots and sherry in a small bowl; cover and let stand 8 hours.
2. Combine water and sugar in a medium saucepan; bring to a boil. Add apricot mixture, honey, and cranberries. Cook over medium heat 8 minutes or until slightly thick. Spoon into a bowl; cover and chill. Yield: 3 cups (serving size: 2 tablespoons).

CALORIES 49 (0% from fat); FAT 0g; PROTEIN 0.2g; CARB 12.7g; FIBER 0.5g; CHOL 0mg; IRON 0.2mg; SODIUM 1mg; CALC 3mg

ROASTED MASHED POTATOES WITH LEEKS

1 leek (about ½ pound)
8½ cups cubed Yukon gold or red potato (about 3 pounds)
Cooking spray
1½ tablespoons olive oil
1½ cups 1% low-fat milk
1 teaspoon salt
½ teaspoon black pepper
1 (8-ounce) carton low-fat sour cream

1. Preheat oven to 425°.
2. Remove roots and outer leaves from leek, leaving 1 inch of green leaves. Discard remaining leaves; rinse with cold water. Remove 1 inch green leaves; cut lengthwise into 1-inch strips. Set aside. Cut white portion into thin slices to measure ½ cup.
3. Combine white portion of leek and potato in a 13 x 9-inch baking dish coated with cooking spray. Drizzle with 1 tablespoon oil; toss well. Place green portion of leek in an 8-inch baking dish. Drizzle with remaining 1½ teaspoons oil; toss well, and set aside.
4. Bake potato mixture at 425° for 20 minutes, stirring once. (Do not remove from oven.) Add baking dish with green leek tops to oven. Bake at 425° for 15 minutes or until potato mixture and green leek tops are tender, stirring both after 8 minutes. Remove baking dishes from oven.
5. Place milk in a large microwave-safe bowl. Microwave at HIGH 2 minutes or until warm. Add potato mixture;

beat at medium speed of a mixer until well-blended. Stir in salt, pepper, and sour cream. Sprinkle potato mixture with green leek tops. Yield: 8 servings (serving size: 1 cup).

CALORIES 213 (20% from fat); FAT 4.8g (sat 1.7g, mono 2.4g, poly 0.5g); PROTEIN 6.5g; CARB 35.7g; FIBER 2.9g; CHOL 7mg; IRON 2.4mg; SODIUM 351mg; CALC 148mg

SAUSAGE-AND-HERB DRESSING

2 tablespoons butter or stick margarine
2 (4-ounce) links sweet Italian turkey sausage, crumbled
2 cups chopped onion
2 cups chopped fennel bulb
½ cup chopped celery
3 garlic cloves, minced
1½ cups fat-free, less-sodium chicken broth
⅓ cup chopped fresh parsley
1½ teaspoons dried thyme
1½ teaspoons dried oregano
½ teaspoon salt
12 cups (1-inch) cubed French bread (about 1 [1-pound] loaf)
1 cup thinly sliced green onions
1 large egg, lightly beaten
Cooking spray

1. Preheat oven to 375°.
2. Melt butter in a Dutch oven over medium-high heat. Add sausage; cook 4 minutes or until browned. Add chopped onion, fennel, celery, and garlic; sauté 8 minutes. Stir in broth and

---

COUNTDOWN TO THE BIG DAY

Saturday
1. Start *Spirited Cranberry-Apricot Sauce* in the morning; soak apricots for 8 hours. Finish sauce; cover and refrigerate.
2. Make *Sausage-and-Herb Dressing.* Bake; then cool completely. Wrap dish tightly in foil; freeze.

Sunday
1. Make dough for *Cornmeal Cloverleaf Rolls.* Follow recipe for shaping dough into balls. Place balls in a large zip-top plastic bag; seal and freeze.

Monday
1. Make *Maple-Glazed Sweet Potatoes.* Spoon into a microwave-safe casserole dish; cover and refrigerate.

Tuesday
1. Make *Roasted Mashed Potatoes with Leeks.* Spoon into a microwave-safe casserole dish; cover and refrigerate.
2. Remove *Sausage-and-Herb Dressing* from freezer, and place in refrigerator to thaw.

Wednesday
1. Cook green beans for *Green Beans and Pan-Roasted Onions;* cover. Cut red onions; place in a separate storage container. Store both in refrigerator.
2. Clean and prepare turkey with seasonings. Place turkey in roasting pan (without broth); cover and refrigerate.
3. Toast breadcrumbs for *Parsnip, Turnip, and Rutabaga Gratin;* cover and store at room temperature. Prepare gratin without breadcrumb topping (do not bake); cover and refrigerate.

next 4 ingredients, scraping pan to loosen browned bits. Remove from heat. Stir in bread, green onions, and egg. Spoon into a 13 x 9-inch baking dish coated with cooking spray. Bake at 375° for 35 minutes. Yield: 13 servings (serving size: ¾ cup).

CALORIES 166 (27% from fat); FAT 5g (sat 1.9g, mono 1.6g, poly 1g); PROTEIN 7.8g; CARB 22.5g; FIBER 2g; CHOL 36mg; IRON 2.1mg; SODIUM 488mg; CALC 64mg

MAPLE-GLAZED SWEET POTATOES

(pictured on page 299)

You'll need to peel and section a lemon for this dish. Take care to use only the flesh by removing the skinlike, white membrane from each section.

    8 cups (1-inch) cubed peeled
          sweet potato (about 3 pounds)
    4 cups water
    ¼ cup lemon sections (about 1
          large lemon)
    ¼ cup packed dark brown sugar
    3 tablespoons maple syrup
    2 tablespoons butter or stick
          margarine
    ½ teaspoon ground cinnamon
    ⅛ teaspoon ground red pepper
    Dash of salt

1. Combine first 3 ingredients in a large saucepan; bring to boil. Cook 20 minutes or until tender, stirring occasionally. Remove sweet potatoes from pan with a slotted spoon, reserving cooking liquid. Bring cooking liquid to a boil; cook until reduced to ⅓ cup (about 12 minutes). Stir in sugar and remaining 5 ingredients. Stir in sweet potatoes; cook 2 minutes or until thoroughly heated. Yield: 12 servings (serving size: ½ cup).

CALORIES 142 (14% from fat); FAT 2.2g (sat 1.3g, mono 0.6g, poly 0.2g); PROTEIN 1.5g; CARB 29.8g; FIBER 2.7g; CHOL 5mg; IRON 0.7mg; SODIUM 46mg; CALC 30mg

TURKEY DAY TIME LINE

Three to four hours ahead:

1. Preheat oven to 350°. Insert meat thermometer into turkey, add broth to pan, and place in oven.

2. Cook turkey neck with shallots and carrots as instructed for the *Wild-Mushroom Gravy.* Remove meat from neck; chop and combine with reserved cooking liquid. Cover and refrigerate.

3. Remove dough balls from freezer. Separate balls, and place 3 in each muffin cup coated with cooking spray. Cover; let thaw and rise 2½ hours.

One hour ahead:

1. Take *Sausage-and-Herb Dressing* from refrigerator, and place in oven on bottom rack (under the turkey). Reheat 25 minutes or until thoroughly heated. Remove from oven; keep warm.

2. Remove *Parsnip, Turnip, and Rutabaga Gratin* from refrigerator, and let stand at room temperature while dressing is reheating. Chop the parsley, and finish making breadcrumb mixture. Sprinkle on gratin, and bake.

Just prior to serving:

1. Remove the turkey from the oven, cover turkey with foil, and let stand at least 15 to 25 minutes; carve turkey.

2. Place rolls in oven, and bake 25 minutes.

3. Prepare gravy.

4. Make *Green Beans and Pan-Roasted Red Onions.*

5. Reheat the *Maple-Glazed Sweet Potatoes* and *Roasted Mashed Potatoes with Leeks* in the microwave at HIGH 3 minutes, and stir well. Continue microwaving until hot, and keep warm.

GREEN BEANS AND PAN-ROASTED RED ONIONS

    5 cups water
    1 pound green beans, trimmed
    1 tablespoon olive oil
    3 red onions, each cut into 8 wedges
    ½ cup fat-free, less-sodium
          chicken broth
    1 tablespoon balsamic vinegar
    2 teaspoons brown sugar
    ¼ teaspoon salt
    ¼ teaspoon black pepper

1. Bring water to a boil in a saucepan; add beans. Cook 6 minutes or until crisp-tender. Drain and keep warm.

2. Heat oil in a large nonstick skillet over medium-high heat. Add onion; sauté 8 minutes or until browned. Add broth; cook 3 minutes, stirring occasionally. Stir in vinegar and remaining 3 ingredients. Stir in beans; cover and cook 2 minutes. Yield: 14 servings (serving size: ½ cup).

Note: Cut beans into small pieces, if desired.

CALORIES 33 (27% from fat); FAT 1g (sat 0.2g, mono 0.7g, poly 0.1g); PROTEIN 1.1g; CARB 5.4g; FIBER 1.2g; CHOL 0mg; IRON 0.4mg; SODIUM 62mg; CALC 19mg

PARSNIP, TURNIP, AND RUTABAGA GRATIN

    1 large rutabaga (about 3
          pounds), peeled, halved, and
          cut into ¼-inch-thick slices
    4 cups (½-inch) cubed peeled
          turnip (about 1 pound)
    2 cups (¼-inch) sliced parsnip
    1 cup (¼-inch) sliced carrot
    2 tablespoons brown sugar
    2 tablespoons lemon juice
    2 teaspoons Worcestershire sauce
    ¼ teaspoon salt
    ¼ teaspoon black pepper
    Cooking spray
    Cheese Sauce
    2 (1-ounce) slices bread
    1 tablespoon butter or stick
          margarine, melted
    2 tablespoons chopped fresh parsley

Continued

1. Cut each rutabaga slice into quarters. Combine rutabaga, turnip, parsnip, and carrot in an 8-quart stockpot; cover with water. Bring to a boil, and cook 30 minutes or until tender. Drain. Stir in sugar and next 4 ingredients. Spoon vegetable mixture into a 13 x 9-inch baking dish coated with cooking spray. Spread Cheese Sauce over vegetable mixture.
2. Preheat oven to 350°.
3. Place bread in a food processor; pulse 10 times or until crumbly to measure 1 cup. Sprinkle crumbs on a baking sheet; bake at 350° for 5 minutes or until golden. Combine breadcrumbs and butter in a small bowl; sprinkle over sauce. Bake at 350° for 25 minutes or until bubbly. Let stand 10 minutes. Sprinkle with parsley. Yield: 10 servings (serving size: 1 cup).

(Totals include Cheese Sauce) CALORIES 178 (28% from fat); FAT 5.5g (sat 3.1g, mono 1.5g, poly 0.4g); PROTEIN 6.3g; CARB 28.9g; FIBER 3.3g; CHOL 15mg; IRON 1.4mg; SODIUM 305mg; CALC 207mg

Cheese Sauce:

1 tablespoon butter or margarine
3 tablespoons all-purpose flour
2½ cups 1% low-fat milk
½ cup (2 ounces) shredded white Cheddar cheese
¼ teaspoon salt
⅛ teaspoon grated whole or dash of ground nutmeg
⅛ teaspoon black pepper

1. Melt butter in a medium saucepan over medium heat. Add flour, stirring with a whisk. Gradually add milk, stirring with a whisk until well-blended. Cook until slightly thick (about 10 minutes), stirring constantly. Remove mixture from heat; add cheese and remaining ingredients, stirring until cheese melts. Yield: 2 cups (serving size: 2 tablespoons).

CALORIES 42 (47% from fat); FAT 2.3g (sat 1.5g, mono 0.7g, poly 0.1g); PROTEIN 2.3g; CARB 3g; FIBER 0g; CHOL 7mg; IRON 0.1mg; SODIUM 85mg; CALC 73mg

CORNMEAL CLOVERLEAF ROLLS

1 package dry yeast (about 2¼ teaspoons)
1 tablespoon sugar
¼ cup warm water (100° to 110°)
1½ cups 2% reduced-fat milk
4⅓ cups all-purpose flour, divided
⅓ cup cornmeal
3 tablespoons butter or stick margarine, melted
1¼ teaspoons salt
1 large egg white, lightly beaten
1 tablespoon water
1 teaspoon cornmeal

1. Dissolve yeast and sugar in warm water in a large bowl; let stand 5 minutes. Stir in milk. Lightly spoon flour into dry measuring cups; level with a knife. Add 4 cups flour, ⅓ cup cornmeal, butter, and salt to yeast mixture; beat at medium speed of a mixer until smooth. Turn dough out onto a floured surface. Knead until smooth and elastic (about 10 minutes); add enough remaining flour, 1 tablespoon at a time, to prevent dough from sticking to hands (dough will feel tacky).
2. Place dough in a large bowl coated with cooking spray, turning to coat top. Cover and let rise in a warm place (85°), free from drafts, 1 hour or until doubled in size. (Press two fingers into dough. If indentation remains, dough has risen enough.) Punch dough down; cover and let rest 10 minutes. Divide into 18 equal portions. Working with 1 portion at a time (cover remaining dough to keep from drying), divide each portion into 3 pieces; shape each piece into a ball. Coat muffin pans with cooking spray; place 3 dough balls in each muffin cup. Cover and let rise 10 minutes or until doubled in size.
3. Preheat oven to 350°.
4. Uncover rolls. Combine egg white and 1 tablespoon water; brush over rolls. Sprinkle with 1 teaspoon cornmeal. Bake at 350° for 25 minutes. Yield: 1½ dozen (serving size: 1 roll).

CALORIES 152 (16% from fat); FAT 2.7g (sat 1.5g, mono 0.7g, poly 0.2g); PROTEIN 4.4g; CARB 26.9g; FIBER 1.1g; CHOL 7mg; IRON 1.6mg; SODIUM 196mg; CALC 30mg

Turkey Day: Take Two

Transform your leftovers into dinners so delicious you'll want to make that first meal all over again.

When the fun food extravaganza known as Thanksgiving is finally over, transform yesterday's dishes into easy-to-prepare meals so tasty that no one will know they're not made from original fare. Just as we guided you through the "Thanksgiving Countdown," (page 302), we offer recipes for what remains. Once you've tasted the creative alternatives, that boring cold turkey sandwich won't be a tradition anymore.

PEPPERCORN PORK MEDALLIONS WITH CRANBERRY SAUCE

Pepper lovers will want to use 2 teaspoons of cracked black pepper. Cut back to 1 teaspoon if you prefer a milder flavor.

1 pound pork tenderloin
1 to 2 teaspoons cracked black pepper
1 teaspoon lemon pepper
1 teaspoon vegetable oil
3 tablespoons balsamic vinegar
2 tablespoons water
1 cup Spirited Cranberry-Apricot Sauce (page 302)
2 teaspoons butter or stick margarine

1. Trim fat from pork; cut crosswise into 8 pieces. Place each piece between 2 sheets of heavy-duty plastic wrap; flatten each piece to ½-inch thickness using a meat mallet or rolling pin. Sprinkle both sides of pork with peppers.
2. Heat oil in a 10-inch cast-iron skillet over medium-high heat. Add pork; cook 5 minutes on each side or until done. Remove from pan; keep warm. Add vinegar and water to pan; cook 30

seconds, stirring constantly. Stir in Spirited Cranberry-Apricot Sauce and butter, and cook 1 minute, stirring constantly. Serve sauce with pork. Yield: 4 servings (serving size: 3 ounces pork and ¼ cup sauce).

CALORIES 256 (21% from fat); FAT 5.9g (sat 2.4g, mono 2.2g, poly 0.9g); PROTEIN 24.4g; CARB 26.6g; FIBER 1.4g; CHOL 79mg; IRON 2.4mg; SODIUM 208mg; CALC 22mg

SHORTCUT CASSOULET

1 (1-ounce) slice white bread
1 teaspoon vegetable oil
3 (3-ounce) smoked turkey and
   duck sausages (such as
   Gerhard's), cut into ½-inch
   slices
1½ cups chopped onion
½ cup sliced celery
½ cup thinly sliced carrot
1 cup fat-free, less-sodium
   chicken broth
2 tablespoons tomato paste
½ teaspoon dried thyme
½ teaspoon dried Italian seasoning
¼ teaspoon black pepper
1 (14.5-ounce) can no-salt-added
   diced tomatoes, undrained
2 (15.8-ounce) cans Great
   Northern beans, drained and
   divided
2 cups coarsely chopped cooked
   turkey
1 tablespoon grated Parmesan
   cheese

1. Preheat oven to 325°.
2. Place bread in a food processor; pulse 5 times or until coarse crumbs form to measure ½ cup. Arrange breadcrumbs on a jelly-roll pan; bake at 325° for 8 minutes or until golden. Set aside.
3. Heat oil in a large saucepan over medium heat until hot. Add sausages, and cook 3 minutes or until browned. Remove from pan; keep warm. Add onion, celery, and carrot to pan; sauté 5 minutes. Return sausages to pan; stir in broth and next 5 ingredients. Bring to a boil. Reduce heat; simmer 30 minutes. Remove from heat.

4. Mash ½ cup beans; stir into sausage mixture. Stir remaining beans into sausage mixture. Spoon half of bean mixture into a 2½-quart casserole dish; top with turkey and remaining bean mixture. Combine breadcrumbs and cheese; sprinkle over bean mixture. Bake at 325° for 30 minutes or until bubbly. Yield: 8 servings (serving size: 1 cup).

CALORIES 226 (19% from fat); FAT 4.8g (sat 1.5g, mono 1.7g, poly 1.3g); PROTEIN 22.2g; CARB 24.1g; FIBER 4.1g; CHOL 53mg; IRON 3.4mg; SODIUM 535mg; CALC 99mg

CARIBBEAN SWEET POTATOES AND BLACK BEANS

1 (5-ounce) package yellow rice
   mix
3 (4-ounce) links hot Italian
   turkey sausage
2 teaspoons butter or stick
   margarine
½ cup thinly sliced onion
1 garlic clove, minced
2 cups Maple-Glazed Sweet
   Potatoes (page 303)
1 cup fat-free, less-sodium
   chicken broth
½ teaspoon ground cumin
⅛ teaspoon ground red pepper
⅛ teaspoon ground cinnamon
¾ cup sliced green onions
1 (15-ounce) can black beans,
   rinsed and drained

1. Remove seasoning packet from rice mix, and discard. Cook rice according to package directions, omitting fat. Keep warm.
2. Crumble sausage into a large non-stick skillet, and stir over medium-high heat until browned (about 8 minutes). Drain sausage, and set aside.
3. Melt butter in pan over medium-high heat. Add ½ cup onion and garlic, and sauté 3 minutes. Stir in Maple-Glazed Sweet Potatoes and next 4 ingredients. Reduce heat to medium; cover and cook 10 minutes. Stir in sausage, green onions, and beans; cover and cook 3 minutes or until thoroughly heated. Serve over rice. Yield: 5

servings (serving size: 1 cup sweet potato mixture and ½ cup rice).

CALORIES 406 (22% from fat); FAT 9.8g (sat 3.9g, mono 4.2g, poly 1.4g); PROTEIN 20.2g; CARB 60.1g; FIBER 5.4g; CHOL 62mg; IRON 3.3mg; SODIUM 637mg; CALC 52mg

CREOLE CAKES WITH SWEET AND SPICY RÉMOULADE SAUCE

Sauce:

⅓ cup plain fat-free yogurt
2 tablespoons minced green onions
2 tablespoons light mayonnaise
1 tablespoon Creole mustard
1 tablespoon sweet pickle relish
Dash of garlic powder
Dash of ground red pepper

Cakes:

2 (1-ounce) slices white bread
3 cups chopped cooked turkey
   breast
⅓ cup minced green onions
¼ cup light mayonnaise
1 tablespoon Worcestershire sauce
1 teaspoon Cajun seasoning
2 large egg whites
1 teaspoon vegetable oil
Cooking spray

1. To prepare sauce, combine first 7 ingredients in a small bowl. Chill.
2. To prepare cakes, place bread in a food processor, and pulse 10 times or until coarse crumbs form to measure 1¼ cups. Set aside. Combine turkey and next 5 ingredients. Stir in breadcrumbs. Divide turkey mixture into 8 equal portions, shaping each into a ½-inch-thick patty. Heat oil in a large nonstick skillet coated with cooking spray over medium heat. Add patties, and cook 5 minutes. Turn patties over; cook 5 minutes or until golden brown. Serve with sauce. Yield: 4 servings (serving size: 2 cakes and 2 tablespoons sauce).

CALORIES 277 (29% from fat); FAT 8.9g (sat 1.5g, mono 2.5g, poly 4.2g); PROTEIN 34.5g; CARB 13.1g; FIBER 0.6g; CHOL 92mg; IRON 2.2mg; SODIUM 746mg; CALC 82mg

TUNA-AND-GREEN BEAN PASTA SALAD

2 cups Green Beans and
    Pan-Roasted Red Onions
    (page 303)
¼ cup fresh lemon juice
2 tablespoons olive oil
2 tablespoons water
¼ teaspoon freshly ground black
    pepper
¼ teaspoon salt
⅛ teaspoon garlic powder
4 cups cooked gemelli (about 2
    cups uncooked short twisted
    pasta)
¼ cup chopped fresh parsley
1½ tablespoons capers
2 (6-ounce) cans albacore tuna in
    water, drained and flaked

1. Cut beans into 1-inch pieces. Combine juice and next 5 ingredients in a large bowl; stir well with a whisk. Add Green Beans and Pan-Roasted Red Onions, pasta, and remaining ingredients; toss well. Yield: 6 servings (serving size: 1⅓ cups).

CALORIES 271 (23% from fat); FAT 7g (sat 1.1g, mono 4.2g, poly 1.1g); PROTEIN 18.4g; CARB 33.1g; FIBER 1.9g; CHOL 20mg; IRON 2.2mg; SODIUM 496mg; CALC 24mg

COUSCOUS-TURKEY SALAD

1 cup water
¾ cup uncooked couscous
2 cups chopped cooked turkey
¾ cup thinly sliced celery
¾ cup frozen green peas, thawed
¼ cup sliced green onions
¼ cup light mayonnaise
¼ cup fat-free sour cream
¼ cup fat-free, less-sodium
    chicken broth
1 teaspoon Dijon mustard
¼ teaspoon salt
¼ teaspoon coarsely ground black
    pepper

1. Bring water to a boil in a medium saucepan, and gradually stir in couscous. Remove from heat; cover and let stand 5 minutes. Fluff with a fork.

Combine couscous, turkey, celery, peas, and green onions in a large bowl. Combine mayonnaise and remaining 5 ingredients; stir well with a whisk. Add to couscous mixture; toss well. Cover and chill at least 2 hours. Yield: 6 servings (serving size: 1 cup).

CALORIES 205 (21% from fat); FAT 4.8g (sat 1.1g, mono 1.1g, poly 1.9g); PROTEIN 21.2g; CARB 18.1g; FIBER 1.8g; CHOL 42mg; IRON 1.5mg; SODIUM 295mg; CALC 24mg

MEXICAN TURKEY-AND-BEAN SOUP

1 teaspoon olive oil
½ cup chopped onion
1 cup coarsely chopped cooked
    turkey
1½ teaspoons ground cumin
¼ teaspoon garlic powder
⅛ teaspoon hot pepper sauce
1 (16-ounce) can navy beans,
    drained
1 (15-ounce) can low-sodium
    chickpeas (garbanzo beans),
    drained
1 (15-ounce) can white
    whole-kernel corn, drained
1 (16-ounce) can fat-free,
    less-sodium chicken broth
1 (4.5-ounce) can chopped green
    chiles, drained
¾ cup quick-cooking wild rice,
    uncooked
7 tablespoons low-fat sour cream

1. Heat oil in a Dutch oven over medium-high heat; add onion, and sauté 5 minutes. Stir in turkey and next 8 ingredients. Bring to a boil; cover, reduce heat, and simmer 15 minutes. Stir in wild rice, and simmer 5 minutes. Serve soup with sour cream. Yield: 7 servings (serving size: 1 cup soup and 1 tablespoon sour cream).

CALORIES 260 (15% from fat); FAT 4.3g (sat 1.6g, mono 1.4g, poly 0.8g); PROTEIN 16g; CARB 37.5g; FIBER 5.2g; CHOL 22mg; IRON 2.5mg; SODIUM 547mg; CALC 61mg

INSPIRED VEGETARIAN

The Specialness of Spuds

The hearty, versatile potato has long been an American favorite—for good reasons.

ROASTED POTATOES, PARSNIPS, AND CARROTS WITH HORSERADISH SAUCE

Horseradish sauce:

1 (8-ounce) carton plain low-fat
    yogurt
2 tablespoons prepared horseradish
¼ teaspoon salt

Vegetables:

1 pound (1-inch-thick) sliced
    carrot
1 pound parsnips, peeled and cut
    into 1-inch pieces
1 pound fingerling potatoes,
    halved lengthwise
1 tablespoon olive oil
2 teaspoons chopped fresh sage
½ teaspoon salt
¼ teaspoon freshly ground black
    pepper
12 garlic cloves, peeled (about 1
    garlic head)
4 large shallots, peeled and
    quartered
4 thyme sprigs
Cooking spray

1. To prepare horseradish sauce, spoon yogurt onto several layers of heavy-duty paper towels; spread to ½-inch thickness. Cover with additional paper towels; let stand 5 minutes. Scrape into a bowl using a rubber spatula; stir in horseradish and ¼ teaspoon salt. Cover and chill.

2. Preheat oven to 450°.

3. To prepare vegetables, cook carrot in boiling water 5 minutes or until tender; drain. Combine carrot, parsnip, and next 8 ingredients in a shallow roasting pan coated with cooking spray. Bake at 450° for 20 minutes; stir. Reduce oven temperature to 400° (do not remove vegetables from oven); bake an additional 30 minutes or until vegetables are tender. Discard thyme. Serve with horseradish sauce. Yield: 6 servings (serving size: 1 cup vegetables and 2 tablespoons sauce).

Note: Substitute small round red potatoes for fingerlings, if desired.

CALORIES 197 (15% from fat); FAT 3.3g (sat 0.8g, mono 1.9g, poly 0.4g); PROTEIN 5.5g; CARB 38.5g; FIBER 5.5g; CHOL 2mg; IRON 2.1mg; SODIUM 371mg; CALC 129mg

SAFFRON POTATOES WITH ALMONDS

2 pounds red potatoes, peeled and quartered
1 tablespoon olive oil, divided
¾ teaspoon salt, divided
¼ teaspoon freshly ground black pepper
1½ cups water
1 tablespoon tomato paste
⅛ teaspoon powdered saffron
1 teaspoon paprika
¼ cup slivered almonds, toasted
¼ cup chopped fresh parsley
1 (1-ounce) slice country or peasant bread, toasted
2 garlic cloves

1. Preheat oven to 400°.

2. Combine potato, 1½ teaspoons oil, ½ teaspoon salt, and pepper in a 13 x 9-inch baking dish; toss well. Arrange potato in a single layer in dish; set aside.

3. Bring water to a boil. Stir in tomato paste and saffron; remove from heat, and let stand 1 minute. Pour tomato mixture over potato. Sprinkle with paprika. Cover and bake at 400° for 40 minutes. Uncover potato mixture; stir. Bake an additional 25 minutes or until tender.

4. Combine 1½ teaspoons oil, ¼ teaspoon salt, almonds, and remaining 3

ingredients in a food processor; process until well-blended. Top potato with almond mixture; toss gently. Yield: 5 servings (serving size: 1 cup).

CALORIES 209 (25% from fat); FAT 5.7g (sat 0.7g, mono 3.7g, poly 0.9g); PROTEIN 5.3g; CARB 35.9g; FIBER 3.8g; CHOL 0mg; IRON 2.1mg; SODIUM 397mg; CALC 40mg

MASHED POTATO CAKES WITH ONIONS AND KALE

12 cups water
1 bunch kale, trimmed (about 4 ounces)
2⅔ cups (1-inch) cubed Yukon gold or red potato (about 1 pound)
¾ teaspoon salt, divided
1 tablespoon olive oil
1 tablespoon butter or stick margarine
3 cups diced onion
2 tablespoons chopped fresh sage
¼ cup sliced green onions
¼ teaspoon freshly ground black pepper
Cooking spray
Sage sprigs (optional)

1. Bring water to a boil in a Dutch oven; add kale. Cover and cook over medium heat 5 minutes or until tender. Remove kale with a slotted spoon, reserving cooking liquid. Chop kale, and set aside.

2. Add potato to reserved cooking liquid in pan; bring to a boil. Reduce heat, and simmer 10 minutes or until tender. Drain; partially mash potato. Stir in kale and ¼ teaspoon salt.

3. Preheat oven to 400°.

4. Heat oil and butter in a large nonstick skillet over medium-high heat. Add remaining ½ teaspoon salt, diced onion, and chopped sage. Cook 13 minutes or until browned. Stir in potato mixture, green onions, and pepper. Remove from heat; cool slightly. Divide potato mixture into 8 equal portions, shaping each into a ½-inch-thick patty. Place patties on a baking sheet coated with cooking spray. Bake at 400° for 20 minutes.

5. Preheat broiler.

6. Broil patties 5 minutes or until browned. Garnish with sage sprigs, if desired. Yield: 4 servings (serving size: 2 patties).

CALORIES 246 (26% from fat); FAT 7g (sat 2.4g, mono 3.4g, poly 0.6g); PROTEIN 5.1g; CARB 43.2g; FIBER 5.1g; CHOL 8mg; IRON 2.6mg; SODIUM 495mg; CALC 87mg

POTATO FRITTATA

¾ pound baking potatoes, peeled, halved lengthwise, and thinly sliced
Cooking spray
1½ cups vertically sliced red onion
½ teaspoon salt, divided
¼ cup chopped fresh parsley
¼ teaspoon paprika
⅛ teaspoon black pepper
4 large egg whites
3 large eggs
1 garlic clove, minced
½ cup (2 ounces) shredded reduced-fat Cheddar cheese

1. Place potato in a saucepan, and cover with water; bring to a boil. Reduce heat, and simmer 8 minutes or until tender; drain and set aside.

2. Place a nonstick skillet coated with cooking spray over medium-high heat. Add onion, and cook 20 minutes or until deep golden brown, stirring frequently. Remove onion from pan, and recoat pan with cooking spray. Return onion to pan; stir in potato and ¼ teaspoon salt.

3. Preheat broiler.

4. Combine remaining ¼ teaspoon salt, parsley, and next 5 ingredients in a bowl, stirring well with a whisk. Pour over onion mixture; sprinkle with cheese. Cook over medium heat 2 minutes or until slightly set. Wrap handle of skillet with foil; broil 3 minutes or until eggs are set and cheese melts. Gently slide frittata onto a platter, and cut into 8 wedges. Yield: 4 servings (serving size: 2 wedges).

CALORIES 213 (30% from fat); FAT 7.1g (sat 2.8g, mono 2.5g, poly 0.7g); PROTEIN 14.7g; CARB 22.2g; FIBER 2.2g; CHOL 175mg; IRON 1.3mg; SODIUM 507mg; CALC 153mg

POTATO-AND-CELERIAC GRATIN

Cooking spray
2 garlic cloves, halved
1 small celeriac (celery root), peeled (about 1½ pounds)
2 pounds Yukon gold or red potatoes, peeled and cut into ¼-inch-thick slices
4 thyme sprigs, divided
3 tablespoons all-purpose flour
½ teaspoon salt
¼ teaspoon black pepper
2 cups 1% low-fat milk
1 cup (4 ounces) grated Gruyère cheese, divided

1. Preheat oven to 350°.
2. Rub sides and bottom of an 11 x 7-inch baking dish coated with cooking spray with garlic halves. Crush garlic halves; set aside.
3. Cut celeriac into ¼-inch-thick slices; cut slices into quarters to measure 2 cups, reserving remaining celeriac for another use. Place 2 cups celeriac, potato, and 3 thyme sprigs in a large saucepan, and cover with water; bring to a boil. Reduce heat, and simmer 10 minutes or until potato is tender; drain and discard 3 thyme sprigs.
4. While vegetables are cooking, combine flour, salt, and pepper in a small saucepan; gradually add milk, stirring with a whisk. Stir in crushed garlic and 1 thyme sprig. Place pan over medium heat, and cook until thick (about 10 minutes), stirring constantly with a whisk. Remove from heat; stir in ¾ cup cheese.
5. Arrange potato and celeriac in prepared baking dish; pour sauce over vegetables. Sprinkle with ¼ cup cheese. Bake at 350° for 30 minutes or until lightly browned. Discard thyme. Yield: 7 servings (serving size: 1 cup).

CALORIES 240 (24% from fat); FAT 6.3g (sat 3.6g, mono 1.9g, poly 0.4g); PROTEIN 10.4g; CARB 35.4g; FIBER 2.4g; CHOL 21mg; IRON 0.9mg; SODIUM 295mg; CALC 272mg

POTATO-FENNEL SOUP

You could use celeriac, turnips, or parsnips, but you may want to try fennel.

1 (½-pound) fennel bulb with stalks
2 baking potatoes, quartered (about 2 pounds)
1 tablespoon butter or stick margarine
2 cups chopped leek (about 3 large)
3 cups water
½ teaspoon salt
1 (14½-ounce) can vegetable broth
½ cup minced fresh parsley
¼ teaspoon freshly ground black pepper
8 teaspoons low-fat sour cream

1. Trim tough outer leaves from fennel; mince feathery fronds to measure 2 tablespoons. Remove and discard stalks. Cut fennel bulb in half lengthwise; discard core. Chop bulb to measure 1 cup.
2. Cut quartered potatoes into ¼-inch-thick slices. Melt butter in a Dutch oven over medium-high heat. Add chopped fennel bulb, potato, and leek; cook 3 minutes. Add water, salt, and broth; bring to a boil. Cover, reduce heat, and simmer 25 minutes or until potato is tender.
3. Remove 2 cups soup from pan. Place in a blender; process until smooth. Return pureed mixture to pan, and stir in minced fennel fronds, parsley, and pepper. Spoon into bowls; top with sour cream. Yield: 8 servings (serving size: 1 cup soup and 1 teaspoon sour cream).

CALORIES 169 (14% from fat); FAT 2.6g (sat 1.4g, mono 0.7g, poly 0.3g); PROTEIN 3.5g; CARB 34.1g; FIBER 2.7g; CHOL 6mg; IRON 2.6mg; SODIUM 431mg; CALC 49mg

AT LAST

Being There

National Geography Awareness Week is a good time to ask yourself where you are. Literally.

ALTUNA MELT

If the citizens of Altoona, Pennsylvania, want to adopt our world-class variation on this classic café sandwich, we grant them full latitude.

½ cup drained canned artichoke hearts, finely chopped
¼ cup sliced green onions
1 tablespoon fresh lemon juice
1 teaspoon olive oil
½ teaspoon dried oregano
⅛ teaspoon black pepper
⅛ teaspoon ground red pepper
1 (6-ounce) can albacore tuna in water, lightly drained and flaked
2 English muffins, split and toasted
6 tablespoons (1½ ounces) grated provolone cheese

1. Preheat broiler.
2. Combine first 8 ingredients in a medium bowl. Divide evenly among muffin halves; sprinkle with cheese. Place on a baking sheet; broil 5 inches from heat 4 minutes or until golden brown. Yield: 2 servings (serving size: 2 muffin halves).

CALORIES 374 (26% from fat); FAT 10.8g (sat 4.7g, mono 4.3g, poly 1.3g); PROTEIN 27.6g; CARB 41.8g; FIBER 0.5g; CHOL 38mg; IRON 3.3mg; SODIUM 845mg; CALC 303mg

DECEMBER

The French Cake Connection

No classic French dessert is easier to make—or as fun to say. Génoise *(pronounced Zhehn-WAHZ) is the start of many a pièce de résistance.*

Génoise is one of the most prized elements in the French pastry chef's repertoire. Brush generous amounts of tasty liquids over the dense, golden cake, and it won't disintegrate. It also holds up to rolling and slicing. The cake is simple, and we've simplified the procedures without altering the ingredients.

CLASSIC GÉNOISE

Génoise is baked in either a 15 x 10-inch jelly-roll pan or a 9-inch spring-form pan. For Sherried Banana-Strawberry Trifle (page 311) *and* Triple Lemon Génoise with Butter-cream and Raspberries (page 312) *you can make it in 2 (9-inch) round cake pans; bake 13 minutes.*

  Cooking spray
  1 tablespoon cake flour
  2 tablespoons butter
  1 cup unsifted cake flour
  ⅛ teaspoon salt
  ½ cup sugar
  1 teaspoon vanilla extract
  4 large eggs

1. Preheat oven to 375°.
2. Coat a 15 x 10-inch jelly-roll pan or a 9-inch springform pan with cooking spray; line with wax paper. Coat paper with cooking spray; dust with 1 tablespoon flour. Set aside.
3. Cook butter in a small saucepan over medium heat until lightly browned (about 4 minutes). Pour into a small bowl; cool and set aside.
4. Lightly spoon 1 cup flour into a dry measuring cup; level with a knife. Combine 1 cup flour and salt in a sifter. Sift flour and salt once; set aside.
5. Beat sugar, vanilla, and eggs at high speed of a mixer until ribbons fall from beaters (about 10 to 15 minutes or until egg mixture holds its shape). Lightly spoon one-third of flour mixture onto egg mixture; quickly fold. Repeat procedure twice with remaining flour mixture.
6. Stir about 1 cup batter into cooled browned butter. Gently fold butter mixture into remaining batter. Spoon batter into prepared pan; spread evenly. Bake at 375° in jelly-roll pan for 12 minutes or in springform pan for 20 minutes, or until a wooden pick comes out clean or cake springs back when touched lightly in center. Loosen from sides of pan; turn out onto a wire rack. Carefully peel off wax paper. Cool completely. Yield: 12 servings.

CALORIES 109 (31% from fat); FAT 3.8g (sat 1.7g, mono 1.2g, poly 0.3g); PROTEIN 2.9g; CARB 15.5g; FIBER 0g; CHOL 79mg; IRON 0.9mg; SODIUM 66mg; CALC 10mg

MINT-CHOCOLATE ICE-CREAM CAKE

(pictured on page 317)

Classic Génoise (see recipe)

Cake:

  4 cups low-fat vanilla ice cream
  2 tablespoons crème de menthe
  12 crème de menthe chocolaty mint thins (such as Andes), finely chopped

Frosting:

  1 cup powdered sugar
  3 tablespoons unsweetened cocoa
  2 tablespoons fat-free milk
  1 tablespoon butter or stick margarine
  ½ teaspoon vanilla extract
  1 teaspoon unsweetened cocoa

1. Prepare Classic Génoise as directed in a 9-inch springform pan. Cool completely.
2. To assemble cake, split génoise into 3 layers horizontally using a serrated knife. Place bottom layer, cut side up, in a 9-inch springform pan; place layer in pan and remaining layers in freezer.
3. Place a large bowl in freezer. Remove ice cream from freezer, and let stand at room temperature until slightly soft. Spoon ice cream into chilled bowl. Stir in crème de menthe and mint thins until well-blended. Spoon half of ice cream mixture onto cake layer in pan; top with middle layer of cake. Repeat procedure, ending with top layer of cake, cut side down. Return cake to freezer.
4. To prepare frosting, combine sugar and 3 tablespoons cocoa in a small bowl. Combine milk and butter in a 1-cup glass measure; microwave at HIGH 30 seconds or until butter melts. Add milk mixture and vanilla to sugar mixture, stirring with a whisk until smooth. Spread frosting over top of cake; freeze 30 minutes. Cover with plastic wrap, and freeze 4 hours or until firm.
5. Place cake in refrigerator 30 minutes before serving to soften. Remove band from springform pan. Sprinkle 1 teaspoon cocoa over cake. Yield: 12 servings (serving size: 1 wedge).

CALORIES 260 (29% from fat); FAT 8.5g (sat 5.1g, mono 2g, poly 0.5g); PROTEIN 5.4g; CARB 40g; FIBER 0.1g; CHOL 88mg; IRON 1.3mg; SODIUM 119mg; CALC 83mg

❶ *Coat the pan with cooking spray; line with wax paper. Then coat the paper with cooking spray; dust with flour. It's important to prepare the pan well so the cake doesn't stick.*

❷ *Cook the butter over medium heat until lightly browned. Margarine will not brown, so it's important to use butter. Watch the butter carefully because it can burn quickly.*

❸ *Sift flour and salt together. This "lightens" the flour, making it easier to incorporate into the beaten eggs, thereby minimizing lumps. A few lumps of flour, though, are typical in génoise.*

❹ *Combine sugar, vanilla, and eggs; beat until the mixture falls in ribbons from the beaters, about 10 to 15 minutes. If ribbons don't form after 15 minutes, continue to beat mixture until they do.*

❺ *Gently fold one-third of flour mixture into the egg mixture. Use a rubber spatula to cut down through the batter in the center of the bowl, and draw the spatula up the side of the bowl. Turn the bowl and repeat the process. Work quickly, but don't stir.*

❻ *Gently stir about one cup of the batter into the cooled browned butter. Then fold back into remaining batter. This helps to disperse the butter.*

Génoise is ideal for a trifle because the cake nicely soaks up the liquid. Orange juice, brandy, or any liqueur can be substituted for the sherry.

Classic Génoise (see recipe on previous page)

Custard:

- ½ cup sugar
- 1½ tablespoons cornstarch
- ⅛ teaspoon salt
- 2 large egg yolks
- 1 large egg
- 2 cups 2% reduced-fat milk
- 1 tablespoon grated lemon rind
- 1 teaspoon vanilla extract

Remaining ingredients:

- ½ cup seedless strawberry jam
- 1 tablespoon lemon juice
- ⅔ cup dry sherry
- 2 cups sliced banana (about 2 large)
- 1½ cups frozen reduced-calorie whipped topping, thawed
- 2 tablespoons sliced almonds, toasted

1. Prepare Classic Génoise as directed in a 15 x 10-inch jelly-roll pan. Cool completely.
2. To prepare custard, combine sugar and next 4 ingredients in a bowl; stir well with a whisk, and set aside. Heat milk over medium-high heat in a small, heavy saucepan to 180° or until tiny bubbles form around edge (do not boil). Gradually add hot milk to sugar mixture, stirring constantly with a whisk. Return milk mixture to pan; cook over medium heat until thick and bubbly (about 5 minutes), stirring constantly. Reduce heat to low; cook 2 minutes. Remove from heat. Place pan in a large ice-filled bowl until milk mixture comes to room temperature, stirring occasionally. Remove pan from ice; stir in lemon rind and vanilla.

Continued

3. Combine jam and juice in a small microwave-safe bowl. Microwave at HIGH 15 seconds; stir until jam dissolves. Set aside.

4. Cut cake crosswise into 5 (3-inch-wide) pieces. Cut cake lengthwise into 8 (1¼-inch) pieces to equal 40 pieces. Arrange 14 cake pieces in a single layer in bottom of a 2-quart trifle bowl or soufflé dish. Lightly brush cake pieces with sherry. Spread half of strawberry mixture over cake in dish; top with 1 cup banana. Spread half of custard over banana. Arrange 13 cake pieces over custard, and brush with sherry. Spread remaining strawberry mixture over cake; top with 1 cup banana and remaining custard. Top with 13 cake pieces, and brush with remaining sherry. Cover and chill for at least 8 hours. Uncover and spread whipped topping over top; sprinkle with almonds. Yield: 12 servings (serving size: about ¾ cup).

CALORIES 277 (25% from fat); FAT 7.6g (sat 3.8g, mono 2.3g, poly 0.7g); PROTEIN 6g; CARB 44g; FIBER 0.8g; CHOL 137mg; IRON 1.3mg; SODIUM 129mg; CALC 78mg

TRIPLE-LEMON GÉNOISE WITH BUTTERCREAM AND RASPBERRIES

Add 1 teaspoon lemon rind to the génoise batter for this decadent-tasting dessert.

Classic Génoise (page 310)
1 teaspoon grated lemon rind

Buttercream frosting:

2 tablespoons butter or stick margarine, softened
1 tablespoon fresh lemon juice
1 teaspoon vanilla extract
1 (8-ounce) block ⅓-less-fat cream cheese, chilled
2 cups powdered sugar

Lemon syrup:

⅓ cup boiling water
¼ cup granulated sugar
2 tablespoons fresh lemon juice

Remaining Ingredients:

1½ cups fresh raspberries

1. Prepare Classic Génoise as directed in a 9-inch springform pan, adding 1 teaspoon lemon rind to batter. Cool completely.

2. To prepare buttercream frosting, beat butter and next 3 ingredients at medium speed of a mixer until smooth. Lightly spoon powdered sugar into dry measuring cups; level with a knife. Gradually add powdered sugar to butter mixture; beat at low speed just until blended (do not overbeat). Cover and chill.

3. To prepare lemon syrup, combine water and granulated sugar in a small bowl; stir until sugar dissolves. Stir in 2 tablespoons lemon juice; cool to room temperature.

4. To assemble cake, split Classic Génoise in half horizontally using a serrated knife. Place bottom layer, cut side up, on a serving platter; brush with half of lemon syrup. Spread with ¾ cup frosting. Arrange ¾ cup raspberries on top of frosting. Top with remaining cake layer, cut side down; brush with remaining syrup. Spread remaining frosting over top and sides of cake. Top with ¾ cup raspberries. Store cake loosely covered in refrigerator. Yield: 12 servings (serving size: 1 slice).

CALORIES 278 (33% from fat); FAT 10.2g (sat 5.7g, mono 3.1g, poly 0.6g); PROTEIN 5g; CARB 42.3g; FIBER 1.1g; CHOL 98mg; IRON 1.1mg; SODIUM 161mg; CALC 29mg

---

A PERFECT GÉNOISE

• Read the recipe before starting. Organize your equipment and ingredients. You have to work quickly before the eggs begin to fall.

• Warm eggs will beat up to a higher volume. Place the eggs in a bowl of warm water 5 minutes.

• Use an oven thermometer to make sure the temperature is accurately 375°.

• Use cake flour (such as Swans Down) for a light, delicate cake.

Playing Chicken

Specialty chicken sausages are what your evening rush hour has been looking for.

Specialty flavored chicken sausages make short work of getting dinner on the table, and they carry as little as one-third the fat and calories of traditional sausages.

PASTA WITH SAUSAGE AND GREENS

Preparation time: 14 minutes
Cooking time: 13 minutes

3 cups uncooked fusilli (about 8 ounces short twisted spaghetti)
12 cups torn escarole (about 1 head)
1 tablespoon olive oil
1 (12-ounce) package basil, pine nut, and chicken sausage (such as Gerhard's), cut into ½-inch-thick slices
1 cup chopped onion
2 teaspoons bottled minced garlic
¼ cup fat-free, less-sodium chicken broth
¼ cup dry white wine
2 tablespoons country-style Dijon mustard
1 (15-ounce) can cannellini beans or other white beans, rinsed and drained
1 cup chopped tomato

1. Cook fusilli in boiling water 7 minutes, omitting salt and fat. Stir in escarole; cook 4 minutes. Drain and set aside.

2. While fusilli is cooking, heat oil in a large nonstick skillet over medium-high heat. Add sausage; sauté 5 minutes. Add onion and garlic; sauté 3 minutes. Add broth and wine; bring

to a boil. Reduce heat; simmer 3 minutes or until liquid almost evaporates. Stir in mustard and beans; cook 2 minutes or until thoroughly heated. Combine pasta mixture, sausage mixture, and tomato in a large bowl; toss well. Serve immediately. Yield: 6 servings (serving size: 1⅓ cups).

CALORIES 381 (28% from fat); FAT 11.7g (sat 2.6g, mono 5g, poly 3.1g); PROTEIN 20.1g; CARB 50.6g; FIBER 5.3g; CHOL 50mg; IRON 4.6mg; SODIUM 643mg; CALC 94mg

SAUSAGE-PEPPER PIZZA

(pictured on page 3)

Preparation time: 5 minutes
Cooking time: 25 minutes

2 cups presliced mushrooms
1 cup thinly sliced onion
1 cup red bell pepper strips
1 cup green bell pepper strips
¼ cup water
1 teaspoon dried basil
½ teaspoon dried oregano
½ teaspoon dried thyme
6 ounces chicken and sun-dried tomato sausage (such as Gerhard's), cut into ¼-inch-thick slices
1 (10-ounce) can refrigerated pizza crust dough
Cooking spray
½ cup commercial pizza sauce
¾ cup (3 ounces) shredded part-skim mozzarella cheese

1. Preheat oven to 425°.
2. Place a large nonstick skillet over medium-high heat until hot. Add first 9 ingredients; cook 10 minutes or until vegetables are tender and liquid almost evaporates. Remove from heat, and set aside.
3. Unroll dough, and press into a 12-inch pizza pan coated with cooking spray. Bake at 425° for 7 minutes or just until crust begins to brown. Spread pizza sauce evenly over crust, leaving a ½-inch border; top with sausage mixture. Sprinkle with cheese. Bake at 425° for 8 minutes or until

crust is golden. Yield: 4 servings (serving size: 2 wedges).

CALORIES 372 (30% from fat); FAT 12.5g (sat 4.4g, mono 4.1g, poly 3.4g); PROTEIN 19.7g; CARB 43g; FIBER 4.2g; CHOL 50mg; IRON 3.9mg; SODIUM 1,011mg; CALC 160mg

BAVARIAN SAUSAGE-AND-KRAUT SUPPER

Preparation time: 8 minutes
Cooking time: 19 minutes

4 cups uncooked medium egg noodles (about 8 ounces)
1 tablespoon olive oil
1 cup sliced onion
1 teaspoon caraway seeds
2 cups sliced peeled Granny Smith apple (about ¾ pound)
1½ cups refrigerated sauerkraut, drained
1 (12-ounce) package chicken apple sausage (such as Gerhard's), cut into ½-inch-thick slices
½ cup fat-free, less-sodium chicken broth
¼ cup sherry

1. Cook noodles according to package directions, omitting salt and fat; drain and set aside.
2. While noodles are cooking, heat oil in a large nonstick skillet over medium-high heat. Add onion and caraway seeds; cook 4 minutes or until lightly browned, stirring constantly. Add apple, sauerkraut, and sausage; cook 5 minutes. Stir in broth and sherry; bring to a boil. Reduce heat to medium; cook 5 minutes. Serve over noodles. Yield: 4 servings (serving size: 1¼ cups noodles and 1 cup sausage-apple mixture).

CALORIES 445 (29% from fat); FAT 14.5g (sat 3.4g, mono 6.9g, poly 3.3g); PROTEIN 20.1g; CARB 59.9g; FIBER 9g; CHOL 114mg; IRON 4.8mg; SODIUM 1,118mg; CALC 31mg

HASH BROWN-SAUSAGE SKILLET

Preparation time: 7 minutes
Cooking time: 14 minutes

Cooking spray
9 ounces chicken sausage with habanero chiles and tequila (such as Gerhard's), cut into ½-inch-thick slices
2 teaspoons vegetable oil
1½ cups shredded peeled sweet potato (about 8 ounces)
½ teaspoon paprika
¼ teaspoon salt
⅛ teaspoon black pepper
1 (24-ounce) package frozen hash brown potatoes with onions and peppers (such as Ore-Ida Potatoes O'Brien)
1 teaspoon dried rubbed sage

1. Place a large nonstick skillet coated with cooking spray over medium-high heat until hot. Add sausage; sauté 4 minutes. Remove sausage from pan, and keep warm. Add oil to pan; heat over medium-high heat until hot. Add sweet potato, paprika, salt, pepper, and hash brown potatoes; cover and cook 4 minutes. Uncover and stir well, breaking up frozen chunks of potato. Stir in sausage; cover and cook 4 minutes. Stir in sage. Yield: 4 servings (serving size: 1½ cups).

CALORIES 312 (30% from fat); FAT 10.5g (sat 2.7g, mono 3.5g, poly 3.4g); PROTEIN 13.1g; CARB 42.5g; FIBER 6.7g; CHOL 56mg; IRON 2.3mg; SODIUM 597mg; CALC 32mg

WHERE'S THE CHICKEN?

You can substitute one flavored sausage for another in these recipes. On average, these chicken sausages contain fewer than 45 calories and 3 grams of fat per ounce. Because Gerhard's is one of the easiest-to-find brands distributed nationally, we used its many varieties in our Test Kitchens, as well as in the nutritional analyses. You can also find excellent regionally made sausages.

Chestnuts Come Home

To call something an "old chestnut" is to link it to a familiar past. But the story of these sweet, starchy nuts lies in the future.

Most modern-day Americans know little about chestnuts or chestnut trees. But there was a time when these trees filled the landscape from New Hampshire to North Carolina. Between 1904 and 1940, the bulk of American chestnut trees succumbed to a blight from Asia. Hoping that this bit of Americana will regain its preeminence, many modern orchards are filled with new, disease-resistant varieties of chestnut trees.

SPICED PEAR SUNDAE WITH SUGARED CHESTNUTS

This dessert serves two, but can easily be doubled.

- 2 cups thinly sliced pear (about 2 pears)
- ¼ cup fresh lemon juice
- 1 cup water
- 5 tablespoons sugar, divided
- 1 teaspoon ground cinnamon
- ¼ teaspoon ground cloves
- 2 tablespoons honey
- 3 tablespoons coarsely chopped cooked shelled chestnuts (about ¼ pound in shell)
- ½ cup vanilla low-fat frozen yogurt

1. Combine pear and lemon juice; set aside. Place water in a skillet; bring to a boil. Stir in 3 tablespoons sugar, cinnamon, and cloves; reduce heat to medium. Add pear mixture; cover and cook 6 minutes or until tender. Remove pear with a slotted spoon; keep warm. Add honey to pan; cook until mixture begins to thicken (about 5 minutes).
2. Combine chestnuts and 2 tablespoons sugar in a small saucepan over medium heat; cook 3 minutes or until sugar coats chestnuts, stirring frequently. Remove chestnuts from pan. Cool on wax paper. Arrange pear on 2 serving plates. Pour sauce over pear; top with frozen yogurt. Sprinkle with chestnuts; serve immediately. Yield: 2 servings (serving size: ⅔ cup pear, ¼ cup sauce, ¼ cup yogurt, and 1½ tablespoons nuts).

CALORIES 364 (4% from fat); FAT 1.8g (sat 0.6g, mono 0.2g, poly 0.5g); PROTEIN 2.4g; CARB 91.1g; FIBER 5.9g; CHOL 4mg; IRON 1.1mg; SODIUM 16mg; CALC 79mg

RICE PILAF WITH CHESTNUTS AND BRUSSELS SPROUTS

- 1 tablespoon olive oil
- 2 tablespoons chopped shallots or onion
- 2 garlic cloves, crushed
- 4 cups trimmed Brussels sprouts, cut into eighths (about 1 pound)
- ¾ cup diced red bell pepper
- ½ cup dry white wine
- ½ cup water
- 2 cups hot cooked long-grain brown rice
- ¾ cup chopped cooked shelled chestnuts (about 1 pound in shells)
- ¾ teaspoon ground cumin
- ½ teaspoon salt
- ⅛ teaspoon freshly ground black pepper
- Dash of ground red pepper

1. Heat oil in a nonstick skillet over medium heat. Add shallots and garlic; sauté 2 minutes. Add Brussels sprouts and bell pepper; sauté 3 minutes. Stir in wine and water; bring mixture to a boil. Cover, reduce heat, and simmer 12 minutes or until half of liquid evaporates, stirring occasionally. Stir in rice and remaining ingredients; cook 2 minutes or until thoroughly heated. Yield: 6 servings (serving size: 1 cup).

CALORIES 172 (19% from fat); FAT 3.6g (sat 0.6g, mono 2.1g, poly 0.7g); PROTEIN 4.6g; CARB 31.9g; FIBER 6.1g; CHOL 0mg; IRON 1.8mg; SODIUM 217mg; CALC 45mg

CHESTNUT TORTE

This rich chestnut torte is a holiday tradition for chestnut-grower Bob Wallace of Chestnut Hill Nursery in Alachua, Florida. We lightened it slightly by decreasing the butter and using fat-free whipped topping in place of whipped cream.

Chestnut puree:

- 1½ cups whole cooked shelled chestnuts (about 2 pounds in shell)
- 1 tablespoon butter or stick margarine, softened

Filling:

- ⅓ cup sugar
- 1 tablespoon hot water
- 1½ teaspoons instant coffee granules
- 2 large egg yolks
- 1½ ounces semisweet chocolate, melted
- ¼ cup butter, softened
- ½ teaspoon vanilla extract

Remaining ingredients:

- 6 large egg yolks
- 1½ cups sugar
- 1½ teaspoons vanilla extract
- 6 large egg whites
- Cooking spray
- 1 (8-ounce) carton frozen fat-free whipped topping, thawed

1. To prepare chestnut puree, process chestnuts in a food processor until finely ground. Add 1 tablespoon butter; process until blended to measure 2½ cups. (Add a few more chestnuts, and puree, if necessary.) Cover and chill.
2. To prepare filling, combine ⅓ cup sugar, water, coffee granules, and 2 egg yolks in food processor; process until smooth. Add chocolate; process until blended. Add ¼ cup butter and ½ teaspoon vanilla; process until blended. Add ½ cup chestnut puree; process until smooth. Cover and chill 8 hours.

3. Preheat oven to 325°.

4. Beat 6 egg yolks in a large bowl at high speed of a mixer 2 minutes. Gradually add 1½ cups sugar, beating until thick and pale (about 5 minutes); beat in 1½ teaspoons vanilla until blended. Gently fold in 2 cups chestnut puree. Beat egg whites at high speed of a mixer until stiff peaks form using clean, dry beaters (do not overbeat). Gently stir one-fourth of egg whites into chestnut mixture; gently fold in remaining egg whites. Pour batter into 2 (8-inch) round cake pans coated with cooking spray. Bake at 325° for 50 minutes. Cool completely on wire racks. Loosen cake layers using a knife or narrow spatula. Place one cake layer on a plate; spread with filling, and top with other cake layer.

5. Spread whipped topping evenly over top and sides of torte. Chill 2 hours before serving. Yield: 12 servings.

CALORIES 299 (30% from fat); FAT 9.9g (sat 4.9g, mono 3.3g, poly 0.9g); PROTEIN 4.3g; CARB 47.7g; FIBER 2.1g; CHOL 158mg; IRON 0.8mg; SODIUM 92mg; CALC 25mg

---

ROOT-VEGETABLE MASHED POTATOES WITH CHESTNUTS

Chervil is an aromatic herb that's a member of the parsley family. It lends a mild anise flavor to this dish.

- 4 cups (1-inch) cubed peeled baking or Yukon gold potato
- 2 cups (1-inch-thick) sliced parsnip
- 5 garlic cloves, peeled
- ¾ cup fat-free, less-sodium chicken broth
- 1 tablespoon butter or stick margarine
- ½ teaspoon salt
- ½ teaspoon dried chervil
- Dash of black pepper
- ½ cup chopped cooked shelled chestnuts (about ½ pound in shell)

1. Place first 3 ingredients in a large saucepan; cover with water. Bring to a boil; cook 20 minutes or until very tender. Drain.

2. Return potato mixture to pan. Add broth and next 4 ingredients; beat at medium speed of a mixer until smooth. Stir in chestnuts. Yield: 10 servings (serving size: ½ cup).

CALORIES 99 (14% from fat); FAT 1.5g (sat 0.8g, mono 0.4g, poly 0.2g); PROTEIN 2.1g; CARB 19.9g; FIBER 2.3g; CHOL 3mg; IRON 0.7mg; SODIUM 172mg; CALC 19mg

---

WINTER STEW WITH CHESTNUTS

- 2 acorn squash (about 1 pound each)
- 4 cups (1-inch) cubed peeled turnips (about 1 pound)
- Cooking spray
- 1 tablespoon olive oil
- 1¾ cups chopped onion
- 1¼ cups (¼-inch-thick) sliced carrot
- ¾ cup chopped green onions
- 2 garlic cloves, minced
- 1 cup chopped cooked shelled chestnuts (about 1 pound in shell)
- 2 (16-ounce) cans fat-free, less-sodium chicken broth
- 1 (28-ounce) can crushed tomatoes, undrained
- 2 tablespoons cornstarch
- 2 tablespoons water
- 3 cups chopped smoked turkey or turkey ham
- ½ teaspoon dried oregano
- ¼ teaspoon dried rosemary, crushed
- ⅛ teaspoon black pepper

1. Preheat oven to 400°.

2. Cut squash in half lengthwise; discard seeds and stringy membrane. Cut each half lengthwise into quarters. Place squash and turnips on a baking sheet coated with cooking spray. Bake at 400° for 25 minutes; cool. Scoop out pulp from each squash piece; discard rind. Cut squash into 1-inch cubes.

3. Heat oil in a Dutch oven over medium heat. Add 1¾ cups onion, carrot, green onions, and garlic to pan; sauté 8 minutes. Add squash, turnips, chestnuts, broth, and tomatoes. Cover and simmer 25 minutes.

4. Combine cornstarch and water in a small bowl. Add cornstarch mixture, turkey, and remaining ingredients to pan; bring to a boil. Reduce heat; simmer 25 minutes. Yield: 8 servings (serving size: 1½ cups).

CALORIES 246 (20% from fat); FAT 5.5g (sat 1.4g, mono 2.1g, poly 1.4g); PROTEIN 15.4g; CARB 35.6g; FIBER 6.2g; CHOL 38mg; IRON 2.2mg; SODIUM 1,133mg; CALC 108mg

---

CURRIED CHESTNUT SOUP

- 1 tablespoon olive oil
- 1 cup chopped onion
- 1½ cups (½-inch) cubed peeled sweet potato
- 1½ teaspoons curry powder
- 2 garlic cloves, crushed
- 1½ cups (1-inch) cut green beans
- 1½ cups coarsely chopped cooked shelled chestnuts (about 1½ pounds in shell)
- 2 (16-ounce) cans fat-free, less-sodium chicken broth
- 1 (15-ounce) can cannellini beans or other white beans, drained
- ½ teaspoon salt
- ¼ teaspoon dried basil
- ¼ teaspoon ground cumin
- ¼ teaspoon black pepper
- 1 (14.5-ounce) can stewed tomatoes, drained

1. Heat oil in a Dutch oven over medium heat. Add onion; sauté 4 minutes. Add sweet potato, curry powder, and garlic; sauté 5 minutes. Add green beans, chestnuts, broth, and cannellini beans; bring to a boil. Cover, reduce heat, and simmer 30 minutes or until potato is tender, stirring occasionally. Place 4 cups vegetable mixture in a blender; process until smooth. Return pureed mixture to pan; stir in salt and remaining ingredients. Cook 5 minutes or until thoroughly heated. Yield: 8 servings (serving size: 1 cup).

CALORIES 202 (15% from fat); FAT 3.4g (sat 0.5g, mono 1.7g, poly 0.9g); PROTEIN 7g; CARB 36.6g; FIBER 6.2g; CHOL 0mg; IRON 2mg; SODIUM 550mg; CALC 58mg

CHESTNUT-AND-SAUSAGE STUFFING

- 1 teaspoon butter or stick margarine
- 8 ounces sweet Italian turkey sausage
- ¾ cup finely chopped onion
- ½ cup finely chopped celery
- 1 cup diced tomato
- 1 teaspoon dried thyme
- ½ teaspoon dried rubbed sage
- ¼ teaspoon salt
- ¼ teaspoon black pepper
- 6 cups (1-inch) cubed French bread (about 8 slices), toasted
- 1½ cups fat-free, less-sodium chicken broth
- 1 cup coarsely chopped cooked shelled chestnuts (about 1 pound in shell)

1. Preheat oven to 350°.
2. Melt butter in a large nonstick skillet over medium-high heat. Add sausage; cook until browned, stirring to crumble. Add onion and celery; sauté 4 minutes. Add tomato and next 4 ingredients; sauté 3 minutes.
3. Combine sausage mixture, bread, broth, and chestnuts in a large bowl. Spoon into an 11 x 7-inch baking dish. Bake at 350° for 40 minutes. Yield: 8 servings (serving size: ½ cup).

CALORIES 209 (20% from fat); FAT 4.6g (sat 1.4g, mono 1.8g, poly 1.2g); PROTEIN 9.6g; CARB 31.8g; FIBER 3.9g; CHOL 24mg; IRON 1.9mg; SODIUM 564mg; CALC 45mg

---

COOKING AND PEELING FRESH CHESTNUTS

Soak chestnuts in a bowl of water for about 30 minutes; drain well. Cut a slit in the shell in the rounded side of the chestnut. To roast in your oven, arrange chestnuts on a baking sheet. Bake at 400° for 25 minutes. Or use your microwave; just arrange chestnuts in a single layer on a microwave-safe dish. Microwave at HIGH 2 minutes (do only 12 chestnuts at a time so they cook evenly). After either method, allow chestnuts to cool; then peel.

LIGHTEN UP

A Must for Madeleine

Mom wants the belt-busting family coffeecake she grew up with to get a healthy makeover for when her daughter begins to bake.

Taia Kaniewski of East Greenbush, New York, wants to be ready to pass down her grandmother's Sour Cream Coffeecake to her daughter Madeleine. But not all the fat.

We had some ideas: First, cut down on the streusel mixture and its high-fat walnuts. We also opted for fat-free sour cream, reduced the butter by a third, cut out an egg, and added fat-free cream cheese for moistness.

The weigh-in? Less than half the fat and nearly 100 fewer calories per slice in the new version.

SOUR CREAM COFFEECAKE

Streusel:

- ¼ cup granulated sugar
- ¼ cup coarsely chopped walnuts
- 1 teaspoon ground cinnamon

Cake:

- 2 cups granulated sugar
- 10 tablespoons butter, softened
- ½ cup (4 ounces) block-style fat-free cream cheese
- 2 large egg whites
- 1 large egg
- 2 cups all-purpose flour
- ½ teaspoon baking powder
- ½ teaspoon baking soda
- ¼ teaspoon salt
- 1 cup fat-free sour cream
- ½ teaspoon vanilla extract
- Cooking spray
- 1 teaspoon powdered sugar

1. Preheat oven to 350°.
2. To prepare streusel, combine first 3 ingredients in a small bowl; set aside.
3. To prepare cake, beat 2 cups sugar, butter, and cream cheese at medium speed of a mixer until well-blended (about 5 minutes). Add egg whites and egg, 1 at a time, beating well after each addition. Lightly spoon flour into dry measuring cups; level with a knife. Combine flour and next 3 ingredients, stirring well with a whisk. Add flour mixture to sugar mixture alternately with sour cream, beginning and ending with flour mixture. Stir in vanilla.
4. Spoon half of batter into bottom of a 12-cup Bundt pan coated with cooking spray; sprinkle with streusel. Spoon remaining batter over streusel, spreading evenly. Bake at 350° for 1 hour or until a wooden pick inserted in center comes out clean. Cool in pan 10 minutes on a wire rack; remove from pan. Cool completely on wire rack. Sprinkle with powdered sugar. Yield 16 servings (serving size: 1 slice).

Note: We also tested this cake substituting 1 cup light butter (such as Land O' Lakes) for 10 tablespoons regular butter. Because total fat was slightly lower using light butter, we discovered we could increase walnuts from ¼ cup to ½ cup and still have about same amount of calories and fat.

CALORIES 265 (30% from fat); FAT 8.8g (sat 4.7g, mono 2.5g, poly 1.1g); PROTEIN 5g; CARB 41.9g; FIBER 0.6g; CHOL 34mg; IRON 0.9mg; SODIUM 228mg; CALC 38mg

BEFORE & AFTER	
SERVING SIZE	
1 slice	
CALORIES PER SERVING	
356	265
FAT	
19.7g	8.8g
PERCENT OF TOTAL CALORIES	
50%	30%
CHOLESTEROL	
65mg	34mg

Mint-Chocolate Ice-Cream Cake, page 310

Fresh Vegetable Rolls, page 328

Cranberry-Glazed Ham,
White Cheddar-Potato Gratin, and
Holiday Green Beans, page 331

Two-Potato Party Latkes, page 326

*Old-Fashioned Caramel
Layer Cake, page 332*

Oyster Stew with Chestnuts,
page 322

New-Tradition Lasagna
with Spinach Noodles,
page 321

The Magical Memories of Holiday Meals

We asked six notable authors from different regions to recount how a meal or certain food became an unforgettable occasion at a holiday home. Join Julia Alvarez in Vermont with her Yankee husband on Noche Buena (below); Clifton Taulbert in Tulsa, Oklahoma, with his wife, her sisters, and their mother's pies (page 323); Annabelle Gurwitch's spiritual quest for, among other things, latkes (page 325); Malachy McCourt's Irish-style goose and Chinese food in Manhattan (page 327); Gretel Ehrlich in Montana with jilted eggs and no electricity (page 329); and Sandra Conroy's memories of her mother's candies (page 331).

Noche Buena, New England

What happens when German Nebraskan meets Spanish Caribbean in the middle of New England?

During my childhood, *Noche Buena* (Christmas Eve) dinner was the apex of a Dominican woman's cooking skills: She put on the table the most splendid meal of the year. In Nebraska, my husband Bill's family always sat down to chili and oyster stew. In snowy Vermont, our Christmas Eve dinner presents something of a challenge.

—Julia Alvarez

JULIA AND BILL'S
*NOCHE BUENA/*CHRISTMAS EVE
DINNER MENU

NEW-TRADITION LASAGNA
WITH SPINACH NOODLES
OR
OYSTER STEW WITH
CHESTNUTS

POTATO-BLACK BEAN
CAKES WITH TROPICAL
DRESSING OVER GREENS

PERSIMMON FLAN
OR
GERMAN CHOCOLATE CAKE
WITH COCONUT-PECAN
SAUCE

NEW-TRADITION LASAGNA WITH SPINACH NOODLES

(pictured on page 320)

You can substitute prepackaged spinach lasagna noodles and a good jarred low-fat marinara sauce. The noodle recipe makes more than you'll need in case some fall apart. You can make the sauce in advance and store it in airtight containers; freeze up to two months or refrigerate up to three days.

½ cup (2 ounces) grated fresh
   Parmesan cheese
1 tablespoon butter or stick
   margarine, softened
¼ teaspoon salt
¼ teaspoon black pepper
⅛ teaspoon grated whole nutmeg
1 (15-ounce) carton fat-free
   ricotta cheese
6 cups Bill's Marinara Sauce
Cooking spray
9 cooked Homemade Spinach
   Lasagna Noodles
¼ cup thinly sliced fresh basil
2 cups (8 ounces) shredded
   part-skim mozzarella cheese

1. Preheat oven to 350°.
2. Combine first 6 ingredients in a bowl. Spoon 1 cup marinara sauce into a 13 x 9-inch baking dish coated with cooking spray. Arrange 3 noodles over sauce; top with 1 cup ricotta mixture, 2 cups marinara sauce, 2 tablespoons basil, and ⅔ cup mozzarella cheese. Repeat layers, ending with noodles. Spread 1 cup marinara sauce over noodles; top with ⅔ cup mozzarella. Cover and bake at 350° for 1 hour. Let stand 15 minutes. Yield: 9 servings.

(Totals include Bill's Marinara Sauce and Homemade Spinach Lasagna Noodles) CALORIES 267 (36% from fat); FAT 10.7g (sat 5g, mono 4g, poly 0.7g); PROTEIN 19.8g; CARB 25.3g; FIBER 1.6g; CHOL 64mg; IRON 2.1mg; SODIUM 827mg; CALC 385mg

Bill's Marinara Sauce:

1 tablespoon olive oil
¼ cup chopped onion
4 garlic cloves, thinly sliced
½ teaspoon salt
½ teaspoon sugar
½ teaspoon black pepper
2 (14.5-ounce) cans diced
   tomatoes, undrained
1 (28-ounce) can crushed
   tomatoes, undrained

1. To prepare sauce, heat oil in a saucepan over medium-high heat. Add onion and garlic. Cook 3 minutes or until tender; stir constantly. Stir in salt and remaining ingredients; bring to a boil. Reduce heat; simmer 30 minutes. Yield: 6 cups (serving size: ⅔ cup).

CALORIES 55 (31% from fat); FAT 1.9g (sat 0.2g, mono 1.2g, poly 0.2g); PROTEIN 1.9g; CARB 8.8g; FIBER 1.1g; CHOL 0mg; IRON 1.1mg; SODIUM 394mg; CALC 56mg

Homemade Spinach Lasagna Noodles:

1½ cups all-purpose flour
3 tablespoons frozen chopped
   spinach, thawed, drained, and
   squeezed dry
½ teaspoon salt
2 teaspoons olive oil
2 large eggs, lightly beaten

1. To prepare noodles, lightly spoon flour into dry measuring cups, and level with a knife. Place flour, spinach, and salt in a food processor; pulse 3 times or until blended. With processor on, slowly pour oil and eggs through food chute; process until dough forms *Continued*

a ball. Turn dough out onto a lightly floured surface, and knead until smooth and elastic (about 10 minutes). Dust dough lightly with flour; let stand 10 minutes.

2. Divide dough into 4 equal portions. Working with 1 portion at a time, pass dough through smooth rollers of pasta machine on widest setting. Continue moving width gauge to narrower settings; pass dough through rollers once at each setting, dusting with flour, if needed. Repeat procedure with remaining dough. Cut each pasta sheet into 3 (11 x 2-inch) strips. Hang pasta on a wooden drying rack 10 minutes. Cook pasta in boiling water 2 minutes or until al dente; drain. Yield: 12 noodles (serving size: 1 noodle).

CALORIES 77 (21% from fat); FAT 1.8g (sat 0.4g, mono 0.9g, poly 0.3g); PROTEIN 2.8g; CARB 12.1g; FIBER 0.5g; CHOL 37mg; IRON 0.9mg; SODIUM 111mg; CALC 9mg

OYSTER STEW WITH CHESTNUTS

(pictured on page 320)

Fresh chestnuts are ideal in this dish, but you can substitute 1 (15-ounce) jar. If so, skip the soaking and microwaving steps; just chop and proceed with the recipe.

   1   pound fresh chestnuts in shells
1½   cups diced peeled baking potato
   2   (12-ounce) containers Standard oysters, undrained
   2   bacon slices
   1   cup chopped onion
   ½   cup chopped celery
   ½   cup chopped green onions
   ¼   cup all-purpose flour
   4   cups 2% reduced-fat milk
   ¾   teaspoon salt
   ½   teaspoon dried thyme
   ⅛   teaspoon white pepper
   2   tablespoons dry sherry

1. Soak chestnuts in a bowl of water 30 minutes.
2. While chestnuts are soaking, place potato in a medium saucepan, and cover with water; bring to a boil. Reduce heat, and simmer 15 minutes or until tender; drain.
3. Drain chestnuts. Cut a slit in shell on rounded side of chestnut. (Make sure slit goes all the way through the shell. If not, they will explode.) Arrange chestnuts in a single layer on a microwave-safe dish. (Microwave a maximum of 12 chestnuts at one time in order to cook evenly). Microwave at HIGH 2 minutes. Cool 5 minutes. Peel and chop to equal 2 cups.
4. Drain oysters in colander over a bowl; reserve ½ cup liquid and oysters.
5. Cook bacon in a Dutch oven over medium heat until crisp. Remove bacon from pan; crumble. Add chestnuts, 1 cup onion, celery, and green onions to bacon drippings in pan; sauté 5 minutes. Spoon flour into a dry measuring cup; level with a knife. Stir flour into chestnut mixture; cook 1 minute. Add potato, reserved oyster liquid, bacon, milk, salt, thyme, and pepper. Bring to a boil; reduce heat, and simmer until thick (about 8 minutes). Stir in sherry and oysters; cook 3 minutes or until edges of oysters curl. Serve immediately. Yield: 6 servings (serving size: 1½ cups).
Note: Try Cuvaison Chardonnay Reserve 1997 (Carneros, $32)—creamy and rich, yet refined—with this dish.

CALORIES 342 (23% from fat); FAT 8.6g (sat 3.4g, mono 2.2g, poly 1.6g); PROTEIN 16.6g; CARB 48.6g; FIBER 7g; CHOL 77mg; IRON 9mg; SODIUM 534mg; CALC 284mg

POTATO-BLACK BEAN CAKES WITH TROPICAL DRESSING OVER GREENS

Potato cakes:

   1   tablespoon olive oil
   ¼   cup chopped onion
   1   tablespoon minced seeded serrano chile or jalapeño pepper
   1   garlic clove, minced
   ⅓   cup 2% reduced-fat milk
   ½   teaspoon salt
   1   (15-ounce) can black beans, drained
   1   large egg white
   2   cups shredded peeled baking potato
Cooking spray

Dressing:

   1   cup pineapple juice
   ½   cup finely chopped onion
   3   tablespoons brown sugar
   2   tablespoons white rum or water
   1   tablespoon fresh lime juice
   1   tablespoon chopped pecans, toasted
   2   bacon slices, cooked and crumbled
   6   cups gourmet salad greens

1. To prepare potato cakes, heat oil in a large nonstick skillet over medium-high heat. Add ¼ cup onion, chile, and garlic; sauté 3 minutes. Combine onion mixture, milk, salt, beans, and egg white in a food processor; process until smooth, scraping sides of bowl once. Stir in potato.
2. Place skillet coated with cooking spray over medium-high heat until hot. For each cake, spoon 1 tablespoon potato mixture into pan, spreading to form a 2-inch circle; cook 2 minutes or until lightly browned. Carefully turn cakes over; cook 2 minutes. Remove from pan, and keep warm. Repeat procedure with remaining potato mixture.
3. To prepare dressing, combine pineapple juice and next 4 ingredients in a saucepan; bring to a boil. Reduce heat; simmer 5 minutes. Stir in pecans and bacon.
4. Arrange 1 cup salad greens on each of 6 plates. Arrange 4 potato cakes around greens on each plate. Drizzle ¼ cup warm dressing over each serving. Yield: 6 servings.

CALORIES 215 (22% from fat); FAT 5.2g (sat 1.1g, mono 2.9g, poly 0.8g); PROTEIN 8.2g; CARB 35.6g; FIBER 4.2g; CHOL 3mg; IRON 2.3mg; SODIUM 377mg; CALC 71mg

PERSIMMON FLAN

1½ cups sugar, divided
¼ cup water
2 ripe persimmons, peeled and quartered (about 10 ounces)
2 tablespoons all-purpose flour
1 (8-ounce) block ⅓-less-fat cream cheese
3 large egg whites
2 large eggs
2 cups 2% reduced-fat milk
½ cup pomegranate seeds
24 thin slices peeled ripe persimmon (about 4 persimmons)

1. Combine 1 cup sugar and water in a small heavy saucepan; cook over medium-high heat until sugar dissolves, stirring frequently. Continue cooking 9 minutes or until golden, stirring constantly. Immediately pour into a 9-inch round cake pan, tipping quickly until sugar coats bottom of pan.
2. Place persimmon quarters in a food processor; process until smooth, scraping sides of bowl once.
3. Preheat oven to 350°.
4. Combine ½ cup sugar and flour. Beat cream cheese at medium speed of a mixer until smooth. Add flour mixture; beat until well-blended. Add egg whites and eggs; beat well. Gradually add milk and ½ cup persimmon puree; beat well. Pour batter into prepared cake pan. Place cake pan in a broiler pan; add hot water to broiler pan to a depth of 1 inch. Bake at 350° for 1½ hours or until a knife inserted in center comes out clean. Remove cake pan from pan; cool completely on a wire rack. Cover and chill 8 hours.
5. Loosen edges of flan with a knife or rubber spatula. Place a serving plate, upside down, on top of pan; invert flan onto plate. Drizzle any remaining caramelized syrup over flan. Sprinkle with pomegranate seeds; garnish with persimmon slices. Yield: 10 servings (serving size: 1 wedge).

CALORIES 282 (24% from fat); FAT 7.4g (sat 4.2g, mono 2.2g, poly 0.3g); PROTEIN 6.8g; CARB 49.2g; FIBER 1.1g; CHOL 65mg; IRON 0.5mg; SODIUM 145mg; CALC 89mg

GERMAN-CHOCOLATE CAKE WITH COCONUT-PECAN SAUCE

⅓ cup butter or stick margarine
1 (4-ounce) bar sweet baking chocolate, chopped
1¼ cups sugar
½ cup water
1½ teaspoons vanilla extract
2 large egg whites
1 large egg
2 cups all-purpose flour
2 teaspoons baking powder
⅛ teaspoon salt
Cooking spray
Coconut-Pecan Sauce

1. Preheat oven to 350°.
2. Place butter and chocolate in a microwave-safe bowl; microwave at HIGH 1 minute or until melted, stirring until smooth. Stir in sugar, water, and vanilla. Add egg whites and egg; stir with a whisk. Lightly spoon flour into dry measuring cups; level with a knife. Combine flour, baking powder, and salt; add to chocolate mixture, stirring with a whisk until smooth. Coat bottom of a 13 x 9-inch baking pan with cooking spray; pour batter into pan. Bake at 350° for 30 minutes or until a wooden pick inserted in center comes out clean. Cool in pan on a wire rack. Serve with Coconut-Pecan Sauce. Yield: 20 servings (serving size: 1 cake piece and 2 tablespoons sauce).

(Totals include Coconut-Pecan Sauce) CALORIES 267 (30% from fat); FAT 8.9g (sat 4.7g, mono 3g, poly 0.7g); PROTEIN 3.7g; CARB 44.5g; FIBER 0.6g; CHOL 25mg; IRON 0.9mg; SODIUM 144mg; CALC 84mg

Coconut-Pecan Sauce:

1½ cups sugar
2½ tablespoons cornstarch
1 (12-ounce) can evaporated low-fat milk
3 tablespoons butter or stick margarine
⅓ cup chopped pecans
¼ cup flaked sweetened coconut
1½ teaspoons vanilla extract

1. Combine sugar and cornstarch in a medium, heavy saucepan. Add milk; stir with a whisk. Add butter. Bring to a boil over medium heat; cook 1 minute, stirring constantly. Remove from heat; stir in pecans, coconut, and vanilla. Serve warm. Yield: 2⅔ cups (serving size: about 2 tablespoons).

CALORIES 110 (29% from fat); FAT 3.5g (sat 1.6g, mono 1.4g, poly 0.4g); PROTEIN 1.5g; CARB 18.8g; FIBER 0.2g; CHOL 5mg; IRON 0.1mg; SODIUM 40mg; CALC 51mg

AT MY HOUSE

Sisters

When seven sisters reunited for the holidays to make pies like their mother's, something loving came out of the oven.

One holiday, my wife Barbara's six sisters drove almost 500 miles to surprise her. After the hugging and kissing, my wife had to ask: "Why are you all here?" The reply was almost in unison: "We've come to make our holiday sweet potato pies." They all just wanted to cook together like they did when they were little girls.

—Clifton Taulbert

CREAM CHEESE PIECRUST

2 tablespoons butter or stick margarine
2 tablespoons (1 ounce) ⅓-less-fat cream cheese
2 tablespoons sugar
1 teaspoon vanilla extract
1 tablespoon 1% low-fat milk
1 large egg yolk
1 cup all-purpose flour
¼ teaspoon baking powder
¼ teaspoon salt
Cooking spray

1. Combine first 4 ingredients in a large bowl; beat at medium speed of a mixer until smooth. Add milk and egg yolk; beat until well-blended. Lightly spoon flour into a dry measuring cup; level with a knife. Add flour, baking

Continued

powder, and salt to milk mixture, stirring until well-blended.

2. Press mixture gently into a 4-inch circle on heavy-duty plastic wrap; cover with additional plastic wrap. Chill 15 minutes. Roll dough, still covered, into an 11-inch circle. Place dough in freezer 5 minutes or until plastic wrap can be easily removed.

3. Remove 1 sheet of plastic wrap; fit dough into a 9-inch pie plate coated with cooking spray. Remove top sheet of plastic wrap. Press dough against bottom and sides of pan. Fold edges under; flute. Fill and bake crust according to recipe directions. Yield: 1 (9-inch) crust.

CALORIES 916 (36% from fat); FAT 37g (sat 20.5g, mono 10.7g, poly 2.3g); PROTEIN 19.3g; CARB 123.1g; FIBER 3.4g; CHOL 302mg; IRON 6.7mg; SODIUM 1,074mg; CALC 158mg

PECAN-CRUSTED SWEET POTATO PIE

1   (9-inch) unbaked Cream Cheese Piecrust (page 323)
1½ cups mashed cooked sweet potato (about ¾ pound)
⅓   cup packed dark brown sugar
3   tablespoons evaporated fat-free milk
¾   teaspoon pumpkin-pie spice
¼   teaspoon salt
1   large egg
½   cup packed dark brown sugar
½   cup light-colored corn syrup
2   teaspoons vanilla extract
¼   teaspoon ground cinnamon
⅛   teaspoon salt
1   large egg
½   cup chopped pecans

1. Prepare Cream Cheese Piecrust in a 9-inch pie plate; set aside.
2. Preheat oven to 350°.
3. Combine sweet potato and next 5 ingredients in a food processor; process until smooth. Spoon into prepared crust. Combine ½ cup brown sugar and next 5 ingredients in a bowl; stir well with a whisk. Stir in pecans. Pour pecan mixture over sweet potato mixture. Bake at 350° for 1 hour or until

almost set; shield edges of piecrust with foil after 20 minutes. Cool on a wire rack. Yield: 10 servings (serving size: 1 wedge).

CALORIES 322 (25% from fat); FAT 8.9g (sat 2.7g, mono 4g, poly 1.4g); PROTEIN 4.9g; CARB 56.1g; FIBER 2.2g; CHOL 75mg; IRON 1.6mg; SODIUM 248mg; CALC 65mg

CLASSIC SWEET POTATO PIE

1   (9-inch) unbaked Cream Cheese Piecrust (page 323)
2   cups mashed cooked sweet potato (about 1¼ pounds)
1   cup evaporated fat-free milk
¾   cup sugar
1   teaspoon vanilla extract
½   teaspoon grated lemon rind
½   teaspoon ground cinnamon
¼   teaspoon salt
¼   teaspoon ground nutmeg
2   large eggs
1¼ cups frozen reduced-calorie whipped topping, thawed
Ground cinnamon (optional)

1. Prepare Cream Cheese Piecrust in a 9-inch pie plate; set aside.
2. Preheat oven to 350°.
3. Combine sweet potato and next 8 ingredients in a food processor; process until smooth. Spoon mixture into prepared crust. Bake at 350° for 45 minutes or until set; shield edges of piecrust with foil after 20 minutes. Cool completely on a wire rack. Top each serving with whipped topping; sprinkle with cinnamon, if desired. Yield: 10 servings (serving size: 1 wedge and 2 tablespoons topping).
Note: Serve with Clos du Bois Late Harvest Semillon 1997 (Knights Valley, $18 per half-bottle), an opulent wine that is long and syrupy in the mouth.

CALORIES 274 (20% from fat); FAT 6.1g (sat 3.5g, mono 1.5g, poly 0.5g); PROTEIN 6.5g; CARB 48.4g; FIBER 2.3g; CHOL 76mg; IRON 1.3mg; SODIUM 223mg; CALC 117mg

COCONUT-RUM SWEET POTATO PIE

1   (9-inch) unbaked Cream Cheese Piecrust (page 323)
2   cups mashed cooked sweet potato (about 1¼ pounds)
½   cup packed dark brown sugar
¼   cup 2% reduced-fat milk
2   tablespoons dark rum
1½ teaspoons vanilla extract
½   teaspoon ground nutmeg
¼   teaspoon salt
3   large eggs
½   cup flaked sweetened coconut

1. Prepare Cream Cheese Piecrust in a 9-inch pie plate; set aside.
2. Preheat oven to 350°.
3. Combine sweet potato and next 7 ingredients in a food processor; process until smooth. Spoon into prepared crust; sprinkle with coconut.
4. Bake at 350° for 1 hour or until set; shield edges of piecrust with foil after 20 minutes. Cool on a wire rack. Yield: 10 servings (serving size: 1 wedge).

CALORIES 254 (26% from fat); FAT 7.3g (sat 4.1g, mono 1.8g, poly 0.6g); PROTEIN 5.3g; CARB 41.8g; FIBER 2.6g; CHOL 97mg; IRON 1.6mg; SODIUM 214mg; CALC 55mg

GRAHAM CRACKER PIECRUST

36 graham crackers (9 full cracker sheets)
¼   cup sugar
1   tablespoon chilled butter or stick margarine, cut into small pieces
1   teaspoon ground cinnamon
1   large egg white
Cooking spray

1. Preheat oven to 350°.
2. Place crackers in a food processor; process until finely ground. Add sugar, butter, and cinnamon; pulse 6 times or until mixture resembles coarse meal. Add egg white; pulse 10 times or just until blended (do not allow mixture to form a ball). Firmly press mixture into bottom and up sides of a 9-inch pie plate coated with cooking spray. Bake

at 350° for 7 minutes; cool on a wire rack. Yield: 1 (9-inch) crust.

CALORIES 863 (26% from fat); FAT 25g (sat 9.2g, mono 8.7g, poly 5.3g); PROTEIN 11.1g; CARB 148.5g; FIBER 4.1g; CHOL 31mg; IRON 5.8mg; SODIUM 984mg; CALC 79mg

SWEET POTATO PIE WITH HAZELNUT STREUSEL

1 (9-inch) Graham Cracker Piecrust (see recipe on previous page)

Filling:

1½ cups mashed cooked sweet potato (about ¾ pound)
⅔ cup granulated sugar
½ cup evaporated fat-free milk
2 teaspoons vanilla extract
½ teaspoon ground nutmeg
¼ teaspoon salt
¼ teaspoon ground mace
3 large eggs

Streusel:

¼ cup hazelnuts
¼ cup all-purpose flour
¼ cup packed dark brown sugar
¾ teaspoon ground cinnamon
2 tablespoons chilled butter or stick margarine, cut into small pieces

1. Prepare and bake Graham Cracker Piecrust in a 9-inch pie plate; cool on a wire rack.
2. Preheat oven to 350°.
3. To prepare filling, combine sweet potato and next 7 ingredients in a food processor; process until smooth. Scrape sides of bowl once. Pour into prepared crust.
4. To prepare streusel, place hazelnuts on a baking sheet. Bake at 350° for 15 minutes, stirring once. Turn nuts out onto a towel. Roll up towel; rub off skins. Chop nuts. Lightly spoon flour into a dry measuring cup; level with a knife. Combine flour, brown sugar, and cinnamon in a bowl; cut in butter with a pastry blender or 2 knives until

mixture resembles coarse meal. Stir in hazelnuts. Sprinkle filling with streusel. Bake pie at 350° for 45 minutes or until set. Cool on a wire rack. Yield: 10 servings (serving size: 1 wedge).

CALORIES 295 (25% from fat); FAT 8.2g (sat 3g, mono 3.4g, poly 1.1g); PROTEIN 5.5g; CARB 50.2g; FIBER 2.1g; CHOL 76mg; IRON 1.5mg; SODIUM 224mg; CALC 76mg

AT MY HOUSE

Nice Jewish Girl Seeks Holiday Spirit

The search for a spiritual home seemed to be an endless and rather flavorless voyage—until the latkes led to home.

I grew up as a Reformed Jew in the '70s. Outside of watching *Star Trek* together, my family didn't cling to a lot of rituals. Eight years ago, I heard a rabbi who recounted the mystical version of the story of Hanukkah.

That year I celebrated my first Hanukkah. Tradition insists on fried foods for Hanukkah, usually latkes, or potato pancakes. I've given up fried foods since then, and my husband doesn't eat meat, so we've come up with a compromise big vegetarian Hanukkah meal.

—Annabelle Gurwitch

ECUMENICAL VEGETARIAN BUFFET

CHOPPED SALAD WITH BLUE CHEESE DRESSING

CREAMY INDIAN LENTILS AND RICE

SHERRY-ROASTED ROOT VEGETABLES

PEPPER-SWIRLED CHICKPEA DIP

TWO-POTATO PARTY LATKES

MEDITERRANEAN STUFFED BREAD

CHALLAH

CHOPPED SALAD WITH BLUE CHEESE DRESSING

Salad:

6 cups chopped iceberg lettuce
2 cups sliced cucumber
1 cup diced plum tomato
1 cup sliced celery
1 cup sliced radishes
1 cup diced red bell pepper
½ cup diced carrot
½ cup thinly sliced green onions
¼ cup chopped fresh parsley
3 tablespoons capers, drained
1 teaspoon dried oregano

Dressing:

⅓ cup low-fat buttermilk
¼ cup crumbled blue cheese
1 tablespoon light mayonnaise
1 tablespoon red wine vinegar
1 teaspoon Worcestershire sauce
½ teaspoon salt
¼ teaspoon black pepper

1. Combine first 11 ingredients in a bowl.
2. To prepare dressing, combine buttermilk and remaining 6 ingredients, stirring with a whisk. Just before serving, drizzle salad with dressing; toss gently to coat. Yield: 12 servings (serving size: 1 cup).

CALORIES 36 (35% from fat); FAT 1.4g (sat 0.5g, mono 0.3g, poly 0.3g); PROTEIN 1.8g; CARB 4.8g; FIBER 1.3g; CHOL 2mg; IRON 0.7mg; SODIUM 334mg; CALC 45mg

CREAMY INDIAN LENTILS AND RICE

1 tablespoon vegetable oil
2 cups thinly sliced onion
1 cup uncooked long-grain brown rice
1 tablespoon curry powder
2 teaspoons mustard seeds
1 teaspoon salt
½ teaspoon black pepper
4 cups water
1 cup dried lentils
1 cup chopped fresh cilantro
½ cup low-fat sour cream

Continued

1. Heat oil in a large Dutch oven over medium-high heat. Add onion; sauté 8 minutes or until golden brown, stirring occasionally. Add rice and next 4 ingredients; sauté 1 minute. Add water and lentils; bring to a boil. Cover, reduce heat, and simmer 1 hour. Remove from heat; stir in cilantro and sour cream. Yield: 6 servings (serving size: 1 cup).

CALORIES 297 (20% from fat); FAT 6.5g (sat 2.1g, mono 2g, poly 1.7g); PROTEIN 13.2g; CARB 48g; FIBER 6.3g; CHOL 8mg; IRON 4.5mg; SODIUM 411mg; CALC 78mg

SHERRY-ROASTED ROOT VEGETABLES

2 cups (¼-inch-thick) sliced parsnip
2 cups baby carrots (about ½ pound)
1 cup thinly sliced fennel bulb (about 1 small bulb)
¼ cup dry sherry
2 tablespoons olive oil
1½ teaspoons salt
1 teaspoon dried thyme
7 shallots, peeled (about ½ pound)
4 red potatoes, cut into ½-inch-thick wedges (about 1 pound)
2 turnips, peeled, quartered, and thinly sliced (about 1 pound)
Cooking spray

1. Preheat oven to 425°.
2. Combine all ingredients except cooking spray in a large bowl; toss well to coat. Place vegetable mixture in a roasting pan coated with cooking spray. Bake at 425° for 1 hour and 15 minutes, turning vegetables occasionally. Yield: 8 servings (serving size: 1 cup).

CALORIES 139 (25% from fat); FAT 3.8g (sat 0.5g, mono 2.5g, poly 0.4g); PROTEIN 3g; CARB 24.8g; FIBER 3.6g; CHOL 0mg; IRON 2mg; SODIUM 491mg; CALC 62mg

PEPPER-SWIRLED CHICKPEA DIP

1 garlic clove, peeled
1 (19-ounce) can chickpeas (garbanzo beans), undrained
¼ cup plain fat-free yogurt
1 tablespoon fresh lemon juice
1 tablespoon olive oil
1 (7-ounce) bottle roasted red bell peppers, drained
1 tablespoon tomato paste
2 teaspoons red wine vinegar
¾ teaspoon paprika
½ teaspoon salt
5 (6-inch) pitas, cut into quarters

1. Place garlic in a food processor; pulse 2 or 3 times. Drain chickpeas in a colander over a bowl, reserving 1 tablespoon liquid. Add chickpeas, reserved liquid, yogurt, juice, and oil to garlic; process until smooth. Spoon mixture into a bowl. Rinse food processor.
2. Process peppers and next 4 ingredients until smooth. Swirl chickpea puree and bell pepper puree together using a knife (do not thoroughly combine). Serve with pita wedges. Yield: 20 servings (serving size: about 1½ tablespoons dip and 1 pita wedge).

CALORIES 80 (16% from fat); FAT 1.4g (sat 0.2g, mono 0.6g, poly 0.4g); PROTEIN 3.1g; CARB 14g; FIBER 1.1g; CHOL 0mg; IRON 1mg; SODIUM 228mg; CALC 29mg

TWO-POTATO PARTY LATKES

(pictured on page 319)

These latkes taste better when the potatoes and onion are shredded on a hand grater, rather than in the food processor.

5 cups shredded peeled sweet potato (about 1 pound)
2 cups shredded peeled baking potato (about ½ pound)
1 cup shredded fresh onion
¼ cup all-purpose flour
¾ teaspoon salt
¼ teaspoon black pepper
3 large egg whites, lightly beaten
4 teaspoons vegetable oil, divided

1. Combine first 6 ingredients in a large bowl. Stir in beaten egg whites. Heat 2 teaspoons oil in a large nonstick skillet over medium heat. Spoon 4 (½-cup) patties into skillet, and flatten slightly with a spatula; sauté 7 minutes. Carefully turn patties over; cook 7 minutes or until golden. Repeat procedure with 2 teaspoons oil and remaining potato mixture. Yield: 8 servings (serving size: 1 latke).

CALORIES 138 (16% from fat); FAT 2.5g (sat 0.5g, mono 0.7g, poly 1.2g); PROTEIN 3.5g; CARB 25.4g; FIBER 2.7g; CHOL 0mg; IRON 0.7mg; SODIUM 248mg; CALC 20mg

MEDITERRANEAN STUFFED BREAD

Olive pâté is sold in small jars next to olives in the supermarket. It's fairly high in sodium, but a little goes a long way.

1 (2-pound) package frozen white bread dough (2 [1-pound] portions)
¾ cup (6 ounces) ⅓-less-fat cream cheese, softened
1 tablespoon olive pâté (such as Alessi)
1 (12-ounce) bottle roasted red bell peppers, drained
1 (10-ounce) package frozen chopped spinach, thawed and drained
Cooking spray
1 large egg white, lightly beaten

1. Thaw dough in refrigerator 12 hours.
2. Combine cream cheese and pâté in a medium bowl, stirring until smooth. Set aside.
3. Working with 1 portion of dough at a time (cover remaining dough to keep from drying), roll each portion into a 12 x 5-inch rectangle on a floured surface. Spread half of cheese mixture over center of each rectangle, leaving ½-inch margins around edges. Arrange pepper pieces over cheese mixture; top with spinach. Roll up each rectangle tightly, starting with a long edge, pressing firmly to eliminate air pockets; pinch seams and ends to seal. Place loaves,

seam sides down, on a large baking sheet coated with cooking spray. Cover and let rise 1 hour or until doubled in size. (Press two fingers into dough. If indentation remains, dough has risen enough.) Brush loaves with egg white.

4. Preheat oven to 375°.

5. Bake at 375° for 35 minutes or until loaves are browned on bottom and sound hollow when tapped. Remove from pan; cool 5 minutes on a wire rack. Yield: 16 servings, 8 servings per loaf (serving size: 1 slice).

CALORIES 193 (25% from fat); FAT 5.3g (sat 2.2g, mono 2.1g, poly 0.6g); PROTEIN 7g; CARB 30g; FIBER 2g; CHOL 9mg; IRON 0.7mg; SODIUM 421mg; CALC 70mg

CHALLAH

1 package dry yeast (about 2¼ teaspoons)
½ teaspoon sugar
¼ cup warm water (100° to 110°)
½ cup water
¼ cup vegetable oil
1 large egg, lightly beaten
3⅓ cups all-purpose flour
1½ teaspoons salt
  Cooking spray
2 teaspoons water
1 large egg yolk, lightly beaten

1. Dissolve yeast and sugar in ¼ cup warm water in a bowl; let stand 10 minutes. Add ½ cup water, oil, and egg; stir with a whisk. Lightly spoon flour into dry measuring cups; level with a knife. Place flour and salt in a food processor; pulse 2 times or until blended. With processor on, slowly add yeast mixture through food chute; process 20 seconds or until dough forms a ball. Process 1 additional minute. Place dough in a large bowl lightly coated with cooking spray, turning to coat top. Cover and let rise in a warm place (85°), free from drafts, 1 hour or until doubled in size. (Press two fingers into dough. If indentation remains, dough has risen enough.)

2. Punch dough down, reshape into a ball, and return to bowl; cover and let rise 1 hour or until doubled in size.

3. Punch dough down; turn dough out onto a lightly floured surface. Let dough rest 15 minutes. Divide dough into 3 equal portions, shaping each portion into a 15-inch rope. Place ropes lengthwise on a baking sheet coated with cooking spray (do not stretch); pinch ends together at one end to seal. Braid ropes; pinch loose ends to seal. Cover and let rise 1 hour until doubled in size.

4. Preheat oven to 375°.

5. Combine 2 teaspoons water and egg yolk. Uncover dough; gently brush loaf with egg yolk mixture. Bake at 375° for 35 minutes or until loaf sounds hollow when tapped. Remove from pan; cool on a wire rack. Yield: 1 loaf, about 16 servings (serving size: 1 [1½-ounce] slice).

CALORIES 128 (30% from fat); FAT 4.3g (sat 0.9g, mono 1.3g, poly 1.8g); PROTEIN 3.2g; CARB 18.6g; FIBER 0.8g; CHOL 27mg; IRON 1.3mg; SODIUM 225mg; CALC 7mg

AT MY HOUSE

Blessed are the Pandemonious

... for they shall survive an Irish holiday feast by ordering Chinese.

One Christmas, my wife, Diana, and self invited some family and friends to the festive table. Instead of turkey, we opted for goose with stuffing.

Dinner was delayed when I forgot to light the oven, wherein reposed the goose. When the blasted goose decided it was cooked, we all trooped to the table to carve the goose. Imagine my astonishment when the knife struck bone on the third slice of the goose. Panic and frantic eye signals to Diana to join me in the kitchen. Be the excuses as they may, we hadn't enough to serve everyone.

When the guests left, Diana, children, and myself went out and had the jolliest Chinese meal in history. Our history, of course.

—Malachy McCourt

SAUCY BEEF LO MEIN

Steak:

1 (1½-pound) flank steak
1 tablespoon sugar
2 tablespoons low-sodium soy sauce
1½ tablespoons rice vinegar
4 garlic cloves, minced

Sauce:

½ cup low-sodium soy sauce
¼ cup water
2½ tablespoons cornstarch
3 tablespoons rice vinegar
1½ teaspoons sugar
1 teaspoon dark sesame oil
¼ teaspoon freshly ground black pepper
1 (16-ounce) can fat-free, less-sodium chicken broth

Remaining ingredients:

1 tablespoon vegetable oil, divided
2 cups (1-inch) sliced green onions
3 tablespoons minced peeled fresh ginger
2 garlic cloves, minced
3 cups fresh bean sprouts, rinsed and drained
6 cups hot cooked wide lo mein noodles or fettuccine (about 12 ounces uncooked)

1. To prepare steak, trim fat. Cut steak diagonally across grain into thin slices. Combine 1 tablespoon sugar, 2 tablespoons soy sauce, 1½ tablespoons vinegar, and 4 garlic cloves in a large zip-top plastic bag. Add steak; seal bag, and marinate in refrigerator 1 hour, turning occasionally. Remove steak from bag; discard marinade.

2. To prepare sauce, combine ½ cup soy sauce and next 7 ingredients; stir with a whisk. Set aside.

3. Heat 1½ teaspoons oil in a large nonstick skillet over medium-high

Continued

heat. Add steak; cook 7 minutes or until steak loses its pink color. Remove steak with a slotted spoon; set aside. Wipe pan clean with a paper towel. Heat 1½ teaspoons oil in pan. Add green onions, ginger, and 2 garlic cloves; stir-fry 1 minute. Stir in sauce and bean sprouts; bring to a boil. Cook 1 minute. Stir in steak and noodles; toss well. Yield: 8 servings (serving size: 1 cup).

CALORIES 375 (27% from fat); FAT 11.1g (sat 4g, mono 4g, poly 1.7g); PROTEIN 25.7g; CARB 42.2g; FIBER 2.1g; CHOL 43mg; IRON 4.5mg; SODIUM 737mg; CALC 41mg

VEGETABLE STIR-FRY OVER CRISP NOODLES

Crisp noodles:

1 (12-ounce) package fine egg noodles
1½ teaspoons dark sesame oil
1 teaspoon vegetable oil

Sauce:

1½ cups fat-free, less-sodium chicken broth
6 tablespoons oyster sauce
¼ cup sake (rice wine)
1½ tablespoons cornstarch
1 teaspoon dark sesame oil
1 teaspoon low-sodium soy sauce

Vegetables:

2 teaspoons vegetable oil
1½ tablespoons minced peeled fresh ginger
4 large garlic cloves, minced
4 cups julienne-cut leek (about 4 small)
3 cups shredded carrot (about 6 small)
2 cups sliced shiitake mushroom caps (about 3 ounces)
4 cups fresh bean sprouts

1. Preheat broiler.
2. To prepare noodles, cook according to package directions, omitting salt and fat. Rinse with cold water; drain well. Combine noodles, 1½ teaspoons sesame oil and 1 teaspoon vegetable oil in a large bowl; toss well to coat. Divide noodle mixture evenly into 6 (1-inch-thick) nests on 2 baking sheets. Place 1 baking sheet on oven rack 3 inches from heat; broil 10 minutes. Carefully turn nests over, and broil 6 minutes or until golden brown. Set aside. Repeat procedure with remaining nests.
3. To prepare sauce, combine broth and next 5 ingredients; stir well with a whisk. Set aside.
4. To prepare vegetables, heat 2 teaspoons vegetable oil in a large nonstick skillet over medium-high heat. Add ginger and garlic; stir-fry 10 seconds. Add leek, carrot, and mushrooms; stir-fry 2 minutes. Add sauce; bring to a boil, and cook 2 minutes or until thick. Stir in sprouts; cook until thoroughly heated. Spoon vegetables over nests. Yield: 6 servings (serving size: 1⅓ cups vegetables and 1 nest).

CALORIES 368 (17% from fat); FAT 7.1g (sat 1.3g, mono 2.2g, poly 2.8g); PROTEIN 13.1g; CARB 65.2g; FIBER 5.2g; CHOL 54mg; IRON 5.2mg; SODIUM 586mg; CALC 92mg

SHRIMP FRIED RICE

Perfect fried rice relies on chilled cooked rice.

3 tablespoons low-sodium soy sauce
2 tablespoons water
2 tablespoons rice vinegar
1 teaspoon sesame oil
¼ teaspoon salt
¼ teaspoon crushed red pepper
3 tablespoons vegetable oil, divided
1½ pounds medium shrimp, peeled and deveined
3 large eggs, lightly beaten
2 cups finely chopped green onions
1 tablespoon minced peeled fresh ginger
4 cups cooked long-grain rice, chilled
1½ cups frozen green peas, thawed

1. Combine first 6 ingredients in a small bowl; set aside.
2. Heat 1 tablespoon vegetable oil in a large nonstick skillet over medium-high heat. Add shrimp; cook 4 minutes or until done. Remove shrimp from pan; keep warm. Heat 2 tablespoons vegetable oil in pan. Add eggs; stir-fry 30 seconds or until soft-scrambled. Stir in green onions and ginger; stir-fry 1 minute. Stir in soy sauce mixture, shrimp, rice, and peas; cook 3 minutes or until thoroughly heated. Yield: 6 servings (serving size: 1⅓ cups).

CALORIES 388 (28% from fat); FAT 12g (sat 2.5g, mono 3.5g, poly 4.6g); PROTEIN 26.1g; CARB 42.3g; FIBER 3.1g; CHOL 240mg; IRON 4.8mg; SODIUM 544mg; CALC 104mg

FRESH VEGETABLE ROLLS

(pictured on page 317)

A food processor does a great job of shredding the vegetables.

Rolls:

5 black dried mushrooms
2 teaspoons vegetable oil
1 tablespoon minced peeled fresh ginger
4 garlic cloves, minced
2 cups shredded bok choy
1 cup shredded carrot
¾ cup fresh bean sprouts, rinsed and drained
½ cup chopped green onions
2 tablespoons sesame seeds
12 (8-inch) round sheets rice paper

Sauce:

½ cup hoisin sauce
3 tablespoons water
3 tablespoons low-sodium soy sauce
1 tablespoon rice vinegar
1½ teaspoons dark sesame oil
⅛ teaspoon crushed red pepper

1. To prepare rolls, combine mushrooms and boiling water to cover in a bowl; cover and let stand 10 minutes. Drain and cut mushrooms into thin slices. Heat vegetable oil in a nonstick

skillet over medium-high heat. Add mushrooms, ginger, and garlic; stir-fry 2 minutes. Remove from heat.

2. Combine mushroom mixture, bok choy, carrot, bean sprouts, onions, and sesame seeds in a large bowl; set aside.

3. Add cold water to a large, shallow dish to a depth of 1 inch. Place 1 rice paper sheet in dish of water. Let stand 2 minutes or until soft. Place rice paper sheet on a flat surface. Spoon about ⅓ cup vegetable mixture in center of sheet. Fold sides of sheet over filling, and roll up jelly-roll fashion. Gently press seam to seal; place, seam side down, on a serving platter (cover to keep from drying). Repeat procedure with remaining rice paper and vegetable mixture. Cut each roll in half crosswise.

4. To prepare sauce, combine hoisin sauce and remaining 5 ingredients in a small bowl. Serve with rolls. Yield: 1 dozen (serving size: 1 vegetable roll and about 1 tablespoon sauce).

CALORIES 90 (26% from fat); FAT 2.6g (sat 0.4g, mono 0.8g, poly 1.1g); PROTEIN 2.3g; CARB 11.1g; FIBER 1.2g; CHOL 0mg; IRON 0.8mg; SODIUM 308mg; CALC 45mg

SEARED ORANGE DUCK BREAST

Like Malachy, we found that goose didn't quite work for our holiday meal, but everyone from Dublin to Beijing can enjoy a tasty Christmas duck.

   3 (12-ounce) frozen duck breasts, thawed
1½ tablespoons grated orange rind
   1 teaspoon salt
  ¼ teaspoon black pepper
   4 garlic cloves, crushed
  ½ cup fresh orange juice (about 2 oranges)
  ¼ cup sake (rice wine)
1½ tablespoons low-sodium soy sauce
   1 tablespoon honey
   1 tablespoon vegetable oil

1. Trim skin and fat from duck; cut each breast in half. Combine duck,

rind, salt, pepper, and garlic in a bowl. Cover and refrigerate 30 minutes.

2. Preheat oven to 400°.

3. Combine juice, sake, soy sauce, and honey in a small saucepan; bring to a boil. Reduce heat to medium-low and simmer until reduced to ⅔ cup (about 10 minutes).

4. Heat oil in a large nonstick skillet over medium-high heat. Add duck; sauté 5 minutes. Turn duck over; drizzle with 3 tablespoons juice mixture. Wrap handle of skillet with foil; bake at 400° for 10 minutes. Remove duck from pan; cut duck into ¼-inch-thick slices. Serve with orange-juice sauce. Yield: 6 servings (serving size: 3 ounces duck and about 2 tablespoons sauce).

Note: Find duck breasts in the frozen poultry section. Try pairing this recipe with Saintsbury Pinot Noir 1998 (Carneros, $22). It's an earthy wine with hints of mandarin orange.

CALORIES 166 (24% from fat); FAT 4.5g (sat 1.3g, mono 1.5g, poly 1.5g); PROTEIN 24.5g; CARB 6.7g; FIBER 0.1g; CHOL 123mg; IRON 4.5mg; SODIUM 562mg; CALC 13mg

GLAZED GREEN BEANS

   1 tablespoon vegetable oil
2½ cups vertically sliced red onion
   2 pounds green beans, trimmed
  ½ cup water
  ¼ cup low-sodium soy sauce
1½ tablespoons sugar
   3 tablespoons sake (rice wine) or rice vinegar

1. Heat oil in a large nonstick skillet over medium heat. Add onion; stir-fry 1 minute. Increase heat to medium-high. Add beans, and stir-fry 1 minute. Stir in water and remaining ingredients; bring to a boil. Cover, reduce heat, and simmer 12 minutes or until beans are tender. Uncover and bring to a boil; cook 10 minutes or until liquid almost evaporates. Toss gently to combine. Yield: 10 servings (serving size: ½ cup).

CALORIES 62 (22% from fat); FAT 1.5g (sat 0.3g, mono 0.4g, poly 0.7g); PROTEIN 2.3g; CARB 11.4g; FIBER 2.4g; CHOL 0mg; IRON 1.1mg; SODIUM 200mg; CALC 41mg

Christmas Stockings

Snowbound on the ranch wasn't so bad, thanks to a well-stocked larder, a positive spirit, and memories of "Jilted Eggs."

The snow began a week before Christmas and didn't stop. The art of living well on a ranch is the art of making do. The electricity went out Christmas morning. I cooked "Jilted Eggs" on a woodstove. It was a recipe given to me by a woman who stole my boyfriend, then felt so badly, she sent care packages of her favorite recipes. That was a good breakfast and a happy Christmas.

—Gretel Ehrlich

JILTED EGGS

   6 large eggs
      Cooking spray
1½ cups diced tomato
   1 tablespoon chopped fresh basil
  ¾ cup 2% reduced-fat milk
  ¾ teaspoon salt
  ¼ teaspoon black pepper
   6 tablespoons (1½ ounces) shredded reduced-fat sharp Cheddar cheese
   3 English muffins, split and toasted

1. Preheat oven to 350°.

2. Break eggs, 1 at a time, into a shallow casserole dish coated with cooking spray. Combine tomato and basil. Top each egg with ¼ cup tomato mixture. Combine milk, salt, and pepper; spoon 2 tablespoons milk mixture over tomato mixture on each egg. Sprinkle each serving with 1 tablespoon cheese. Bake at 350° for 20 minutes or until eggs are set. Serve with English muffins. Yield: 6 servings (serving size: 1 egg with toppings and 1 muffin half).

Note: Eggs can also be baked individually. Break 1 egg into each of 6 (6-ounce) custard cups coated with

Continued

cooking spray. Top as directed in recipe. Place cups on a baking sheet, and bake as directed.

CALORIES 209 (34% from fat); FAT 7.9g (sat 2.7g, mono 2.5g, poly 0.8g); PROTEIN 12.4g; CARB 21.8g; FIBER 0.5g; CHOL 220mg; IRON 2mg; SODIUM 594mg; CALC 181mg

VENISON TENDERLOIN WITH WILD-MUSHROOM SAUCE

  2 pounds venison tenderloin
Cooking spray
  ¾ teaspoon salt, divided
  ¼ teaspoon black pepper, divided
  2 (3½-ounce) packages fresh shiitake mushrooms
  ¼ cup minced shallots
  ¾ cup port or other sweet red wine
  1 cup beef broth
  2¼ teaspoons cornstarch

1. Preheat oven to 425°.
2. Trim fat from venison; place on a rack coated with cooking spray. Sprinkle with ½ teaspoon salt and ⅛ teaspoon pepper; insert a meat thermometer into thickest part of venison. Bake at 425° for 30 minutes or until thermometer registers 145° (medium-rare) to 160° (medium). Cover loosely with foil; let stand 10 minutes.
3. Remove stems from mushrooms and discard; cut caps into thin slices. Place a large nonstick skillet coated with cooking spray over medium-high heat until hot. Add mushrooms and shallots; sauté 4 minutes or until tender. Add ¼ teaspoon salt, ⅛ teaspoon pepper, and port; cook 2 minutes. Combine broth and cornstarch in a small bowl. Add to skillet; bring to a boil, and cook 1 minute or until thick, stirring constantly. Serve with venison. Yield: 8 servings (serving size: 3 ounces venison and 3 tablespoons sauce).
Note: You can substitute beef tenderloin for venison.

CALORIES 156 (17% from fat); FAT 2.9g (sat 1.1g, mono 0.8g, poly 0.6g); PROTEIN 27.7g; CARB 3.3g; FIBER 0.3g; CHOL 95mg; IRON 4.4mg; SODIUM 429mg; CALC 13mg

RUSTIC POTATO CHOWDER

Parsley butter:

  1 cup fresh parsley leaves (about 1 bunch)
  1 tablespoon butter or stick margarine

Soup:

  6 cups water
  3½ cups fresh parsley sprigs (about 1½ bunches)
  4½ cups cubed peeled Yukon gold or red potato (about 2 pounds)
  ¾ cup cubed carrot
  1 teaspoon salt

1. To prepare parsley butter, process parsley leaves and butter in a food processor until well-blended.
2. To prepare soup, combine water and parsley sprigs in a large saucepan; bring to a boil. Reduce heat; simmer 15 minutes. Strain mixture through a sieve over a large bowl, reserving broth; discard solids. Return broth to pan; add potato, carrot, and salt. Bring to a boil. Reduce heat; simmer 15 minutes or until vegetables are tender. Remove 1½ cups vegetables from soup with a slotted spoon. Place remaining soup and vegetables in a food processor; process until smooth, and pour into pan. Return 1½ cups vegetables to soup. Bring to a boil; stir in parsley butter. Yield: 6 servings (serving size: 1 cup).

CALORIES 115 (16% from fat); FAT 2.1g (sat 1.2g, mono 0.6g, poly 0.1g); PROTEIN 2.7g; CARB 22.2g; FIBER 2.7g; CHOL 5mg; IRON 1.5mg; SODIUM 427mg; CALC 26mg

SWEET POTATO BISCUITS

  2 cups all-purpose flour
  ⅓ cup yellow cornmeal
  2½ teaspoons baking powder
  ½ teaspoon salt
  ⅓ cup chilled butter or stick margarine, cut into small pieces
  1 cup mashed cooked sweet potato
  ½ cup fat-free milk
  2 tablespoons honey

1. Preheat oven to 400°.
2. Lightly spoon flour into dry measuring cups; level with a knife. Combine flour, cornmeal, baking powder, and salt in a bowl; cut in butter with a pastry blender or 2 knives until mixture resembles coarse meal. Add sweet potato, milk, and honey; stir just until moist.
3. Turn dough out onto a heavily floured surface; knead lightly 5 times. Pat dough into a 9-inch square; cut into 16 squares. Place biscuits on a baking sheet. Bake at 400° for 20 minutes or until golden. Yield: 16 biscuits (serving size: 1 biscuit).

CALORIES 134 (28% from fat); FAT 4.1g (sat 2.4g, mono 1.1g, poly 0.3g); PROTEIN 2.5g; CARB 21.9g; FIBER 1.2g; CHOL 11mg; IRON 1.1mg; SODIUM 196mg; CALC 60mg

BRAISED RED CABBAGE AND PEARS

  1 teaspoon olive oil
  1½ cups thinly sliced onion, separated into rings
  6 cups sliced red cabbage
  ⅓ cup red wine vinegar
  2 tablespoons sugar
  2 bay leaves
  1 (3-inch) cinnamon stick
  1½ cups thinly sliced peeled Anjou pear (about 2 pears)
  ½ teaspoon salt
  ¼ teaspoon black pepper

1. Heat oil in a Dutch oven over medium-high heat. Add onion; sauté 5 minutes. Stir in cabbage, vinegar, sugar, bay leaves, and cinnamon stick; cover, reduce heat, and simmer 15 minutes or until cabbage is tender. Stir in pear, salt, and pepper; cover and cook 5 minutes. Discard bay leaves and cinnamon stick. Yield: 8 servings (serving size: ¾ cup).

CALORIES 59 (13% from fat); FAT 0.9g (sat 0.1g, mono 0.5g, poly 0.2g); PROTEIN 1.1g; CARB 13.2g; FIBER 2.2g; CHOL 0mg; IRON 0.4mg; SODIUM 153mg; CALC 35mg

Teacher's Pet

It wasn't her grades—it was her mom's special Christmas treats that had teachers scrambling to get a young Southern farm girl into their classes.

In south Alabama, like most farm wives, my mother was a superb cook. I assumed it was because I was such a good student that my grammar-school teachers wanted me in their rooms. I found out that it actually was my mother's Christmas candy boxes.

—Sandra Conroy

MENU

CRANBERRY-GLAZED HAM

WHITE CHEDDAR-POTATO GRATIN

HOLIDAY GREEN BEANS

WINTER SALAD

BUTTERMILK-CHIVE BISCUITS

OLD-FASHIONED CARAMEL LAYER CAKE

about 876 calories per menu serving

CRANBERRY-GLAZED HAM

(pictured on page 318)

1 (7-pound) 33%-less-sodium smoked, fully cooked ham half
½ cup whole-berry cranberry sauce
3 tablespoons brown sugar
1 tablespoon spicy brown mustard

1. Preheat oven to 325°.
2. Place ham on a broiler pan lined with foil. Insert meat thermometer into thickest portion of pork. Bake at 325° for 1 hour. Score outside of ham in a diamond pattern. Combine cranberry sauce, sugar, and mustard; brush over ham. Bake an additional 35 minutes or until thermometer registers 140°. Transfer ham to a platter; let stand 10 minutes before slicing. Yield: 25 servings (serving size: 3 ounces).

CALORIES 173 (57% from fat); FAT 11g (sat 4g, mono 5.2g, poly 1.7g); PROTEIN 13g; CARB 5.2g; FIBER 0g; CHOL 46mg; IRON 0.8mg; SODIUM 96mg; CALC 2mg

WHITE CHEDDAR-POTATO GRATIN

(pictured on page 318)

2 pounds baking potatoes, peeled and cut into ¼-inch-thick slices (about 5 cups)
1 garlic clove, minced
1 (1-ounce) slice rye bread
1 tablespoon butter or stick margarine, melted
¼ cup all-purpose flour
2 cups 1% low-fat milk
1 cup (4 ounces) shredded white Cheddar cheese
¾ teaspoon salt
⅛ teaspoon ground red pepper
Cooking spray

1. Place potato and garlic in a saucepan, and cover with water. Bring to a boil, and cook 8 minutes or just until tender. Drain.
2. Place bread in food processor; pulse 10 times or until coarse crumbs form to measure ½ cup. Combine breadcrumbs and butter; set aside.
3. Preheat oven to 350°.
4. Lightly spoon flour into a dry measuring cup; level with a knife. Place flour in a medium, heavy saucepan; gradually add milk, stirring well with a whisk. Place over medium heat; cook until thick (about 8 minutes), stirring constantly. Remove from heat; add cheese, salt, and pepper, stirring until cheese melts. Arrange potato mixture in an 11 x 7-inch baking dish coated with cooking spray. Pour cheese sauce over potato. Sprinkle with breadcrumb mixture. Bake at 350° for 35 minutes or until bubbly. Let stand 10 minutes. Yield: 10 servings (serving size: ½ cup).

CALORIES 173 (30% from fat); FAT 5.7g (sat 3.5g, mono 1.6g, poly 0.2g); PROTEIN 6.6g; CARB 23.6g; FIBER 1.5g; CHOL 17mg; IRON 0.6mg; SODIUM 307mg; CALC 150mg

HOLIDAY GREEN BEANS

(pictured on page 318)

2½ tablespoons Dijon mustard
¼ teaspoon salt
¼ teaspoon freshly ground black pepper
¼ teaspoon dried tarragon
1½ pounds green beans, trimmed
2 teaspoons butter or stick margarine
¾ cup thinly sliced shallots
2 tablespoons low-fat sour cream

1. Combine first 4 ingredients; set aside.
2. Steam green beans, covered, 5 minutes or until tender. Keep warm. Melt butter in a Dutch oven over medium heat. Add shallots; sauté 3 minutes. Stir in mustard mixture and green beans; toss well. Cook 2 minutes or until thoroughly heated. Stir in sour cream; remove from heat. Serve immediately. Yield: 10 servings (serving size: ½ cup).

CALORIES 45 (29% from fat); FAT 1.5g (sat 0.8g, mono 0.5g, poly 0.1g); PROTEIN 1.6g; CARB 7.3g; FIBER 1.5g; CHOL 3mg; IRON 0.9mg; SODIUM 185mg; CALC 33mg

WINTER SALAD

2 tablespoons raspberry vinegar
1 tablespoon fresh orange juice
1 tablespoon balsamic vinegar
2 teaspoons extra-virgin olive oil
½ teaspoon sugar
¼ teaspoon black pepper
½ teaspoon low-sodium soy sauce
¼ teaspoon Dijon mustard
⅛ teaspoon salt
8 cups mixed salad greens
1 cup grapefruit sections
1 cup thinly sliced red onion
¼ cup coarsely chopped walnuts

1. Combine first 9 ingredients. Combine salad greens, grapefruit, onion, and walnuts in a large bowl. Drizzle with vinegar mixture; toss. Yield: 6 servings (serving size: 1½ cups).

CALORIES 80 (53% from fat); FAT 4.7g (sat 0.4g, mono 1.8g, poly 2.2g); PROTEIN 3g; CARB 8.1g; FIBER 2.4g; CHOL 0mg; IRON 1.1mg; SODIUM 75mg; CALC 39mg

BUTTERMILK-CHIVE BISCUITS

3 cups all-purpose flour
½ cup chopped fresh chives
4 teaspoons baking powder
2 teaspoons sugar
1 teaspoon baking soda
¾ teaspoon salt
⅓ cup chilled butter or stick margarine, cut into small pieces
1½ cups low-fat buttermilk
Cooking spray

1. Preheat oven to 425°.
2. Lightly spoon flour into dry measuring cups; level with a knife. Combine flour and next 5 ingredients in a bowl; cut in butter with a pastry blender or 2 knives until mixture resembles coarse meal. Add buttermilk; stir just until moist.
3. Turn dough out onto a lightly floured surface; knead lightly 4 times. Roll dough to a ¾-inch thickness; cut with a 2½-inch biscuit cutter. Place on a baking sheet. Lightly coat tops with cooking spray. Bake at 425° for 13 minutes or until golden. Yield: 1 dozen (serving size: 1 biscuit).

CALORIES 178 (29% from fat); FAT 5.9g (sat 3.2g, mono 1.5g, poly 0.3g); PROTEIN 4.5g; CARB 26.6g; FIBER 0.9g; CHOL 14mg; IRON 1.7mg; SODIUM 482mg; CALC 136mg

OLD-FASHIONED CARAMEL LAYER CAKE

(pictured on page 319)

Cake:

Cooking spray
1 tablespoon all-purpose flour
1½ cups granulated sugar
½ cup butter or stick margarine, softened
2 large eggs
1 large egg white
2¼ cups all-purpose flour
2½ teaspoons baking powder
½ teaspoon salt
1¼ cups fat-free milk
2 teaspoons vanilla extract

Frosting:

1 cup packed dark brown sugar
½ cup evaporated fat-free milk
2½ tablespoons butter or stick margarine
2 teaspoons light-colored corn syrup
Dash of salt
2 cups powdered sugar
2½ teaspoons vanilla extract

1. Preheat oven to 350°.
2. To prepare cake, coat 2 (9-inch) round cake pans with cooking spray; line bottoms with wax paper. Coat wax paper with cooking spray; dust with 1 tablespoon flour.
3. Beat granulated sugar and ½ cup butter at medium speed of a mixer until well-blended (about 5 minutes). Add eggs and egg white, 1 at a time, beating well after each addition. Lightly spoon 2¼ cups flour into dry measuring cups; level with a knife. Combine 2¼ cups flour, baking powder, and salt; stir well with a whisk. Add flour mixture to sugar mixture alternately with 1¼ cups milk, beginning and ending with flour mixture. Stir in 2 teaspoons vanilla.
4. Pour batter into pans; tap pans once on counter to remove air bubbles. Bake at 350° for 30 minutes or until a wooden pick inserted in center comes out clean. Cool in pans 10 minutes on a wire rack; remove from pans. Peel off wax paper; cool completely on wire rack.
5. To prepare frosting, combine brown sugar and next 4 ingredients in saucepan. Bring to a boil over medium-high heat; stir constantly. Reduce heat; simmer until thick (about 5 minutes), stirring occasionally. Remove from heat. Add powdered sugar and 2½ teaspoons vanilla; beat at medium speed until smooth and slightly warm. Cool 2 to 3 minutes (frosting will be thin but thickens as it cools).
6. Place 1 cake layer on a plate; spread with ½ cup frosting. Top with remaining cake layer. Frost top and sides of cake. Store loosely covered in refrigerator. Yield: 18 servings (serving size: 1 slice).

CALORIES 307 (22% from fat); FAT 7.5g (sat 4.4g, mono 2.2g, poly 0.4g); PROTEIN 3.8g; CARB 56.7g; FIBER 0.4g; CHOL 43mg; IRON 1.2mg; SODIUM 251mg; CALC 97mg

A Good Day for Soup

Nothing melts winter and warms the soul better than a steaming bowl of soup.

Soup is one of the perfect foods—particularly for dinner and especially in winter. It's economical, easy to make, usually gets better with time, and tends to be naturally low in fat.

VEGETABLE STOCK

While making homemade stock does add an extra step, the big flavor it produces is well worth it. You can make the stock in advance and freeze until ready to use, if desired.

1 teaspoon olive oil
3 cups coarsely chopped onion
1 cup chopped carrot
3 large leeks (about 2 pounds)
1 cup sliced mushrooms
1 cup (2-inch) parsley stems
½ teaspoon salt
5 thyme sprigs
2 bay leaves
8 cups water

1. Heat oil in a large Dutch oven over medium-high heat. Add onion and carrot; sauté 8 minutes or until onion begins to brown.
2. Remove roots, outer leaves, and top 6 inches from leeks. Rinse well, and drain. Reserve remaining portion for another use. Chop leek outer leaves and tops. Add roots, chopped leek, mushrooms, and remaining 5 ingredients to onion mixture; bring to a boil. Reduce heat, and simmer until reduced to 6 cups (about 30 minutes). Strain stock through a sieve over a bowl; discard solids. Yield: 6 cups (serving size: 1 cup).

CALORIES 5 (0% from fat); FAT 0g; PROTEIN 0g; CARB 2g; FIBER 0g; CHOL 0mg; IRON 0mg; SODIUM 195mg; CALC 0mg

MIXED-BEAN CHILI WITH TOFU

This recipe makes use of canned beans for a quicker meal. Use pure ground chiles instead of chili powder, which is laced with garlic.

  7 ounces firm tofu, drained and crumbled (about 1 cup)
1½ teaspoons ground cumin, divided
1½ tablespoons low-sodium soy sauce
  2 teaspoons vegetable oil
1½ cups chopped onion
  ½ teaspoon ground coriander
  ½ teaspoon dried oregano
1½ tablespoons tomato paste
1½ tablespoons hot chili powder or regular chili powder
  1 teaspoon minced drained canned chipotle chile in adobo sauce
  ½ teaspoon black pepper
  ¼ teaspoon salt
  2 garlic cloves, minced
1½ cups water
  1 (15-ounce) can pinto beans
  1 (15-ounce) can red kidney beans
  1 (14.5-ounce) can no-salt-added diced tomatoes, undrained
  ½ teaspoon cider vinegar
  ¼ cup chopped fresh cilantro
  ¼ cup low-fat sour cream

1. Heat a large Dutch oven over medium-high heat. Add tofu and ¾ teaspoon cumin; sauté 3 minutes. Stir in soy sauce; cook 1 minute or until liquid evaporates. Remove tofu mixture from pan.
2. Heat oil in pan; add ¾ teaspoon cumin, onion, coriander, and oregano; sauté 4 minutes. Stir in tofu mixture, tomato paste, and next 5 ingredients. Add water, beans, and tomatoes; bring to a boil. Cover, reduce heat, and simmer 30 minutes. Stir in vinegar. Spoon chili into bowls; top each serving with cilantro and sour cream. Yield: 4 servings (serving size: 2 cups chili, 1 tablespoon cilantro, and 1 tablespoon sour cream).

CALORIES 256 (19% from fat); FAT 5.4g (sat 1.7g, mono 1.5g, poly 1.7g); PROTEIN 12.2g; CARB 42.8g; FIBER 9.6g; CHOL 6mg; IRON 4.7mg; SODIUM 807mg; CALC 145mg

WINTER SQUASH-AND-WHITE BEAN SOUP

You might think of this soup as a winter squash minestrone. We've called for canned beans to make it more doable for busy people, but the soup will be better if you cook your own beans.

  1 tablespoon olive oil
  4 cups (½-inch) cubed peeled butternut squash
  2 cups chopped leek (about 3 leeks)
  ¾ cup diced carrot
  ½ cup diced celery
  2 teaspoons chopped fresh or ½ teaspoon dried rubbed sage
  ¼ teaspoon salt
  1 garlic clove, minced
1¾ cups Vegetable Stock (see recipe on previous page) or 1 (14½-ounce) can vegetable broth, divided
  5 cups water
  2 cups chopped green cabbage
  ¼ teaspoon black pepper
  2 (15½-ounce) cans cannellini beans or other white beans, drained
  ½ cup chopped fresh parsley
  3 garlic cloves, minced

1. Heat oil in a Dutch oven over medium heat until hot. Add squash and next 6 ingredients; sauté 10 minutes. Stir in 1 cup Vegetable Stock, scraping pan to loosen browned bits. Add ¾ cup stock and water; bring to a boil. Partially cover, reduce heat, and simmer 30 minutes or until vegetables are tender. Stir in cabbage; simmer, partially covered, 12 minutes. Stir in pepper and beans; cook 1 minute or until thoroughly heated. Spoon soup into bowls. Combine parsley and 3 garlic cloves; sprinkle over each serving. Yield: 7 servings (serving size: 1½ cups soup and 1 tablespoon topping).
Note: If you decide to use canned vegetable broth instead of Vegetable Stock, omit added salt.

CALORIES 231 (17% from fat); FAT 4.4g (sat 0.6g, mono 2g, poly 1.3g); PROTEIN 9.8g; CARB 41.6g; FIBER 5.8g; CHOL 0mg; IRON 4.1mg; SODIUM 339mg; CALC 126mg

QUINOA CHOWDER WITH SPINACH, FETA CHEESE, AND GREEN ONIONS

The inspiration for this recipe comes from a soup in Felipe Rojas-Lombardi's book, The Art of South American Cooking *(Harpercollins, 1991).*

  8 cups water
  ¾ cup uncooked quinoa
  2 teaspoons olive oil
  2 tablespoons finely chopped seeded jalapeño pepper
  1 garlic clove, minced
2½ cups diced peeled baking potato (about 1 pound)
  1 teaspoon salt
  1 teaspoon ground cumin
  ¼ teaspoon freshly ground black pepper
  ⅔ cup thinly sliced green onions, divided
  3 cups thinly sliced spinach
  1 cup (4 ounces) crumbled feta cheese
  ⅓ cup chopped fresh cilantro

1. Combine water and quinoa in a Dutch oven; bring to a boil. Cover, reduce heat, and simmer 20 minutes. Remove from heat. Drain in a sieve over a bowl, reserving cooking liquid; add enough water to cooking liquid to measure 6 cups. Set quinoa aside.
2. Heat oil in pan over medium heat. Add jalapeño and garlic; cook 30 seconds. Stir in potato, salt, cumin, and black pepper; cook 5 minutes, stirring frequently. Stir in 6 cups cooking liquid, quinoa, and ⅓ cup green onions; bring to a boil. Reduce heat, and simmer 10 minutes or until potato is tender. Stir in ⅓ cup green onions and spinach; cook 3 minutes. Remove from heat. Stir in cheese and cilantro. Yield: 8 servings (serving size: 1¼ cups).

CALORIES 165 (29% from fat); FAT 5.3g (sat 2.4g, mono 1.8g, poly 0.7g); PROTEIN 6g; CARB 24.2g; FIBER 4.1g; CHOL 13mg; IRON 2.8mg; SODIUM 484mg; CALC 116mg

Spelt-and-Wild Mushroom Soup with Pasta

Find spelt, *an ancient whole grain slightly higher in protein than wheat, in health food stores.*

- 1 cup uncooked spelt or wheatberries
- 2 cups boiling water
- ½ cup dried porcini or shiitake mushrooms (about ¾ ounce)
- ½ cup finely chopped fresh parsley
- 3 garlic cloves, minced
- 1 tablespoon olive oil, divided
- 3 cups thinly sliced leek (about 3 large)
- 6 cups Vegetable Stock (page 332) or canned vegetable broth
- ½ cup dry white wine
- 1 tablespoon tomato paste
- 1½ cups hot cooked farfalle (about 1 cup uncooked bow tie pasta)
- ½ teaspoon salt
- ¼ teaspoon black pepper
- 6 tablespoons (1½ ounces) grated fresh Parmesan cheese

1. Place spelt in a medium saucepan; cover with water to 2 inches above spelt. Bring to a boil; reduce heat, and cook, uncovered, 1 hour or until tender. Drain.
2. Combine 2 cups boiling water and mushrooms in a bowl; cover and let stand 30 minutes. Drain mushrooms through a colander, reserving soaking liquid. Discard mushroom stems; cut mushroom caps into thin slices.
3. Combine parsley and garlic; divide into 2 (¼-cup) portions.
4. Heat 1½ teaspoons oil in a large Dutch oven over medium-high heat. Add spelt, mushrooms, ¼ cup parsley mixture, and leek; sauté 5 minutes. Stir in reserved mushroom liquid, Vegetable Stock, wine, and tomato paste; bring to a boil. Cover, reduce heat, and simmer 30 minutes. Add pasta; sprinkle with salt and pepper. Cook 1 minute or until thoroughly heated. Stir in reserved ¼ cup parsley mixture. Spoon soup into bowls; sprinkle with cheese, and drizzle with 1½ teaspoons oil. Yield: 6 servings (serving size: 1⅓ cups soup, 1 tablespoon cheese, and ¼ teaspoon olive oil).
Note: If you decide to use canned vegetable broth instead of Vegetable Stock, omit added salt.

CALORIES 245 (18% from fat); FAT 4.9g (sat 1.6g, mono 2.3g, poly 0.5g); PROTEIN 9.7g; CARB 42.7g; FIBER 3.3g; CHOL 5mg; IRON 3.1mg; SODIUM 522mg; CALC 130mg

Split Pea Soup with Rosemary

- 1½ cups green split peas
- 2 teaspoons olive oil, divided
- 2 cups chopped onion
- 1 cup diced carrot
- 1 bay leaf
- 1 tablespoon minced garlic cloves (about 3 cloves), divided
- 1 tablespoon minced fresh rosemary, divided
- 1 teaspoon paprika
- ¼ teaspoon black pepper
- 1 tablespoon tomato paste
- 1 tablespoon low-sodium soy sauce
- 4 cups water
- 2 cups Vegetable Stock (page 332) or 1 (14½-ounce) can vegetable broth
- 1 teaspoon salt
- ¼ cup chopped fresh parsley
- ¼ cup low-fat sour cream

1. Sort and wash peas; cover with water to 2 inches above peas, and set aside. Heat 1 teaspoon oil in a Dutch oven over medium-high heat. Add onion, carrot, and bay leaf; sauté 5 minutes, stirring frequently. Add 2 teaspoons garlic, 1 teaspoon rosemary, paprika, and pepper; cook 3 minutes. Add tomato paste and soy sauce; cook until liquid evaporates, scraping pan to loosen browned bits.
2. Drain peas. Add peas, 4 cups water, Vegetable Stock, and salt to onion mixture; bring to a boil. Cover, reduce heat to medium-low, and simmer 1 hour, stirring often. Discard bay leaf. Place half of soup in a blender or food processor; process until smooth. Pour pureed soup into a large bowl. Repeat procedure with remaining soup.
3. Combine 1 teaspoon oil, 1 teaspoon garlic, 2 teaspoons rosemary, and parsley. Stir parsley mixture into soup. Spoon soup into bowls; top with sour cream. Yield: 6 servings (serving size: about 1 cup soup and 2 teaspoons sour cream).
Note: If you decide to use canned vegetable broth instead of Vegetable Stock, omit added salt.

CALORIES 233 (14% from fat); FAT 3.5g (sat 1.1g, mono 1.6g, poly 0.5g); PROTEIN 13.7g; CARB 38.7g; FIBER 4.8g; CHOL 4mg; IRON 2.9mg; SODIUM 559mg; CALC 65mg

AT LAST

Beyond the Brain

Orzo with Spinach and Feta

Popeye might have downed spinach to get big muscles, but the leafy green gets its real punch from antioxidants, which keep you thinking sharply.

- 5 cups water
- 2 cups uncooked orzo (rice-shaped pasta)
- 5 cups coarsely chopped spinach
- 1 cup (4 ounces) crumbled feta cheese
- 1 tablespoon extra-virgin olive oil
- 1 teaspoon grated lemon rind
- 1 tablespoon fresh lemon juice
- ½ teaspoon salt

1. Bring water to a boil in a medium saucepan. Add orzo. Cook 10 minutes; drain. Rinse with cold water; drain.
2. Combine pasta, spinach, and feta in a large bowl. Combine oil and remaining 3 ingredients in a small bowl. Drizzle lemon mixture over pasta mixture; toss well to coat. Yield: 8 servings (serving size: 1 cup).

CALORIES 244 (23% from fat); FAT 5.5g (sat 2.5g, mono 2g, poly 0.6g); PROTEIN 8.5g; CARB 33.8g; FIBER 2.4g; CHOL 13mg; IRON 2.7mg; SODIUM 335mg; CALC 113mg

It's Dough Easy

Take a shortcut to yummy yeast breads and rolls for the holidays with ready-to-use dough from your grocer's freezer case.

CITRUS-CREAM CHEESE PULL-APARTS

The cream cheese mixture sinks to the bottom of the rolls. Place a piece of foil under the pan in case the sugar mixture runs over.

1   (25-ounce) package frozen roll dough
Cooking spray
¼   cup butter or stick margarine, melted
½   cup sweetened dried cranberries (such as Craisins) or chopped dried apricots
1   cup granulated sugar, divided
⅔   cup (6 ounces) ⅓-less-fat cream cheese, softened
2   tablespoons fresh orange juice
1   large egg
1   tablespoon grated lemon rind
1   tablespoon grated orange rind
1   cup powdered sugar
5   teaspoons fresh lemon juice

1. Thaw roll dough at room temperature 30 minutes.
2. Cut rolls in half. Place 24 halves, cut sides down, in bottom of each of 2 (9-inch) round cake pans coated with cooking spray. Brush butter evenly over rolls. Cover and let rise in a warm place (85°), free from drafts, 30 minutes. Sprinkle with dried cranberries. Combine ¼ cup granulated sugar, cream cheese, orange juice, and egg in a bowl; beat at medium speed of a mixer until well-blended. Pour cream cheese mixture evenly over rolls. Combine ¾ cup granulated sugar and rinds. Sprinkle evenly over rolls. Cover and let rise 1 hour or until doubled in size.
3. Preheat oven to 350°.

4. Bake at 350° for 20 minutes. Cover with foil. Bake an additional 5 minutes or until rolls in center are done. Remove from oven; cool 15 minutes. Combine powdered sugar and lemon juice. Drizzle over rolls. Yield: 4 dozen (serving size: 2 rolls).
Overnight Variation: After pouring cream cheese mixture over rolls, cover with plastic wrap and refrigerate 12 hours. Gently remove plastic wrap from rolls; sprinkle with rind mixture. Let stand at room temperature 30 minutes or until dough has doubled in size. Proceed with recipe as directed.

CALORIES 174 (29% from fat); FAT 5.6g (sat 2.8g, mono 1.9g, poly 0.6g); PROTEIN 3.6g; CARB 27.7g; FIBER 0.6g; CHOL 20mg; IRON 0.3mg; SODIUM 203mg; CALC 10mg

APPLE-BRIE BRAID WITH ALMONDS

If Brie isn't the cheese for you, substitute your favorite kind. Cheddar, smoked gouda, or Swiss also would be nice.

1   (1-pound) loaf frozen white bread dough
2   tablespoons butter or stick margarine, divided
4   cups finely chopped peeled Granny Smith apple (about 1¼ pounds)
½   cup packed brown sugar, divided
3   tablespoons chopped slivered almonds
Cooking spray
4   ounces Brie cheese
1   teaspoon all-purpose flour

1. Thaw dough in refrigerator 12 hours.
2. Melt 1 tablespoon butter in a medium nonstick skillet over medium-high heat. Add apple; sauté 10 minutes. Add ¼ cup brown sugar; cook 5 minutes. Remove from heat; stir in almonds.
3. Roll dough into a 15 x 12-inch rectangle on a lightly floured surface. Place on a baking sheet coated with cooking spray. Spread apple mixture lengthwise down center of dough. Remove rind from cheese; cube. Arrange

cheese on apple mixture. Make diagonal cuts, 1½ inches apart, on both sides of filling to within ½ inch of filling. Fold strips alternately over filling from each side, overlapping at an angle. Cover and let rise in a warm place (85°), free from drafts, 1½ hours or until doubled in size.
4. Preheat oven to 350°.
5. Combine ¼ cup brown sugar and flour in a medium bowl; cut in 1 tablespoon butter with a pastry blender or 2 knives until combined. Sprinkle over top of loaf. Bake at 350° for 30 minutes or until golden. Yield: 16 servings (serving size: 1 slice).

CALORIES 169 (25% from fat); FAT 4.7g (sat 2.4g, mono 1.6g, poly 0.4g); PROTEIN 5.1g; CARB 27.4g; FIBER 1.3g; CHOL 41mg; IRON 1.2mg; SODIUM 321mg; CALC 43mg

SPINACH-FETA BREAD

1   (1-pound) loaf frozen white bread dough
1   cup (4 ounces) crumbled feta cheese
⅓   cup (3 ounces) ⅓-less-fat cream cheese
½   teaspoon dried oregano
¼   teaspoon salt
1   (14-ounce) can artichoke hearts, drained and chopped
1   (10-ounce) package frozen chopped spinach, thawed, drained, and squeezed dry
3   garlic cloves, minced
1   large egg white
Cooking spray
2   tablespoons (½ ounce) grated fresh Parmesan cheese

1. Thaw dough in refrigerator 12 hours.
2. Combine feta and next 7 ingredients in a bowl.
3. Roll dough into a 16 x 10-inch rectangle on a lightly floured surface. Spread spinach mixture over dough, leaving a ½-inch border. Beginning with a long side, roll up dough, jelly-roll fashion; pinch seam and ends to seal. Place roll, seam side down, on a baking sheet coated with cooking spray.
Continued

Cut diagonal slits into top of roll using a sharp knife. Cover roll, and let rise in a warm place (85°), free from drafts, 1 hour or until doubled in size.

4. Preheat oven to 350°.

5. Sprinkle Parmesan cheese over top of roll. Bake at 350° for 45 minutes or until golden. Yield: 16 servings (serving size: 1 slice).

CALORIES 143 (23% from fat); FAT 3.7g (sat 2.2g, mono 1g, poly 0.3g); PROTEIN 6.4g; CARB 21.7g; FIBER 1.2g; CHOL 14mg; IRON 1.7mg; SODIUM 461mg; CALC 99mg

READER RECIPES

Is That Fish Sober?

A decade in the restaurant business left a Washington state reader with at least one intoxicating (figuratively) seafood favorite.

SHEILA'S FISH WITH TEQUILA SAUCE

"This sauce is great on just about any white fish and even chicken."
—Sheila Geraghty Leek, Spokane, Washington

½ teaspoon black pepper, divided
1½ cups chopped tomato
½ cup sliced green onions
1 teaspoon grated lime rind
¼ cup fresh lime juice
1 tablespoon tequila
¼ cup all-purpose flour
½ teaspoon salt
2 (6-ounce) sea bass fillets (about 1½ inches thick)
1 tablespoon olive oil

1. Combine ¼ teaspoon pepper, tomato, and next 4 ingredients in a small bowl. Cover and chill 2 hours.

2. Preheat oven to 350°.

3. Combine ¼ teaspoon pepper, flour, and salt in a shallow bowl; dredge fish in flour mixture. Heat oil in a medium nonstick skillet over medium-high heat. Add fish; cook 5 minutes on one side or until browned. Turn fish over; top with tomato mixture. Wrap handle of skillet with foil; bake at 350° for 15 minutes or until fish flakes easily when tested with a fork. Yield: 2 servings (serving size: 1 fillet and ⅔ cup sauce).

CALORIES 320 (30% from fat); FAT 10.8g (sat 2g, mono 5.9g, poly 2.4g); PROTEIN 34.7g; CARB 20.6g; FIBER 2.7g; CHOL 70mg; IRON 2.4mg; SODIUM 718mg; CALC 48mg

TACO PIZZA

—Reneé Mahoney, Rochester, New York

1 (1-pound) loaf frozen white bread dough, thawed
Cooking spray
½ pound ground turkey
1 (1-ounce) package taco seasoning
1 cup bottled salsa
1 (2¼-ounce) can sliced ripe olives, drained
1 cup (4 ounces) shredded reduced-fat sharp Cheddar cheese
1 cup chopped iceberg lettuce
6 tablespoons fat-free sour cream

1. Preheat oven to 450°.

2. Roll dough into a 12-inch circle on a floured surface. Place dough on a 12-inch pizza pan or baking sheet coated with cooking spray. Crimp edges of dough with fingers to form a rim. Set aside.

3. Cook turkey in a nonstick skillet over medium-high heat until browned; stir to crumble. Stir in 1½ tablespoons taco seasoning; reserve remaining seasoning for another use. Spread turkey mixture over dough, leaving a 1-inch border. Spread salsa over turkey mixture; sprinkle with olives and cheese. Bake at 450° for 20 minutes or until cheese melts. Top with lettuce. Let stand 5 minutes. Top each slice with sour cream. Yield: 6 servings (serving size: 1 pizza slice and 1 tablespoon sour cream).

CALORIES 316 (23% from fat); FAT 8.2g (sat 3.2g, mono 3.2g, poly 1.2g); PROTEIN 21.5g; CARB 38.3g; FIBER 1.1g; CHOL 37mg; IRON 2.9mg; SODIUM 900mg; CALC 235mg

VEGETABLE SALSA

—Linda Salter, Richmond Hill, Georgia

2 tablespoons olive oil
2 tablespoons red wine vinegar
3 garlic cloves, minced
1 cup chopped plum tomato
⅓ cup chopped green onions
1 teaspoon chopped fresh cilantro
1 (15-ounce) can black beans, rinsed and drained
1 (11-ounce) can shoepeg white corn, drained
1 (4.5-ounce) can chopped green chiles, drained
4 ounces baked tortilla chips

1. Combine first 3 ingredients in a large bowl; stir well with a whisk. Stir in tomato and next 5 ingredients. Serve with chips. Yield: 8 servings (serving size: ½ cup salsa and 5 chips).

CALORIES 164 (24% from fat); FAT 4.4g (sat 0.6g, mono 2.8g, poly 0.7g); PROTEIN 5.1g; CARB 28.7g; FIBER 3.2g; CHOL 0mg; IRON 1.3mg; SODIUM 447mg; CALC 38mg

BLACK-BEAN ENCHILADA CASSEROLE

—Kathi Galloway, Santa Maria, California

1 cup (4 ounces) shredded reduced-fat Monterey Jack cheese, divided
1 cup cooked brown basmati rice or long-grain rice
1 cup fat-free sour cream
½ cup chopped fresh cilantro
⅓ cup chopped green onions
1 teaspoon ground cumin
1 teaspoon chili powder
1 (15-ounce) can black beans, rinsed and drained
1 jalapeño pepper, seeded and chopped
1 (19-ounce) can red enchilada sauce
Cooking spray
12 (6-inch) corn tortillas

1. Preheat oven to 350°.

2. Combine ½ cup cheese, rice, and next 7 ingredients in a large bowl.

Spread ¼ cup enchilada sauce in an 11 x 7-inch baking dish coated with cooking spray. Heat remaining enchilada sauce in a skillet 2 minutes or until warm; remove from heat. Dredge both sides of 6 tortillas in warm sauce; arrange tortillas, overlapping, over sauce in baking dish. Top with 1¾ cups bean mixture. Dredge both sides of remaining tortillas in warm sauce; arrange tortillas, overlapping, over bean mixture. Top with remaining bean mixture, remaining sauce, and ½ cup cheese. Bake at 350° for 40 minutes or until bubbly. Yield: 6 servings (serving size: 1 [3½-inch] square).

CALORIES 323 (20% from fat); FAT 7.2g (sat 2.4g, mono 2.6g, poly 1.7g); PROTEIN 16.1g; CARB 49.5g; FIBER 5.5g; CHOL 12mg; IRON 2.5mg; SODIUM 683mg; CALC 269mg

"BARBECUED" CHICKEN-AND-BLACK BEAN BURRITOS

—*Julie Ungashick, Kansas City, Missouri*

 1   tablespoon olive oil
 ¾   pound skinned, boned chicken breast, cut into bite-size pieces
 ½   cup chopped onion
 3   garlic cloves, minced
 ⅓   cup bottled barbecue sauce
 1   (15-ounce) can black beans, drained
 ½   cup (2 ounces) shredded reduced-fat sharp Cheddar cheese
 4   (10-inch) flour tortillas
 ¼   cup low-fat sour cream

1. Heat oil in a nonstick skillet over medium heat. Add chicken, onion, and garlic; cook 8 minutes or until chicken is done, stirring constantly. Stir in barbecue sauce and beans. Sprinkle with cheese; cook 5 minutes. Warm tortillas according to package directions. Spoon about ½ cup chicken mixture down center of each tortilla; top each with 1 tablespoon sour cream, and roll up. Yield: 4 servings (serving size: 1 burrito).

CALORIES 458 (26% from fat); FAT 13.3g (sat 4.1g, mono 5.6g, poly 2.4g); PROTEIN 34.9g; CARB 49.1g; FIBER 4.8g; CHOL 65mg; IRON 3.9mg; SODIUM 744mg; CALC 243mg

The Ultimate New Year's Eve

It can be at your house this year, with our sophisticated but simple step-by-step guide.

If you plan to ring in this momentous new year with sophisticated style, bring the celebration home with a dazzling sit-down dinner party. With our step-by-step guide, preparing a meal worthy of the occasion is so much easier than fighting the crowds.

NEW YEAR'S EVE DINNER PARTY FOR 8

BUTTERNUT BISQUE WITH CIDER SYRUP

CAESAR SALAD WITH PEPPERS

PORCINI-CRUSTED BEEF TENDERLOIN WITH WILD-MUSHROOM SAUCE

SHERRY VINEGAR-GLAZED PEARL ONIONS

WILD RICE WITH WALNUT OIL AND GREEN ONIONS

CHOCOLATE-HAZELNUT TORTE

about 1,036 calories (27% from fat) per serving

BUTTERNUT BISQUE WITH CIDER SYRUP

Extracting juice from ginger is easy and adds a distinct flavor. If you don't have fresh ginger, you can substitute 2 tablespoons orange juice.

 4   cups apple cider, divided
 2   large butternut squash (about 4½ pounds)
 ½   cup grated peeled fresh ginger
 3   cups water
 2½ cups thinly sliced leek (about 4 large)
 ½   teaspoon salt
 1   cup whole milk

1. Bring 2½ cups cider to a boil in a saucepan over medium-high heat. Cook until reduced to ½ cup (about 20 minutes); cool. Cover and chill.

2. Preheat oven to 400°.

3. Cut squash in half lengthwise; discard seeds and membrane. Place squash halves on a baking sheet; bake at 400° for 1 hour or until tender. Cool. Remove pulp, and set aside. Discard rind.

4. Place ginger on several layers of paper towel. Gather edges of paper towel together; squeeze paper towel bag over a small bowl, reserving ginger juice. Discard solids. Set aside.

5. Combine 1½ cups cider, water, leek, and salt in a Dutch oven. Bring to a boil. Cover, reduce heat, and simmer 40 minutes or until leek is soft.

6. Add squash, ginger juice, and milk to leek mixture, stirring well. Cook 15 minutes. Place half of squash mixture in a blender or food processor; process until smooth. Pour pureed squash

Continued

mixture into a large bowl. Repeat procedure with remaining squash mixture. Return pureed squash mixture to pan. Cook until thoroughly heated. Ladle soup into bowls; drizzle with cider syrup. Yield: 8 servings (serving size: 1 cup soup and 1 tablespoon syrup).

CALORIES 149 (8% from fat); FAT 1.4g (sat 0.7g, mono 0.3g, poly 0.2g); PROTEIN 3.3g; CARB 34.5g; FIBER 2.9g; CHOL 4mg; IRON 2mg; SODIUM 177mg; CALC 147mg

CAESAR SALAD WITH PEPPERS

Dressing:

2 large whole garlic heads
¼ cup fat-free mayonnaise
1½ teaspoons Dijon mustard
1 teaspoon anchovy paste
Dash of black pepper
3 tablespoons red wine vinegar
1 tablespoon olive oil

Salad:

2 yellow bell peppers
2 red bell peppers
14 cups torn romaine lettuce
¼ cup (1 ounce) finely grated fresh Parmesan cheese, divided
4 (1-ounce) slices rye bread, cubed and toasted

1. Preheat oven to 400°.
2. To prepare dressing, remove white papery skin from garlic heads (do not peel or separate cloves). Wrap each head separately in foil. Bake at 400° for 1 hour; cool. Cut crosswise; squeeze to extract garlic pulp to measure 3 tablespoons. Discard skins. Place garlic, mayonnaise, mustard, anchovy paste, and black pepper in a food processor; process until smooth. With food processor on, slowly pour vinegar and oil through food chute; process until well-blended.
3. Preheat broiler.
4. To prepare salad, cut bell peppers in half lengthwise; discard seeds and membranes. Place pepper halves, skin

sides up, on a foil-lined baking sheet; flatten with hand. Broil 15 minutes or until blackened. Place in a zip-top plastic bag; seal. Let stand 15 minutes. Peel and cut into 1-inch strips. Combine dressing, lettuce, 2 tablespoons cheese, and bread cubes in a large bowl; toss gently to coat. Divide salad evenly among 8 salad plates. Arrange yellow and red bell pepper strips on top of salads. Sprinkle evenly with 2 tablespoons cheese. Yield: 8 servings (serving size: 2 cups).

CALORIES 111 (30% from fat); FAT 3.7g (sat 1g, mono 1.7g, poly 0.5g); PROTEIN 5g; CARB 15.3g; FIBER 3.4g; CHOL 2mg; IRON 2.2mg; SODIUM 378mg; CALC 98mg

PORCINI-CRUSTED BEEF TENDERLOIN WITH WILD-MUSHROOM SAUCE

Be sure to ask the butcher for a center-cut piece of tenderloin.

1½ cups dried porcini mushrooms (about 1½ ounces), divided
1 (3½-pound) center-cut beef tenderloin
¾ teaspoon salt, divided
¼ teaspoon white pepper, divided
2 teaspoons vegetable oil
Cooking spray
2 cups boiling water
2 tablespoons chilled butter or stick margarine, cut into small pieces

1. Preheat oven to 400°.
2. Place ½ cup mushrooms in a blender; process until finely ground. Trim fat from tenderloin. Sprinkle beef with ground mushrooms, ½ teaspoon salt, and ⅛ teaspoon pepper. Heat oil in large nonstick skillet over medium-high heat until hot. Add beef; cook 1 minute on all sides or until browned. Place tenderloin on a broiler pan coated with cooking spray. Insert meat thermometer into thickest portion of tenderloin. Bake at 400° for 30 minutes or until thermometer registers 145° (medium-rare) to 160° (medium).

3. Place tenderloin on a platter; cover with foil. Let stand 10 minutes.
4. Combine boiling water and 1 cup mushrooms in a bowl; cover and let stand 30 minutes. Drain mushrooms through a cheesecloth-lined sieve into a medium saucepan, reserving soaking liquid; coarsely chop mushrooms. Bring reserved soaking liquid to a boil; add chopped mushrooms. Reduce heat, and simmer until reduced to 1 cup (about 12 minutes). Add ¼ teaspoon salt, ⅛ teaspoon pepper, and butter, stirring with a whisk until butter melts. Serve with tenderloin. Yield: 8 servings (serving size: 3 ounces beef and 2 tablespoons sauce).

CALORIES 226 (48% from fat); FAT 12g (sat 5.1g, mono 4.3g, poly 1g); PROTEIN 24.6g; CARB 4.1g; FIBER 0.6g; CHOL 79mg; IRON 3.1mg; SODIUM 303mg; CALC 8mg

SHERRY VINEGAR-GLAZED PEARL ONIONS

8 cups water
2 pounds pearl onions, peeled
Cooking spray
¾ cup sherry vinegar or red wine vinegar
¼ cup honey
¼ teaspoon salt
¼ teaspoon freshly ground black pepper

1. Preheat oven to 400°.
2. Bring water to a boil in a large saucepan; add onions. Cook 3 minutes or until tender; drain. Place onions in a 13 x 9-inch baking dish coated with cooking spray. Combine vinegar, honey, salt, and pepper. Pour vinegar mixture over onions. Bake at 400° for 1 hour and 15 minutes or until golden brown, stirring occasionally. Yield: 8 servings (serving size: ¼ cup).

CALORIES 73 (1% from fat); FAT 0.1g (sat 0g, mono 0.1g, poly 0g); PROTEIN 1g; CARB 18.9g; FIBER 0.7g; CHOL 0mg; IRON 0.4mg; SODIUM 83mg; CALC 39mg

WILD RICE WITH WALNUT OIL AND GREEN ONIONS

Walnut oil adds a nutty flavor to the wild rice, but you can use olive oil instead.

6 cups water
2 cups uncooked wild rice (about 12 ounces)
1 teaspoon salt
½ cup dried currants
2 tablespoons walnut oil or olive oil, divided
1 cup chopped green onions, divided
1 teaspoon grated lemon rind, divided

1. Bring water to a boil in a large saucepan. Add wild rice and salt; cover, reduce heat, and simmer 50 minutes. Stir in currants; cover and cook an additional 10 minutes or until rice is tender and liquid is absorbed. Drain; spoon into a large bowl.
2. Heat 1½ tablespoons oil in a nonstick skillet over medium-low heat. Add ¾ cup onions; cook 10 minutes or until soft. Stir 1½ teaspoons oil, onion mixture, and ½ teaspoon rind into rice mixture. Sprinkle with ¼ cup green onions and ½ teaspoon rind. Yield: 8 servings (serving size: ¾ cup).

CALORIES 202 (18% from fat); FAT 4.1g (sat 0.4g, mono 2.5g, poly 0.9g); PROTEIN 6.4g; CARB 37g; FIBER 2.5g; CHOL 0mg; IRON 1.2mg; SODIUM 301mg; CALC 26mg

ON THE VINE

Start the evening with a top-notch Champagne as an apéritif. *Billecart-Salmon Brut Rosé* (nonvintage, $55) is lively and elegant. After the bubbly, move to a sensual, full-bodied white. *Flora Springs Chardonnay Reserve 1997* (Napa Valley, $24) is rich and stylish. Finally, with the main course, a soft, concentrated Merlot would be terrific. *Stags' Leap Winery Merlot 1997* (Napa Valley, $30) is an outrageously good accompaniment to the *Porcini-Crusted Beef Tenderloin with Wild-Mushroom Sauce* (page 338).

—*Karen MacNeil-Fife*

CHOCOLATE-HAZELNUT TORTE

Cooking spray
2 teaspoons all-purpose flour
½ cup hazelnuts (about 2 ounces)
3 tablespoons all-purpose flour
1 cup granulated sugar
⅔ cup unsweetened cocoa
3 tablespoons cold strongly brewed coffee
2½ tablespoons butter or stick margarine, melted
1 teaspoon vanilla extract
½ teaspoon grated orange rind
3 large egg whites
7 large egg whites
3 tablespoons granulated sugar
2 cups fresh raspberries
1 teaspoon powdered sugar

1. Coat a 9-inch springform pan with cooking spray; sprinkle with 2 teaspoons flour.
2. Place hazelnuts in a medium nonstick skillet. Cook over medium heat 6 minutes or until lightly toasted, stirring frequently. Turn nuts out onto a towel. Roll up towel; rub off skins. Cool. Place hazelnuts in a food processor; process until coarsely ground. Add 3 tablespoons flour; process until finely ground.
3. Preheat oven to 350°.
4. Combine 1 cup granulated sugar and next 6 ingredients in a large bowl; stir well with a whisk. Stir in hazelnut mixture. Beat 7 egg whites at high speed of a mixer until soft peaks form. Gradually add 3 tablespoons granulated sugar, 1 tablespoon at a time, beating until stiff peaks form. Fold one-third of egg white mixture into cocoa mixture; gently fold in remaining egg white mixture. Spoon into prepared springform pan.
5. Bake at 350° for 40 minutes or until set; cool on a wire rack. Remove sides of pan. Arrange raspberries on top of torte; sift powdered sugar over raspberries. Yield: 8 servings (serving size: 1 wedge).

CALORIES 275 (30% from fat); FAT 9.3g (sat 3.2g, mono 4.9g, poly 0.7g); PROTEIN 7.9g; CARB 41.4g; FIBER 2.5g; CHOL 10mg; IRON 1.9mg; SODIUM 106mg; CALC 36mg

Recipe Title Index

An alphabetical listing of every recipe title that appeared in the magazine in 1999. See page 351 for the General Recipe Index.

Month-by-Month Index

A month-by-month listing of every food story with recipe titles that appeared in the magazine in 1999. See page 351 for the General Recipe Index.

General Recipe Index

*A listing by major ingredient, food category, and/or regular column
for every recipe that appeared in the magazine in 1999.*

Credits

CONTRIBUTING RECIPE DEVELOPERS:

Bruce Aidells
Mark Bittman
Cinda Chavich
Ying Chang Compestine
Martha Condra
Terry Conlan
Meredith Deeds
Abby Duchin Dinces
Dave DiResta
Jane Doerfer
Patrick Earvolino
Linda West Eckhardt
Jim Fobel
Michael Foley
Joanne Foran

Maggie Glezer
Rozanne Gold
Jessica B. Harris
Scott Haulman
Nancy Hughes
Jeanne Jones
Jeanne Thiel Kelley
Jean Kressy
Cynthia Nicholson LaGrone
Theresa V. Laursen
Jeanne Lemlin
Karen A. Levin
Kathi Long
Susan Herrmann Loomis
Deborah Madison
Marianne Marinelli
Melissa Monosoff
Greg Patent

Leslie Glover Pendleton
Marge Perry
Steven Petusevsky
Steven Raichlen
Victoria Abbott Riccardi
Nina Simonds
Lisë Stern
Elizabeth Taliaferro
John Martin Taylor
Jim Thornton
Robin Vitetta-Miller
Kenneth Wapner

CONTRIBUTING PHOTOGRAPHER:

Howard L. Puckett, pages 37, 39 (top), 57 (bottom)

METRIC EQUIVALENTS

The recipes that appear in this cookbook use the standard United States method
for measuring liquid and dry or solid ingredients (teaspoons, tablespoons, and cups).
The information in the following charts is provided to help cooks outside the U.S.
successfully use these recipes. All equivalents are approximate.

EQUIVALENTS FOR DIFFERENT TYPES OF INGREDIENTS

A standard cup measure of a dry or solid ingredient will
vary in weight depending on the type of ingredient.
A standard cup of liquid is the same volume for any type of
liquid. Use the following chart when converting standard
cup measures to grams (weight) or milliliters (volume).

Standard Cup	Fine Powder (ex. flour)	Grain (ex. rice)	Granular (ex. sugar)	Liquid Solids (ex. butter)	Liquid (ex. milk)
1	140 g	150 g	190 g	200 g	240 ml
¾	105 g	113 g	143 g	150 g	180 ml
⅔	93 g	100 g	125 g	133 g	160 ml
½	70 g	75 g	95 g	100 g	120 ml
⅓	47 g	50 g	63 g	67 g	80 ml
¼	35 g	38 g	48 g	50 g	60 ml
⅛	18 g	19 g	24 g	25 g	30 ml

DRY INGREDIENTS BY WEIGHT
(To convert ounces to grams,
multiply the number of ounces by 30.)

1 oz	=	1/16 lb	=	30 g
4 oz	=	¼ lb	=	120 g
8 oz	=	½ lb	=	240 g
12 oz	=	¾ lb	=	360 g
16 oz	=	1 lb	=	480 g

LENGTH
(To convert inches to centimeters,
multiply the number of inches by 2.5.)

1 in			=	2.5 cm		
6 in	=	½ ft	=	15 cm		
12 in	=	1 ft	=	30 cm		
36 in	=	3 ft	= 1 yd	=	90 cm		
40 in			=	100 cm	=	1 m

LIQUID INGREDIENTS BY VOLUME

¼ tsp					=	1 ml	
½ tsp					=	2 ml	
1 tsp					=	5 ml	
3 tsp	=	1 tbls		=	½ fl oz	=	15 ml
		2 tbls	=	⅛ cup	=	1 fl oz	=	30 ml
		4 tbls	=	¼ cup	=	2 fl oz	=	60 ml
		5⅓ tbls	=	⅓ cup	=	3 fl oz	=	80 ml
		8 tbls	=	½ cup	=	4 fl oz	=	120 ml
		10⅔ tbls	=	⅔ cup	=	5 fl oz	=	160 ml
		12 tbls	=	¾ cup	=	6 fl oz	=	180 ml
		16 tbls	=	1 cup	=	8 fl oz	=	240 ml
		1 pt	=	2 cups	=	16 fl oz	=	480 ml
		1 qt	=	4 cups	=	32 fl oz	=	960 ml
					33 fl oz	=	1000 ml	= 1l

COOKING/OVEN TEMPERATURES

	Fahrenheit	Celsius	Gas Mark
Freeze Water	32° F	0° C	
Room Temperature	68° F	20° C	
Boil Water	212° F	100° C	
Bake	325° F	160° C	3
	350° F	180° C	4
	375° F	190° C	5
	400° F	200° C	6
	425° F	220° C	7
	450° F	230° C	8
Broil			Grill